THE EU LAW DUTY OF CONSISTENT INTERPRETATION IN GERMAN, IRISH AND DUTCH COURTS

AF776604

THE EU LAW DUTY OF CONSISTENT INTERPRETATION IN GERMAN, IRISH AND DUTCH COURTS

Sim HAKET

intersentia
Cambridge – Antwerp – Chicago

Intersentia Ltd
8 Wellington Mews | Wellington Street
Cambridge | CB1 1HW | United Kingdom
Tel.: +44 1223 736 170
Email: mail@intersentia.co.uk
www.intersentia.com | www.intersentia.co.uk

Distribution for the UK and Ireland:
NBN International
Airport Business Centre, 10 Thornbury Road
Plymouth, PL6 7 PP
United Kingdom
Tel.: +44 1752 202 301 | Fax: +44 1752 202 331
Email: orders@nbninternational.com

Distribution for Europe and all other countries:
Intersentia Publishing nv
Groenstraat 31
2640 Mortsel
Belgium
Tel.: +32 3 680 15 50 | Fax: +32 3 658 71 21
Email: mail@intersentia.be

Distribution for the USA and Canada:
Independent Publishers Group
Order Department
814 North Franklin Street
Chicago, IL60610
USA
Tel.: +1 800 888 4741 (toll free) | Fax: +1312 337 5985

The EU Law Duty of Consistent Interpretation in German, Irish and Dutch Courts
© 2019 S.W. Haket

The author has asserted the right under the Copyright, Designs and Patents Act 1988, to be identified as author of this work.

No part of this book may be reproduced, stored in a retrieval system, or transmitted, in any form, or by any means, without prior written permission from Intersentia, or as expressly permitted by law or under the terms agreed with the appropriate reprographic rights organisation. Enquiries concerning reproduction which may not be covered by the above should be addressed to Intersentia at the address above.

Cover artwork: F.J. Ramaker

ISBN 978-1-78068-879-4
ISBN 978-1-78068-880-0 (pdf)
D/2019/7849/109
NUR 828

British Library Cataloguing in Publication Data. A catalogue record for this book is available from the British Library.

ACKNOWLEDGEMENTS

In the first place I would like to thank my supervisors Professor Rob Widdershoven and dr. Hanneke van Eijken. Rob has the unique talent that he can point out the most detailed nuances of a particular legal issue and then seemingly effortlessly switches to telling you what the guiding threads are of the chapter that you just submitted – often leaving you surprised at the coherent structure of your work that you had not yet discovered yourself. His comments contributed significantly to the quality of the legal analyses in this book. Hanneke encouraged me to strengthen the theoretical component of my analysis of the duty of consistent interpretation which inadvertently (or subtly?) led me to theories that also played a key role in her own dissertation. Her enthusiasm and support have meant, and mean, a lot to me. I should also thank dr. Herman van Harten who played a crucial role at the start of the project by suggesting that my ideas on the dual mandate of national courts could be given more focus by concentrating on a particular area of EU law that is situated at the interface between EU and national law: the duty of consistent interpretation. I was given the opportunity to carry out part of my research at Heidelberg University and University College Dublin, for which I wish to thank Professor Müller-Graff and Professor Barrett. And I also briefly visited the European Court of Justice, which was made possible by Professor Sacha Prechal. All three of them later became members of the reading committee, and were joined by Professor Elaine Mak and Professor Mark Wissink, for which I am very grateful.

Despite my visits abroad, most of the work was of course carried out in Utrecht. I wish to thank all the colleagues for making Achter Sint Pieter and Newtonlaan enjoyable and stimulating places to work. I wish to thank in particular my roommates, and former roommates, Claire, Elif, Lukas, Paulien, Sander and Tim for their kindness, contagious work ethic and hearing me out while I ramble on about my views on the duty of consistent interpretation. I thank Klaartje Hoeberechts for preparing the manuscript and Freddy Ramaker for the beautiful cover design.

Pim, I am thankful for the relationship that we have as father and son; you have always supported me and gave me the freedom to find my own path. I am sure Jetteke is proud of both of us. Céline, I realise that the final stages of writing the dissertation will sometimes have been rough for you as well. Perhaps I am mistaken, but I do not believe that you mentioned this even once. Your devotion to us and our family are not taken for granted. Esmée and Sophia, you both came into my life when the dissertation was still a work in progress. It is now finished and I suspect that I have an even more interesting and surprising road ahead of me as you evolve into your 'final version'.

CONTENTS

LIST OF ABBREVIATIONS

AB	Administratiefrechtelijke beslissingen
AC	Appeal Cases
ABRvS	Afdeling Bestuursrechtspraak van de Raad van State
AG	Advocate General
ArbG	Arbeitsgericht
BAG	Bundesarbeitsgericht
BAGE	Entscheidungen des Bundesarbeitsgerichts
BFH	Bundesfinanzhof
BFHE	Entscheidungen des Bundesfinanzhof
BGH	Bundesgerichtshof
BGHZ	Bundesgerichtshof für Zivilsachen
BGHSt	Bundesgerichtshof für Strafsachen
BJu	Boom Juridische uitgevers
BNB	Beslissingen in belastingzaken
BSG	Bundessozialgericht
BVerfG	Bundesverfassungsgericht
BVerfGE	Entscheidungen des Bundesverfassungsgerichts
BVerfGK	Kammerentscheidungen des Bundesverfassungsgerichts
BVerwG	Bundesverwaltungsgericht
BVerwGE	Entscheidungen des Bundesverwaltungsgerichts
CBb	College van Beroep voor het bedrijfsleven
CJ	Chief Justice
CMLR	Common Market Law Reports
CMLRev	Common Market Law Review
DB	Der Betrieb
DÖV	Die Öffentliche Verwaltung
DStR	Deutsches Steuerrecht
ECHR	European Convention on Human Rights
ECJ	European Court of Justice
EHRC	European Human Rights Cases
ELJ	European Law Journal
ELR	European Law Reports
ELRev	European Law Review
EU	European Union
EuR	Europarecht
EuZW	Europäische Zeitschrift für Wirtschaftsrecht

GPR	Zeitschrift für das Privatrecht der Europäischen Union
HR	Hoge Raad
ICR	Industrial Cases Reports
IEHC	High Court of Ireland Decisions
IER	Intellectuele Eigendom en Reclamerecht
IESC	Supreme Court of Ireland Decisions
ILRM	Irish Law Reports Monthly
IR	Irish Reports
IRLR	Industrial Relations Law Reports
J	Justice
JGR	Jurisprudentie Geneesmiddelenrecht
JIC	Justis Irish Cases
JM	Jurisprudentie Milieurecht
JOR	Jurisprudentie Onderneming & Recht
JZ	JuristenZeitung
LG	Landgericht
M en R	Milieu en Recht
MJ	Maastricht Journal of European and Comparative Law
MLR	Modern Law Review
NJ	Nederlandse Jurisprudentie
NJW	Neue Juristische Wochenschrift
NVwZ	Neue Zeitschrift für Verwaltungsrecht
NZA	Neue Zeitschrift für Arbeitsrecht
OJLS	Oxford Journal of Legal Studies
OLG	Oberlandesgericht
OUP	Oxford University Press
RAwb	Rechtspraak Algemene wet bestuursrecht
RIW	Recht der internationalen Wirtschaft
TEU	Treaty on European Union
TFEU	Treaty on the Functioning of the European Union
UK	United Kingdom
WLR	Weekly Law Reports
YEL	Yearbook of European Law
ZIP	Zeitschrift für Wirtschaftsrecht

CHAPTER 1
INTRODUCTION

1. WHAT IS THIS BOOK ABOUT?

1.1. FROM HAMM TO LUXEMBOURG AND BACK

It was on 6 December 1982 that the Labour Court (Arbeitsgericht) Hamm decided to stay the proceedings before it and refer preliminary questions to the European Court of Justice (ECJ). While it did not doubt that the applicants had been discriminated against on grounds of their sex when pursuing an employment relationship as social workers at Werl prison, it nevertheless considered that, in the present circumstances, German law only permitted the award of compensation corresponding to damages incurred as a result of the applicants' reliance on the expectation that the establishment of the employment relationship would not be obstructed as a result of discriminatory treatment (*'Vertrauensschaden'*). In the case of the applicants this amounted to approximately € 3,90 as compensation for travelling expenses. The referring court wanted to know whether such slight compensation was in conformity with the Equal Treatment Directive.[1] It followed from the ECJ's preliminary ruling, which would become known as the *Von Colson and Kamann* judgment, that there was an incompatibility with the directive. Be that as it may, it also pointed out that this could not be remedied by means of direct effect as the provision in the directive was not sufficiently precise and unconditional. However, in a passage that would subsequently make its way to the textbooks on EU law, it established the duty to interpret national law in conformity with an EU law directive.[2] The obligation has been further developed in subsequent case law and its current formulation requires the national court to interpret national law, so far as possible, in the light of the wording and the purpose of the directive concerned in order to achieve the result sought by the directive and consequently comply with the third paragraph of Article 288

1 Council Directive 76/207/EEC of 9 February 1976 on the implementation of the principle of equal treatment for men and women as regards access to employment, vocational training and promotion, and working conditions, *OJ* 1976, L39/40.

2 Case 14/83 *Von Colson and Kamann*, ECLI:EU:C:1984:153. The most common alternative designations for the duty of consistent interpretation are 'indirect effect' and 'harmonious interpretation'.

TFEU.[3] Frequently, a treatise on the duty of consistent interpretation ends as soon as the ECJ's case law has been pointed out. However, would not it be interesting to learn what the ECJ's interlocutors, on this occasion the Labour Court Hamm, actually decided? It considered that, seemingly for the first time, the ECJ had stated a duty to interpret national law in conformity with the directive. But could national law accommodate such an interpretation? The Labour Court Hamm considered that, according to national interpretative rules, German courts are required to respect the wording of the provision at issue, the spirit of the measure and the legislature's intention. In principle, these limits would be exceeded if a more extensive compensation was awarded (I interpret this as a reflection on what would have been possible in a purely internal context). However, it derived from the duty of consistent interpretation the requirement to disregard the historical and systematic arguments. Since the provision's text – which the court was not prepared to relinquish – could be read in a way that complied with the directive, it found a way to allow the award of a more appropriate amount of compensation.[4]

How did the Labour Court Hamm determine what the ECJ's *Von Colson and Kamann* judgment required? Was there a conflict between the duty of consistent interpretation and one or more national interpretative methods or rules in its follow-up decision? And, if so, was a preliminary ruling from the ECJ sufficient reason to set aside or disregard the opposing methods or rules? Moreover, did courts in other Member States adopt an equally accommodating position with regard to this new obligation under EU law? In fact, a series of subsequent judgments addressing the same point as the Labour Court Hamm's judgment showed that it was already difficult enough for the German courts to determine the scope for adopting a consistent interpretation among themselves.

1.2. RESEARCH QUESTION

The research pursues two objectives. First, is there any kind of underlying rule coordinating the claims made by the duty of consistent interpretation and opposing claims made by national law (more specifically the national interpretative rules)? Or does such a rule exist, but is it so broadly defined that it is still unclear to what extent, and when, it circumscribes the interpretative freedom of the national courts? This would in my opinion be undesirable, not least from the perspective of predictability of judicial decisions. Of course, the duty of consistent interpretation

3 See e.g. Case C-106/89 *Marleasing*, ECLI:EU:C:1990:395, para. 8; Case C-334/92 *Wagner Miret*, ECLI:EU:C:1993:945, para. 20; Joined Cases C-240/98 to C-244/98 *Océano*, ECLI:EU:C:2000:346, para. 30; Case C-456/98 *Centrosteel*, ECLI:EU:C:2000:402, para. 16; Joined Cases C-397/01 to C-403/01 *Pfeiffer*, ECLI:EU:C:2004:584, para. 113; Case C-282/10 *Dominguez*, ECLI:EU:C:2012:33, para. 24.

4 ArbG Hamm 6 September 1984, ZIP 1984, 1525, 1528-9.

as such already provides a coordinating rule by holding that national law must be interpreted, so far as possible, in conformity with EU law. Yet, 'so far as possible' is not a phrase that always makes it clear just how far the obligation requires the national courts to go. I recall the example of the Labour Court Hamm's judgment: to what extent was the court required to strive for an interpretation that seemed to lie beyond the confines of what a traditional application of the national interpretative methods enabled? It is submitted that, in order to better understand the 'firepower' of 'so far as possible', it is necessary to examine what kind of effect the latter has on the relationship between EU and national law. When the question of the relationship between EU and national law is raised, it is logical to search for an answer by looking at established theories on this relationship, i.e. supremacy of EU law, national constitutionalism and constitutional pluralism. For this purpose, the research looks at case law concerning the duty of consistent interpretation and examines whether the judgment's considerations and/or the adopted interpretation are adequately explained by one or more of the theories. The second objective is to determine the explanatory value of those theories beyond the context in which they were initially developed and in which they have primarily been discussed, i.e. where provisions of EU law are invoked by means of direct effect and where they conflict with national law. This is aimed at acquiring an enriched understanding of supremacy of EU law, national constitutionalism and constitutional pluralism.

The research question addressed in this book is as follows:

> To what extent are supremacy of EU law, national constitutionalism, or constitutional pluralism adequate theories for understanding the relationship between EU and national law under the duty of consistent interpretation, taking into consideration, first, the requirements that are imposed by EU law on national courts and, secondly, the approach adopted by superior courts in Germany, Ireland and the Netherlands to determine whether it is possible to interpret national law in conformity with an EU law directive?

It is apparent from the description of the duty of consistent interpretation that, inherently, it encompasses both an EU and national law dimension. Therefore, in order to answer the question what kind of relationship exists between EU and national law under the duty of consistent interpretation, logically, two further questions must be addressed: what does the EU law dimension and what does the national law dimension entail? For the first dimension it is necessary to look at the case law in which the ECJ provided the framework for the duty of consistent interpretation and further explicated what EU law requires from national courts when they operate within that framework. The second dimension focuses on the German, Irish and Dutch superior courts' approach to the duty of consistent interpretation. It is necessary, in particular, to determine whether this confirms or undermines the conception of the ECJ, but it also complements the comprehension of the relationship between EU and national law on the basis of the ECJ's case law by revealing how the national courts deal with aspects of the duty of consistent interpretation that leave a measure of discretion to the national court, as well as aspects that come up before the national courts but have not yet been considered by the ECJ at all.

1.3. THEORIES ON THE RELATIONSHIP BETWEEN EU AND NATIONAL LAW

The main research question is based on an underlying presumption that there is an interaction between EU and national law in the context of the duty of consistent interpretation and that existing theories on the relationship between EU and national law can help understand how this interaction works. As explained, the case law concerning the duty of consistent interpretation also provides an opportunity to say something about the explanatory value of the theories themselves as regards the application of EU law remedies before national courts. For these purposes, this part of the introduction sketches the spectrum of theories and the views on those theories that have been expressed in the existing literature. This provides the background and a point of reference for the chapters discussing the case law of the ECJ and the superior courts in Germany, Ireland and the Netherlands.

1.3.1. Supremacy of EU law

At least as far as the ECJ's perspective is concerned, supremacy of EU law is the only correct way to look at the relationship between EU and national law. De Witte defines supremacy as the capacity of an EU law norm '(...) to overrule inconsistent norms of national law (...)'.[5] The definition provided by Prechal is similar, yet it has the benefit that it also mentions the duty of consistent interpretation:

> '(...) supremacy entails the obligation to resolve the conflict in favour of the Community law provision, either by setting aside the conflicting rule of national law, or by national law being consistently interpreted with Community law'.[6]

These definitions contain the essence of a vision on supremacy as a conflict rule model: when a substantive conflict between EU and national law is identified, the latter must yield to the former.

5 B. De Witte, 'Direct Effect, Primacy, and the Nature of the Legal Order', in: G. De Búrca and P.P. Craig (Eds.), *The Evolution of EU Law* (OUP 2011), p. 323.

6 S. Prechal, 'Direct Effect, Indirect Effect, Supremacy and the Evolving Constitution of the European Union', in: C. Barnard (Ed.), *The Fundamentals of EU Law Revisited* (OUP 2007), p. 38.

> It is noted that the ECJ's *Simmenthal* judgment stated that '(…) any provision of a national legal system and any legislative, administrative or judicial practice which might impair the effectiveness of Community law by withholding from the national court having jurisdiction to apply such law the power to do everything necessary at the moment of its application to set aside national legislative provisions which might prevent Community rules from having full force and effect are incompatible with those requirements which are the very essence of Community law'.[7] This could be viewed as establishing a kind of structural or procedural supremacy which deviates from the normal use of supremacy which, as stated above, entails that national law must yield to EU law if there is a substantive conflict between the two. Structural supremacy then extends to national procedural rules that stand in the way of the full effectiveness of the substantive EU law provisions. For example, in the *Simmenthal* judgment an Italian judge-made rule reserving to the Italian Constitutional Court the jurisdiction to set aside national law contrary to EU law had to be disapplied and in the equally renowned *Factortame* judgment structural supremacy was applied to the lack of jurisdiction to grant interim relief in order to give effect to EU law.[8] A recent example is found in the judgment in *Minister for Justice and Equality and Commissioner of the Garda Síochána* concerning the power to disapply national legislation that conflicts with EU law.[9] It has been argued that *Simmenthal* should not be understood as transforming the meaning of supremacy by extending it to all rules belonging to the national legal environment conditioning the operation of EU law,[10] or that this version of supremacy needs to be viewed as being only applicable in exceptional cases where the EU law mandate of national courts (or administrative authorities) is at stake.[11] The topics with which the referred to judgments were concerned certainly confirm these arguments.

The conflict rule model addresses the *rank* of EU law. It does not per se address the preceding question how EU law becomes *applicable* in the national legal orders in the first place, i.e. its legal effect. These can be viewed as two separate questions.[12] Supremacy can also be approached as a hierarchical model.[13] The rank of EU law and its applicability are then inextricably bound up with each other. Since there was also a linkage between the two in the ECJ's *Costa v ENEL* judgment pronouncing the supremacy of EU law, this has something to say for it – from

---

7 Case 106/77 *Simmenthal*, ECLI:EU:C:1978:49, para. 22.

8 Case C-213/89 *Factortame*, ECLI:EU:C:1990:257.

9 Case C-378/17 *Minister for Justice and Equality and Commissioner of the Garda Síochána*, ECLI:EU:C:2018:979, para. 36.

10 S. Prechal, 'Community Law in National Courts: The Lessons from *Van Schijndel*' (1998/3) *CMLRev*, p. 685.

11 M. Claes, *The National Courts' Mandate in the European Constitution* (Hart Publishing 2006), p. 133.

12 M.H. Wissink, *Richtlijnconforme interpretatie van burgerlijk recht* (Kluwer 2001), p. 122-3; S. Prechal, *Directives in EC Law* (OUP 2005), p. 94.

13 An analysis applying the distinction between supremacy as a conflict rule and hierarchical model was already conducted in L.F.M. Besselink, 'Curing a "Childhood Sickness"? On Direct Effect, Internal Effect, Primacy and Derogation from Civil Rights' (1996/2) *MJ*, p. 168.

an EU law perspective.[14] The model provides that EU law is integrated into the national legal orders and that they, together, constitute, a unitary legal order in which all EU law (including directives) is hierarchically superior.[15] This means that incompatible norms are invalidated or that they cannot be validly adopted in the first place. It should be noted in particular that under this model the duty of consistent interpretation is simply viewed as a corollary of supremacy, requiring that inferior national law is interpreted in conformity with supreme EU law.[16] A wholly different view, which Dougan calls the 'trigger model' provides that EU law can only create a linkage between both legal systems if it satisfies the conditions for direct effect.[17]

Notwithstanding the identified differences regarding the conceptualisation of supremacy of EU law, the above models have in common that, in line with the ECJ's *Internationale Handelsgesellschaft* judgment, EU law (when applicable) must be given precedence, even if it runs counter to provisions of a Member State's constitution.[18] This is called 'full supremacy' by De Witte.[19] Yet, it is primarily on this point that Avbelj draws a distinction under what he calls the 'primacy model'. *While supremacy and primacy are often used interchangeably*, Avbelj separates the two and confers a *considerably different* meaning on the latter. First, only when there is a conflict between the two legal orders, does the primacy model coordinate the relationship between them and this requires the EU law rule to have direct effect. In this sense some of its characteristics are a mix of the conflict rule and trigger models. However, secondly, primacy denotes a heterarchical model and the primacy of EU law is subject to compliance with a Member State's own irreducible epistemic core (standing for 'the essential formal and substantive features in whose absence it cannot exist qua a specific autonomous legal order').[20]

While they do not discuss the consequences for the duty of consistent interpretation in detail – in fact this is often not at all considered – the above sketch of the main

---

14 Case 6/64 *Costa v ENEL*, ECLI:EU:C:1964:66. See previously Case 26/62 *Van Gend & Loos*, ECLI:EU:C:1963:1 regarding direct effect.

15 For a description see M. Dougan, 'When Worlds Collide! Competing Visions of the Relationship between Direct Effect and Supremacy' (2007/4) *CMLRev*, p. 943; M. Avbelj, 'Supremacy or Primacy of EU Law – (Why) Does it Matter?' (2011/6) *ELJ*, p. 746-50. Support for the hierarchical model is provided in M. Lenz, 'Horizontal What? Back to Basics' (2000/5) *ELRev*, p. 509; T. Tridimas, 'Black, White and Shades of Grey: Horizontality of Directives Revisited' (2001/1) *YEL*, p. 327; Claes (n. 11), p. 115; K. Lenaerts and T. Corthaut, 'Of Birds and Hedges: The Role of Primacy in Invoking Norms of EU Law' (2006/3) *ELRev*, p. 287.

16 See also the Opinion of AG Van Gerven in Case C-106/89 *Marleasing*, ECLI:EU:C:1990:310, para. 9.

17 Dougan (n. 15), p. 942.

18 Case 11/70 *Internationale Handelsgesellschaft*, ECLI:EU:C:1970:114, para. 3.

19 De Witte (n. 5), p. 342. Cf. Claes (n. 11), p. 561, who uses the term 'ultimate supremacy'. Both De Witte and Claes distinguish the type of supremacy claimed by EU law from 'ordinary supremacy' which is limited to supremacy of EU law over statutes and anything inferior to the constitution.

20 Avbelj (n. 15), p. 750-3, 762.

visions in relation to the meaning of supremacy of EU law already raises some questions as regards the legal basis for the duty of consistent interpretation (is it a corollary of the conflict between the directive and national law or does it have an independent legal basis?) and the rank *vis-à-vis* national law (some of the definitions view the supremacy of EU law as absolute and unconditional, but is this compatible with the requirement to interpret national law in conformity with the directive 'so far as possible'?).

1.3.2. National Constitutionalism

The theory of national constitutionalism differs from supremacy of EU law as regards the *source* of 'ordinary' supremacy and in its rejection of *full* supremacy. As regards the former, this theory rejects the idea that EU law autonomously determines its legal effect in the national legal orders; a Member State's constitution, or other national acts of similar authority, remain the ultimate source of application of EU law.[21] It is noted that it shares this feature with the just discussed primacy model envisaged by Avbelj. As De Witte explains, the identification of different sources from which EU law flows into the national legal orders is not problematic as long as no conflict arises, or if the conflict concerns ordinary national provisions. However, this changes when the conflict concerns a norm of constitutional rank:

> '[i]f the national courts (...) think that European law ultimately derives its validity in the domestic legal order from the authority of the constitution, then they are unlikely to recognize that EU law might simply prevail over the very foundation from which its legal force derives'.[22]

The theory of national constitutionalism describes the attitudes to the claim of supremacy of EU law in most Member States. They accept that EU law takes precedence over 'ordinary' national law and perhaps even certain constitutional provisions, but not over the fundamental provisions of the constitution (again, the similarities with primacy as envisaged by Avbelj are noted).[23] If, hypothetically speaking, this second theory indeed underpins the relationship between EU and national law when national courts apply the duty of consistent interpretation, it seems to entail that they would give precedence to constitutional provisions, or national rules of interpretation if they are of a constitutional nature, that conflict with an interpretation in conformity with EU law. In that regard it is interesting to point out that Claes argues that the duty of consistent interpretation does not pose

21 M. Kumm, 'Who is the Final Arbiter of Constitutionality in Europe?: Three Conceptions of the Relationship between the German Federal Constitutional Court and the European Court of Justice' (1999/2) *CMLRev*, p. 366; M. Poiares Maduro, 'Contrapunctual Law: Europe's Constitutional Pluralism in Action', in: N. Walker (Ed.), *Sovereignty in Transition* (Hart Publishing 2003), p. 505; De Witte (n. 5), p. 356.

22 De Witte (n. 5), p. 352.

23 Ibid, p. 355-6.

any problems of a constitutional nature.[24] However, in the present research it needs to be examined whether this is indeed correct.

1.3.3. Constitutional Pluralism

In a sense, the third theory resulted from the dissatisfaction with the explanatory value of the first and second theory.[25] The German Federal Constitutional Court's (BVerfG) *Maastricht* judgment had highlighted the risk of an occurrence of constitutional conflict as a result of the incommensurable claims of ultimate authority of EU law and national constitutional law.[26] This gave rise to the view that, since both would not subordinate themselves to the other, supremacy of EU law and national constitutionalism could not explain the reality of the existence of such a conflict, let alone resolve it. The BVerfG's judgment increased the interest in a new theory which would become known as constitutional pluralism, whose foundations had already been provided by MacCormick shortly before the judgment.

> In MacCormick's classic article entitled 'Beyond the Sovereign State' he theorised the conflicting supremacy claims. Pointing out that both the EU and Member States approached the question of ultimate authority from their own legal orders and that this in fact led to the incommensurability of their claims. There was no neutral framework to mediate the opposing claims and no final solution. In this sense, MacCormick's approach was one of systemic, or radical, pluralism.[27] However, he would subsequently soften his approach and point to international law as an overarching framework through which the conflicting positions might be reconciled. This vision required both the EU and the Member States to make *substantive concessions,* in the sense that the former can only claim ultimate authority within the scope of EU competence, and the latter see their sovereignty restricted to the topics for which they retain the possibility to exercise it.[28]

Three other influential authors, who provided a foundational contribution to the debate on constitutional pluralism, must be mentioned. First, there is Walker who introduced the vision of epistemic pluralism:

> He argues that the claims of the EU and the Member States exist alongside each other. They are valid from the point of view of the internal logic of the respective legal orders only. The relationship between the legal orders is heterarchical rather than hierarchical. There is not a common point from which both claims can be reviewed, and their incommensurability must simply be accepted. The concessions are therefore of a procedural nature: while the scope of the claim

24 Claes (n. 11), p. 44.
25 De Witte (n. 5), p. 356.
26 BVerfG 12 October 1993 *Maastricht,* BVerfGE 89, 155.
27 N. MacCormick, 'Beyond the Sovereign State' (1993/1) *MLR.*
28 N. MacCormick, 'Risking Constitutional Collision in Europe?' (1998/3) *OJLS.* See also N. MacCormick, 'Questioning Post-Sovereignty' (2004/6) *ELRev.*

> of ultimate authority is not limited, both the EU and the Member States must accept that this claim is only recognised internally as opposed to externally.[29]

Secondly, Kumm's vision on constitutional pluralism is based on the aim to provide a solution that takes into account the principles underlying the conflict between the first and second theory.

> On the one hand, there is the interest of extending the rule of law to the EU legal order which, in his view, requires a uniform application of EU law and, on the other hand, there is the interest of achieving the highest possible level of fundamental rights protection and democratic legitimacy. Kumm proposes that the best solution is the one that realises the two underlying principles to the highest extent possible.[30]

Thirdly, there is the vision of Maduro's contrapunctual law which puts more focus on principles to avoid conflict.

> Maduro recognises the virtues of a pluralist, non-hierarchical, conception of the relationship between EU and national law. However, he is also aware of the dangers emanating from constitutional conflict which, he accepts, is not a mere theoretical possibility but can be the result of the incompatible positions as to who has the final say. By proposing the principles of contrapunctual law, he focusses on the question how to avoid such conflicts while the virtues of pluralism are maintained.[31] The principles highlight the importance of (i) respect for the identity of the other's legal order, (ii) an obligation to reason and justify decisions in the context of a coherent and integrated legal order, and (iii) an obligation to reason and justify decisions in a manner that could be universalisable, for which it must be based on reasoning that could be applied by any other national court.

The above is merely a brief excursion into the extensive debate concerning constitutional pluralism. It is best not to get lost in the details of this discussion – at least not in the introductory part of this book. For the sake of clarity, I conclude this part by looking at Jaklic's description of what he believes constitutes the essence of the different theories of constitutional pluralism, which he arrived at after a thorough analysis of the leading visions:

> '(...) two or more constitutional orders and their sources coexist over a shared piece of territory as ultimately self-standing and equal, so that now neither, or none, of them is any longer the single ultimate superior order/source of authority over a given territory. Secondly, in the *most abstract general* sense,

29 N. Walker, 'The Idea of Constitutional Pluralism' (2002/3) *MLR*.
30 Kumm (n. 21), p. 375-6.
31 Maduro (n. 21), p. 524-30.

this thinnest pluralist principle also implies the need for concessions by such overlapping constitutional orders and their sources'.[32]

1.3.4. *A Conflict of Norms as a Prerequisite?*

It appears from the above sketch of the existing theories on the relationship between EU and national law that they are all premised on the identification of a conflict of norms – or, in the context of constitutional pluralism, perhaps a potential conflict of norms as well.[33] Traditionally this denotes a conflict between two substantive norms. For example, the directive provides that a contract is void and national law does not. Can it be said that there is a conflict of this kind at the stage of consistent interpretation which, after all, intends to reconcile the two norms? If there is not yet such a conflict, could the existing theories on the relationship between EU and national law still have explanatory value for how that obligation works? In addition to a conflict of norms, legal scholarship has also recognised the possibility of a conflict of interpretations, i.e. a conflict operating at the level of interpretations instead of norms, and rules of priority providing how such a conflict is to be resolved.[34] What is the value of this perspective for the duty of consistent interpretation? All of these questions will be addressed in the following chapters.

1.4. NATIONAL INTERPRETATIVE RULES AND METHODS

Regardless of whether the focal point should be a conflict of norms or otherwise, it is in any event clear that interpretative rules fulfil an essential role for the present research. I use a notion of national interpretative rules which intends to catch a broad array of rules impacting interpretation, also encompassing unwritten principles and customs which, in some legal systems, are probably primarily considered as guidelines.[35] National interpretative methods are part of the national interpretative rules and broadly refer to grammatical, historical, systematic and teleological interpretation. Certain legal systems may prefer to refer to one or more of these methods by using different terminology and of course the four methods

32 K. Jaklic, *Constitutional Pluralism in the EU* (OUP 2014), p. 170. Cf. the idea of multilevel constitutionalism, I. Pernice, 'Multilevel Constitutionalism in the European Union' (2002/5) *ELRev*. This starts from the idea that citizens are the source of authority at both the EU and national level. *For that reason* no *a priori* hierarchy exists between them, but they are both part of a single system which must produce a single answer to a legal issue. However, on account of the necessity to preserve the functioning of the EU legal system and the requirement of equal application of the law, EU law does enjoy a functional supremacy. See also L.F.M. Besselink, *A Composite European Constitution* (Europa Law Publishing 2007).

33 See also Claes (n. 11), p. 37.

34 See C.-W. Canaris, '*Die richtlinienkonforme Auslegung und Rechtsfortbildung im System der juristischen Methodenlehre*', in: H. Koziol and P. Rummel (Eds.), *Im Dienste der Gerechtigkeit* (Springer Verlag 2002), p. 68-9.

35 See Prechal (n. 12), p. 194.

require elaboration and specification. Accordingly, a further discussion is provided in the chapters examining the national courts' perspectives. In addition to the interpretative methods, interpretative rules also cover matters such as the objectives of interpretation, the relative weight of a particular method, interpretative maxims and presumptions, relevant principles such as legality, legal certainty and non-retroactivity.

1.5. THE BROADER LEGAL LANDSCAPE WITHIN WHICH THE RESEARCH IS SITUATED

1.5.1. Direct Effect and State Liability

In order to better understand the nature of the duty of consistent interpretation, it is useful to look at the broader context of the effects of EU law in the Member States' legal orders. For this purpose, direct effect and State liability are briefly discussed.[36] A discussion of the former doctrine is also important as the conceptualisation of supremacy has been influenced by it.

The *Van Gend & Loos* judgment established the doctrine of direct effect in EU law, and in the *Van Duyn* judgment the ECJ ruled that directives are capable of having direct effect too.[37] Prechal defines direct effect as 'the obligation of a court or another authority to apply the relevant provision of Community law, either as a norm which governs the case or as a standard for legal review'.[38] As direct effect is concerned with the effect of EU law in the Member States' legal orders, it can be said that direct effect has, at least to some extent, the same function as the duty of consistent interpretation. It is also clear, however, that this effect is accomplished in different ways. Under the duty of consistent interpretation it is national law that is applied in the national proceedings, whereas, in case of direct effect, it is EU law whose application is sought. Also, while the precise role of the national court under the duty of consistent interpretation will be examined in the subsequent chapters, it seems safe to say that it has less discretion in determining whether EU law can be effectuated in the national proceedings when it applies the remedy of direct effect.[39]

Three further explanations regarding the relationship between the duty of consistent interpretation and direct effect are warranted. First, the direct effect of *directives*

36 See, further, J.M. Prinssen, *Doorwerking van Europees recht. De verhouding tussen directe werking, conforme interpretatie en overheidsaansprakelijkheid* (Kluwer 2004), chapter 5.

37 Case 41/74 *Van Duyn*, ECLI:EU:C:1974:133, para. 12.

38 Prechal (n. 6), p. 37-8.

39 See, as regards the discretion of national courts when applying the remedy of direct effect, J.H. Jans and J.M. Prinssen, 'Direct Effect: Convergence or Divergence?', in: J.M. Prinssen and A. Schrauwen (Eds.), *Direct Effect: Rethinking a Classic of EC Legal Doctrine* (Europa Law Publishing 2002), p. 114.

cannot be invoked against an individual. This has become known as the prohibition of horizontal,[40] and inverse vertical,[41] direct effect. The ECJ's case law shows that a similar restriction does not apply to the duty of consistent interpretation.[42] Secondly, the applicability of the duty of consistent interpretation does not depend on the concerned provision of EU law having direct effect. For example, in the *Von Colson and Kamann* judgment the ECJ concluded that Article 6 of the Equal Treatment Directive did not meet the conditions for direct effect, and then proceeded to introduce the duty of consistent interpretation as an alternative remedy. In the light of the above mentioned discussion whether supremacy is only activated in case of direct effect, it is important to emphasise that the question whether supremacy applies to the duty of consistent interpretation must be separated from the question whether that duty is applicable in the first place. Thirdly, the ECJ's *Dominguez* judgment provided that national courts should first attempt to interpret national law in conformity with the directive before applying the remedy of direct effect.[43]

The principle of State liability entails that a Member State must pay compensation for a breach of EU law if (i) EU law confers rights upon an individual, (ii) there is a sufficiently serious breach, and (iii) a causal link between the breach and damage to the individual.[44] It is important to point out that State liability does not perform the same function as the duty of consistent interpretation (or direct effect): it does not accomplish that EU law has effect in the national legal order but only offers compensation instead. Arguably, this explains why the *Dominguez* judgment mentioned State liability as a last resort for situations in which both the duty of consistent interpretation and direct effect cannot be applied.[45]

1.5.2. The Duty of Consistent Interpretation and Other Instruments of EU Law than Directives

This book only concerns the duty to interpret national law in conformity with EU law directives. This focus results from the fact that the issue of consistent interpretation is particularly relevant for directives.[46] They always require

40 Case 152/84 *Marshall I*, ECLI:EU:C:1986:84, para. 48; Case C-91/92 *Faccini Dori*, ECLI:EU:C:1994:292, para. 20; Joined Cases C-397/01 to C-403/01 *Pfeiffer*, ECLI:EU:C:2004:584, para. 108.

41 Case 14/86 *Pretore di Salò*, ECLI:EU:C:1987:275, para. 19.

42 Case C-321/05 *Kofoed*, ECLI:EU:C:2007:408, para. 45; Case C-53/10 *Mücksch*, ECLI:EU:C:2011:585, para. 34.

43 Case C-282/10 *Dominguez*, ECLI:EU:C:2012:33, para. 23.

44 These requirements were stipulated in Case C-46/93 *Brasserie du Pêcheur*, ECLI:EU:C:1996:79, para. 51. The principle of State liability was introduced in Joined Cases C-6/90 and C-9/90 *Francovich*, ECLI:EU:C:1991:428.

45 Case C-282/10 *Dominguez*, ECLI:EU:C:2012:33, paras. 43-4. See also the case note by Widdershoven in *AB* 2012/48.

46 W. Brechmann, *Die richtlinienkonforme Auslegung* (C.H. Beck'sche Verlagsbuchhandlung 1994), p. 3; M.H. Wissink, 'Interpretation of Private Law in Conformity with EU Directives', in: A.S. Hartkamp and others (Eds.), *The Influence of EU Law on National Private Law* (Kluwer 2014), p. 121; J.H. Jans and M.J.M. Verhoeven, 'Europeanisation via Consistent Interpretation

transposition (i.e. translation of the directive into national law, the Member State's choice of 'form and methods' as it is called in Article 288 TFEU, which is a phase of the process of implementation, which in addition encompasses operationalisation, application and enforcement),[47] which creates the risk that the national legislature misinterprets what the directive requires, leading to an incompatibility between the directive and the national implementing legislation. At the same time, direct effect cannot always solve this issue due to the specific limitations of the direct effect of directives. However, it should be mentioned that the duty of consistent interpretation is not limited to directives. The ECJ has stated that national law must be interpreted in conformity with general principles of EU law,[48] the Treaties,[49] regulations,[50] and soft law.[51] The ECJ's *Pupino* judgment extended the application of the duty of consistent interpretation to framework decisions (this separate category of EU law instruments ceased to exist after the Lisbon Treaty).[52] Although this did not come as a complete surprise, the ECJ's recent *Bauer* judgment made it clear that national courts are also required to interpret national law in conformity with the Charter.[53]

1.5.3. Administrative Authorities

Verhoeven argues that the ECJ's case law on the duty of consistent interpretation also covers administrative authorities.[54] Such a view might be supported by the fact that, on account of the *Costanzo* judgment, the scope of direct effect extends to administrative authorities.[55] Therefore, it would be logical to require them to apply the duty of consistent interpretation as well. However, the question if, or to what extent, administrative authorities are required to take into account the duty of consistent interpretation, is not completely settled.[56] In any event, the research does

---

and Direct Effect', in: J.H. Jans, S. Prechal and R.J.G.M. Widdershoven (Eds.), *Europeanisation of Public Law* (Europa Law Publishing 2015), p. 77.

47 S. Prechal, R.J.G.M. Widdershoven and J.H. Jans, 'Introduction', in: J.H. Jans, S. Prechal and R.J.G.M. Widdershoven (Eds.), *Europeanisation of Public Law* (Europa Law Publishing 2015), p. 13-18.

48 Case C-246/06 *Navarro*, ECLI:EU:C:2008:19, para. 35.

49 Case C-165/91 *Van Munster*, ECLI:EU:C:1994:359, para. 34; Joined Cases C-270/97 and C-271/97 *Sievers*, ECLI:EU:C:2000:76, para. 64; Case C-262/97 *Engelbrecht*, ECLI:EU:C:2000:492, para. 39; Case C-8/02 *Leichtle*, ECLI:EU:C:2004:161, para. 58; Case C-208/05 *ITC*, ECLI:EU:C:2007:16, para. 68.

50 Case C-60/02 *Criminal proceedings against X*, ECLI:EU:C:2004:10, paras. 59-60; Joined Cases C-383/06, C-384/06 and C-385/06 *Vereniging Nationaal Overlegorgaan Sociale Werkvoorziening*, ECLI:EU:C:2008:165, para. 59.

51 Case C-322/88 *Grimaldi*, ECLI:EU:C:1989:646, para. 18; Case C-207/01 *Altair Chimica*, ECLI:EU:C:2003:451, para. 41; Case C-55/06 *Arcor*, ECLI:EU:C:2008:244, para. 94.

52 Case C-105/03 *Pupino*, ECLI:EU:C:2005:386, para. 43.

53 Joined Cases C-569/16 and C-570/16 *Bauer*, ECLI:EU:C:2018:871, paras. 64, 91. See also Case C-684/16 *Max-Planck-Gesellschaft*, ECLI:EU:C:2018:874, paras. 62, 80.

54 M.J.M. Verhoeven, *The Costanzo Obligation* (Intersentia 2011), p. 31.

55 Case 103/88 *Costanzo*, ECLI:EU:C:1989:256, para. 31.

56 Jans and Verhoeven (n. 46), p. 127-8.

not include the decisions of administrative authorities for this would lead to a less attractive research design. In relation to the administrative authorities, only legal areas dealing with relationships between the Member State and individuals could be covered; even for those legal areas access to decisions would not be unlimited; it is presumed that the decisions of administrative authorities are not the best place to discover elaborate considerations giving a further interpretation as to what is required under the duty of consistent interpretation or what the relationship is between EU and national law; the decisions of administrative authorities are subject to an appeal to the court, who therefore have the last word on the application of the duty of consistent interpretation.

2. WHY IS THIS BOOK OF ADDED VALUE?

The added value of this book is that it brings together three aspects that have not yet been sufficiently dealt with or could be further explored. First, direct effect has traditionally always been the main focus when it comes to the effects of directives in the Member States' legal orders whereas the duty of consistent interpretation has received considerably less attention.[57] This is surprising since a number of authors have observed that, in cases of incorrect transposition of directives, the duty of consistent interpretation is the primary tool for ensuring the effect of directives in the Member States' legal orders.[58] Two recent studies reduced the difference in the interest for direct effect and the duty of consistent interpretation, and highlighted the latter's importance: Brenncke's 'Judicial Law-Making in English and German Courts' and a collection of national reports edited by Franklin examining 'The Effectiveness and Application of EU and EEA Law in National Courts'. While the object of these studies to some extent overlap with the present one, it is submitted that the three studies look at the relevant materials from a different perspective. In particular, the present study asks what kind of relationship exists between EU and national law in the context of the duty of consistent interpretation and looks at theories intended to coordinate that relationship. Secondly, it has been observed that EU legal scholarship focusses primarily on the case law of the ECJ whereas far less attention is devoted to national case law applying EU law.[59] This limited attention is problematic. National courts are responsible for the day-to-day application of EU law and if this is not sufficiently taken into account there is the risk of presenting a picture that does not reflect reality.[60] As Claes observed:

---

57 See also G. Betlem, 'The Doctrine of Consistent Interpretation – Managing Legal Uncertainty' (2002/3) *OJLS*, p. 399. Craig and De Búrca devote 29 pages to direct effect compared to 7 on the duty of consistent interpretation, P. Craig and G. De Búrca, *EU Law* (OUP 2015), chapter 7.

58 U. Everling, 'Zur Auslegung des durch EG-Richtlinien angeglichenen Rechts' (1992/3) *Zeitschrift für Unternehmens- und Gesellschaftsrecht*, p. 395; Wissink (n. 12), p. 49; Betlem (n. 57), p. 399.

59 H. Van Harten, *Autonomie van de nationale rechter in het Europees recht* (BJu 2011), p. 13.

60 Maduro (n. 21), p. 518; S. Prechal, 'National Courts in EU Judicial Structures' (2006/1) *YEL*, p. 432; Van Harten (n. 59), p. 11-3.

> '[t]he study of European Union law is far too one-sided if it is only looked at from the European perspective: the picture emerging from the case-law of the Court of Justice may well be misleading. In order to gain a better understanding of the functioning of Union law, it must be looked at from a double perspective: top-down from the Community perspective and bottom-up from the national angle'.[61]

Claes's observations acquire additional prominence in the context of the duty of consistent interpretation as it encompasses both an EU and national law dimension. Thirdly, the inclusion of theories on the relationship between EU and national law does not only have the potential of enhancing our understanding of the duty of consistent interpretation, but it *also* tells us something about the value of these theories. Are these judgments explained by, or do they reveal a gap in, those theories?

3. WHAT IS THE APPROACH OF THIS BOOK?

Having set out what the research question is and having explained why it is of added value to answer that question, let me outline how I intend to do this.

3.1. THE SCOPE OF THE RESEARCH: WHICH MEMBER STATES, LEGAL AREAS, AND COURTS?

First, the part of the research that looks at the national application of the duty of consistent interpretation includes Germany, Ireland and the Netherlands. Germany had to be included in the research for there is an extensive application of the duty of consistent interpretation and the national courts are familiar with, and perhaps influenced by, *verfassungskonforme Auslegung* (the requirement to adopt an interpretation that is in conformity with the German Constitution if a lower-ranking provision allows more than one interpretation). Also, the German Constitution, in Article 20(3), contains a provision that states that the judiciary shall be bound by law and justice. This provision has had an impact on the approach to interpretation of the law by German courts.[62] Finally, it is well known that the BVerfG, primarily in its *Solange I and II, Maastricht* and *Lisbon* judgments, establishing the fundamental rights, competence, and constitutional identity locks respectively, formulated its own vision as regards the relationship between EU and national law that has had a lasting impact, even

---

61 Claes (n. 11), p. 14.

62 Questions of interpretation are constitutional questions, B. Rüthers, 'Methodenrealismus in Jurisprudenz und Justiz' (2006/2) *JZ*, p. 56, 60.

beyond Germany.[63] It is often assumed that there is a distinction in the approach to statutory interpretation between Member States' courts belonging to common law and civil law systems.[64] Simply put, the former are strictly bound by the wording of the concerned provision whereas the latter adopt a more teleological approach. Although this may be an oversimplification,[65] it would be interesting to see if the application of the duty of consistent interpretation is different in a common law Member State. The UK is traditionally the usual suspect for this purpose, but I feared that a discussion on the English courts' approach may not be sufficiently future-proof in light of Brexit.

> To be sure, consistent interpretation will not disappear with Brexit.[66] In order to prevent a large number of legal gaps on and after exit day, the European Union (Withdrawal) Act 2018 makes provision for retaining UK legislation that derives from EU law. And through section 5(2) of the same Act a duty of consistent interpretation is maintained, requiring EU-derived UK legislation, *and even all other pre-exit legislation*, to be interpreted in conformity with applicable directives. It also provides that the principle of supremacy of EU law continues to apply for this purpose. This, of course, creates an oddity as such is no longer required by EU law itself, the exact consequences of which are difficult to predict at this point. But even if there may be reasons to believe that this will not lead to larger or smaller divergences in approach, the self-imposed duty of consistent interpretation will become less and less relevant in practice as it does not apply to legislation adopted after Brexit and modifications made to pre-existing legislation.

I therefore choose Ireland instead. In addition to Ireland belonging to the family of common law systems, it should also be mentioned that the Irish constitution contains a provision recognising, yet seemingly also authorising, the supremacy of

---

63 BVerfG 29 May 1974 *Solange I*, BVerfGE 37, 271; BVerfG 22 October 1986 *Solange II*, BVerfGE 73, 339; BVerfG 12 October 1993 *Maastricht*, BVerfGE 89, 155; BVerfG 30 June 2009 *Lisbon*, BVerfGE 123, 267. For comments on the *Solange II* judgment see J.A. Frowein, 'Solange II (BVerfGE 73, 339). Constitutional complaint Firma W.' (1988/1) *CMLRev*. See U. Everling, 'The *Maastricht* Judgment of the German Federal Constitutional Court and its Significance for the Development of the European Union' (1994/1) *YEL*; M. Herdegen, 'Maastricht and the German Constitutional Court: Constitutional Restraints for an "Ever Closer Union"' (1994/2) *CMLRev*; N. MacCormick, 'The Maastricht-Urteil: Sovereignty Now' (1995/3) *ELJ*; J.H.H. Weiler, 'Does Europe Need a Constitution? Reflections on Demos, Telos and the German *Maastricht* Decision' (1995/3) *ELJ* for the *Maastricht* judgment. And, finally, see D. Halberstam and C. Möllers, 'The German Constitutional Court says "*Ja zu Deutschland!*"' (2009/8) *German Law Journal*; D. Thym, 'In the Name of Sovereign Statehood: A Critical Introduction to the *Lisbon* Judgment of the German Constitutional Court' (2009/6) *CMLRev* for the *Lisbon* judgment.

64 See, for example, R.C. Van Caenegem, *Judges, Legislators and Professors* (Cambridge University Press 1987), p. 17; B. Grossfeld and K. Bilda, 'Europäische Rechtsangleichung' (1992) *Zeitschrift für Europarecht, Internationales Privatrecht und Rechtsvergleichung*, p. 429.

65 Cf. S. Vogenauer, *Die Auslegung von Gesetzen in England und auf dem Kontinent* (Mohr Siebeck 2001), p. 1300, who argues that the approach in the UK and in continental Europe is largely identical.

66 The discussion on the legal situation pertaining post-Brexit is based on the analysis provided in M. Brenncke, *Judicial Law-Making in English and German Courts* (Intersentia 2018), p. 396-421.

EU law, and that the Interpretation Act 2005 gives specific instructions to the Irish courts for the approach to interpretation. Finally, the Netherlands was a logical choice as this is the legal system from which the author originates and which he therefore knows best. Also, the Dutch constitutional system has a rather open, monistic, attitude towards international law, and in particular towards EU law.

Secondly, the research looks at all legal areas except criminal and social security law and, thirdly, only the case law of the Member States' superior courts is examined. It is primarily because of the impossibility to look at all the legal areas and all national courts within the framework of a PhD thesis, that these limitations were necessary. Also, criminal law is considered to be of a considerably different nature compared to the other legal areas when it comes to the approach to statutory interpretation. In the area of social security law there was simply a shortage of case law in Germany and the Netherlands, with no cases in this area in Ireland, so that it was decided to leave it out entirely.

For Germany, the above entails that I look at the Federal Court of Justice (BGH), Federal Labour Court (BAG), Federal Administrative Court (BVerwG) and the Federal Fiscal Court (BFH), and that the Federal Social Court (BSG) as well as the BGH case law in the area of criminal law are not included. In principle, the BGH has – in addition to criminal law disputes – jurisdiction over civil law disputes, but it should be noted that it has a wide jurisdiction, covering all matters that fall outside the remit of the specialised courts. The BAG was set up to deal with the specific category of labour law cases. The BVerwG has jurisdiction over public law disputes, with the exception of purely constitutional matters (they can consider constitutional elements in a dispute, unless the constitutional validity of legislation is challenged[67]), social security law and tax law. The latter is dealt with by the BFH and comprises disputes regarding tax, revenue, succession and customs law. With a few exceptions, these courts decide upon appeals on points of law against judgments of the lower ranking courts. There is one further federal superior court, which occupies a kind of special position: the BVerfG. The BVerfG acts as the guardian of the German Constitution, it is the ultimate authority for its interpretation, and it can review whether ordinary legislation, but also individual decisions and judgments, are compatible with it.[68] However, the BVerfG does not deal with the application and interpretation of ordinary legislation as such. Finally, it should be noted that the BVerfG also has jurisdiction over inter-institutional, electoral and international law disputes, as well as matters concerning the authority and competences of the various constitutional institutions and political parties. The BVerfG's case law is included in the research, but it must be noted that it has only addressed the duty of consistent interpretation in a limited number of cases.

67 N. Foster and S. Sule, *German Legal System and Laws* (OUP 2010), p. 87.
68 See section 13 of the Act on the Federal Constitutional Court for a catalogue of its jurisdiction.

This is probably because most cases do not reach the BVerfG, of which an even smaller portion raises questions regarding the duty of consistent interpretation. In addition to this, it must be made clear that the BVerfG has not so far applied the duty of consistent interpretation itself (i.e. in the sense of interpreting the German Constitution in conformity with a directive) but has only examined whether the approach to interpretation adopted by other courts is compatible with the German Constitution, in which regard a high threshold is applied, namely whether the approach is not unsustainable, that it is not arbitrary.[69]

For Ireland, the case law of the High Court, Court of Appeal and the Supreme Court is included. The High Court has full original jurisdiction in criminal and civil matters. The High Court's jurisdiction also includes constitutional matters. An appeal on a point of law can be made from the High Court to the Court of Appeal (which was only established in 2014) and subsequently to the Supreme Court. 'Full' jurisdiction means that no restrictions are placed on the type of cases that can be brought before the High Court (and consequently the stated appellate courts). But note that, on account of their subject matter or monetary value, original jurisdiction for certain cases may be assigned to the lower ranking district and circuit courts, which only have local and limited jurisdiction (i.e. the jurisdiction is regional and only exists in as far as it was explicitly assigned to them by legislation). These courts are not included, as well as adjudicative bodies that do not exercise judicial power in the sense of the Irish Constitution.[70]

While precedent is of significance for both civil and common law systems, it has greater significance for the latter, which adhere to the principle of *stare decisis*. In short, this means that judges must decide a case on the basis of prior decisions. However, not all parts of a judgment necessarily have the same significance. A distinction is made between the *ratio decidendi* and *obiter dicta*. The former is defined by Byrne and others as '(…) being the reason for the decision; it consists of the principle of law applied to the facts of the case,' and the latter is defined as '[o]ther statements of law which are contained in the case (…)'.[71] While the former have binding authority for subsequent decisions, the latter only have persuasive authority.[72]

69 BVerfG 26 September 2011, BVerfGK 19, 89, para. 43.

70 An Bord Pleanála, the Irish planning appeals board but also – perhaps more surprisingly if only its name is considered – the Labour Court, fall within this category. Such bodies are comprised of specialists in a particular field and given the task of dispute settlement in that area. Their decisions are in principle subject to judicial review (which is a kind of supervision of inferior courts or bodies, aimed at ensuring that their decisions are reached in an appropriate manner and are in accordance with the law), and exceptionally subject to an appeal on a point of law (which concerns the issue central to a decision).

71 Byrne and others, *Byrne and McCutcheon on the Irish Legal System* (Bloomsbury 2014), p. 478.

72 Ibid, p. 476-8.

For the Netherlands, the Supreme Court (HR), the Administrative Jurisdiction Division of the Council of State (ABRvS), and the Trade and Industry Appeals Tribunal (CBb) are discussed. The HR carries out review in cassation of judgments by the lower ranking courts in civil, criminal and tax disputes – it is, again, pointed out that I only look at the former and the latter. Review in cassation connotes a review in last instance on points of law only (infringements of procedural rules or the law, see Article 79 of the Judiciary Organisation Act). The HR must accept the facts as they were determined by the court whose judgment is under review. The ABRvS is the highest appeal court having general jurisdiction in administrative law disputes.[73] Unless one of the two specialised administrative law appeal courts has jurisdiction, the ABRvS is the competent court. One of these specialised courts is the CBb, entertaining jurisdiction in socioeconomic administrative law. The other specialised court, the Central Appeals Tribunal is not included in the research as it is primarily concerned with social security law, which is not included in the scope of the research. Unlike the review in cassation before the HR, appeals before the ABRvS and CBb are devolutive (i.e. there is a complete rehearing of the case). Although this may already be deduced from the above, it is emphasised that judgments delivered by the ABRvS and CBb are not open to review in cassation.

Although the book does every now and then look at judgments from lower national courts in order to clarify the corresponding superior court's judgment on appeal, I regret that this could not be done more often. It was mentioned above that a more realistic picture of EU law adjudication is obtained if one does not only look at the ECJ but also at the national courts. The same applies, I think, in the relationship between a Member State's superior court and the lower courts. At the same time, the superior courts' judgments provide the most guidance within a national legal order so that, if limitations are necessary, their judgments are the most important to examine for understanding the national application of the duty of consistent interpretation.

3.2. HOW DOES THE REST OF THIS BOOK PROCEED?

The next chapter discusses the ECJ's case law on the duty of consistent interpretation. This provides a framework for the three separate chapters analysing the case law of the superior courts in Germany, Ireland and the Netherlands. As will be seen, although there are a lot of similarities between the Member States, there are also a number of important differences. This, together with the fact that the national case law must often be viewed in the context of the characteristics of a Member

---

73 For the sake of completeness, it is pointed out that the ABRvS sometimes also acts as a court of first, and final, instance (particularly in cases concerning educational and environmental law). The same applies for the CBb.

State's legal system, makes a separate discussion more appropriate. However, the separation is only temporary, because the different analyses will be put together in the conclusion, which also contains my answer to the question what the relationship is between EU and national law under the duty of consistent interpretation and how this reflects on our understanding of theories on the relationship between EU and national law.

CHAPTER 2

THE EUROPEAN COURT OF JUSTICE'S COMPOSITION OF A FRAMEWORK FOR THE DUTY OF CONSISTENT INTERPRETATION

1. INTRODUCTION

There is the well known technique whereby lower ranking norms are interpreted in conformity with hierarchically superior norms. This does not usually raise questions if it is applied within a single legal order. An example is the requirement to adopt an interpretation that is in conformity with the Constitution if a lower-ranking provision allows more than one interpretation.[1]

Another example is the requirement to interpret EU secondary law, wherever possible, in conformity with the Treaties.[2] However, as will be further discussed in paragraph 2.3, it must be asked whether the duty of consistent interpretation, as established in the *Von Colson and Kamann* judgment and further developed in subsequent judgments,[3] is similarly based on the *rationale* that there is a *substantive norm* that is recognised as being *superior* in a legal order. In any event, it is clear that the duty to interpret national law in conformity with directives is different from the above two examples as both the EU and national legal order are involved. Yet, it is not unique in this sense, as there are already other obligations aimed at preventing a conflict between two legal orders. In international law, for example, it is a common technique to prevent a conflict with obligations agreed to by contracting parties under international treaties.[4] Also, EU law must itself be interpreted in conformity with the international obligations of the EU.[5] However, the latter two examples (and perhaps even all, or some, of the interpretative obligations within a national legal order) as well as the interpretative obligations

1 The prime example of this is the *verfassungskonforme Auslegung* in Germany.

2 Joined Cases C-201/85 and C-202/85 *Klensch*, ECLI:EU:C:1986:439, para. 21; Case C-12/00 *Commission v Spain*, ECLI:EU:C:2003:21, para. 97.

3 Case 14/83 *Von Colson and Kamann*, ECLI:EU:C:1984:153.

4 See, further, A. Nollkaemper, *National Courts and the International Rule of Law* (OUP 2011), p. 140 *et seq.*

5 Case C-53/96 *Hermès*, ECLI:EU:C:1998:292, para. 28; Case C-284/95 *Safety Hi-Tech*, ECLI:EU:C:1998:352, para. 22.

within a single legal order), seem to be less demanding than the duty of consistent interpretation that is discussed in this chapter.[6]

This chapter's analysis is divided into five parts, looking, first, at the legal basis for the duty of consistent interpretation, secondly, its temporal scope, thirdly, what *so far as possible* requires the national courts to do, fourthly, what it does not require them to do (i.e. the limits to the duty of consistent interpretation), and fifthly, the role played by consistent interpretation for the requirement of adequate implementation of directives.

2. THE LEGAL BASIS FOR THE DUTY OF CONSISTENT INTERPRETATION

The *Von Colson and Kamann* judgment referred to Articles 288 TFEU (ex Article 249 EC Treaty and Article 189 EEC Treaty) and 4(3) TEU (ex Article 10 EC Treaty and Article 5 EEC Treaty) as the legal basis for the duty of consistent interpretation. It first appeared from the *Pfeiffer* judgment that the duty of consistent interpretation is regarded by the ECJ as being inherent in the system of the TFEU as it ensures the full effectiveness of EU law. At the end of this paragraph, it is examined to what extent the supremacy of directives can be seen as the legal basis for the duty of consistent interpretation.

2.1. ARTICLES 288 TFEU AND 4(3) TEU

The *Von Colson and Kamann* judgment provided that:

> '(…) the Member States' obligation arising from a directive to achieve the result envisaged by the directive and their duty under Article 5 of the Treaty to take all appropriate measures, whether general or particular, to ensure the fulfilment of that obligation, is binding on all the authorities of Member States including, for matters within their jurisdiction, the courts. It follows that, in applying the national law and in particular the provisions of a national law specifically introduced in order to implement Directive No 76/207, national

6 For example, it will be seen, in particular in paragraph 2.4, that, in order to enhance the effectiveness of directives, the duty of consistent interpretation can be quite demanding, requiring national courts to stretch the scope of national provisions and sometimes interfering with national rules of interpretation. By contrast, the *verfassungskonforme Auslegung* only requires courts to choose an interpretation that is in conformity with the Constitution if the lower-ranking provision allows more than one interpretation. Another example: UK Supreme Court 30 May 2012 *Assange v Sweden* [2012] 2 AC 471 (Lord Mance), para. 203, after having emphasised the far-reaching requirements imposed by the duty of consistent interpretation in EU law, added that '[i]n this light, considerable significance may attach to whether the European legal duty of conforming interpretation applies or whether the case is subject only to the common law presumption that Parliament intends to give effect to the United Kingdom's international obligations'.

> courts are required to interpret their national law in the light of the wording and the purpose of the directive in order to achieve the result referred to in the third paragraph of Article 189'.[7]

Similar considerations can be found in numerous subsequent judgments.[8] According to these judgments, Articles 288 TFEU and 4(3) TEU, both binding on the Member States, provide the legal basis for the duty of consistent interpretation. The former contains the obligation to implement directives and the latter provides for the principle of sincere cooperation. The dominant view is that the duty of consistent interpretation contributes to the fulfilment of the Member States' obligation to correctly implement directives into national law, and can thus be described as 'an extension of the implementation obligation'.[9] In that regard it appears logical to give Article 288 TFEU a dominant role for the establishment of the duty of consistent interpretation.

What is then the role played by Article 4(3) TEU? This is a multifaceted provision of EU law and that characteristic is confirmed in the context of the duty of consistent interpretation. It has been described as being merely auxiliary in relation to the duty of consistent interpretation since the implementation obligation provided by Article 288 TFEU can be seen as a specific expression of the general obligation stipulated in Article 4(3) TEU that '[t]he Member States shall take any appropriate measure, general or particular, to ensure fulfilment of the obligations arising out of the Treaties or resulting from the acts of the institutions of the Union'.[10] This is correct, but in my opinion the provision has a more meaningful role for the duty of consistent interpretation. Klamert formulates that role as contributing the 'conflictive side' to the duty of consistent interpretation.[11]

> I should first explain the context in which Klamert discusses Article 4(3) TEU and supremacy. He argues that, for the duty of consistent interpretation, the relevant context is not a conflict of norms in the sense that EU and national law apply to the same facts but provide a different solution (e.g. where the directive provides that a contract is void and national law does not). Instead he believes that supremacy manifests itself by means of the less intrusive requirement to disapply national rules of interpretation in order to attain the objective of the directive. This interventionist aspect is in Klamert's view appropriately based on the principle of sincere cooperation stipulated in Article 4(3) TEU. It is in

7 Ibid, para. 26.

8 For example Case C-106/89 *Marleasing*, ECLI:EU:C:1990:395, para. 8; Case C-91/92 *Faccini Dori*, ECLI:EU:C:1994:292, para. 26; Case C-212/04 *Adeneler*, ECLI:EU:C:2006:443, para. 113.

9 C.-W. Canaris, '*Die richtlinienkonforme Auslegung und Rechtsfortbildung im System der juristischen Methodenlehre*', in: H. Koziol and P. Rummel (Eds.), *Im Dienste der Gerechtigkeit* (Springer Verlag 2002), p. 56; M. Klamert, 'Judicial Implementation of Directives and Anticipatory Indirect Effect' (2006/5) *CMLRev*, p. 1261. See also W. Brechmann, *Die richtlinienkonforme Auslegung* (C.H. Beck'sche Verlagsbuchhandlung 1994), p. 256-7.

10 Brechmann (n. 9), p. 257-8.

11 M. Klamert, *The Principle of Loyalty in EU Law* (OUP 2014), p. 78.

> that regard important to note that Klamert believes that that provision was the main foundation for the establishment of supremacy in *Costa v ENEL* where the ECJ considered that '[t]he executive force of Community law cannot vary from one State to another in deference to subsequent domestic laws, without jeopardizing the attainment of the objectives of the Treaty set out in Article 5(2) [now Article 4(3) TEU; SWH] and giving rise to the discrimination prohibited by Article 7'.[12] Notwithstanding the above, Klamert does not consider Article 4(3) TEU as the primary legal basis for the duty of consistent interpretation – but instead accords this role to Article 288 TFEU.[13]

It is thus clear that, effectively, the more important role ascribed by Klamert to Article 4(3) TEU, whereby it is seen as a more appropriate basis for the 'interventionist aspect' of the duty of consistent interpretation, derives from the further proposition that that provision is the main foundation for supremacy itself. This is based on the role that this provision played in the *Costa v ENEL* judgment. Actually, a number of authors have already confirmed the supremacy of the obligation to implement the directive into national law laid down in Article 288 TFEU and, as a corollary of this, confer supremacy on the duty of consistent interpretation.[14] This does not seem to be controversial. But the more difficult question is what the *source* of this supremacy is. It could be argued that supremacy is inherent to Article 288 TFEU, simply because it is a binding provision of EU law. However, it seems that Klamert deems it more appropriate to rely on the written provision of Article 4(3) TEU. If this is correct, the ECJ's reference to Article 4(3) TEU would be more than merely auxiliary and provides a justification for a potential interference by the duty of consistent interpretation with the interpretation of national law.

As the ECJ has not elaborated the exact division of labour between Articles 288 TFEU and 4(3) TEU for the establishment of the duty of consistent interpretation,[15] it is difficult to be absolutely certain about the role played by the latter provision. Be that as it may, I am inclined to agree with Klamert that the more 'interventionist aspects' of the duty of consistent interpretation are more appropriately based on Article 4(3) TEU, instead of Article 288 TFEU itself (which merely states the implementation obligation and does not determine the hierarchy between EU and national law).

---

12 Case 6/64 *Costa v ENEL*, ECLI:EU:C:1964:66.

13 Klamert (n. 11), p. 77-8.

14 See, for example, Canaris (n. 9), p. 69; M. Brenncke, 'Europäisierung der Methodik richtlinienkonformer Rechtsfindung' (2015/4) *EuR*, p. 452.

15 Klamert (n. 9), p. 1253.

2.2. THE FULL EFFECTIVENESS OF EU LAW

While De Witte does not address the question what the legal basis for the duty of consistent interpretation might be, he does say something about the origins of supremacy. It was seen in the previous subparagraph that this is not entirely unimportant for the legal basis for the duty of consistent interpretation as it might tell something about the role played by Article 4(3) TEU. Although sceptical about the ECJ's reasoning in *Costa v ENEL,* he nevertheless provides that effectiveness might have been the most convincing argument.[16] Interestingly, the *Pfeiffer* judgment added the further point of guidance regarding the legal basis for the duty of consistent interpretation:

> '[t]he requirement for national law to be interpreted in conformity with Community law is inherent in the system of the Treaty, since it permits the national court, for the matters within its jurisdiction, to ensure the full effectiveness of Community law when it determines the dispute before it'.[17]

What is meant with the reference to effectiveness? It should be emphasised that the *Pfeiffer* judgment did not refer to effectiveness in the sense of the *Rewe* judgment.[18] Instead the reference to effectiveness in the *Pfeiffer* judgment is arguably a reference to the idea that the authorities of Member States are required to ensure 'the effective protection of Community rights and, more generally, the effective enforcement of Community law in national courts'.[19] Indeed, the *Pfeiffer* judgment stipulated that:

> '[i]t is the responsibility of the national courts in particular to provide the legal protection which individuals derive from the rules of Community law and to ensure that those rules are fully effective'.[20]

At this juncture, it must be pointed out that there is a certain degree of overlap between the requirement of effectiveness of EU law and Article 4(3) TEU. The latter requires Member States to '(...) take any appropriate measure, general or particular, to ensure fulfilment of the obligations arising out of the Treaties or resulting from the acts of the institutions of the Union'. This clearly resembles the description of effectiveness just mentioned. In fact, there is broad support for

---

16 B. De Witte, 'Direct Effect, Primacy, and the Nature of the Legal Order', in: G. De Búrca and P.P. Craig (Eds.), *The Evolution of EU Law* (OUP 2011), p. 329.

17 Joined Cases C-397/01 to C-403/01 *Pfeiffer*, ECLI:EU:C:2004:584, para. 114.

18 The *Rewe* judgment provided that national procedural rules that render the exercise of individuals' rights under EU law practically impossible or excessively difficult are prohibited, see Case 33/76 *Rewe*, ECLI:EU:C:1976:188, para. 5. See also Case 45/76 *Comet*, ECLI:EU:C:1976:191, paras. 13-6; Case C-312/93 *Peterbroeck*, ECLI:EU:C:1995:437, para. 12; Case C-432/05 *Unibet*, ECLI:EU:C:2007:163, para. 43; Joined Cases C-222/05 to C-225/05 *Van der Weerd and Others*, ECLI:EU:C:2007:318, para. 28.

19 T. Tridimas 2006, *The General Principles of EU Law* (OUP 2006), p. 418.

20 Joined Cases C-397/01 to C-403/01 *Pfeiffer*, ECLI:EU:C:2004:584, para. 111.

the view that the principle of effectiveness of EU law is derived from Article 4(3) TEU.[21] In the *Brasserie du Pêcheur* judgment, the description of the legal basis for State liability put together the principle of effectiveness, the effective protection of rights and Article 4(3) TEU.[22]

On the basis of the above, my conclusion is that when the principle of effectiveness and Article 4(3) TEU are invoked in the specific context of the duty of consistent interpretation, they largely perform the same function. This also means that, if effectiveness is viewed as the basis for supremacy in the *Costa v ENEL* judgment, this does not undermine, but rather confirms, Klamert's suggestion regarding the role played by Article 4(3) TEU in the context of the duty of consistent interpretation.

It may nevertheless be asked why it was necessary to include a reference to effectiveness in the *Pfeiffer* judgment if it largely performs the same function as Article 4(3) TEU. The answer is twofold. First, Drake put forward that the reliance on the principle of effectiveness 'bolstered' the legal basis for the duty of consistent interpretation, '(…) and signifies the Court's commitment to the principle of indirect effect as a characteristic of the principle of effective judicial protection (…)'.[23] Secondly, reference to effectiveness enabled a broadening of the scope of the duty of consistent interpretation so that it could also be applied to Third Pillar framework decisions. This actually materialised in the *Pupino* judgment.[24]

> It is recalled that the predecessor of Article 4(3) TEU was Article 10 of the EC Treaty. That provision did not apply to framework decisions. The ECJ considered it necessary to transplant the duty of sincere cooperation from the EC Treaty to the Third Pillar to enable the extension of the duty of consistent interpretation to framework decisions. This was possible by relying on the principle of effectiveness, which has a broader scope as it applies to every part of EU law.[25] On account of its similarities to what is now Article 4(3) TEU, effectiveness was an obvious candidate for transplanting the principle of sincere cooperation, and, as a consequence, the duty of consistent interpretation, to the Third Pillar.

---

21 J. Temple Lang, 'The Development by the Court of Justice of the Duties of Cooperation of National Authorities and Community Institutions under Article 10 EC' (2007/5) *Fordham International Law Journal*, p. 1489; Klamert (n. 11), p. 138, 271. See also R. Caranta, 'Judicial Protection against Member States: A New *Jus Commune* Takes Shape' (1995/3) *CMLRev*, p. 704, where it is provided that the requirement of effective judicial protection is derived from Article 4(3) TEU.

22 Joined Cases C-46/93 and C-48/93 *Brasserie du Pêcheur*, ECLI:EU:C:1996:79, para. 39. Similarly, the seminal judgment in *Francovich* mentioned effectiveness together with the necessity that individuals must be able to enforce their EU law rights before the national courts, Joined Cases C-6/90 and C-9/90 *Francovich*, ECLI:EU:C:1991:428, para. 34.

23 S. Drake, 'Twenty Years after *Von Colson*: The Impact of "Indirect Effect" on the Protection of the Individual's Community Rights' (2005/3) *ELRev*, p. 334.

24 Case C-105/03 *Pupino*, ECLI:EU:C:2005:386.

25 See also Caranta (n. 21), p. 704.

2.3. SUPREMACY OF DIRECTIVES AS THE LEGAL BASIS UNDER THE HIERARCHICAL MODEL

In chapter 1, subparagraph 1.3.1, one of the approaches to supremacy of EU law was described as the hierarchical model, which views the EU and national legal orders as part of a single legal order wherein all EU law (including directives) is superior. An interesting feature of this model is that it views the duty of consistent interpretation as a self-evident corollary of the supreme nature of directives. The inquiry is therefore slightly different from the previous one: the validity of the position that the duty of consistent interpretation can be based on the supremacy of directives, hinges on the assumption that directives actually enjoy supremacy. Although the above discussion also touched upon the question of supremacy (which was viewed as primarily deriving from Article 4(3) TEU), the answer to that question would not make or break the validity of the position that the duty of consistent interpretation is based on Articles 288 TFEU and 4(3) TEU, with the inclusion of effectiveness.

The applicability and rank of EU law in the national legal orders are inextricably bound up with each other under the hierarchical model. While under the hierarchical model the applicability and rank (i.e. supremacy) of EU law are considered inherent facets of the autonomous and integrated nature of the EU legal order, and can both be premised on this characteristic, I already put forward that applicability and rank of EU law should not necessarily be viewed as coinciding.[26] The first step is then obviously that EU law must apply in the national legal orders and only then is it appropriate to consider its rank. However, the applicability and rank of directives in national law is still, after all these years, a controversial topic in EU law and the debate on this point seems to remain unresolved.[27] Assuming that this question can be solved in the first place, it is not within the scope of this research to do so since this requires a broader perspective than the duty of consistent interpretation with regard to the position of directives in the national legal orders. Admittedly, as far as concerns the *applicability* of directives in the national legal orders, the EU law perspective is relatively unambiguous:

> First, the EU legal order is autonomous and at the same time integrated into the legal orders of the Member States and national courts are bound to apply EU law. This point was first made in a context that was primarily concerned with the interpretation of the Treaties[28] but, importantly, was repeated in the *Francovich*

26 M.H. Wissink, *Richtlijnconforme interpretatie van burgerlijk recht* (Kluwer 2001), p. 122-3; S. Prechal, *Directives in EC Law* (OUP 2005), p. 94.
27 On this issue, see M. Dougan, 'When Worlds Collide! Competing Visions of the Relationship between Direct Effect and Supremacy' (2007/4) *CMLRev.* See also J. Dickson, 'Directives in EU Legal Systems: Whose Norms Are They Anyway?' (2011/2) *ELJ.* For an earlier contribution, see Brechmann (n. 9), p. 191-4, 247-9, 251-2, 255-6.
28 Case 14/68 *Walt Wilhelm*, ECLI:EU:C:1969:4.

judgment, which was concerned with the interpretation of a directive and immediately preceded the considerations mentioning the indispensability of an alternative remedy (in that case State liability) for directives that have not been implemented and do not have direct effect.[29] The fact that the autonomous nature of the EU legal order and the integration into the national legal orders was mentioned in the *Francovich* judgment clearly implies that these characteristics are also regarded as being applicable in the context of directives. Secondly, and related to the first point, the *Inter-Environnement Wallonie* judgment clarified '(...) that a directive has legal effect with respect to the Member State to which it is addressed from the moment of its notification'.[30] See also, more generally, the *Becker* judgment, which also stresses the binding nature of directives.[31] Taking these two points into consideration, it is difficult to deny that, even though they depend on implementation by the national legislature to acquire their full effect, directives produce a certain legal effect in national law.

However, even if it is accepted that directives are applicable (again, I believe that a less tentative answer to that question requires a more comprehensive analysis), in any event, confirmation of the hierarchical model's view on the legal basis still hinges on a finding that directives take the position of a supreme self-standing norm in the national legal orders. It is clear that they can have this effect – admittedly, such is the case where they have direct effect. But if the supremacy of directives is to be a comprehensive legal basis, it must also apply to the duty of consistent interpretation where the provisions of the concerned directive do not have direct effect. I am not aware of any ECJ case law which explicitly confirms the overall supremacy of directives. This part of the hierarchical model's claim therefore seems shaky from an empirical point of view.[32]

29 Joined Cases C-6/90 and C-9/90 *Francovich*, ECLI:EU:C:1991:428, paras. 31, 34.

30 Case C-129/96 *Inter-Environnement Wallonie*, ECLI:EU:C:1997:628, para. 41.

31 Case 8/81 *Becker*, ECLI:EU:C:1982:7, para. 22.

32 See, however, the Opinion of AG Van Gerven in Case C-106/89 *Marleasing*, ECLI:EU:C:1990:310, para. 9. See also K. Lenaerts and T. Corthaut, 'Of Birds and Hedges: The Role of Primacy in Invoking Norms of EU Law' (2006/3) *ELRev*, p. 293. To some extent, the view whereby consistent interpretation is based on the supremacy of directives, is similar to the one adopted by primarily German legal scholars, who draw an analogy between the duty of consistent interpretation and *verfassungskonforme Auslegung* in German law, which requires the adoption of an interpretation that is in conformity with the German Constitution if a lower-ranking provision allows more than one interpretation, M. Weber, *Grenzen EU-rechtskonformer Auslegung und Rechtsfortbildung* (Nomos 2010), p. 90. See also M. Claes, *The National Courts' Mandate in the European Constitution* (Hart Publishing 2006), p. 116, who shares the view that supremacy can be invoked as the legal basis for the duty of consistent interpretation. Although she does not link this explicitly to the nature of directives in national law, it appears that she also subscribes to a hierarchical vision on supremacy (p. 115).

2.4. CONCLUSION: ARTICLES 288 TFEU AND 4(3) TEU (WITH THE INCLUSION OF THE PRINCIPLE OF EFFECTIVENESS)

I conclude that the legal basis for the duty of consistent interpretation is best viewed as being provided by Articles 288 TFEU and 4(3) TEU (with the inclusion of the principle of effectiveness). This view ties in with consistent ECJ case law referring to those provisions and conceptualises the duty of consistent interpretation as an extension of the implementing obligation. The alternative legal basis provided under the hierarchical model of supremacy, which conceptualises the duty of consistent interpretation as a corollary of the superiority of directives over national law, was argued to be less attractive. While the applicability of directives in the national legal order may still be a point of debate, but seems to correspond to the ECJ's view, this legal basis hinges in particular on the assumption that directives are in general to be treated as the hierarchically superior norm in the national legal orders. However, if I am correct, there is currently no explicit authority supporting such a view.

The fact that the duty of consistent interpretation cannot be based on the supremacy of directives, does not mean that supremacy cannot be an adequate theory for understanding the relationship between EU and national law under the duty of consistent interpretation – just as national constitutionalism and constitutional pluralism do not become irrelevant as they are not the legal basis for the duty of consistent interpretation. It was seen that the inclusion of Article 4(3) TEU (and in line with this the principle of effectiveness) in the legal basis for the duty of consistent interpretation indicate that it may interfere with national law and is in principle capable of making an appeal to supremacy in this regard.

3. THE TEMPORAL SCOPE OF THE DUTY OF CONSISTENT INTERPRETATION

The *Adeneler* judgment made clear that the duty of consistent interpretation does not apply before the directive's transposition period has expired. In support of this conclusion the ECJ provided, in the first place, that the duty of consistent interpretation '(...) has been imposed in particular where a provision of a directive lacks direct effect (...)',[33] apparently referring to the restriction that directives can

33 It could be asked whether this position is in line with the position adopted in the *Dominguez* judgment, where it was held that '(...) the question whether a national provision must be disapplied in as much as it conflicts with European Union law arises only if no compatible interpretation of that provision proves possible', Case C-282/10 *Dominguez*, ECLI:EU:C:2012:33, para. 23. The two positions could be made compatible if the relevant sentence from the *Adeneler* judgment is interpreted as merely saying that the duty of consistent interpretation is primarily of added value if direct effect is not available.

only have direct effect once the transposition period has expired, which must then also apply to the duty of consistent interpretation, and, secondly, that Member States cannot be reproached for not having adopted implementing measures before the transposition period has expired.[34] However, relying on Articles 288 TFEU and 4(3) TEU and the national court's obligation to ensure the full effect of EU law, the ECJ added that:

> '(…) from the date upon which a directive has entered into force, the courts of the Member States must refrain as far as possible from interpreting domestic law in a manner which might seriously compromise, after the period for transposition has expired, attainment of the objective pursued by that directive'.[35]

The ECJ thereby extended the obligation to refrain established in the *Inter-Environnement Wallonie* judgment beyond the specific facts of that case, which related to the adoption of legislative provisions that could seriously compromise the result prescribed by the directive.

> The *Inter-Environnement Wallonie* judgment concerned the question whether EU law prohibited the adoption of legislative measures during the transposition period that are incompatible with the directive. It was provided that Member States cannot be faulted for not having adopted the necessary measures before expiry of the transposition period. However, in addition to this positive obligation, it stated a negative obligation, based on Articles 288 TFEU and 4(3) TEU, to refrain from taking any measures during the transposition period that could seriously compromise the result prescribed by the directive.[36]

The obligation to refrain is distinct from the duty of consistent interpretation that applies after expiry of the transposition period.[37] It aims to prevent an interpretation adopted by a national court that would seriously compromise, after expiry of the transposition period, the result prescribed by the directive. It is difficult to imagine a situation in which this would occur and the practical use of the rule adopted in the *Adeneler* judgment has therefore been questioned.[38] A consistent interpretation neither relieves nor prevents the adoption of legislative measures required to transpose the directive (see also paragraph 6).

---

34 Case C-212/04 *Adeneler*, ECLI:EU:C:2006:443, paras. 113-5.

35 Ibid, paras. 122-3.

36 Case C-129/96 *Inter-Environnement Wallonie*, ECLI:EU:C:1997:628, paras. 43, 45.

37 M. Franzen, 'EuGH, 4. 7. 2006 – Rs. C-212/04 Adeneler u.a../. ELOG. Zum Beginn der Pflicht zu richtlinienkonformer Auslegung durch innerstaatliche Gerichte bei verspäteter Richtlinienumsetzung' (2007/4) *JZ*, p. 192; W.-H. Roth and C. Jopen, '*Die richtlinienkonforme Auslegung*', in: K. Riesenhuber (Ed.), *Europäische Methodenlehre* (De Gruyter 2015), p. 269.

38 M.H. Wissink, 'Interpretation of Private Law in Conformity with EU Directives', in: A.S. Hartkamp and others (Eds.), *The Influence of EU Law on National Private Law* (Kluwer 2014), p. 128; Roth and Jopen (n. 37), p. 269.

The ECJ's *Adeneler* judgment did not follow the Opinion of Advocate General Kokott, who argued that the obligation as to the result to be achieved exists once directives have entered into force. From that moment, national courts would be required to contribute to the implementation of directives by interpreting national law in conformity with directives.[39]

In my opinion, the necessity to ensure the implementation of directives (Articles 288 TFEU and 4(3) TEU) and the principle of effectiveness clearly surfaced in the *Adeneler* judgment. The judgment clarified that the task to correctly implement directives and secure their effectiveness primarily becomes an issue if the transposition period has expired. Before that time, directives only produce certain legal effects in national law by precluding actions that could imperil the implementing objective and the directive's effectiveness. For the existence of this obligation the ECJ relied on primary EU law. It also confirmed that not only legislatures, but also national courts, have their own role to play for the implementation of directives.

4. WHAT DOES 'SO FAR AS POSSIBLE' REQUIRE THE NATIONAL COURTS TO DO?

The title of this paragraph refers to what is the most important and difficult question with regard to consistent interpretation. The case law discussed in this paragraph is likely to convey something about the kind of relationship between EU and national law that is envisaged under the duty of consistent interpretation from the perspective of the case law of the ECJ. Unfortunately, so far as possible is not a particularly enlightening expression. This has given rise to various interpretations as to what so far as possible requires. Some argued that it requires that supremacy is conferred on the duty of consistent interpretation:

> According to Lutter a consistent interpretation has supremacy over national rules of interpretation. The main argument in support of this conclusion is that national courts must comply with the principle of sincere cooperation which in turn implies supremacy which also governs the application of the duty of consistent interpretation.[40]
>
> A kind of absolute supremacy of the duty of consistent interpretation has often been based on the *Marleasing* judgment. There, the ECJ omitted the reference to the discretion provided under national law and furthermore reformulated the duty of consistent interpretation for the first time as requiring that national

39 Opinion of AG Kokott in Case C-212/04 *Adeneler*, ECLI:EU:C:2006:443, paras. 46-53.

40 M. Lutter, 'Die Auslegung angeglichenen Rechts' (1992/12) *JZ*, p. 604-5. See also E. Spetzler, 'Die richtlinienkonforme Auslegung als vorrangige Methode steuerjuristischer Hermeneutik' (1991/7) *RIW*, p. 580.

> law is 'as far as possible' interpreted in conformity with directives.[41] This is the duty's current formulation (since the *Wagner Miret* judgment, a preference for 'so far as possible' can be detected but this does not signify any change in substance). However, the formulation of the duty of consistent interpretation in the *Marleasing* judgment should not be interpreted as indicating a more far-reaching obligation on behalf of national courts.[42] Indeed, on further consideration, 'as far as possible' is not so fundamentally different from 'in so far as it is given discretion to do so under national law'. Some support for this conclusion can be found in the Opinion of Advocate General Slynn for the *Marshall I* judgment, which was delivered before the *Marleasing* judgment, since he already used the formulation 'so far as possible', simply as shorthand when discussing the requirements imposed through the *Von Colson and Kamann* judgment.[43]

However, it seems to be clear that the duty of consistent interpretation cannot be understood as having absolute supremacy, in the sense that in any situation conflicting national rules of interpretation must be set aside. The ECJ's case law explicitly recognises the fundamental role played by national courts and national rules of interpretation for deciding whether a consistent interpretation can be adopted:

> '(…) it is for the national court to interpret the national law, so far as possible, in the light of the wording and the purpose of the directive concerned in order to achieve the result sought by the directive, which requires that national court to do whatever lies within its jurisdiction, taking the whole body of domestic law into consideration and applying the interpretative methods recognised by that law'.[44]

The reason why this is necessary can be found in the following observations by Prechal:

> '(…) as consistent interpretation is interpretation of *national* law, it is within the competence of the national courts and not within that of the Court of Justice (…).
>
> When searching for an answer to the question whether consistent interpretation is possible or not, and thus when addressing the issue of the discretion of the national courts under national law, the crucial factor is the approach, or methods or rules of interpretation or construction prevailing within the Member State concerned'.[45]

---

41 Case C-106/89 *Marleasing*, ECLI:EU:C:1990:395, para. 8.

42 Cf. M. Klamert, *Die richtlinienkonforme Auslegung nationalen Rechts* (Manz 2001), p. 41.

43 Opinion of AG Slynn in Case 152/84 *Marshall I*, ECLI:EU:C:1985:345, p. 733.

44 Joined Cases C-131/13, C-163/13 and C-164/13 *Italmoda*, ECLI:EU:C:2014:2455, para. 52; Case C-441/14 *Ajos*, ECLI:EU:C:2016:278, para. 31; Case C-187/15 *Pöpperl*, ECLI:EU:C:2016:550, para. 43.

45 Prechal (n. 26), p. 194.

However, some authors seem to take the role occupied by national courts and rules of interpretation too far, reducing the scope of the duty of consistent interpretation entirely to what is possible under national law:

> Jarass argues that national rules of interpretation determine the possibility of a consistent interpretation. The decision what national rules of interpretation permit lies entirely in the domain of national law. It follows directly from the *Von Colson and Kamann* judgment that national courts must remain within the limits of their jurisdiction under national law when they make that decision (this is supported by the sentence 'in so far as it is given discretion to do so under national law).[46] According to Jarass, this approach is necessary to ensure that the duty of consistent interpretation does not result in a violation of the limits in relation to direct effect. This approach is also required to prevent that national courts invoke imprecise provisions of EU law to the detriment of national law, violating the separation of powers between the judiciary and the legislature.[47]
>
> Brechmann also submits that the duty of consistent interpretation must respect the limits that follow from national interpretative rules. Importantly, those limits cannot be influenced by EU law.[48]

If national rules of interpretation fully determined the scope of the duty of consistent interpretation, it is unlikely that the theory of supremacy accurately reflects how the relationship between EU and national law is to be understood in the context of that obligation. However, things might not be that simple. After the just referred to observations, Prechal continues to explain that:

> '[s]oon after the judgment in *Von Colson* it became obvious, particularly from the UK experience, that the national rules of construction may form a very serious and perhaps too far-reaching restriction upon the doctrine of consistent interpretation'. By way of example, Prechal refers to a number of judgments decided by the English courts that rejected a consistent interpretation for which one of the main arguments was that the national provisions had been adopted prior to the directive and therefore did not have an implementing objective.[49]
>
> Also, in his Opinion for the *Barber* judgment, Advocate General Van Gerven points out that upon receipt of the requested preliminary ruling in the *Von Colson and Kamann* judgment, the referring court decided that '(...) it was not empowered to interpret a specific provision of German law in accordance with the normal methods of interpretation customarily applied under the German

46 Case 14/83 *Von Colson and Kamann*, ECLI:EU:C:1984:153, paras. 26, 28.

47 H.D. Jarass, 'Richtlinienkonforme bzw. EG-rechtskonforme Auslegung nationalen Rechts' (1991/3) *EuR*, p. 217-8. See further on this discussion, Wissink (n. 26), p. 88.

48 Brechmann (n. 9), p. 273, 284. See also U. Di Fabio, 'Richtlinienkonformität als ranghöchstes Normauslegungsprinzip? Überlegungen zum Einfluß des indirekten Gemeinschaftsrechts auf die nationale Rechtsordnung' (1990/15) *NJW*, p. 953.

49 Prechal (n. 26), p. 194. This concerns first and foremost House of Lords 11 February 1988 *Duke v Reliance Systems Ltd* [1988] AC 618 (Lord Templeman), 638-9, 641.

> legal system (...). Hence, it would appear that Community law may set limits to certain methods of interpretation applied under a national legal system (...)'.[50]

In other words, the effectiveness of the duty of consistent interpretation as a means to enforce directives before national courts was felt to be under threat. This is where a series of judgments that further shaped the meaning of 'so far as possible', and, as a result, the task of the national courts under the duty of consistent interpretation, come into the picture. The main focus of this paragraph is to analyse these judgments and determine carefully the meaning that can be ascribed to them. I do so by dividing them into three themes: object, methodological instructions, and prescribing specific outcomes.

4.1. THE OBJECT OF THE DUTY OF CONSISTENT INTERPRETATION

While the temporal scope of the duty of consistent interpretation was already addressed in the previous paragraph, it was felt that it would be more appropriate to examine the object of the duty of consistent interpretation *vis-à-vis* national law in this paragraph, as it tells something about the reach of so far as possible.

The *Von Colson and Kamann* judgment remained a bit ambiguous on the question whether the duty of consistent interpretation applied to implementing measures only, or whether other provisions of national law were also affected.[51] In his Opinion for the *Marshall I* judgment, Advocate General Slynn contended that the *Von Colson and Kamann* judgment had not established a rule that pre-existing national law must be interpreted in conformity with directives. It is interesting to see that he appears to struggle with the idea that national courts would be required to apply the duty of consistent interpretation in relation to national provisions that were not adopted by the legislature (who, on the basis of Article 288 TFEU, is left the choice of form and methods regarding implementation) to implement a directive.[52] The same view was adopted by Advocate General Mischo.[53]

The *Marleasing* judgment adopted a different position and made clear that the duty of consistent interpretation applies to national law '(...) whether the provisions in question were adopted before or after the directive (...)'.[54] It is clear that the ECJ does not see the duty of consistent interpretation as being limited to legislation

50 Opinion of AG Van Gerven in Case C-262/88 *Barber*, ECLI:EU:C:1990:34, para. 50. His remarks concern the Labour Court Hamm's judgment of 6 September 1984 discussed at the beginning of the introduction to this book.

51 Brechmann (n. 9), p. 50.

52 Opinion of AG Slynn in Case 152/84 *Marshall I*, ECLI:EU:C:1985:345, p. 732-3.

53 Opinion of AG Mischo in Case 80/86 *Kolpinghuis*, ECLI:EU:C:1987:138, paras. 21-2.

54 Case C-106/89 *Marleasing*, ECLI:EU:C:1990:395, para. 8.

that was adopted for the specific purpose of implementing directives. It does not require further explanation that the judgment enhanced the effectiveness of the duty of consistent interpretation. For the urgency to do so, two circumstances must be mentioned. First, the *Marshall I* judgment's clarification that directives do not have horizontal direct effect,[55] was delivered in between the *Von Colson and Kamann* and *Marleasing* judgments. If the scope of the doctrine of direct effect is limited, the duty of consistent interpretation takes over. This is logical from a perspective of effectiveness. Secondly, it was also not long before the ECJ's judgment that the House of Lords delivered its *Duke* judgment, which rejected a consistent interpretation, primarily because the national provisions had been adopted prior to the directive and therefore did not have an implementing objective.[56] As I explained at the beginning of this paragraph, this can be seen as raising the ECJ's awareness that the unqualified application of certain national rules of interpretation could pose a serious threat to the duty of consistent interpretation. Another important principle, supremacy, has primarily been the subject of discussion in relation to another passage of the *Marleasing* judgment (see further subparagraph 4.3), but has also been related to the considerations regarding the object of the duty of consistent interpretation. In his Opinion for the *Marleasing* judgment, Advocate General Van Gerven argued that there is no reason to restrict the duty of consistent interpretation to implementing legislation which, in his view, followed from, among others, the principle that directives, as part of EU law, take precedence over all provisions of national law.[57] However, in my opinion, the broader scope does not depend on a finding that directives enjoy supremacy: the applicability of Articles 288 TFEU and 4(3) TEU in the national legal orders suffices, and, after expiry of the transposition period, there is no need to limit the judiciary's contribution to implementation to measures that were adopted specifically in pursuit of the directive's implementation (in so far as they are available at all) as the legislature can choose to implement directives through pre-existing legislation. This explanation is to be preferred on account of the observations made in subparagraph 2.3 regarding directives and supremacy.

Similar to the *Marleasing* judgment, the *Pfeiffer* judgment provided that the duty of consistent interpretation '(...) requires the national court to consider national law as a whole in order to assess to what extent it may be applied so as not to produce a result contrary to that sought by the directive'.[58] Although the *Pfeiffer* judgment differed from the *Marleasing* judgment as the incompatibility actually

55 Case 152/84 *Marshall I*, ECLI:EU:C:1986:84, para. 48.

56 House of Lords 11 February 1988 *Duke v Reliance Systems Ltd* [1988] AC 618 (Lord Templeman), 638-9, 641.

57 Opinion of AG Van Gerven in Case C-106/89 *Marleasing*, ECLI:EU:C:1990:310, para. 9.

58 Joined Cases C-397/01 to C-403/01 *Pfeiffer*, ECLI:EU:C:2004:584, para. 115, referring to Case C-131/97 *Carbonari*, ECLI:EU:C:1999:98, paras. 49-50, where the same point was made, albeit by using different words.

resulted from a very detailed implementing provision (whereas there were no implementing measures whatsoever in the *Marleasing* judgment), both judgments made clear that national courts must include any suitable provision in their attempt to adopt a consistent interpretation.

4.2. METHODOLOGICAL INSTRUCTIONS ON THE APPLICATION OF THE DUTY OF CONSISTENT INTERPRETATION

4.2.1. The Interpretative Selection Rule

The *Océano* judgment introduced an interpretative selection rule in favour of a consistent interpretation,[59] which was confirmed in the following words in, among others, the *Adeneler* judgment:

> '(...) the national courts are bound to interpret domestic law so far as possible (...) in the light of the wording and the purpose of the directive concerned with a view to achieving the results sought by the directive, favouring the interpretation of the national rules which is the most consistent with that purpose in order thereby to achieve an outcome compatible with the provisions of the directive'.[60]

Brenncke provides three important points of clarification regarding the interpretative selection rule. First, the rule does not of itself influence the application of national interpretative rules and the interpretations that can be given to a particular provision of national law. Secondly, it does not establish a hierarchy between the applicable national interpretative methods. Thirdly, what the rule does do is prescribe that, if the provision of national law is open to more than one interpretation, priority must be given to the one that is in conformity with the directive.[61] This is even so if that may not have been the preferred interpretation if the national interpretative rules were applied in isolation of the duty of consistent interpretation.[62] If the operation of the interpretative selection rule is considered, it is clear that it resembles the *verfassungskonforme Auslegung* (a doctrine under German law which requires the adoption of an interpretation that is in conformity with the German Constitution if a lower-ranking provision allows more than one interpretation). Similar to the

59 Joined Cases C-240/98 to C-244/98 *Océano*, ECLI:EU:C:2000:346, para. 32.

60 Case C-212/04 *Adeneler*, ECLI:EU:C:2006:443, para. 124. See also Case C-414/07 *Magoora*, ECLI:EU:C:2008:766, para. 44; Case C-305/08 *CoNISMa*, ECLI:EU:C:2009:807, para. 50; Case C-594/10 *Van Laarhoven*, ECLI:EU:C:2012:92, para. 37; Case C-124/12 *AES-3C Maritza East 1*, ECLI:EU:C:2013:488, para. 53.

61 M. Brenncke, 'Hybrid Methodology for the EU Principle of Consistent Interpretation' (2017/2) *Statute Law Review*, p. 138. The same conclusion is adopted in R. Widdershoven, 'De doorwerking van richtlijnen in een samengestelde Europese rechtsorde', in: H.R.B.M. Kummeling and others (Eds.), *De samengestelde Besselink* (Wolf Legal Publishers 2012), p. 214.

62 Canaris (n. 9), p. 72.

latter, the rule contains an element of supremacy as it requires the adoption of the interpretation that is in conformity with the directive. A further similarity, that must be reiterated, is that the rule is applied subsequently to, and does not of itself influence, the national courts' determination of what is possible on the basis of the national interpretative rules. However, in what follows, it will be seen that, unlike the *verfassungskonforme Auslegung*, sometimes, the methodological instructions on the application of the duty of consistent interpretation also have the potential to affect the way in which the national rules of interpretation are applied themselves.

4.2.2. The Presumption of the Intention to Comply

The *Wagner Miret* judgment provided that:

> '(…) it should be borne in mind that when it interprets and applies national law, every national court must presume that the State had the intention of fulfilling entirely the obligations arising from the directive concerned (…).'[63]

This presumption that the legislature intends to comply with directives was reformulated in the *Pfeiffer* judgment. The ECJ reiterated the national courts' task to provide legal protection for individuals' their EU law rights and to ensure that those rules are fully effective, and added that:

> '[t]hat is *a fortiori* the case when the national court is seised of a dispute concerning the application of domestic provisions which, as here, have been specifically enacted for the purpose of transposing a directive intended to confer rights on individuals. The national court must, in the light of the third paragraph of Article 249 EC, presume that the Member State, following its exercise of the discretion afforded it under that provision, had the intention of fulfilling entirely the obligations arising from the directive concerned'.[64]

The passages from the *Wagner Miret* and *Pfeiffer* judgments raise two questions. First, what is the scope of the presumption of the intention to comply? And secondly, what is the effect of this presumption on the national rules of interpretation?

The scope of the *Pfeiffer* judgment's description can only be interpreted in one way: the presumption applies where the legislature has carried out its task to implement the directive under Article 288 TFEU. The scope of the description in the *Wagner Miret* judgment is less obvious. An isolated interpretation of the paragraph providing the presumption would lead one to understand it as encompassing national law in its entirety and regardless of whether it can be established that the legislature took the view that he complied with his obligation to implement

63 Case C-334/92 *Wagner Miret*, ECLI:EU:C:1993:945, para. 20.
64 Joined Cases C-397/01 to C-403/01 *Pfeiffer*, ECLI:EU:C:2004:584, para. 112.

the directive.[65] However, that paragraph was followed by the consideration that the duty of consistent interpretation applies in particular to a situation such as the present case, i.e. where the Member State considered that the pre-existing provisions of its national law satisfy the requirements of the directive concerned.[66] The presumption formulated in the *Wagner Miret* judgment must probably be read in the light of this subsequent paragraph, and limited accordingly to situations in which the Member State considered that the pre-existing provisions of national law satisfy the requirements of the directive.[67] This interpretation fits better with the *Pfeiffer* judgment, and confers upon the two judgments a consistent meaning, namely that, each time that there is an actual indication of legislative intent to comply with the directive, the presumption applies.

What is then the effect of the presumption? It does not seem difficult to agree that a presumption refers to something that is in principle accepted as true, but is not certain to be true,[68] and can be rebutted by arguments of a certain weight. In this sense it is a rule of evidence (*praesumptio juris*): the presumption stands until one of the parties to the proceedings furnishes sufficient evidence that the legislature had not intended to follow the directive. Also, the integrity of the presumed implementing objective must be respected, which in my opinion entails that such an objective may not be partitioned into several sub-objectives, some of which fit in better with a traditional approach (i.e. the approach adopted in a purely internal context) to the national legislation than others. I also believe that an implementing objective has an impact on the application of the national interpretative methods. It seems obvious that the courts will take this into account in the context of the historical and/or teleological interpretative method, where the legislature's intent or the legislation's purpose must be determined. In relation to these interpretative methods, there is in my opinion a very strong *prima facie* priority for the legislature's implementing objective, if such an objective can be established through the use of the historical and/or teleological methods. In principle, the reconciliation of the implementing objective in relation to other, incompatible, objectives, should then

---

65 This interpretation of the passage in *Wagner Miret* can be found in N. Baldauf, *Richtlinienverstoß und Verschiebung der Contra-legem-Grenze im Privatrechtsverhältnis* (Mohr Siebeck 2013), p. 91.

66 Case C-334/92 *Wagner Miret*, ECLI:EU:C:1993:945, para. 21. Note that the English version of the judgment mentions 'national court'. However, taking into account the original Spanish version, and the French, German and Dutch version, as well as paragraph 5 of the judgment mentioning that Spain did not consider amendment of national law necessary, it is clear that it should be read as 'Member State' instead.

67 See also Wissink (n. 26), p. 94; Brenncke (n. 61), p. 139. For a different interpretation which is, however, a less natural reading of the relevant passages, see J. Suhr, *Richtlinienkonforme Auslegung im Privatrecht und nationale Auslegungsmethodik* (Nomos 2011), p. 60, who argues that the judgment must be read as establishing that for the application of the presumption the inactivity of the legislature is converted into a fictional intention to implement the directive once the transposition period has expired.

68 See, however, M. Amstutz, 'In-Between Worlds: *Marleasing* and the Emergence of Interlegality in Legal Reasoning' (2005/6) *ELJ*, p. 773, who interprets the presumption as establishing an absolute priority of an intention to implement the directive over incompatible, more specific, intentions.

be in favour of the former. The strength of an overriding counter-argument must presumably be significant if the presumption is applied *vis-à-vis* contradictory intentions or purposes. In particular, the threshold for overriding the presumption does not seem to be reached if, for example, the content of a provision concerning the nullity of contracts is further explained and discussed in the explanatory memorandum in a way that indicates the rule's incompatibility with the directive. This concerns an ordinary feature of explanatory memoranda and the presumption would become meaningless if it could be so easily overridden. However, there is something to say for the view that the presumption is rebutted in the situation where the legislature unequivocally expressed a conscious intention to depart from the directive.[69] Admittedly, this appears to be a rather theoretical possibility. Apart from this unlikely scenario, I think that other interpretative criteria than the historical and/or teleological method must come into play before the presumption can be set aside. If the historical and/or teleological method contradict the presumption and this is also supported by compelling grammatical or systematic arguments, it becomes difficult to expect the courts to hold on to the presumption. Arguably, this would come very close to a *contra legem* interpretation (see subparagraph 5.2). However, it is important to point out that the presumption also extends to the grammatical and systematic interpretative methods as such. In particular the *Wagner Miret* judgment made clear that the presumption applies when the national court 'interprets and applies national law'. This does not seem to restrict the scope of the presumption to one or more specific interpretative methods. In my opinion this does not differ from the use of intent or purpose in a non-EU law context: they indicate what the provision wants to achieve which informs the interpreter on the meaning of the words used. Nevertheless, there is an important difference with the effect of the presumption *vis-à-vis* the historical and/or teleological methods: if, despite having considered that the national provision was meant to have a meaning that follows the directive, a grammatical or systematic interpretation still exclude a consistent interpretation, it does not seem reasonable to expect the national courts to override this by means of the presumption.[70]

The *Wagner Miret* and *Pfeiffer* judgments have been linked to the *Björnekulla* judgment,[71] which reiterated the national courts' duty of consistent interpretation, adding that '[t]hat applies notwithstanding any contrary interpretation which may arise from the *travaux préparatoires* for the national rule'.[72] It should first be noted that the applicable national provision had an implementing objective. Secondly,

69 I should point out that other authors have also recognised this exception to the rule laid down in *Wagner Miret* and *Pfeiffer*, see Weber (n. 32), p. 99; Widdershoven (n. 61), p. 214; Roth and Jopen (n. 37), p. 276; Brenncke (n. 61), p. 140.

70 See also L. Michael and M. Payandeh, 'Richtlinienkonforme Rechtsfortbildung zwischen Unionsrecht und Verfassungsrecht' (2015/33) *NJW*, p. 2396.

71 Wissink (n. 38), p. 143; Roth and Jopen (n. 37), p. 276.

72 Case C-371/02 *Björnekulla*, ECLI:EU:C:2004:275, para. 13.

the relevant passage has not been repeated since. Thirdly, the instruction to adopt a consistent interpretation 'so far as possible', a phrase that requires that it is taken into consideration what is still possible on account of national interpretative rules, was also reiterated in the *Björnekulla* judgment. I therefore suggest a moderate interpretation of the judgment. It does not directly address the role of the national *travaux préparatoires* if the rule does not have an implementing objective. However, if an implementing objective can be identified, the *travaux préparatoires* must be set aside provided that there are otherwise sufficient connecting points in national law supporting a consistent interpretation. So while the *Björnekulla* judgment was criticised for potentially paying insufficient attention to national interpretative rules,[73] in my opinion the above discussed presumption formulated in the *Wagner Miret* and *Pfeiffer* judgments is more far-reaching.

In summary, it can be said that the presumption provided in the *Wagner Miret* and *Pfeiffer* judgments applies whenever there is an actual indication of legislative intent to comply with the directive. At a minimum, national courts are required to apply the presumption in the context of the historical and/or teleological interpretative method, but presumably also the grammatical and systematic interpretative method. In relation to the former, the effects of the presumption probably go much further as there appears to be less scope – presumably no scope whatsoever most of the time – to arrive at the conclusion that the presumption is overridden by other intentions or purposes (which would entail that the presumption of the intention to comply is set aside as a whole).[74] This means that, normally, incompatible, more specific intentions, must be disregarded, even if this would not have been the result of a traditional application of the national rules of interpretation. Therefore, within the scope of its application, the presumption interferes with national rules of interpretation to the extent that certain outcomes of the application of an interpretative method are excluded. The presumption enhances the effectiveness of the duty of consistent interpretation: acting as a kind of 'dynamic reference', it aligns the national legislature's intentions with the evolving meaning of directives as determined by the ECJ.[75] However, this does not mean that national courts are forced to adopt a consistent interpretation if the presumption applies: the other interpretative methods also come into the equation and it will depend on the force of those arguments whether they are outweighed by the presumption. Finally, I proposed a moderate interpretation of the *Björnekulla* judgment: in line with the *Wagner Miret* and *Pfeiffer* judgments, the rule that incompatible intentions arising from the *travaux préparatoires* must be set aside only applies to implementing

73 J.H. Jans and M.J.M. Verhoeven, 'Europeanisation via Consistent Interpretation and Direct Effect', in: J.H. Jans, S. Prechal and R.J.G.M. Widdershoven (Eds.), *Europeanisation of Public Law* (Europa Law Publishing 2015), p. 86-7.

74 See also Klamert (n. 42), p. 48; Klamert (n. 9), p. 1258-9.

75 Brenncke (n. 61), p. 139.

legislation and requires that there are otherwise sufficient connecting points in national law supporting a consistent interpretation.

4.2.3. *A Reinforced Obligation when Interpreting Implementing Legislation?*

As the paragraphs of the *Wagner Miret* and *Pfeiffer* judgments mentioning the presumption of the intention to comply were immediately followed by paragraphs that held that the duty of consistent interpretation applies in particular to implementing legislation, this may give the false impression that the first paragraph was the immediate cause for the second paragraph.[76] Although there is a connection between them, the meaning of the consideration that the duty of consistent interpretation applies in particular to implementing legislation must be interpreted separately from the presumption. This follows from the fact that that consideration is normally not mentioned together with, and was already part of the ECJ's case law before the introduction of, the presumption.[77]

What is then the meaning of the observation that the duty of consistent interpretation applies 'in particular' to implementing legislation? It must be seen as a prognosis: it is expected that, all other things being equal, it is easier to adopt a consistent interpretation of implementing legislation.[78] It is, for example, more likely that the wording of the implementing legislation goes in the same direction as that of the directive. Also, it can be presumed that the historical or teleological interpretative method is favourable to a consistent interpretation. This is where the consideration that the duty of consistent interpretation applies in particular to implementing legislation connects with the presumption. However, unlike the presumption, it does not interfere with national interpretative rules. It also does not entail a kind of reinforced obligation for implementing legislation. This would not make sense, since it should normally be easier for a national court to come to a consistent interpretation when it interprets implementing legislation.[79]

76 Case C-334/92 *Wagner Miret*, ECLI:EU:C:1993:945, para. 21; Joined Cases C-397/01 to C-403/01 *Pfeiffer*, ECLI:EU:C:2004:584, para. 113.

77 In fact it was already mentioned in Case 14/83 *Von Colson and Kamann*, ECLI:EU:C:1984:153, para. 26. See further Case 80/86 *Kolpinghuis*, ECLI:EU:C:1987:431, para. 12; Case C-131/97 *Carbonari*, ECLI:EU:C:1999:98, para. 48; Case C-185/97 *Coote*, ECLI:EU:C:1998:424, para. 28; Case C-316/04 *Stichting Zuid-Hollandse Milieufederatie*, ECLI:EU:C:2005:678, para. 78; Case C-356/05 *Farrell*, ECLI:EU:C:2007:229, para. 42; Case C-268/06 *Impact*, ECLI:EU:C:2008:223, para. 98.

78 Wissink (n. 26), p. 93.

79 Ibid.

4.2.4. *Option under National Law Becomes an Obligation Qua EU Law*

The *Pfeiffer* judgment stated that:

> '(…) if the application of interpretative methods recognised by national law enables, in certain circumstances, a provision of domestic law to be construed in such a way as to avoid conflict with another rule of domestic law or the scope of that provision to be restricted to that end by applying it only in so far as it is compatible with the rule concerned, the national court is bound to use those methods in order to achieve the result sought by the directive'.[80]

The exact meaning of this paragraph is further explored here. In order to better understand this slightly cryptic paragraph, it must be read in the light of the facts underlying the *Pfeiffer* judgment. This is important because the sentence is first and foremost applicable to this specific situation. The main proceedings concerned the interpretation of the Working Time Directive,[81] of which Article 6 required Member States to take measures necessary to ensure that the average working time for each 7-day period, including overtime, did not exceed 48 hours. The German Law on working time made provision for a corresponding maximum working time. However, it also contained a provision allowing for certain exceptions by way of a collective agreement, which was utilised for emergency workers. The provision enabling certain exceptions was found to be incompatible with the Working Time Directive. This explains why the judgment suggested an approach to the interpretation of German law aimed at enabling the application of one provision instead of the other.

Admittedly, the idea is not entirely new: in the *Von Colson and Kamann* judgment the referring court indicated that the national provision adopted for the purpose of implementing Article 6 of the Equal Treatment Directive[82] could not accommodate a consistent interpretation, which did not stop the ECJ from alluding to the possibility to obtain the result prescribed by the directive via general rules regarding compensation. Nevertheless, the *Pfeiffer* judgment went one step further as it made the use of the technique compulsory. The methodological instruction provided by the ECJ raises the question whether the *Pfeiffer* judgment does not blur the lines between the duty of consistent interpretation and direct effect and/or must be seen as a sign of supremacy of the duty of consistent interpretation. In my opinion such is not the case once four qualifications to the seemingly intrusive paragraph of the judgment are

---

80 Joined Cases C-397/01 to C-403/01 *Pfeiffer*, ECLI:EU:C:2004:584, para. 116. Confirmed by Case C-12/08 *Mono Car Styling*, ECLI:EU:C:2009:466, para. 63.

81 Council Directive 93/104/EC of 23 November 1993 concerning certain aspects of the organization of working time, *OJ* 1993, L307/18.

82 Council Directive 76/207/EEC of 9 February 1976 on the implementation of the principle of equal treatment for men and women as regards access to employment, vocational training and promotion, and working conditions, *OJ* 1976, L39/40.

taken into consideration. First, the part which stated that '(...) the national court is bound to use those methods in order to achieve the result sought by the directive' should not be interpreted as an interpretative selection rule comparable to the one established in the *Océano* judgment. It tells national courts that they should not exclude a technique that is normally available under national interpretative rules and, as such, it is situated prior to the point at which national courts must make a choice between two or more possible interpretations. In other words, it determines the range of interpretative arguments that must be taken into consideration when examining whether a consistent interpretation is possible instead of determining the interpretative outcome. Secondly, the judgment only required national courts to use the solution proposed by the ECJ, *provided that recognised national rules of interpretation enabled the application of the technique*. Thirdly, and confirming the first two points, the judgment reiterated that national courts are only required to apply the duty of consistent interpretation 'so far as possible'. Fourthly, it is pointed out that German interpretative rules do in principle recognise the technique described by the ECJ, i.e. teleological reduction, whereby a provision is given a restrictive interpretation.[83] To be sure, a quick look at the underlying legal framework of the case learns that a consistent interpretation would require a significant reduction of the scope of the national provision containing the exception (perhaps even to virtually zero).[84] Yet, as I just explained, this is subject to what is possible according to national rules of interpretation. The ECJ probably had this in mind when it delivered its judgment. While the technique as such might appear to some to go quite far in this respect, it is not something the ECJ invented and decided to impose on national courts.

It has been deduced from this passage of the judgment that if national law allows a particular interpretative technique to be applied, national courts are bound to use it if this helps them to resolve a conflict between national law and the directive via a consistent interpretation.[85] Although such a general rule does not literally follow from the text of the *Pfeiffer* judgment itself, it is a logical implication of the above discussed paragraph. The four qualifications that were just mentioned then also apply to this further implication.

4.3. PRESCRIBING SPECIFIC OUTCOMES?

This subparagraph analyses whether the ECJ sometimes prescribes a specific interpretative outcome to the national courts, leaving virtually no discretion to them to adopt a different interpretation of national law than one that is

83 Klamert (n. 9), p. 1259-60.
84 See also S. Prechal, 'Joined Cases C-397/01 to C-403/01, *Bernhard Pfeiffer et al*' (2005/5) *CMLRev*, p. 1458.
85 Prechal (n. 26), p. 199; Widdershoven (n. 61), p. 214; Brenncke (n. 61), p. 136.

in conformity with the directive. As a preliminary point, I must explain that it is necessary to carefully distinguish between judgments that merely provide a further interpretation of the directive applicable to the national proceedings, and judgments that provide guidance or instructions to national courts on the required interpretation in the context of the duty of consistent interpretation. As the first category of judgments does not actually tell something about the duty of consistent interpretation, they will not be dealt with here. The *Dekker* judgment is an example of the first category.[86]

> It provided that any infringement of the prohibition of discrimination laid down in the Equal Treatment Directive '(…) suffices in itself to make the person guilty of it fully liable, and no regard may be had to the grounds of exemption envisaged by national law'.[87] This has been interpreted as compelling the national court to disregard the grounds of exemption provided under national law by adopting a consistent interpretation.[88] However, the judgment did not directly address the application of the duty of consistent interpretation.[89] The only question that was directly addressed concerned the interpretation of the Equal Treatment Directive.

4.3.1. *A Specification of the Required Interpretation and a Prognosis of the Outcome*

In the *Marleasing* judgment, the duty of consistent interpretation was undeniably addressed. For the purpose of this subparagraph the following paragraph is further analysed:

> '[i]t follows that the requirement that national law must be interpreted in conformity with Article 11 of Directive 68/151 precludes the interpretation of provisions of national law relating to public limited companies in such a manner that the nullity of a public limited company may be ordered on grounds other than those exhaustively listed in Article 11 of the directive in question'.[90]

Different opinions were expressed regarding the consequences of this paragraph for our understanding of the duty of consistent interpretation. On the one hand, it was put forward that the instructions given to the referring court can hardly be distinguished from the horizontal direct effect of directives. Also, in their opinion, this part of the *Marleasing* judgment can only be explained as being based on supremacy.[91] Wissink, on the other hand, argues that, at most, the cited paragraph

86 See also Wissink (n. 26), p. 94-5.
87 Case C-177/88 *Dekker*, ECLI:EU:C:1990:383, para. 25.
88 G. Betlem, 'The Doctrine of Consistent Interpretation – Managing Legal Uncertainty' (2002/3) *OJLS*, p. 401.
89 See, however, the Opinion of AG Darmon in Case C-177/88 *Dekker*, ECLI:EU:C:1989:424, paras. 11-5, who did discuss the duty of consistent interpretation as a solution.
90 Case C-106/89 *Marleasing*, ECLI:EU:C:1990:395, para. 9.
91 V. Götz, 'Europäische Gesetzgebung durch Richtlinien – Zusammenwirken von Gemeinschaft und Staat' (1992/30) *NJW*, p. 1854; Brechmann (n. 9), p. 72-4. See also, with regard to horizontal

specified the interpretation required by the directive and contained a prognosis that a consistent interpretation would be possible.[92] The consequences that can be derived from the *Marleasing* judgment – and thus the usefulness of the expressed opinions – are determined by the meaning of the cited paragraph. Admittedly, the concerned paragraph gave the impression that the referring court was prohibited to adopt any other interpretation than one that complied with the directive, regardless of the possibilities to do so according to national interpretative rules: it provided a very detailed description of the interpretative result that was required by the directive, added that the duty of consistent interpretation 'precludes' divergent interpretations, and similar considerations were found in one of the subsequent paragraphs. Yet, Wissink cogently explains why such a far-reaching interpretation must be rejected. First, the cited paragraph is the logical conclusion of a syllogism: it was preceded by the well known major premise that national courts are required to interpret national law so far as possible in conformity with directives (paragraph 8), and followed by the minor premise which provided what an interpretation in conformity with the directive entailed in this specific instance, i.e. Article 11 of the directive prohibited a judicial declaration of nullity on grounds other than those exhaustively listed in the directive (paragraph 10).[93] Secondly, the use of the verb 'preclude' perhaps gave the wrong impression; as the directive provided that the grounds are exhaustively listed, it is a necessary corollary that it is precluded that other grounds are used. Thirdly, the ECJ did not pre-empt the national court's competence to interpret national law by prescribing a specific solution. Unlike, for example, the situation in the *Von Colson and Kamann* judgment, here, there was only one solution to adopt a consistent interpretation, namely not applying the general provision of the Spanish Civil Code. Indeed, and this is the fourth point, the judgment stipulated that the referring court must so far as possible apply the duty of consistent interpretation. At no point is it mentioned that the national court must adopt the proposed interpretation, regardless of the possibilities to do so according to national interpretative rules.[94]

To be sure, the adoption of a consistent interpretation required that the general provision of the Spanish Civil Code was not applied in the proceedings before the referring court (but note that it has been argued that this result was certainly

direct effect, Klamert (n. 42), p. 42. Cf. P.-C. Müller-Graff, 'Europäisches Gemeinschaftsrecht und Privatrecht – Das Privatrecht in der europäischen Integration' (1993/1) *NJW*, p. 20-2, who, referring to, among others, the principle of effectiveness, criticises the lack of horizontal direct effect of directives and, in that light, does not consider the solution adopted in the *Marleasing* judgment unreasonable.

92 Wissink (n. 26), p. 103.

93 Wissink refers to the *Habermann-Beltermann* and *Bellone* judgments which largely adopted the same approach as the *Marleasing* judgment, but did not contain the perhaps superfluous observation what a consistent interpretation required, taking into account the ascertained content of the directive – thereby avoiding any misunderstandings, Case C-421/92 *Habermann-Beltermann,* ECLI:EU:C:1994:187; Case C-215/97 *Bellone,* ECLI:EU:C:1998:189.

94 Wissink (n. 26), p. 99-104.

not impossible by means of interpretation).[95] But this is not the point that is of concern here (subparagraph 4.2.4 showed that the *Von Colson and Kamann* and *Pfeiffer* judgments also contained the idea that a particular provision of national law can be an obstacle that must, if possible, be circumvented to enable a consistent interpretation). On the basis of the above arguments, I agree with Wissink that the *Marleasing* judgment did not establish that national courts must adopt a consistent interpretation, regardless of the possibilities to do so according to national interpretative rules. This means that the *Marleasing* judgment does not support the far-reaching conclusions that the duty of consistent interpretation can hardly be distinguished from the horizontal direct effect of directives, and that it is a manifestation of supremacy.

A similar point occurred in the *Océano* judgment, where it was held that:

> '[t]he requirement for an interpretation in conformity with the Directive requires the national court, in particular, to favour the interpretation that would allow it to decline of its own motion the jurisdiction conferred on it by virtue of an unfair term'.[96]

The judgment again made explicit the interpretation required by the directive. But also here, this should not be understood as forcing the adoption of a consistent interpretation.[97] Also, note that, unlike the *Marleasing* judgment, the judgment positively formulated what a consistent interpretation requires – but, as I explained, this is rather a difference in drafting style instead of substance. The *Pfeiffer* judgment is particularly instructive for understanding the ECJ's intentions when it discusses the interpretative outcome in more detail. In this judgment the interpretation required by the directive was explicated as well, but added what seemed to have been taken for granted in judgments drafted in the style of the *Marleasing* judgment, namely that that result must still be possible on the basis of national interpretative rules:

> '[i]n this instance, the principle of interpretation in conformity with Community law thus requires the referring court to do whatever lies within its jurisdiction, having regard to the whole body of rules of national law, to ensure that Directive 93/104 is fully effective, in order to prevent the maximum weekly working time laid down in Article 6(2) of the directive from being exceeded'.[98]

---

95 Opinion of AG Van Gerven in Case C-106/89 *Marleasing*, ECLI:EU:C:1990:310, para. 20; Prechal (n. 26), p. 198.

96 Joined Cases C-240/98 to C-244/98 *Océano*, ECLI:EU:C:2000:346, para. 32.

97 J.M. Prinssen, *Doorwerking van Europees recht. De verhouding tussen directe werking, conforme interpretatie en overheidsaansprakelijkheid* (Kluwer 2004), p. 208.

98 Joined Cases C-397/01 to C-403/01 *Pfeiffer*, ECLI:EU:C:2004:584, para. 118.

Interestingly, the above cited paragraph referred to two paragraphs of the *Marleasing* judgment, of which the first contained the reformulation of the preliminary question in that case (which, in my opinion, cannot have been very relevant for the proceedings in the *Pfeiffer* judgment), and the second one mentioned the considerations that were mistakenly understood as prescribing a specific outcome. The reference in the relevant paragraph of the *Pfeiffer* judgment indicates that the position is considered to be the same as in the *Marleasing* judgment, despite the fact that the latter did not explicitly include a statement that in order to obtain the explicated interpretative outcome national courts must still take national interpretative rules into account.

4.3.2. Requiring the Reconsideration of the National Court's Analysis

Compared to the above judgments, the *Dominguez* judgment went one step further. The judgment concerned the question whether it is allowed to make the entitlement to paid annual leave conditional on a minimum of one month's actual work during a reference period that was determined by the Member State. The condition was stipulated in Article L. 223-2 of the French Labour Code and the referring French court had indicated that that provision was not amenable to an interpretation that is compatible with the Working Time Directive.[99] The ECJ went on to suggest that the duty of consistent interpretation requires:

> 'national courts to do whatever lies within their jurisdiction, taking the whole body of domestic law into consideration and applying the interpretative methods recognised by domestic law, with a view to ensuring that the directive in question is fully effective (...)'.[100]

The ECJ then departed from its usual approach by holding that, notwithstanding the referring court's indication of a limitation, it might nevertheless be able to adopt a consistent interpretation if the scope of Article L. 223-4 of the Labour Code, which provided an exemption for the requirement of actual work during the reference period, was extended so as to apply to the concerned proceedings.[101] To be sure, the judgment subsequently recognised that it is still for the referring court to determine whether it can come to such an interpretation of national law.[102] Nevertheless, the judgment made it clear that, if a national court's approach to interpretation is considered to be unsuitable in terms of effectiveness, the duty of consistent interpretation can intervene in this approach. This can even go so far as suggesting to national courts that they should, taking into account the interpretative methods recognised by national law, reconsider their approach

99 Directive 2003/88/EC of the European Parliament and of the Council of 4 November 2003 concerning certain aspects of the organisation of working time, *OJ* 2003, L299/9.
100 Case C-282/10 *Dominguez*, ECLI:EU:C:2012:33, para. 27.
101 Ibid, paras. 28-30.
102 Ibid, para. 31.

to interpretation.[103] The *Dominguez* judgment's approach was confirmed by the *Klausner Holz Niedersachsen* judgment (it is noted that this judgment did not pertain to a directive):

> This judgment concerned an obstacle to rectify the consequences of an infringement of the rules on state aid derived from the principle of *res judicata*. The referring court indicated that a consistent interpretation was impossible. Nevertheless, the ECJ provided a detailed analysis of national law and, accordingly, the national court was also requested to reconsider its position.[104] In the context of directives, the *Amia* judgment could, to some extent, be interpreted as confirming the *Dominguez* judgment's approach. However, the referring Italian court did not explicitly state that a consistent interpretation was impossible. It only stated that the relevant provisions of national law were incompatible. Referring to the submissions made by the Italian Government, the ECJ then put forward that there might yet be a possibility to adopt a consistent interpretation if other provisions of national law were taken into account. This could be interpreted as an interference with the referring court's analysis of national law, but it is equally possible that the option of solving the incompatibility through a consistent interpretation was simply overlooked.[105]

4.3.3. *Verbatim Transposition*

Last but not least, there is the application of the duty of consistent interpretation to a provision of national law that transposed the directive almost *verbatim*. This situation occurred in the *Spedition Welter* judgment. With regard to the interpretation of the concerned national provision the ECJ considered that:

> '[i]n the case in the main proceedings, it is not disputed that Paragraph 7b(2) of the VAG transposes, word for word, Article 21(5) of Directive 2009/103. Those provisions of national law therefore require an interpretation which is consistent with European Union law to the effect that the claims representative is authorised to accept service of judicial documents'.[106]

It must be pointed out that the legal framework that applied to the *Spedition Welter* judgment was more complicated than the cited paragraph suggests: it was not so much the provision of national law providing for the *verbatim* transposition but rather a general provision contained in the German Code of Civil Procedure, that also applied to the proceedings, that caused the interpretation issue. On account of that provision, it was not at all self-evident that German law could accommodate a consistent interpretation.

---

103 See also the case note by Widdershoven in *AB* 2012/48, para. 3, who points out that the ECJ departed from its usual approach to the duty of consistent interpretation and notes the far-reaching interference by the ECJ regarding the possibilities for a consistent interpretation under French law.

104 Case C-505/14 *Klausner Holz Niedersachsen*, ECLI:EU:C:2015:742, paras. 33-7.

105 Case C-97/11 *Amia*, ECLI:EU:C:2012:306, paras. 25-31.

106 Case C-306/12 *Spedition Welter*, ECLI:EU:C:2013:650, para. 31.

Leaving aside, for the moment, the provision contained in the German Code of Civil Procedure, the first question that arises is whether the *Spedition Welter* judgment must indeed, as the clear wording of the judgment seemed to indicate, be interpreted as requiring the absolute supremacy of a consistent interpretation of national law providing for a *verbatim* transposition over other interpretations, regardless of the possibilities to do so according to national interpretative rules. Surely, the basic underlying assumption that implicitly appeared in the *Spedition Welter* judgment is reasonable: if national law literally reproduces a provision of EU law, a uniform interpretation is required, and the ECJ is the only court that can provide authoritative guidance in this respect.[107] This could provide a justification for the requirement of absolute supremacy, and for differentiating the judgment from other judgments concerning the duty of consistent interpretation. Yet, the judgment contained three points that cast doubt on the correctness of this far-reaching interpretation. First, the judgment reiterated that national law must only be interpreted so far as possible in conformity with directives. In his Opinion for the judgment, Advocate General Cruz Villalón also emphasised that, while he was clearly convinced that the implementing provision, being a *verbatim* transposition, had to be given a consistent interpretation, that decision was to be made by the referring court.[108] Secondly, in line with the division of competences between the ECJ and national courts, a plausible interpretation of the first part of the second sentence (as national law transposes the directive word for word, '[t]hose provisions of national law therefore require an interpretation which is consistent with European Union law') would be that it explains why a consistent interpretation must in particular be followed in the present proceedings, without depriving the national court of the right to take a final decision on the interpretation of national law. The prognosis that, in principle, a consistent interpretation must be followed in particular where the directive is transposed *verbatim* is logical since there is an implementing objective and the wording of the national provision is in line with the directive. Thirdly, the second part of the second sentence ('to the effect that the claims representative is authorised to accept service of judicial documents'), similar to the *Marleasing* judgment, provided a specification of the interpretation required by the directive.

---

107 See also the Opinion of AG Cruz Villalón in Case C-306/12 *Spedition Welter*, ECLI:EU:C:2013:359, para. 38. This concern is also mentioned in C.N.K. Franklin, 'Limits to the Limits of the Principle of Consistent Interpretation? Commentary on the Court's Decision in Spedition Welter' (2015/6) *ELRev*, p. 917 as a possible way to understand the judgment. The same concern underlies the position that in situations where the facts are outside of the scope of EU law (internal situations), but where the same approach as that provided under EU law is adopted, provisions or concepts taken from EU law should be interpreted uniformly, irrespective of the circumstances in which they are to apply, Joined Cases C-297/88 and C-197/89 *Dzodzi*, ECLI:EU:C:1990:360, para. 37; Case C-28/95 *Leur-Bloem*, ECLI:EU:C:1997:369, paras. 27, 32. However, it should be noted that those judgments explicitly recognise the division of competences between the ECJ and national courts in interpreting EU and national law respectively. See further M. Franzen, *Privatrechtsangleichung durch die Europäische Gemeinschaft* (De Gruyter 1999), p. 392-3.

108 Opinion of AG Cruz Villalón in Case C-306/12 *Spedition Welter*, ECLI:EU:C:2013:359, paras. 38, 40.

The more narrow interpretation of the *Spedition Welter* judgment suggested here[109] is further supported if it is taken into account that it was the German Code of Civil Procedure that actually caused the interpretation issue. Advocate General Cruz Villalón explained why, in his opinion, also the provision in the German Code of Civil Procedure could be interpreted in a way that enabled a consistent interpretation.[110] By contrast, that provision was not at all mentioned in the part of the judgment answering the preliminary question. In my opinion, this confirms the view that no final statement was made by the ECJ as to the interpretation of national law.[111] In other words, although it is obvious that national courts are expected to have less difficulties in adopting a consistent interpretation where there has been *verbatim* transposition, the *Spedition Welter* judgment did not seem to have had the intention to prevent the referring court from rejecting a consistent interpretation on account of the provision of the German Code of Civil Procedure.

Nevertheless, in my opinion one important caveat applies. On the basis of the *Spedition Welter* judgment, there is no longer the possibility for national courts to claim that the national provision's wording cannot accommodate a consistent interpretation if the directive was transposed *verbatim*. This may seem self-evident but entails an important restriction of the national courts' competences, similar to what was seen in the context of the historical and teleological interpretative methods once an implementing objective is established. Yet, it is reiterated that this does not mean that a consistent interpretation is imposed on the national courts, as they must still weigh this interpretation against the other methods (such as the fact that another provision contained in the same piece of legislation casts significant doubt on the viability of a consistent interpretation).

4.4. THE DUTY OF CONSISTENT INTERPRETATION AS A SUPERIOR METHODOLOGICAL STANDARD

Which conclusions can be drawn from this paragraph with regard to the nature of the duty of consistent interpretation and its meaning for the relationship between EU and national law? It is clear that national rules of interpretation play a fundamental role as it is ultimately national law that is being interpreted. At a minimum, national courts are required to make an effort to examine whether national law can accommodate the result prescribed by the directive.[112] However,

109 Cf. Wissink (n. 38), p. 145; Roth and Jopen (n. 37), p. 279; Franklin (n. 107), p. 910.

110 Opinion of AG Cruz Villalón in Case C-306/12 *Spedition Welter*, ECLI:EU:C:2013:359, para. 39.

111 In Franklin (n. 107), p. 919, it is put forward that the absence of any treatment of the provision of the German Code of Civil Procedure could be understood as a recognition on behalf of the ECJ that a consistent interpretation of that provision was not as straightforward as the Advocate General made it look.

112 Wissink (n. 26), p. 144; J. Altena-Davidsen, 'The Netherlands', in: C.N.K. Franklin (Ed.), *The Effectiveness and Application of EU and EEA Law in National Courts* (Intersentia 2018), p. 77.

the duty of consistent interpretation does not stop there as it was felt that this alone could not ensure the effectiveness of its application. Hence, the ECJ proceeded to provide more detailed instructions that national courts must take into account, e.g. the obligation to consider national law as a whole and the presumption that the legislature intends to comply with his obligation to implement the directive. It cannot be determined *in abstracto* to what degree these instructions might conflict with national rules of interpretation. Some instructions leave a larger potential scope of application for those national rules than others – but I have not identified a methodological instruction that made national interpretative rules entirely obsolete. However, as the duty of consistent interpretation can claim supremacy (derived from Article 4(3) TEU), national interpretative rules must be disapplied to the extent that they conflict with the ECJ's instructions. Also, it was seen in the *Dominguez* judgment that, if the ECJ believes that a national court has not tried hard enough to adopt a consistent interpretation, it is not afraid to interfere and overrule the national court's conclusion that such an interpretation is not possible. A further question is of course whether national courts proceed to such a reconsideration and whether they comply with instructions from the ECJ that interfere with their national interpretative rules. From this point of view, the ECJ's case law is only a potential claim to supremacy. Be that as it may, from the perspective of EU law, the preceding observations lead to the provisional conclusion that the duty of consistent interpretation must be understood as a superior methodological standard (as a result of the potential disapplication of national interpretative rules and where the national court's appraisal of the forcefulness of the examination required by so far as possible is being overruled).

5. THE LIMITS TO THE DUTY OF CONSISTENT INTERPRETATION

The previous parts of this chapter showed that the duty of consistent interpretation plays an important role in securing the effectiveness of directives. Nevertheless, the duty of consistent interpretation is restricted by general principles of law, in particular by the principles of legal certainty and non-retroactivity. A first question that arises is whether the limits are based on EU or national law principles. I should point out that, most of the time, the ECJ does not explicitly address the question of the origin of the general principle but simply refers to general principles of law.[113] However, in the ECJ's *Kolpinghuis* judgment – a groundbreaking judgment as far as concerns the limits to consistent interpretation and to which many subsequent judgments refer – reference was made to '(...) general principles of law which

113 Case C-105/03 *Pupino*, ECLI:EU:C:2005:386, para. 50; Case C-212/04 *Adeneler*, ECLI:EU:C:2006:443, para. 110; Case C-282/10 *Dominguez*, ECLI:EU:C:2012:33, para. 25; Case C-441/14 *Ajos*, ECLI:EU:C:2016:278, para. 32.

form part of Community law (...)'.[114] Other judgments have also emphasised the importance of there being a link to the EU legal order.[115] Moreover, it is pointed out that the limits were established in the ECJ's case law and therefore can only have their basis in EU law as the ECJ does not have competence to further interpret national law principles. Finally, it has been observed that, since the duty of consistent interpretation has its legal basis in EU law, it follows from the rule of supremacy that it can only be limited through rules belonging to that legal order.[116] Since the limits are therefore based on EU law, this also means that their scope and precise meaning are controlled by EU law.[117] This does not at all mean that national law is irrelevant: it will often provide the ingredients for the application of the limitation (e.g. the legal provision and the scope for its interpretation for the purpose of applying the *contra legem* limitation, or a national procedural rule conferring *res judicata* on a judicial decision).

Since the principle of legal certainty plays a key role, it is useful to mention some of the general characteristics of this principle in EU law. Tridimas defines the principle as expressing '(...) the fundamental premise that those subject to the law must know what the law is so as to be able to plan their actions accordingly'.[118] He provides at the same time that its precise content is difficult to pin down and that it rarely dictates a specific, single, result. Also, it must sometimes give way to other, overriding, arguments.[119] But I should point out that the diffuse nature of the principle of legal certainty is less pertinent in relation to some of the specific requirements that derive from the principle. This brings me to an important point, namely that the principle of legal certainty is a broad principle which encapsulates several corollaries, among which is the principle of non-retroactivity (if, hereinafter, reference is made to the principle of legal certainty this includes the principle of non-retroactivity unless stated otherwise).[120] The legality principle, of which the criminal law variant is of primary importance for the limitation discussed in the

114 Case 80/86 *Kolpinghuis*, ECLI:EU:C:1987:431, para. 13.

115 Case C-268/06 *Impact*, ECLI:EU:C:2008:223, para. 103; Case C-167/17 *Klohn*, ECLI:EU:C:2018:833, para. 63.

116 Prechal (n. 26), p. 204. See also A. Sagan, 'Nationaler Vertrauensschutz nach Junk: Das Ende eines deutschen Alleingangs' (2015/6) *NZA*, p. 342.

117 This is apparent from the statement by AG Jacobs, as it refers to the general principles of EU law as the legal basis for the restrictions. This point is confirmed more explicitly in the Opinion of AG Van Gerven in Case C-106/89 *Marleasing*, ECLI:EU:C:1990:310, para. 8. In Joined Cases C-383/06 to C-385/06 *Vereniging Nationaal Overlegorgaan Sociale Werkvoorziening*, ECLI:EU:C:2008:165, para. 57, which was admittedly delivered in proceedings concerning the interpretation of a regulation, the ECJ considered that the national court had to examine whether the principles of legal certainty and the protection of legitimate expectations could be relied upon as a defence and that this should be approached on the basis of the understanding of those principles under EU law.

118 Tridimas (n. 19), p. 242.

119 Ibid, p. 243.

120 Wissink (n. 26), p. 175; X. Groussot, *General Principles of Community Law* (Europa Law Publishing 2006), p. 194; Tridimas (n. 19), p. 252.

next subparagraph, also traces back to legal certainty. The principle of legal certainty (including its several corollaries) can be a ground of review, but it is mostly invoked as a rule of interpretation.[121] The function which legal certainty performs in relation to the limits to the duty of consistent interpretation does not clearly belong to one of the two categories. On the one hand it further stipulates the extent to which national courts are bound to interpret national law in conformity with directives on the basis of Articles 288 TFEU and 4(3) TEU (with the inclusion of the principle of effectiveness). In other words: it further defines the obligations deriving from those provisions. At the same time it is clearly a self-standing limitation and not merely an interpretative tool. The prominent role of the principle in the context of consistent interpretation is not surprising as it is one of the major concerns of courts when interpreting the law.[122]

In his Opinion for the *Centrosteel* judgment, Advocate General Jacobs provided the following statement:

> 'General principles of law recognised by the Court do, however, impose certain limitations on the obligation to interpret national law in the light of directives. On the one hand, as the Court ruled in *Pretore di Salò*, the interpretation of national law must not create a new, or aggravate an existing, criminal liability which would not have existed but for the Directive. On the other hand, the national court is not required to interpret national law in a way which is contrary to the express terms of the relevant legislation'.[123]

This paragraph first discusses the question to what extent a consistent interpretation can result in the imposition of obligations on an individual, which includes, as a separate category, the discussion on the restriction regarding criminal liability. Next, the second limitation referred to by Advocate General Jacobs, i.e. that there is no requirement to adopt a *contra legem* interpretation, is analysed. By the way, one of the conclusions that will be drawn from this analysis is that it is not sufficiently accurate to describe the *contra legem* limitation as not requiring an interpretation 'which is contrary to the express terms of the relevant legislation' (compare Advocate General Jacobs's definition above, but also take into account that he made these remarks before the ECJ itself formally introduced the *contra legem* limitation). For a long time, this limitation, and the one regarding criminal liability, were indeed the only restrictions that have been unambiguously confirmed by the ECJ's case law. However, in its *Klohn* judgment the ECJ also recognised the principle of *res judicata* as a limitation to the duty of consistent interpretation and, albeit that this remains a more ambiguous point, also seemed to recognise, in principle, the possibility of invoking the principle of legitimate expectations against the duty

121 Tridimas (n. 19), p. 244.
122 Prechal (n. 26), p. 208.
123 Opinion of AG Jacobs in Case C-456/98 *Centrosteel*, ECLI:EU:C:2000:137, para. 32.

of consistent interpretation. Both limits also derive from the principle of legal certainty. This paragraph also discusses whether it is conceivable that other limits than the ones that have so far been explicitly discussed by the ECJ in the context of the duty of consistent interpretation, and in particular fundamental rights, could be invoked as a limitation to that obligation.

5.1. IMPOSING AN OBLIGATION ON AN INDIVIDUAL AS A RESULT OF A CONSISTENT INTERPRETATION

5.1.1. *Determining or Aggravating Criminal Liability*

Starting in the specific context of criminal law, the *Kolpinghuis* judgment introduced the following limitation to the duty of consistent interpretation:

> '(...) that obligation on the national court to refer to the content of the directive when interpreting the relevant rules of its national law is limited by the general principles of law which form part of Community law and in particular the principles of legal certainty and non-retroactivity. Thus the Court ruled in its judgment of 11 June 1987 in Case 14/86 *Pretore di Salò v X* (…) that a directive cannot, of itself and independently of a national law adopted by a Member State for its implementation, have the effect of determining or aggravating the liability in criminal law of persons who act in contravention of the provisions of that directive'.[124]

The *Pretore di Salò* judgment, to which reference was made, was delivered in the context of criminal proceedings and provided the prohibition to determine or aggravate criminal liability where the directive is directly relied upon by a Member State against an individual.[125] That is in line with the *Marshall I* judgment which prohibited that a directive is relied upon against an individual, whether in criminal proceedings or otherwise.[126] However, the limitation in the *Kolpinghuis* judgment is not the same. First, consider the following clarification in the *Criminal proceedings against X* judgment regarding the origins of this limitation:

> 'More specifically, in a case such as that in the main proceedings, which concerns the extent of liability in criminal law arising under legislation adopted for the specific purpose of implementing a directive, the principle that a provision of the criminal law may not be applied extensively to the detriment of the defendant, which is the corollary of the principle of legality in relation to crime and punishment and more generally of the principle of legal certainty, precludes bringing criminal proceedings in respect of conduct not clearly defined as culpable by law. That principle, which is one of the general legal principles underlying the constitutional traditions common to the

124 Case 80/86 *Kolpinghuis*, ECLI:EU:C:1987:431, para. 13.

125 Case 14/86 *Pretore di Salò*, ECLI:EU:C:1987:275, paras. 18-20.

126 Case 152/84 *Marshall I*, ECLI:EU:C:1986:84, para. 48.

> Member States, has also been enshrined in various international treaties, in particular in Article 7 of the Convention for the Protection of Human Rights and Fundamental Freedoms (...)'.[127]

It is thus clear that the limitation is based on EU law itself, more specifically the principle that a provision of the criminal law may not be applied extensively to the detriment of the defendant (*nullum crimen, nulla poena sine lege*), which is the corollary of the principle of legality in relation to crime and punishment and more generally of the principle of legal certainty. The conduct giving rise to criminal liability must be stipulated in the law in a sufficiently specific and clear manner; it must satisfy the requirement of *lex certa*. In the *Criminal proceedings against X* judgment, the ECJ does not refer to the principle of non-retroactivity, but it is clear that this is the second element to which the limitation from the *Kolpinghuis* judgment refers. This principle is again derivative of legal certainty,[128] and imposes a strict limitation when at the material time certain behaviour did not yet constitute a violation. It should be noted that, after the introduction of the Charter, the ECJ has also referred to Article 49(1) of this instrument (enshrining the principle of legality of criminal offences).[129] It follows that the reasoning behind this limitation is specific to criminal law whereas the reasoning in the *Marshall I* judgment referred to the wording of Article 288 TFEU and the characteristics of directives and was therefore not confined to a particular area of law (indeed, the prohibition that a directive is relied upon against an individual applies regardless of the area of law to which it is applied).

Secondly, the limitation from the *Kolpinghuis* judgment only concerns the determination or aggravation of criminal liability and does not apply to other aspects of criminal proceedings. The *Pupino* judgment, delivered in the context of a framework decision, concerned criminal proceedings against Mrs Pupino, a nursery school teacher charged with inflicting injuries on pupils. The judgment provided that the limitation identified in the *Kolpinghuis* judgment did not apply as the material question concerned the conduct of the proceedings and the means of taking evidence instead of the extent of Mrs Pupino's criminal liability.[130] By

---

127 Joined Cases C-74/95 and C-129/95 *Criminal proceedings against X*, ECLI:EU:C:1996:491, para. 25. See also Opinion of AG Jacobs in Joined Cases C-206/88 and C-207/88 *Vessoso and Zanetti*, ECLI:EU:C:1989:644, para. 25; Opinion of AG Elmer in Case C-168/95 *Arcaro*, ECLI:EU:C:1996:107, para. 41; Opinion of AG Ruiz-Jarabo Colomer in Joined Cases C-74/95 and C-129/95 *Criminal proceedings against X*, ECLI:EU:C:1996:239, paras. 43-4.

128 J.E. Van den Brink and others, 'General Principles of Law', in: J.H. Jans, S. Prechal and R.J.G.M. Widdershoven (Eds.), *Europeanisation of Public Law* (Europa Law Publishing 2015), p. 208.

129 Case C-7/11 *Caronna*, ECLI:EU:C:2012:396, para. 55. The reference to Article 49 of the Charter is quite logical on account of the reference to the corresponding Article 7 ECHR in Joined Cases C-74/95 and C-129/95 *Criminal proceedings against X*, ECLI:EU:C:1996:491, para. 25 (delivered before the introduction of the Charter and hence referring to the ECHR).

130 Case C-105/03 *Pupino*, ECLI:EU:C:2005:386, para. 46. The procedural point concerned the taking of testimonies of the victims, who were pupils of less than five years at the time that the

contrast, it is immaterial for the limitation laid down in the *Marshall I* judgment what kind of obligation is imposed.

Thirdly, as far as concerns the *lex certa* component of the limitation established in the *Kolpinghuis* judgment, the difficulty lies in determing at what point a directive 'of itself and independently of a national law' determines or aggravates criminal liability. Surely, just like any other provision of national law, provisions of criminal law usually require a certain degree of interpretation.[131] It is therefore, to a certain extent, an open question at what point the consistent interpretation as such established criminal liability.[132] Unlike the limitation established in the *Marshall I* and *Pretore di Salò* judgments, the limitation established in the *Kolpinghuis* judgment does not wholly exclude that a directive is relied upon against individuals. As Betlem explains:

> 'It will be remembered that the ECJ had first decided in [the *Kolpinghuis* judgment; SWH] that also in the context of criminal liability where the state sought to invoke EC law to the detriment of an individual the courts are obliged to give indirect effect to a directive (the preliminary question also asked whether a court *was allowed* to do so). By contrast, it ruled out any possibility for the State to rely on direct effect as against an individual (so-called inverse vertical direct effect)'.[133]

By contrast, the second component, i.e. the prohibition of retroactivity, imposes an unambiguous limitation; it should normally be clear whether or not criminal law is applied retrospectively, and in that case the prohibition applies.[134]

Since the effect of the *lex certa* limitation is less straightforward, a few more comments are devoted to this component. Notwithstanding the fact that, in principle, the duty of consistent interpretation also applies in the context of criminal liability, it seems to me that the *Kolpinghuis* judgment signalled to national courts that the influence of the duty of consistent interpretation will be more modest when criminal liability is concerned. So while national courts should still follow an interpretation that is in conformity with the directive where more than one interpretation is possible, it is assumed that the principle that a provision of the criminal law must be stated in a sufficiently clear manner, increases the degree of autonomy for the national court to decide that a definition in criminal law cannot accommodate a consistent interpretation. Generally speaking, this means that the duty of consistent

offences were committed, under special arrangements instead of in court, which would have harmful effects on the children's well-being.

131 Opinion of AG Ruiz-Jarabo Colomer in Joined Cases C-74/95 and C-129/95 *Criminal proceedings against X*, ECLI:EU:C:1996:239, para. 58.

132 See also J.G.H. Altena-Davidsen, *Het legaliteitsbeginsel en de doorwerking van Europees recht in het Nederlandse materiële strafrecht* (Kluwer 2016), p. 125.

133 Betlem (n. 88), p. 406.

134 Altena-Davidsen (n. 132), p. 302.

interpretation must defer to whatever is considered possible according to national rules of interpretation. It cannot require them to go further than this. This *also* translates, to some extent, to the methodological instructions on the application of the duty of consistent interpretation mentioned in subparagraph 4.2. I think, for example, that it must be accepted that national courts will sooner come to the conclusion that national interpretative rules do not permit one provision to be applied instead of another, even though the former might lead to a consistent interpretation. Also, if it was unforeseeable that, as a result of an application of the presumption that the legislature intends to comply with directives, certain behaviour would come within the scope of a provision of criminal law, the national court is in my view not obliged to comply with the presumption. This is what I mean when I point out that the national courts' autonomy increases. This seems to put national law first, but it should not be overlooked that this window is only opened as a result of the approval by EU law to do so.

Since the basis of the principle is found in EU law, it must in any event be taken into account as a limitation to the duty of consistent interpretation, whose influence is arguably more limited. A related question is whether national courts could, if this is possible on the basis of national interpretative rules, push the interpretation of a national provision of criminal law to the point where this would be incompatible with the EU law principle that a provision of the criminal law may not be applied extensively to the detriment of the defendant. This actually turns out to be an irrelevant question:

> The above discussion made clear that the limitation from the *Kolpinghuis* judgment conferred an additional degree of autonomy to national courts when the question of consistent interpretation concerns the determination or aggravation of criminal liability. The idea is therefore to leave more, and not less, to the decision of the national courts. Although this limitation has its origins in EU law upholding the principle that a provision of the criminal law may not be applied extensively to the detriment of the defendant, no substantive criteria are provided for determining whether the interpretation of national law complies with this principle. Instead, it was seen that, at least in the context of the duty of consistent interpretation, this matter is left to be decided by national courts. The only parameters are the remaining requirement to interpret national law so far as possible in conformity with EU law, whose effect will be more modest in the context of criminal liability, and the *contra legem* limitation. Within those parameters national courts cannot be faulted for adopting a particular interpretation. By the way, a violation of the *contra legem* limitation stands on its own and should be separated from the present discussion.

The principle that a provision of criminal law may not be applied extensively to the detriment of the defendant operates in the specific context of criminal law. It is recalled that this area of law is not included in the research. However, as will be seen in chapters 3 and 5, the limitations established in the *Kolpinghuis* judgment, national courts consider this limitation to be relevant for certain administrative law cases as well.

5.1.2. Obligations Imposed on Individuals Outside the Area of Criminal Law

The starting point for this discussion is the *Arcaro* judgment, which stated that the duty of consistent interpretation:

> '(...) reaches a limit where such an interpretation leads to the imposition on an individual of an obligation laid down by a directive which has not been transposed or, more especially, where it has the effect of determining or aggravating, on the basis of the directive and in the absence of a law enacted for its implementation, the liability in criminal law of persons who act in contravention of that directive's provisions'.[135]

The first sentence of this paragraph perhaps gives the impression that a consistent interpretation is not possible whenever an obligation is imposed on individuals. This would have been a major setback for the enforcement of directives through the duty of consistent interpretation and would clearly be incompatible with both pre-existing and subsequent case law showing that a consistent interpretation can entail disadvantages for individuals.[136] In my opinion, a different interpretation must therefore be sought. In Advocate-General Elmer's Opinion for this judgment, he reiterated that a direct effect, whereby the directive 'of itself' imposes obligations on individuals, is not permitted. He also mentioned that the duty of consistent interpretation cannot be applied in a way '[t]hat would be tantamount to introducing the direct effect of provisions of a directive imposing obligations on individuals by the back door'.[137] As it cannot be accommodated by national law anymore, it seems that it was felt that a too far-reaching application of the duty of consistent interpretation would entail that the obligation is imposed by the directive itself.[138] The explanation for the difference in the scope of application

---

135 Case C-168/95 *Arcaro*, ECLI:EU:C:1996:363, para. 42.

136 For example, in Case C-106/89 *Marleasing*, ECLI:EU:C:1990:395, the result would be that a ground for invoking the nullity of a contract establishing a public limited company, provided by national law, could not be invoked; in Case C-91/92 *Faccini Dori*, ECLI:EU:C:1994:292, the nullity of the contract could be invoked; in Joined Cases C-240/98 to C-244/98 *Océano*, ECLI:EU:C:2000:346, an undertaking was deprived of the benefit under national law to enforce contracts before a particular court.

137 Opinion of AG Elmer in the *Arcaro* judgment, ECLI:EU:C:1996:107, paras. 30, 39.

138 See also Case C-235/03 *QDQ Media*, ECLI:EU:C:2005:147, paras. 15-6, where the referring court indicated that a result in conformity with the directive could not be attained by the application of national law. The ECJ considered that '[i]n such a case, which relates to a dispute between individuals, as in the main proceedings, a directive cannot of itself impose obligations on an individual and cannot be relied upon as such against an individual'. See further P. Craig, 'The Legal Effect of Directives: Policy, Rules and Exceptions' (2009/3) *ELRev*, p. 363: '[t]he "correct characterisation" will depend on the change to pre-existing national law from reading it with the Directive'.

between the duty of consistent interpretation and direct effect indeed always relied on the argument that the former was based on an interpretation that could still be accommodated by national law, so that it was actually the latter which affected the legal position of individuals. On this interpretation, the concerned paragraph of the *Arcaro* judgment reminded that, once a certain point is crossed, the justification for this distinction no longer applies – this is done, moreover, in a way that highlights the coherence of the effects produced by the duty of consistent interpretation and direct effect. For the sake of completeness, I should add that the duty of consistent interpretation can also not be applied in a way that goes beyond what is possible in terms of interpretation in the situation where the directive favours the position of an individual. This will of course be less of an issue as individuals can then in principle rely on the direct effect of directives.

The proposed interpretation is confirmed by the subsequent *Kofoed* judgment, which referred to the relevant paragraph of the *Arcaro* judgment, and stated that:

> '(...) although it is true that the requirement of a directive-compliant interpretation cannot reach the point where a directive, by itself and without national implementing legislation, may create obligations for individuals or determine or aggravate the liability in criminal law of persons who act in contravention of its provisions, a Member State may nevertheless, in principle, impose a directive-compliant interpretation of national law on individuals'.[139]

In the first place, this confirmed that the duty of consistent interpretation does not cease to apply whenever this could result in a disadvantage for individuals. Secondly, the final part of the sentence accurately pointed out that it is national law, interpreted in conformity with the directive, that imposes the obligation on the individuals, and this is contrasted with the situation described in the first part of the sentence, where interpretation crosses a certain point and where it is the directive 'by itself and without national implementing legislation', that then imposes an obligation on individuals.

Alternative interpretations of the first part of the sentence of the concerned paragraph from the *Arcaro* judgment are less compelling. First, it could be interpreted very narrowly as only applying to the judgment's criminal law context, and as merely confirming the limitation introduced in the *Kolpinghuis* judgment. However, this is difficult to reconcile with the actual text of the judgment, which clearly suggests a distinction between imposing obligations on individuals in general and the specific prohibition to determine or aggravate criminal liability; the second part of the sentence of the cited paragraph concerning criminal liability would become redundant. Secondly, after the *Arcaro* judgment, *but*

139 Case C-321/05 *Kofoed*, ECLI:EU:C:2007:408, para. 45. Confirmed in Case C-53/10 *Mücksch*, ECLI:EU:C:2011:585, para. 34.

before delivery of the Kofoed judgment, it was suggested that obligations could not be imposed on individuals through a consistent interpretation on the basis of an unimplemented directive where this confers a corresponding advantage on a Member State (i.e. in so-called inverse vertical relationships).[140] This would be a broader limitation than the one laid down in the *Kolpinghuis* judgment – and therefore would remove the incongruity with the wording of the judgment – but still accepts that in horizontal relationships a consistent interpretation can result in a disadvantage for individuals – so that it would also be compatible with both pre-existing and subsequent case law to that effect. Yet, the *Kofoed* judgment, which held that a consistent interpretation can be imposed on individuals, related to a vertical dispute regarding taxes, where the directive favoured the position of the Member State. The point that a consistent interpretation can also result in the imposition of obligations on individuals in so-called inverse vertical situations was explicitly confirmed in the ECJ's *Mücksch* judgment.[141] This second, alternative, interpretation, must therefore also be rejected.

It can therefore be concluded from the *Arcaro* judgment that: on the basis of a consistent interpretation of national law, obligations can be imposed on individuals (whether in horizontal or inverse vertical relationships, but note the specific limitation already introduced in the *Kolpinghuis* judgment if the latter category concerns criminal proceedings) as long as it cannot be said that this result is produced by the directive only.[142] The ECJ's case law does not explicitly provide when the point is reached where it can no longer be said that the obligation follows from national law itself. In that sense it is just as ambiguous as the expression that national courts are only required to interpret national law 'so far as possible'. Be that as it may, from a more fundamental point of view, it is to be welcomed that the *Arcaro* judgment clarified that 'so far as possible' entails that national law must offer some scope for accommodating the consistent interpretation and that, at a certain point, the duty of consistent interpretation no longer applies. It could be argued that this is inherent to the formulation 'so far as possible', but in that case the *Arcaro* judgment explicated what was previously only implicated. The *Arcaro* judgment was delivered some time before the introduction of the *contra legem* limitation. It can be said that the conception of the limits to the duty of consistent interpretation that surfaced in the *Arcaro* judgment, further matured in the case law concerning *contra legem,* which is discussed next.

---

140 Klamert (n. 42), p. 57-8; T. Tridimas, 'Black, White and Shades of Grey: Horizontality of Directives Revisited' (2001/1) *YEL*, p. 349; Drake (n. 23), p. 338.

141 Case C-53/10 *Mücksch,* ECLI:EU:C:2011:585.

142 This is also the approach adopted in the Opinion of AG Kokott in Case C-321/05 *Kofoed,* ECLI:EU:C:2007:86, paras. 65-6, which emphasised that it is permitted that, through national law, that is to say, indirectly, EU law is applied to the detriment of an individual, which must be distinguished from the situation in which a directive of itself imposes the obligation and is relied upon as such against an individual, which is not permitted.

5.2. NO REQUIREMENT TO ADOPT A *CONTRA LEGEM* INTERPRETATION

In relation to directives, the limitation of a *contra legem* interpretation was first mentioned in the *Adeneler* judgment, providing that the duty of consistent interpretation '(...) is limited by general principles of law, particularly those of legal certainty and non-retroactivity, and that obligation cannot serve as the basis for an interpretation of national law *contra legem*'.[143] This is an important limitation, which is not confined to a particular area of the law. Broadly speaking, it marks out an area in which an interpretation of the law deviates from what is normally considered to be acceptable. The question is of course when this can be said to be the case.

The *contra legem* limitation has been invoked as evidence that the duty of consistent interpretation only operates within the limits set by national interpretative rules.[144] In other words, could it perhaps be so that, whatever positive requirements the duty to interpret national law 'so far as possible' imposes on national courts (see the previous paragraph), can be counteracted by invoking limits set by national interpretative rules under the *contra legem* limitation?[145] In a similar vein, Dougan puts forward that, when it comes to explaining the *contra legem* limitation, the theory of supremacy of EU law is not persuasive, and contends, more generally, that the *contra legem* limitation contradicts an approach to the duty of consistent interpretation based on supremacy.[146] In order to asses these statements, and to understand what the *contra legem* limitation says about the relationship between EU and national law, it is examined what its origins are and what *contra legem* means.

5.2.1. *The Origins of the* Contra Legem *Limitation*

The paragraph from the Opinion of Advocate General Jacobs in the *Centrosteel* judgment, cited at the beginning of this paragraph, which was delivered before the *Adeneler* judgment, saw the *contra legem* limitation as being derived from general principles of EU law. The above excerpt from the *Adeneler* judgment also referred to general principles of EU law and pointed to the principle of legal certainty in

143 Case C-212/04 *Adeneler*, ECLI:EU:C:2006:443, para. 110, referring to Case C-105/03 *Pupino*, ECLI:EU:C:2005:386, para. 47.

144 M. Auer, 'Neues zu Umfang und Grenzen der richtlinienkonformen Auslegung' (2007/16) *NJW*, p. 1107.

145 This possibility is suggested in Canaris (n. 9), p. 95. Note, however, that this suggestion was made before the *Adeneler* judgment, and subsequent case law, were delivered.

146 Dougan (n. 27), p. 947.

particular.[147] Opinions of Advocates General and legal scholarship have adopted the same view.[148]

It is pointed out that the *Adeneler* judgment stated that the duty of consistent interpretation '(...) cannot serve as the basis for an interpretation of national law *contra legem*'. This has been understood as not obliging, but at the same time not prohibiting, national courts to adopt an interpretation *contra legem*.[149] Is it sustainable that EU law does not prohibit national courts to proceed to a *contra legem* interpretation, even though such an interpretation is believed to be to the detriment of the general principle of EU law regarding legal certainty? One answer could be that this is not an obstacle as the *Adeneler* and subsequent judgments clearly state legal certainty as a limitation to the duty of consistent interpretation itself and not in relation to whatever interpretation is adopted by the national court. So when the national court goes further than required, this is no longer a consequence or concern of the duty of consistent interpretation – although it could be argued that they are nevertheless acting within the scope of EU law and therefore should abide by the general principles of EU law, but that is another matter.[150] Yet, this answer presupposes that the ECJ's case law regarding the *contra legem* limitation concerns itself with supervising the national courts to ensure that they do not take the duty of consistent interpretation too far. As will be discussed further below, the ECJ may, exceptionally, interfere with the national court's interpretation of *contra legem*, but it will only do so to prevent national courts from taking recourse to this limitation too quickly. Apart from that, it rather leaves it to the national courts to make an appeal to the *contra legem* limitation, and accepts that the meaning of *contra legem* does not have to be identical for all the Member States. This is not really a surprise, taking into account that consistent interpretation is about the interpretation of national law, for which the national rules of interpretation are, in principle, the decisive factor. It is also not inconsistent since legal certainty is a flexible principle, whose impact can depend on the specific circumstances, which justifies that the different national contexts within which the duty of consistent interpretation is applied are taken into account.[151] The point is, and this could be a second affirmative answer to the question posed, that, in the context of the duty of consistent interpretation, legal certainty does not function as a means to supervise the national courts, but rather offers them an optional dispensation that can be invoked when a consistent interpretation would be unacceptable in their legal

147 See also e.g. Case C-605/15 *Aviva*, ECLI:EU:C:2017:718, paras. 37-8.

148 Opinion of AG Trstenjak in Case C-282/10 *Dominguez*, ECLI:EU:C:2011:559, para. 67; Opinion of AG Sharpston in Case C-79/11 *Giovanardi*, ECLI:EU:C:2012:297, para. 65; Opinion of AG Kokott in Case C-151/12 *Commission v Spain*, ECLI:EU:C:2013:354, para. 25. See also Prechal (n. 26), p. 207.

149 Suhr (n. 67), p. 93; Brenncke (n. 61), p. 143.

150 Cf. Prechal (n. 26), p. 208.

151 Ibid, p. 207.

order. If the first and second affirmative answer are taken into account, it does not seem to be inconsistent that no prohibition is imposed, so that it does not stand in the way of accepting legal certainty as requiring the *contra legem* limitation.

Finally, can the origins of the *contra legem* limitation also be found elsewhere? Could it be said that the *contra legem* limitation is inherent in the expression 'so far as possible'?[152] Indeed, a close relationship cannot be denied. In addition to this, the *contra legem* limitation of course touches upon the separation of powers between the legislature and the judiciary. Does any of this qualify my position that the origins are to be found in the principle of legal certainty? I do not believe that this is so, since it does not alter the fact that from the perspective of the ECJ's case law, the strongest indication for the origins of the *contra legem* limitation is found in the principle of legal certainty. Also, it seems more compelling to derive a limitation on the duty of consistent interpretation from a general principle of EU law, instead of the notion of separation of powers, or Articles 288 TFEU and 4(3) TEU and the principle of effectiveness (providing the legal basis for the duty to interpret national law so far as possible in conformity with EU law).

5.2.2. The Meaning of Contra Legem

What does *contra legem* mean, and who decides? The *Adeneler* judgment did not reveal whether the *contra legem* limitation is considered to be an autonomous EU law concept with a confined meaning or a catchall for limits imposed by national interpretative rules. At first sight, the previous *Pupino* judgment seems to be more instructive in this regard. The referring Italian court had stated that, on the basis of the relevant national legislation referred to in the judgment, it was not possible to make use of special procedures that could guarantee the protection of minors that give testimony, as the facts of the case did not fall within the scope of the relevant national provisions. Moreover, one of the arguments put forward by the Italian Government for denying the jurisdiction of the ECJ to give a preliminary ruling, was that it cannot have an impact on the solution of the dispute in the main proceedings on account of the limits inherent to the duty of consistent interpretation. Nonetheless, in the Opinion of Advocate General Kokott, it was argued that it was not inconceivable that a consistent interpretation might be possible. Importantly, it also mentioned that – despite the observations regarding the interpretation of the applicable national legislation – the referring court itself did not seem to exclude the possibility of a consistent interpretation entirely.[153] This must be taken into account when reading the ECJ's response which, in addition to stating the *contra legem* limitation, in a subsequent paragraph concluded that '(…) it is not obvious that an interpretation of national law in conformity with the framework decision

152 Wissink (n. 26), p. 201, 203.
153 Opinion of AG Kokott in Case C-105/03 *Pupino*, ECLI:EU:C:2004:712, para. 40.

is impossible'.[154] This was followed by the acknowledgement that it is ultimately for the national court to determine whether a consistent interpretation is possible. While it might be argued that the *Pupino* judgment indicated that the ECJ did not consider it obvious that the *contra legem* limitation applied as it continued to rule on the substance of the preliminary question (presupposing, of course, contrary to what was argued above, that the *contra legem* limitation would have entailed an absolute obstacle to proceeding to a consistent interpretation, i.e. constituting a prohibition, making any answer to the question referred obsolete), no direct reference to the *contra legem* limitation was made in the cited paragraph of the judgment. It does not therefore support the view that the ECJ prescribed to the national court how it should apply the *contra legem* limitation. A more cautious interpretation would be that the ECJ merely had to determine whether it had jurisdiction, for which it sufficed that the national court did not itself seem to reject the possibility of a consistent interpretation entirely, and that such a possibility was further substantiated by the suggestions made by Advocate General Kokott in relation to the interpretation of the applicable national law. The reference to the *contra legem* limitation was a general observation regarding the limits that attach to the duty of consistent interpretation, that was triggered by the Italian Government's submission, but was left unapplied when the ECJ turned to the facts of the case before it. I am therefore hesitant to ascribe a meaning to the *contra legem* limitation on the basis of the *Pupino* judgment.

In the *Quelle* judgment it was also brought to the ECJ's attention that national law could not be given a consistent interpretation. This time, however, the national court explicitly referred to the *contra legem* limitation. The referring court pointed out that if the interpretation of the directive advocated by the applicant was correct, a consistent interpretation would be at odds with the wording of the provision of national law and the clear intention of the legislature, and therefore prohibited by the German Constitution.[155] Against that background, the ECJ reiterated that it is for the national court to determine the necessity and relevance of submitting a preliminary question, and that it will only refuse such a request in a limited number of circumstances, which did not apply in the present case. Uncertainty whether it is possible, in the main proceedings before the referring court, to adopt a consistent interpretation (taking into account, among others, the *contra legem* limitation provided in the *Adeneler* judgment), cannot affect the ECJ's obligation to answer the preliminary question.[156] The ECJ's binary approach towards its own task and that of the national courts, seemed to have been inspired by Advocate General Trstenjak's observation that the *contra legem* limitation only comes into

154 Case C-105/03 *Pupino*, ECLI:EU:C:2005:386, para. 48.

155 Reference was made to Paragraph 20(3) of the German Constitution, which provides that the judiciary is bound by law and justice. See further chapter 3, subparagraph 3.1.

156 Case C-404/06 *Quelle*, ECLI:EU:C:2008:231, paras. 18-22.

play when the *national* court applies the duty of consistent interpretation in the *national* proceedings.[157] Although it follows from the next two judgments that this is not entirely correct, it shows the ECJ's preference to see *contra legem* as a matter that is first and foremost decided by the national courts.

Unlike the previous two judgments, the *Impact* judgment, originating in a preliminary reference from the Irish Labour Court, included the discussion on the *contra legem* limitation in the answer to the preliminary question itself. The reason for this is probably that one of the questions of the referring court asked whether it was required, on account of the duty of consistent interpretation, to give implementing legislation that entered into force after expiry of the transposition period retrospective effect to the date by which the directive should have been transposed. Such was not explicitly excluded by the wording of the relevant provisions of national law but a national interpretative rule did preclude the retrospective application of legislation unless there was a clear and unambiguous indication to the contrary. The ECJ observed that the national court should determine whether the relevant provisions of national law can provide such an indication. However, if this were not the case:

> '(…) Community law – in particular the requirement for national law to be interpreted in conformity with Community law – cannot be interpreted as requiring the referring court to give section 6 of the 2003 Act retrospective effect to the date by which Directive 1999/70 should have been transposed, as the referring court would otherwise be constrained to interpret national law *contra legem*'.[158]

Although this time the ECJ's ruling explicitly included the meaning of the *contra legem* limitation, its considerations resemble the hands-off approach to the question when an interpretation is *contra legem*, that was already seen in the *Quelle* judgment.[159] Although there is something to be said for not applying legislation retroactively through the duty of consistent interpretation, it is interesting to see that, in principle, the *contra legem* limitation can also encompass a national rule regarding the interpretation of legislation. Moreover, I should add that in Irish law the rule against retroactive effect is unwritten.[160] It should be noted that the *contra legem* limitation has also been discussed by the ECJ in the context of the principle of *res judicata* in the *Klohn* judgment – and it is noted that the preliminary reference again originated from an Irish court.[161]

---

157 Opinion of AG Trstenjak in Case C-404/06 *Quelle*, ECLI:EU:C:2007:682, para. 39.

158 Case C-268/06 *Impact*, ECLI:EU:C:2008:223, para. 103.

159 See also A. Arnull, 'The Principle of Effective Judicial Protection in EU Law: An Unruly Horse?' (2011/1) *ELRev*, p. 60; Michael and Payandeh (n. 70), p. 2396.

160 Byrne and others, *Byrne and McCutcheon on the Irish Legal System* (Bloomsbury 2014), p. 677-9.

161 Case C-167/17 *Klohn*, ECLI:EU:C:2018:833, para. 65.

The two rulings originating in preliminary questions submitted by Irish courts appear to entail that the meaning of *contra legem* cannot be confined to an interpretation against the clear wording of a provision, which had been a commonly held view, espoused in, among others, the Opinion of Advocate General Jacobs in the *Centrosteel* judgment, cited at the beginning of this paragraph.[162] This does not change the fact that where the wording of a provision is clearly incompatible with the directive, this is likely to be a situation in which the *contra legem* limitation becomes relevant. For example, in the *AMS* judgment, the ECJ considered that it was apparent from the referring court's judgment asking the preliminary questions that the relevant provision of national law could not accommodate a consistent interpretation and that this would be *contra legem*.[163] This seemed to be a result of the wording of that provision.

> The ECJ concluded that Article 3(1) of Directive 2002/14[164] precludes that workers with assisted contracts (apprentices, employees with an employment-initiative contract or accompanied-employment contract and employees with a professional training contract) were excluded from the calculation of the number of employees in an undertaking when determining the thresholds for the establishment of bodies representing employees. Article L. 1111-3 of the French Labour Code explicitly excluded this category of workers from the calculation of the number of employees.

One might object that the *AMS* judgment is difficult to reconcile with the *Quelle* judgment, as the national court had discussed the difficulties of adopting a consistent interpretation more elaborately in the latter judgment but the ECJ did not provide any guidance as to whether the *contra legem* limitation applied, leaving this matter entirely to the national court. However, in the *AMS* judgment the preliminary questions clearly asked whether the provisions of EU law had direct effect, implying that it did not consider it possible to adopt a consistent interpretation, whereas the preliminary question in the *Quelle* judgment only asked the ECJ how the directive had to be interpreted. It can therefore be concluded that the formulation of the preliminary question is a relevant factor and that additional

---

162 See, further, the Opinion of AG Van Gerven in Case C-271/91 *Marshall II*, ECLI:EU:C:1993:30, para. 41; Opinion of AG Elmer in Case C-168/95 *Arcaro*, ECLI:EU:C:1996:107, paras. 39-41; Opinion of AG Bot in Case C-441/14 *Ajos*, ECLI:EU:C:2015:776, para. 68. See also Prechal (n. 26), p 207. But see also, for example, Wissink (n. 38), p. 146, who proposes a broader understanding of *contra legem* whereby this limit is reached when national courts, after having balanced all the available arguments with the objective to come to a consistent interpretation, conclude that this is simply not possible.

163 Case C-176/12 *AMS*, ECLI:EU:C:2014:2, paras. 39-40. See also, albeit before the introduction of the limitation that a *contra legem* interpretation is not required, and thus using different terminology, Case C-111/97 *EvoBus Austria*, ECLI:EU:C:1998:434, para. 20. Another example is provided by Case C-193/17 *Cresco Investigation*, ECLI:EU:C:2019:43, para. 21.

164 Directive 2002/14/EC of the European Parliament and of the Council of 11 March 2002 establishing a general framework for informing and consulting employees in the European Community - Joint declaration of the European Parliament, the Council and the Commission on employee representation, *OJ* 2002, L80/29.

clarifications do not in itself induce the ECJ to extend the scope of its answer. The fact that the aspect concerning the *contra legem* limitation must be included in the preliminary questions is further supported by the *Mücksch* judgment, where national law did not initially seem to provide any discretion for the public authority to take the directive into account. Nevertheless, the ECJ referred to the duty of consistent interpretation as a possible way to resolve the incompatibility with the directive but did not go into the question whether a consistent interpretation might be *contra legem*. The silence of the *Mücksch* judgment in this regard has been questioned.[165] But also here, the preliminary questions themselves only addressed the interpretation of the directive, and not the question of how the preliminary ruling can be implemented by the national court in the main proceedings.[166] Whether or not further guidance on the application of the *contra legem* limitation may have been useful for the referring court, it is clear that the approach in the *Mücksch* judgment is entirely in line with the preference of the ECJ to leave the meaning of *contra legem* to the national courts, unless it is clearly invited to assist the national court in this matter. A final example confirming this approach is the *Smith* judgment: in its preliminary question, the Irish Court of Appeal explicitly stated its position that it had found that a consistent interpretation was not possible and the ECJ appeared to accept this position in its answer to the court.[167]

Similar to the *AMS* judgment, the preliminary questions in the *Dominguez* and *Ajos* judgments addressed the direct effect of EU law. In both cases it appeared from the judgment making a reference for a preliminary ruling that the national court had taken recourse to the remedy of direct effect as it considered that the *contra legem* limitation was applicable in the case before it. However, unlike the previously discussed case law, the ECJ did not simply accept the national courts' determination whether a consistent interpretation was possible without going beyond the *contra legem* limitation.[168] It is submitted that the ECJ's involvement is, in principle, legitimated as the *contra legem* limitation was identified by the ECJ itself and has its origins in EU law.[169] I will look at the relevant considerations of the

165 Jans and Verhoeven (n. 73), p. 85.

166 In Case C-395/14 *Vodafone*, ECLI:EU:C:2016:9, it was clear that, according to the referring court, on the basis of national law alone, the applicant's action were to succeed. Nevertheless, it asked the ECJ for a preliminary ruling on the interpretation of the concerned directive. The ECJ's preliminary ruling implied that the position under national law was incompatible with the directive, but it did not discuss the resulting interpretative difficulties for the implementation of its interpretation of the directive in the main proceedings. However, again the preliminary question did not address this matter.

167 Case C-122/17 *Smith*, ECLI:EU:C:2018:631, para. 49.

168 It would be interesting to see whether the ECJ would take a more active approach if the preliminary questions do not at all address the consequences of the interpretation of the directive for the national proceedings, but where the ECJ believes it is clear from the judgment making a reference for a preliminary ruling that the referring court interpreted the scope of the *contra legem* limitation too extensively. To my knowledge, this situation has not yet occurred.

169 Opinion of AG Bot in Case C-441/14 *Ajos*, ECLI:EU:C:2015:776, para. 53.

ECJ in both judgments to determine whether, and if so to what extent, the national courts' discretion over the meaning of *contra legem* is restricted. In the *Dominguez* judgment, the ECJ actually prevented a direct confrontation, providing that the referring court encountered the *contra legem* limitation in respect of Article L. 223-2 of the French Labour Code, but that it might nevertheless be possible to adopt a consistent interpretation through Article L. 223-4 (this is in line with the obligation to consider national law as a whole, see further subparagraphs 4.1 and 4.3).[170] Although it might be said that, as the preliminary question only addressed the possibility to give effect to EU law by means of direct effect, the referring court had ruled out the possibility of a consistent interpretation entirely, the ECJ's approach avoided a dispute over the referring court's finding that a consistent interpretation of Article L. 223-2 of the French Labour Code would be *contra legem*.[171] It should be emphasised that the final decision whether a consistent interpretation could be adopted was left to the referring court.[172] In the *Ajos* judgment the ECJ stated that:

> '(...) the requirement to interpret national law in conformity with EU law entails the obligation for national courts to change its established case-law, where necessary, if it is based on an interpretation of national law that is incompatible with the objectives of a directive.
>
> Accordingly, the national court cannot validly claim in the main proceedings that it is impossible for it to interpret the national provision at issue in a manner that is consistent with EU law by mere reason of the fact that it has consistently interpreted that provision in a manner that is incompatible with EU law'.[173]

It is clear from the judgment making the reference for a preliminary ruling that the referring court formulated the impossibility to adopt a consistent interpretation in the terms of the *contra legem* limitation (so that the ECJ's considerations must be understood as being related to this concept). Three remarks must be made here. First, in the judgment making a reference for a preliminary ruling, the conclusion that a consistent interpretation would be *contra legem* was only based on settled national case law. It is clear from the second part of the excerpt that it is only in that specific scenario that the national courts' discretion to determine whether a consistent interpretation is possible, in particular whether such an interpretation would be *contra legem*, is limited. Secondly, the first part of the excerpt does not in my opinion entail that settled case law can never be relevant for determining the meaning of *contra legem*. This paragraph repeated the position previously adopted in the *Centrosteel* judgment.[174] It seems clear that, in that judgment, as well as the

170 Case C-282/10 *Dominguez*, ECLI:EU:C:2012:33, paras. 26-9. See also the case note by Widdershoven in *AB* 2012/48, para. 3.

171 Cf. the Opinion of AG Trstenjak in Case C-282/10 *Dominguez*, ECLI:EU:C:2011:559, para. 68.

172 Case C-282/10 *Dominguez*, ECLI:EU:C:2012:33, paras. 31-2.

173 Case C-441/14 *Ajos*, ECLI:EU:C:2016:278, paras. 33-4. Subsequently confirmed in Case C-414/16 *Egenberger*, ECLI:EU:C:2018:257, paras. 72-3; Case C-68/17 *IR*, ECLI:EU:C:2018:696, para. 64.

174 Case C-456/98 *Centrosteel*, ECLI:EU:C:2000:402, para. 17.

Ajos judgment, the obligation to change settled case law must be read in the light of the qualification that national courts are only required to do so if this is possible. The point seemed to be that if a provision has been interpreted in a certain way in settled case law this, in itself, does not exclude the possibility of a consistent interpretation. From this point of view, the first and second paragraph cited, fit in well with each other. Thirdly, although the national court in *Ajos* was required to comply with the ECJ's instructions regarding the *contra legem* limitation, the final decision whether a consistent interpretation could be adopted was left to the referring court.[175] So to put it briefly: the ECJ distinguished between the qualified obligation (i.e. so far as possible) to change settled case law based on an interpretation incompatible with EU law, and the unqualified prohibition to dismiss a consistent interpretation *merely because* the relevant provision has consistently been interpreted in a manner inconsistent with EU law. The *Bauer* judgment confirmed the *Ajos* judgment,[176] but on account of differences in the reasoning in the judgments making a reference for a preliminary ruling, the reference is not self-evident.

> I already noted that in the judgment making a reference for a preliminary ruling in the *Ajos* proceedings, the impossibility of a consistent interpretation was only justified by reference to settled case law. However, in the judgment making a reference for a preliminary ruling in the *Bauer* proceedings, it was submitted that the relevant national provisions could not accommodate a consistent interpretation. And the national case law that was mentioned by the referring court for this purpose shows that the incompatible interpretation is based on a grammatical and systematic interpretation.[177] So it would have been useful if the ECJ elaborated why it considered it appropriate to mention the considerations provided in the *Ajos* judgment here as well. An explanation for this can perhaps be found in the Opinion of Advocate General Bot – but since the ECJ does not explicitly refer to the Opinion, it remains speculative whether this is indeed the correct explanation. The Advocate General recalled the concerned paragraphs from the *Ajos* judgment and appeared to question, albeit indirectly, whether the *contra legem* limitation applied in the case of *Bauer*. In this regard it is interesting that he observed that: '(…) the orders for reference themselves seem to indicate that the incompatibility of the national legislation with EU law is based on the interpretation (…) of those provisions'.[178] It seems that he uses 'interpretation' to denote the application of interpretative methods other than a grammatical interpretation here. In my view the *Ajos* judgment did not state a prohibition to rely on the *contra legem* limitation if the impossibility to adopt a consistent interpretation results from a further interpretation (i.e. one that does not, or does not only, rely on a grammatical interpretation but depends on the application of other interpretative criteria)

175 Case C-441/14 *Ajos*, ECLI:EU:C:2016:278, para. 35.

176 Joined Cases C-569/16 and C-570/16 *Bauer*, ECLI:EU:C:2018:871, para. 68.

177 BAG 18 October 2016, Beck online Rechtsprechung 2016, 74836, para. 14, and see in particular paras. 19-23 of BAG 20 September 2011, NZA 2012, 326, to which the judgment making the reference refers.

178 Opinion of AG Bot in Joined Cases C-569/16 and C-570/16 *Bauer*, ECLI:EU:C:2018:337, para. 42.

> of the national provision.[179] Whether such a development would be desirable is of course another matter. It is recalled that the *Impact* and *Klohn* judgments appeared to indicate a willingness to accept an understanding of the scope of *contra legem* that is not confined to incompatibilities with the wording of the concerned provision. The *Bauer* judgment did not reverse that position, but it does leave room for speculation that the ECJ might be less generous in accepting arguments that a consistent interpretation is not possible because such an interpretation is allegedly *contra legem* in future cases.

As I observed elsewhere, the position adopted in the *Ajos* judgment is hardly surprising. If the referring court's reliance on the *contra legem* limitation, as described in the judgment making a reference for a preliminary ruling, would have been accepted, the cause of the incompatibility of national law with the directive would also provide the justification for its continued existence. This would have entailed a serious impediment to the effectiveness of the duty of consistent interpretation.[180]

If further guidance on the relevance of national case law for the meaning of the *contra legem* limitation is provided, this will probably be done on a case-by-case basis. National courts will probably take the lead in this discussion as they are most likely to submit to the ECJ cases in which they believe the *contra legem* limitation applies. Also in this context, they must submit to the ECJ all relevant information, in particular regarding the extent to which case law limits their interpretative freedom. I discuss three examples to assess to what extent national case law might be relevant for the meaning of *contra legem*. First, I think that national case law is most likely to be relevant if this refers to an unwritten rule with a broader scope of application than interpretations of individual national provisions. An example of this would be an interpretative rule precluding the retrospective application of legislation that was mentioned by the referring court in the *Impact* judgment.[181] Another example would be the jurisprudential rule that some commentators considered to be applicable in the *Von Colson and Kamann* judgment, namely that a limitation on contractual liability also applied to quasi-contractual liability (*Sperrwirkung*).[182] Secondly, if a provision appears to be incompatible with the directive, settled national case law can confirm this incompatibility. However, the applicability of the *contra legem* limitation cannot be based primarily on case law and requires justification by other arguments. Also, the national interpretative rules must have been applied in a way that takes into account the requirements

---

179 That view was explicitly adopted in AG Bot's Opinion in Case C-441/14 *Ajos*, ECLI:EU:C:2015:776, para. 68.

180 S.W. Haket, '*Dansk Industri: nadere afbakening grenzen aan richtlijnconforme interpretatie en horizontale werking algemeen Unierechtelijk beginsel*' (2016/7) *Nederlands tijdschrift voor Europees recht*, p. 240-1. Cf. Wissink (n. 26), p. 203.

181 See further, Byrne and McCutcheon (n. 160), p. 677-9.

182 L. Van den Hende, 'Overzicht van rechtspraak. Europees gemeenschapsrecht: rechtsbescherming (1979-1994)' (1995) *Tijdschrift voor Privaatrecht*, p. 181.

imposed by the duty of consistent interpretation discussed in paragraph 4. Finally, if an ambiguous provision has been given a specific, incompatible, meaning through settled case law, it is in my opinion less convincing that this falls within the scope of the *contra legem* limitation. First, on account of the *Ajos* and *Centrosteel* judgments, it would seem that the mere fact that a particular interpretation represents settled case law, does not easily persuade the ECJ that this stands in the way of a consistent interpretation. Secondly, it is logical to assume that it is in particular in relation to incompatible provisions that are open to more than one interpretation that a consistent interpretation can be adopted.[183] If this would be excluded as a result of settled case law, this would reduce the effectiveness of the duty of consistent interpretation. Thirdly, national courts might consider that the principle of legal certainty prevents a departure from settled case law, but an argument based on legal certainty is in my opinion not as convincing as in situations where that principle is relied upon as a result of the clear wording of the national provisions or a settled, self-standing, jurisprudential rule. This is so since either a particular, incompatible, interpretation has been developed before the entry into force of the directive and this must now be viewed in a different light and one cannot rely on the certainty that previously existed or, in the unlikely scenario that a long-standing, incompatible, interpretation develops after the entry into force of the directive, that interpretation should have been questioned from the very start. An exception to this could perhaps be justified if a national court pointed out that a national rule concerning precedent limits the possibility to decide a case differently by distinguishing it from previous case law concerning the same provision. This might fall within the scope of the *contra legem* limitation. It would then not be the settled case law in itself, but the rule concerning precedent, on which the appeal to legal certainty is based. Finally, it should be noted that the *Klohn* judgment, which is discussed next, showed a strict approach when the principle of legitimate expectations is invoked in the context of the duty of consistent interpretation. Although the judgment did not concern the complaint that a consistent interpretation would depart from settled case law, it does seem to indicate that such an argument is to be treated under the principle of legitimate expectations and in my opinion it is questionable that the ECJ would adopt a more flexible approach in that situation.

5.3. OTHER LIMITS: THE *KLOHN*, *MAKS PEN* AND *PUPINO* JUDGMENTS

In the *Klohn* judgment, the ECJ discussed two new limitations to the duty of consistent interpretation. First, it was recognised that, in principle, the requirement of legitimate expectations can impose limits to the duty of consistent interpretation.

183 Jans and Verhoeven (n. 73), p. 79.

However, in a manner consistent with its approach to this principle (in particular the temporal effect of legislation), the argument was rejected.

> One of the parties to the main proceedings argued that the immediate applicability of the new rule concerning prohibitively expensive costs for judicial proceedings in environmental matters[184] to ongoing proceedings violated the principle of legitimate expectations. While the ECJ did not dismiss the possibility to rely on this principle entirely, it held that, first, no assurances had been given to the concerned party that the former rule would remain applicable, secondly, taking into account the starting date of the proceedings and the implementing deadline of the concerned directive, it was not unforeseeable that that rule would have to be amended before the conclusion of the proceedings and, thirdly, as the concerned party was an Irish public authority it could not rely on a legitimate expectation that the existing rule would remain in force notwithstanding the Member State's implementing obligation. The ECJ also pointed out, more generally, that the principle of legitimate expectations '(…) cannot be extended to the point of generally preventing a new rule from applying to the future effects of situations which arose under the earlier rule'.[185]

Following these considerations, the ECJ *precluded* the invocation of this principle in the specific circumstances of the case, leaving no scope for the referring court to make its own assessment. It should be noted that in the *Klohn* judgment it was not the unexpectedness of the interpretation of the directive (which would find its way to national law through a consistent interpretation) that was the issue, but rather the potential immediate application of new rules based on an interpretation in conformity with the directive that had been transposed belatedly. While the ECJ clearly dismissed the argument based on legitimate expectations, the examination of the merits of the argument indicates that it could, on another occasion, constitute a relevant limitation to the duty of consistent interpretation. The second limitation discussed in the *Klohn* judgment is again derived from the principle of legal certainty and concerns the rule that judicial decisions which have become final can no longer be called into question (the principle of *res judicata*). Although a novelty in the context of consistent interpretation, it cannot be said that it was very surprising that the duty of consistent interpretation must be applied in a manner which takes into account the requirements imposed by this principle. In fact, it is even somewhat odd that it is presented as a limit to the interpretative process. Surely, consistent interpretation must also respect the principle of *res judicata*; before this limitation was discussed in the context of consistent interpretation, it was already well-established and the ECJ has generally left it to the national courts to determine

184 Article 10a of Council Directive 85/337/EEC of 27 June 1985 on the assessment of the effects of certain public and private projects on the environment, *OJ* 1985, L175/40, as amended by Directive 2003/35/EC of the European Parliament and of the Council of 26 May 2003 providing for public participation in respect of the drawing up of certain plans and programmes relating to the environment and amending with regard to public participation and access to justice Council Directives 85/337/EEC and 96/61/EC, *OJ* 2003, L156/17.

185 Case C-167/17 *Klohn*, ECLI:EU:C:2018:833, paras. 49-53.

whether the principle would be violated.[186] But arguably the same applies in respect of for example time limits for bringing national proceedings; these are not simply set aside because of the requirement of consistent interpretation. At the same time such limits do not seem to impose constraints on the scope for interpretation as such. Are they not simply limitations on the result prescribed by EU law (and a confirmation of EU law's deference to national procedural autonomy), which apply irrespective of whether it is consistent interpretation or direct effect which is relied upon to remedy the incompatibility between EU and national law? As a final remark it is noted that the ECJ, despite having recognised the national court's final say in the matter, deemed it appropriate to provide to the referring court some guidance for the assessment whether the principle of *res judicata* prevented a consistent interpretation. At the very least, this provided some incentives for the referring court to find a way to conclude that the principle was not violated. However, looking at the details of the judgment making a preliminary reference, I am not sure whether the national court will be able to come to such a conclusion.[187] The follow-up judgment will have to be awaited to learn more about this.

Remaining within the sphere of legal certainty, the *Maks Pen* judgment required the national court to examine to what extent national law, that seemed to be contrary to the requirement imposed by EU law that the national court examine on its own motion the existence of tax evasion, could be given a consistent interpretation, adding that EU law cannot oblige the national court to disregard the principle, enshrined in national procedural law, of the prohibition of *reformatio in peius*.[188] However, I must add that, in this case it was not clear whether a limitation is imposed on the duty of consistent interpretation, or the effect of the relevant substantive provisions of EU law. From the latter point of view, the *Maks Pen* judgment could be interpreted as limiting the requirement for the national court to examine of its own motion the existence of tax evasion.

Some judgments refer to general principles of EU law as a limitation, without specifying the principle of legal certainty, from which the earlier discussed limitations are derived.[189] This raises the question whether it would be possible that the duty of consistent interpretation is limited by other general principles of EU law.[190] The *Pupino* judgment could be interpreted as providing some authority

186 For a further discussion see R. Ortlep and R.J.G.M. Widdershoven, 'Judicial Protection', in: J.H. Jans, S. Prechal and R.J.G.M. Widdershoven (Eds.), *Europeanisation of Public Law* (Europa Law Publishing 2015), p. 396-9.
187 Case C-167/17 *Klohn,* ECLI:EU:C:2018:833, para. 62 *et seq.*
188 Case C-18/13 *Maks Pen,* ECLI:EU:C:2014:69, paras. 36-7.
189 See, for example, Case C-282/10 *Dominguez,* ECLI:EU:C:2012:33, para. 25; Case C-187/15 *Pöpperl,* ECLI:EU:C:2016:550, para. 44.
190 See also Prechal (n. 26), p. 204-5. In M.J.M. Verhoeven and J.H. Jans, 'Doorwerking via conforme interpretatie en rechtstreekse werking', in: S. Prechal and R.J.G.M. Widdershoven (Eds.), *Inleiding tot het Europees bestuursrecht* (Ars Aequi Libri 2017), p. 71, it is provided that the ECJ's case law

for this. It made it clear that, although the framework decision required that the national court should seek an interpretation of national law enabling the use of special procedures that could guarantee the protection of minors, the national court was also required to ensure that application of such procedures respects the fundamental rights of the defendant, and would not cause the criminal proceedings to become unfair within the meaning of Article 6 ECHR.[191] However, also on this occasion it may be asked whether the judgment should not be interpreted as imposing a limitation on the scope of the broadly formulated objective, stated in the framework decision, to provide protection through special procedures.

Whatever the correct characterisation of the limitations mentioned in the *Pupino* (i.e. complying with Article 6 ECHR, *not* the above discussed *contra legem* limitation) and *Maks Pen* judgments must be, from the point of view of scale, the limitations in respect of the determination or aggravation of criminal liability and *contra legem* remain far more important for understanding the duty of consistent interpretation. Also, both judgments, as well as the *Klohn* judgment, cannot change the conclusion that EU law ultimately controls the role played by limitations to the duty of consistent interpretation.

5.4. FUNDAMENTAL RIGHTS AS A SEPARATE LIMITATION?

Especially the reference to Article 6 ECHR in the *Pupino* judgment raises the question whether fundamental rights should be acknowledged as a separate limitation to the duty of consistent interpretation. It is important to point out that the ECJ's case law has not yet directly addressed this question. However, it follows from for example the *Kolpinghuis, Adeneler* and *Dominguez* judgments that general principles of EU law can impose limitations on the duty of consistent interpretation. This makes sense for the reason that conflicts between the Treaties, on which the duty of consistent interpretation is based, and general principles of EU law, should be avoided by means of interpretation.[192] I should furthermore add that it is settled case law that fundamental rights form an integral part of the general principles of law whose observance is ensured by the ECJ. It appears from the case law concerning interpretations of secondary EU law in conformity with fundamental rights that the same position is adopted in relation to the Charter.[193] The net result is that fundamental rights, either as general principles of law or on the basis of the

---

has not so far recognised other general principles of EU law than the principles of legal certainty and non-retroactivity as limits to the duty of consistent interpretation.

191 Case C-105/03 *Pupino*, ECLI:EU:C:2005:386, paras. 56-60.

192 See, for an example outside the context of the duty of consistent interpretation, Case C-368/95 *Familiapress*, ECLI:EU:C:1997:325. See also S. Prechal, R.J.G.M. Widdershoven and J.H. Jans, 'Introduction', in: J.H. Jans, S. Prechal and R.J.G.M. Widdershoven (Eds.), *Europeanisation of Public Law* (Europa Law Publishing 2015), p. 10.

193 Case C-131/12 *Google Spain*, ECLI:EU:C:2014:317, para. 68.

Charter, could be a relevant limitation to the duty of consistent interpretation in the sense that the scope of that obligation should be molded to fit the requirements derived from fundamental rights. In principle, such a further interpretation of the scope of the duty of consistent interpretation is quite conceivable since Articles 288 TFEU and 4(3) TEU hardly circumscribe the ECJ's discretion to further define the contours of that obligation.

A more difficult question is which fundamental rights would be suitable for that purpose. As far as concerns fundamental rights that directly concern the interpretative process, I can only think of Article 49 of the Charter enshrining the principle of legality of criminal offences. The effect of Article 49 of the Charter coincides with the limits established in the *Kolpinghuis* judgment (see subparagraph 5.1.1). One way of looking at this would be that this shows that fundamental rights indeed already provide a limitation to the duty of consistent interpretation. But what about fundamental rights that are not clearly linked to interpretative questions, e.g. right for private and family life or the right to property? They can of course play a role if it is first necessary to determine the correct interpretation of a provision of a directive in the light of EU fundamental rights, which is then followed by an examination whether national law can be read in conformity with the just-arrived-at meaning of the directive (as I pointed out above, the *Pupino* judgment could be read as an example of this). But fundamental rights here function as a correction on the directive and this should therefore not be seen as setting limits to the duty of consistent interpretation itself. Yet, it seems that rights that do not directly address the interpretative process itself, can be relevant in another, more important, way. Article 52(1) of the Charter stipulates the specific requirement that '[a]ny limitation on the exercise of the rights and freedoms recognised by this Charter must be provided for by law (...)'. It follows from Article 51(1) that this requirement also applies to the Member States when they are implementing EU law. And if a national court interprets national law in conformity with a directive it is certainly acting within the scope of EU law meaning that the provisions of the Charter, including Article 52(1), apply. Article 52(1) does not only stipulate the formal requirement that a limitation is introduced by law, but also a 'quality of the law' test, i.e. it must be clear and accessible, and should meet the requirement of foreseeability. This of course resonates the requirement known from the law of the ECHR. Interestingly, with some exceptions,[194] the ECJ rarely referred to that requirement when it ruled on limitations to general principles of EU law protecting fundamental rights that corresponded to rights protected by the ECHR. It has to be conceded that this has not really changed with the introduction of the Charter, but it now seems that there can be little doubt that the requirement is as such

194 For example Case C-368/95 *Familiapress*, ECLI:EU:C:1997:325, para. 26; Case C-274/99 P *Connolly*, ECLI:EU:C:2001:127, para. 42; Joined Cases C-465/00, C-138/01 and C-139/01 Österreichischer Rundfunk, ECLI:EU:C:2003:294, para. 76 *et seq.*

applicable.[195] It is submitted that when national courts apply the duty of consistent interpretation and where it is found that the interpretation required by the directive entails a limitation of fundamental rights protected by EU law, they are obliged to examine whether the requirements of Article 52(1) of the Charter are fulfilled. The test of foreseeability is then immediately relevant for the interpretative process itself as it raises the threshold for the adoption of a consistent interpretation. Only interpretations of which it can be said that they were foreseeable are permitted. If a consistent interpretation is, as a consequence of this, excluded, the national court must conclude that it is not possible to interpret national law in conformity with the directive. Since the test of foreseeability raises the threshold, the scope for adopting a consistent interpretation is more narrow compared to situations where fundamental rights are not at stake. As it concerns the interpretation of national law, the national courts are in principle best placed to determine whether the test of foreseeability is met.[196]

Apart from the fact that the ECJ is of course competent to further interpret Article 52 as it is a provision of EU law, another important qualification applies to the rule that it is for the national courts to make the assessment whether the test of foreseeability is met. If the national provision allegedly impinging upon a fundamental right is not – in a significant way – different from the provision in the directive, a national court cannot simply reject the possibility of a consistent interpretation if it believes that the limitation of the concerned fundamental right was not sufficiently foreseeable. This position follows from the instruction provided in the ECJ's case law concerning a *verbatim* transposition (see subparagraph 4.3.3), considered together with the rule that national courts do not themselves have jurisdiction to declare EU legislation invalid (which national courts would *de facto* do if they refused a consistent interpretation in the described situation for the reason that there is a limitation to a fundamental right that cannot be justified).[197] The correct procedural route for the national courts would be to ask preliminary questions to the ECJ concerning the compatibility of the corresponding provision in the directive with Article 52(1) of the Charter, the outcome of which then also determines the fate of the national provision.

The identified restriction on the national courts' power to make the assessment concerning foreseeability cannot be rebutted by the argument that national courts should be free to apply a higher national rights standard. This follows from the *Melloni* judgment:

---

195 S. Peers and S. Prechal, 'Article 52 – Scope and Interpretation of Rights and Principles', in: S. Peers and others (Eds.), *The EU Charter of Fundamental Rights: A Commentary* (Hart Publishing 2014), p. 1470.

196 Ibid, p. 1474.

197 Case 314/85 *Foto-Frost*, ECLI:EU:C:1987:452, para. 15.

> '[i]t is true that Article 53 of the Charter confirms that, where an EU legal act calls for national implementing measures, national authorities and courts remain free to apply national standards of protection of fundamental rights, provided that the level of protection provided for by the Charter, as interpreted by the Court, and the primacy, unity and effectiveness of EU law are not thereby compromised'.[198]

The sting of this consideration is in the tail and makes it clear that the Charter does not simply offer – in relation to national fundamental rights standards – a minimum level of protection, but establishes a maximum standard if an application of the national fundamental right would compromise the supremacy, unity and effectiveness of EU law. More generally, it follows from this sentence of the *Melloni* judgment that when national courts act within the scope of EU law and are asked to adjudicate upon the compatibility of national provisions with fundamental rights that are also protected by the Charter, they cannot apply higher standards when it comes to the scope of the fundamental right. This could be relevant in a context of consistent interpretation as well since the interpretative question regarding the appropriate degree of foreseeability only arises once it is found that there exists a limitation to a fundamental right in the first place. However, it should be noted that in *Melloni* the relevant issue (i.e. conditions for the surrender of persons convicted in *absentia*) had been regulated exhaustively by EU law. It remains to be seen what room is left for the application of national fundamental rights if a matter is not dealt with at the level of EU law. The *M.A.S. and M.B.* judgment could be interpreted as providing that there is scope to offer protection on the basis of national fundamental rights standards where the relevant matter is *not* harmonised.[199] However, it is not entirely clear whether the judgment concerned the priority of the legality principle in EU or national law over provisions contained in the directive.[200] In the situation where the Member States need to implement EU law and can do so in more than one way and one of these ways enables the protection of higher national fundamental rights standards, there should in principle not be a conflict with the *Melloni* judgment. And also if derogations from EU law are not applied or interpreted restrictively on account of national fundamental rights, hence strengthening the application of the EU law provisions to which the derogation pertains, the higher national standard is not problematic.[201] Nevertheless, it has been argued that, as long as the situation falls within the scope of EU law, the application of national fundamental rights must in any event meet the requirements of unity and effectiveness stated in the *Melloni* judgment (but supremacy of EU law would then not come into play since there is not a conflict between an EU and national law provision).[202]

198 Case C-399/11 *Melloni*, ECLI:EU:C:2013:107, para. 60.
199 Case C-42/17 *M.A.S. and M.B.*, ECLI:EU:C:2017:936.
200 Case note by Krommendijk in *EHRC* 2018/34, para. 12.
201 N. De Boer, 'Addressing rights divergences under the Charter: *Melloni*' (2013/4) *CMLRev*, p. 1096.
202 See Van den Brink and others (n. 128), p. 160; Case note by Widdershoven in *AB* 2013/132, para. 5.

5.5. DISCRETIONARY DISPENSATION CONFERRED AND CONTROLLED BY EU LAW

The *Arcaro* judgment did not establish that a consistent interpretation is not possible if it would lead to the imposition of an obligation on individuals. The tenor of the judgment was instead that a consistent interpretation is not possible if it can no longer be accommodated by national law. This can be seen as an explication of what is already implicit in the requirement to interpret national law so far as possible. Indeed, the requirement to interpret national law *so far as possible* is inherently a requirement that at some point reaches a limit. It is important to take this into account when the national superior courts' case law is examined. A rejection of a consistent interpretation does not imply a violation of EU law but could just as well be a faithful interpretation of what is no longer possible and required under that obligation. The more interesting question – and on this point the *Arcaro* judgment does not offer much more guidance than the nebulous phrase 'so far as possible' – is how much autonomy the EU law framework confers on the national courts when making this determination. The more specific limitations that have been recognised in the ECJ's case law are based on the principles of legal certainty and non-retroactivity and, in the case of the determination or aggravation of criminal liability, the principle that a provision of the criminal law may not be applied extensively to the detriment of the defendant, which is the corollary of the principle of legality which, in turn, traces back to legal certainty. It should be pointed out that this refers to general principles of EU law, and not a national variant.

The establishment of the *contra legem* limitation in the *Adeneler* judgment can be viewed as a further specification of the *Arcaro* judgment. At the beginning of this subparagraph two statements concerning the limitation that a *contra legem* interpretation is not required, were mentioned. First, that it entails that the duty of consistent interpretation only operates within the limits set by national interpretative rules. Secondly, that it undermines the adequacy of the theory of supremacy of EU law for understanding the duty of consistent interpretation. As the first statement is a relevant factor for determining the second statement, I will start there. The ECJ's case law does not explain the relationship between the methodological instructions that national courts must take into account when applying the duty of consistent interpretation, discussed in paragraph 4, and the limitation that a *contra legem* interpretation is not required. However, I believe that the answer is twofold here. In my opinion it would not make a lot of sense if national courts were permitted to rely on the *contra legem* limitation in order to disregard those methodological instructions. Two arguments are provided to justify the necessity and appropriateness of considering the instructions discussed in paragraph 4 and the *contra legem* limitation together. First, if the *contra legem* limitation unconditionally limited what was discussed in the previous paragraph, this would sometimes leave no meaningful scope of application for the specific instruction. For example, it would be inconsistent to impose the instruction that, when applying the duty of consistent interpretation, national courts should consider the whole body of national law, and subsequently allow national courts to do the opposite as soon as they claim that they are prevented from doing so since that would be *contra legem*. In a way, the *Dominguez* judgment could be interpreted as confirming that the *contra legem* limitation does not interfere with positive methodological requirements (i.e. if the referring court's recourse to direct effect is interpreted as excluding not only a consistent interpretation of the provision that it mentioned in its reference for a preliminary ruling but as excluding a consistent interpretation in general). Secondly, there are the instructions that already acknowledge that national interpretative rules set limits to the application of the duty of consistent interpretation, so that there should not be a conflict. An example of this is the interpretative selection rule. The *contra legem* limitation can be relevant for how that rule is applied and this is possible without disregarding the ECJ's case law on the interpretative selection rule. Ultimately, the *contra legem* limitation and the instructions discussed in the previous paragraph address the same point and must therefore be considered jointly and not as conflicting instructions. So how *does contra legem* work then? This brings me to the second limb of my two-folded response. With the consideration that national courts are not required to interpret national law *contra legem* it is acknowledged that the seemingly open-ended requirement to interpret national law 'so far as possible' does not require them to go beyond the limits of what the national courts can do in terms of interpretation. Where this point lies exactly will usually be left to the national courts as it depends on matters such as the wording of the concerned provision of national law and the scope of national interpretative rules. The national courts, and not the ECJ, have competence over these matters, and it is in principle the former court that determines the meaning of *contra legem*. However, since the *contra legem* limitation has its legal basis in EU law, the ECJ can, taking into account the division of competences, provide instructions to the national courts.[203] On the basis of the existing case law, it appears that the ECJ will only intervene if a national court applies the *contra legem* limitation too extensively. This was seen in the *Ajos* judgment (and perhaps in the *Dominguez* judgment as well). While interference on behalf of the ECJ, correcting a finding that a consistent interpretation would be *contra legem*, is clearly the exception, it confirmed that the limitation's outer limits are ultimately controlled by the ECJ. This can be interpreted as an indication that the duty of consistent interpretation enjoys supremacy but it should not be forgotten that, similar to what was said with regard to the methodological instructions discussed under paragraph 4, as long

203 See previously Haket (n. 180), p. 239-40.

as it is not clear whether the national courts follow suit, this merely constitutes a claim to supremacy.

If my response to the first statement (concerning the question whether the duty of consistent interpretation only operates within the limits set by national interpretative rules) is considered, it cannot be a surprise that I do not think that the second statement (concerning the question whether the adequacy of the theory of supremacy of EU law is undermined) is correct. I recall that, from the perspective of the ECJ's case law, applying the *contra legem* limitation is authorised and controlled by EU law itself (more specifically: the general principle of EU law concerning legal certainty). So it is EU law that grants the national courts discretion to determine the meaning of *contra legem*. Things would of course be different if national courts would reject this view and claim to have the final say over the *contra legem* limitation, or if that limitation was used in a way that *de facto* conferred supremacy to national interpretative rules in a large number of situations. The above discussed case law does not provide an indication that national courts would pursue such a course of action. They already enjoy an important measure of discretion as things currently stand, and the *contra legem* limitation is usually only invoked when national courts are faced with a serious obstacle to adopt a consistent interpretation. However, the above discussed judgments represent only a fraction of the case law in which the limitation is applied, and it must be examined whether the subsequent chapters concerning its application before the national courts confirm this impression.

A final remark that is made with regard to the *contra legem* limitation is that it is not yet clear from the ECJ's case law whether it views this limitation as a synonym for the impossibility to adopt a consistent interpretation or whether it has a more self-standing and confined meaning. The latter view would be logical if the limitation only applied to interpretations that are incompatible with the outer limits of a provision's text. But the *Impact* and *Klohn* judgments are indicative of a broader meaning (yet, the *Bauer* judgment raises some questions in this regard). Also, the conclusion that the ECJ usually leaves it to the national courts to determine whether the *contra legem* limitation applies might be relevant for this matter – but it should be noted that on nearly all occasions this concerned the question whether the text of the provision constituted an obstacle. If future case law further increases the scope of *contra legem* by permitting all kinds of interpretative obstacles that are encountered by the national courts to be brought within its scope, at some point, *contra legem* and the dispensational side to so far as possible will indeed become synonyms (note that this matter does not touch upon and is without prejudice to the positive methodological instructions!). However, on the basis of the existing case law, such a conclusion appears premature. An important consequence of this is that if the *contra legem* limitation does not apply, this does not automatically mean that national courts are forced to adopt a consistent interpretation (perhaps an exception applies to national courts whose interpretative freedom is so broad that the limits to consistent interpretation coincide with the ECJ's case law on the meaning of *contra legem*); the question what is required of national courts under the duty of consistent interpretation is then not replaced, but only narrowed down to some extent, by this limitation.

The *Kolpinghuis* judgment made it clear that a consistent interpretation may not provide the basis for the determination or aggravation of criminal liability. This has two components. First, in line with the requirements of *lex certa*, generally speaking, the duty of consistent interpretation must defer to whatever is considered possible according to national rules of interpretation. Secondly, criminal liability cannot be based on a retroactive application of the law. Both components *also* override the specific positive methodological instructions. In that sense the position under the *contra legem* limitation is different from that under the limitation regarding criminal liability. In my view this outcome is not inconsistent since the *contra legem* limitation is far more related to the general question what must be undertaken by national courts and how far they must go to reach a consistent interpretation whereas the limitation regarding criminal liability is based on specific considerations concerning legality that apply in the area of criminal law. Since, similar to the limitation regarding criminal liability, the limitation concerning legitimate expectations discussed in the *Klohn* judgment is of a more self-standing nature, i.e. compared to the *contra legem* limitation it is less intertwined with the question how far national interpretative rules can be stretched in order to interpret national law so far as possible in conformity with the directive, I think that it is to be treated similar to the limitation laid down in the ECJ's *Kolpinghuis* judgment (by the way, another similarity is that, similar to the second component of the *Kolpinghuis* judgment, legitimate expectations also addresses the question of the temporal effect of EU law). In principle, the same applies for the limitation concerning the principle of *res judicata,* which was also discussed in the *Klohn* judgment, but it was argued that this is more a limitation on the result prescribed by EU law than a limitation on the interpretative process. While the prohibition from the *Kolpinghuis* judgment seems to put national law first, it should (again) not be overlooked that this window is only opened as a result of the approval by EU law to do so.

Finally, it was examined whether fundamental rights could act as a separate limitation to the duty of consistent interpretation. The ECJ has not yet delivered an explicit ruling on this point, but it seems to follow from the protection of fundamental rights as general principles of EU law and the Charter that the duty of consistent interpretation should take into account limits deriving from fundamental rights. I identified two different ways in which fundamental rights protected by EU law could limit the duty of consistent interpretation. Both limits derive from EU law and are thus self-imposed. They cannot therefore challenge the theory of supremacy of EU law. While it is less clear what the scope is for applying higher national fundamental rights standards, it follows from the *Melloni* judgment that this must respect the supremacy, unity and effectiveness of EU law.

6. CONSISTENT INTERPRETATION AND ADEQUATE IMPLEMENTATION

The implementation of directives in national law must guarantee that:

> '(...) the national authorities will effectively apply the directive in full, that the legal position under national law should be sufficiently precise and clear and that individuals are made fully aware of their rights and, where appropriate, may rely on them before the national courts'.[204]

As I characterised the duty of consistent interpretation as an extension of the implementation obligation (see paragraph 2), what are the consequences of the adoption or rejection of a consistent interpretation for the determination whether the directive has been adequately implemented in national law? The case law regarding infringement procedures on the basis of Article 258 TFEU for inadequate legislative implementation offers useful guidance for the answer to this question. Three different situations can be distinguished in which the duty of consistent interpretation plays a role. First, national court decisions can, to a limited degree, remove doubts as to the national legislation's compatibility. In *Commission v Italy*, for example, the Italian Government could point to several judgments of the Italian Constitutional Court showing that the provisions of national law could be applied in a manner satisfying the directive's requirements, and therefore it was not established that there had been an infringement.[205] Two judgments in which infringement procedures were brought against the United Kingdom showed that, if it can reasonably be assumed that provisions that are not clearly incompatible with the directive will be given a consistent interpretation, this must be refuted by judgments to the contrary in order to establish an infringement.[206] Secondly, national court decisions can also be an indication that the national provisions do not comply. This can be because a provision that is in principle neutral as regards its compatibility with the directive is, opposite to the first situation described, widely interpreted in a way that makes it incompatible, and the law was not changed to

204 Case C-365/93 *Commission v Greece*, ECLI:EU:C:1995:76, para. 9; Case C-144/99 *Commission v Netherlands*, ECLI:EU:C:2001:257, para. 17.

205 Case 235/84 *Commission v Italy*, ECLI:EU:C:1986:303, para. 14.

206 Case C-382/92 *Commission v United Kingdom*, ECLI:EU:C:1994:233, paras. 32-9; Case C-300/95 *Commission v United Kingdom*, ECLI:EU:C:1997:255, paras. 37-8.

overcome this.[207] Unsurprisingly, decisions by national courts of final instance play a key role in determining the legal position in a given Member State.[208] In addition to this, if a national provision has been interpreted differently by national courts, some of which are compatible with the directive whereas others are not, this provides an indication that, apparently, that provision was not sufficiently clear and does not satisfy the requirements of adequate transposition.[209] From the first and second situation it is thus clear that, since national court decisions reveal how national provisions are actually interpreted, they provide an important touchstone for determining the compatibility of those provisions. But, in my view, the function of national court decisions can go further than this. This is where I arrive at the third situation. As Prechal pointed out in her extensive study of directives, '(...) legislation, by the nature of things, is cast at a certain level of abstraction. This is equally true with respect to legislative measures transposing a directive'.[210] She also argues that, in addition to being a touchstone for legislation adopted by the Member States, '(...) national courts have a distinct role in the process of achieving the result prescribed by the directive'.[211] In this regard she refers to consistent interpretation in the context of 'judicial implementation'.

> Prechal describes judicial implementation as a subcategory of the duty of consistent interpretation. If directives have, in principle, been implemented into national law correctly, they remain relevant as a standard for interpretation, and the national court must ensure that its interpretation of the implementing measures remains in line with the interpretation of the directives.[212]

The necessity to ensure that the interpretation of national implementing legislation remains in line with the directive does not only result from the level of abstraction at which national legislation is cast. The meaning of the directive's provisions will also be further clarified by the ECJ over the course of time. Indeed, it is apparent from the ECJ's case law on the duty of consistent interpretation that this is always preceded by a question concerning the further clarification of one or more provisions of a directive. In this setting, it is the primary responsibility of national courts to ensure that, after transposition by the legislature, national law remains, or becomes, compatible with the directive. In the third situation, the duty of consistent interpretation fulfils an independent role in the implementation process. In the *Steenhorst-Neerings* judgment the national provisions were clearly incompatible with the directive, nevertheless the national courts had interpreted those provisions

207 See Case C-129/00 *Commission v Italy*, ECLI:EU:C:2003:656, paras. 34, 41, where the incompatible interpretation was adopted by the Italian Supreme Court and a substantial number of Italian lower courts.
208 Ibid, para. 32. See also M. Taborowski, 'Infringement Proceedings and Non-Compliant National Courts' (2012/6) *CMLRev*, p. 1887.
209 Case C-129/00 *Commission v Italy*, ECLI:EU:C:2003:656, para. 33.
210 Prechal (n. 26), p. 188.
211 Ibid, p. 190.
212 Ibid, p. 188.

in conformity with the directive, and the ECJ invited them to continue doing so, '(...) for so long as the Member State has not yet adopted the legislation necessary to implement it in full'.[213] This situation can no longer be characterised as a simple continuation of the legislature's action or judicial implementation but this is an example of what Prechal has labelled 'remedial interpretation'.

> Remedial interpretation is described by Prechal with reference to the situation in which directives have not been correctly implemented. A consistent interpretation then *temporarily*[214] bridges the gap between national law and directives.[215] Since the remedial interpretation requires a more corrective application of the duty of consistent interpretation *vis-à-vis* national law, it is conceivable that, generally speaking, the relationship between EU and national law can be more tense compared to judicial implementation.

Since the duty of consistent interpretation also applies to this type of situation, and since one of the provisions constituting its legal basis is Article 288 TFEU, it seems to be clear that the duty of consistent interpretation can sometimes have an independent role in the implementation process – despite the fact that, as the *Steenhorst-Neerings* judgment explicitly stated, full implementation requires the adoption of legislation.

If one thing is clear from the above discussion it is that, in order to successfully implement directives, legislation cannot do without national court decisions confirming their compliance with the directive, but, conversely, a consistent interpretation will also not suffice in itself to fully implement the directive if the underlying provisions are clearly not in line with the directive.[216] The consequences of the adoption or rejection of a consistent interpretation for the determination whether the directive has been adequately implemented (in the broad sense) confirms that national courts have an important, sometimes independent, task in carrying out the binding obligation stipulated in Article 288 TFEU.

7. CONCLUSION

The simple idea introduced in the *Von Colson and Kamann* judgment that national courts are required to interpret national law so far as possible in conformity with directives has by now evolved into a complex body of case law. Some issues have been resolved. It appeared from the analysis of the legal basis for the duty of consistent interpretation that this obligation primarily contributes to the

213 Case C-338/91 *Steenhorst-Neerings*, ECLI:EU:C:1993:857, para. 34.
214 Prechal mentions this important disclaimer to emphasise that a consistent interpretation does not remove the need to adopt adequate implementing measures to cure the non-compliance.
215 Prechal (n. 26), p. 191-2.
216 See also Klamert (n. 9), p. 1270.

effectiveness of directives and their implementation in national law (this view was confirmed in the previous paragraph concerning requirements in respect of the implementation of directives), which is prescribed by Article 288 TFEU, and that through the inclusion of Article 4(3) TEU, the duty of consistent interpretation is in principle capable of enjoying supremacy. The temporal scope and the object of the duty of consistent interpretation were clarified in the *Adeneler*, and *Marleasing* and *Pfeiffer* judgments respectively.

Some issues have only partly been resolved and often the ECJ's case law provides little more than a few rough sketches. In my opinion this is the result of the imperative to find a balance between the EU and national law component that are inherent to the duty of consistent interpretation. As I explained at the beginning of paragraph 4, on the one hand, the ECJ's case law recognises that, since the duty of consistent interpretation is about the interpretation of national law, and since national courts are made responsible for applying it in proceedings in which EU law rights are invoked, national rules of interpretation are a crucial factor. On the other hand, the ECJ also attempts to ensure the effectiveness of directives through the duty of consistent interpretation. In that regard it has imposed specific instructions on methodological rules of interpretation that must be taken into account by the national courts and that have supremacy over national interpretative rules to the extent that those rules are incompatible with the ECJ's instructions. The ECJ's attempt to further effectiveness while remaining within the limits of its own competences, and not doing too much damage to the national interpretative rules, permeates many aspects of the duty of consistent interpretation. This means, in the first place, that one has to very carefully determine what the scope is of the 'positive' requirements and the limitations (negative requirements) to the duty of consistent interpretation (discussed in paragraphs 4 and 5 respectively), and what this means for national interpretative rules. As regards the instructions discussed in paragraph 4, while the interpretative selection rule, the presumption that the legislature intends to comply with the directive, and the pre-emption of the grammatical interpretation in relation to *verbatim* implementing measures, are a clear indication that, at least to some extent, the duty of consistent interpretation has the potential of interfering with national interpretative rules (and from the EU law perspective then enjoys supremacy), I explained that national interpretative rules are not completely set aside but still remain an important and necessary tool when these instructions have to be applied by the national courts. In paragraph 5 it was seen that the ECJ's case law has also accepted three, or perhaps four, limitations to the duty of consistent interpretation. The two most important limitations are that it cannot have the effect of determining or aggravating criminal liability (prohibiting the establishment of criminal liability that is not clearly foreseen in the law, as well as a retroactive application of criminal law) and that a *contra legem* interpretation is not required. Additionally, the *Klohn* judgment recognised that, in principle, the requirement of legitimate expectations might be a relevant limitation to the duty of consistent interpretation. It also referred to the principle of *res judicata*. Surely, this principle must also be respected in the context of consistent interpretation, but I argued that it is rather a limit on the result prescribed by EU law – and something which must be viewed in the context of procedural autonomy – than a limit on the interpretative process. Finally, although the ECJ has not yet entered into an explicit discussion on the question whether fundamental rights limit the duty of consistent interpretation, I argued why it is plausible that this is the case (and that it is in fact already protecting a fundamental right in the context of the *Kolpinghuis* limitation). In particular with regard to the *contra legem* limitation it is in principle left to the national courts to determine the exact scope of this limitation. This is probably so because – broadly speaking – the limitation refers to an interpretation of the law that deviates from what is normally considered to be acceptable when national law is being interpreted – something which is more appropriately decided by the national court, who is also better equipped to carry out this assessment. However, sometimes EU law plays a far more prominent role: see for example the approach to the principle of legitimate expectations in the *Klohn* judgment. The ECJ is legitimated to do so as the concerned limitations all have their origins in, and are ultimately controlled by, EU law (also the *contra legem* limitation). These limitations therefore do not necessarily invalidate the adequacy of the theory of supremacy. In the second place, the complex balance between national rules of interpretation and effectiveness can be found in the relationship between the positive methodological instructions imposed by the ECJ and the limits to the duty of consistent interpretation. Do the limits apply to those specific instructions or do they, similar to those instructions, further shape the seemingly open-ended requirement to interpret national law so far as possible, leaving those instructions unaffected? I argued that the limitation regarding criminal liability, as well as the limitations discussed in the *Klohn* judgment, can affect those specific instructions, but that I do not think that this is the case for the *contra legem* limitation.

It is submitted that it follows from the above characterisation of the duty of consistent interpretation that it constitutes an interpretative rule based on the legally binding norms contained in Articles 288 TFEU and 4(3) TEU (with the inclusion of the principle of effectiveness). In that sense it is more accurate to speak of a conflict of interpretative rules than of a conflict of interpretations. This characterisation has two important implications. First, the duty of consistent interpretation is understood as a methodological standard.[217] National courts are obliged to make an effort to find a route through which national law can be given the meaning required by the directive. The substantive meaning that is to be conferred upon national law is prescribed through the directives (e.g. the contract is not void). Subparagraph 4.3

217 Wissink (n. 26), p. 129; Klamert (n. 42), p. 182; Canaris (n. 9), p. 68-9. Cf. Altena-Davidsen (n. 112), p. 78-9.

showed that the ECJ, in its preliminary rulings, provides a further interpretation of the result required by the directive, yet this must be separated from the question how, and to what extent, that result can be implemented in the main proceedings before the national court (which is done through the duty of consistent interpretation or direct effect). But the duty of consistent interpretation goes further: there are also binding obligations when it comes to the steps that must be taken in the course of this examination. These steps refer to the positive and negative methodological instructions that further substantiate the mere requirement to pursue a particular result. The second implication concerns the usefulness of existing theories on the relationship between EU and national law. Besselink submits that supremacy must be understood as being connected to cases in which a conflict of substantive norms (e.g. where the directive provides that a contract is void and national law does not) has been established: '(...) so not situations of "consistent interpretation" of which the purpose is primarily to avoid any conflict'.[218] I agree that there is not, or at least not yet, the kind of conflict of substantive norms envisaged by Besselink in the context of the duty of consistent interpretation. It is only once the national courts conclude that national law cannot be made compatible with the directive, that there is a conflict of norms. This seems to raise a difficulty of applying the existing theories to the duty of consistent interpretation. However, it is argued that this is not necessarily so if the duty of consistent interpretation is viewed as an interpretative rule making its own normative claim.[219] In this connection I also want to point out that it is not necessary to have recourse to a version of supremacy that deviates from its ordinary meaning, in particular the idea of structural supremacy (see chapter 1, subparagraph 1.3.1). Admittedly, the latter version could be interpreted as providing support for the view that, in order to give full effect to EU law, supremacy extends beyond the national provision that causes the substantive conflict and increases the scope of national rules that must yield to the supremacy of EU law. Hence, it could also encompass national rules of interpretation. However, it still takes a conflict between substantive norms as its starting point. It is also pointed out that the part of the *Simmenthal* judgment that could be interpreted as laying down the principle of structural supremacy has only been stated in cases where national procedural rules were concerned and there are no indications that it was intended to cover national interpretative rules too. Apart from that, the issue of unravelling the meaning of the rule established by Articles 288 TFEU and 4(3) TEU has more to do with understanding its nuanced

218 L.F.M. Besselink, *A Composite European Constitution* (Europa Law Publishing 2007), p. 7-8. See further M. Fletcher, 'Extending "Indirect Effect" to the Third Pillar: The Significance of Pupino?' (2005/6) *ELRev*, p. 876.

219 Cf. Canaris (n. 9), p. 46-7, who argues that consistent interpretation is not concerned with a conflict of norms, but operates on the level of interpretations. The duty of consistent interpretation is viewed as requiring a concrete interpretative result which must then, under conditions identical to *verfassungskonforme Auslegung*, be favoured over opposing interpretations. Canaris does not, however, go into the details of the individual methodological instructions that have been provided by the ECJ.

implications for the interpretation of national law than that it is contested that national interpretative rules are subject to its effects (which might be supremacy or otherwise) – compared to substantive national law, interpretative rules are in principle of a less absolute nature and I do not see why there should be a higher threshold to subject these rules to supremacy *in as far as they are in conflict with EU law*.

On the basis of the analysis in paragraphs 4 and 5 the large open space that was created by the *Von Colson and Kamann* judgment's instruction to interpret national law so far as possible in conformity with EU law, was narrowed down by determining the consequences that can be derived from the ECJ's case law that further developed this obligation. This fixates, to some extent, the autonomous space enjoyed by national courts, which is then the sum of the positive requirements imposed minus the discretion conferred by the limits to the duty of consistent interpretation. Brenncke identifies this constellation as 'bounded *internal* European legal pluralism'. Brenncke explains that this kind of legal pluralism is bounded as it is managed by methodological rules controlled by EU law.[220] I want to add that this kind of legal pluralism is internal as it is not the result of incompatible conflicting positions derived from two or more legal orders without it being clear who has the final say – which is usually the situation in theories on constitutional pluralism – but is rather the result of the discretion unilaterally afforded by EU law. However, even though I agree with Brenncke's characterisation, the question remains how 'bounded' things are. This brings me to my next point, which is that, although the ECJ's case law provided methodological rules, they still leave a large measure of discretion. To be fair, this is understandable since, arguably, some flexibility is required to do justice to the different national contexts within which the duty of consistent interpretation is applied. In any case it should be clear that national courts still enjoy a significant degree of autonomy when they carry out the duty of consistent interpretation. This will be further explored in the subsequent chapters. On the basis of this chapter, the following questions seem to be of particular relevance:

- as the supremacy enjoyed by the duty of consistent interpretation is derived from its legal basis in EU law, as provided by the ECJ, do national courts also view the legal basis for the duty of consistent interpretation as originating from EU law;
- in which situations is the presumption that the legislature intends to comply with the directive applied and when is that presumption rebutted;
- how extensively is the *contra legem* limitation applied;

220 See further, Brenncke (n. 61), p. 19. See also G. Davies, 'Constitutional Disagreement in Europe and the Search for Pluralism', in: M. Avbelj and J. Komárek (Eds.), *Constitutional Pluralism in the European Union and Beyond* (Hart Publishing 2012), p. 272 who uses the term 'internal EU pluralism' in the context of scope for diversity as a result of the proportionality principle.

- are additional limitations (i.e. other than the limitation regarding criminal liability and the *contra legem* limitation) derived from the general principles of EU law and/or fundamental rights? It should be noted that the limitations discussed in the *Klohn* judgment were introduced relatively recently, and it may be asked whether precursors existed in national case law.

With the exception of fundamental rights (admittedly, the ECJ's case law contains some indications of the course that it would follow if fundamental rights were to be considered in the context of consistent interpretation, but it has never dealt with the matter explicitly), the above points all refer to matters in relation to which the ECJ has provided a clarification. But as far as concerns the latter three points, the precise application of the instruction is to a greater or lesser extent left to the national courts. Furthermore, it cannot be said that the ECJ's case law exhaustively deals with each question that may arise before a national court when applying the obligation. The precise scope of the obligation and hence the meaning of so far as possible therefore also depends on the national courts own further interpretation. In this area the national courts logically enjoy autonomy as well. These areas of the national courts' case law must be scrutinised extra carefully for their compliance with the outer limits established by the ECJ's framework.

CHAPTER 3
THE GERMAN SUPERIOR COURTS' PERSPECTIVE

1. INTRODUCTION

It was already in 1974 that the German Federal Court of Justice (Bundesgerichtshof, hereinafter BGH) decided that, since the meaning of the relevant national provisions were unclear and intended to implement the First Directive on Company Law,[1] it was necessary to ask the ECJ how the underlying provisions in the directive were to be interpreted so that national law could be given a consistent interpretation.[2] However, the necessity to adopt a consistent interpretation was exclusively based on the intentions of the German legislature. A year later, the German Federal Administrative Court (Bundesverwaltungsgericht, hereinafter BVerwG) interpreted national law in conformity with a directive.[3] Yet, on account of the reasoning of the decision, it can be asked whether it was not primarily based on the direct effect of EU law. But the existence of some divergences between the German superior courts' early case law and the subsequently developed duty of consistent interpretation in EU law is not surprising and does not alter the fact that the German courts were prepared to take the initiative to look at directives for determining the meaning of national law. This was perhaps explained by their experience with the requirement of a *verfassungskonforme Auslegung* (a technique that is further discussed in subparagraphs 3.1.3 and 3.3). However, it is important not to overlook the differences between the two interpretative obligations.

This chapter examines the German superior courts' (i.e. the BGH, BVerwG, Federal Labour Court (Bundesarbeitsgericht; hereinafter BAG) and the Federal Fiscal Court (Bundesfinanzhof; hereinafter BFH)) perspective on the relationship between EU and national law under the duty of consistent interpretation.

---

1 First Council Directive 68/151/EEC of 9 March 1968 on co-ordination of safeguards which, for the protection of the interests of members and others, are required by Member States of companies within the meaning of the second paragraph of Article 58 of the Treaty, with a view to making such safeguards equivalent throughout the Community, *OJ* 1968, L65/8.

2 BGH 14 February 1974, DB 1974, 1280.

3 BVerwG 2 July 1975, BVerwGE 49, 60.

The jurisdiction of these superior federal courts was discussed in detail in the introductory part of this book. Here it is briefly recalled that the BGH has jurisdiction over civil and criminal law disputes (the latter is not part of the analysis); the BVerwG has jurisdiction over public law disputes; tax law is, however, dealt with by the BFH; the BAG has jurisdiction over labour law disputes. The BVerfG has dealt with the duty of consistent interpretation in a limited number of cases but is the ultimate authority for the German Constitution's interpretation and it can review whether ordinary legislation, but also individual decisions and judgments, are compatible with it. In that regard it has delivered a large number of judgments that complete the picture of the German superior courts' courts case law examined in this chapter.

It does so by looking at, first, the legal basis for applying the duty of consistent interpretation. Secondly, the scope for a consistent interpretation from the perspective of the German interpretative rules is examined. It should be noted that this consists of two parts: in line with the approach in German legal scholarship and jurisprudence, a distinction is drawn between *Auslegung* and *Rechtsfortbildung* (for this distinction see further subparagraph 3.1). For both parts I first look at judgments successfully adopting a consistent interpretation, followed by a discussion of judgments that point out the limitations that are applied to the duty of consistent interpretation. In addition to this, I consider – by way of an afterthought – the role played by the preliminary reference procedure.

2. THE LEGAL BASIS FOR THE APPLICATION OF THE DUTY OF CONSISTENT INTERPRETATION

There are two reasons why the perspective on the legal basis for the duty of consistent interpretation is relevant. First, it is as such an argument in favour of a particular theory for the relationship between EU and national law. Secondly, it can be an indication for an approach to the duty of consistent interpretation that further supports, or challenges, a particular theory.

After its introduction in the ECJ's *Von Colson and Kamann* judgment, the German superior courts initially justified the application of the duty of consistent interpretation in different ways. Over time, their positions have converged. It is pointed out that, technically, the provisions of EU law discussed below entered the German legal order through the Law approving the Treaty of Lisbon. This is a result of Germany's dualist approach to international law. However, once EU law has passed through this conduit, its applicability and supremacy are recognised and the German courts directly rely on the EU law provisions.

2.1. AN INCOHERENT APPROACH IN THE BEGINNING...

In one of the judgments that ensued from the ECJ's *Von Colson and Kamann* judgment's considerations regarding the kind of sanction that the Equal Treatment Directive[4] required if discrimination has been established, and in a decision of 21 May 1992, the BAG considered that the duty of consistent interpretation had its legal basis in Article 288 TFEU, stipulating the obligation to implement directives into national law, and Article 4(3) TEU.[5] This was consistent with the ECJ's case law (see chapter 2, paragraph 2). The BVerwG did not seem to concern itself with the question of the legal basis for the duty of consistent interpretation, although on one occasion it justified its application by referring to the need to adopt a uniform interpretation.[6] Initially, the BGH, and in particular the BFH, adopted an approach that departed from the legal basis under EU law. Spetzler explains that the duty of consistent interpretation was merely used by the BFH to determine the legislature's intention and that it was incorporated into the teleological interpretative method where the national provisions had been adopted for the purpose of implementing a directive.[7] For example, in a judgment of 30 July 1992, the BFH stated that, since the Law on turnover tax intended to implement the Sixth Directive,[8] its provisions must be given a consistent interpretation.[9] In a previous judgment the BFH did refer to Article 4(3) TEU but as the explanatory memorandum clearly stated the implementing objective, it was deemed unnecessary to determine whether that provision always provided the legal basis for the duty of consistent interpretation.[10] Although it is more difficult to identify a consistent approach in the BGH's case law, it occasionally also justified the application of the duty of consistent interpretation by relying on the legislature's intention.[11]

2.2. ...WHICH HAS BEEN CONVERGING TOWARDS THE POSITION UNDER EU LAW

However, it should be mentioned that the German superior courts' approach to the legal basis for the duty of consistent interpretation has changed over time.

4 Council Directive 76/207/EEC of 9 February 1976 on the implementation of the principle of equal treatment for men and women as regards access to employment, vocational training and promotion, and working conditions, *OJ* 1976, L39/40.
5 BAG 14 March 1989, NJW 1990, 65; BAG 21 May 1992, BAGE 70, 238.
6 BVerwG 23 January 1992, BVerwGE 89, 320.
7 E. Spetzler, 'Die richtlinienkonforme Auslegung als vorrangige Methode steuerjuristischer Hermeneutik' (1991/7) *RIW*, p. 579.
8 Sixth Council Directive 77/388/EEC of 17 May 1977 on the harmonization of the laws of the Member States relating to turnover taxes - Common system of value added tax: uniform basis of assessment, *OJ* 1977, L145/1.
9 BFH 30 July 1992, Beck online Rechtsprechung 1992, 7770.
10 BFH 20 January 1988, BFHE 152, 556, 557.
11 BGH 9 March 1993, NJW 1993, 1594, 1595.

The approaches have, to some extent, converged. The BGH now consistently provides that the duty of consistent interpretation has its legal basis in Articles 288 TFEU and 4(3) TEU,[12] bringing it in line with the position adopted in the ECJ's case law. The BAG often refers to Article 288 TFEU,[13] sometimes in combination with the full effectiveness of EU law.[14] The BVerwG has referred to Articles 288 TFEU and 4(3) TEU,[15] only Article 288 TFEU,[16] only Article 4(3) TEU,[17] and the full effectiveness of EU law.[18] The BFH still justifies the application of the duty of consistent interpretation by relying on the legislature's intention to implement the directive,[19] but it has also become more common to see a reference to Article 288 TFEU and/or Article 4(3) TEU.[20] On balance, the German courts often take the exact same view as the ECJ, referring to both Articles 288 TFEU and 4(3) TEU. However, there are also quite a few judgments that mentioned only Article 288 TFEU, Article 4(3) TEU, or the full effectiveness of EU law (the latter is sometimes mentioned together with Article 288 TFEU). From a conceptual point of view, this is not flawless. Nevertheless, it can be asked whether it is reasonable to expect the national courts to meticulously refer to Articles 288 TFEU and 4(3) TEU for the duty of consistent interpretation's legal basis all the time. Moreover, a closer analysis of the German courts' judgments that did not mention both articles reveals that, in most cases, they have simply taken over an incomplete description of the legal basis contained in the ECJ's judgment to which the German court's judgment referred. For these reasons, it is appropriate to also see those judgments as adhering to the legal basis stated by the ECJ.

In particular the inclusion of Article 4(3) TEU for the duty of consistent interpretation's legal basis justified the conclusion that the duty of consistent interpretation is in principle capable of relying on the supremacy of EU law. If national courts adhere to the position under EU law, this is as such an argument in favour of supremacy of EU law. Secondly, it can be an indication for an approach to the duty of consistent interpretation that further supports this theory. This applies to the BGH, BVerwG and BAG.

12 BGH 9 April 2002 *Heininger*, BGHZ 150, 248; BGH 26 November 2008 *Quelle*, BGHZ 179, 27, para. 19; BGH 21 December 2011 *Bodenfliesen*, BGHZ 192, 148, para. 24; BGH 16 May 2013 *Interprofessionelle Sozietät*, NJW 2013, 2674, para. 40; BGH 28 October 2015 *Gasversorgung II*, BGHZ 207, 209, para. 36.

13 BAG 23 March 2006, BAGE 117, 281, para. 23; BAG 17 November 2009 *Urlaubsentgelt*, BAGE 132, 247, para. 25.

14 BAG 24 March 2009, BAGE 130, 119, para. 58.

15 BVerwG 29 January 2004, Beck online Rechtsprechung 2004, 21828; BVerwG 21 August 2018, DÖV 2019, 79, para. 27.

16 BVerwG 31 January 2017, Beck online Rechtsprechung 2017, 103948, para. 27.

17 BVerwG 5 September 2013, BVerwGE 147, 312, para. 46.

18 BVerwG 20 December 2012 *Mücksch*, NVwZ 2013, 719, 723.

19 BFH 12 March 1998, BFHE 185, 308; BFH 29 June 2011, BFHE 233, 470, paras. 20-2; BFH 12 October 2016, BFHE 255, 457, paras. 32-3; BFH 26 July 2017, DB 2017, 2395, para. 24.

20 BFH 2 April 1998, BFHE 185, 536; BFH 23 October 2003, BFHE 203, 531; BFH 19 January 2016, ZIP 2016, 1378, para. 81.

The BFH's prevailing approach to the legal basis for the duty of consistent interpretation tends to go in another direction and is more in line with the theory of national constitutionalism. Consider, for example, the BFH's judgment of 26 July 2017. It provided that, according to the legislature, the concerned provision contained in the Law on turnover tax implemented the directive and for that reason a consistent interpretation is required.[21]

> The BFH has also provided that a provision's purpose must be determined in the light of its systematic-teleological context, adding that national law on turnover tax must be interpreted in accordance with the applicable EU law provisions.[22] Since the BFH's application of the duty of consistent interpretation is based on systematic-teleological arguments, the legal basis is also found in national law. Also, as the judgments that contain this reference to a systematic-teleological interpretation all concerned implementing legislation, it does not seem to differ that much from the approach adopted in the judgment of 26 July 2017: in both situations the focal point was the objective to implement the directive.

First, the BFH's use of a legal basis that derives from national law is as such an argument supporting the theory of national constitutionalism. Secondly, it is an *indication* that that theory adequately describes the BFH's approach to the duty of consistent interpretation. Spetzler argues that with this kind of approach the BFH seemingly distances itself from the duty of consistent interpretation's binding nature and autonomous position under EU law and that it has as a consequence that the duty of consistent interpretation is treated as being auxiliary and cannot have supremacy over conflicting national interpretative rules.[23] Also, Franzen points out that national interpretative methods do not possess the normative force to oblige national courts to interpret national law in conformity with directives.[24] The duty of consistent interpretation would thus become the 'option' of a consistent interpretation. However, it remains to be seen in the next paragraph, whether all this has also materialised in the BFH's case law regarding the duty of consistent interpretation.

Subject to the BFH's more nationally-oriented approach, that has been in use to this day, it is reiterated that, in general, the German superior courts' current approach to the legal basis for the duty of consistent interpretation is identical or similar to

---

21 BFH 26 July 2017, DB 2017, 2395, para. 24.

22 BFH 8 September 2010, BFHE 231, 343, para. 25; BFH 15 February 2012, BFHE 236, 267, para. 17; BFH 16 May 2012, BFHE 238, 468, para. 41; BFH 2 July 2014, Beck online Rechtsprechung 2014, 96183, para. 30 (albeit that this latter judgment also appears to recognise that the duty of consistent interpretation follows on from the imperative of the effectiveness of EU law).

23 Spetzler (n. 7), p. 579-80. See also C.-W. Canaris, '*Die richtlinienkonforme Auslegung und Rechtsfortbildung im System der juristischen Methodenlehre*', in: H. Koziol and P. Rummel (Eds.), *Im Dienste der Gerechtigkeit* (Springer Verlag 2002), p. 50.

24 M. Franzen, *Privatrechtsangleichung durch die Europäische Gemeinschaft* (De Gruyter 1999), p. 313. See also M. Weber, *Grenzen EU-rechtskonformer Auslegung und Rechtsfortbildung* (Nomos 2010), p. 89.

the ECJ's position described in chapter 2. This is further supported by the BVerfG, which has adopted a position that corresponds with this:

> 'Gemäß Art. 288 Abs. 3 AEUV obliegt es vielmehr den Mitgliedstaaten und im Rahmen ihrer Zuständigkeiten den nationalen Gerichten, das in der Richtlinie vorgesehene Ziel zu verwirklichen. Dabei sind sie gemäß Art. 4 Abs. 3 EUV verpflichtet, alle ihnen zur Verfügung stehenden geeigneten Maßnahmen zur Erfüllung dieser Verpflichtung zu treffen (...). Den nationalen Gerichten obliegt es, den Rechtsschutz zu gewährleisten, der sich für den Einzelnen aus den unionsrechtlichen Bestimmungen ergibt, und dabei die volle Wirksamkeit des Unionsrechts sicherzustellen. Bei der Anwendung des innerstaatlichen Rechts, insbesondere einer speziell zur Umsetzung einer Richtlinie erlassenen Norm, müssen sie das innerstaatliche Recht daher so weit wie möglich anhand des Wortlauts und des Zwecks der Richtlinie auslegen, um der Verpflichtung aus Art. 288 Abs. 3 AEUV nachzukommen'.[25]
>
> Actually, in my opinion this did not only confirm the ECJ's judgments regarding the legal basis for the duty of consistent interpretation but explained the reasoning behind the stated legal basis even more clearly and in a way that is in line with what I contended in chapter 2. It showed that, first, there is the requirement to implement directives into national law, which in my opinion confirmed that the duty of consistent interpretation is seen as an extension of, and flows from, the obligation to implement the directive. Secondly, it is on the basis of Article 4(3) TEU that national courts must take the appropriate measures that are available to them to ensure that this objective is accomplished, which in my opinion confirmed that the interventionist aspects that make an appeal to the supremacy of EU law, are more appropriately based on Article 4(3) TEU.

3. THE SCOPE FOR, AND LIMITS TO, A CONSISTENT INTERPRETATION FROM THE PERSPECTIVE OF THE GERMAN SUPERIOR COURTS

On the one hand, the duty of consistent interpretation was characterised as an interpretative rule. On the other hand, the existing theories on the relationship between EU and national law require that there is a conflict or, in the context of constitutional pluralism, perhaps a potential or looming conflict. If the two are combined, this means that a conflict on the level of interpretative rules needs to be identified for the existing theories to come into play. The existence of a conflict can be the result of either an incompatibility with the obligation to interpret national law so far as possible, or the national interpretative rules. The scope and meaning of the former were already discussed in chapter 2. In this chapter I discuss the latter to acquire a better understanding of the German superior courts' traditional

25 BVerfG 10 December 2014, ZIP 2015, 335, para. 30. Confirmed by BVerfG 17 November 2017, NJW-RR 2018, 305, para. 36.

approach to interpretation (i.e. the approach adopted in a purely internal context). I then proceed to the main part of this paragraph which examines when a conflict of interpretative rules arises, how the German courts resolve such a conflict, and which theory most adequately explains the adopted solution. Before proceeding to this analysis, it is first pointed out, by way of example, that there is not a conflict if a consistent interpretation turns out to be identical to the interpretation that follows from a traditional approach to interpretation:

> In a judgment of the BGH it was examined which requirements must be met by merger reports. The applicants had argued that the report that was the subject matter of the dispute fell short of the statutory requirements. The BGH examined the wording of the relevant statutory context and agreed with the applicants. It added that this outcome was also in conformity with the directive.[26] However, this merely confirmed what already followed from a traditional approach to interpretation.[27] There is no independent influence of the duty of consistent interpretation and no tension whatsoever between this obligation and the traditional approach.
>
> A similar approach can be found in a decision regarding the registration of persons authorised to represent a company. The BGH first examined what the traditional approach to interpretation entailed and only mentioned the directive at the very end, concluding that the found interpretation was also in conformity with the directive.[28]
>
> A further example is the BVerwG's judgment of 31 March 2011, in which the interpretation whereby refugee status could also be withdrawn on the basis of the retrospective applicability of grounds of exclusion resulted from a traditional approach to interpretation. The BVerwG added that this outcome was also in line with the directive.[29]
>
> Finally, in the BFH's judgment of 22 November 2018 it followed from a traditional interpretation of national law that the applicant was not entitled to claim the reduced rate of turnover tax. The directive confirmed this interpretation.[30]

But also if the national courts go a little bit further, and even if the adopted consistent interpretation entailed an adaptation of a traditional interpretation, this does not automatically mean that there was a conflict. While the identification of a conflict presupposes some kind of adaptation, this does not hold true the other way around. Hence, it is necessary to acquire a precise understanding of the

---

26 BGH 22 May 1989 *Kochs Adler*, BGHZ 107, 296.
27 W. Brechmann, *Die richtlinienkonforme Auslegung* (C.H. Beck'sche Verlagsbuchhandlung 1994), p. 100-1.
28 BGH 10 November 1997, NJW 1998, 1071.
29 BVerwG 31 March 2011, BVerwGE 139, 272.
30 BFH 22 November 2018, DStR 2019, 265, para. 41.

interpretative scope, more specifically the interpretative discretion, that is available in a traditional context.

3.1. THE TRADITIONAL APPROACH TO INTERPRETATION

It is often said that there is no consistency in the German courts' traditional approach to interpretation; that there is no reliable methodology underlying their approach. Rüthers, for example, complains that the predictable application of interpretative methods by the German superior courts is in a state of decline.[31] Larenz and Canaris are less dismissive of the courts' use of interpretative methods, pointing out that interpretative questions cannot be solved mathematically.[32] They have two things in common. First, they agree that the German courts apply the interpretative methods with a considerable degree of discretion. Secondly, they agree that the interpretation of the law cannot be completely unrestricted. At some level it should be possible to verify the application of the interpretative methods' compliance with certain standards.[33]

The necessity to exercise some degree of control over the courts' approach to interpretation is also indispensable from a constitutional point of view: '*Methodenfragen sind Verfassungsfragen*'. This is a well known proverb in German legal scholarship, providing that the German courts' approach to interpretation is a question governed by the German Constitution (which will hereinafter simply be referred to as the Constitution), of which Article 20(3) provides that the judiciary shall be bound by law and justice, and Article 97(1) provides that judges shall be independent and subject only to the law. These fundamental provisions would become meaningless if the courts were free to do whatever they want. Accordingly, the BVerfG has concerned itself with the stipulation of rules for the approach to interpretation. It is settled case law that the very objective of interpretation is to ascertain the intent of the legislature which is objectified in the provision and manifested in the wording and the context of the provision. On the face of it, the BVerfG thus endorses what has been labelled as an 'objective' approach to interpretation.[34] In contrast to the 'subjective' approach, this does not view the historical legislative intention as the key element guiding the interpretative process, but aims to find out what the objective, contemporary, purpose of the legislation is. The BVerfG has, for example, provided that a historical interpretation is not

31 B. Rüthers, 'Methodenrealismus in Jurisprudenz und Justiz' (2006/2) *JZ*, p. 54. For an overwhelming overview of critical assessments of the methodology applied by German courts, see S. Vogenauer, *Die Auslegung von Gesetzen in England und auf dem Kontinent* (Mohr Siebeck 2001), p. 157-8.

32 K. Larenz and C.-W. Canaris, *Methodenlehre der Rechtswissenschaft* (Springer 1995), p. 166.

33 Ibid, p. 167; B. Rüthers, C. Fischer and A. Birk, *Rechtstheorie* (C.H. Beck 2018), p. 431 *et seq.*

34 This theory was explicitly endorsed in BVerfG 17 May 1960, BVerfGE 11, 126, 130.

decisive and only has an auxiliary role to play.[35] However, in other judgments it was admitted that the historical interpretation provides a not unimportant indication for the determination of the legislation's purpose.[36] It has also expressed a kind of conciliatory approach, providing that the relevance of the historical interpretation depends on the age of the legislation.[37] Also, it has been pointed out that, contrary to its theoretical observations, the BVerfG's actual application of the historical interpretative method confers a significant, often decisive, importance upon it.[38]

There are thus differences in the German courts' approach to interpretation, and German legal scholarship has also proposed different interpretative theories, mainly along the lines of the 'objective-subjective' divide. Assuming these issues can be solved in the first place, it is not within the scope of this book to do so. Instead I will – in addition to what was said above – limit myself to a number of relatively uncontroversial observations. These are divided into three categories. German legal scholarship as well as judicial practice distinguishes between, on the one hand, *Auslegung*, which is probably closest to the English term 'interpretation' and, on the other, *Rechtsfortbildung*, for which there is no equivalent in English but which denotes a further development of the law by the courts. These comprise the first two categories. This is followed by a discussion on *verfassungskonforme Auslegung* and *Rechtsfortbildung* (interpretation and a further development of the law in conformity with the Constitution).

3.1.1. *Conventional* Auslegung

In the context of *Auslegung*, the legislature's objectivised intention is determined through the grammatical, historical, systematic and teleological interpretative methods. They are complementary; methods neither operate to the exclusion of the other nor do they enjoy absolute priority.[39] The relative weight of the criteria is influenced by the circumstances of the case.[40]

First, it is clear that the purpose of the legislation is the key element for interpretation. This is not undermined by discussions on how that purpose is to be identified. It might seem obvious to attach the most weight to a teleological interpretation in that regard, but I am hesitant to do so. First, Vogenauer submits that, on the

---

35 BVerfG 17 May 1960, BVerfGE 11, 126, 130; BVerfG 17 January 2017, BVerfGE 144, 20, para. 155.

36 BVerfG 19 March 2013, BVerfGE 133, 168, para. 66. Confirmed in BVerfG 26 August 2014, NJW 2014, 3504, paras. 15-6.

37 BVerfG 11 June 1980, BVerfGE 54, 277, 297.

38 C. Walz, 'Das Ziel der Auslegung und die Rangfolge der Auslegungskriterien' (2010/3) *Zeitschrift für das Juristische Studium*, p. 485; Rüthers, Fischer and Birk (n. 33), p. 491.

39 BVerfG 17 May 1960, BVerfGE 11, 126, 130. See further BVerfG 20 March 2002, BVerfGE 105, 135, 157; BVerfG 19 March 2013, BVerfGE 133, 168, para. 66; BVerfG 17 January 2017, BVerfGE 144, 20, para. 555. See also Larenz and Canaris (n. 32), p. 140, 166.

40 M. Brenncke, *Judicial Law-Making in English and German Courts* (Intersentia 2018), p. 56 with further references to literature.

basis of its use in the German courts' case law, a teleological interpretation is often actually based on grammatical, historical and systematic arguments.[41] In those circumstances, it would be inaccurate to say that the teleological interpretation is the most important interpretative method. Secondly, where the teleological interpretation *is* used in a way that does not coincide with one or more of the other interpretative methods, it covers matters such as the requirement to reach a fair decision and finding a solution for the case whereby the relevant provision is applied in a manner that duly takes into account the concerned interests. Vogenauer views this use of the teleological interpretative method as a way to incorporate extra-legal (*Zweckmäßigkeits- und Gerechtigkeitserwägungen*) arguments – adding that such use is found first and foremost when the national interpretative methods do not clearly provide which interpretation must be followed.[42] As will be seen below, this way of applying the teleological interpretative method is not without discussion.

Secondly, a provision's wording is the starting point for determining its purpose. A more difficult question is then how much weight must be attributed to this criterion. Höpfner, and Rüthers, Fischer and Birk, who subscribe to the 'subjective' theory, are sceptical in this regard and relativize the role played by the grammatical interpretative method, emphasising that words can only be understood if the intention of the author is understood and that a provision's wording is only 'clear' if confirmed by the other interpretative methods.[43] Other authors adopt the point of view that only interpretations that remain within the established outer limits of the provision's wording are permitted.[44] I am not sure to what extent these two positions are in conflict with one another. There is something to be said for the Federal Social Court's following consideration, which is perhaps suitable as a rule of thumb: the less doubt there is on account of a grammatical interpretation, the more weighty must be the reasons that result from the other interpretative methods, if they are to justify a divergent interpretation.[45] When a balance is struck between grammatical and other interpretative methods, it seems clear that the exact weight conferred upon a grammatical interpretation depends on the circumstances of the case. There is broad consensus, both among supporters of the 'objective' as well as the 'subjective' approach, that, actually, most of the time, a provision's wording will leave open several interpretations.[46] This suggests that, at least *de*

41 Vogenauer (n. 31), p. 137-8, 154.

42 Ibid, p. 154. He provides that those extra-legal arguments are often disguised as teleological interpretation. Reference is made to case law and further case law studies showing a tendency to favour interpretations that are believed to be just and fair.

43 C. Höpfner, *Die systemkonforme Auslegung* (Mohr Siebeck 2008), p. 146; Rüthers, Fischer and Birk (n. 33), p. 449, 495. See also S. Pötters and R. Christensen, 'Richtlinienkonforme Rechtsfortbildung und Wortlautgrenze' (2011/8) *JZ*, p. 389-91.

44 F. Bydlinski, *Juristische Methodenlehre und Rechtsbegriff* (Springer 1991), p. 467 *et seq*, who spoke of the 'möglichen Wortsinn' of the provision. See also Larenz and Canaris (n. 32), p. 163-5; Walz (n. 38), p. 487.

45 BSG 23 October 1958, NJW 1959, 167, 168.

46 See, for example, Rüthers (n. 31), p. 59 and Larenz and Canaris (n. 32), p. 140.

facto, a grammatical interpretation will often leave room for further interpretation. Nevertheless, if the wording is clear-cut, and the provision is intended as an exhaustive and exclusive rule, it will be a more compelling argument leaving less room for the other interpretative methods.[47] The same applies when the provision belongs to the area of criminal law,[48] but also tax law, although there are again exceptions to the rule.[49]

> Legal scholarship does also not provide an unambiguous answer on this point. On the one hand, an absolute rejection of the possibility to interpret (i.e. by means of *Auslegung*) tax law to the detriment of an individual if this is not covered by the grammatical scope of the provision has been advocated.[50] On the other hand, it has been contended that the limits of interpretation are to be found in the wording of the provision *and* its context and clear purpose, and that a deviation from a provision's wording is only permitted under strict conditions – which, nevertheless, confirms, that in principle this possibility is recognised.[51]

Thirdly, the fact that, in principle, the grammatical interpretation must be considered in the light of the other interpretative methods, also ties in with the BVerfG's consideration that the determination of the legislature's objectivised intention requires that all interpretative methods are considered, and that they complement each other. This means that the historical and systematic interpretative method also provide relevant criteria. Their force is less evident than for the grammatical interpretation. Nevertheless, especially the historical interpretation is often an important criterion. Arguably, its force will diminish as the age of the concerned materials increases.

Finally, some concluding remarks are submitted. It is beyond dispute that there is an important degree of discretion in the German courts' approach to interpretation. It seems to me that the interpretative rules rarely strictly prescribe one single interpretation only. Surely, since the interpretative rules developed by the BVerfG are directly deduced from the Constitution, they are of a normative character. Yet, an actual finding of a violation of Article 20(3) of the Constitution is unlikely to occur if the lower court put forward a reasonable argumentation that is based on one or more of the recognised interpretative methods. The standard of review applied by the BVerfG to these matters is very lenient and merely examines whether the approach is not unsustainable, that it is not arbitrary.[52] The ordinary

47 Vogenauer (n. 31), p. 61.

48 Rüthers, Fischer and Birk (n. 33), p. 450. See in particular, BVerfG 23 October 1985, BVerfGE 71, 108, 116; BVerfG 20 October 1992, BVerfGE 87, 209, 224.

49 Vogenauer (n. 31), p. 98-9, 153; R.P. Schenke, *Die Rechtsfindung im Steuerrecht* (Mohr Siebeck 2007), p. 228-9.

50 Klein/Gersch AO § 4, paras. 26-8.

51 Koenig/Koenig AO § 4, para. 89.

52 BVerfG 10 July 1990, BVerfGE 82, 286, 300-1. See also BVerfG 3 April 1990, BVerfGE 82, 6, 11.

courts have of course also developed their own practices within the confines set by the BVerfG when it comes to interpretation, but these will often function more as guidelines instead of strict interpretative rules.

3.1.2. Conventional Rechtsfortbildung

The requirement of a *Rechtsfortbildung* can be linked to Article 20(3) of the Constitution, according to which the judiciary is not only bound by law, but also to the broader notion of justice.[53] Three points require further explanation. First, there is the question of the boundary between *Auslegung* and *Rechtsfortbildung*. Here, the 'objective/subjective' divide re-emerges, and the discussion regarding the appropriate boundary largely coincides with the different limits drawn by those theories in relation to *Auslegung*. As Rüthers, Fischer and Birk explain, supporters of the objective theory regard the limits of a provision's wording as the limits of an *Auslegung*, beyond which one must speak of a *Rechtsfortbildung*. Supporters of the subjective theory rather emphasise that, as *Auslegung* requires determining the legislature's intent using all the available interpretative methods, it is incorrect to draw the line by means of the grammatical interpretation only.[54] A further example is to be found in the use of systematic-teleological arguments. It is uncontroversial that a systematic interpretation requires the courts to take into account matters such as how the relevant provision relates to other provisions, and inferences that can be drawn from the categorisation of the relevant provision. For example, if section 842 of the Civil Code is being interpreted, it is necessary to understand that it is part of the title on torts, which is in turn part of book 2 on the law of obligations, and so on. Additionally, both supporters of the objective and subjective theory accept, albeit in varying degrees, that it can be required to take into account legal principles as they are part of the larger legal complex, which is relevant as well. This is referred to as systematic-teleological interpretation,[55] or teleological interpretation.[56] The point is that, within the limits set by the provision's wording, supporters of the objective theory permit 'objective purposes' of the law (e.g. the requirement to reach a fair decision; finding a solution for the case whereby the relevant provision is applied in a manner that duly takes into account the concerned interests) to impact a provision's *Auslegung*, whereas supporters of the subjective theory regard any departure from the legislature's historical intent as a *Rechtsfortbildung*.[57] These two examples show that the sharp edges of the methodological discussion between supporters of the objective and subjective theory can be softened since, to some extent, they accept the same approach but characterise this as either *Auslegung* or *Rechtsfortbildung*. Admittedly, this is not just a semantical issue. This brings

53 BVerfG 26 September 2011, BVerfGK 19, 89, para. 57.
54 Rüthers, Fischer and Birk (n. 33), p. 450-1.
55 Höpfner (n. 43), p. 91; Rüthers, Fischer and Birk (n. 33), p. 457 *et seq.*
56 Larenz and Canaris (n. 32), p. 153 *et seq.*
57 Rüthers, Fischer and Birk (n. 33), p. 447.

me to the second point that requires further consideration. *Rechtsfortbildung* is subject to specific requirements (and, depending on the limits that are applied to an *Auslegung,* these requirements are, or are not yet, applicable). It requires the identification of a *Regelungslücke* (a legislative gap or lacuna).[58]

> The BVerfG's judgment of 3 April 1990, for example, addressed the question whether a non-married partner could invoke a right to continue a residential tenancy agreement which, according to the relevant provision of German law, was conferred upon spouses and other family members that had a joint household with the deceased tenant. Although non-married partners did not come within the scope of that provision, the BVerfG considered that it was only near the end of the 1970s that such households had become more and more familiar, so that this could not have been taken into account by the legislature when the drafted the relevant provision. It referred to social and legal developments that had occurred since and concluded that the provision must be applied by analogy to non-married partners.

In the above example the *Regelungslücke* was the result of the larger legal complex and principles, and social developments, that are external to the legislation (*gesetzesübersteigende Rechtsfortbildung*). In addition, the *Regelungslücke* can follow from the legislation itself (*gesetzesimmanente Rechtsfortbildung*).[59]

Thirdly, a *Rechtsfortbildung* is also subject to limitations.[60] First, there are limits that derive from Article 20(3) of the Constitution. In a decision of 19 June 1973, the BVerfG held that a *Rechtsfortbildung* would be *contra legem,* and thereby prohibited, if the legislative intent would be contravened on an essential point ('*das gesetzgeberische Ziel in einem wesentlichen Punkt verfehlender oder verfälschender Sinn*').[61] Also, in its *Delisting* judgment, the BVerfG prohibited a *Rechtsfortbildung* whereby the legislative intent would be replaced by a judge's own weighing of interests.[62] Similarly, there is the requirement to respect the legislature's '*Grundentscheidung*'.[63] Also derived from Article 20(3) of the Constitution, but of a slightly different nature, is the prohibition to adopt a *Rechtsfortbildung* which reduces the scope of application for a legal rule to zero.[64] Secondly, a *Rechtsfortbildung* may not violate fundamental rights protected under the Constitution. A *Rechtsfortbildung* will, for

58 BAG 30 August 1989, BAGE 62, 338, 345; BVerfG 3 April 1990, BVerfGE 82, 6, 12; BGH 20 January 2005, NJW 2005, 1508, 1510; BVerwG 18 April 2013, NJW 2013, 2457, para. 22; BFH 13 May 2013, BFHE 241, 1.

59 For this distinction see Larenz and Canaris (n. 32), p. 187.

60 BVerfG 11 October 1978, BVerfGE 49, 304, 318.

61 BVerfG 19 June 1973, BVerfGE 35, 263, 280. See also BVerfG 10 January 2012 *Delisting,* BVerfGE 132, 99, para. 75.

62 BVerfG 10 January 2012 *Delisting,* BVerfGE 132, 99, para. 75. Also BVerfG 3 April 1990, BVerfGE 82, 6, 12; BVerfG 25 January 2011, BVerfGE 128, 193, para. 52.

63 BVerfG 25 January 2011, BVerfGE 128, 193, para. 53; BVerfG 4 April 2011, NJW 2011, 1723, para. 17; BVerfG 10 January 2012 *Delisting,* BVerfGE 132, 99, para. 76.

64 BVerfG 30 June 1964, BVerfGE 18, 97, 111; Canaris (n. 23), p. 94.

example, be rejected if it violates the right to property,[65] or the equality principle.[66] This second category of limitations is different from the first since it does not concern the separation of powers between the judiciary and the legislature, but examines whether the outcome of the *Rechtsfortbildung* is still compatible with the catalogue of fundamental rights in the Constitution.

While it is uncontroversial that a *Rechtsfortbildung* is part and parcel of the German courts' tools, it is not always clear when a *Regelungslücke* can be identified (in particular the degree to which factors that are more remote to the concerned legislation are relevant),[67] or at what point the limits attached to this instrument are exceeded.[68] It is also clear that this is no small matter as a *Rechtsfortbildung* allows a determination of when the written law requires a further development by the judiciary, thus raising difficult legal-political questions concerning the demarcation of its own competences and those of the legislature. It is self-evident that there is the risk of an usurpation of the latter's powers, a risk that is not merely hypothetical.[69] The dividing line between a legitimate *Rechtsfortbildung* and judicial activism is again primarily guided by Article 20(3) of the Constitution.

3.1.3. Verfassungskonforme Auslegung *and* Rechtsfortbildung

Prior to the EU law duty of consistent interpretation there already existed an interpretative obligation in the German legal order to interpret ordinary law in conformity with the Constitution. This requirement has been based both on the supreme rank of the Constitution as well as respect *vis-à-vis* the national legislature by finding a way to uphold the enactment instead of setting it aside.[70]

The relationship between *verfassungskonforme Auslegung* and the above discussed conventional approach to interpretation has been a matter of debate. It is accepted that *verfassungskonforme Auslegung* requires that a provision is, in a first step, interpreted in the true sense of the word (i.e. by applying the traditional interpretative methods). Only if this leaves open more than one interpretation, of which at least one is in conformity with the Constitution, do the courts move on to the second step, by which the interpretation in conformity with the Constitution is to be given priority.[71] However, while the prevailing view in legal scholarship seems to be that the requirement of *verfassungskonforme Auslegung* cannot in

---

65 BVerfG 3 October 1989, BVerfGE 81, 29, 31 *et seq.*

66 BVerfG 14 January 1986, BVerfGE 71, 354, 362.

67 Cf., on the one hand, Canaris (n. 23), p. 84, Bydlinski (n. 44), p. 473 and, on the other hand, K. Larenz, *Methodenlehre der Rechtswissenschaft* (Springer 1991), p. 375 *et seq.*

68 See also W.-H. Roth, 'Die richtlinienkonforme Auslegung' (2005/9) *Europäisches Wirtschafts- und Steuerrecht*, p. 393; Brenncke (n. 40), p. 102, 348.

69 Rüthers, Fischer and Birk (n. 33), p. 535.

70 Brenncke (n. 40), p. 142-3.

71 Höpfner (n. 43), p. 152-3.

any way modify the interpretative process taking place under the first step,[72] the BVerfG has also adopted a *verfassungskonforme Auslegung* where an application of the interpretative methods clearly identified a different outcome and did not leave room for further interpretation.[73] The BVerfG has also recognised the requirement to proceed to a *verfassungskonforme Rechtsfortbildung.*[74]

3.2. THE ADOPTION OF A CONSISTENT INTERPRETATION BY MEANS OF AN *AUSLEGUNG*

3.2.1. Negative Test Approach

In the context of conventional interpretation, the German courts use well established interpretative methods to determine the most accurate meaning of a national provision. A different approach can be discerned in some of the judgments applying the duty of consistent interpretation. The BGH's *Heininger* judgment is a prime example of a negative test approach – a term introduced by Brenncke[75] – which takes a particular result as its starting point (i.e. the interpretation prescribed by the directive) and, instead of asking what the most accurate interpretation of the national provision is, asks whether that provision does not oppose the desired interpretation.

The key issue was whether a person who – in the context of a doorstep sale – had taken out a loan and had offered security for the loan by way of a charge on the property that they sought to buy, could rely on the provisions of the Law on the Cancellation of Doorstep Sales to cancel the agreement, or that this was to be dealt with in accordance with the provisions of the Consumer Credit Law. In a decision of 29 November 1999, the BGH had stated that it followed from section 5 of the Law on the Cancellation of Doorstep Sales that the only condition for the Consumer Credit Law to apply and take precedence was that a situation came within the latter's scope. This interpretation followed from, among others, a grammatical interpretation. In particular, it rejected the argument that the Consumer Credit Law only applied depending on whether all or part

72 Ibid. See also M. Schmidt, 'Privatrechtsangleichende EU-Richtlinien und nationale Auslegungsmethoden' (1995) *Rabels Zeitschrift für ausländisches und internationales Privatrecht*, p. 588-90.

73 See M.H. Wissink, *Richtlijnconforme interpretatie van burgerlijk recht* (Kluwer 2001), p. 117-8; Brenncke (n. 40), p. 155, 180, referring, among others, to BVerfG 23 October 1991 *Eilversammlungen*, BVerfGE 85, 69.

74 See for a detailed discussion C.-W. Canaris, 'Gemeinsamkeiten zwischen verfassungs- und richtlinienkonformer Rechtsfindung', in: H. Bauer and others (Eds.), *Wirtschaft im offenen Verfassungsstaat* (C.H. Beck 2006), p. 53 *et seq*, with reference to BVerfG 17 June 1953 *Armenanwalt*, BVerfGE 2, 336, 340 *et seq*; BVerfG 15 December 1965 *Wencker*, BVerfGE 19, 342, 351 *et seq*; BVerfG 3 June 1992, BVerfGE 86, 288, 320 *et seq*; BVerfG 30 March 2004 *Geldwächse*, BVerfGE 110, 226, para. 147 *et seq*; BGH 19 May 1981, BGHSt 30, 105, 121.

75 Brenncke (n. 40), p. 291.

of its provisions protecting consumers could actually be invoked in the specific circumstances of the case.[76] Although it presumed that the underlying Doorstep-Selling Directive[77] would provide the same outcome, it considered that this was not completely beyond dispute, so that it referred preliminary questions to the ECJ. It followed from the ECJ's preliminary ruling that the outcome of the BGH's decision of 29 November 1999 was incompatible.[78] The BGH had the unenviable task of either establishing the national provision's incompatibility with the directive, or – despite the considerations in its previous decision – to find a way to adopt a consistent interpretation. It opted for the second alternative, thus clearly deviating from its earlier interpretation. One of the main challenges for this consisted of justifying the possibility of a consistent interpretation from the point of view of the provision's wording (the other main challenge consisted of surmounting its previous considerations regarding a historical interpretation, which is discussed in the next subparagraph). To this end, it provided the following argumentation. It stated that the starting point for the enquiry whether a consistent interpretation could be adopted from a grammatical point of view was whether the wording of section 5 of the Law on the Cancellation of Doorstep Sales (and section 3 of the Consumer Credit Law) *excluded* a consistent interpretation. From there, it went on to provide that, while an isolated grammatical interpretation of section 5 of the Law on the Cancellation of Doorstep Sales is more in favour of the interpretation adopted in the decision of 29 November 1999, that interpretation, which was incompatible with the directive, was not peremptory as the provision's wording was not unambiguous. In other words, the provision was open to more than one interpretation, thus also keeping the door open for a consistent interpretation. It then went on to substantiate the alleged ambiguity. It pointed out that section 5 of the Law on the Cancellation of Doorstep Sales stated that the provisions of the Consumer Credit Law were to apply if a transaction at the same time fulfilled the '*Voraussetzungen*' of the latter. The most natural reading of '*Voraussetzungen*' was that it meant 'scope of application', which was the interpretation that the BGH initially adopted in its decision of 29 November 1999. But in its final judgment it provided that it could also be interpreted so as to mean that the Consumer Credit Law only applied to the situation as long as it offered a protection equivalent to that of the Law on the Cancellation of Doorstep Sales (which condition was not fulfilled in the present proceedings). This interpretation (i.e. the requirement of equivalent protection so not the intention to implement the directive) was in particular supported by the argument based on a historical interpretation.[79] Finally, reference was made to several scholarly contributions, as well as case law of some of the lower ranking courts, which supported the interpretation in conformity with the

76 BGH 29 November 1999, NJW 2000, 521, 522.
77 Council Directive 85/577/EEC of 20 December 1985 to protect the consumer in respect of contracts negotiated away from business premises, *OJ* 1985, L372/31.
78 Case C-481/99 *Heininger*, ECLI:EU:C:2001:684, para. 40.
79 BGH 9 April 2002 *Heininger* BGHZ 150, 248, 254.

directive, adding that it can only be said that there is no possibility whatsoever to adopt a consistent interpretation, if these positions were found to be manifestly untenable.[80]

Two subsequent BGH judgments that confirmed the interpretation that, in a situation such as the *Heininger* case, the Law on the Cancellation of Doorstep Sales was to be applied led to constitutional complaints before the BVerfG. The BVerfG concluded that the complaints were unfounded and that there had not been a violation of Article 20(3) of the Constitution.[81] Nevertheless, it is not entirely clear from the decision whether the BVerfG saw the solution adopted in the *Heininger* and similar subsequent judgments, which it characterised as a teleological reduction, as an *Auslegung* or *Rechtsfortbildung*.[82]

One of the main criticisms with respect to the *Heininger* judgment was the BGH's change of mind regarding the grammatical interpretation. It was argued that the provision's wording clearly pointed in a different direction, corresponding to the position adopted in the BGH's previous decision of 29 November 1999.[83] Or that it was simply inconsistent that the BGH first held that the provision's wording supported one interpretation and then, subsequently, took the opposite view.[84] These points of criticism lay bare the BGH's change in attitude: it openly acknowledged that it departed from its previous position, which it justified by providing that that position had been the result of an isolated, traditional approach, which did not take into account the directive and the duty of consistent interpretation.[85] In its final judgment the focus shifted and the grammatical interpretative method was applied as an outer limit.

---

80 Ibid, 256. Cf. M. Herdegen, 'Richtlinienkonforme Auslegung im Bankrecht: Schranken nach Europa- und Verfassungsrecht' (2005/41) *Wertpapier-Mitteilungen, Zeitschrift für Wirtschafts- und Bankrecht*, p. 1923, who argues that the provision's clear wording was set aside by the presumption that the legislature intended to fully implement the directive. However, that argument cannot be found in the part of the judgment that discussed the possibility to adopt a consistent interpretation in the light of its wording, but is only mentioned subsequently in the judgment when it had to be determined what a historical interpretation entailed.

81 BVerfG 26 September 2011, BVerfGK 19, 89, para. 42.

82 Ibid, cf. paras. 45 and 56 on the one hand, and para. 58 on the other. In the former paragraphs the rules for the adoption of a *Rechtsfortbildung* were examined, which implies that this was a relevant benchmark. M. Franzen, '"Heininger" und die Folgen: ein Lehrstück zum Gemeinschaftsprivatrecht' (2003/7) *JZ*, p. 327; W.-H. Roth and C. Jopen, '*Die richtlinienkonforme Auslegung*', in: K. Riesenhuber (Ed.), *Europäische Methodenlehre* (De Gruyter 2015), p. 285, view the *Heininger* judgment as an example of a *Rechtsfortbildung*. Nevertheless, in para. 58, the *Heininger* judgment is characterised by the BVerfG as an *Auslegung*.

83 Franzen (n. 82), p. 324.

84 Herdegen (n. 80), p. 1922; Roth and Jopen (n. 82), p. 285.

85 BGH 9 April 2002 *Heininger*, BGHZ 150, 248, 253.

A similar approach can be seen in the BGH's *Bodenfliesen* judgment, albeit that there was perhaps less of a volte-face than in the *Heininger* judgment.[86] Nevertheless, initially, the BGH tended towards a grammatical interpretation which, upon receipt of the requested preliminary ruling from the ECJ, turned out to be incompatible with the concerned directive. In the follow-up judgment, it went along with the ECJ, which it justified by holding that the required interpretation was still possible on account of the wording of the provision,[87] which was open to more than one interpretation. It should be pointed out that this was further supported by a historical and systematic interpretation.[88] Also, in the BVerwG's judgment of 7 July 2016 it had to be determined what 'in the course of business' (*gewerbsmäßig*) meant, and in particular whether this required that the activities are performed to make a profit. The ECJ had pointed out that this is not a necessary requirement. The BVerwG considered that, while legal scholarship and also certain case law made clear that the intention to make a profit was a necessary requirement and that this was indeed the most natural reading of the provision, the duty of consistent interpretation required the opposite conclusion. It held that this would not exceed the limits of what was still a permissible interpretation and that 'in the course of business' was not further defined and open to a further interpretation in line with the provision's purpose, which was the implementation of the directive.[89]

Do the above judgments indicate a conflict of interpretations that was resolved in favour of the duty of consistent interpretation? After all, the judgments more or less transform the traditional objective of interpretation (ascertaining the intent of the legislature as accurately as possible). There is a close similarity here with the *verfassungskonforme Auslegung*. After the ECJ delivered its *Von Colson and Kamann* judgment, the majority of German legal scholarship supported the view that the duty of consistent interpretation must be treated on the same footing as *verfassungskonforme Auslegung*.[90] The BVerfG's first statement on the newly introduced obligation also went in that direction.[91] Importantly, *verfassungskonforme Auslegung* also takes as its starting point the objective to obtain a result that is in

86 BGH 21 December 2011 *Bodenfliesen*, BGHZ 192, 148.

87 See also BGH 12 October 2016, NJW 2017, 1093, paras. 40, 50.

88 This aspect of the judgment related to the question whether the seller's obligation to provide cure in relation to defective goods by supplying replacement goods, also requires him to uninstall and remove the defective goods. The natural meaning of supply did not seem to include the latter, but it appeared from the historical and systematic interpretation that the legislature had used an understanding of 'supply' that also envisaged an exchange of goods.

89 BVerwG 7 July 2016, BVerwGE 155, 381, para. 20 *et seq.*

90 Brechmann (n. 27), p. 259-62, 272-3; Canaris (n. 23), p. 79; Canaris (n. 74), p. 46, 48-51; Höpfner (n. 43), p. 272, 274-5; Weber (n. 24), p. 122-7; Roth and Jopen (n. 82), p. 283-94. However, if the different positions are compared, it becomes clear that they often draw different conclusions on what such an analogy entails for the approach to the duty of consistent interpretation. Cf. Schmidt (n. 72), p. 590-1, who rejects *verfassungskonforme Auslegung* as a paradigm for the duty of consistent interpretation.

91 BVerfG 8 April 1987 *Kloppenburg*, BVerfGE 75, 223, 237.

conformity with the Constitution.[92] Moreover, I pointed out in subparagraph 3.1.3 that it is not always reduced to a tool to choose between whatever interpretations remain after having applied well established interpretative methods. So it would be tempting to conclude that the German courts do nothing 'extra' when they proceed in the same manner in the context of the duty of consistent interpretation. Yet, this overlooks that *verfassungskonforme Auslegung* is partly based on the supreme rank of the Constitution and that the negative test approach contrasts sharply with the conventional approach to interpretation. Accordingly, to permit the same approach for the duty of consistent interpretation indicates that this obligation is viewed as having supremacy in relation to the conventional interpretative rules as well. So it is the change in approach, combined with the identified rationale urging such change, that provides the indication for supremacy.[93] It is also pointed out that the discussed judgments made it clear that the negative test approach is not reduced to an inquiry which interpretations remain after a conventional application of the national interpretative methods, but that the objective to obtain a result that is in conformity with the directive has the capacity to push the scope available under the interpretative methods to their outer limits.

3.2.2. The Intention to Implement the Directive

It must be pointed out that, often, supporters of the view that the duty of consistent interpretation cannot affect the traditional interpretative approach nevertheless consider that an implementing objective must be taken into account by means of a historical, systematic or teleological *traditional* interpretation. This is then clearly distinguished from any autonomous influence of the duty of consistent interpretation.[94] When it comes to the identification of a conflict, use of the argument that the legislation was intended to implement the directive must be approached with some suspicion because it is woven into the fabric of these three interpretative methods that a provision's intention or purpose to implement the directive, or its genealogical place in the legal order, is taken into account. If this is done, it will obviously be favourable to the chances of the adoption of a consistent interpretation, but does not require the national courts to do something extra.[95]

---

92 Canaris (n. 74), p. 46; Brenncke (n. 40), p. 154.

93 Cf. Wissink (n. 73), p. 150-1, who does not draw a link with the theory of supremacy when discussing the negative test approach. However, it is noted that his contribution did not focus on the specific context of German law.

94 See, for example, Weber (n. 24), p. 123.

95 See also BGH 14 February 1974, DB 1974, 1280, mentioned in the introduction of this chapter, which was delivered before the establishment of the duty of consistent interpretation in the ECJ's case law and where the BGH pointed to the provision's implementing objective for the necessity to adopt an interpretation in conformity with the directive. Jarass is also very clear on this point: a consistent interpretation can also be adopted as a matter of national law if there was an implementing objective. This must in his opinion be separated from the duty of consistent interpretation under EU law, H.D. Jarass, *Grundfragen der innerstaatlichen Bedeutung des EG-Rechts* (Carl Heymanns 1994), p. 89-90.

The German superior courts' case law contains a number of judgment where the adopted consistent interpretation, on an initial reading, appears to go beyond the limits set by national interpretative rules, but where, on closer inspection, it cannot be said that this conclusion is justified if the role played by the legislature's implementing objective is taken into account:

> The legislature's intention to implement the directive can be invoked in order to question a proposed interpretation, and subsequently impose one that is consistent with the directive. After all, the very objective of interpretation is to ascertain the intent of the legislature, so that for example the provision's wording must be considered in the light of those intentions. When the courts proceed in this way, usually reference is made to the legislation's explanatory memorandum which states the implementing objective. In its judgment of 7 July 2016, for example, the BVerwG departed from a particular interpretation, dictated by the prevailing view in the German legal order, to adopt a consistent interpretation. It mentioned the duty of consistent interpretation and its legal basis in EU law, which at first sight might seem to support the idea that the adopted interpretation was the result of the supremacy of the requirement to interpret national law in conformity with the directive. But the primary reason for the adoption of a more expansive interpretation, that deviated from the prevailing view, seemed to be that the latter would not be compatible with the provision's purpose, i.e. the implementation of the directive.[96] Also consider the judgment of 14 February 2006 concerning the question whether a contract could be cancelled if the doorstep sale had been negotiated through a third party and not directly with the contracting party, In settled case law, the BGH had dismissed this view.[97] The BGH did not really have to make an effort to find interpretative scope in the provision's wording. The previous interpretation resulted in particular from systematic-historical arguments. However, after subsequent ECJ case law, the earlier interpretation turned out to be incompatible with the directive. The BGH put forward the argument that the provision was intended to implement the directive and that the systematic-historical arguments had not found expression in the provision's wording and proceeded to a consistent interpretation.[98] The Higher Regional Court (Oberlandesgericht) Karlsruhe's judgment, which preceded the BGH's final judgment in the *Heinrich Heine* case,[99] provided that a consistent interpretation must in principle be adopted because the legislature had intended to fully implement the directive.[100] In the BGH's tersely reasoned final judgment those considerations were not repeated but the overall conclusion was that the Higher Regional Court Karlsruhe's judgment should be upheld.

These judgments have in common that they retreated from an earlier interpretation which had not taken into account new developments in the ECJ's case law. Since clarity about the precise scope of a provision of a directive often follows on the basis

96 BVerwG 7 July 2016, BVerwGE 155, 381, paras. 21-4.
97 See BGH 14 February 2006, NJW 2006, 1340, para. 13 for extensive references to case law.
98 Ibid, para. 14.
99 BGH 7 July 2010 *Heinrich Heine*, NJW 2010, 2651.
100 OLG Karlsruhe 5 September 2007, NJW-RR 2008, 1016, 1017.

of ECJ case law delivered after the introduction of implementing measures, and because the German courts are required to take into account a provision's changing context[101] – which also includes directives, as interpreted by the ECJ[102] – it actually seems quite normal that, once they become aware that a previous interpretation turned out to be incompatible with the directive, that factor is taken into account by means of a 'contextualised application' of particular traditional interpretative methods. Importantly, there does also not seem to be a kind of absolute priority of the implementing objective in those situations. Although it provides a strong argument, the courts can also prioritise other intentions.[103]

However, there is an indication of supremacy of the duty of consistent interpretation if the intention to implement the directive is systematically prioritised, or enjoys a kind of *prima facie* supremacy, over opposing intentions. So contrary to the above discussed situation, here it concerns the determination of legislative intent as such instead of the relationship with other interpretative criteria. I refer to the *Heininger* judgment again to further illustrate this. In addition to a reconsideration of the grammatical interpretation, it was also necessary to explain why a historical interpretation did not stand in the way of a consistent interpretation: the legislature had explicitly provided, albeit in the explanatory memorandum of the Consumer Credit Law and not the Law on the Cancellation of Doorstep Sales, that it was not deemed appropriate if a right of cancellation could be invoked in relation to secured-credit agreements. However, the BGH gave priority to the fact that it cannot be presumed that the legislature intended to violate the directive when he drafted the provisions of the Law on the Cancellation of Doorstep Sales – which had occurred just prior to the introduction of the directive and anticipated its entry into force.[104] Another approach favourable to a prioritisation of the implementing objective can be found in the BGH's judgment of 12 October 2016. While the explanatory memorandum made clear that the legislature intended to implement a rule introduced by the directive concerning the burden of proof in relation to lack of conformity of consumer goods, it was not clear whether he had intended to depart from the general national rules regarding burden of proof to the extent required by the directive. However, it was sufficient that the explanatory memorandum contained no indication that the legislature had intended to draft a provision that was incompatible with the directive, as interpreted by the ECJ.[105] Also in light of the legislation's overall objective to enhance consumer protection, it

101 Rüthers, Fischer and Birk (n. 33), p. 440.
102 C. Herresthal, *Rechtsfortbildung im europarechtlichen Bezugsrahmen* (C.H. Beck 2006), p. 183 *et seq.*
103 This can be seen in BFH 18 April 1991, RIW 1991, 782, 782; BVerwG 18 December 1997, NJW 1998, 3433, 3435; BAG 18 February 2003, DB 2003, 1387.
104 BGH 9 April 2002 *Heininger*, BGHZ 150, 248, 256.
105 The BGH's judgment was prompted by Case C-497/13 *Faber*, ECLI:EU:C:2015:357. Arguably, before the ECJ's judgment it was difficult to predict what the exact scope of the rule concerning the burden of proof was, see the case note by Koch in *JZ* 2015, p. 835.

had to be presumed that the legislature intended to duly implement the directive.[106] It should be noted that this judgment, as well as the *Heininger* judgment, did not refer to any of the ECJ's case law regarding the presumption that the legislature intends to comply with the directive. The BAG's judgment of 23 March 2006 *did* state the ECJ's *Pfeiffer* judgment's requirement that it must be presumed that the legislature intends to comply with the directive but it appears from the judgment's reasoning that the main obstacles to a consistent interpretation were set aside on other grounds so that it is not entirely clear what the impact of the presumption was for the BAG's decision to adopt a consistent interpretation.[107]

The absence of a reference to EU law could be interpreted as an indication that in the *Heininger* judgment and the judgment of 12 October 2016 the duty of consistent interpretation was not decisive and did not conflict with national interpretative rules. Moreover, was it not just pointed out that it must be presumed that there was not a conflict if the key reason relied upon was the legislation's implementing objective? Yet, in my opinion this overlooks that there was a fixation of the interpretative approach in these judgments, which goes against the German courts' traditional approach to interpretation whereby a single interpretative method cannot have the effect of fixating an otherwise flexible system. I therefore think that the answer to the question whether or not there was a conflict depends on the extent to which the approach entailed a fixation of the weight of historical interpretation. In that regard it is submitted that the judgments convey the message that the intention to implement the directive in principle sets aside incompatible arguments derived from parliamentary history. Furthermore, I want to point out that other judgments, among which is the BAG's judgment of 23 March 2006,[108] discussed when the intention to implement the directive should no longer be prioritised. It follows from this case law that this is so if the legislature unequivocally expressed a conscious intention to depart from the directive. Arguably, it is not very likely that this exception applies so that, on balance, the priority of the implementing objective stands. I conclude that there is indeed a *structural* prioritisation and that it supports the theory of supremacy of EU law.

3.2.3. Transgressions of the National Interpretative Rules?

The above identified conflicts all concerned examples of supremacy of the duty of consistent interpretation as a result of a change to the interpretative process (the negative test approach and a structural prioritisation). At the beginning of the previous subparagraph I argued that there is in principle not a conflict of interpretative rules when a seemingly far-reaching consistent interpretation is based on the argument that the provision has an implementing objective. This does

---

106 BGH 12 October 2016, NJW 2017, 1093, paras. 41-5, see also para. 51.
107 BAG 23 March 2006, BAGE 117, 281, paras. 24-5, 27.
108 Ibid, para. 25. See also BGH 7 May 2014, BGHZ 201, 101, para. 23.

not concern the interpretative process but asks whether the interpretative *outcome* can be reconciled with the outer limits set by national interpretative rules. This subparagraph is also devoted to this subject.

It is pointed out that a conflict is unlikely if the duty of consistent interpretation is applied to provisions that are of a flexible *casu quo* general nature. These provisions normally have the intrinsic characteristic that they are open to new developments. Two judgments of the BAG and BGH confirm that such provisions can more easily accommodate a consistent interpretation.[109]

> One of the relevant aspects of a judgment of the BAG which formed part of a series of judgments that ensued from the ECJ's *Von Colson and Kamann* judgment, was that it adopted the required consistent interpretation in relation to sanctions imposed for breaches of the prohibition of discrimination by allowing more extensive compensation based on a violation of the 'right of personality', which is protected under section 823 of the Civil Code regarding liability in damages.[110] That provision is of a general nature and open to new developments,[111] thus providing considerable scope for a consistent interpretation.
>
> In the *Testpreis-Angebot* judgment, the BGH identified an incompatibility with the directive but considered that this could be resolved as the relevant national provision was a broadly formulated 'general clause'.[112]

It can be presumed that it is also more easy to adopt a consistent interpretation in a situation of so-called *verbatim* transposition, i.e. where the national implementing provisions have literally taken over the directive's provisions.[113] However, it remains to be seen whether the German superior courts automatically follow the ECJ's interpretation of the directive if it has been transposed *verbatim*.

> In the previous chapter I already addressed the ECJ's *Spedition Welter* judgment,[114] which is perhaps the best known example of this category of cases. I concluded that, while it is logical that a consistent interpretation must be followed in particular where the directive is transposed verbatim since there is an implementing objective and on account of the proximity of the national provision's wording, the ECJ's judgment should in my opinion not be interpreted as leaving the national court no discretion whatsoever when taking the final decision. So what did the referring court decide? It repeated the most important part of the ECJ's judgment and then simply concluded that, accordingly, the claims representative was authorised to accept service of

109 See also, in general, Canaris (n. 23), p. 71.
110 This 'right of personality' encompasses the right to the free development of his or her personality, which was believed to be harmed by the concerned breaches of the prohibition of discrimination, see BAG 14 March 1989, NJW 1990, 65, 65.
111 T.C.W. Beyer and T.M.J. Möllers, 'Die Europäisierung des Arbeitsrechts' (1991/1) *JZ*, p. 28.
112 BGH 5 February 1998, NJW 1998, 2208, 2211.
113 See also Franzen (n. 24), p. 390, 392-3.
114 Case C-306/12 *Spedition Welter*, ECLI:EU:C:2013:650.

judicial documents (which was the result prescribed by the directive).[115] The argumentation is not particularly elaborate, but it seems to be clear that it did not find any difficulty in adopting a consistent interpretation. I must point out that, since the preliminary reference was made by a lower ranked court (the Landgericht Saarbrücken), this requires the qualification that it is not representative for the German superior courts' approach.

In the BAG's judgment of 23 March 2006 a consistent interpretation was adopted and the concerned provision did not belong to one of the just described categories. The proceedings revolved around the interpretation of the concept 'redundancy'. There was settled case law, supported by systematic-teleological arguments, that followed an interpretation that turned out to be incompatible with the directive. The BAG retreated from its previous position.

The key question was whether 'redundancy' must be understood as the declaration intended to terminate the contract of employment, or the actual cessation of the employment relationship. This was essential for determining the moment at which the employer must carry out his obligation under the Law on Employment Protection to notify to the labour office his intention of carrying out redundancies. In settled case law, the BAG interpreted the term '*Entlassung*' – which was used in the Law on Employment Protection implementing the directive – to refer to the actual cessation of the employment relationship.[116] However, it followed from the ECJ's *Junk* judgment that this was incorrect and that the labour office had to be notified prior to the declaration intended to terminate the contract of employment.[117] When the BAG received a case with regard to this subject, it took the opportunity to examine whether it could adopt a consistent interpretation. It provided that, on account of a grammatical interpretation, such an interpretation was not *a priori* excluded; it did not go beyond the provision's wording.[118] However, there were two substantial counter-arguments. First, the scope of application of parts of another, related provision, contained in the same legislation, would have been considerably reduced as a result of a consistent interpretation.[119] Secondly, the consistent interpretation lay bare the difficulties that arise if a directive is implemented through provisions that were originally enacted for different purposes. The directive primarily aimed to protect the workers, whereas the relevant part of the Law on Employment Protection was originally primarily a measure of labour market policy, intended to enable the labour office to anticipate an increase in unemployed people (although it must be pointed

115 LG Saarbrücken 15 November 2013, not reported.

116 See BAG 23 March 2006, BAGE 117, 281, para.19 for extensive references to case law.

117 Case C-188/03 *Junk*, ECLI:EU:C:2005:59, paras. 39, 54.

118 Note that the BAG also supported that conclusion through systematic arguments: on a number of occasions the legislation did not clearly separate between the declaration intended to terminate the contract of employment and the cessation of the employment relationship when using the term '*Entlassung*'.

119 S. Naber, 'Richtlinienkonforme Rechtsfindung am Beispiel des Massenentlassungsrechts' (2007/7) *Juristische Schulung*, p. 616-7.

out that the objective to protect workers was not entirely alien to it).[120] The consistent interpretation clearly enhanced the former objective but, as there was only an obligation to notify the labour office of planned redundancies, it would not be informed when those redundancies actually took effect, even though that is the moment that is most relevant to the labour office as it must then make payments and assist the unemployed persons.[121] It is pointed out that this has negative consequences for the pursuit of the labour market policy.[122] Nevertheless, the systematic-teleological counter-arguments were dismissed by the BAG.[123] This may have been influenced by some of its more general considerations regarding the force of the duty of consistent interpretation when it is applied in a context of implementing legislation, although the judgment is not really clear in that regard.

It must be noted that, in the end, a consistent interpretation was rejected on account of the principle of the protection of legitimate expectations (which did not alter the fact that, in principle, the BAG considered that the provision could be given a consistent interpretation). This, and the subsequent constitutional complaint before the BVerfG, will be discussed in subparagraph 3.4.

While the BAG adapted its previous interpretation, it is submitted that this did not go so far that it can be said that there was a conflict. The BAG pointed out that a consistent interpretation was grammatically possible and explained why the systematic-teleological arguments were not decisive. It must therefore be presumed that national law did not preclude the adoption of a consistent interpretation.

Next, there is the BVerwG's *Mücksch* judgment. In the decision making a reference for a preliminary ruling it was stated that, *on the basis of national law*, permission had to be granted for the building project (thus, again, clearly identifying a particular interpretation). However, it submitted that this raised some questions in respect of the compatibility with the directive.[124] And, again, the obtained preliminary ruling showed that this hesitation was justified, and the BVerwG had to find an appropriate solution. The key to this was provided by a criterion contained in the relevant national legislation, which required that the building project had to be in keeping with the features of its immediate surroundings. This was found by the BVerwG to be a criterion that could accommodate several interests, including the requirements imposed by the directive.[125] It should be noted that the

120 Ibid, p. 616. The point that the relevant part of the Law on Employment Protection is also to some extent concerned with the protection of workers is made in K. Riesenhuber and R. Domröse, 'Die "Entlassung" nach der Massenentlassungsrichtlinie' (2005/3) *Europäisches Wirtschafts- und Steuerrecht*, p. 97-103, although the authors also regard the objectives regarding labour market policy to be dominant.

121 Riesenhuber and Domröse (n. 120), p. 97-103.

122 Naber (n. 119), p. 616.

123 BAG 23 March 2006, BAGE 117, 281, para. 29 *et seq.*

124 BVerwG 3 December 2009, Zeitschrift für deutsches und internationales Bau- und Vergaberecht 2010, 262, 263-4.

125 BVerwG 20 December 2012 *Mücksch*, NVwZ 2013, 719, 723.

relevant national provision did not have an implementing objective.[126] Hence, it was not possible to argue that the other interpretative arguments now required a contextualised application in light of the finding that the previous interpretation had not been in line with the provision's objective to implement the directive. Be that as it may, similar to the BAG's judgment of 23 March 2006, the BVerwG explained why national law could accommodate a consistent interpretation even though this departed from the earlier interpretation adopted. Taking into account the degree of flexibility that is available to the German courts when they interpret the law, I believe that there is not a conflict with national interpretative rules as long as such an interpretation is not unreasonable.

> The BFH's case law also provides two examples where there was a clear deviation from the previous interpretation, but where the adopted consistent interpretation fell short of a conflict with national interpretative rules. In the first case the consistent interpretation was difficult to reconcile with the provision's wording; the outcome was primarily guided by historical arguments (unrelated to the finding of an implementing objective) and the principle of fiscal neutrality.[127] And in another judgment the BFH was inclined to reject the possibility of a consistent interpretation in the decision making a reference for a preliminary ruling on account of the provision's wording, but in its final judgment adopted such an interpretation on the basis of the conceptualisation of the term 'legal person' in the German legal order.[128] Finally, there is a judgment from the BAG concerning the question when there is a transfer of an undertaking.[129]

It transpires in particular from the BAG's judgment of 23 March 2006 and the BVerwG's *Mücksch* judgment that an adequate justification facilitates the conclusion that there was not yet a conflict. This applies first and foremost to the situation where the adaptation came close to a transgression of the interpretative rules. By contrast, in the *Heinrich Heine* judgment, the BGH forgot to provide such an explanation, which raises the suspicion that the court was itself not entirely sure how it managed to arrive at the adopted consistent interpretation.[130] And in a judgment delivered by the BVerwG, a ground invalidating decisions for which no environmental impact assessment was carried out at all was simply extended to situations in which such an assessment was carried out inadequately.[131] It is difficult to determine whether such judgments violated national interpretative rules since there is not really any discussion on this point in the judgment which means that

126 BVerwG 3 December 2009, Zeitschrift für deutsches und internationales Bau- und Vergaberecht 2010, 262 para. 25.

127 BFH 29 June 2011, BFHE 233, 470, paras. 32-5.

128 BFH 19 January 2016, ZIP 2016, 1378, para. 82 *et seq.*

129 BAG 11 December 1997, BAGE 87, 303.

130 BGH 7 July 2010 *Heinrich Heine,* NJW 2010, 2651.

131 BVerwG 22 October 2015, NVwZ 2016, 308. An inadequate reasoning is also found in BAG 11 December 1997, BAGE 87, 303. However, in relation to the latter, Canaris, points out that the adopted interpretation was nonetheless *sustainable*, Canaris (n. 74), p. 50-1.

often only experts in the concerned area of law will be able to form a more or less conclusive view on this matter. Also, even if limits were transgressed in the context of *Auslegung*, there is still the further question whether the adopted consistent interpretation is also inexplainable if the scope for a consistent interpretation in the context of *Rechtsfortbildung* is taken into account.

It can be concluded that, while there were adaptations of the traditional interpretation, this was in most of the judgments supported by an adequate explanation. For those judgments it can be said that there was not a conflict between the duty of consistent interpretation and national interpretative rules. Hence, they cannot provide support for one of the theories on the relationship between EU and national law. However, I also mentioned two judgments that clearly deviated from a traditional interpretation without it being explained how this could be reconciled with national interpretative rules. It is difficult to be certain here that there was not a conflict with national interpretative rules.

3.3. THE ANALOGY WITH VERFASSUNGSKONFORME AUSLEGUNG

I already pointed out that the prevailing view in German legal scholarship believed that the approach to the duty of consistent should be analogous to the one adopted for the *verfassungskonforme Auslegung*. A possible explanation for scholarship's preference might be found in the fact that the BVerfG's *Kloppenburg* decision, which was the court's first statement regarding the duty of consistent interpretation, provided that courts must adopt the interpretation that is in conformity with the directive, which seemed to imply that, similar to the *verfassungskonforme Auslegung*, the duty of consistent interpretation only comes into play once there is more than one possible interpretation.[132] According to the prevailing view, this entailed that it must first be determined which interpretations are possible on account of the national interpretative methods, and only subsequently, if more than one interpretation remains, it must be determined which interpretations are in conformity with the directive. However, different conclusions were drawn as regards the further consequences deriving from the suggested analogy[133] and it is necessary to determine the position that emerges from the German superior courts' case law, and what this entails for the possibilities to adopt a consistent interpretation.

---

132 BVerfG 8 April 1987 *Kloppenburg*, BVerfGE 75, 223, 237. For this interpretation see also Brechmann (n. 27), p. 79.

133 Cf. Brechmann (n. 27), p. 259-62, 272-3; Canaris (n. 23), p. 79; Canaris (n. 74), p. 46, 48-51; Höpfner (n. 43), p. 272, 274-5; Weber (n. 24), p. 122-7; Roth and Jopen (n. 82), p. 283-94.

Approximately two years after the BVerfG's *Kloppenburg* decision, the BAG delivered a judgment that settled the controversial question whether the ECJ's *Von Colson and Kamann* judgment's stipulations as regards the requirements for sanctions under the Equal Treatment Directive, could be read into national law. Although it adopted a consistent interpretation on the basis of section 823 of the Civil Code, it also pointed out that a consistent interpretation of section 611a(2) of the Civil Code (which had actually been adopted to implement the directive) was not possible as a result of a grammatical and historical interpretation. In this regard it stated that even a *verfassungskonforme Auslegung* is not possible where it is incompatible with the provision's wording and clear legislative intent (those limits are indeed referred to by the BVerfG for the *verfassungskonforme Auslegung*[134]) and that the same applies for the duty of consistent interpretation.[135] Another judgment of the BAG also approached the duty of consistent interpretation in the same way as *verfassungskonforme Auslegung.* Similar to the latter, the duty of consistent interpretation was subjected to 'the general rules of interpretation'. However, compared to its judgment of 14 March 1989, it is remarkable that the BAG here indicated that the grammatical interpretative method does not always impose strict limits, whereas a consistent interpretation may not depart from the clear legislative intent.[136] The reference to 'the general rules of interpretation' was repeated in a decision of 18 February 2003, which also drew the analogy, and concerned the classification of on-call duty. There, the BAG provided a more detailed explanation as to the scope for a consistent interpretation, which has been repeated on two other occasions.[137] If I am correct, the BAG's considerations essentially provided that, *on balance*, all the interpretative methods must allow more than one interpretation of which at least one is in conformity with the directive, yet it would seem that a historical interpretation does not as such impede a consistent interpretation whereas the provision's wording and clear legislative intent impose a hard limit.[138] This is reminiscent of Brechmann's views on the approach to the duty of consistent interpretation that is required if it is applied by analogy to *verfassungskonforme Auslegung,* which provides that, after it has been established that the provision is open to more than one interpretation of which at least one is in conformity with the directive so that, in principle, that interpretation must be favoured, the national courts can only proceed in this way after it has been checked that this does not

134 BVerfG 30 June 1964, BVerfGE 18, 97, 111; BVerfG 22 October 1985, BVerfGE 71, 81, 105; BVerfG 24 May 1995, BVerfGE 93, 37, 81.

135 BAG 14 March 1989, NJW 1990, 65, 66.

136 BAG 5 March 1996, NJW 1996, 2529, 2532. See also BVerfG 30 March 1993, NJW 1993, 2861.

137 BAG 30 March 2004, BAGE 110, 122, para. 47; BAG 23 June 2010, BAGE 135, 34, para. 35.

138 This interpretation is in particular confirmed by the reference to the approach adopted in BVerfG 24 May 1995, BVerfGE 93, 37, 81. There, a further remark was inserted which was not explicitly stated in the BAG's decision, providing that, if a *verfassungskonforme Auslegung* is possible, this is not changed because another, incompatible, interpretation would have corresponded more closely to the legislature's intention expressed in the explanatory memorandum. Similar to the BAG's decision, the BVerfG's decision does consider the provision's wording and clear legislative intent as imposing hard limits.

conflict with the legislature's intention and, exceptionally, the clear wording of the provision (i.e. certain interpretative rules act as a corrective on the consistent interpretation).[139] When it proceeded to apply these principles to the case before it, the BAG arrived at the conclusion that a consistent interpretation was not possible. This did not result from a grammatical interpretation of the provision contained in the Working Time Act – which has an implementing objective – that directly concerned the matter of whether on-call duty had to be considered as working time, but rather from a systematic interpretation: two other provisions contained in the Working Time Act were practically repealed if on-call duty was classified as working time. It was in particular in this regard that the BAG considered that a consistent interpretation was also impeded by Article 20(3) of the Constitution (providing that the judiciary shall be bound by law and justice, which limits the German courts' discretion when they interpret the law). The explanatory memorandum also clearly stated that on-call duty was not considered as working time.[140] This shows that, although the BAG only identified the provision's wording and clear legislative intent as imposing hard limits, when it is found that both a historical and systematic interpretation oppose a consistent interpretation, this can be a reason to reject such an interpretation. To be sure, it is difficult to separate legislative intent from the other interpretative criteria, as the latter must be considered when determining the former. Nevertheless, since the rule had an implementing objective, it is remarkable that it was not further examined whether the presumption to comply with the directive could be maintained in the light of the opposing arguments. Also, although this is more a matter of internal coherence, the weight attributed to a systematic interpretation differed considerably from the use of this method in the BAG's judgment of 23 March 2006 concerning the concept redundancy (which I discussed above).

It appears from the above discussion that the analogy with the *verfassungskonforme Auslegung* has been drawn in the case law of the BAG most often, but there is also an interesting BFH judgment of 15 February 2012, which drew an analogy with the *verfassungskonforme Auslegung* and rejected a consistent interpretation. It held that a provision's purpose must be determined in the light of its systematic-teleological context.[141] This is not only regarded as the legal basis for the duty of consistent interpretation (see paragraph 2) but also has the effect of incorporating the duty of consistent interpretation into a specific national interpretative method – and limiting it to the effect that this method can exert on the interpretative process. As regards the principles underlying the court's approach to the duty of consistent interpretation, it provided that a consistent interpretation must only be adopted if

139 Brechmann (n. 27), p. 259-62, 272-3.
140 BAG 18 February 2003, DB 2003, 1387, 1389-90.
141 See also BFH 8 September 2010, BFHE 231, 343, para. 25; BFH 16 May 2012, BFHE 238, 468, para. 41; BFH 2 July 2014, Beck online Rechtsprechung 2014, 96183, para. 30.

the provision is open to more than one interpretation. The provision's wording and the purpose expressed therein were found to be clear and therefore not open to further interpretation so that a consistent interpretation was not possible. I should point out that, after the BFH concluded that the provision's wording was clear, it primarily seemed to examine the purpose of the provision in relation to the question whether a *Rechtsfortbildung* (a '*teleologischen Extension*') could be adopted, which was dismissed since the legislature had not implemented the concerned part of the directive, which conclusion was based on the fact that it was clear that he had for some time been aware of the incompatibility with the directive but had not made any amendments. It is, in the first place, interesting to see that, in addition to an explicit choice to make a provision that departs from the directive, the absence of legislative activity sufficed here to rebut the presumption that the legislature intends to comply with the directive. Secondly, in my opinion the role played by purpose is not identical for the context of *Auslegung* and *Rechtsfortbildung* and it does not seem to be correct to skip an examination of its influence (e.g. *vis-à-vis* the alleged clarity of the wording) in the former context.[142] This exemplifies why it can be problematic to incorporate the duty of consistent interpretation into one of the interpretative criteria: its influence (in this case in particular the presumption) can then logically not have an affect on the other criteria, e.g. a grammatical interpretation. To be fair, this may not have changed the outcome of this specific case: the provision's wording clearly opposed a consistent interpretation and it is unlikely that an application of the presumption would have resulted in a different outcome.

Another example of the analogy is found in the BVerfG's decision of 26 September 2011 (addressing the constitutional complaints following from the BGH's *Heininger* case law), which repeated the considerations of the *Kloppenburg* decision (which, as mentioned above, were interpreted by me as referring to the approach under the *verfassungskonforme Auslegung*). The BVerfG's decision of 26 September 2011 discussed the scope for a consistent interpretation in more detail, and this was clearly not confined to whatever room is left by the national interpretative methods considered in isolation. Instead it was emphasised that, if '*Auslegungsspielraum*' (room for further interpretation) exists, this must be optimised to the benefit of a consistent interpretation. Accordingly, *the various interpretative methods must, to the fullest extent possible, be applied in order to achieve the directive's objective.*[143] This was also repeated in the BFH's judgment of 19 January 2016, which adopted a consistent interpretation.[144]

---

142 BFH 15 February 2012, BFHE 236, 267, paras. 17-9. See para. 20 *et seq* for the BFH's considerations regarding the determination of the national provision's purpose.

143 BVerfG 26 September 2011, BVerfGK 19, 89, para. 46.

144 BFH 19 January 2016, ZIP 2016, 1378, para. 81.

Most of the above case law drawing an analogy with the *verfassungskonforme Auslegung* provided statements to the effect that the duty of consistent interpretation is subject to the general rules of interpretation, the national provision being open to more than one interpretation, or there being room for further interpretation. While this offers some direction for the courts' approach to the duty of consistent interpretation, a more concrete indication for this approach is that, most of the time, the scope for a consistent interpretation is restricted by the provision's clear wording and legislative intent. I do not think that these general statements, or the more concrete limits, can be seen as an indication that the analogy with *verfassungskonforme Auslegung* entails a more restrictive application of the duty of consistent interpretation (albeit that it is of course not equally beneficial for a consistent interpretation as the negative test and structural prioritisation approaches, but the latter represent just a segment, albeit an important one, of the overall case law). Besides the fact that these statements still leave open a variety of approaches to the duty of consistent interpretation, these, or similar, statements, are also found in judgments that did not make the analogy with *verfassungskonforme Auslegung* (see further below). Wissink argues that the analogy with the *verfassungskonforme Auslegung* does not need to result in a more restrictive approach. His main objection against this approach to the duty of consistent interpretation is that there is the risk that it does not force the national courts to apply the national interpretative methods to the fullest extent possible in order to adopt a consistent interpretation, and that they, instead, focus on the traditional interpretation only, sidelining the duty of consistent interpretation with the claim that the national provision is not open to further interpretation.[145] In this regard it must be mentioned that in nearly all cases the courts examined the possibility of a consistent interpretation and provided a plausible justification why such an interpretation was not possible. Turning to the approach adopted in individual decisions, it is submitted that the BVerwG's judgment of 18 February 2003 raises a question as regards the compatibility with the instruction that it must be presumed that the legislature intends to comply with the directive, yet, at the same time, I do not doubt that the court encountered some significant obstacles here that made the adoption of a consistent interpretation more difficult. Although the final decision was understandable on account of the clearly incompatible wording of the concerned provision, the approach adopted in the BFH's judgment of 15 February 2012 seems difficult to reconcile with the duty of consistent interpretation.

Admittedly, it is striking that five out of the six discussed/referred to cases rejected a consistent interpretation. Yet, an explanation for the frequent rejection of a consistent interpretation might be that the courts consider it as a part of their justification for rejecting a consistent interpretation when they point out that they would have done the same thing if they were required to examine, in a purely

145 Wissink (n. 73), p. 119-21.

internal context, a question that is considered to be of a similar nature, namely whether a lower-ranking provision can be interpreted in conformity with the higher-ranking Constitution. So when the German superior courts encounter a limitation preventing a consistent interpretation, it is at that point that they consider it useful to refer to the *verfassungskonforme Auslegung*. On balance, it can thus be said that a reference to *verfassungskonforme Auslegung* is a sign that a consistent interpretation will not be adopted, but it is not a sign that the court falls short of its obligations under the duty of consistent interpretation. The latter does not imply the former if there were good reasons not to adopt a consistent interpretation.

3.4. LIMITS IN THE CONTEXT OF *AUSLEGUNG*

Franzen provides that German legal scholarship's determination of the limits to the duty of consistent interpretation was primarily inspired by the traditional limits to interpretation.[146] Under the traditional approach to interpretation, these limits primarily concern the separation of powers between the judiciary and the legislature and the protection of fundamental rights. This is of course very broad. It is therefore not surprising that this also fits the German superior courts' application of limits to the duty of consistent interpretation.

3.4.1. *Limits of the Judicial Function*

There are, in the first place, limits that are based on the courts' interpretative discretion, and which therefore relate to Article 20(3) of the Constitution, providing that the judiciary shall be bound by law and justice, and Article 97(1), providing that judges shall be independent and subject only to the law.[147] In a decision of 18 April 1991, the BFH was asked whether the private use of a motor car belonging to the business of the taxable person was subject to turnover tax.

> The imposition of turnover tax for the private use of business goods is based on the idea that final consumption of goods must be made subject to turnover tax.[148] According to section 1(1)(2)(b) of the Law on turnover tax, the taxability of the use for private purposes was not made dependant on the possibility to deduct input taxes.[149] However, the directive stated the condition that the turnover tax must be wholly or partly deductible.

---

146 Franzen (n. 24), p. 374.
147 See also Weber (n. 24), p. 172.
148 Bunjes/Leonard UStG § 3, para. 261.
149 Gormley explains that, '[t]axable persons are authorized to deduct from the value added tax for which they are liable the value added tax which the goods have already borne', L. Gormley, *EU Taxation Law* (OUP 2005), p. 55.

The BFH held that a consistent interpretation could not be adopted since this would be incompatible with a grammatical interpretation and the legislation's purpose. A consistent interpretation would exceed the limits of the judicial function. Referring to the ECJ's *Kolpinghuis* judgment (the choice for this particular judgment is not entirely clear to me), the BFH takes the position that this outcome does not violate the ECJ's case law. It must be pointed out that the relevant provision of the Law on turnover tax had an implementing objective. This is also mentioned in the judgment, but the BFH explained that the legislature had interpreted the directive differently and, albeit that this interpretation turned out to be erroneous, the implementing objective did not override the legislature's divergent position.[150] This argumentation does not seem to be satisfactory in light of the presumption of the intention to comply, which was formulated in the *Wagner Miret* and *Pfeiffer* judgments and, in my opinion, entails that it is *par excellence* in a situation such as the one occurring in the BFH's decision that the national court must prioritise the implementing objective. But since the ECJ's judgments were delivered after the BFH's decision, these further instructions could not have been taken into account. The BVerwG has also emphasised the importance of a grammatical interpretation and the legislation's purpose as limits to the duty of consistent interpretation in a judgment of 29 September 2011 rejecting a consistent interpretation.[151] Again, the relevant national provision had an implementing objective.[152] But this is not discussed at all by the BVerwG, let alone that it was explained why a consistent interpretation was nevertheless not adopted. Since the judgment was delivered well after the formulation of the presumption of the intention to comply with the directive in the *Wagner Miret* and *Pfeiffer* judgments, this cannot explain that a presumption to comply with the directive was not mentioned. At the same time, the BVerwG considered that practically all relevant interpretative criteria opposed a consistent interpretation, so in the end it is not likely that a presumption would have persisted. Finally, the above discussed BAG's judgment of 23 March 2006, which aligned the meaning of the concept redundancy in national law with the directive, also emphasised the importance of the grammatical interpretation and the legislation's purpose as limits to the duty of consistent interpretation.[153] There, the consequences of the ECJ's *Pfeiffer* judgment, and in particular the presumption of the intention to comply, were discussed in detail. In subparagraph 3.2 concerning possible transgressions of the national interpretative rules, it was seen that the judgment was ambiguous with regard to the force of this presumption, but it is nevertheless important to point out the difference in approach.

---

150 BFH 18 April 1991, RIW 1991, 782, 782.

151 BVerwG 29 September 2011, NVwZ 2012, 176, para. 28. The proceedings before the BVerwG took place against the background of the judgment in Case C-115/09 *Trianel*, ECLI:EU:C:2011:289, which had revealed an inconsistency between the relevant national provisions and the directive.

152 BT-Drucks. 16/2495, 1.

153 BAG 23 March 2006, BAGE 117, 281, para. 25.

The grammatical interpretation and the legislation's purpose appear to be the main focus of the limits to the duty of consistent interpretation.[154] It is not very surprising that the legislation's purpose is an important limitation, as it was seen at the beginning of this paragraph that this is the key element for the traditional approach to interpretation. A provision's clear wording facilitates identifying a clear legislative intention but will only produce a relevant limit if it provides a clear direction. Legislative intent can also be based on the other interpretative criteria. For example, in the BVerwG's judgment of 18 December 1997, a grammatical interpretation did not provide any real guidance. The meaning of the relevant national provision was therefore determined by means of a historical and systematic interpretation. Having identified the legislature's intention, it was concluded that a consistent interpretation should be rejected as it would be contrary to the legislation's '*Sinngehalt*' (by the way, despite the presence of an implementing objective, again, no mention was made of the presumption).[155] Another question is whether, if the grammatical interpretation is unambiguous and *does* provide a clear direction, this is as such sufficient to refuse a consistent interpretation. Two judgments of the BGH from 2004, which only referred to the provision's wording to reject a consistent interpretation, appear to support such a view. In both cases there was an implementing objective, but this was apparently not a sufficient reason to change the outcome.[156] However, these two judgments must now be viewed in light of the subsequent BGH's *Quelle* judgment. This judgment made it clear that, in accordance with the objective approach to interpretation, the limits of a provision's wording are also the limits of an *Auslegung, but national courts are also required to examine the possibility of a consistent interpretation by means of a Rechtsfortbildung* (see subparagraph 3.1.2).[157] It also held that the *contra legem* threshold is not reached merely because an interpretation would be incompatible with the provision's wording. So while, after the *Quelle* judgment, the BGH and BAG have stated on a number of occasions that, as far as *Auslegung* is concerned, the duty of consistent interpretation is indeed limited by the provision's wording, they also recognised the technique of *Rechtsfortbildung*.[158] The finding that an *Auslegung* is not possible is merely a provisional step for the overall determination whether a consistent interpretation can be adopted.[159] Yet, a surprisingly different approach can be found in a judgment of 10 August 2016. There, the BFH simply provided

154 See also Jarass (n. 47), p. 218; Brechmann (n. 27), p. 270-3; Canaris (n. 74), p. 58.

155 BVerwG 18 December 1997, NJW 1998, 3433, 3434 *et seq.*

156 BGH 29 April 2003, ZIP 2003, 1692; BGH 19 October 2004, ZIP 2004, 2373.

157 BGH 26 November 2008 *Quelle*, BGHZ 179, 27, para. 20.

158 BAG 24 March 2009, BAGE 130, 119, para. 60; BGH 21 December 2011 *Bodenfliesen*, BGHZ 192, 148, para. 28; BGH 8 January 2014, NVwZ 2014, 1111, para. 10; BGH 7 May 2014, BGHZ 201, 101, para. 21.

159 This was already pointed out long before *Rechtsfortbildung* was extended to the duty of consistent interpretation in Brechmann (n. 27), p. 266. See also Canaris (n. 23), p. 81, 94; J. Schürnbrand, 'Die Grenzen richtlinienkonformer Rechtsfortbildung im Privatrecht' (2007/19) *JZ*, p. 911-2; Weber (n. 24), p. 36; Roth and Jopen (n. 82), p. 285-6.

that the grammatical interpretation was unambiguous and that the concerned provision was therefore not open to a divergent consistent interpretation.[160] The correctness of this judgment can be questioned as the BFH has also acknowledged the requirement to proceed to a *Rechtsfortbildung* in the context of the duty of consistent interpretation (see subparagraph 3.6), there seemed to be an implementing objective,[161] and there were no apparent reasons justifying the restrained approach.[162] In addition to this, there is the BGH's *Gasversorgung II* judgment. The case concerned the question which transparency requirements applied to price adjustments imposed by an energy supplier. It followed from the ECJ's *Schulz* judgment that the German provisions did not provide the required guarantees in this regard.[163] It was examined whether the requirements could be inserted into national law, either by means of an *Auslegung* or *Rechtsfortbildung* in conformity with the directive. The BGH rejected both options because the legislature had neither implemented the relevant part of the directive on which the ECJ's ruling was based nor was it possible to identify such an intention. Instead it had been the legislature's intention that the transparency issues would be further dealt with at the level of a regulation. However, this had not happened.[164] The BGH appeared to be satisfied that the requirements could not be inserted into national law because of the absence of an implementing objective.[165] As will be seen in the subparagraph 3.6.2, this may perhaps have justified the rejection of the possibility of a *Rechtsfortbildung*, but it is questionable whether this meets the requirement imposed on national courts to interpret national law so far as possible in conformity with the directive by means of an *Auslegung*. First, an implementing objective was not completely absent, albeit that this was not expressed in the regulation that formed the primary basis for the enquiry whether a consistent interpretation could be adopted. Secondly, leaving aside the question whether this approach is sustainable from the perspective of the German traditional approach

160 BFH 10 August 2016, BFHE 255, 300, para. 30.

161 BT-Drucks. 8/1779, 1, 29.

162 It is, in particular, pointed out that a consistent interpretation would have benefitted the applicant, so that the outcome cannot have been influenced by the consideration that, in an area such as tax law, the legality principle and the grammatical interpretation must be given extra consideration if a consistent interpretation has negative consequences for an individual. Apart from that, also in tax law, there is no strict priority of the grammatical interpretation. Vogenauer (n. 31), p. 153.

163 Joined Cases C-359/11 and C-400/11 *Schulz*, ECLI:EU:C:2014:2317.

164 BGH 28 October 2015 *Gasversorgung II*, BGHZ 207, 209, para. 44.

165 However, it should be noted that the BGH in the end seemed to arrive at an outcome that was compatible with the directive (albeit that this was not characterised by the BGH as a consistent interpretation). Two points are relevant in this regard. First, the directive did not require the introduction of a price adjustment right (see also Joined Cases C-359/11 and C-400/11 *Schulz*, ECLI:EU:C:2014:2317, paras. 39-40). Secondly, the existence of such a right in German law had been unclear for some time but was confirmed through an interpretation of the regulation. So the BGH solved the issue by holding that, since it was not possible to compose a price adjustment right on the basis of the regulation that met the directive's transparency requirements, the interpretation adopted in settled case law which conferred this right on the supplier, had to be rejected.

to interpretation, it may be asked whether there was not a *de facto* violation of the ECJ's *Marleasing* and *Pfeiffer* judgments, which made it clear that the duty of consistent interpretation applies regardless of whether the national provisions have an implementing objective.[166] The second argument becomes even more compelling if it is taken into account that, as far as transparency requirements were concerned, the directive was not that much more specific than the regulation's provision.[167] Notwithstanding this, the BVerfG endorsed a similar judgment, also as regards the rejection of the possibility to read the concerned requirements into the regulation.[168]

3.4.2. *Fundamental Rights*

In the second place, there is a different category of limitations which are based on rights protected under the Constitution. This issue surfaced in the BAG's judgment of 23 March 2006 concerning the concept 'redundancy' used in the Law on Employment Protection which implemented the Collective Redundancies Directive.

> The first part of this judgment was already discussed in subparagraph 3.2.3. It is briefly recalled that the proceedings revolved around the question whether 'redundancy' must be understood as the declaration intended to terminate the contract of employment, or the actual cessation of the employment relationship. In settled case law, the BAG adopted the latter interpretation.[169]

While the BAG provided that it followed from the ECJ's *Junk* judgment that its previous interpretation of the concept redundancy had been incorrect, and that a consistent interpretation was actually methodologically possible,[170] it nevertheless insisted that this could not be relied on against the other party to the dispute, i.e. the employer, as this would entail a retroactive application of the revised interpretation of the national provision contrary to the principle of legitimate expectations; the ECJ's *Junk* judgment was delivered on 27 January 2005, so that the employer, when he announced the redundancies on 30 July 2004, could not have foreseen a revision of the BAG's settled case law. The BAG pointed out that its previous interpretation had been confirmed in a judgment of 18 September 2003 (i.e. not long before the employer's announcement – but before the ECJ's judgment), on which occasion

166 Case C-106/89 *Marleasing*, ECLI:EU:C:1990:395, para. 8; Joined Cases C-397/01 to C-403/01 *Pfeiffer*, ECLI:EU:C:2004:584, para. 115.

167 Cf. Article 3(3) and Annex A(b) of Directive 2003/55/EC of the European Parliament and of the Council of 26 June 2003 concerning common rules for the internal market in natural gas and repealing Directive 98/30/EC, *OJ* 2003, L176/57, on the one hand, and section 4(1) and (2) of the Regulation on general terms and conditions for the supply of gas to standard rate customers, on the other. Both did not state the specific requirement that followed from the ECJ's *Schulz* judgment to give notice of the reasons and preconditions for a price adjustment and its scope.

168 BVerfG 17 November 2017, NJW-RR 2018, 305, paras. 38, 40.

169 See BAG 23 March 2006, BAGE 117, 281, para.19 for extensive references to case law.

170 Ibid, para. 26.

it explicitly addressed the Collective Redundancies Directive, but rejected the possibility of the interpretation that would subsequently be prescribed in the ECJ's *Junk* judgment.[171] That interpretation also corresponded to the prevailing view in legal scholarship and the labour office's practice. The BAG observed that it is not deprived of the competence to take a decision with regard to the point of the protection of legitimate expectations. In particular, it argued that no preliminary reference was required under Article 267 TFEU as it had only adjusted its previous case law, and the interpretation of the *national* provisions, to the Collective Redundancies Directive. It had not interpreted any EU law provisions.[172] By the way, these considerations also made it clear that the BAG applied the *national* principle of legitimate expectations.[173]

I have so far only spoken of the principle of legitimate expectations, which is normally understood as requiring that authorities act, as far as possible, in conformity with expectations raised by them. It is pointed out that this principle is a logical extension of the principle of legal certainty. Sometimes, the retroactive operation of the law is considered first and foremost in the light of the latter principle,[174] but other authors indeed consider it more appropriate to refer directly to the principle of legitimate expectations, pointing out that, compared to legal certainty, it more clearly has the characteristics of a self-standing substantive norm than an interpretative rule.[175] In any event, the BAG's judgments of 23 March 2006 and 1 February 2007 only referred to the principle of legitimate expectations, and although the BVerfG also mentioned the principle of legal certainty, it primarily referred to legitimate expectations. This should be kept in mind when reading the cases and my analysis, which follows the formulation used by the German courts.

The BAG's argumentation and conclusion was maintained in a judgment of 1 February 2007.[176] That case became the subject of a constitutional complaint before the BVerfG alleging a violation of Article 101 of the Constitution, enshrining the right that '[n]o one may be removed from the jurisdiction of his lawful judge'. It is explained in the BVerfG's decision that, in accordance with settled case law, the

171 BAG 18 September 2003, BAGE 107, 318.

172 See BAG 23 March 2006, BAGE 117, 281, para. 32 *et seq* for the BAG's reasoning on these points. The BAG's subsequent follow-up judgment to Case C-144/04 *Mangold*, ECLI:EU:C:2005:709 provided that in relation to the direct effect of EU law, the BAG does consider it necessary to ask the ECJ about the effect of the principle of legitimate expectations under EU law, BAG 26 April 2006, BAGE 118, 76, para. 40. However, in BAG 22 March 2007, NZA 2007, 1101, para. 17, that case was distinguished as it concerned the direct effect of EU law and not the interpretation of national law.

173 See also A. Sagan, 'Nationaler Vertrauensschutz nach Junk: Das Ende eines deutschen Alleingangs' (2015/6) *NZA*, p. 341.

174 J.E. Van den Brink and others, 'General Principles of Law', in: J.H. Jans, S. Prechal and R.J.G.M. Widdershoven (Eds.), *Europeanisation of Public Law* (Europa Law Publishing 2015), p. 208.

175 T. Tridimas, *The General Principles of EU Law* (OUP 2006), p. 251-2.

176 BAG 1 February 2007, Beck online Rechtsprechung 2011, 72103.

ECJ is also 'lawful judge' in the sense of Article 101 of the Constitution,[177] so that, if a court fails to adhere to the conditions for referring preliminary questions to the ECJ under Article 267 TFEU, an individual may be deprived of the jurisdiction of his lawful judge. The BVerfG concluded, unanimously, that there had been a violation of Article 101 of the Constitution by the BAG's judgment. The reason for this was that the BAG had, by invoking the principle of legitimate expectations, which is protected under Article 20(3) of the Constitution, decided the case on the basis of its prior interpretation of the Law on Employment Protection, without having previously consulted the ECJ through the preliminary reference procedure to obtain clarification as to whether the offering of protection through the principle of legitimate expectations was compatible with the EU law obligation of consistent interpretation and whether the restrictions placed on the effect of the ECJ's *Junk* judgment did not violate EU law. The high threshold set for the conclusion that the non-referral also violates Article 101 of the Constitution was met: the BAG's judgment entailed an evidently untenable application of Article 267 TFEU.[178]

It is clear from the BVerfG's decision that the duty of consistent interpretation played a vital role in arriving at this conclusion. The principle of legitimate expectations was first and foremost applied by the BAG to limit an unforeseen interpretation of the provision of the Law on Employment Protection. As that unforeseen interpretation was acquired through the duty of consistent interpretation, any restrictions placed thereon, also restricted the application of the duty of consistent interpretation. That restriction may potentially violate the national courts' requirements under that obligation, which is a matter governed by EU law (that point was overseen in the BAG's case law holding that the principle of legitimate expectations concerned the interpretation of national law only), and therefore the matter clearly fell within the scope of Article 267 TFEU.

Sagan interprets the BVerfG's decision as providing that the national constitutional principle of legitimate expectations cannot be applied to limit the duty of consistent interpretation, and that such a limitation can only be based on the principle of legitimate expectations in EU law.[179] If this interpretation is correct, this would actually be a further argument in favour of supremacy of EU law. Yet, in my opinion, the BVerfG's decision did not provide a definitive answer to that question. It considered that the offering of protection through the principle of legitimate expectations and the connected rejection of a consistent interpretation were, at least also ('*zumindest auch*'), a question of EU law. This seems to leave open the

177 Reference is made to BVerfG 22 October 1986 *Solange II*, BVerfGE 73, 339, 366 *et seq*; BVerfG 8 April 1987 *Kloppenburg*, BVerfGE 75, 223, 233; BVerfG 31 May 1990, BVerfGE 82, 159, 192; BVerfG 6 July 2010 *Honeywell*, BVerfGE 126, 286, 315; BVerfG 25 January 2011, BVerfGE 128, 157, 186 *et seq*; BVerfG 19 July 2011, BVerfGE 129, 78, 105.

178 BVerfG 10 December 2014, ZIP 2015, 335, paras. 14, 37 *et seq*.

179 Sagan (n. 173), p. 342.

possibility to allow the matter to be solely governed by the EU law principle, but it also seems to imply that the national principle is not irrelevant, even if the EU law principle is, to a greater or lesser extent, applicable as well. It added that it is not generally excluded to fall back on national constitutional law, even if EU law is applicable. However, this is subject to the specific requirement that EU law does not offer the minimum constitutional protection as required under the German Constitution.[180] The BVerfG's unwillingness to accept the unconditional supremacy of EU law is nothing new and is in line with the well known limitation requiring that EU law must respect the minimum constitutional protection as required under the German Constitution.[181]

What do the BAG's judgment of 23 March 2006 and the subsequent BVerfG judgment mean for the relationship between EU and national law under the duty of consistent interpretation? It should first and foremost be made clear that it is incompatible with the theory of supremacy of EU law where national constitutional law is given priority over EU law. Does that mean that the BAG's judgment of 23 March 2006 supported the theory of national constitutionalism? A difficulty that arises here is that no final answer can be provided as the ECJ's case law has not yet directly addressed the question whether national fundamental rights can be applied as a limit to the duty of consistent interpretation – instead as a limitation to substantive provisions contained in for example a directive. Nevertheless, there are three reasons which in my opinion make it unlikely that the ECJ would accept this kind of limitation. First, as the duty of consistent interpretation is prescribed by EU law, limits to that obligation must also derive from EU law (as is the case for the limits recognised in the ECJ's *Kolpinghuis* judgment and the *contra legem* limitation).[182] It was more particularly in the *Klohn* judgment that the ECJ reserved for itself the right to determine whether the EU law principle of legitimate expectations could limit the requirements under the duty of consistent interpretation. At the same time, the ECJ did not seem to dismiss the possibility of invoking legitimate expectations entirely.[183] This means that, although a complaint based on this principle should be based on the general principle in EU law, there does not seem to be a categorical rejection of such arguments either. It is noted that in EU law legitimate expectations are protected as a general principle of law but to my knowledge it does not – contrary to German law – have the status of a fundamental right. I will not, therefore, consider the admissibility of the judgments

180 BVerfG 10 December 2014, ZIP 2015, 335, paras. 40-1.

181 See BVerfG 29 May 1974 *Solange I*, BVerfGE 37, 271; BVerfG 22 October 1986 *Solange II*, BVerfGE 73, 339.

182 In a commentary on the BAG's judgments and the subsequent BVerfG's decision, Sagan observed that, since the duty of consistent interpretation has its legal basis in EU law, it can only be limited through rules belonging to that legal order, Sagan (n. 173), p. 342. See also, in general, S. Prechal, *Directives in EC Law* (OUP 2005), p. 204.

183 Case C-167/17 *Klohn*, ECLI:EU:C:2018:833, paras. 48-54.

from the perspective of the potential protection offered by EU fundamental rights (see, further, chapter 2, subparagraph 5.4).

> It should be noted that another BAG judgment referred to the ECJ's *Adeneler* judgment's considerations that the duty of consistent interpretation '(...) is limited by general principles of law, particularly those of legal certainty and non-retroactivity (...)',[184] to justify that, in that regard, Article 20(3) of the Constitution, from which the principle of legitimate expectations is derived, can be applied when determining whether a consistent interpretation can be adopted.[185] I want to point out here that the reliance on Article 20(3) of the Constitution in the context of the *Adeneler* judgment's reference to general principles of law is clearly incorrect. The ECJ referred to general principles of *EU law and* did not have in mind national general principles of law. Höpfner's assertion that the BVerfG has in fact followed the same line of reasoning is incorrect and overlooks that the cited decision explicitly linked the principle of legal certainty to the *contra legem* limitation. This complies with the ECJ's case law which views the *EU law* principles of legal certainty and non-retroactivity as the legal basis for this limitation. The *contra legem* limitation is concerned with what is methodologically possible whereas the BAG's position was that a consistent interpretation could be adopted; it only took issue with the retrospective effect of that interpretation.[186]

One might object that the impossibility of invoking national principles is not consistent since national interpretative rules in fact already limit the scope to adopt a consistent interpretation. However, this refers to the national methodology for interpreting legislation, which constitutes a different category over which the ECJ clearly has no competence and for which it is uncontroversial that this sometimes produces limits to consistent interpretation (whether labelled *contra legem* or otherwise). In this regard it is recalled that the BAG had made it clear that it considered a consistent interpretation possible from a methodological point of view. This is the second reason. Thirdly, and presumably most importantly, the restriction placed by the BAG on the retroactive application of the law raises a more fundamental concern as far as the duty of consistent interpretation is involved. It will not be uncommon that the necessity of consistent interpretation was inspired by new developments in the ECJ's case law which had not yet occurred when the facts giving rise to the proceedings occurred. If this provides a reason to limit the application of the duty of consistent interpretation, the effectiveness of this remedy would arguably diminish considerably. If, hypothetically speaking, the ECJ would have considered the situation occurring before the BAG (i.e. on the basis of the EU law principle), I believe that the possibility to protect legitimate expectations would depend on whether this is viewed as a limitation of the temporal scope of its

184 Case C-212/04 *Adeneler*, ECLI:EU:C:2006:443, para. 110.

185 BAG 22 March 2007, NZA 2007, 1101, para. 18.

186 C. Höpfner, 'Das deutsche Urlaubsrecht in Europa – Zwischen Vollharmonisierung und Koexistenz – Teil 1' (2013/1) *Recht der Arbeit*, p. 26-7, citing BVerfG 26 September 2011, BVerfGK 19, 89, para. 47.

Junk judgment. If so, it is probably unlikely that a consistent interpretation would not have been required as a result of the EU law principle.[187] Whether there would be any remaining scope to apply the national principle in such a situation is, from the perspective of EU law, simple: the national principle cannot go beyond the requirements under EU law, so that the former would have to yield to the latter.[188] Also, although it did not address the exact same question, the *Klohn* judgment indicates a rather dismissive approach by the Luxembourg court as far as concerns arguments based on legitimate expectations (the difference is that, in that case, it was not an unforeseen interpretation of the directive, but rather the application of rights based on the directive, as a result of a consistent interpretation, to the domestic proceedings as such, that formed the basis of the complaint). The ECJ there provided that the principle of legitimate expectations '(…) cannot be extended to the point of generally preventing a new rule from applying to the future effects of situations which arose under the earlier rule'.[189]

The BAG's judgment of 23 March 2006 was of course annulled by the BVerfG. This means that it is not representative of the German superior courts' current position anymore. However, I already pointed out that the BVerfG did not clearly reject the possibility to apply the *national* principle of legitimate expectations itself. In as far as I am correct in this regard, the above identified reasons questioning the compatibility of this position with EU law equally apply to the BVerfG's judgment. Yet, unlike the BAG's judgment, acceptance of those reasons does not lead to the conclusion that the judgment supports the theory of national constitutionalism. I think that the theory of constitutional pluralism more adequately describes the position adopted by the BVerfG. The thrust of the BVerfG's decision was that the BAG should have first consulted the ECJ as the matter was *also* governed by EU law, and it did not yet take a final position on the application of the national principle of legitimate expectations. These features fit in well with the idea of conflict avoidance

187 In Case C-441/14 *Ajos*, ECLI:EU:C:2016:278, paras. 38-41, the ECJ set strict conditions for relying on the principle of legitimate expectations to oppose the application of EU law. It took a broad view of when an application of the principle of legitimate expectations limits the temporal scope of one of its judgments. Adding that this is in principle not permitted '(…) unless there are truly exceptional circumstances'. On the other hand, it should be noted that an application of the principle of legitimate expectations in the *Ajos* judgment would have reduced the effect of the ECJ's case law to a presumably much larger group of cases in comparison to the application foreseen in the BAG's case law. See also S.W. Haket, 'Dansk Industri: nadere afbakening grenzen aan richtlijnconforme interpretatie en horizontale werking algemeen Unierechtelijk beginsel' (2016/7) *Nederlands tijdschrift voor Europees recht*, p. 241-2.

188 In a commentary on the BAG's judgments and the subsequent BVerfG's decision, Sagan observed that, since the duty of consistent interpretation has its legal basis in EU law, it can only be limited through rules belonging to that legal order, Sagan (n. 173), p. 342. See also, in general, Prechal (n. 182), p. 204.

189 Case C-167/17 *Klohn*, ECLI:EU:C:2018:833, para. 53.

under the theory of constitutional pluralism in case of a potential conflict between the EU and national legal orders.[190]

In a judgement delivered after the BAG's judgments of 23 March 2006 and 1 February 2007, but before the BVerfG's decision, the BAG, in an unrelated matter, considered that, as at the material time a preliminary reference had been made to the ECJ, it should have been taken into account that the interpretation of the national provision that prevailed at that moment, was not free from doubt. It also provided that the ECJ had not placed any restrictions on the temporal scope of its ensuing judgment.[191] On these grounds the BAG came to the conclusion that a consistent interpretation did not violate the principle of legitimate expectations.[192]

Finally, I want to briefly address the question whether the German superior courts' case law sets stricter limits when the duty of consistent interpretation is applied in relation to provisions whose violation can be sanctioned with a fine. If, in the areas of administrative and tax law, a fine is imposed when a rule is violated while it was, at the material time, not clear that certain behaviour constituted a violation, the requirement of *lex certa* may provide an argument against such an interpretation. It is interesting to look at the judgment of 7 July 2016 for this point. There, the BVerwG held that, since a violation of the relevant provision could lead to an administrative fine, the limits of the provision's wording require extra consideration – but the BVerwG came to the conclusion that a consistent interpretation did not exceed those limits.[193] A judgment of one of the lower ranking courts supports the view that certain limits require extra consideration if the duty of consistent interpretation is applied to expand the scope of a provision whose violation can be sanctioned through an administrative fine.[194] At the same time it seems to follow from these judgments that there is not a principled exclusion of consistent interpretation if it is applied to such provisions. It should be pointed out that in German law administrative authorities can impose fines for minor offences (*Ordnungswidrigkeiten*). If a complaint is brought before a court against a decision imposing such a fine, German law provides that the provisions regarding criminal proceedings apply and appeals must be brought before the senate of the BGH dealing with criminal law cases.[195] Since this part of the BGH's

190 M. Poiares Maduro, 'Contrapunctual Law: Europe's Constitutional Pluralism in Action', in: N. Walker (Ed.), *Sovereignty in Transition* (Hart Publishing 2003), p. 535; M. Claes, *The National Courts' Mandate in the European Constitution* (Hart Publishing 2006), p. 37.

191 See also K. Riesenhuber and R. Domröse, 'Richtlinienkonforme Auslegung der §§ 17, 18 KSchG und Rechtsfolgen fehlerhafter Massenentlassungen' (2005/10) *NZA*, p. 569, confirming the importance of this aspect.

192 BAG 24 March 2009, BAGE 130, 119, para. 69 *et seq.*

193 BVerwG 7 July 2016, BVerwGE 155, 381, para. 26.

194 OLG München 8 December 2016, Beck online Rechtsprechung 2016, 21199.

195 See section 46(7) of the Act on Regulatory Offences and p. 22 of the BGH's case allocation plan 2018.

jurisdiction has not been examined in detail in the current research, it is only possible to draw highly tentative conclusions on this point. Having said that, there appears to be scholarly support for the position that the limitations established in the ECJ's *Kolpinghuis* judgment regarding criminal liability also apply to the area of administrative fines. At the same time this is not understood as requiring that a consistent interpretation of criminal law is wholly excluded. Instead, the view is adopted that the obligation has a more modest impact for this area of the law. The question at what point a consistent interpretation is deemed inadmissible requires a more detailed examination that goes beyond the scope of this research.[196] The correctness of the link between the ECJ's *Kolpinghuis* judgment and administrative fines will be further discussed in chapter 5, subparagraph 3.5.2, as the Dutch case law provides an actual example of this analogous application.

3.5. PRIORITY OF CONSISTENT INTERPRETATION AND SOME EXCEPTIONS TO THE MAIN RULE

If national courts adopt a consistent interpretation, it must first be determined whether there actually was a conflict of interpretations. If that question is answered in the negative, it is of little use to look at the theories on the relationship between EU and national law, since they all envisage some type of conflict. The above analysis of the case law applying the duty of consistent interpretation in the context of *Auslegung* pointed out two lines that support the theory of supremacy of EU law. First, the negative test approach takes the result prescribed by the directive as its starting point and asks whether the national provision does not oppose the desired interpretation. This relegates the national interpretative rules and methods to outer limits. Secondly, there is the structural prioritisation of the intention to implement the directive over opposing legislative intentions.

In contrast to these two examples, there is not a conflict of interpretative rules if the provision's implementing objective played a decisive role for the adoption of a consistent interpretation. This is rather something that is taken into account as part of a contextualised approach of a historical, systematic or teleological *traditional* interpretation and is not unfamiliar for the German courts. This may very well lead to a consistent interpretation but does not normally signal that there was a conflict. Similar considerations apply if a consistent interpretation was adopted through a provision that is intended to be open to new developments in the law. It is quite normal that a changed legal context (i.e. the entry into force of a new directive, or its further interpretation by the ECJ) is taken into account through such provisions. It must be presumed that there is not a conflict in these circumstances. Finally, despite the fact that there may have been a considerable

196 B. Hecker, *Europäisches Strafrecht* (Springer 2015), p. 344, 348-50, 358.

adaptation of the traditional interpretation of the concerned provision, if it cannot be said that the adopted consistent interpretation is untenable on account of the national interpretative rules, there is also not a conflict. Arguably, since the interpretative rules confer an important measure of discretion on the national courts, a significant degree of restraint is required when it comes to determining whether the court transgressed the limits of interpretation. In most of the examples for which such a transgression was examined, I concluded that this threshold was not yet reached for there was in my opinion an adequate explanation why opposing arguments did not force a different conclusion and/or which arguments pertaining to the national provision could carry the adopted consistent interpretation. However, I also discussed a number of judgments that clearly deviated from a traditional interpretation without it being explained how this could be reconciled with national interpretative rules. It is difficult to be certain here that there was not a conflict with national interpretative rules.

So while it can be said that on the basis of the above analysis the theory of supremacy of EU law seems to be the most adequate theory for how the German superior courts resolve a conflict, this preliminary conclusion has two important open flanks: it does not yet take into consideration the discussion regarding the analogy with the *verfassungskonforme Auslegung,* and the limits to the duty of consistent interpretation.

As regards the analogy with *verfassungskonforme Auslegung,* I concluded that, when the approaches adopted under this label are examined, this does not in principle signify a stricter approach to the duty of consistent interpretation. Also, with a few exceptions (the BAG's judgment of 18 February 2003 and the BFH's judgment of 15 February 2012), most of the individual decisions convincingly explained why a consistent interpretation was not possible. While it was remarkable to see that there is a relative large number of rejections of a consistent interpretation in judgments proposing to apply the obligation analogous to *verfassungskonforme Auslegung,* I concluded that, accordingly a reference to *verfassungskonforme Auslegung* is a sign that a consistent interpretation will not be adopted, yet it is not a sign that the court falls short of its obligations under the duty of consistent interpretation. It was suggested that the reference to *verfassungskonforme Auslegung* is perhaps used to make it clear that, even interpretations in conformity with the Constitution cannot go beyond the point which the national court would have to exceed to obtain a consistent interpretation. This could explain the large number of references to *verfassungskonforme Auslegung* in judgments rejecting a consistent interpretation.

Turning to the limits to the duty of consistent interpretation, it is reiterated that a national court does not fall short of its obligations under the duty of consistent interpretation (i.e. there is not a conflict with EU law) if there were good reasons not to adopt such an interpretation. I will first consider the limits that are derived from Article 20(3) of the Constitution. It is not surprising to see that grammatical interpretation and the legislation's purpose – criteria that ultimately derive from Article 20(3) of the Constitution – are used for determining to what extent a consistent interpretation violates national interpretative rules. It was seen that these criteria were also the most frequently relied upon limits in case law drawing an analogy with the *verfassungskonforme Auslegung*. In my opinion there is in principle no conflict here with the duty of consistent interpretation. However, I already observed that the BAG's judgment of 18 February 2003 (which made an express reference to Article 20(3) of the Constitution) and the BFH's judgment of 15 February 2012 did not adopt a very satisfactory approach by not applying the presumption. Especially with regard to the former judgment, where the relevant national provision was open to a consistent interpretation from a grammatical point of view, it is difficult to see why the intention to implement the directive was not weighed against the opposing arguments. The BFH's judgment of 10 August 2016 cannot be squared with the scope for a consistent interpretation that seems to be available according to German rules of interpretation as it did not examine the possibility of a *Rechtsfortbildung*. Conversely, there was the BGH's *Gasversorgung II* judgment, which did not seem to be compatible with the ECJ's *Marleasing* and *Pfeiffer* judgments and unduly restricted the scope for a consistent interpretation by means of *Auslegung*. In my opinion it are in particular the final two judgments that are difficult to reconcile with the requirements under Articles 288 TFEU and 4(3) TEU. They fit in with the theory of national constitutionalism. However, the *Gasversorgung II* judgment fits in even better with the theory of constitutional pluralism. In the context of the latter, there is also the adoption of a position that is incompatible with EU law, but it is at the same time emphasised that courts should reason and justify their decisions in a way that attempts to reconcile the conflicting position as far as possible.[197] Contrary to the BFH's judgment, the BGH at least appeared to make an attempt to do so by connecting its justification for rejecting a consistent interpretation to the framework developed in the ECJ's case law.

Another challenge to the theory of supremacy of EU law was found in the BAG's judgments of 23 March 2006 and 1 February 2007, which rejected a consistent interpretation on the basis of the *national* principle of legitimate expectations – even though it explicitly considered that such an interpretation was methodologically possible – and clearly supported the theory of national constitutionalism. However, those judgments became the subject of a successful constitutional complaint before the BVerfG. Therefore, also from the perspective of German law, they are no longer good law. The thrust of the BVerfG's decision was that the BAG should have first consulted the ECJ, and it did not yet take a final position on the application of the national principle of legitimate expectations. I submitted that the BVerfG did

197 Maduro (n. 190), p. 527-9.

not unambiguously reject the possibility to apply the national principle and put forward reasons why I believe that such a potential application would probably be incorrect under EU law. If I am correct in this regard, the theory of supremacy of EU law would be undermined. I also argued that the approach adopted by the BVerfG is, unlike the preceding BAG judgment, more in line with the idea of conflict avoidance under the theory of constitutional pluralism in case of a potential conflict between the EU and national legal orders.

On balance, it can be said that if, in the context of *Auslegung*, a conflict is identified, the theory of supremacy of EU law finds the most support taking into account that there is consistent case law adopting a line that grants priority to a consistent interpretation. This is the main position, but there is also a secondary narrative wherein the theories of national constitutionalism and constitutional pluralism come into play. In principle, these theories do not lose their explanatory value on account of judgments conferring supremacy on the duty of consistent interpretation over ordinary law. In this regard it is recalled that national constitutionalism only rejects the supremacy of EU law if there is a conflict with norms of a constitutional rank. However, in as far as my analysis has been correct, and there is indeed a conflict with national interpretative rules, it is in the German setting, whereby limits imposed by interpretative rules clearly have a constitutional connotation, difficult to reconcile the examples of supremacy of EU law with national constitutionalism and constitutional pluralism.

3.6. THE ADOPTION OF A CONSISTENT INTERPRETATION BY MEANS OF A *RECHTSFORTBILDUNG*

An analysis of the German superior courts' case law concerning the duty of consistent interpretation and *Rechtsfortbildung* must start with the BGH's *Quelle* judgment. Ms Brüning had bought a stove-set from the defendant. Nearly a year and a half later the stove-set turned out to be defective. Since repair was not possible, the good was replaced and she was provided with a new one. However, the defendant claimed entitlement to compensation for the prior use of the defective stove-set. The central question before the BGH was whether the defendant was entitled to such compensation on the basis of section 439(4) in conjunction with section 346 of the Civil Code, when viewed in the light of the Consumer Sales Directive.[198] In the decision making a reference for a preliminary ruling the BGH adopted the position that an *Auslegung* whereby the defendant's entitlement to compensation would be refused was not possible. This followed from the wording of section 439(4) in conjunction with section 346 and the clear intention of the

198 Directive 1999/44/EC of the European Parliament and of the Council of 25 May 1999 on certain aspects of the sale of consumer goods and associated guarantees, *OJ* 1999, L171/12.

legislature. However, it also expressed doubt whether this would be compatible with the directive.[199]

The ECJ held that the directive precluded a national provision (such as section 439(4) of the Civil Code) under which a consumer may be required to pay for the use of the defective good.[200] Again, the BGH had the unenviable task of either establishing the national provision's incompatibility with the directive, or – despite the considerations in its previous decision – to find a way to adopt a consistent interpretation. In the BGH's follow-up judgment it confirmed its previous position that a consistent interpretation was not possible by means of an *Auslegung*. However, it proceeded as follows:

> 'Der von der Rechtsprechung des *EuGH* geprägte Grundsatz der richtlinienkonformen Auslegung verlangt von den nationalen Gerichten aber mehr als bloße Auslegung im engeren Sinne. Der *Gerichtshof* ist bei der Verwendung des Begriffs "Auslegung" nicht von der im deutschen Rechtskreis – anders als in anderen europäischen Rechtsordnungen – üblichen Unterscheidung zwischen Auslegung (im engeren Sinne) und Rechtsfortbildung ausgegangen. Auch die vom *EuGH* formulierte Einschränkung, nach der die richtlinienkonforme Auslegung nicht als Grundlage für eine Auslegung des nationalen Rechts contra legem dienen darf (…) bezieht sich nicht auf die Wortlautgrenze. Der Begriff des Contra-legem-Judizierens ist vielmehr funktionell zu verstehen; er bezeichnet den Bereich, in dem eine richterliche Rechtsfindung nach nationalen Methoden unzulässig ist (…). Der Grundsatz der richtlinienkonformen Auslegung fordert deshalb auch, das nationale Recht, wo dies nötig und möglich ist, richtlinienkonform fortzubilden (…). Daraus folgt hier das Gebot einer richtlinienkonformen Rechtsfortbildung durch teleologische Reduktion (…) des § 439 IV BGB auf einen mit Art. 3 der Richtlinie zu vereinbarenden Inhalt'.
>
> Eine Rechtsfortbildung im Wege der teleologischen Reduktion setzt eine verdeckte Regelungslücke im Sinne einer planwidrigen Unvollständigkeit des Gesetzes voraus.[201]

With the above considerations the BGH established that it is also required to examine whether national law can be made compatible with the directive by means of a *Rechtsfortbildung* (which, from a methodological viewpoint, must be separated from *Auslegung* and, broadly speaking, denotes a further development of the law by the courts). The BGH also provided that the *contra legem* limitation does not refer to the limits of a provision's wording – which is not very surprising since it had, just prior to that, indicated that the duty of consistent interpretation requires more than merely an *Auslegung* within the confines of the provision's wording. The position adopted in the *Quelle* judgment may also explain why the

199 BGH 16 August 2006, NJW 2006, 3200.
200 Case C-404/06 *Quelle*, ECLI:EU:C:2008:231, para. 43.
201 BGH 26 November 2008 *Quelle*, BGHZ 179, 27, paras. 21-2.

subparagraph on *Auslegung* did not really provide any judgments discussing the *contra legem* limitation: the judgment was delivered in 2008 and the ECJ only formally recognised the *contra legem* limitation for the first time in 2003 in relation to framework decisions[202] and in 2006 in relation to directives.[203] It should be noted that the BGH speaks of a *prohibition* to interpret national law *contra legem,* whereas the ECJ only considered that such an interpretation is not *required.* Some of the other statements require further consideration. First, the BGH considered that the duty of consistent interpretation does not distinguish between *Auslegung* and *Rechtsfortbildung* and also requires the latter to be applied if this can remove an incompatibility with the directive. This raises the question on which grounds the BGH considers itself obliged to extend the duty of consistent interpretation into the area of *Rechtsfortbildung.* Secondly, it held that a *Rechtsfortbildung* must be based on a *Regelungslücke* (a legislative gap or lacuna). Further on in the judgment, the BGH also discussed the limits that must be taken into account when a *Rechtsfortbildung* in conformity with the directive is pursed: a *Rechtsfortbildung* in conformity with the directive may not (a) lead to a *de facto* repeal of the concerned provision, or violate (b) the judiciary's boundedness to law and justice, (c) the principle of legal certainty, (d) the prohibition of horizontal direct effect.[204] This is the third element that will be further discussed.

It must be pointed out that the other German superior courts, including the BVerfG, have also confirmed the requirement of a *Rechtsfortbildung* in the context of the duty of consistent interpretation.[205]

3.6.1. *The Basis for Proceeding to* Rechtsfortbildung

Does the justification provided by the BGH for proceeding to a *Rechtsfortbildung* in the *Quelle* judgment lend support to one of the theories for understanding the relationship between EU and national law under the duty of consistent interpretation? I believe that this is not so. The first part of the above excerpt of the BGH's *Quelle* judgment stated that *the duty of consistent interpretation* requires more than *Auslegung* only and that when the ECJ uses the term 'interpretation' (*Auslegung*), it does not actually intend to distinguish between *Auslegung* in a narrow sense (i.e. as being limited by the provision's wording) and *Rechtsfortbildung.* Yet, to this it added that a *Rechtsfortbildung* is required where this is necessary *and possible.* Also, in the subsequent paragraphs of the judgment the BGH looks at

202 Case C-105/03 *Pupino,* ECLI:EU:C:2005:386, para. 47.

203 Case C-212/04 *Adeneler,* ECLI:EU:C:2006:443, para. 110.

204 BGH 26 November 2008 *Quelle,* BGHZ 179, 27, paras. 29-35.

205 BAG 24 March 2009, BAGE 130, 119; BAG 17 November 2009 *Urlaubsentgelt,* BAGE 132, 247, para. 29; BVerfG 26 September 2011, BVerfGK 19, 89, para. 57; BFH 22 August 2013, DStR 2013, 2757, para. 26; BFH 19 January 2016, ZIP 2016, 1378, 81; BVerwG 31 January 2017, Beck online Rechtsprechung 2017, 103948, para. 27 *et seq*; BVerwG 21 August 2018, DÖV 2019, 79, paras. 27-8. See also, albeit implicitly, BVerwG 5 September 2013, BVerwGE 147, 312, para. 36.

criteria that were originally developed in German law for this. The justification in the *Quelle* judgment for proceeding to a *Rechtsfortbildung* has been confirmed in subsequent case law of the BGH.[206] Although the BVerwG has only adopted a *Rechtsfortbildung* once, it referred to the same justification.[207] That also seems to be the position of the BAG and BFH.[208] A decision of the BVerfG delivered before the BGH's *Quelle* judgment can also be interpreted in that way.[209]

In my opinion it can be said that the duty of consistent interpretation only indirectly requires the German courts to pursue a consistent interpretation by means of a *Rechtsfortbildung*. There are no indications that it has been, or will be, the intention of the ECJ to force the national courts of all the Member States to also use a technique such as *Rechtsfortbildung*. The actual position adopted in the BGH's *Quelle* judgment is probably most accurately described by Roth and Jopen. They point out that the duty of consistent interpretation requires national courts to interpret national law so far as possible in conformity with the directive. This refers to the possibilities that are available to the national courts in account of national interpretative rules. This means, for the German courts, that they are also required to examine the possibility of a *Rechtsfortbildung*.[210]

> The technique of *Rechtsfortbildung* goes back to at least 1919, when the Supreme Court of the German Empire considered that the judge 'created' a rule of public law, and has been in use ever since.[211] Even if the view were to be adopted that the duty of consistent interpretation must follow the approach to the *verfassungskonforme Rechtsfindung*, this would also encompass *Rechtsfortbildung*, which has been applied to bring lower-ranking provisions in conformity with the Constitution.[212]

In other words: the duty of consistent interpretation did not create the possibility of a *Rechtsfortbildung*, which derives from the German legal order, but the sweeping statement to interpret national law so far as possible entails that it *must* also be

206 BGH 21 December 2011 *Bodenfliesen*, BGHZ 192, 148, para. 30; BGH 7 May 2014, BGHZ 201, 101, para. 20; BGH 28 October 2015 *Gasversorgung II*, BGHZ 207, 209, para. 40. Similar: BGH 8 January 2014, NVwZ 2014, 1111, para. 10.

207 BVerwG 31 January 2017, Beck online Rechtsprechung 2017, 103948, para. 27.

208 BAG 24 March 2009, BAGE 130, 119, para. 65; BFH 22 August 2013, DStR 2013, 2757, para. 26.

209 BVerfG 26 September 2011, BVerfGK 19, 89, para. 57.

210 Roth and Jopen (n. 82), p. 286. See also Canaris (n. 23), p. 82; C. Herresthal, 'Voraussetzungen und Grenzen der Gemeinschaftsrechtskonformen Auslegung' (2007/13) *EuZW*, p. 397; T. Pfeiffer, 'Richtlinienkonforme Auslegung gegen den Wortlaut des nationalen Gesetzes – Die Quelle-Folgeentscheidung des BGH' (2009/7) *NJW*, p. 413.

211 RG 28 October 1919, RGZ 97, 43, 44. BVerfG 14 February 1973 *Soraya*, BVerfGE 34, 269, 287 *et seq*, is normally viewed as the official acknowledgement of the courts' authority to proceed to a *Rechtsfortbildung*.

212 See for a detailed discussion Canaris (n. 74), p. 53 *et seq*, with reference to BVerfG 17 June 1953 *Armenanwalt*, BVerfGE 2, 336, 340 *et seq*; BVerfG 15 December 1965 *Wencker*, BVerfGE 19, 342, 351 *et seq*; BVerfG 3 June 1992, BVerfGE 86, 288, 320 *et seq*; BVerfG 30 March 2004 *Geldwächse*, BVerfGE 110, 226, para. 147 *et seq*; BGH 19 May 1981, BGHSt 30, 105, 121.

included in the courts' tool box. Also, since it can be said that it implicitly follows from the ECJ's *Pfeiffer* judgment that if, in accordance with national interpretative rules, a particular interpretative technique is available to the national courts, they are bound to use it if this helps them to resolve a conflict between national law and the directive via a consistent interpretation,[213] this is a further argument justifying the inclusion of *Rechtsfortbildung*. Since it is a well-established technique that is available to the German courts, there is no *a priori* reason why it should not be applied in the context of the duty of consistent interpretation.[214] At the same time this means that, in principle, a *Rechtsfortbildung* in conformity with directives should not interfere with, but rather follows, the traditional approach. Therefore, the requirement of a *Rechtsfortbildung* in conformity with the directive is as such not an argument that supremacy of EU law is the most adequate theory.

> Admittedly, one might be tempted to conclude that there *was* a conflict when the decision making a reference for a preliminary ruling is compared with the follow-up judgment. The BGH severely cornered itself when it initially seemed to unambiguously conclude that a consistent interpretation could not be adopted. However, all the same it cannot be denied that *Rechtsfortbildung* is a technique which, under certain circumstances, is also available to the German courts. While the BGH might be criticised for not being clear about this in the decision making a reference for a preliminary ruling[215] – and perhaps also for the subsequent approach to the specific conditions and limits for *Rechtsfortbildung* (which will be examined in the next part) – that does not mean that the different positions adopted on these two occasions as regards the methodological tools available to the German courts entails that there was a conflict.

Nevertheless, it needs to be examined whether the approach to the establishment of a *Regelungslücke* and the limits to *Rechtsfortbildung*, when applied in the context of the duty of consistent interpretation, support one or more of the theories on the relationship between EU and national law.

3.6.2. *The Establishment of a* Regelungslücke

The decisive requirement for a *Rechtsfortbildung* is whether a *Regelungslücke* can be established. This first requires the designation of a legislative gap, and it must be

---

213 Prechal (n. 182), p. 199; R. Widdershoven, 'De doorwerking van richtlijnen in een samengestelde Europese rechtsorde', in: H.R.B.M. Kummeling and others (Eds.), *De samengestelde Besselink* (Wolf Legal Publishers 2012), p. 214; M. Brenncke, 'Hybrid Methodology for the EU Principle of Consistent Interpretation' (2017/2) *Statute Law Review*, p. 136.

214 H.D. Jarass and S. Beljin, 'Unmittelbare Anwendung des EG-Rechts und EG-rechtskonforme Auslegung' (2003/15/16), p. 774; K. Riesenhuber and R. Domröse, 'Richtlinienkonforme Rechtsfindung und nationale Methodenlehre' (2005/1) *RIW*, p. 50; Canaris (n. 74), p. 54; Weber (n. 24), p. 132.

215 See also J. Suhr, *Richtlinienkonforme Auslegung im Privatrecht und nationale Auslegungsmethodik* (Nomos 2011), p. 238.

shown that this gap was also unintended.[216] This is also recalled in the BGH's *Quelle* judgment. The legislative gap as such was simply based on the incompatibility between section 439(4) of the Civil Code and the directive.[217] The finding that this gap was also unintended was less straightforward. The BGH saw itself confronted with a 'split' legislative intent. On the one hand, the legislature clearly wanted to confer an entitlement to compensation for the prior use of the defective goods if they are replaced by the seller for the purposes of cure (i.e. the concrete intention). On the other hand, however, the provision was intended to implement the directive (i.e. the general intention to implement the directive). Moreover, the legislature had indicated that the provision made in pursuit of the concrete intention would be compatible with the directive (one could perhaps call this the specific intention to implement the directive[218]).[219] On the basis of this discrepancy (i.e. the discrepancy between the concrete intention to confer an entitlement to compensation and the *concrete* implementing objective), the BGH reasoned that it can be excluded that the legislature would have formulated section 439(4) of the Civil Code in the same way, if it had been aware of the incompatibility with the directive, adding that this presumption ('*Annahme*') is further supported by the fact that the legislature had initiated legislative amendments to take into account the ECJ's *Quelle* judgment.[220] The key argument for the finding that the legislative gap was also unintended was therefore a presumption.[221] Nevertheless, this presumption takes the intention to implement the directive as a starting point.

---

216 In Larenz and Canaris (n. 32), p. 194, it is for example explained that, since this had been a conscious decision of the legislature, there was not an *unintended* legislative gap when a previous version of the Civil Code did not provide for rules regarding home ownership.

217 This approach has been endorsed in, among others, Franzen (n. 24), p. 416; Canaris (n. 23), p. 85. Leading to a similar outcome: C. Sperber, 'Die Grundlage richtlinienkonformer Rechtsfortbildung im Zivilrecht' (2009/9) *Europäisches Wirtschafts- und Steuerrecht*, p. 361. Cf. C. Höpfner, 'Über Sinn und Unsinn der sogenannten "richtlinienkonformen Rechtsfortbildung"' (2009/8) *JZ*, p. 404, who argues that directives can only be relevant for establishing a legislative gap where the relevant provisions have direct effect. But then again, see K. Kroll-Ludwigs and M. Ludwigs, 'Die richtlinienkonforme Rechtsfortbildung im Gesamtsystem der Richtlinienwirkungen' (2009/2) *Zeitschrift für das Juristische Studium*, p. 125; A.J. Kaiser, 'Richtlinienkonforme Rechtsfortbildung – unionsrechtliche und nationale Methodik der Rechtsfindung' (2010/2) *Zeitschrift für Europarechtliche studien*, p. 231, who argue that there cannot be a legislative gap if the provisions of the directive can be directly applied.

218 M. Gebauer, 'Der Durchbruch zur richtlinienkonformen Rechtsfortbildung: Anmerkung zu BGH, Urteil vom 26.11.2008, VIII ZR 200-05 – *Quelle*' (2009/2) *GPR*, p. 83.

219 BT-Drucks. 14/6040, 232 *et seq.*

220 BGH 26 November 2008 *Quelle*, BGHZ 179, 27, paras. 24-5, with reference to BT-Drucks. 16/10607, 4-5 *et seq.* For a critical comment on the BGH's approach to the legislature's intent, see Höpfner (n. 217), p. 405.

221 See also Gebauer (n. 218), p. 83-4; T. Kruis and W. Michl, 'Und es geht doch?! Zur richtlinienkonformen Reduktion durch den BGH als Antwort auf das "Quelle"-Urteil des EuGH' (2009/2) *EuZW*, p. v; Pfeiffer (n. 210), p. 413.

The same approach is found in a judgment of the BGH of 8 January 2014[222] and the BFH's judgment of 22 August 2013.[223] An interesting aspect of the latter judgment is that it concerned a *Rechtsfortbildung* in tax law. In paragraph 3.1 I pointed out that a provision's wording may impose stricter limits in an area such as tax law. In line with this, German legal scholarship tends to approach the possibility of a *Rechtsfortbildung* with more caution for this area of the law.[224] This relates to concerns about legal certainty and legality. But this primarily concerns the situation in which, through a *Rechtsfortbildung*, an individual would become liable to taxes, and the same concerns do not apply when a *Rechtsfortbildung* is adopted in favour of the individual.[225] Since the adopted *Rechtsfortbildung* in the BFH's judgment of 22 August 2013 was in favour of the individual, it seems that further case law is necessary to test the limits of a *Rechtsfortbildung* in conformity with the directive in tax cases where this would be to the detriment of the individual.

More or less the same approach is found in the BGH's *Bodenfliesen* judgment – although there was a minor difference that I will discuss in a moment. This judgment was already briefly referred to in the previous subparagraph. In the final judgment the BGH concluded that an *Auslegung* in conformity with the directive needed to be adopted with the result that section 439(1) of the Civil Code must be interpreted as providing that, when a buyer is entitled to cure of defective goods and demands delivery of goods free from defects, the latter also includes removing the defective goods. For the relevant dispute this entailed that the defendant was not only required to deliver new polished Italian tiles, but he also needed to remove the defective tiles, so that the complete replacement would become far more expensive. This raised a further question concerning the interpretation of Article 3(3) of the Consumer Sales Directive, and in particular the possibility for the seller to refuse to provide a remedy on account of lack of proportionality. That provision conferred the right to repair or replacement of defective goods '(...) unless this is impossible or disproportionate', adding that '[a] remedy shall be deemed to be disproportionate if it imposes costs on the seller which, in comparison with the alternative remedy, are unreasonable [this is followed by a list of criteria indicating a disproportionality; SWH]'. The key point was whether this only covered cases where requiring one remedy is, in terms of costs, disproportionate to the other (i.e. relative lack of proportionality), or also cases where only one remedy is possible in the first place but this entails costs that are as such unreasonable (i.e. absolute lack

222 See BGH 8 January 2014, NVwZ 2014, 1111, para. 11, which also followed after the delivery of a preliminary ruling by the ECJ revealing an incompatibility with the directive. With the exception of forthcoming legislative amendments, the exact same reasoning was applied for the establishment of a *Regelungslücke*.

223 BFH 22 August 2013, DStR 2013, 2757, para. 26 *et seq.*

224 See further Koenig/Koenig AO § 4, para. 112 *et seq*; Klein/Gersch AO § 4, para. 36 *et seq.* See also the comprehensive discussion in Schenke (n. 49) (in particular p. 229-35).

225 Koenig/Koenig AO § 4, para. 117.

of proportionality). In the decision making a reference for a preliminary ruling the BGH made it clear that, while it followed from a traditional interpretation of section 439(3) of the Civil Code that the seller could also refuse to provide cure in a case of absolute lack of proportionality, this might be incompatible with Article 3(3) of the Consumer Sales Directive. It also contemplated how this incompatibility might be resolved, mentioning among others the option of a *Rechtsfortbildung*.[226] The ECJ clarified that the directive only provided an exception in cases of relative lack of proportionality,[227] and it was for the BGH to determine whether national law could be brought in conformity with the directive. It held that this could not be achieved by means of an *Auslegung*, but that this was possible through a *Rechtsfortbildung* – a move that was arguably not entirely surprising after the previous *Quelle* judgment and since it was already more or less anticipated in the decision making a reference. The first requirement of a legislative gap was again based on the incompatibility between section 439(3) of the Civil Code and the directive. This gap was found to be unintended since there was an incompatibility between the intention to confer upon the seller a right to refuse to provide cure in a case of absolute lack of proportionality and statements in the explanatory memorandum confirming the existence of an implementing objective in relation to section 439(4) specifically (note that I also qualify this as a *specific* intention to implement the directive). The only difference with the BGH's *Quelle* judgment was accordingly that the legislature had not explicitly elaborated on the question whether including cases of absolute lack of proportionality would be compatible with the directive. However, the BGH considered that this did not stand in the way of the establishment of a *Regelungslücke*, for which it was only decisive that there was an incompatibility with the directive and that it can be excluded that the national provision would have been formulated in the same way, if the legislature had been aware of this incompatibility.[228] So, again, the key to finding that the legislative gap was unintended seems to have been a presumption. With regard to the distinction that there was no explicit elaboration of the provision's compatibility with the directive, I agree that this cannot be relevant.[229] First, it does not seem reasonable to expect the legislature to discuss the compatibility with the directive for each provision individually. Secondly, the most logical explanation for the absence of such a discussion is probably that the legislature did not really doubt

226 BGH 14 January 2009, NJW 2009, 1660, paras. 14, 17-18.

227 Joined Cases C-65/09 and C-87/09 *Weber*, ECLI:EU:C:2011:396, para. 78.

228 BGH 21 December 2011 *Bodenfliesen*, BGHZ 192, 148, paras. 31-4.

229 But see S. Lorenz, 'Ein- und Ausbauverpflichtung des Verkäufers bei der kaufrechtlichen Nacherfüllung' (2011/31) *NJW*, p. 2244, who considers that a *Rechtsfortbildung* would not be possible in the *Bodenfliesen* judgment since, unlike the situation in the *Quelle* judgment, the legislature had not explicitly discussed the provision's compatibility in the light of the directive, coming to the erroneous viewpoint that there had not been an issue. However, this presumes that the BGH's *Quelle* judgment exhaustively prescribed when the courts can proceed to a *Rechtsfortbildung*. There are no indications that this was the intention. Pfeiffer, in a comment on the *Quelle* judgment, also seems to require that the legislature actively engages with legal questions regarding the directive, see Pfeiffer (n. 210), p. 412.

the provision's compatibility. This can hardly be seen as a sign that it can no longer be presumed that the legislature would have adopted a different provision had he been aware of the incompatibility with the directive.[230] One might even argue that this presumption becomes weaker if the legislature expressed serious doubts as to the provision's compatibility with the directive as this can be seen as an indication that he was prepared to live with a potential risk of violating the directive.[231]

A *Rechtsfortbildung* was also adopted in the BVerwG's judgment of 21 August 2018 (for an earlier *Rechtsfortbildung*, see the court's judgment of 31 January 2017 which is discussed at the end of this subparagraph). While the grammatical interpretation indeed provided support for the view that the legislature had envisaged a provision that turned out to be incompatible with the directive, it was again emphasised that it was clear that the legislature had intended to implement the directive. Hence, adopting a consistent interpretation by means of a *Rechtsfortbildung* did not violate the legislature's intentions.[232]

A divergent decision was adopted by the BGH in its judgment of 5 October 2017. There was again a clear incompatibility with the directive on the basis of a grammatical and historical interpretation, as well as an implementing objective. Yet, this time the BGH held that the rule was unambiguous so that no *Regelungslücke* existed. The case concerned the question who was responsible for issuing an energy performance certificate, more specifically whether estate agents had such a responsibility.[233] Admittedly, the explanatory memorandum specifically discussed the situation with which the national proceedings were concerned, i.e. where the estate agent had issued an advertisement for the property, and made it clear that in such a situation the obligation rested on the seller only. Perhaps it was the identicality of the question addressed in the explanatory memorandum and the dispute before the BGH that explained the difference in approach. Nevertheless, it seems to me that this does not change that the considerations in the explanatory memorandum were provided without the knowledge that the position would be incompatible with the directive and therefore the explicit discussion of the concerned situation does not automatically invalidate the implementing objective and it says rather little about the choice the legislature would have made had he been aware of the incompatibility. The BGH's judgment of 3 July 2018 also adopted a more restrictive approach. While there was an implementing objective, a grammatical, historical and systematic interpretation provided arguments against a consistent interpretation. The BGH noted in particular that the national provision's compatibility with the directive had been questioned in legal scholarship but that

230 Gebauer (n. 218), p. 84.
231 Case note by Gsell in *JZ* 2009, p. 523.
232 BVerwG 21 August 2018, DÖV 2019, 79, paras. 27-8.
233 BGH 5 October 2017, MDR 2017, 13, para. 20.

the legislature had nevertheless not proceeded to any amendments of the relevant part of national law when it introduced amendments.[234]

Compared to the *Quelle* and *Bodenfliesen* judgments, things were clearly taken a step further in the BAG's judgment of 24 March 2009 and the BGH's judgment of 7 May 2014. The first judgment concerned the question whether a worker is entitled to an allowance in lieu of paid annual leave when his employment relationship is terminated in the situation where he had been absent from work due to sick leave and could therefore not enjoy the paid annual leave. There were basically two aspects to the finding of a *Regelungslücke.* First, it was argued that the legislature's considerations in the explanatory memorandum for the relevant national legislation, which had been adopted before the directive was adopted and did not have an implementing objective, did not touch upon the material point whether a worker could be deprived of his right to paid annual leave in case of incapacity to work. Secondly, the BGH added the further argument that a subsequent legislative amendment showed that, similar to the directive, the legislature also intended to take into account public health concerns. This was followed by what seems to be the thrust of the argument,[235] namely that the explanatory memorandum did not contain any indications that the legislature had intended to pursue objectives incompatible with the directive.[236] Perhaps this must be read in the light of the BAG's foregoing reference to the sentence of the ECJ's *Pfeiffer* judgment providing that it must be presumed that the legislature intends to comply with the directive.[237] If the BAG implicitly relied on the *Pfeiffer* judgment for the establishment of a *Regelungslücke* based on legislative intent, this does not seem to me to be correct since it was in the ECJ's judgment the presumption that followed from the presence of an implementing objective, and not the other way around (see subparagraph 4.2.2). Either way, the BAG's approach entailed a significant loosening of the conditions for the establishment of a *Regelungslücke.* Not only was the requirement of a concrete implementing objective (creating room for the argument that in light of the legislature's irreconcilable intentions, it must be presumed that he would have given priority to the implementing objective) disposed of, but it now seemed that no implementing objective whatsoever needed to be established. It is difficult to interpret this in any other way than an embracement of the theory of supremacy of EU law – and, from the perspective of some authors, it was first and foremost a clear violation of the rules for *Rechtsfortbildung.*[238] In the second judgment, the BGH also took a more far-reaching approach to the establishment of a *Regelungslücke,* but it was clear that it also attempted to fit this into the *Quelle* and *Bodenfliesen* judgments' line of reasoning (the relevant paragraphs of which

234 BGH 3 July 2018, NJW-RR 2018, 1204, para. 14.
235 See also Pötters and Christensen (n. 43), p. 392.
236 BAG 24 March 2009, BAGE 130, 119, para. 67.
237 Ibid, para. 58.
238 Pötters and Christensen (n. 43), p. 392; Höpfner (n. 186), p. 23.

were cited by the BGH – as well as the BGH's judgment of 8 January 2014): it held that, if an explicit implementing objective can be identified but with hindsight it turns out that the relevant national provision did not fulfil this objective, it must be presumed that the legislature would have given priority to the implementing objective. Under the approach adopted in the *Quelle* and *Bodenfliesen* judgments, the key was the identification of a clear implementing objective. Yet, in this regard the BGH's judgment of 7 May 2014 goes a step further. The judgment concerned the right of cancellation of life assurance contracts under the Law on insurance contracts, which did not have an explicit implementing objective. However, the BGH attempted to obviate this obstacle by emphasising that the relevant provision contained in the Law on insurance contracts was indispensable for the operation of a provision contained in another piece of legislation which *did* have an implementing objective. It held that these two provisions represented a unity by which the directive had been implemented in German law.[239] This position was maintained notwithstanding specific considerations of the legislature in relation to the Law on insurance contracts which were clearly incompatible with adopting a *Rechtsfortbildung* in conformity with the directive.[240] Nevertheless, the BGH concluded that the intention to implement the directive must be given priority in such circumstances.[241] The BGH relied on the ECJ's *Pfeiffer* judgment for reaching this conclusion, recalling the presumption that the legislature intends to comply with the directive. Interestingly, the BGH points out that it interprets this presumption as requiring that, save where the legislature unequivocally expressed a conscious intention to make a provision that departs from the directive, the provision's purpose is determined by the implementing objective. This is in my opinion a correct interpretation of the ECJ's *Pfeiffer* judgment.

It may be asked whether the BAG's judgment of 24 March 2009 is still good law in light of a judgment delivered only eight months later. The BAG's *Urlaubsentgelt* judgment denied the existence of a *Regelungslücke*, providing that a clear legislative intention emerged on the basis of all the relevant interpretative criteria, *including the grammatical interpretation*. It was also stated that a consistent interpretation would be *contra legem* under these circumstances.[242] It is interesting to see the recurrence of the grammatical interpretation in a context of *Rechtsfortbildung*. It could be argued that this is methodologically unsound since the idea of a *Rechtsfortbildung* is – as was seen in the previous subparagraph discussing the limits to *Auslegung* – that it is permitted to go beyond the provision's wording.[243] The *Quelle* judgment also provided that the threshold for concluding that an

239 BGH 7 May 2014, BGHZ 201, 101, para. 23 *et seq.*

240 L. Michael and M. Payandeh, 'Richtlinienkonforme Rechtsfortbildung zwischen Unionsrecht und Verfassungsrecht' (2015/33) *NJW*, p. 2397.

241 BGH 7 May 2014, BGHZ 201, 101, para. 26.

242 See BAG 17 November 2009 *Urlaubsentgelt*, BAGE 132, 247, paras. 26-7, 30.

243 See further Brechmann (n. 27), p. 266; Franzen (n. 24), p. 374; Herresthal (n. 210), p. 399.

interpretation would be *contra legem* has not yet been reached by the mere fact that an interpretation goes beyond the provision's text. This is a clear signal that the courts should not shy away from proceeding to a consistent interpretation merely because of a grammatical interpretation and that there is additional scope to do so. Michael and Payandeh, on the other hand, argue that, while the transgression of the provision's wording is a fundamental characteristic of *Rechtsfortbildung*, it is nevertheless the overall balance on the basis of all relevant arguments that must be looked at for determining whether a *Rechtsfortbildung* is permitted, in which regard also *the degree* to which the grammatical limits are exceeded is a relevant factor.[244] It will be seen in the next part discussing the limits in the context of *Rechtsfortbildung* that, in any event, the grammatical interpretation does not become entirely obsolete as one of the commonly referred to limits to *Rechtsfortbildung* is the prohibition of a *de facto* repeal of the concerned provision. Be that as it may, an important aspect to the BAG's *Urlaubsentgelt* judgment – albeit that this was not explicitly mentioned by it – which must not be overlooked was that there was not an implementing objective. If this judgment is compared to some of the above case law, it becomes questionable whether the German superior courts would also dismiss the existence of a *Regelungslücke* if an implementing objective has been identified. After all, with the addition of the latter it would have been more difficult to maintain that an equally clear legislative intention emerged on the basis of all the relevant interpretative criteria. This also has implications for the meaning of *contra legem*. Surely, in a first yet insufficient step, it must be established that the required interpretation is incompatible with the provision's wording, and then the main other point of attention will be legislative intent. If the legislation has an implementing objective, this second point will often not stand in the way of a *Rechtsfortbildung* and will not lead to a finding that the interpretation would be *contra legem*. However, if the potent argument of the legislation's implementing objective is not available, the application of the traditional criteria for establishing legislative intent are unlikely to support a *Rechtsfortbildung* and the adoption of a consistent interpretation is in these circumstances considered to be *contra legem*. The same approach to *contra legem* in the context of non-implementing legislation is found in the BGH's *Interprofessionele Sozietät* judgment.[245] Finally, the *Urlaubsentgelt* judgment provided a useful clarification in that it removed some of the sharp edges of the judgment of 24 March 2009. There, it had been possible to maintain that the material point was not explicitly addressed by the legislature, but the question remained: under which circumstances? The later judgment made it clear that, in the absence of an implementing objective, a clear intention, that turned out to be incompatible with the directive, is not set aside through a presumption of compliance with the directive and excludes a *Regelungslücke*, even if the legislature

244 Michael and Payandeh (n. 240), p. 2397-8.
245 BGH 16 May 2013 *Interprofessionelle Sozietät*, NJW 2013, 2674, paras. 36, 42-3.

did not explicitly provide an intention to act in a manner incompatible with the directive.

The BGH's judgment of 7 May 2014 was confirmed in another judgment by the BGH delivered on 29 July 2015.[246] That case became the subject of a constitutional complaint before the BVerfG. Relying on Article 20(3) of the Constitution the applicant argued that the BGH's judgment had transgressed the outer limits of *Rechtsfortbildung* and violated the principle of legitimate expectations. Both claims were rejected by the BVerfG. First, it was held that the BGH could reasonably take the view that the Law on insurance contracts was indispensable for the operation of a provision contained in another piece of legislation, so that the latter's implementing objective should apply with regard to the former law as well and provided the basis for a *Rechtsfortbildung*. In this regard the BVerfG also takes into account the presumption that the legislature intends to comply with the directive (it refers to the ECJ's *Pfeiffer* judgment for this point). The BGH had not exceeded the outer limits of interpretation (including *Rechtsfortbildung*). Secondly, in as far as the applicant argued that it was entitled to expect the relevant national provision to be applied in accordance with its wording, it only takes into account a single interpretative method whereas the BGH was permitted to apply other interpretative techniques, such as the teleological reduction. It is important to point out that the BVerfG applied its usual lenient standard of review, which entails that the ordinary courts approach is preserved unless it is found to be unsustainable or arbitrary.[247] While the broad approach to establishing an implementing objective was thus approved by the BVerfG, limits to this exercise can be identified on account of the BGH's *Gasversorgung II* judgment concerning transparency requirements for price adjustments made by energy suppliers.[248] In that judgment there was also a whiff of an implementing objective but the BGH nevertheless denied the existence of a *Regelungslücke*: it had been the legislature's intention that specific transparency requirements imposed by the directive would be further dealt with at the level of a regulation – however, this had not happened. A similar case was endorsed in a decision of the BVerfG.[249] In my opinion the distinction between the BGH's judgments of 7 May 2014 and its *Gasversorgung II* judgment is that there was in the latter case an explicit indication that the legislation was not intended to implement the directive.

The considerations in the BGH's judgment of 7 May 2014 providing first that, if an explicit implementing objective can be identified but a later incompatibility with the directive is found, it must be presumed that the legislature would have

246 BGH 29 July 2015, ZIP 2015, 61.
247 BVerfG 23 May 2016, ZIP 2016, 55, see in particular paras. 33, 40, 44-6, 58.
248 BGH 28 October 2015 *Gasversorgung II*, BGHZ 207, 209.
249 BVerfG 17 November 2017, NJW-RR 2018, 305.

given priority to the implementing objective and, secondly, the ECJ's *Pfeiffer* judgment must be interpreted as providing that an implementing objective takes priority over other intentions, were reiterated in the BVerwG's judgment of 31 January 2017, which adopted a *Rechtsfortbildung* in conformity with the directive. Two points must be made in relation to the latter judgment. First and foremost, the relevant national provision did have a clear implementing objective and the BVerwG explained in some detail why it was reasonable to presume that, if the legislature had been aware of the irreconcilability of his intentions, he would have enacted a different provision. So in that regard the reasoning was more straightforward compared to the BGH's judgment. Secondly, the judgment made it clear that, according to the BVerwG, the latter presumption is not undermined in the situation where there was ongoing discussion regarding the national provision's compatibility with the directive whereas the legislature did not proceed to any amendments. In other words: this does not show that, had the legislature been aware of the incompatibility, he would still have enacted the same, incompatible, provision.[250]

3.7. LIMITS IN THE CONTEXT OF *RECHTSFORTBILDUNG*

If the conditions for establishing a *Regelungslücke* are fulfilled, a *Rechtsfortbildung* can in principle be adopted *unless this would exceed the limits to Rechtsfortbildung.* These are two separate questions. But note that both are relevant for the determination of whether a *Rechtsfortbildung* would be *contra legem* (and note the distinction drawn between implementing and non-implementing legislation in this regard for the establishment of a *Regelungslücke* and the consequences this has for the *contra legem* limitation).[251] The question what constitutes the limits to the duty of consistent interpretation in the context of *Rechtsfortbildung* is again primarily governed by Article 20(3) of the Constitution, in particular the requirement that the judiciary shall be bound by law and justice.[252] In this respect, the starting point is the same for *Auslegung* and *Rechtsfortbildung.* Yet, it will be seen that, in comparison to *Auslegung,* the question when a *Rechtsfortbildung* violates the separation of powers between the judiciary and the legislature has been discussed more extensively. This is not surprising if it is taken into account that a *Rechtsfortbildung* directly concerns the demarcation of the competences of the judiciary and the legislature. It should also be pointed out that the BFH has so far not discussed any limits to a *Rechtsfortbildung* in conformity with the directive. The

250 BVerwG 31 January 2017, Beck online Rechtsprechung 2017, 103948, paras. 29-32.

251 This can be deduced from, for example, BGH 26 November 2008 *Quelle,* BGHZ 179, 27, para. 21: both the requirements for a *Regelungslücke* and the limits to a *Rechtsfortbildung* are part of national methodology.

252 BAG 24 March 2009, BAGE 130, 119, para. 65; BGH 28 October 2015 *Gasversorgung II,* BGHZ 207, 209, para. 41; BVerwG 31 January 2017, Beck online Rechtsprechung 2017, 103948, para. 27. See also Herresthal (n. 210), p. 400; Michael and Payandeh (n. 240), p. 2396.

German superior courts' case law shows that, once a *Regelungslücke* is established, a *Rechtsfortbildung* has so far hardly ever been rejected as a result of one of the limitations. This means that the limits to a *Rechtsfortbildung* in conformity with the directive are most of the time only discussed in a general way, i.e. without actually finding a violation of these limits.

As I mentioned above, the BGH's *Quelle* judgment provided that a *Rechtsfortbildung* may not (a) lead to a *de facto* repeal of the concerned provision, or violate (b) the judiciary's boundedness to law and justice, (c) the principle of legal certainty, (d) the prohibition of horizontal direct effect. Subsequent judgments of the BGH stated the same or similar limits.[253] This broad list actually covers all the limits that have been stated in relation to a *Rechtsfortbildung* in conformity with the directive by the German superior courts.

Although some of them require more elaboration than others, a few further comments can be made in relation to those limits. First, a violation of the prohibition of a *de facto* repeal – which is also derived from Article 20(3) of the Constitution – is usually rejected with the argument that other parts of the provision are maintained, or that the provision still applies in situations not covered by the directive.[254]

Secondly, because of its dominant role for demarcating the competences of the judiciary and the legislature and perhaps also because its meaning is the most difficult to pin down, the restrictions deriving from the provision that the judiciary shall be bound by law and justice, requires a slightly more detailed discussion. Despite different formulations, two common elements can be identified in the German superior courts' case law with regard to the meaning of this limitation. First, it is required that a clear legislative intent can be identified. Secondly, the *Rechtsfortbildung* would depart from this clear intention, which is then replaced by the judge's own weighing of the concerned interests,[255] or the judge's own legal-political viewpoint.[256] This approach was consolidated in the BVerfG's decision of 26 September 2011. It first provided a similar description of the limits deriving from the judiciary's boundedness by law and justice:

---

253 See BGH 21 December 2011 *Bodenfliesen*, BGHZ 192, 148, paras. 45-7; BGH 7 May 2014, BGHZ 201, 101, paras. 31-4.

254 See, for example, BGH 17 December 2014, NJW 2015, 1023, para. 23, where an entire sentence from a subparagraph was disapplied but it was argued that the same rule was provided in other subsections and that they together constituted a unitary complex, so that a meaningful scope of application remained.

255 BVerwG 31 January 2017, Beck online Rechtsprechung 2017, 103948, para. 27; BVerwG 21 August 2018, DÖV 2019, 79, para. 27.

256 BGH 26 November 2008 *Quelle*, BGHZ 179, 27, para. 31; BAG 24 March 2009, BAGE 130, 119, para. 65; BAG 17 November 2009 *Urlaubsentgelt*, BAGE 132, 247, para. 29; BGH 8 January 2014, NVwZ 2014, 1111, para. 10.

> 'Richterliche Rechtsfortbildung darf nicht dazu führen, dass der Richter seine eigene materielle Gerechtigkeitsvorstellung an die Stelle derjenigen des Gesetzgebers setzt (...). Ein Richterspruch setzt sich über die aus Art. 20 Abs. 3 GG folgende Gesetzesbindung hinweg, wenn die vom Gericht zur Begründung seiner Entscheidung angestellten Erwägungen eindeutig erkennen lassen, dass es sich aus der Rolle des Normanwenders in die einer normsetzenden Instanz begeben hat, also objektiv nicht bereit war, sich Recht und Gesetz zu unterwerfen (...)'.[257]

Subsequently, it was added that these limits are safeguarded by the BVerfG to the same extent, irrespective of whether the national law does or does not implement a directive. Indeed, the BVerfG has formulated the same limits in cases without an EU law context.[258] Importantly, the BVerfG also considered this position to be in line with the ECJ's case law on the duty of consistent interpretation, pointing out that national courts are only required to interpret national law 'so far as possible' in conformity with the directive, thereby not exceeding the interpretative limits derived from national law. In this regard it also referred to the acknowledgment of the *contra legem* limitation in the ECJ's *Pfeiffer* judgment.[259]

The limitation was applied in the BAG's judgment of 10 December 2013.

> The applicant claimed entitlement to a contract of employment as the work carried out under a temporary-work contract had not been of a temporary nature. This specific sanction is not prescribed by the applicable directive, which leaves it to the Member States to adopt appropriate measures in the event of a violation of the directive. However, the German legislation did not provide for sanctions to remedy the violation at all. The BAG mentioned a number of measures that the legislature might adopt to this end, that national law provided no objective indicators which measure should be chosen, and considered that, on account of the variety of options available, it was for the legislature, and not the courts, to act.[260]

However, usually the German superior courts are less cautious when it comes to this limitation and they have frequently adopted a *Rechtsfortbildung* that involved the making of policy choices. This applies equally to situations where a *Rechtsfortbildung* brings national law in conformity with a directive and a *Rechtsfortbildung* in purely internal situations.[261]

---

257 BVerfG 26 September 2011, BVerfGK 19, 89, para. 45.

258 In addition to the case law cited in the BVerfG's decision of 26 September 2011 under para. 45, see, in particular, BVerfG 10 January 2012 *Delisting*, BVerfGE 132, 99, para. 75. See further BVerfG 3 April 1990, BVerfGE 82, 6, 12; BVerfG 25 January 2011, BVerfGE 128, 193, para. 52.

259 BVerfG 26 September 2011, BVerfGK 19, 89, paras. 46-7.

260 BAG 10 December 2013, BAGE 146, 384, paras. 32-4.

261 Brenncke (n. 40), p. 354-5.

Thirdly, I must point out that Article 20(3) of the Constitution also provides the legal basis for the German superior court's examination of a potential violation of the principle of legal certainty. It was already provided in the *Quelle* judgment that this limitation concerns first and foremost the protection of legitimate expectations and subsequent case law has taken the same approach. The BAG's judgment of 24 March 2009 contained the most elaborate discussion on whether the *Rechtsfortbildung* in conformity with the directive violated this principle, but the BAG concluded that this was not the case. There, it was provided that the interpretation that was found to be incompatible with the directive was not free from doubt since there had been a preliminary reference to the ECJ on the relevant point. Also, the ECJ had not placed any restrictions on the temporal scope of its subsequent ruling.[262] The BGH's case law consistently rejects a violation of this principle for the reason that the incompatible interpretation was not free from doubt as a result of scholarly controversy,[263] which is sometimes further supported through a reference to case law.[264] Although this is an interesting question, I will not further explore the sustainability of the BGH's reasoning here. Since the ECJ's *Klohn* judgment, there seems to be some support for the view that the principle of legitimate expectations may not be entirely irrelevant as a limitation to the duty of consistent interpretation. However, the scope for invoking this principle appears to be restrictive and, in any case, the national court should rely on the EU law principle and not the national variant. Since the German superior courts have so far also taken a restrictive approach to this third limitation, I am inclined to say that there is not a discrepancy here with the ECJ's position. However, they have so far only referred to the national principle and not the EU law principle of legitimate expectations. The reference to legitimate expectations also gives rise to another interesting question. Can it be said that, irrespective of the compatibility with the ECJ 's case law, because the technique of *Rechtsfortbildung* probably goes further than what most national courts would permit when it is attempted to adopt a consistent interpretation, the German superior courts therefore already go beyond what EU law requires and are therefore free to arrange the limits to this technique as they see fit? It can be presumed that differences exist between the national courts in terms of how far they can go to adopt a consistent interpretation. I do not think that the requirement to pursue such an interpretation as far as possible ceases to apply as soon as a national court has gone further than the common denominator. So while it can be presumed that a large number of national courts will reject the possibility of a consistent interpretation that is grammatically impossible – and, as was seen in chapter 2, subparagraph 5.2.2, the ECJ will not normally interfere if this reason is invoked – this does not prevent the development of a different view

262 BAG 24 March 2009, BAGE 130, 119, para. 69 *et seq.*

263 BGH 21 December 2011 *Bodenfliesen,* BGHZ 192, 148, para. 47; BGH 7 May 2014, BGHZ 201, 101, para. 32.

264 BGH 26 November 2008 *Quelle,* BGHZ 179, 27, para. 33.

on what so far as possible requires by another national court in another domestic legal (interpretative) context. And in this regard the BGH's *Quelle* judgment makes it crystal-clear that, in the German legal context, the courts believe that they should not, if an implementing objective can be identified, stop at the limits of a provision's text. Accordingly, if the principle of legitimate expectations would be applied, this would be a limitation to the requirements imposed by EU law as interpreted by the German courts. They cannot freely decide such matters by themselves. Hence, the conclusion drawn in the BVerfG's judgment of 10 December 2014 that the German courts should first refer preliminary questions to the ECJ (see subparagraph 3.4.2) before rejecting a consistent interpretation on the basis of the principle of legitimate expectations, equally applies when that principle is relied upon in the context of *Rechtsfortbildung*.

Finally, the inclusion of the prohibition of horizontal direct effect does not really add something in my opinion and, frankly, does not seem to make sense. Consider, for example, the reasoning provided in the BGH's *Quelle* judgment for rejecting a violation of this limitation. The BGH held that the prohibition of horizontal direct effect was not violated since the adopted *Rechtsfortbildung* was compatible with German interpretative rules. But this raises the question what the added value of the inclusion of the prohibition of horizontal direct effect is. It rather seems to be a different way of labelling a consistent interpretation that exceeds the national interpretative limits: if, in a horizontal dispute, it can be established that a consistent interpretation actually violated interpretative limits, the outcome should be considered as a manifestation of direct effect instead of interpretation. While I agree with the BGH's determination of the dividing line between the duty of consistent interpretation and direct effect, since mentioning the prohibition of horizontal direct effect does not add an additional requirement, the label is better preserved for situations that concern the application of the remedy of direct effect. By the way, the latter two limitations have so far only been stated in the BGH's case law.

3.8. THE INTENTION TO IMPLEMENT THE DIRECTIVE AS THE PIVOT OF RECHTSFORTBILDUNG

I explained that, while the German superior courts point to the duty of consistent interpretation for proceeding to a *Rechtsfortbildung*, the obligation under EU law is only indirectly relevant. The requirement to interpret national law so far as possible in conformity with the directive refers to national interpretative rules and for the German courts this means that they are also required to examine the possibility of a *Rechtsfortbildung*. This means that no additional arguments for understanding the relationship between EU and national law can appropriately be derived from the legal basis as such. In my opinion, the same applies for the limits to *Rechtsfortbildung*, but for a different reason, namely that there does not seem to be a conflict of interpretations. While the ECJ's case law does not clearly define when an interpretation is *contra legem*, it does not seem difficult to agree that it would not consider that national courts fall short of their obligations under the duty of consistent interpretation when they reject a consistent interpretation if the clear legislative intent would be replaced by the judge's own weighing of the concerned interests, or the judge's own legal-political viewpoint. The same applies for the prohibition of a *de facto* repeal. These limitations are very reasonable. It should be noted that the ECJ's case law also seems to have recognised that, in principle, the principle of legitimate expectations can be relevant with regard to the limits of the duty of consistent interpretation. So far, the German superior courts have not yet applied this particular exception,[265] but it follows from the BVerfG's judgment of 10 December 2014 that they cannot do so before having referred preliminary questions to the ECJ. They should then primarily base their argument on the EU law principle of legitimate expectations. The prohibition of horizontal direct effect is of course also acknowledged in the ECJ's case law but, as I explained, it does not seem to have any purpose in the context of the duty of consistent interpretation. The limits to a *Rechtsfortbildung* set a rather high threshold for concluding that a *Rechtsfortbildung* in conformity with the directive is prohibited. That is probably also the reason why they have not been applied very often. The *contra legem* limitation encompasses these limits as well as the requirements for a *Regelungslücke*. Since the limits have not been applied very often, the pivot of *Rechtsfortbildung* is the question whether a *Regelungslücke* can be established.

It must thus be examined whether there is a conflict of interpretations in relation to the German superior courts' approach to the establishment of a *Regelungslücke* in the context of the duty of consistent interpretation. There is not a conflict from the perspective of EU law if the existence of a *Regelungslücke* is denied where the provision did not have an implementing objective and both its wording and nearly all other criteria oppose a consistent interpretation. It is not surprising that the court does not then proceed to a consistent interpretation and relies on the *contra legem* limitation. But what about the judgments that *did* establish a *Regelungslücke*, can it be said that there is a conflict with national interpretative rules? This is first examined for the *relatively* less far-reaching judgments such as *Quelle* and *Bodenfliesen*, where the court used a concrete implementing objective to create room for the argument that in light of the legislature's irreconcilable intentions, it must be presumed that he would have given priority to the implementing objective. Gsell, Höpfner and Kaiser already consider this a violation of the German interpretative rules for *Rechtsfortbildung* – and, accordingly, there would thus have been a conflict for the purposes of the present analysis. They argue that there is not

265 On account of BAG 23 March 2006, BAGE 117, 281 this is not entirely true, but note that the BAG's judgment was overturned in BVerfG 10 December 2014, ZIP 2015, 335.

a *Regelungslücke* if, on the basis of the traditional approach, the concrete legislative intent with regard to the provision is clear; this cannot be set aside because of an incompatibility with the objective to implement the directive. If this were different, the establishment of a *Regelungslücke* would violate Article 20(3) of the Constitution; the national provision would become a kind of '*dynamischen Verweisung*' (dynamic reference), an empty shell which assumes whatever the evolving meaning of the directive as determined by the ECJ provides; and there would – again – be a *de facto* violation of the prohibition of horizontal direct effect.[266] Gsell and Kaiser suggest an alternative approach whereby a *Regelungslücke* can only be established if it follows from national law considered in isolation (for example: in the situation in the *Quelle* judgment, Gsell suggests that a *Regelungslücke* might have been based on section 439(4) of the Civil Code's incompatibility with general principles of sales law and the law concerning breaches of contractual obligations.[267] Also Höpfner proposes an approach whereby the scope for establishing a *Regelungslücke* is reduced to situations where the legislature has not expressed any ideas of his own about the enacted provision, but limited his observations to making clear that it is intended to fully implement the directive. In the context of a '*gesetzesübersteigende Rechtsfortbildung*' he also considers it possible to base a *Regelungslücke* on the directive itself as being part of the larger legal complex and principles, external to the concerned legislation ('*Gesammtrechtsordnung*'). The *Regelungslücke* is then based on the incompatibility with the directive. However, this is only possible if the relevant provision has direct effect.[268]

Both approaches are completely understandable if one looks at the phenomenon of a *Rechtsfortbildung* in conformity with the directive from the perspective of national law. They reflect the two ways to a *Regelungslücke* in German law: it can follow from an incompatibility between the legislative intent and the actually enacted provision or from the just referred to '*Gesammtrechtsordnung*'. In both situations a *Rechtsfortbildung* in conformity with the directive that was seen in the *Quelle* and *Bodenfliesen* judgments is the 'odd one out'. In cases without an EU law dimension, if a *Regelungslücke* is based on legislative intent, this intent actually offers concrete criteria that as such point out the incompatibility. What happens in an EU law context? The legislature will normally express his ideas *vis-à-vis* the national provision in a more elaborate way (which then correspond to the substance of the enacted provision: see the *Quelle* and *Bodenfliesen* judgments, as well as the BFH's judgment of 22 August 2013 and the BGH's judgment of 8 January 2014) whereas, even if he does not merely state the provisions' implementing objective but elaborates

266 Gsell (n. 231), p. 524-5; Höpfner (n. 217), p. 404-5; D. Kaiser, 'EuGH zum Austausch mangelhafter eingebauter Verbrauchsgüter' (2011/20) *JZ*, p. 980, 986; B. Gsell, 'Die Reichweite der Ersatzlieferungspflicht nach Einbau der mangelhaften Kaufsache durch den Verbraucher' (2012/3) *Zeitschrift für das Juristische Studium*, p. 374; Case note by Höpfner in *JZ* 2012, p. 475-6.

267 Gsell (n. 231), p. 525. See also Kaiser (n. 266), p. 980-1; Gsell (n. 266), p. 374.

268 Höpfner (n. 217), p. 404; Höpfner (n. 266), p. 476.

on the correct interpretation of the directive, the latter will probably have been an incorrect assessment which cannot guide the way to a *Rechtsfortbildung* – otherwise there would presumably not have been an incompatibility in the first place. In addition to this, yet still with regard to legislative intent, it may be asked whether, from the traditional perspective, a presumption also suffices for the establishment of a *Regelungslücke* where the legislative intent is contradictory. It has been argued that for the interpretation of international treaties there is an interpretation maxim requiring that it must be presumed that the legislature intended to comply with the international obligations if the legislature's intentions are contradictory, and that the same must apply with regard to the duty of consistent interpretation.[269] In general, such presumptions do not seem to be uncommon in German law.[270] However, this seems to be a point of discussion. A counter-argument would be that in as far as the establishment of a *Regelungslücke* is concerned, only clearly stated legislative intentions can play a role.[271] In my opinion, it is not clear whether the intention to comply with international obligations can also be used by the German courts to set aside a provision's clear wording and proceed to a *Rechtsfortbildung.* So as regards the first option, i.e. legislative intent, it can be said that if, under the just described circumstances, a *Regelungslücke* is nevertheless adopted, either directly on the basis of an implementing objective or through a presumption, it is understandable that critical observers view this as being *de facto* based on the directive itself. Is it then more legitimate to acknowledge that the directive is considered to be part of the '*Gesammtrechtsordnung*' and to derive a *Regelungslücke* from this? It was seen that this route is also followed for the *verfassungskonforme Rechtsfortbildung.* But the crucial difference here is that the Constitution is obviously part of the national legal order and superior to lower-ranking rules. One might object that, if there is really a difference on this point for directives, it would not be consistent to permit the national courts to remove a potential incompatibility between national law and the directive in the context of *Auslegung* as well. Is this not also based on the idea that the directive produces a certain legal effect in the national legal order, even before it is implemented correctly? In my opinion this would, in the first place, be a misconception of how the duty of consistent interpretation works, which is based on Articles 288 TFEU and 4(3) TEU (with the inclusion of effectiveness), i.e. it is not based on supremacy of the directive itself. It is rather 'an extension of the implementation obligation'. Even more importantly, it also overlooks the specific requirements for finding a *Regelungslücke* in light of the *Gesammtrechtsordnung,* which can only be based on a conflict with a provision or principle that has full effect in the national legal order. Neither the directive itself nor the duty of consistent interpretation on the basis of Articles 288 TFEU and 4(3) TEU can

269 C.-H. Witt, 'Nutzungsersatz bei Nachlieferung – BGH-Vorlage an den EuGH' (2006/46) *NJW*, p. 3325. See also Sperber (n. 217), p. 360.

270 M. Brenncke, 'Europäisierung der Methodik richtlinienkonformer Rechtsfindung' (2015/4) *EuR*, p. 458. See also Schenke (n. 49), p. 221-2.

271 Schürnbrand (n. 159), p. 916.

directly set aside incompatible national substantive provisions (with the exception of directly effective provisions, but it seems to me that it would then be more logical to apply the remedy of direct effect and not the duty of consistent interpretation – compare the above position adopted by Höpfner).[272] Accordingly, the idea of a *Regelungslücke* in light of the *Gesammtrechtsordnung* does also not make sense from the perspective of the traditional approach to *Rechtsfortbildung* and, frankly, I do not think that it can be the basis for a *Rechtsfortbildung*.[273]

The departure from the traditional approach to *Rechtsfortbildung* may explain some of the apprehension about a *Rechtsfortbildung* in conformity with directives. The question remains, however, whether this also means that there is a conflict of interpretations. I believe this is so, but not because the legislature's implementing objective is taken into account for the establishment of a *Regelungslücke,* not even because the German superior courts use a presumption in this regard, but rather as a result of the principled prioritisation of the implementing objective over an incompatible, specific, legislative intention (which I address in a moment). It must be pointed out that the finding of an implementing objective was on nearly every occasion the key to the establishment of a *Regelungslücke* in the German superior courts' case law[274] – I also pointed out judgments where no implementing objective could be identified and which denied the existence of a *Regelungslücke.* And in that regard it is recalled that I concluded in subparagraph 3.2.2 that it must be presumed that there was not a conflict of interpretations if the national legislature's intention to implement the directive was applied through traditional interpretative methods and was decisive for the adoption of a consistent interpretation. Nevertheless, matters are not that straightforward in the context of *Rechtsfortbildung.* There, the national courts do not simply make a choice among different interpretations – among which there is in principle no strict hierarchical relationship – but they go beyond a provision's wording entering into an area characterised by legal-political tensions concerning the demarcation of the judiciary's and the legislature's competences which is subject to the specific requirement of the presence of a *Regelungslücke.* However, at the same time, it is controversial when that requirement is fulfilled.[275] It is therefore difficult to say to what extent there was already a conflict of interpretations in judgments such as

272 See also Schürnbrand (n. 159), p. 917.

273 For the stated reasons, BVerfG 30 March 2004 *Geldwächse,* BVerfGE 110, 226, para. 151, where a *Rechtsfortbildung* was adopted, dismissing incompatible historical arguments with the presumption that the legislature in principle intends to comply with the Constitution, cannot justify a *Rechtsfortbildung* in conformity with the directive. The opposite view does not, in my opinion, sufficiently take into account the different positions that the Constitution and directives occupy in the German legal order. Cf. Brenncke (n. 40), p. 334.

274 Admittedly, BAG 24 March 2009, BAGE 130, 119, points in a different direction, but see the subsequent judgment in BAG 17 November 2009 *Urlaubsentgelt,* BAGE 132, 247.

275 Gsell (n. 231), p. 523-4; W. Durner, *Verfassungsrechtliche Grenzen richtlinienkonformer Rechtsfortbildung* (Rheinische Friedrich-Wilhelms-Universität Bonn 2010), p. 13.

Quelle and *Bodenfliesen*. Be that as it may, I am inclined to conclude that there is not yet a conflict because it departs from the traditional approach to *Rechtsfortbildung* that an implementing objective plays a decisive role. The opposite opinion does not sufficiently take into account the unique context within which national courts act when they have to interpret national law that incorrectly implemented a directive. The fact that directives always require implementation into national law, and that this can lead to a split legislative intent,[276] indicates that a *Rechtsfortbildung* in conformity with directives cannot be compared to a traditional *Rechtsfortbildung*.[277] This means, in turn, that there was not a conflict of interpretations in the *Quelle* and *Bodenfliesen* judgments, simply because the BGH departed from the traditional approach. What about the fact that a presumption was used? Although I am not sure to what extent the presumption that the legislature intends to comply with international obligations can also be used by the German courts to proceed to a *Rechtsfortbildung*, this matter can be left undecided. On account of the unique context of the split legislative intent in relation to directives, that issue can also not be decisive. However, what *does* support the theory of supremacy of EU law is that, when the German superior courts are confronted with a discrepancy as regards the legislature's intention, they normally favour the objective to implement the directive for the determination of the legislature's overriding intention (but see, however, the BGH's judgments of 5 October 2017 and 3 July 2018). This is a fixed prioritisation, similar to what was seen in subparagraph 3.2.2 with the BGH's *Heininger* judgment (it cannot be presumed that the legislature intended to violate the directive) and the BGH's judgment of 12 October 2016 (the explanatory memorandum contained no indication that the legislature had intended to draft a provision that was incompatible with the directive).

Arguably the line of argumentation adopted in the *Quelle* and *Bodenfliesen* judgments set the standard for the German superior courts' approach to *Rechtsfortbildung* in conformity with directives. From this perspective, the BAG's judgment of 24 March 2009, which implied that a *Regelungslücke* could be established as soon as there were no clear indications that the legislature intended to make a provision contrary to the directive, is situated outside the construct created by the BGH to accommodate the duty of consistent interpretation and the requirements for a *Rechtsfortbildung*. However, that judgment must now be considered in the light of the subsequent *Urlaubsentgelt* judgment, which made it clear that, in the absence of an implementing objective, a clear intention, that turned out to be incompatible with the directive, is not set aside through a presumption of compliance with the directive and excludes a *Regelungslücke*, even if the legislature

---

276 See also Gebauer (n. 218), p. 83; Pfeiffer (n. 210), p. 413.

277 BGH 7 May 2014, BGHZ 201, 101, para. 23, where it was provided that the situations in which a *Regelungslücke* can be found, cannot be restricted to contradictions arising from two incompatible rules of *national* law.

did not explicitly provide an intention to act in a manner incompatible with the directive. The BGH's judgment of 7 May 2014 (broad approach to the finding of an implementing objective) strains the coherence of the construct created by the BGH. Be that as it may, the judgment of 7 May 2014 attempts to justify the approach to *Rechtsfortbildung* by aligning it as far as possible with the conventional construct (requiring the establishment of an implementing objective and using a presumption to identify a *Regelungslücke*) putting forward circumstances to show that in the current situation the similarities were greater than the differences. In that sense, it becomes less interesting to ask whether the BGH's judgment of 7 May 2014 as such provides support for the theory of supremacy of EU law. If it is viewed as falling within the line of reasoning adopted in the *Quelle* judgment, supremacy of consistent interpretation follows from the above analysis and it is not really necessary to examine whether the judgment provides a ground for supremacy of its own. If it does not, then this necessarily means that the judgment goes a step further, in which case it still supports the supremacy of consistent interpretation. Finally, the subsequent *Gasversorgung II* judgment can also be placed in the construct established by the *Quelle* judgment. It shows that the establishment of a *Regelungslücke*, the pivot of *Rechtsfortbildung*, is not a hollow phrase.[278]

4. AN AFTERTHOUGHT: THE ROLE PLAYED BY THE PRELIMINARY RULING PROCEDURE

In most of the cases applying the duty of consistent interpretation that were preceded by a preliminary ruling, the German superior courts emphasise that the ECJ's interpretation is binding upon them. Sometimes, this can give the impression that the preliminary ruling itself brought about the adoption of a consistent interpretation. For example, in its judgment of 7 July 2016, the BVerwG pointed out that the ECJ had interpreted 'dealers engaging in intra-Community trade' in a way that also encompassed the applicant, adding that, accordingly, the national provision had to be given an interpretation whereby the applicant was also brought within its scope.[279] However, I think that it is important to recall that the ECJ only provides a binding interpretation of the directive. This must be separated from the subsequent implementation of the preliminary ruling in national law.[280] Therefore it is better to see the preliminary ruling as the immediate cause to examine whether a revised interpretation of national law can be adopted, which must still be

278 Note that the BGH's judgment of 28 October 2015 was upheld in BVerfG 17 November 2017, NJW-RR 2018, 305.

279 BVerwG 7 July 2016, BVerwGE 155, 381, para. 23.

280 From the perspective of the ECJ see, for example, Case 52/76 *Benedetti*, ECLI:EU:C:1977:16, para. 25; Case C-212/04 *Adeneler*, ECLI:EU:C:2006:443; Joined Cases C-378/07 to C-380/07 *Angelidaki and Others*, ECLI:EU:C:2009:250, para. 63. From the perspective of the BVerfG, see BVerfG 17 November 2017, NJW-RR 2018, 305, para. 36.

obtained through the duty of consistent interpretation. The BVerwG's judgment, as well as other judgments emphasising the binding force of the preliminary ruling,[281] can certainly also be interpreted in that way. I also believe that the influence of a preliminary ruling should not be exaggerated. Surely, the courts may go just a little further when the ECJ's preliminary ruling made it clear that national law is in violation of the directive unless it is given a consistent interpretation. However, the BGH's *Gasversorgung II* judgment was also preceded by a preliminary ruling but the BGH nevertheless refused to adopt a consistent interpretation even though there were some connecting points in national law supporting a consistent interpretation. Importantly, unlike for example the *Heininger, Quelle* and *Bodenfliesen* judgments the national provision did not have an implementing objective. Brenncke correctly points out that:

> '[a] key factor, which in the end had a stronger pull than the CJEU's preliminary reference ruling, seems to be that the contested legislation in *Gasversorgung II* was non-implementing and preceded the applicable directive'.[282]

Nevertheless, it was seen in this chapter that the finding that national law is incompatible with the directive can have a profound impact on the application of the historical and teleological interpretative method if the legislature intended to implement the directive. Particularly in these situations, a preliminary ruling that indicates that national law is incompatible can give rise to a significant shift in the approach to interpretation.[283] I therefore do not agree with authors who criticise a reference for a preliminary ruling after the court has given a detailed explanation as to why national law does not seem to be in line with the directive.[284] Clearly, the judge was uncertain what the directive actually provided, why else would it refer questions for a preliminary ruling? When the judge discusses the meaning of the domestic legal framework in the decision making a reference for a preliminary ruling – which it is required to do under Article 267 TFEU – this can only be a *provisional* conclusion regarding the meaning that must be attributed to the national provisions since the judge cannot yet have taken into account which interpretation is required by the directive. After the ECJ has delivered its preliminary ruling, two things can happen. First, it is possible that there was not an incompatibility with the directive. There is then obviously no need to revise the earlier interpretation. However, often the referring court's feeling that a particular interpretation sits uneasily with the directive turned out to be justified. It is then very important what the directive stipulates exactly, and how far this is removed from earlier interpretations of national law. By the way, the latter point is often

---

281 See, for example, BGH 9 April 2002 *Heininger*, BGHZ 150, 248; BGH 14 February 2006, NJW 2006, 1340, para. 14; BGH 12 October 2016, NJW 2017, 1093, para. 36.

282 Brenncke (n. 40), p. 358.

283 The same conclusion is reached in Brenncke (n. 40), p. 341.

284 Franzen (n. 82), p. 325; case note by Lorenz in *NJW* 2006, p. 3200; Schürnbrand (n. 159), p. 917.

overlooked by authors who are critical of what in their eyes are 'unnecessary' preliminary references: before the ECJ's preliminary ruling there may be broad agreement that there might be an incompatibility but often divergent views exist on what the directive requires exactly, and which solutions are available under national law.

In its *Mücksch* judgment, the BVerwG pointed out that it considered it possible to adopt a consistent interpretation through section 34 of the Building Code. However, it also referred to potentially other routes leading to a consistent interpretation.[285] In the *Heininger* case, there was not only the question whether the Law on the Cancellation of Doorstep Sales applied if, at the same time, a matter fell within the scope of the Consumer Credit Law, but also the questions whether, due to certain exceptions contained therein, the relevant situation came within the scope of the Doorstep-Selling Directive in the first place and whether the directive permitted a national provision which entailed that the right of cancellation must in any event be exercised within a period of one year. It depended on the answers to these questions how difficult it would be to adopt a consistent interpretation. In its decision making a reference for a preliminary ruling in the *Bodenfliesen* case, the BGH explained that perhaps the right to refuse to provide cure in a case of absolute lack of proportionality could fall under the exception provided in the directive that no remedy needs to be provided if this is 'impossible'.[286] This solution was dismissed by the ECJ. In the BGH's follow-up judgment a large number of possible ways to bring national law in conformity with the directive were assessed from the perspective of the requirements imposed by the directive.

In my opinion it can thus be said that national courts cannot easily conclude that it is not necessary to make a reference to decide the dispute before it, because national law can in any event not be interpreted in conformity with the directive.[287] Logically, the question whether a consistent interpretation is possible can only be accurately determined *after* the delivery of the ECJ's preliminary ruling.[288]

5. CONCLUSION

The debate concerning the correct approach to interpretation under German law is already confusing enough without the addition of the duty of consistent interpretation. It is nevertheless clear that this is a matter governed by the Constitution (Article 20(3) stipulating that the judiciary shall be bound by law and justice and Article 97(1) providing that judges shall be independent and subject to

285 BVerwG 20 December 2012 *Mücksch*, NVwZ 2013, 719, 723.

286 BGH 14 January 2009, NJW 2009, 1660, para. 17.

287 BGH 29 April 2003, ZIP 2003, 1692; BGH 19 October 2004, ZIP 2004, 2373; BAG 23 June 2010, BAGE 135, 34, para. 38.

288 T.M.J. Möllers and A. Möhring, 'Recht und Pflicht zur richtlinienkonformen Rechtsfortbildung bei generellem Umsetzungswillen des Gesetzgebers' (2008/19) *JZ*, p. 919-20. See also Pfeiffer (n. 210), p. 413.

the law only). The overriding objective is to ascertain the intent of the legislature which is objectified in the provision and manifested in the wording and the context of the provision. This intention is determined through the grammatical, historical, systematic and teleological interpretative methods. These methods are applied with a considerable degree of discretion and the constitutional provisions only set outer limits. It is important to point out that German law distinguishes between *Auslegung*, which is probably closest to the English term 'interpretation', and *Rechtsfortbildung*, for which there is no equivalent in English but which denotes a further development of the law by the courts.

In the context of *Auslegung* as well as *Rechtsfortbildung*, it is only possible to find support for a particular theory for the relationship between EU and national law under the duty of consistent interpretation once a conflict between the latter and the national interpretative rules can be established. A conflict can arise from an incompatibility with national interpretative rules or the duty of consistent interpretation. There is a peaceful co-existence between the duty of consistent interpretation and national interpretative rules in as far as they both point to the same interpretative outcome or if the duty of consistent interpretation is merely used to make a choice if the concerned provision is open to more than one interpretation. I also referred to a number of judgments where the duty of consistent interpretation was applied in a more interfering way, adapting the traditional approach, but where this did not go so far as to warrant the conclusion that there was a conflict. Hence, an adaptation and a conflict are connected but separate concepts. It must be emphasised that, most of the time, the incompatibility between the directive and national law can be resolved in a harmonious way through the duty of consistent interpretation.

In this chapter I first encountered a conflict of interpretative rules that was resolved to the benefit of supremacy of the duty of consistent interpretation as a result of the negative test approach, which takes the result prescribed by the directive as its starting point and asks whether the national provision does not oppose the desired interpretation. Secondly, there has been a structural prioritisation of the intention to implement the directive over opposing legislative intentions. I did not only encounter such a prioritisation in the context of *Auslegung*, but also in relation to *Rechtsfortbildung*. The pivot of *Rechtsfortbildung* is whether a *Regelungslücke* (an unintended legislative gap) can be established. It was seen that, in nearly all cases, the German superior courts saw themselves confronted with a 'split' legislative intent, resulting from an incompatibility between the intention to implement the directive on the one hand, and an opposing intention on the other hand. When reconciling these intentions, the German superior courts nearly always presume that the legislature intended to give priority to the implementation of the directive. It is argued that such a prioritisation is a good indication of a conflict in the German interpretative context in particular, where there is traditionally not a hierarchical relationship between different interpretative arguments. The two examples both concern the *process* of interpretation. As far as concerns the *outcome* of the interpretative process in individual cases, I did not really find any examples where the adopted consistent interpretation transgressed the outer limits of the national interpretative rules – but note that this is subject to the qualification that the reasoning of some of the judgments was so thin that this could not be established with the required degree of certainty. It was seen that the German courts often adopt a far-reaching consistent interpretation on the basis of methods that are normally intended to accommodate a provision's implementing objective (primarily the historical and teleological interpretative method and perhaps also a systematic interpretation). It must then be presumed that the consistent interpretation was *not* the result of the requirement under EU law to interpret national law so far as possible in conformity with directives, but rather ensued from a 'contextualised application' of the traditional interpretative methods which often took into account new developments in the ECJ's case law regarding the correct interpretation of the concerned directive. Similar considerations apply when the relevant national provision is intended to be open to new developments in the law.

The judgments supporting supremacy of EU law tie in with, and are further supported by, the fact that the German superior courts' prevailing view is that Articles 288 TFEU and 4(3) TEU (and often reference is made to the full effectiveness of EU law as well), provide the legal basis for the duty of consistent interpretation.

It was seen that the prevailing view in German legal scholarship suggested that the duty of consistent interpretation should be approached analogous to *verfassungskonforme Auslegung* (an interpretation in conformity with the Constitution). However, this does not undermine the theory of supremacy of EU law. While the approach analogous to *verfassungskonforme Auslegung* seemed to support a more national law-oriented approach to the duty of consistent interpretation, it was seen that the *verfassungskonforme Auslegung* is itself often applied in a flexible manner and that it represents only a part of the case law (the analogy with *verfassungskonforme Auslegung* is primarily drawn by the BAG). Moreover, if a consistent interpretation is rejected in a case referring to *verfassungskonforme Auslegung,* the approach does not in general appear to be more or less restrictive than otherwise and such a rejection is normally adequately reasoned.

Since many aspects of the duty of consistent interpretation leave discretion to the national courts and the obligation is inherently not unlimited, a rejection of a consistent interpretation does not mean that there is automatically a violation of the duty of consistent interpretation. If it is based on good reasons, there is not a conflict with Articles 288 TFEU and 4(3) TEU, but the national courts simply apply, or perhaps one can even say 'further interpret', the scope of 'so far as possible'. Most of the German superior courts' case law rejecting a consistent interpretation (primarily on the basis of the provision's wording and legislative intent) can be qualified in this way. However, I also encountered four decisions that were difficult to reconcile with the requirements imposed by Articles 288 TFEU and 4(3) TEU. In the first two cases this was the result of a failure to duly take into account the requirements deriving from the presumption that the legislature intends to comply with the directive (see the ECJ's *Wagner Miret* and *Pfeiffer* judgments). Yet, it should be noted that – taking into account the arguments opposing a consistent interpretation – there was not a manifest violation of the duty of consistent interpretation and I am hesitant to conclude that these judgments support the theory of national constitutionalism. In the latter two cases the scope for *Auslegung* and *Rechtsfortbildung* was not sufficiently explored. Both judgments fit in with the theory of national constitutionalism, but I concluded that the theory of constitutional pluralism offers an even more adequate model in case a judgment clearly attempts – albeit unsuccessfully – to justify the rejection of a consistent interpretation by referring to the limits to the duty of consistent interpretation recognised by EU law (this description applied to one of the two judgments). It is noted that two of the four concerned judgments were delivered by the BFH. I showed that this court views the duty of consistent interpretation as being based primarily on the national legislature's implementing objective, thus pointing to a legal basis in national law. However, on the basis of the analysis in this chapter there is not sufficient support to conclude that the divergent view regarding the obligation's legal basis results in an application of the duty of consistent interpretation whereby conflicts are in principle resolved to the detriment of supremacy of EU law. The matter is also not entirely straightforward: the BFH has acknowledged the requirement to pursue a consistent interpretation by means of a *Rechtsfortbildung* and on two occasions departed from a traditional approach to interpretation to adopt a consistent interpretation. Nevertheless, it is clear that, compared to the other German superior courts, the grammatical interpretation is given more emphasis. But this is not necessarily a violation of the duty of consistent interpretation.

When the wording of a provision gives rise to an incompatibility with the directive, this does not yet mean that a consistent interpretation would be *contra legem* if the legislation has an implementing objective. If it can be established that the prevailing intention of the legislature had been to implement the directive, there is in principle scope to proceed to a *Rechtsfortbildung*. The possibility to adopt a consistent interpretation by means of a *Rechtsfortbildung* is then only subject to a set of specific limitations – which have, however, rarely been invoked – and this then constitutes the *contra legem* limitation. However, it was also seen that, if such an objective cannot be established, this potent argument cannot be applied and if the interpretation based on a grammatical interpretation is supported by one or more of the other interpretative criteria, there is a clear legislative intent opposing a consistent interpretation and the adoption of such an interpretation is in that situation considered as a violation of the *contra legem* limitation. For both scenarios it cannot be said that the German superior courts' interpretation of the *contra legem* limitation is incompatible with EU law.

A challenge to the theory of supremacy of EU law does, however, follow from the invocation of the national principle of legal certainty and the principle of legitimate expectations as a limit to *Auslegung*. Admittedly the BAG's judgment of 23 March 2006 (rejecting a consistent interpretation of the concept redundancy on account of the national principle of legitimate expectations, despite the acknowledgment that such an interpretation would be methodologically possible) cannot provide authority for this position as it was overturned by the BVerfG which annulled a similar judgment. The BVerfG's judgment itself can be seen as an example supporting the theory of constitutional pluralism. On the one hand, the BVerfG made it clear that the rejection of a consistent interpretation on the basis of the principle of legitimate expectations is not only a matter of national law, and that this requires consideration of the position under EU law. This spirit of cooperation regarding constitutional issues is reminiscent of theories on constitutional pluralism. But the BVerfG's attitude also reminded of a less positive feature of constitutional pluralism, namely the potential threat of constitutional conflict, as it did not clearly reject the possibility to apply the national principle of legitimate expectations (and I argued that such an application would probably be incompatible with EU law). The BVerfG's unwillingness to accept the unconditional supremacy of EU law is nothing new and is in line with the well known limitation requiring that EU law must respect the minimum constitutional protection as required under the German Constitution. The principle of legitimate expectations also reoccurred as a limitation to a *Rechtsfortbildung*, although it has never been applied by the German superior courts in that regard. Be that as it may, it is clear that it is considered possible to apply this limitation. The ECJ's *Klohn* judgment seems to recognise that, in principle, the protection of legitimate expectations may be relevant with regard to the limits to the duty of consistent interpretation. Accordingly, there is, in the future, scope for reconciliation if German courts intend to rely on this principle. They should then adopt a substantive test that is more strict than the one adopted in the BAG's judgment of 23 March 2006 (the substantive test applied in the context of *Rechtsfortbildung* could be a source of inspiration here, as it seems to be more in line with EU law requirements) and, importantly, they need to rely on the EU law principle of legitimate expectations instead of the national variant.

The German superior courts' perspective shows that 'so far as possible' is interpreted as going quite far. Even though the national interpretative rules confer a considerable degree of discretion, pushing their boundaries has regularly led to a conflict. If the duty of consistent interpretation interferes with national interpretative rules, such conflicts are predominantly resolved in favour of the former. In the paragraph discussing the German superior courts' approach to *Auslegung* I already concluded that this indeed provides the main position when it comes to the relationship between EU and national law, albeit that this is supplemented by a small number of judgments that reflect that the theories of national constitutionalism and constitutional pluralism also have a role to play. The paragraph discussing the approach to *Rechtsfortbildung* also produced an argument in favour of supremacy of EU law so that, on balance, this remains the centre of gravity for explaining the German superior courts' approach to a conflict between the duty of consistent interpretation and national interpretative rules.

CHAPTER 4
THE IRISH SUPERIOR COURTS' PERSPECTIVE

1. INTRODUCTION

The EU's first experiences with the common law came with the accession of Ireland and the United Kingdom in 1973. This also entailed the introduction of the 'common law method of legal reasoning' when the courts of these Member States applied EU law. In relation to the United Kingdom, it has been observed that this method – whose nature has been described as 'pragmatic and non-doctrinaire' and as containing a degree of flexibility and room for further development of the rules,[1] but also as being representative of 'strict textualism and judicial formalism'[2] – is better suited to the application of directly effective provisions of EU law than the duty of consistent interpretation. If the ECJ, as the competent court to determine this, provided that a provision of EU law has direct effect, the UK courts would act accordingly. It was observed that this method of legal reasoning is by nature not tailored to an appraisal of the extent to which a national provision can be made compatible with the directive while ensuring that the line between the judiciary's competences *vis-à-vis* the legislature is not crossed.[3] Nevertheless, even before the formal recognition of the duty of consistent interpretation in the ECJ's *Von Colson and Kamann* judgment,[4] the UK courts eagerly applied principles of interpretation presuming that it had not been Parliament's intention to make an enactment violating EU law obligations. This was done for pragmatic reasons to circumvent another, even more problematic and fundamental, issue under the UK legal system: the incompatibility of the traditional understanding of the constitutional principle of parliamentary sovereignty with the supremacy of EU

---

1 P.P. Craig, 'Report on the United Kingdom', in: A.-M. Slaughter, A. Stone Sweet and J.H.H. Weiler (Eds.), *The European Courts & National Courts – Doctrine and Jurisprudence* (Hart Publishing 1998), p. 218-9; R. Byrne and others, *Byrne and McCutcheon on the Irish Legal System* (Bloomsbury 2014), p. 636.

2 S.P. Donlan and R. Kennedy, 'A Flood of Light?: Comments on the Interpretation Act 2005' (2006/1) *Judicial Studies Institute Journal*, p. 95.

3 See Craig (n. 1), p. 218-9. The application of the remedy of direct effect is authorised by section 2(1) of the UK European Communities Act 1972 which, until the United Kingdom will leave the EU, makes the remedy a part of the UK legal system. Post-Brexit, rights recognised as having direct effect immediately before exit day are domesticated and continue to be available in national law (see section 4 of the European Union (Withdrawal) Act 2018.

4 Case 14/83 *Von Colson and Kamann*, ECLI:EU:C:1984:153.

law.[5] The details of this matter will not be addressed further here, but the threat to supremacy of EU law derived from the point that the most recent will of Parliament is decisive so that supremacy should be conferred upon legislation enacted after contradictory measures implementing a directive (implied repeal).[6] With the delivery of the ECJ's *Von Colson and Kamann* judgment, consistent interpretation became an obligation *qua* EU law, and there were concerns about the UK courts' approach. The clearest example of this is provided by the House of Lords' *Duke* judgment, which rejected a consistent interpretation, primarily because the national provisions had been adopted before the directive and therefore did not have an implementing objective.[7] The restrictive approach was criticised at the relevant time,[8] and rightly so, since it would significantly hamper the effectiveness of the duty of consistent interpretation. Nevertheless, before the ECJ's *Marleasing* judgment it was not free from doubt whether the duty of consistent interpretation also extended to provisions that did not have an implementing objective.[9] And once this further clarification was provided, the 'pragmatic and flexible' side of the common law method of legal reasoning resurfaced with the UK courts conforming their approach to the ECJ's case law.[10]

But it is now time to turn the discussion to Ireland, as this is the subject of the chapter. Arguably, as far as the domestic operation of EU law was concerned, the starting position was more favourable for the Irish legal system. Ireland did not have to reconcile a dominant constitutional principle such as parliamentary sovereignty with the supremacy of EU law; it has moved away from the traditional model of absolute parliamentary sovereignty adhered to in the United Kingdom, which is clear from the introduction of a system of judicial review, more particularly the courts' power to determine the validity of laws in light of the Constitution (Article 34(3)(2) of the Constitution).[11] But this does not mean that there was a natural fit between EU law and the Irish legal system. The difference with the United Kingdom is that Ireland decided to remove these obstacles *ex ante*. After Ireland decided that it wanted to accede to the EU, the Irish Constitution (hereinafter simply referred to as the 'Constitution') was amended through a referendum in order to ensure a smooth operation of EU law in the Irish legal order. One of the amendments

---

5 With regard to reconciliatory interpretations prior to the ECJ's *Von Colson and Kamann* judgment, see UK Court of Appeal 27 April 1978 *Shields v E Coomes (Holdings) Ltd* [1978] 1 WLR 1408, 1415; UK Court of Appeal 25 July 1979 *Macarthys Ltd v Smith* [1979] ICR 785, 789; House of Lords 22 April 1982 *Garland v British Rail Engineering Ltd* [1983] 2 AC 751, 771.

6 For detailed discussion see Craig (n. 1), p. 195 *et seq.*

7 House of Lords 11 February 1988 *Duke v Reliance Systems Ltd* [1988] AC 618, 638-9, 641.

8 A. Arnull, 'The Duke Case: An Unreliable Precedent' (1988/3) *Public Law*, p. 316-7.

9 Case C-106/89 *Marleasing*, ECLI:EU:C:1990:395, para. 8.

10 House of Lords 19 October 1995 *Webb v Emo Air Cargo (U.K.) Ltd (No 2)* [1995] 1 WLR 1454.

11 B. McMahon and F. Murphy, *European Community Law in Ireland* (Butterworths 1989), p. 264; L. Cahillane, *Drafting the Irish Free State Constitution* (Manchester University Press 2016), p. 173.

introduced a 'constitutional immunity clause', and the updated version of that provisions now reads, in Article 29(4)(6), that:

> 'No provision of this Constitution invalidates laws enacted, acts done or measures adopted by the State, before, on or after the entry into force of the Treaty of Lisbon, that are necessitated by the obligations of membership of the European Union (...), or prevents laws enacted, acts done or measures adopted by [the EU and its institutions; SWH] from having the force of law in this State'.

This provision is described by Barrett as the 'constitutional door' to Europe: it offered a 'shield of immunity' preventing, on the one hand, the otherwise unavoidable conflicts occurring between Irish law 'necessitated'[12] by membership of the EU and the Constitution and,[13] on the other, that EU measures would be deprived of their legal force in the Irish legal order. It seems that the Supreme Court's judgment in *Campus Oil Ltd v Minister for Industry and Energy* confirmed that the Constitution would normally not be invoked against the supremacy of EU law.[14] However, the question whether the same applies if EU law would require the setting aside of fundamental values protected under the Constitution, is more difficult to answer as the Supreme Court's judgment in *SPUC (Ireland) Ltd v Grogan* made clear.

> The proceedings concerned an injunction sought against the distribution of information regarding abortion services available abroad. The plaintiff invoked the fundamental right to life, and in the course of the proceedings before the Supreme Court the question arose whether this constitutionally guaranteed right violated the freedom to provide services, protected by the Treaties and therefore by what is now Article 29(4)(6) of the Constitution. It needs to be emphasised that at the moment that the Supreme Court pronounced its judgment, it was not yet known whether there actually was an incompatibility with EU law (ultimately, a constitutional clash was averted as the ECJ's judgment provided that in the circumstances of the case the activity was not sufficiently linked to an economic operator from another Member State and therefore outside the scope of the freedom to provide services,[15] and as a

---

12 The term 'necessitated' is essential for the scope of this provision. The Irish superior courts' case law has not yet provided a clear answer to how necessitated should be interpreted exactly, cf. High Court 2 October 1987 *Lawlor v Minister for Agriculture* [1990] 1 IR 356 at 377; High Court 14 April 1989 *Greene v Minister for Agriculture* [1990] 2 IR 17 at 25; High Court 12 October 1990 *Condon v Minister for Agriculture* [1993] Irish Journal of European Law 151 at 156. It seems to be clear, however, that it is not confined to the minimum of what is required by EU law, but extends to matters for which a sufficiently close link exists with the implementation of EU law.

13 In G. Barrett, 'The Evolving Door to Europe: Reflections on an Eventful Forty Years for Article 29.4 of the Irish Constitution' (2012/48) *Irish Jurist*, p. 139, the following constitutional provisions are identified: Article 6 (confining governmental powers to the organs of the Irish State); Article 15(2)(1) (vesting sole and exclusive law-making power in the Oireachtas); Article 28(2) (providing that the executive power of the State be exercised by or on the authority of the Government); Article 34(1) (requiring justice to be administered by judges appointed in the manner provided by the Constitution); and Article 34(3)(1) (providing for a High Court with full original jurisdiction).

14 Supreme Court 17 June 1983 *Campus Oil Ltd v Minister for Industry and Energy* [1983] IR 82 at 87.

15 Case C-159/90 *SPUC*, ECLI:EU:C:1991:378.

> result of an amendment of the Irish Constitution providing exceptions for the right to travel to another Member State and the dissemination of information regarding services lawfully available abroad[16]). In those circumstances Finlay C.J. considered that '[i]f and when a decision of the European Court of Justice rules that some aspect of European Community law affects the activities of the defendants impugned in this case, the consequence of that decision on these constitutionally guaranteed rights [i.e. the right to life of an unborn child; SWH] and their protection by the Courts will then fall to be considered by these Courts [note that the latter referred to the *Irish* courts as provided in the Constitution; SWH]'.[17] The other judgments delivered in this case also made it clear that, if necessary, the Supreme Court intended to uphold the Constitution against any incompatible rights claimed under EU law.[18]

It is useful to point out that Article 29(4)(6) of the Constitution only prevents a constitutional conflict whereas it is section 2 of the European Communities Act 1972 that provides for the incorporation of EU law into the Irish legal order and the supremacy of EU law (or, to again use a metaphor, the former provides a canopy for national measures, necessitated by membership, and EU measures, whereas the latter is the perch on which they stand[19]).[20] There is a caveat to this constellation. Phelan explains that it has as a consequence that there is no rule of Irish law preventing the possibility that the Oireachtas (the Irish Parliament) would explicitly legislate against EU law, thereby amending the European Communities Act 1972, which does not enjoy any kind of special protection under Irish law. Article 29(4)(6) of the Constitution could not be invoked to prevent this as it merely immunises EU law against the other existing constitutional provisions but *does not* apply to the situation where subsequent ordinary legislation explicitly rejects the supremacy of EU law stipulated in the European Communities Act 1972.[21]

So while it is clear that the general Irish legal framework has been very accommodating towards the operation of EU law in the national legal order and intended to structurally prevent a conflict with EU law, it is now necessary to examine to what extent this is also reflected in the Irish superior courts' (i.e. the High Court, Court of Appeal and the Supreme Court) perspective on the relationship between EU and national law under the duty of consistent interpretation.

---

16 See Article 40(3)(3) of the Constitution.

17 Supreme Court 19 December 1989 *SPUC (Ireland) Ltd v Grogan* [1990] 1 CMLR 689 at 699.

18 See further M. Cahill, 'Constitutional Exclusion Clauses, Article 29.4.6, and the Constitutional Reception of European Law' (2011/34) *Dublin University Law Journal*, p. 96-7. See also J. Sterck, 'The Nation's Own Genius: A European View of Irish Constitutional Identity' (2014/37) *Dublin University Law Journal*, p. 114.

19 High Court 12 February 1987 *Crotty v An Taoiseach* [1987] IR 713 at 758.

20 Barrett (n. 13), p. 132-3.

21 W. Phelan, 'Can Ireland Legislate Contrary to European Community Law?' (2008/4) *ELRev*, p. 539-47.

> The jurisdiction of the Irish superior courts was discussed in detail in the introductory part of this book. Here it is briefly recalled that the High Court has full original jurisdiction in criminal and civil matters. For the purposes of this research the former is not included. An appeal on a point of law can be made from the High Court to the Court of Appeal and subsequently to the Supreme Court.

Assuming that the description of the common law method of legal reasoning with regard to the United Kingdom bears some relevance to the Irish superior courts' approach to interpretation as well: is the latter also representative of strict textualism and judicial formalism, or is it rather the pragmatic and flexible side that prevails when they must apply the duty of consistent interpretation? I first examine on which legal basis the Irish superior courts proceed when they apply the duty of consistent interpretation. Secondly, the scope for, and limits to, a consistent interpretation from the perspective of the Irish interpretative rules is examined. In addition to this, and by way of an afterthought, I focus on the potential impact of the Interpretation Act 2005 and the ECJ's *Pupino* and *Adeneler* judgments for the application of the duty of consistent interpretation.

2. THE LEGAL BASIS FOR THE APPLICATION OF THE DUTY OF CONSISTENT INTERPRETATION

There are two reasons why the perspective on the legal basis for the duty of consistent interpretation is relevant. First, it is as such an argument in favour of a particular theory for the relationship between EU and national law. Secondly, it can be an indication for an approach to the duty of consistent interpretation that further supports, or challenges, a particular theory.

The High Court's judgment in *Murphy v An Bord Telecom* Éireann was the first occasion on which the duty of consistent interpretation was considered by an Irish superior court. The judgment hinted at a legal basis derived from either the supremacy of EU law or a presumption that the Oireachtas cannot have intended to legislate in a manner that would violate EU law obligations. The latter was viewed as a necessary corollary that national legislation is presumed to be constitutional unless it is shown to be otherwise.[22] In that regard it is again pointed out that national legislation explicitly contradicting EU law is not unconstitutional, so that it is not entirely clear why the presumption of compatibility with EU law obligations was viewed by the High Court as being the direct result of the presumption of constitutionality. As far as the reference to supremacy of EU law is concerned,

22 High Court 11 April 1988 *Murphy v An Bord Telecom* Éireann [1989] ILRM 53 at 59-60.

it must be mentioned that, while the Equal Treatment Directive[23] was initially relevant for the domestic proceedings, this changed after the ECJ's preliminary ruling in the case had made it clear that the matter could be resolved on the basis of (now) Article 157 TFEU (equal pay for men and women) only. It is submitted that, since the High Court's considerations regarding supremacy were thus delivered in the context of primary EU law, it cannot simply be assumed that the same view is taken in relation to directives. The same two points were discussed in the judgment of Barrett J. in *EPA v Harte Peat Ltd*, for which a directive provided the relevant EU legal framework. Barrett J. only hesitantly linked the duty of consistent interpretation to the supremacy of EU law. He seemed to be more in favour of premising the obligation on the interpretative rule that it is presumed that the Oireachtas intends to comply with its international legal obligations[24] – note that this is slightly different from the position adopted in *Murphy v An Bord Telecom* Éireann, which characterised the presumption as a corollary of the presumption of constitutionality.

However, it is important to point out that the above described views regarding the legal basis for the duty of consistent interpretation have not been confirmed in other Irish case law. In the Supreme Court's judgment in *Nathan v Bailey Gibson Ltd*, Hamilton C.J., referring to the ECJ's *Von Colson and Kamann* and *Marleasing* judgments and the legal basis stated therein, provided the following commonly expressed view:

> '(...) national or domestic courts in interpreting a provision of national law designed to implement the provisions of a directive, should interpret their national law in the light of the wording and the purpose of the directive in order to achieve the result envisaged by the directive'.[25]

There is no explicit consideration of what must be regarded as the legal basis but the statement contained two indications in this regard. First, it is possible to interpret 'national law designed to implement the provisions of a directive' as a reference to the legislation's implementing objective providing the legal basis. Secondly, the reference to the ECJ's *Von Colson and Kamann* and *Marleasing* judgments can be interpreted as endorsing the view whereby Articles 288 TFEU and 4(3) TEU provide the relevant legal basis. Moreover, the sentence 'in order to achieve the result envisaged by the directive' also copies the text of those judgments and

23 Council Directive 76/207/EEC of 9 February 1976 on the implementation of the principle of equal treatment for men and women as regards access to employment, vocational training and promotion, and working conditions, *OJ* 1976, L39/40.

24 High Court 30 May 2014 *EPA v Harte Peat Ltd* [2015] 1 IR 462 at para. 12.

25 Supreme Court 29 February 1996 *Nathan v Bailey Gibson Ltd* [1998] 2 IR 162 at 174. See further Supreme Court 4 February 1998 *Telecom* Éireann *v O'Grady* [1998] 3 IR 432 at 442; High Court 16 December 1999 *Coastal Line Container Terminal Ltd v Services Industrial Professional Technical Union* [2000] 1 IR 549 at 559.

confirms in particular the relevance of Article 288 TFEU as a legal basis for the application of the duty of consistent interpretation.

Some of the subsequent case law emphasised the objective of aligning an interpretation with the national legislature's intention as the rationale to apply the duty of consistent interpretation. In the High Court's judgment in *Sandymount and Merrion Residents Association v An Bord Pleanála*, for example, Charleton J. held that '[w]here a national measure is passed in order to give effect to an obligation of the State which arises from European law, such national legislation must be construed so as to conform to that legislative purpose'. But also here the ECJ's *Marleasing* judgment was referred to, and the requirement to achieve the result pursued by the directive was stated.[26] The High Court judgments in *Hanrahan Farms Ltd v EPA* and *EPA v Neiphin Trading Ltd* both unambiguously provided that the duty of loyal cooperation must be understood as underpinning the Irish courts' duty of consistent interpretation.[27] Yet, the latter judgment also pointed out that in the majority of cases, the duty of consistent interpretation was applied by the Irish courts in relation to implementing legislation, and that in those circumstances it can be presumed that the national legislature's intentions ran parallel to those of the European legislature, which made it completely legitimate to apply the duty of consistent interpretation in the context of a teleological approach to the national provisions.[28]

Having considered the above case law – which either explicitly or more implicitly addressed the question what the legal basis is for the duty of consistent interpretation – the most satisfactory point of view is in my opinion that the Irish superior courts recognise that the duty of consistent interpretation has its legal basis in EU law, more specifically Articles 288 TFEU and 4(3) TEU while, in as far as the provisions were adopted by the legislature to implement the directive, a further reason to apply the obligation is found in the traditional teleological approach to interpretation. So when the Irish courts interpret implementing provisions, the legislature's intentions provide an 'extra' argument, but it would be wrong to hold that the Irish superior courts only proceed to a consistent interpretation for that reason. If this were otherwise, it cannot be explained why the Irish superior courts have consistently acknowledged the requirement to also apply the duty of consistent interpretation to legislation that does not have an implementing objective.[29] Admittedly, the Irish

26 High Court 19 November 2013 *Sandymount and Merrion Residents Association v An Bord Pleanála* [2013] 11 JIC 1904 at para. 4.4.

27 High Court 21 July 2005 *Hanrahan Farms Ltd v EPA* [2012] 3 IR 417 at para. 39; High Court 3 March 2011 *EPA v Neiphin Trading Ltd* [2011] 2 IR 575 at para. 64.

28 High Court 3 March 2011 *EPA v Neiphin Trading Ltd* [2011] 2 IR 575 at para. 71.

29 Supreme Court 21 February 2003 *O'Connell v EPA* [2003] 1 IR 530 at 555; High Court 21 July 2005 *Hanrahan Farms Ltd v EPA* [2012] 3 IR 417 at para. 39; High Court 11 October 2010 *EMI Records (Ireland) Ltd v UPC Communications Ireland Ltd* [2010] IEHC 377; High Court 30 May 2014 *EPA v Harte Peat Ltd* [2015] 1 IR 462 at para. 17.

superior courts do not consequently state both Articles 288 TFEU and 4(3) TEU (ideally also with a reference to the full effectiveness of EU law) as the legal basis, but neither does the ECJ.[30] Another point that must be briefly addressed here is that, technically, the provisions referred to only enter the Irish legal order through section 2 of the European Communities Act 1972. However, similar to what was observed in relation to the German position regarding the legal basis for the duty of consistent interpretation, it can be said that, once EU law has passed through this conduit, its applicability and supremacy are no longer called into question and the Irish courts directly refer to the legal basis in EU law.[31]

Since the Irish courts recognise the legal basis for the duty of consistent interpretation provided by EU law, there seems to be a willingness to accept the obligation's binding nature and autonomous position under EU law – presumably also as far as more intervening aspects of that obligation are concerned. Their perspective on the legal basis is therefore in line with the theory of supremacy of EU law.

3. THE SCOPE FOR, AND LIMITS TO, A CONSISTENT INTERPRETATION FROM THE PERSPECTIVE OF THE IRISH SUPERIOR COURTS

On the one hand, the duty of consistent interpretation was characterised as an interpretative rule. On the other hand, the existing theories on the relationship between EU and national law require that there is a conflict or, in the context of constitutional pluralism, perhaps a potential or looming conflict. If the two are combined, this means that a conflict on the level of interpretative rules needs to be identified for the existing theories to come into play. The existence of a conflict can be the result of either an incompatibility with the obligation to interpret national law so far as possible, or the national interpretative rules. The scope and meaning of the former were already discussed in chapter 2. In this chapter I discuss the latter to acquire a better understanding of the Irish superior courts' traditional approach to interpretation (i.e. the approach adopted in a purely internal context). I then proceed to the main part of this paragraph which examines when a conflict of interpretative rules arises, how the Irish courts resolve such a conflict, and which

30 See, for example, Case C-12/08 *Mono Car Styling*, ECLI:EU:C:2009:466, para. 60; Case C-53/10 *Mücksch*, ECLI:EU:C:2011:585, para. 32.

31 Cf. the UK European Communities Act 1972 which in section 2(4) makes special provision for a legal basis to apply the duty of consistent interpretation. The judgment in UK Supreme Court 30 May 2012 *Assange v Swedish Prosecution Authority* [2012] 2 AC 471 demonstrates the kind of difficulties to which this approach can give rise as it was concluded that section 2(4) of the Act could not be applied to EU framework decisions. See further S. Haket, 'Coherence in the Application of the Duty of Consistent Interpretation in EU Law' (2015/2) *Review of European Administrative Law*, p. 229. A similar provision is not found in the Irish pendant of the law.

theory most adequately explains the adopted solution. Before proceeding to this analysis, it is first pointed out, by way of example, that there is not a conflict if a consistent interpretation turns out to be identical to the interpretation that follows from a traditional approach to interpretation:

> What is a pig? More particularly, does that term also include weaners and finishers?[32] That was the question that the High Court had to determine in *Maher v An Bord Pleanála.* A purposive interpretation of the national provisions mandated the conclusion that the weaners and finishers also qualified as pigs, so that they had to be included for the determination whether certain environmental requirements applied. That outcome was in particular confirmed if the objective of the directive (pollution or nuisances are best prevented at their source), which the national provisions implemented, was taken into account.[33]
>
> The judgment in *Hanrahan Farms Ltd v EPA* concerned, among others, the question whether the respondent had a power to impose a condition of de-stocking of animal numbers for controlling pollution. The High Court adopted the position that this power was already conferred upon the respondent – either explicitly or implicitly – on the basis of the national provisions as such. However, it was added that, even if this would not have been correct (which was explicitly not the position taken by the High Court), it would have been possible to arrive at the same result through a consistent interpretation (without interfering with national interpretative rules).[34]

But also if the national courts go a little bit further, and even if the adopted consistent interpretation entailed an adaptation of a traditional interpretation, this does not automatically mean that there was a conflict. While the identification of a conflict presupposes some kind of adaptation, this does not hold true the other way around. Hence, it is necessary to acquire a precise understanding of the interpretative scope, more specifically the interpretative discretion, that is available in a traditional context.

3.1. THE TRADITIONAL APPROACH TO INTERPRETATION

The Irish superior courts' 'traditional approach to interpretation' is aimed at the identification of the legislature's intention.[35] This points to the principle constraint placed on the courts for the approach to interpretation, namely that they should not perform legislative functions, a role which, under the Constitution, is reserved

32 Young pigs recently separated from the sow and grower pigs over 70 kg respectively.
33 High Court 7 May 1999 *Maher v An Bord Pleanála* [1999] 2 ILRM 198.
34 High Court 21 July 2005 *Hanrahan Farms Ltd v EPA* [2012] 3 IR 417 at paras. 36-40.
35 See, for example, High Court 6 May 1997 *Ni Eili v EPA* [1997] 2 ILRM 458; High Court 2 March 2012 *Dowling v Minister for Finance* [2012] IEHC 89 at para. 22.

to the Oireachtas.[36] It is therefore ultimately a constitutional limitation.[37] The key question is how, from the perspective of the Irish superior courts, this is to be achieved. Traditionally, from the perspective of the rules at common law, the view had always been that the literal approach best reflects the legislature's intention. Arguably, this has not changed with the introduction of the Interpretation Act 2005, which introduced a number of rules that the Irish courts must heed when interpreting the law. Nevertheless, this act clarified that the courts are permitted, under certain circumstances, to apply schematic or teleological criteria (these criteria resemble a purposive approach, which is the term that I will use henceforth). However, the modalities for proceeding to the latter may have had a negative impact on the scope to adopt a consistent interpretation (this matter is discussed in detail in subparagraph 3.3.3).

3.1.1. Conventional Approach under the Rules at Common Law

Initially, the only available guidance for the approach to interpretation was provided by the rules at common law. Under the rules at common law, the Irish courts adhere to the literal approach. This means that if a provision's wording is clear and unambiguous, it has to be applied in accordance with its ordinary meaning (the plain meaning rule).[38] Does this mean that other interpretative criteria become redundant in that situation?[39] It is clear that, under the rules at common law, a departure from the literal approach requires that the provision would otherwise have a meaning that would be ambiguous or absurd.[40] Whether a purposive approach can be used to identify a latent ambiguity or absurdity is subject to different views.[41] The more narrow approach contends that the courts must follow a two staged approach whereby the first step is a literal interpretation and only if this produces an ambiguity or absurdity do the courts move on to apply

36 The doctrine of separation of powers is laid down in Article 15(2) of the Constitution. When concluding that it was not possible to adopt the desired consistent interpretation, the High Court's judgment of 11 October 2010 in *EMI Records (Ireland) Ltd v UPC Communications Ireland Ltd* [2010] IEHC 377 referred (at para. 138) to the doctrine of separation of powers. See also D. Dodd, *Statutory Interpretation in Ireland* (Tottel Publishing 2008), p. 281 *et seq*; S. O'Reilly, 'The Private Enforcement of European Community Laws in the Irish Superior Courts' (2009/31) *Dublin University Law Journal*, p. 343; Byrne and others (n. 1), p. 633.

37 See also C. Curran and E. Daly, 'Reappraising the Constitutional Justification for Intentionalism and Literalism in Statutory Interpretation (2013/36) *Dublin University Law Journal*, p. 155: '[i]t is a truism that principles of statutory interpretation are derivative of constitutional theory'.

38 Supreme Court 26 May 1993 *Howard v Commissioners of Public Works* [1994] 1 IR 101 at 151, 162. See further Dodd (n. 36), p. 40; Curran and Daly (n. 37), p. 157.

39 To be sure, as a result of the submissions made by the parties to the proceedings, or otherwise, judges will obviously be aware of any arguments that potentially undermine an apparently clear literal interpretation. But under the far-reaching interpretation of the plain meaning rule, the point seems to be that this cannot be of any relevance if the rule applies.

40 High Court 6 October 2008 *Monahan v Legal Aid Board* [2009] 3 IR 458.

41 See also Law Reform Commission, *Report on Statutory Drafting and Interpretation: Plain Language and the Law* (2000), p. 10-6.

a purposive approach.[42] While I agree that it is uncontroversial that ambiguity or absurdity can derive from a literal interpretation, and that there may be some case law in support of the strict two staged approach,[43] there is also case law in which a purposive approach was taken into account for the determination whether a literal interpretation accurately reflected the legislature's intention. The judgment in *The People (Attorney General) v Kennedy* (per Black J.) contains the most eloquent formulation of the concerned point: '[a] small section of a picture, if looked at close-up, may indicate something quite clearly; but when one stands back and views the whole canvas, the close-up view of the small section is often found to have given a wholly wrong view of what it really represented'.[44] There is of course a paradox here: 'literal meaning is supposed to convey legislative intent unless, in context, it appears contrary to the legislature's aims – yet this requires an appraisal of legislative aims antecedent to the statute's literal meaning'.[45] On balance, my impression is that there will be situations in which courts are more but also situations in which they are less likely to engage with more purposive criteria; the prevailing view seems to be that it may *sometimes* be appropriate to do so.[46]

Nevertheless, the threshold for engaging with purposive criteria is quite high: it is not sufficient that a literal interpretation would produce an unjust or anomalous consequence.[47] The courts have to be satisfied that the outcome would be so absurd or ambiguous that it must be presumed that it cannot have been the Oireachtas's intention.[48] For the appraisal whether that is the case, a number of factors can be relevant, such as the degree of clarity of the text and the degree to which a particular

42 O'Reilly (n. 36), p. 343-4.

43 McGuinness J.'s considerations in Supreme Court 11 April 2002 *Maguire v Ardagh* [2002] 1 IR 385 at 640-1, could be interpreted in that way. She endorsed the view that a provision's words must be looked at first and that if they are clear, it is not appropriate to look any further. However, sometimes considerations can be misconceiving. For example, in High Court 2 March 2012 *Dowling v Minister for Finance* [2012] IEHC 89 at paras. 21-6, it was first emphasised that if a provision is clear on a literal interpretation, that is the meaning that must be adopted and courts should look no further. However, if one examines the actual approach of the court, it becomes clear that the approach to interpretation included contextual and purposive arguments.

44 Adding that the same applies to a single word or phrase, and that consideration of the context and other provisions is required, Supreme Court 31 January 1946 *The People (Attorney General) v Kennedy* [1946] IR 517 at 536. See also Supreme Court 27 July 1970 *East Donegal Co-op Livestock Mart Ltd v Attorney General* [1970] 1 IR 317 at 341. The judgment in High Court 26 October 2012 *Minister for Justice and Equality v Doyle (No 2)* [2012] IEHC 451 seemed to imply that, even if a provision's wording is found to be plain and unambiguous, a certain scope to apply purposive criteria remains. The Supreme Court has also made it clear that, while a literal rule is dominant, it is only to be enforced if it is not undermined by a clear indication from the Act as a whole that the legislature intended something else, see Supreme Court 1 April 1971 *Rahill v Brady* [1971] IR 69 at 86; Supreme Court 11 July 2001 *Crilly v T & J Farrington Ltd* [2001] 3 IR 251 at 295-6.

45 Curran and Daly (n. 37), p. 162.

46 See also Dodd (n. 36), p. 41.

47 High Court 4 November 1994 *Mulcahy v Minister for the Marine*, not reported.

48 Byrne and others (n. 1), p. 650.

result cannot be presumed to have been intended,[49] as well as the extent to which a departure from the text is necessitated.[50] As regards the latter: there is well established case law that, regardless of the degree of ambiguity or absurdity, courts may in any event not '(...) rewrite a section, supplement provisions, substitute a legislative provision for another provision with a different context or do violence to the language or text of an enactment'.[51] Courts are also not permitted to enter into policy considerations.[52] So whether they are used to circumscribe room for further interpretation *ex ante*, or applied *ex post* to scrutinise a particular interpretation, grammatical criteria play a dominant role.

A final factor that needs to be pointed out is the presumption of constitutionality. Applying the presumption, courts can attribute more weight to factors favouring an interpretation in conformity with the Constitution. However, if the provision is absolutely clear on a literal interpretation, courts cannot but conclude that an interpretation in conformity with the constitution is not possible and must make a declaration of unconstitutionality.[53]

It is submitted that, if it is taken into account that the application of the above criteria is inevitably coupled with a degree of subjectivity, as well as the divergent authorities regarding the scope to depart from the literal approach, there is, at least *de facto, some* flexibility in the use of the literal and purposive criteria[54] – albeit that the former is clearly dominant. The subordinate character also follows from a feature that has not yet been mentioned: if it is permitted to apply purposive criteria, the approach is nevertheless rather limited and rarely goes beyond arguments that are derived from the legislation itself. Irish courts will typically look at matters such as the structure of the legislation of which the relevant provision is a part, related provisions, but also the long title of the legislation, which often provides information regarding the legislation's background, purpose and scope. The legislature's intention is not to be ascertained on the basis of Oireachtas debates,[55]

---

49 Which also requires that the legislature's intention is sufficiently clear. In the judgment in Supreme Court 15 May 1997 *Re The Employment Equality Bill 1996* [1997] 2 IR 321 at 363, Hamilton C.J. discussed the possibility to depart from a literal interpretation which would create an absurdity, emphasising the requirement that the intention of the legislature is plain on the construction of the legislation as a whole. The Supreme Court's judgment of 29 July 1998 in *DPP (Ivers) v Murphy* [1999] 1 IR 98 at 111, rejected a literal interpretation since this would have defeated the explicit purpose of the provision.

50 See also Dodd (n. 36), p. 188.

51 Ibid, p. 317-8, with references to case law.

52 Supreme Court 26 May 1993 *Howard v Commissioners of Public Works* [1994] 1 IR 101 at 125. Also, to some extent, Supreme Court 7 July 1988 *McGrath v McDermott* [1988] IR 258 at 277.

53 A useful summary of the approach to the presumption of constitutionality is provided in Dodd (n. 36), p. 304.

54 In Byrne and others (n. 1), p. 636 it is argued that the national interpretative rules must be viewed as general guidelines, describing different roads which can legitimately be taken by the courts.

55 Supreme Court 11 July 2001 *Crilly v T & J Farrington Ltd* [2001] 3 IR 251. An important reason to exclude these materials is that it is only the intention expressed by the legislature in the legislation

i.e. the parliamentary history, which must be distinguished from legislative history (explanatory memoranda, the original bill, amendments; note that the term legislative history is not used here to describe the historical evolution of a rule from the perspective of previous versions), which may in principle be taken into account, albeit that it mostly has a modest, auxiliary, role.

3.1.2. The Interpretation Act 2005

Importantly, there has been a legislative intervention in the form of the Interpretation Act 2005. The Interpretation Act 2005 was inspired by a report published by the Law Reform Commission. Interestingly, one of the Commission's observations concerned the influence of EU law on the approach to interpretation:

> '(...) the strict literal approach is very much a creature with a common law pedigree. A major factor in the move towards a more purposive approach has been the increasingly important interface between domestic and European Union law'.[56] The Commission noticed that this style of approach had now also become more accepted in cases with a purely internal context.[57] The Commission's recommendations with regard to the approach to interpretation were to a large extent influenced by the following passage of the judgment in *Mulcahy v Minister for the Marine* (which it considered to be a good example of the more purposive approach): '[w]hile the Court is not, in the absence of a constitutional challenge, entitled to do violence to the plain language of an enactment in order to avoid an unjust or anomalous consequence, that does not preclude the Court from departing from the literal construction of an enactment and adopting in its place a teleological or purposive approach, if that would more faithfully reflect the true legislative intention gathered from the Act as a whole'.[58]

When the Oireachtas introduced section 5 of the Interpretation Act 2005, addressing the approach to interpretation, it was clear that the literal rule remained the dominant interpretative method, but it was also clarified that it was permitted to apply a purposive approach if a literal interpretation failed to reflect the plain intention of the Oireachtas, which had to be ascertained on the basis of the act as a whole. Admittedly, an exception to the literal approach where it would fail to

itself that is authoritative, and not individual statements expressed during parliamentary debates. It is thus a separation of powers issue. The other main reason relates to rule of law concerns: the citizen must know in advance what legal consequences flow from a particular course of action, for which he should be able to rely on the wording of the legislation as such and cannot be expected to examine other sources. Interestingly, Irish courts go less far than the UK courts. For the latter see S. Vogenauer, 'A Retreat From *Pepper* v *Hart*? A Reply to Lord Steyn' (2005/4) *OJLS*, p. 634 *et seq*, commenting on the House of Lords' landmark judgment of 26 November 1992 in *Pepper v Hart* [1993] AC 593.

56 Law Reform Commission (n. 41), p. 18.

57 Ibid.

58 High Court 4 November 1994 *Mulcahy v Minister for the Marine*, not reported.

reflect the plain intention of the Oireachtas was not a complete novelty,[59] but it was not yet commonplace. Section 5 provides that:

> '(1) In construing a provision of any Act (other than a provision that relates to the imposition of a penal or other sanction) –
>
> (a) that is obscure or ambiguous, or
>
> (b) that on a literal interpretation would be absurd or would fail to reflect the plain intention of –
>
> (i) in the case of an Act to which paragraph (a) of the definition of "Act" in section 2(1) relates, the Oireachtas, or
>
> (ii) in the case of an Act to which paragraph (b) of that definition relates, the parliament concerned,
>
> the provision shall be given a construction that reflects the plain intention of the Oireachtas or parliament concerned, as the case may be, where that intention can be ascertained from the Act as a whole.
>
> (2) [the same approach is prescribed for statutory instruments; SWH]'.

The requirement that the intention must be sufficiently plain and the direction that a purposive approach allows the courts to look at the Act as a whole, make it clear that section 5 reflects a 'moderate purposive approach'. On three points, section 5 raises some further questions. First, the first paragraph stipulates that the restriction of the scope applies for provisions that relate to the imposition of a penal or other sanction. If this is interpreted broadly, also provisions concerning procedure, jurisdiction or evidence are covered (as provisions relating to such sanctions).[60] However, the reference to sanctions specifically, makes it clear that areas such as criminal law, but also taxation law, for which it could be argued that the legality principle should set stricter conditions regarding the clarity with which obligations are stipulated in the law, are not as such subject to stricter interpretative rules but only in as far as sanctions are actually being imposed. For taxation law, this position is clearly confirmed by the Supreme Court's judgment in *O'Flynn Construction Ltd v Revenue Commissioners*.[61] Additionally, the scope of 'other sanctions' is not clear to me. From the perspective of Irish law, financial penalties which are either prosecuted, for example by the Environmental Protection Agency for offences under environmental law, or sometimes even directly imposed, for example by the Revenue Commissioners, meet the key condition that distinguishes criminal from civil actions, namely that it is intended to punish the offender.[62] If this is

---

59 Supreme Court 4 February 1998 *Telecom* Éireann *v O'Grady* [1998] 3 IR 432 at 450.

60 Dodd (n. 36), p. 264.

61 Supreme Court 14 December 2011 *O'Flynn Construction Ltd v Revenue Commissioners* [2011] IESC 47 at paras. 69-70. See also High Court 6 July 2016 *Revenue Commissioners v Canada Life Ltd* [2016] IEHC 499 at para. 6. Cf. the earlier position adopted in Supreme Court 4 December 1981 *Inspector of Taxes v Kiernan* [1981] IR 117.

62 Byrne and others (n. 1), p. 278. See also their discussion of enforcement by regulators, where they characterise the imposition of a fine by such regulators as belonging to the sphere of criminal sanctions (p. 457).

also viewed as belonging to the sphere of criminal sanctions, it may be asked what meaning must be ascribed to 'other sanctions'.

Secondly, it could be argued that section 5 only tells the courts when they can proceed to a more purposive approach, but that it does not restrict the courts' interpretative discretion when they consider that a provision is entirely unambiguous. Are they at liberty to decide that they are then simply to give effect to the clear meaning of the text? In my opinion it can be derived from the Law Reform Commission's suggestions leading up to the Interpretation Act 2005 that it had been the intention to provide *more* room to apply a purposive approach, also if the text is clear on a literal reading. Interestingly, the High Court has considered the correct approach under the Interpretation Act 2005 if it is found that the provision's text is unambiguous, pointing out that:

> '[w]here a provision is obscure, ambiguous, or a literal interpretation would be absurd, or would fail to reflect the plain intention of the Oireachtas, that intention should be ascertained from the Act itself, in order to give effect to the purpose of the legislature; s. 5 of the Interpretation Act 2005. If the meaning of the text is, however, unambiguous, the task of the court is to give effect to that literal meaning'.[63]

This seems to contradict the position that I adopted on account of the rationale behind the introduction of section 5. However, it must be noted that the excerpt from the High Court's judgment was immediately preceded by the observation that the relevant provision must be construed within its context. Also, it was followed by the consideration that courts are not to enter into policy considerations and '[e]ven though a deviation from the plain meaning expressed may be desirable, the court has no authority to pursue any course which would involve rewriting the text', which was viewed as being incompatible with the principle of separation of powers. If these two further statements are considered, the following position emerges: notwithstanding an apparently clear literal meaning, this must be viewed in its context, and an absolute prohibition to depart from an unambiguous meaning primarily concerns cases where there would be such a manifest violation of the text that the judge transgresses his own competences. In essence, the approach then largely resembles the above identified position under the rules at common law whereby it may sometimes be permitted to depart from the literal approach while one of the aspects that needs to be taken into account for this determination is that, regardless of the degree of ambiguity or absurdity, the gap that must be bridged grammatically may sometimes simply be too large.

---

63 High Court 11 October 2010 *EMI Records (Ireland) Ltd v UPC Communications Ireland Ltd* [2010] IEHC 377 at para. 96. Also, in High Court 2 March 2012 *Dowling v Minister for Finance* [2012] IEHC 89 at para. 22, it is considered that section 5 of the Interpretation Act 2005 provides relevant guidance '[i]n circumstances where the literal approach is not capable by itself of resolving all doubts as to the interpretation and meaning of a statute (...)'.

Thirdly, it is also less clear whether section 5 overrides interpretative rules at common law that are not expressly discussed. On the one hand, the provision seemed to have been intended to clarify and supplement, instead of supplant, the rules at common law.[64] On the other hand, the direction to look at the Act as a whole for the purposive approach, seemingly reinforces an objective approach and excludes the use of parliamentary history, but perhaps also legislative history.[65] Yet, the provision's silence could also be interpreted to mean that the legislature wanted to leave it to the courts to further develop these aspects – and, as I explained above, the current position under the rules at common law seems to be more nuanced. In other words, on such a view, section 5 only makes explicit what the courts may do, and one has to be careful in drawing conclusions from that as to what the courts may not do.[66] This certainly seems true for a number of presumptions and aids that operated under the rules at common law, such as the aforementioned presumption of constitutionality.[67] Subparagraph 3.3.3 examines in a more detailed way to what extent the introduction of the Interpretation Act 2005 has perhaps brought changes to the approach of the Irish superior courts to the duty of consistent interpretation.

3.2. A SHIFT TO A PURPOSIVE APPROACH IN CONFORMITY WITH THE DIRECTIVE

The judgment of Edwards J. in *EPA v Neiphin Trading Ltd* mentioned a fundamental development in the Irish courts' approach to the duty of consistent interpretation. It was pointed out that the Irish courts face a dual, now and then, conflicting task. They have to interpret national law in accordance with well established traditional interpretative rules and, in as far as the duty of consistent interpretation applies, they simultaneously have to do so with due regard to that obligation. So while, as seen in the introduction to this paragraph, a literal interpretation is normally the dominant approach used by the Irish courts, Edwards J. considered that, particularly in situations where national law was intended to implement the directive, a '*de facto* shift in approach' could be witnessed: '[i]n such cases the Irish courts began to adopt a purposive or teleological approach to interpreting national implementing legislation, notwithstanding any clear literal meaning and/or the absence of any ambiguity or absurdity'.[68] He subsequently referred to a large

64 Law Reform Commission (n. 41), p. 7.

65 High Court 23 November 2006 *BUPA Ireland Ltd v Health Insurance Authority* [2006] IEHC 431 at para. 82; High Court 6 October 2008 *Monahan v Legal Aid Board* [2009] 3 IR 458. See also Dodd (n. 36), p. 235, 260.

66 The High Court's judgment of 12 May 2016, i.e. after the introduction of the Interpretation Act 2005, in *KRA v Minister for Justice and Equality* [2016] IEHC 289 at para. 35, showed that the court was prepared to look at legislative history, albeit that it was concluded that this did not provide the guidance the court was looking for.

67 Dodd (n. 36), p. 263.

68 High Court 3 March 2011 *EPA v Neiphin Trading Ltd* [2011] 2 IR 575 at para. 67.

number of decisions from the Irish superior courts, arguing that this is now a well established point in the Irish courts' jurisprudence. His views also dovetail with the developments identified in the Law Reform Commission's report.

In order to better understand this shift in approach, the High Court's judgment in *Murphy v An Bord Telecom* Éireann must be looked at. This judgment provided the first occasion on which an Irish superior court had to deal with the question of the relationship between the duty of consistent interpretation and national interpretative rules. Proceedings were brought by Mary Murphy and a number of other women against their employer, the Irish Telecommunications Board. The appellants invoked section 2 of the Anti-Discrimination (Pay) Act 1974, which provided that if male and female employees are engaged in 'like work', they must receive the same rate of pay. It was clear that the work of the female employees was actually superior in nature to that of the specified male employee but, since it was not possible to claim pay reflecting this superiority, the aim was to at least partly remove the injustice to which they were subject. To achieve this, it had to be established that the female employees were engaged in like work which, according to section 3(c) of the Act, required that the work be of equal value in terms of the demands it makes. Initially, Keane J., adopting a traditional approach, considered that:

> '[t]he words used in a statute must be construed in their ordinary and natural meaning. So construed, there is no ambiguity in the expression "equal in value" and it cannot apply to the circumstances in the present case'. Keane J. also cited, among others, the following passage of Henchy J.'s judgment in *DPP v Flanagan*, '(...) the province of the courts in interpreting a statute is not to divine what intention parliament had when passing the particular statute but, by the application of the relevant canons of interpretation, to ascertain what intention is evinced by the actual statutory words used'. The adoption of a purposive approach was explicitly rejected as inappropriate since the legislature could have availed himself of other words but, intentionally or by an oversight, had not done so. Since there was no ambiguity in the provision's wording, it was not possible to rely on an interpretation in conformity with the provisions of EU law that the appellants had invoked in their support.[69]

This clear rejection of a consistent interpretation limited the scope of that obligation to a finding of any ambiguity following the traditional approach to interpretation which, according to Keane J., entailed that such ambiguity must follow from the text of the provision itself.[70] But it was also observed that national law might be in violation of Article 157 TFEU and the Equal Treatment Directive and preliminary questions were referred to the ECJ. After the preliminary ruling

69 High Court 4 March 1986 *Murphy v An Bord Telecom* Éireann [1986] ILRM 483 at 486-7, citing Supreme Court 19 January 1979 *DPP v Flanagan* [1979] IR 265 at 282.

70 McMahon and Murphy (n. 11), p. 289.

stated the obvious point that there was an *a fortiori* example of discrimination in the sense of Article 157 TFEU if the female employees are paid less for work of superior value,[71] Keane J. had the unenviable task of either establishing the national provision's incompatibility with Article 157 TFEU (the matter could now be resolved without recourse to the directive), or to reverse his earlier position regarding the possibility to adopt a consistent interpretation. He opted for the second alternative. It was emphasised that on the basis of a traditional approach to interpretation, the relevant provision of national law could not be made compatible with EU law. Yet, a consistent interpretation needed to be adopted to guarantee the supremacy of EU law and the efficacy of Article 157 TFEU. Keane J. explicitly came back to his previous judgment, explaining that it had been misleading in as far as it was asserted that only a literal interpretation was possible.[72] It is submitted that, while the judgment making a reference for a preliminary ruling reflected the strict textualist and formalist side of the common law method of legal reasoning, the follow-up judgment showed its pragmatic and flexible side by permitting structural changes to the interpretative framework as such.

The more purposive approach to interpretation applied in the follow-up judgment in *Murphy v An Bord Telecom* Éireann was also followed in the High Court judgment in *Lawlor v Minister for Agriculture*, where national law was interpreted in accordance with an EU law regulation (note that when I refer in this chapter to 'regulation' without the addition of 'EU law', this refers to a form of Irish secondary law and not EU law). There, some further light was shed on what motivated the court to follow a more purposive approach. Referring to a paper by Kutscher (who was at the time of its delivery the president of the ECJ) on the interpretative methods applied by the ECJ, it was provided that the same approach needed to be adopted by national courts interpreting the EU law regulation, but also in relation to national law where it concerns the application of EU law regulations.[73] The same principle was reiterated in a subsequent judgment, and on that occasion not only mentioned in relation to EU law regulations, with which the particular case was concerned, but the court indicated that the same applied in relation to directives.[74]

This subparagraph further examines the consequences which the identified shift in approach had for the application of the duty of consistent interpretation. This can be divided into two parts. First, it is asked whether the shift in approach leading to a more purposive approach also means that the duty of consistent interpretation is structurally prioritised. Secondly, taking as a starting point that the shift in approach has, similar to the judgment in *Murphy v An Bord Telecom*

71 Case 157/86 *Murphy*, ECLI:EU:C:1988:62 at para. 6 *et seq.*
72 High Court 11 April 1988 *Murphy v An Bord Telecom* Éireann [1989] ILRM 53 at 59, 61.
73 High Court 2 October 1987 *Lawlor v Minister for Agriculture* [1990] IR 356 at 375.
74 High Court 21 June 1994 *Bosphorus Hava v Minister for Transport* [1994] 3 CMLR 464 at 469-70.

Éireann, not only resulted in a theoretical shift, but also impacted the approach to interpretation, it is examined when this can be seen to take place in the context of an interpretation of national law in conformity with directives (it is recalled that the judgment in *Murphy v An Bord Telecom* Éireann concerned an interpretation in conformity with the Treaties) and in particular to what extent this has motivated the Irish courts to go beyond the outer limits of the national interpretative rules.

Before proceeding to the indicated analysis, it is observed, as a preliminary point, that it is in my opinion also possible to derive a further consequence from Edwards J.'s statement, namely that if there is a clear literal meaning that is in line with a consistent interpretation, or if a grammatical interpretation produces an ambiguity or absurdity, it would be quite natural for the Irish courts to consider the directive. The Irish superior courts' case law indeed provides some authority for the position that, if the text clearly reproduces a provision of the directive (this appears to come close to, but does not yet require the level of similarity of a *verbatim* transposition), the meaning of the directive will be followed (but see the judgment in *Albatros Feeds Ltd v Minister for Agriculture and Food,* discussed in subparagraph 3.3.4, although I do not believe that this principally undermines the stated position as the case can be distinguished). In such a situation, it is presumed that, if the legislature had the intention to depart from or go beyond the directive, it would have clearly expressed this intention so as to remove any doubt.[75] This is even so notwithstanding any interpretative doubt cast upon the interpretation of the concerned provision by other provisions of the same law.[76] Be that as it may, I do not believe that this must be viewed as a 'structural prioritisation' of consistent interpretation that supports the theory of supremacy of EU law. The reason for this is that the judges based their approach on objective criteria derived from the national legislation (e.g. following the details and layout of the directive) indicating that the legislature intended to follow the directive, and there was no incongruity between the *prima facie* meaning of the national provisions' wording and the directives. In those circumstances it is in my opinion quite natural that the interpretation is approached on the basis of the presumption that the legislature intended the national provisions to have the same meaning as the directive. It is also submitted that the kind of presumption applied here is different from the presumption that the legislature intends to comply with the directive, as formulated in the ECJ's *Wagner Miret* and *Pfeiffer* judgments.[77] There, it was sufficient that an implementing objective was identified, which as such entailed the requirement to confer a strong *prima facie* priority on the legislature's implementing objective over other interpretations. In the examples from the Irish courts' case law, a similarity between the directive and the national provisions was

---

75 See Supreme Court 5 March 2015 *Thompson v Dublin Bus* [2015] 3 JIC 503.

76 High Court 16 December 1999 *Coastal Line Container Terminal Ltd v Services Industrial Professional Technical Union* [2000] 1 IR 549 at 561.

77 Case C-334/92 *Wagner Miret*, ECLI:EU:C:1993:945, para. 20; Joined Cases C-397/01 to C-403/01 *Pfeiffer*, ECLI:EU:C:2004:584, para. 112.

identified, which then provided the basis for presuming that, in the absence of a clear contrary expression, it was intended to follow the former. Additionally, the High Court's judgment in *Sweetman v An Bord Pleanála* illustrates that it may be easier for the Irish courts to adopt a consistent interpretation if the national provision is not unambiguous.[78] The case concerned a provision for standing and the judge made standard of review in environmental and planning law cases. Clarke J. agreed that the national rules complied with the directive, taking into account that they were sufficiently flexible to accommodate, if necessary, an interpretation that he considered to be consistent with the directive. It is important to note the observation of O'Reilly that the requirement for standing as laid down in the relevant national provision was 'inherently malleable'. As the standard for review was judge made there was, in a similar vein, albeit for different reasons, also no grammatical curtailment. According to O'Reilly, these aspects aided the adoption of a consistent interpretation.[79] It should be observed, however, that the approach to the requirement for standing must now be viewed in the light of the subsequent Supreme Court judgment in *Harding v Cork County Council (No 5)*, where a stricter approach was adopted regarding standing (the Supreme Court's judgment is analysed in detail in subparagraph 3.3.2). But again, for present purposes, the more important point is that the judgment in *Sweetman v An Bord Pleanála* should not be viewed as an adaptation of the traditional approach or as an example of supremacy of EU law.

3.2.1. *A Structural Prioritisation or* Prima Facie *Supremacy of Consistent Interpretation?*

The judgment of Barrett J. in *EPA v Harte Peat Ltd* made two contentions. First, for national provisions that have their genesis in EU law, the starting point for interpretation must be the requirements of EU law, with all other national interpretative rules being subject to those requirements. Secondly, for the relationship between the duty of consistent interpretation and the literal approach specifically, this means that, 'when it comes to measures that derive from European Union law', the former enjoys supremacy, and if the latter produces an incompatible result the courts must seek an alternative meaning to be ascribed to the relevant provision.[80] It is in my opinion clear that both contentions put the duty of consistent interpretation before national interpretative rules. It can be qualified as a structural prioritisation of a consistent interpretation, supporting the supremacy of EU law. However, this is subject to the reservation that Barrett considered that, although the first contention might be seen as a facet of supremacy of EU law, it was probably more appropriately based on the presumption that the

78 High Court 26 April 2007 *Sweetman v An Bord Pleanála* [2008] 1 IR 277.
79 O'Reilly (n. 36), p. 341.
80 High Court 30 May 2014 *EPA v Harte Peat Ltd* [2015] 1 IR 462 at paras. 12, 26.

Oireachtas intends to comply with its international legal obligations, thus referring to a national principle.[81]

When the interpretative principles were applied to the dispute before the High Court, the literal approach was primarily applied as an additional argument in support of the meaning that was arrived at by considering the intention of the Oireachtas and the directive.[82] For the matters that the High Court had to determine, the national interpretative rules and the duty of consistent interpretation largely pointed in the same direction. Therefore, the case under consideration was not an occasion at which it could be tested in what manner the interpretative questions are approached if there is an incompatibility with the wording of the relevant provisions or the Oireachtas's intention.

Both statements of principle were repeated by the same judge on the same day in the judgment in *OCS One Complete Solution Ltd v Dublin Airport Authority PLC*.[83] However, when I look at the application of the stated principles to the case, which again concerned the interpretation of implementing legislation, I do not really see an approach that principally differed from a traditional approach to interpretation – but perhaps, on balance, in that particular case the order of application of the interpretative rules may have been less important for the outcome.

In addition to the above, it is necessary to ask whether a structural prioritisation can be established on the basis of the Irish superior courts' application of the presumption that the legislature intends to comply with the directive, as formulated in the ECJ's *Wagner Miret* and *Pfeiffer* judgments. Without in fact referring to these judgments, the High Court has stated that where national law was adopted to implement a directive '(…) the Court must presume, in the absence of explicit wording to contrary effect, that the legislative purpose is to give full and accurate effect to the provisions of the Community measure and no more'.[84]

> If I am correct, the words 'and no more', at the end of the excerpt, are of no relevance for understanding the court's views on the presumption formulated in the ECJ's *Wagner Miret* and *Pfeiffer* judgments, but concerned another question that arose in the proceedings, namely whether the insertion of additional words in the national legislation, unnecessary to fulfil its objective to implement the directive and going further than the requirements under EU law, are covered by section 3 of the European Communities Act 1972. That provision permits a Minister to make regulations to implement a directive, which may also '(…)

81 Ibid, at para. 12.
82 Ibid, at para. 34.
83 High Court 30 May 2014 *OCS One Complete Solution Ltd v Dublin Airport Authority PLC* [2014] IEHC 306 at paras. 5, 19.
84 High Court 4 December 2009 *MST v Minister for Justice, Equality and Law Reform* [2009] 12 JIC 403 at para. 27.

contain such incidental, supplementary and consequential provisions as appear to the Minister making the regulations to be necessary for the purposes of the regulations (…)'. I will not further discuss the interesting question of the exact scope of that provision. The point is that the final part of the excerpt expressed that the legislature is normally presumed not to go further than what the directive requires.

So far, the presumption has only played a limited role. In the High Court's judgment its firepower was not really tested since no incompatibility with the directive was found. And in the Supreme Court's judgment in *National Asset Management Agency (NAMA) v Commissioner for Environmental Information,* O'Donnell J. considered the presumption briefly, commenting that the presumption could, in an appropriate case be rebutted, and characterising it as a 'starting point for analysis' and 'a rule of thumb'.[85]

Barrett J.'s statements in *EPA v Harte Peat Ltd* clearly conferred a structural priority on a consistent interpretation. Yet, a reservation is in order as it is less clear whether this was the result of the duty of consistent interpretation as such or a, perhaps reinforced, national presumption that the Oireachtas intends to comply with its international legal obligations. The statements made by Barrett J. have also not been repeated elsewhere. This adds a second qualification to the consequences that can be drawn from that judgment for understanding the relationship between EU and national law under the duty of consistent interpretation. I do not consider the statements made so far in relation to the presumption that the legislature intends to comply with the directive as providing support for supremacy of EU law, albeit that they are also not incompatible with it.

3.2.2. Going Beyond the Traditional Limits to Interpretation as a Consequence of the Shift in Approach

The judgment in *Nathan v Bailey Gibson Ltd* concerned the rejection of Ms Nathan for a post that had become vacant in the respondent's undertaking. Initially, it had been the intention to employ her, but this was obstructed by a 'closed shop' agreement with the trade union. This meant that if a vacancy resulted from a union member leaving, the respondent was required to attempt to fill the vacancy by offering it to union members before non-members. The area of work was traditionally dominated by men and they were also the overwhelming majority of the union's members. It had to be determined whether the decision not to employ Ms Nathan for the reason that she was not a member of the concerned trade union had been based on grounds that were indirectly discriminatory (it was common case that there was no direct discrimination). In the High Court's

85 Supreme Court 23 June 2015 *National Asset Management Agency (NAMA) v Commissioner for Environmental Information* [2015] 2 ILRM 165 at paras. 42-3.

judgment, leading up to the subsequent Supreme Court's judgment in the case, a consistent interpretation was impeded by a literal interpretation of section 2(c) of the Employment Equality Act 1977. The subsection provided the following definition of discrimination:

> 'where because of his sex (...) a person is obliged to comply with a requirement, relating to employment [or membership of certain bodies, including trade unions; SWH] (...) in respect of which the proportion of persons of the other sex (...) able to comply is substantially higher'.

While it was conceded that it was not required that the obligation be imposed because of a person's sex, it was found that section 2(c) could not be interpreted as being applicable simply because, on account of another criterion than sex, a difference in treatment between two groups, of which one was predominantly female, was established. On account of the plain meaning of the words 'because of his sex', the High Court considered that some causal link had to exist between the treatment afforded to a person and that person's sex. This could be established if, for example, women would be excluded from membership of the trade union, or if such membership was more difficult to acquire for them. In other words, there had to be some link between the obligation and the quality of being a woman that could as such explain the adverse treatment. But according to the High Court no such causal link existed in the case of Ms Nathan.[86] When her case reached the Supreme Court, the High Court's judgment was overturned. It concluded that the more broadly formulated provision of section 3 of the same Act, prohibiting discrimination by employers (instead of defining it), had to be read so as to include cases of indirect discrimination and as not being confined by section 2, which provided definitions of discrimination but was accordingly interpreted as only covering, and merely being relevant for, cases of direct discrimination. Express reference was made to the duty of consistent interpretation when the Supreme Court proceeded to this conclusion.[87] The Supreme Court's judgment has been characterised as an example of 'extraordinary interpretative dexterity'.[88] This does not so much seem to be the result of the broad reading of section 3, so that it also encompasses cases of indirect discrimination, but rather the circumvention of the clear wording contained in section 2(c) by denying its relevance for section 3 in cases other than direct discrimination. Section 2 clearly provided a further definition of what constituted discrimination for the purposes of the other provisions in the Act,[89] and, even more importantly, subsection (c) had for a long time been

86 High Court 7 October 1992 *Nathan v Bailey Gibson Ltd* [1993] ELR 106 at 110-1.
87 Supreme Court 29 February 1996 *Nathan v Bailey Gibson Ltd* [1998] 2 IR 162 at 174-8.
88 L. Flynn, '*Nathan v. Bailey Gibson Ltd* (Irish Supreme Court, 29 February 1996, unreported)' (1997/3) *International Journal of Discrimination and the Law*, p. 228.
89 Ibid.

considered as the relevant framework for forms of *indirect* discrimination.[90] This indicated an adaptation of the provision's traditional understanding, which resulted from an interference by the duty of consistent interpretation and supports the theory of supremacy of EU law (to which theory the Supreme Court explicitly referred at the start of the operative part of the judgment). It should also be noted that the technique applied by the Supreme Court is in line with the part of the ECJ's *Pfeiffer* judgment mentioning the possibility to reduce the scope of application of one provision in favour of another.[91]

A second judgment that can be placed in that category was delivered by the High Court in *Health Service Executive v Sallam*. The aspect of the judgment relevant for the duty of consistent interpretation concerned the discrepancy between successive and continuous employment, used in the Fixed-Term Work Directive[92] and the national implementing provisions respectively. On the face of it, it is clear that the former is broader than the latter as it is also capable of including contracts that followed on from each other, even if there has been some time in between. For a good understanding of the High Court's decision, it is necessary to look at the previous determination by the Labour Court that was under appeal before the High Court. The Labour Court had resolved the definitional issue through a consistent interpretation which relied on guidance offered by the term 'lay-off' (a temporary interruption of work), contained in another piece of legislation to which the implementing provisions explicitly referred. To enable a consistent interpretation, lay-off was given a meaning that deviated from a literal interpretation. It is this part of the judgment that I consider to be important. The Labour Court's approach to the matter can be summarised as follows:

> The term lay-off is contained in the first schedule to the Minimum Notice and Terms of Employment Act 1973. The first schedule further defines continuous employment as well as termination. It provides that employment continues and is not terminated as a result of a lay-off. However, this was not yet sufficient to secure an outcome that would be compatible with the directive, for which an extensive interpretation of lay-off was necessary. A previous Labour Court determination showed the way to such an interpretation.
>
> There, the Labour Court endorsed the statement made in *Murphy v An Bord Telecom* Éireann that, where a literal interpretation produces a result that is incompatible with the directive, a teleological interpretation in conformity with the directive must be adopted. As I explained, that judgment should be

90 D. Curtin, *Irish Employment Equality Law* (Roundhall Press 1989), p. 236-40 (with references to case law); C. Maguire, 'Nathan v. Bailey Gibson: Curing Past Injustices?' (1996/10) *Irish Law Times*, p. 232-4.

91 Joined Cases C-397/01 to C-403/01 *Pfeiffer*, ECLI:EU:C:2004:584, para. 116. Confirmed by Case C-12/08 *Mono Car Styling*, ECLI:EU:C:2009:466, para. 63.

92 Council Directive 1999/70/EC of 28 June 1999 concerning the framework agreement on fixed-term work concluded by ETUC, UNICE and CEEP, *OJ* 1999, L175/43.

> seen as fundamental for the shift in approach and also showed that there was a conflict of interpretations that was resolved in favour of the supremacy of the duty of consistent interpretation. The Labour Court considered that it was required to adopt a consistent interpretation unless this was 'plainly impossible'. It referred to a judgment from the UK Employment Appeal Tribunal to confirm that the duty of consistent interpretation required an approach of this kind.[93] The Labour Court concluded that, while a literal interpretation entailed that when a fixed-term contract ends there is automatically a termination of the employment relationship, an interpretation in line with the objective of the directive nevertheless required that lay-off is extensively interpreted so that 'where a person's employment is terminated because there is no longer work available for him or her to do, and it is envisaged at the time of the terminations that his or her service will be required again in the future, and they are in fact re-engaged, the employment could be regarded as continuous'.[94]
>
> Applying such an extensive interpretation enabled the Labour Court to adopt a consistent interpretation – aligning continuous employment with successive employment – in its determination leading up to the subsequent High Court judgment in *Health Service Executive v Sallam.*[95]

When the case came before the High Court, the above part of the Labour Court's determination was upheld, and the use of its previous determination was also endorsed. This does not mean that the latter's outlook (i.e. the determination to which the Labour Court itself referred) on the scope of the duty of consistent interpretation can be ascribed to the High Court as well. What it does mean, however, is that the High Court saw no error of law in the departure from the literal interpretation of the term lay-off in favour of a consistent interpretation.[96] When the correctness of the Labour Court's determination on this point was examined, the High Court did point out that the national provisions have an implementing objective but there is no evidence that it was only, or primarily, for this reason that the conclusion that a consistent interpretation would be possible was upheld.

3.2.3. *The Duty of Consistent Interpretation as* Sine Qua Non *for the Adopted Interpretation?*

There were not really compelling alternative explanations for the shift in approach in the judgments in *Nathan v Bailey Gibson Ltd* and *Health Service Executive v Sallam* other than the duty of consistent interpretation. But sometimes it is significantly more difficult to determine whether a particular decision was forced by the duty of consistent interpretation, or whether it is more appropriately viewed as remaining within the confines of the traditional interpretative rules. This is especially true

---

93 UK Employment Appeal Tribunal 30 October 2009 *EBR Attridge Law LLP v Coleman* [2010] IRLR 10, where it was provided that '[t]he court may add words to a statute so as to depart from the unambiguous meaning that the legislation would otherwise bear'.

94 Labour Court 28 January 2011, FTD2/2011.

95 Labour Court 17 January 2013, FTD2/2013.

96 High Court 9 May 2014 *Health Service Executive v Sallam* [2014] 5 JIC 905 at paras. 23, 28.

for cases in which the court relied on the duty of consistent interpretation in combination with arguments that are habitually applied in a purely internal context. This will not be of any concern to the judge: he must decide the case before him and will be pleased if the duty of consistent interpretation and national interpretative rules point in the same direction. However, the point becomes relevant if one must determine whether the adopted consistent interpretation is a genuine or a fallacious example underpinning the theory of supremacy of EU law. The judgment in *Watson v EPA* is an example of a case that I find difficult to place on one side or the other of the dividing line. However, O'Sullivan J. seemed to take the position that there was not a conflict and I am inclined to follow his judgment.

> The relevant national provision, Article 33(4) of the Genetically Modified Organisms Regulations 1994, stated that '[t]he Agency shall not consent to a deliberate release [of genetically modified organisms; SWH] unless it is satisfied that the deliberate release will not result in adverse effects on human health or the environment'. The applicant submitted that this meant that the risk of adverse effects should be 'effectively zero'. Yet, the High Court believed that the applicable directive did not impose such a strict standard. With regard to the applicant's submission it held that it '(…) is based on a literal construction of art. 33(4) which places an exclusive and out of context burden of interpretation on this sub-article, which assigns minimalist or nugatory significance to other portions of the Regulations (for example those that refer to risk evaluation) and perhaps most importantly conflicts with the objective of the Directive (…)'.[97] While it is clear that there was a departure from the literal approach and particular emphasis was placed on the directive, O'Sullivan J.'s reasoning also relied on the immediate national legal context of the concerned provision and found that this showed that the national legislation intended to take the same approach as the directive. In my opinion there was not a conflict of interpretations *per se*.

In the judgment in *Eircom Ltd v ComReg* an isolated interpretation of one of the relevant provisions may have given the impression that the adopted consistent interpretation must have been the result of a conflict of interpretative rules. However, on closer inspection I am convinced – more so in comparison to the previous example – that this conclusion would be incorrect.

> There was a discrepancy in the Framework Regulations 2003 and Access Regulations 2003, which implemented the Framework Directive and Access Directive respectively.[98] The former conferred a right to appeal a decision taken by the respondent and the possibility of applying for a suspension, including decisions taken under regulation 17 of the Access Regulations, on which basis

97 High Court 6 October 1998 *Watson v EPA* [2000] 2 IR 454 at 478.

98 Directive 2002/21/EC of the European Parliament and of the Council of 7 March 2002 on a common regulatory framework for electronic communications networks and services (Framework Directive), *OJ* 2002, L108/33; Directive 2002/19/EC of the European Parliament and of the Council of 7 March 2002 on access to, and interconnection of, electronic communications networks and associated facilities (Access Directive), *OJ* 2002, L108/7.

> the *original* decision relevant for the proceedings had been issued. However, the Framework Regulations excluded decisions taken on the basis of regulation 18 of the Access Regulations, by which a decision taken under regulation 17 was *enforced*, and if regulation 18(10) was invoked – as the respondent had done in this case – immediate compliance was required without this being subject to the previous conclusion of an appeal against the original decision. The question that arose before the High Court was whether the absence of an appeal against enforcement decisions and the requirement of immediate compliance should be interpreted as having the effect of rendering the right to appeal and the possibility to suspend the original decision *de facto* nugatory. McKechnie J. concluded that, on a correct interpretation of the relevant provisions, the appellant should not be deprived of his right to appeal, and the possibility to ask for a suspension of, the original decision. Any other conclusion would not meet the demands of both Article 4(1) of the Framework Directive, demanding an effective appeal mechanism, as well as national requirements of fair procedures and constitutional justice.[99] Unlike the judgment in *SIAC Construction Ltd v National Roads Authority* (which I discuss next), there can be no doubt that the requirements of the directive were the immediate cause to examine how the right to an appeal and regulation 18 could be reconciled. However, I do not think that the outcome of this reconciliation was the result of a conflict. As I already mentioned, the Framework Regulations clearly included decisions taken under regulation 17. The latter provision itself was silent on the matter. The only real obstacle was the effect of the enforcement decision. McKechnie J. resolved this in a manner that left intact the exclusion of enforcement decisions – he considered that the relevant national provisions could not be interpreted in any other way than to exclude an appeal of such decisions, for which there were good reasons as well – yet considered that the exclusion must have been based on the assumption that there had previously been a right of appeal in respect of the underlying original decision – which was accordingly also left intact.[100] This was in my opinion a cogent arrangement of, instead of interference with, the different provisions, which ensured that national law accommodated the requirements of the directive.[101]

While there is again room for some discussion I think, albeit with some hesitation, that, unlike the previous two examples, the High Court's judgment in *SIAC Construction Ltd v National Roads Authority*[102] is an example where there *was* a conflict of interpretations.

> The judgment concerned the interpretation of Order 84A(4) of the Rules of the Superior Courts 1986, which provided that: '[a]n application for the review of a decision to award or the award of a public contract shall be made at the earliest opportunity and in any event within three months from the date when grounds for the application first arose unless the Court considers that there is good

---

99 High Court 29 July 2005 *Eircom Ltd v ComReg* [2007] 1 IR 1 at paras. 32, 39.

100 Ibid, at paras. 33, 37.

101 See also the comment in N. Connery, 'Right of appeal under the electronic communications regulatory framework' (2005/7) *Law Society Gazette*, p. 53.

102 High Court 16 July 2004 *SIAC Construction Ltd v National Roads Authority* [2004] IEHC 128.

reason for extending such period'.[103] A literal interpretation of Order 84A(4) conferred a clear meaning on that provision, entailing that the time limit to submit complaints regarding the award procedure only began to run from the date of the decision to award the contract. But there were three arguments that undermined such an interpretation, and the High Court departed from the literal interpretation to adopt a consistent interpretation. The difficulty in determining whether there was a conflict of interpretations lies in the fact that the court did not only rely on the obligation to adopt an interpretation in conformity with the directive, but also two traditional arguments. It is therefore necessary to determine whether the latter were by themselves capable of carrying the High Court's decision, or whether it is more appropriately viewed as an interference on behalf of the duty of consistent interpretation. The literal interpretation was clearly incompatible with another rule in Order 84A(4) (rule 9), and it could be argued that this required, as a matter of national rules of interpretation, a broader approach. Also, the High Court pointed out that the literal interpretation would have absurd consequences, and it was seen at the beginning of this paragraph that the Irish superior courts accept a departure from the literal approach in such a situation. However, if one looks at the High Court's reasoning, it is clear that the requirement to adopt a consistent interpretation was the main reason for its decision. Also, leaving aside whether rule 9 and/or the finding of an absurdity had the capacity to create the interpretative doubt necessary to require a reconsideration of the literal interpretation and the need to consider a purposive interpretation,[104] it would still be necessary to take into account the gap between the provision's wording and the desired alternative interpretation, which is a separate issue.[105] In the present case, there was a significant departure from the express wording of Order 84A(4), causing the time limit to be applied by analogy to, and to start running immediately after, decisions taken interim the award procedure. I am therefore inclined to take the position that there was a conflict – and that this was resolved to the benefit of the duty of consistent interpretation – in the judgment in *SIAC Construction Ltd v National Roads Authority* as the traditional arguments alone could not in my opinion have justified such a far-reaching departure from the provision's clear text.

---

103 It is noted that this provision was inserted in order to implement Council Directive 89/665/EEC of 21 December 1989 on the coordination of the laws, regulations and administrative provisions relating to the application of review procedures to the award of public supply and public works contracts, *OJ* 1989, L395/33.

104 Cf. D. Fairgrieve and F. Lichère, *Public Procurement Law: Damages as an Effective Remedy* (Hart Publishing 2011), p. 127, where it is argued that the High Court relied 'in particular' on rule 9 for reaching its decision, which is difficult to reconcile, however, with for example the judgment's consideration that '[i]t follows, therefore [i.e. after having referred to the duty of consistent interpretation; SWH], that O. 84(A) in order to be in accord with applicable community law, must be interpreted as applying not merely to a decision to award a contract, or award of a contract, but also to decisions taken by contracting authorities regarding contract award procedures'.

105 See the discussion of the approach to interpretation under both the rules at common law and section 5 of the Interpretation Act 2005 in subparagraphs 3.1.1 and 3.1.2. With regard to the latter, the Supreme Court's judgment (per Clarke J.) of 10 May 2012 in *Kadri v Governor of Wheatfield Prison* [2012] IESC 27 at para. 3.4, confirmed that the mandate given to the courts under section 5 is one of construction or interpretation rather than rewriting. In my opinion this makes it clear that, even if there is interpretative doubt, this still needs to be weighed against other relevant criteria, in particular the extent to which the text is departed from.

After having lost the case, the applicant submitted a complaint to the Commission, which led to infringement proceedings before the ECJ. There, Ireland relied among others on the adopted consistent interpretation to argue that Order 84A(4) did not violate the Member State's obligations under EU law. The ECJ nevertheless found that there had been an infringement as the national provision did not meet the standard that implementing measures must be sufficiently clear and precise. Pointing out that decisions adopted in the course of the award procedure were not at all mentioned, the ECJ provided that '[t]he resulting legal situation is not sufficiently clear and precise to exclude the risk that concerned candidates and tenderers may be deprived of their right to challenge decisions in public procurement matters handed down by a national court on the basis of its own interpretation of that provision'.[106] Advocate General Kokott even questioned whether the adopted consistent interpretation was compatible with the requirement to interpret national law 'so far as possible' or, more specifically, the limits attached to that obligation, pointing out that the interpretation exceeded the provision's wording and had the consequence of prescribing a time limit for situations not clearly envisaged by the legislature.[107] Although the issue of adequate transposition should not be conflated with the question whether national rules of interpretation are interfered with (although consistent interpretation and adequate implementation are not entirely unrelated, see chapter 2, paragraph 6), and while Advocates General of the ECJ do not determine the scope of national interpretative rules, the ECJ's ruling and the Opinion of Advocate General Kokott support the view that there was a significant departure from the text and that, from a grammatical point of view, it would be everything but unusual to read the concerned provision in a different way than was done by the High Court in *SIAC Construction Ltd v National Roads Authority*.

The evaluation whether a consistent interpretation is a genuine or fallacious example underpinning the theory of supremacy of EU law is not always simple and often rather case-specific. Nevertheless, the following general observations can be made. The first point is derived from the judgment in *Watson v EPA*. If it is accepted that it is sometimes permitted to apply purposive criteria notwithstanding a provision's clear wording, there is *not* a conflict of interpretations if an interpretation is based on the duty of consistent interpretation and criteria derived from the domestic context of the concerned national provision *if such context is entirely in line with and points in the same direction as the directive*. The qualification concerning the issue at what point purposive criteria can become relevant is now less pertinent with the Interpretation Act 2005 having increased the scope to do so. Secondly, on the basis of *Eircom Ltd v ComReg* it can be said that, if there is an incongruity as a result of two seemingly contradictory provisions of national law, but this can be resolved without doing violence to the wording of either of them, there is also

106 Case C-456/08 *Commission v Ireland*, ECLI:EU:C:2010:46, para. 66. Interestingly, Ireland also relied on the different role played by case law under the common law system, emphasising that, in addition to statutory law, this also determines the relevant legal framework. However, this did not persuade the ECJ to adapt its requirements regarding implementing measures.

107 Opinion of AG Kokott in Case C-456/08 *Commission v Ireland*, ECLI:EU:C:2009:679, paras. 62-3.

not a conflict of interpretations. Thirdly, there *is* a conflict of interpretations if the distance between the literal meaning and the interpretation that is believed to be demanded by the directive, is simply too large. It is submitted that the difference between the judgments in *Watson v EPA* and *SIAC Construction Ltd v National Roads Authority* is that in the latter judgment time limits in respect of decisions taken interim the award procedure were inserted into the provision while its wording showed no indication that this had been envisaged by the legislature whereas the former judgment involved the relaxation of the threshold stated in the national provision.

3.3. LIMITS TO THE APPLICATION OF THE DUTY OF CONSISTENT INTERPRETATION

I already explained at the beginning of this paragraph that when the Irish courts interpret the law, the principle restriction placed upon them is that they should not perform legislative functions, a role which, under the Constitution, is reserved to the Oireachtas. The Irish superior courts have mainly discussed the limits that derive from this principal restriction to the duty of consistent interpretation by referring to the *contra legem* limitation. I first discuss the Irish superior courts' general approach to the *contra legem* limitation. This is followed by a discussion of three aspects that may give rise to complications: the threshold for concluding that an interpretation would be *contra legem,* divergences between the directive's objectives and the positivised intention of the Oireachtas, and the protection of fundamental rights under the Constitution.

Before I explore the Irish superior courts' interpretation of the *contra legem* limitation, I would like to make a more general remark. The Irish superior courts view the *contra legem* limitation as a further elaboration of the requirement to interpret national law 'so far as is possible' in conformity with directives. In principle, this point of view is correct: the limitation obviously concerns the question how far national courts should go when they apply the duty of consistent interpretation and marks out an area that is shielded from interference by EU law, giving national courts the possibility to prevent too far-reaching interferences with national law. However, it was argued in chapter 2, subparagraph 5.5, that a view whereby the *contra legem* limitation is equated with the obligation to interpret national law so far as possible is probably premature on account of the current position in the ECJ's case law. While the ECJ leaves a significant measure of discretion to the national courts for determining the precise meaning of *contra legem,* so far, this has usually been interpreted as an incompatibility with the national provision's text – albeit that an exception to this is the ECJ's *Impact* and *Klohn* judgments which, perhaps not completely by coincidence, originated in a preliminary reference from the Irish Labour Court and Supreme Court respectively.[108] If I am correct in this regard, it means that, even if the *contra legem* limitation does not apply, this does not automatically have as a consequence that national courts are forced to adopt a consistent interpretation. The large open space created by the establishment of the duty of consistent interpretation in the ECJ's *Von Colson and Kamann* judgment has under this position only partly been filled through the further elaboration of the *contra legem* limitation in the *Pupino* and *Adeneler* judgments,[109] leaving room within which national courts are to find out for themselves how far Articles 288 TFEU and 4(3) TEU require them to go, taking into account national rules of interpretation. Yet, it is in any event clear, and this is the more important point for the current discussion, that 'so far as possible' is more than a mere constraint on the duty of consistent interpretation and has a broader meaning than the *contra legem* limitation. Judgments from the High Court as well as the Supreme Court sometimes seem to pay insufficient attention to this, and appear to place more emphasis on the 'dispensational' than on the 'exploratory' aspect of 'so far as possible'[110]

3.3.1. Contra Legem *as a Prohibition to Do Violence to the National Provision's Wording*

In principle, the Irish courts' prevailing view on *contra legem* ties in with the more confined interpretation linking this limitation to the provision's text only. In *Smith v Meade,* the Court of Appeal considered that it was not possible to adopt a consistent interpretation as this was an interpretation that would be *contra legem* '(...) and which would do violence to the actual wording of both provisions'.[111] It is clear that this is seen as a *prohibition,* to which no exceptions have been formulated so far. This quasi-definition indicated that the determination whether an interpretation would be *contra legem* looks at the *wording* of the concerned national provisions. The Irish superior courts' case law regularly links the *contra legem* limitation to the text of a provision.

> So, for example, in *EMI Records (Ireland) Ltd v UPC Communications Ireland Ltd,* the High Court linked the *contra legem* limitation to its statement that the duty of consistent interpretation '(...) cannot be used beyond the scope of its

108 Case C-268/06 *Impact,* ECLI:EU:C:2008:223, para. 103; Case C-167/17 *Klohn,* ECLI:EU:C:2018:833, para. 65.

109 Case C-105/03 *Pupino,* ECLI:EU:C:2005:386, para. 47; Case C-212/04 *Adeneler,* ECLI:EU:C:2006:443, para. 110.

110 Supreme Court 26 July 2006 *Albatros Feeds Ltd v Minister for Agriculture and Food* [2007] 1 IR 221 at para. 59; High Court 3 March 2011 *EPA v Neiphin Trading Ltd* [2011] 2 IR 575 at para. 65; High Court 22 November 2011 *JC Savage Supermarket Ltd v An Bord Pleanála* [2011] IEHC 488 at para. 3.10; High Court 19 November 2013 *Sandymount and Merrion Residents Association v An Bord Pleanála* [2013] 11 JIC 1904 at para. 4.5. A notable exception to this is the judgment in High Court 30 May 2014 *EPA v Harte Peat Ltd* [2015] 1 IR 462 at para. 20.

111 Court of Appeal 16 December 2016 *Smith v Meade* [2016] 12 JIC 1608 at para. 51.

proper purpose so as impose a solution which, though in conformity with an obligation under a directive, contradicts the plain terms of national law'.[112]

The Irish superior courts have on two occasions defined the *contra legem* limitation as referring to an interpretation that would be incompatible with the relevant national legislation.[113] This seems to confer a broader meaning to *contra legem* that does not merely refer to an incompatibility with a provision's text only, but could also potentially encompass an incompatibility that arises on the basis of other interpretative criteria that must be taken into account for the determination of the meaning of the relevant provision. Yet, while one of these judgments showed a broadening of the *contra legem* limitation in the sense that a consistent interpretation was rejected as a result of what the national provision did *not* say, the examination whether a consistent interpretation remained within the limits of what is interpretatively possible nevertheless focussed on the provision's text (see further subparagraph 3.3.4). And in the other judgment there were not any clear indications that the court envisaged a broader meaning of the *contra legem* limitation. Moreover, similar to the statement delivered on these two occasions, the Irish superior courts have also held that the *contra legem* limitation refers to an interpretation that would distort the meaning of the enactment. However, there, the court simultaneously referred to a contradiction of the plain terms of national law.[114] This can be interpreted to mean that the courts do not intend the two statements to have entirely different meanings.

While the ECJ has so far not provided a clear definition of the *contra legem* limitation, it was seen that its case law is favourable to an approach that links this limitation to the clear wording of the text.[115]

112 High Court 11 October 2010 *EMI Records (Ireland) Ltd v UPC Communications Ireland Ltd* [2010] IEHC 377 at para. 103.

113 Supreme Court 26 July 2006 *Albatros Feeds Ltd v Minister for Agriculture and Food* [2007] 1 IR 221 at para. 60; High Court 9 May 2014 *Health Service Executive v Sallam* [2014] 5 JIC 905 at para. 26.

114 High Court 22 November 2011 *JC Savage Supermarket Ltd v An Bord Pleanála* [2011] IEHC 488 at para. 3.10; High Court 19 November 2013 *Sandymount and Merrion Residents Association v An Bord Pleanála* [2013] 11 JIC 1904 at para. 4.5.

115 In Case C-176/12 *AMS*, ECLI:EU:C:2014:2, paras. 39-40, for example, the ECJ did not question that the *contra legem* limitation was invoked, which seemed to have been the result of the wording of the relevant national provision. See also, albeit before the introduction of the limitation that a *contra legem* interpretation is not required, Case C-111/97 *EvoBus Austria*, ECLI:EU:C:1998:434, para. 20. The ECJ's Advocates General, as well as EU legal scholarship, have predominantly interpreted the *contra legem* limitation as referring to the limits of the provision's text: Opinion of AG Jacobs in Case C-456/98 *Centrosteel*, ECLI:EU:C:2000:137, para. 32; Opinion of AG Van Gerven in Case C-271/91 *Marshall II*, ECLI:EU:C:1993:30, para. 41; Opinion of AG Elmer in Case C-168/95 *Arcaro*, ECLI:EU:C:1996:107, paras. 39-41; Opinion of AG Bot in Case C-441/14 *Ajos*, ECLI:EU:C:2015:776, para. 68. See also S. Prechal, *Directives in EC Law* (OUP 2005), p. 207. Cf. M.H. Wissink, 'Interpretation of Private Law in Conformity with EU Directives', in: A.S. Hartkamp and others (Eds.), *The Influence of EU Law on National Private Law* (Kluwer 2014), p. 146.

3.3.2. A Broadening of the Contra Legem *Limitation?*

Although Kearns J.'s judgment in *Harding v Cork County Council (No 5)* mentioned the same benchmark for the *contra legem* limitation – linking it to 'the terms of the Act itself'[116] – its application in the specific case was quite restrictive so that it needs to be asked whether there was not actually a broadening of the *contra legem* limitation.

> The appellant, Mr Harding, requested the setting aside of a decision granting planning permission for a golf and leisure resort that would be situated at the Ballymacus area (the southern coast of Ireland). The legal issue was whether he had standing to apply for 'leave' to bring judicial review.[117] Section 50 of the Planning and Development Act 2000, which was considered by Ireland to be compatible with the directive, so that no specific implementing measures had been introduced, provided that the granting of leave was conditional on having a 'substantial interest in the matter which is the subject of the application'. In subparagraph 3.2, it was seen that in *Sweetman v An Bord Pleanála* the High Court deemed it possible to interpret that provision in a manner that did not conflict with the requirement stipulated by the directive that persons having a 'sufficient interest' shall have access to judicial review procedures and, more generally, that the national rules should provide 'wide access to justice'. However, Kearns J. adopted the stricter approach to the test as adopted in the judgment in *O'Shea v Kerry County Council*,[118] and confirmed in, among others, the High Court judgment leading up to the proceedings before the Supreme Court. Briefly put, it is under this approach required that the interest is 'peculiar or personal' to the appellant. Applying this test, the appellant was refused standing.

Kearns J.'s conclusion that the appellant did not meet the threshold for standing in environmental and planning cases has been criticised by a number of commentators.[119] However, as this concerns the details of the requirements that are imposed upon the interest that someone must have in a proposed development, it will not be further discussed here. The relevant aspect of the judgment concerns Kearns J.'s considerations with regard to the question whether the directive might

---

116 Supreme Court 2 May 2008 *Harding v Cork County Council (No 5)* [2008] 2 ILRM 251 at 279.

117 Before the actual judicial review proceedings (which reviews whether a decision of an administrative body, or inferior court, was reached in an appropriate manner and in accordance with the law; see also chapter 1, subparagraph 3.1) can commence, it is first necessary to submit an application to the relevant court for leave to proceed, setting out the grounds on which relief is sought. The judge must at this stage be satisfied that there is some ground to continue to the actual examination of the complaints. But if the application for leave is granted, this does not have any bearing on the ensuing determination by the judge. See Byrne and others (n. 1), p. 461.

118 High Court 1 September 2003 *O'Shea v Kerry County Council* [2003] 4 IR 143 at 160.

119 See, for example, B. Conroy, 'Harding v Cork County Council: No Standing Room in Public Interest Environmental Litigation?' (2008/3) *Irish Planning and Environmental Law Journal*, p. 95-101; R. Kennedy, '"Substantial Interest Requirement" for Judicial Review of Planning Decisions' (2009/11) *Environmental Law Review*, p. 52. See also, albeit prior to the Supreme Court's judgment in *Harding v Cork County Council (No 5)*, G. Simons, 'Locus Standi, Public Interest and the EIA Directive' (2007/1) *Irish Planning and Environmental Law Journal*, p. 21-5.

require a more yielding test for standing, which had to be obtained through a consistent interpretation of the requirement of having a 'substantial interest in the matter which is the subject of the application'. In this regard he observed that:

> '[a]ccepting that the Act falls to be interpreted in the light of the terms and objectives of the Directive in question it is also an established principle that such an interpretative approach does not mean that the Act be interpreted contra legem. The interpretation which I have given to the meaning of "substantial interest" in the context of this case flows directly from the terms of the Act itself. That being in my view the plainly correct interpretation of s. 50, no issue as to community law arises'.[120]

Ryall characterises this aspect of the decision as 'perplexing'. She points out that the test of substantial interest is not defined with any degree of rigour in the Planning and Development Act, so that it would be difficult to see why it cannot be given a flexible interpretation.[121] She also pointed out that section 50, in which the test was prescribed, envisaged that the courts perform an important function in fleshing out its exact meaning in a particular case.[122] Murray C.J., in the same judgment, while concurring with Kearns J., noted that the terms of the provision were '(...) imprecise and likely to generate further litigation (...)'.[123]

I am not convinced that the words 'substantial interest' were not open to further interpretation whatsoever and that such would be *contra legem*. However, I am also not convinced that Kearns J.'s judgment must necessarily be read in that way. For determining the kind of test to be applied in the dispute, Kearns J. also took into account the legislature's reasons behind the introduction of the standard of substantial interest. Ironically, the test for standing in judicial review procedures had always been one of establishing a sufficient interest, but the Planning and Development Act 2000 had willingly introduced a higher standard for standing in environmental and planning cases. That point was also explicitly mentioned in Kearns J.'s judgment and he mentioned a number of aspects of the Planning and Development Act 2000 that in his view confirmed this purpose.[124] So the reference to the 'terms of the Act itself' must surely be understood as referring to 'substantial' (which admittedly differs from 'sufficient') but probably also to the broader scheme within which that standard was introduced and which confirmed the stricter approach to standing. If this is correct, Kearns J.'s understanding of the *contra legem*

---

120 Supreme Court 2 May 2008 *Harding v Cork County Council (No 5)* [2008] 2 ILRM 251 at 279.

121 A. Ryall, *Effective Judicial Protection and the Environmental Impact Assessment Directive in Ireland* (Hart Publishing 2009), p. 253. Other authors have also provided critical comments in response to the conclusion that substantial interest was not open to further interpretation, see for example the characterisations of the concerned national provision in Simons (n. 119), p. 21-5 (nebulous); Conroy (n. 119), p. 95-101 (vague and open-textured); O'Reilly (n. 36), p. 347-8 (not set in stone).

122 Ryall (n. 121), p. 253.

123 Supreme Court 2 May 2008 *Harding v Cork County Council (No 5)* [2008] 2 ILRM 251 at 259.

124 Ibid, at 268.

limitation would then depart from the prevailing view discussed above where it was linked to the provision's text. His interpretation would be broader, equating *contra legem* to an interpretation that is not possible on the basis of national interpretative rules. To be sure, from the perspective of an effective application of the duty of consistent interpretation this is somewhat disappointing. First, the scheme of the legislation was not unequivocally in support of viewing its purpose as imposing a strict standard: section 50(4) stated that substantial interest is not limited to an interest in land or other financial interest, which rather pointed in the direction of a more *lenient* approach to standing.[125] Secondly, under the traditional approach to interpretation the courts are not normally forced to follow an argument based on a systematic interpretation. It may thus be asked whether the Supreme Court tried hard enough to adopt an interpretation in conformity with the directive; even if the broader notion of *contra legem* was applied, it remains difficult to see why that limitation prevented a consistent interpretation. However, in my opinion there was not a clear violation of the duty of consistent interpretation.

Two final remarks are necessary. First, as the directive was not relied upon in arguments before the Supreme Court, Kearns J.'s considerations regarding the duty of consistent interpretation were *obiter* (and therefore did not have binding authority, see further chapter 1, subparagraph 3.1). This also justifies the Supreme Court not asking the ECJ to further clarify the meaning of the standard of 'sufficient interest' contained in the directive, so that it could subsequently be compared to the test of substantial interest. Secondly, it is pointed out that the Planning and Development Act 2000, through Article 50A(3)(b)(i), has reinstated the test of *sufficient* interest, so that any further case law on standing is more likely to be in line with the directive. Although the latter point certainly cannot affect the above discussion of Kearns J.'s judgment, the first point must be taken into account for the overall picture of the Irish superior courts' case law interpreting the *contra legem* limitation.

3.3.3. *Divergences between the Directive's Objectives and the Positivised Intention of the Oireachtas*

An interesting example of how the question whether an interpretation would be *contra legem* could be approached, is offered by the High Court's judgment in *EMI Records (Ireland) Ltd v UPC Communications Ireland Ltd,* where this matter was addressed in a more contextualised manner:

> Charleton J. first applied a traditional literal approach, which produced a clear meaning of the national provision. However, he then asked whether '(...) the

125 See also Conroy (n. 119), p. 95-101.

> legislation can be looked at differently in the context of the European law'.[126] Although, the comparison with the applicable directive – as well as the measures adopted in some of the other jurisdictions – in the end did not undermine the interpretation based on a literal approach, but only strengthened Charleton J.'s opinion that national law did not provide the remedies required by the plaintiffs, it is submitted that his willingness to look at the directive despite a clear literal meaning must mean that the *contra legem* question should not be considered in the abstract, but must be viewed in relation to the provisions of the directive, i.e. in a contextualised manner.[127]

However, even if a more contextualised approach is adopted, it may be asked what constitutes this context, and how much room there is to look at the directive. O'Reilly identified a potential issue here as a result of the approach prescribed for a purposive interpretation in section 5 of the Interpretation Act 2005. While section 5 was in part inspired by the Irish courts' approach to the interpretation in conformity with EU law, he pointed out that there is an important distinction. For the former, the courts are instructed to look at the plain intention of the Oireachtas, and where that intention can be ascertained from the Act as a whole whereas, for the latter, the directive itself is paramount. As a result of this distinction, difficulties might arise if the Oireachtas has not clearly taken over particular aspects of the directive.[128] Especially if it is taken into account that often certain provisions contained in a directive are further clarified by the ECJ over the course of time, it is not unlikely that it turns out that there exists an inadvertent divergence between the directive and the intention of the Oireachtas as expressed in national law.

In his judgment in *EPA v Neiphin Trading Ltd*, Edwards J. referred to the distinction identified by O'Reilly and agreed with his analysis. The approach to the question whether the applicable provisions, in particular section 57 of the Waste Management Act 1996 – which had an implementing objective – could accommodate the polluter pays principle (those responsible for pollution should bear the costs for the ensuing damage to the environment) so that orders concerning civil liability could be made against four individuals who, together with the company of which they were the directors, were the respondents, clearly showed what repercussions this had for the decision in that case.

> It is noted that section 57 provides, among others, that if it is established that activities regarding waste cause, or are likely to cause, environmental pollution the High Court may '(…) make such other provision, including provision in relation to the payment of costs (…), as the Court considers appropriate'. That section also mentions that provisions can be made against the 'holder' of the waste which is defined in another piece of legislation as 'the producer of the

126 High Court 11 October 2010 *EMI Records (Ireland) Ltd v UPC Communications Ireland Ltd* [2010] IEHC 377 at para. 100.

127 Ibid, see in particular paras. 110, 131, 138.

128 O'Reilly (n. 36), p. 345.

waste or the natural or legal person who is in possession of it'. This differed from the previous definition which had also encompassed persons in charge, such as a manager, supervisor or operator.

The previous High Court judgment in *Wicklow County Council v Fenton (No 2)*, permitted that an action concerning civil liability was taken against individuals on the basis of an interpretation of national law in light of the directive, which was on that occasion found to contain the polluter pays principle.[129] However, as Edwards J. pointed out, that judgment was delivered *before* the introduction of section 5 of the Interpretation Act 2005. While he admitted that it followed from the directive that an effective enforcement system, premised on the polluter pays principle, needed to be established, he disagreed that the national provisions could accommodate this, adding that the previous judgment 'in the application of a purposive and teleological approach to the interpretation of ss. 57 and 58 of the Act of 1996, focussed unduly on the intention of the European legislators and insufficiently upon the intention of the Oireachtas's.[130] In the opinion of Edwards J., the previous High Court judgment had adopted a *contra legem* interpretation.[131] That conclusion seemed to be based not only on the text of the relevant national provisions, on which the applicant had relied for the action against the individual directors, but also on a consideration of the Act as a whole and on the conditions developed in jurisprudence that must be fulfilled in order to 'lift the corporate veil'.[132] As regards the latter, a subsequent High Court judgment observed in relation to the judgment in *EPA v Neiphin Trading Ltd*, that the principle of separate corporate personality was the main obstacle to a consistent interpretation.[133]

It may be asked whether Edwards J. was correct in the conclusions that he drew from the introduction of section 5 of the Interpretation Act 2005 – which to his mind necessitated a more restrictive approach to purposive interpretation in light of the directive. More specifically, does it follow that the pre-existing approach to the duty of consistent interpretation under the rules at common law was set aside? This issue was implicitly addressed in the judgment, which held that the more flexible approach to the duty of consistent interpretation, applied under the rules at common law, had been possible because the interpretative rules were not fixated by legislation, which seems to indicate that things have changed now that such legislation does exist.[134] I already mentioned at the beginning of this paragraph that I think that this matter is not entirely clear. However, if for the sake

129 High Court 31 July 2002 *Wicklow County Council v Fenton (No 2)* [2002] 4 IR 44.
130 High Court 3 March 2011 *EPA v Neiphin Trading Ltd* [2011] 2 IR 575 at para. 106.
131 Ibid, at para. 108. This was a rare departure from the doctrine of *stare decisis*, C. Linehan, 'Environmental Regulation and Insolvency: Two Divergent Regimes – Part II' (2012/1) *Irish Planning and Environmental Law Journal*, p. 20.
132 Ibid, at paras. 110-5.
133 High Court 14 October 2016 *Bookfinders Ltd v Revenue Commissioners* [2016] IEHC 569 at para. 29.
134 High Court 3 March 2011 *EPA v Neiphin Trading Ltd* [2011] 2 IR 575 at para. 67.

of argument it is presumed that Edwards J. was correct in this respect, the further question arises whether it is compatible with the duty of consistent interpretation that courts first look at the Act as a whole to identify the legislature's intention and whether this coincides with particular points derived from the directive (e.g. the intention to establish an enforcement system based on the polluter pays principle), which then determines the scope to consider an interpretation in light of the objective to implement the directive. In my opinion it cannot be excluded that the duty of consistent interpretation permits courts to not only advance arguments based on the national provision's wording, but also arguments based on for example a systematic interpretation, or even important principles in national law for the purpose of determining whether the *contra legem* limitation applies. Also, it seems entirely reasonable to me that national courts do not adopt a consistent interpretation if it appears from the Act as a whole that it cannot support a consistent interpretation. However, that conclusion must be reached in a manner which duly takes into account the requirements under the duty of consistent interpretation. In *EPA v Neiphin Trading Ltd* the national provisions were interpreted on the basis of a traditional approach only. It was asked whether it followed from the text and the Act as a whole that the legislature had envisaged an enforcement system based on the polluter pays principle. Arguably, if that answer would have been affirmative, there would have been no need to resort to the interpretative obligation in the first place. Wissink observes that such an approach falls short of the duty of consistent interpretation: '(…) the court should not approach harmonious interpretation as a two-staged-exercise, that is first interpreting national law in the traditional way and after that comparing the outcome, or perhaps several outcomes, with the requirements of the directive'.[135] In addition to this, the approach adopted in *EPA v Neiphin Trading Ltd* also fell short of the specific methodological instruction stipulated in the ECJ's *Wagner Miret* and *Pfeiffer* judgments that it must be presumed that the legislature intended to comply with the directive. I argued that this establishes a very strong *prima facie* priority for the legislature's implementing objective and that the reconciliation of the implementing objective in relation to other, incompatible, objectives, should normally be in favour of the former. Also, the integrity of the implementing objective must be respected, which in my opinion entails that such an objective may not be partitioned into several sub-objectives, some of which fit in better with a traditional approach to the national legislation than others (see chapter 2, subparagraph 4.2.2). In the judgment in *EPA v Neiphin Trading Ltd*, which was concerned with the interpretation of implementing legislation, no compelling competing objectives were identified.[136] It may then be asked whether, applying the presumption, the national provisions truly made

135 Wissink (n. 115), p. 145.

136 Apart from, perhaps, the observance of the principle of separate corporate personality, in relation to which it was not, however, examined whether that principle *did* find clear expression in the concerned provisions (note that it was mentioned in High Court 14 October 2016 *Bookfinders Ltd v Revenue Commissioners* [2016] IEHC 569 at para. 29, that this had been the main obstacle

it impossible to adopt a consistent interpretation. But even if this were so, the steps taken to reach such an outcome in *EPA v Neiphin Trading Ltd* were flawed as they had the effect of partitioning the implementing objective; the Oireachtas had the intention to implement the directive, and once it was established that the directive intended to provide for an enforcement system based on the polluter pays principle, it should be presumed that this had also been the intention of the Oireachtas. This was not the route followed by the High Court, which required positive confirmation in national law for ascribing this objective to the Oireachtas. Therefore, the judgment was in any event incompatible with the duty of consistent interpretation from a more procedural instead of substantive point of view, i.e. the national court reached its conclusion without taking the steps prescribed by EU law that aim to increase the scope for national courts to find a route to a consistent interpretation. It thus concerns the line of argumentation followed.

3.3.4. *Protection of Fundamental Rights under the Constitution*

The final aspect that is relevant for the Irish superior courts' application of the *contra legem* limitation is discussed by reference to the Supreme Court's judgment in *Albatros Feeds Ltd v Minister for Agriculture and Food.* In order to prevent a potential spread of BSE, the applicant had been the subject of seizure, detention and recall notices in respect of imported animal feed, which notices the respondent had based on the national European Communities (Processed Animal Products) Regulations 2000 only. It was clear that the relevant EU law provisions required that the defendant was empowered to take such action. However, Fennelly J. (with whom the other judges agreed) pointed out that the notices interfered with the applicant's constitutionally protected right to property. This led to the following observation:

> '[i]n the application of [the duty of consistent interpretation; SWH] to the facts of the present case, it is of the first importance to note that the powers claimed by the first respondent entail a drastic incursion into the fundamental property rights of the affected trader. Such action must be justified, if at all, by clear words. There are no words in the Regulations of 2000, which are capable, on even the most extended and generous interpretation, of justifying the first respondent's actions'. This was followed by these concluding remarks: 'I am fully conscious of the obligation of "conforming interpretation" (…). I am equally conscious of the need for severe action to prevent the spread of B.S.E. Severe action may be indispensable and it may be necessary to infringe fundamental rights including property rights. However, clear words are necessary where fundamental rights are at issue. I do not accept that our courts are obliged to interpret our laws so as to confer drastic powers by vague or indirect words or, indeed, by none. In

---

for Edwards J. to adopt a consistent interpretation), or the contrived objective *not* to implement the polluter pays principle.

> the present case such a result cannot be achieved by any normal process of legal reasoning'.[137]

So it was the interference with the fundamental right to property protected under the Constitution that gave rise to the consideration that the sought-after powers could only be applied if they were clearly foreseen by national law.

The first route to a consistent interpretation that was rejected by the Supreme Court was based on a combined reading of regulation 9 of the Regulations of 2000 and regulation 7 of the European Communities (Animal Nutrition Inspections) Regulations 2003 (it is again emphasised that the Regulations of 2003 were not stated on the concerned notices). I will not discuss this route further here as I agree with the Supreme Court that there was not a sufficiently clear reference in the former provision to the powers contained in the latter. However, in view of the discussion of the second route it may be useful to point out that Fennelly J. did not seem to clearly dismiss the possibility that Regulation 7 of the Regulations of 2003 could potentially provide for the powers sought after by the defendant and that this provision stated that the Minister shall prohibit entry and order re-dispatch of non-compliant products.

The second route was barely considered by the Supreme Court as it considered that it was clearly impossible. It would be based on Regulation 4 of the Regulations of 2000, which provided that:

> '[w]here processed animal proteins intended for feeding to farmed animals were put into circulation prior to the 1st January 2001, the person responsible for putting the material into circulation shall, unless otherwise authorised, ensure that all remaining stock of such material is withdrawn immediately from the market, from distribution channels and from on-farm storage'.

In terms of the sought-after powers, that provision does not seem to me to be fundamentally less appropriate than Regulation 7 of the Regulations of 2003. But even if I am incorrect about this, it is important to point out that Regulation 4 was rather similar to, and implemented, Article 3 of Decision 2000/766.[138] As the Supreme Court itself noted, it was decided in the ECJ's *Bellio* judgment (which

---

137 Supreme Court 26 July 2006 *Albatros Feeds Ltd v Minister for Agriculture and Food* [2007] 1 IR 221 at paras. 61, 63.

138 Council Decision of 4 December 2000 concerning certain protection measures with regard to transmissible spongiform encephalopathies and the feeding of animal protein, *OJ* 2000, L306/32, Article 3(1) of which provided that Member States shall '(...) ensure that all processed animal proteins intended for the feeding of farmed animals which are kept, fattened or bred for the production of food are withdrawn from the market, distribution channels and from on-farm storage'. Although it follows that the two provisions are not completely identical, it is submitted that, in as far as the adoption of certain measures is prescribed (which is the material point), there is no distinction.

originated in a reference by an Italian court) that '[w]ith regard to the destruction of the contaminated consignments, it should be noted that this is a measure provided for by Article 3(1) of Decision 2000/766'.[139] By the way, I also point out here that in the *Bellio* case Ireland submitted before the ECJ that the destruction of the product was justified. Fennelly J. expressed surprise at the ECJ's ruling. Be that as it may, on account of the close proximity between the two provisions, the ECJ's *Spedition Welter* judgment comes into the picture.[140] In chapter 2, subparagraph 4.3.3, I argued that that judgment must not be understood as removing all discretion from the national courts to take a final decision as to whether a consistent interpretation can be adopted. Nevertheless, I submitted that one caveat applies: it follows from the judgment that, in a situation of *verbatim* transposition, national courts cannot claim that a consistent interpretation is not possible as a result of the national provision's wording. Yet, it seems that this was exactly the argument made by Fennelly J. To be more precise, it was the absence of clear words conferring the sought-after powers that led to the rejection of a consistent interpretation. This means that the judgment did not only indicate that there may be less scope to proceed to a consistent interpretation if this would interfere with a national fundamental right, but also that reliance on the *contra legem* limitation can relate to the situation where there is a clear contradiction as a result of what national legislation does *not* say.

> It also needs to be asked how this part of the judgment relates to the decisions adopted in *Coastal Line Container Terminal Ltd v Services Industrial Professional Technical Union* and *Thompson v Dublin Bus* (note that the latter was also delivered by the Supreme Court and subsequent to the judgment in *Albatros Feeds Ltd v Minister for Agriculture and Food*).[141] These two judgments provide authority for the position that, if the text clearly reproduces the directive, the meaning of the latter will be followed, unless the legislature has clearly expressed a different intention. However, it seems to me that an important distinction between these two cases and *Albatros Feeds Ltd v Minister for Agriculture and Food* is that the latter would involve the adoption of an interpretation infringing upon the fundamental right to property as protected under the Constitution.

What does the Supreme Court's judgment in *Albatros Feeds Ltd v Minister for Agriculture and Food* mean for the relationship between EU and national law under the duty of consistent interpretation? It should first and foremost be made clear that it is incompatible with the theory of supremacy of EU law where national constitutional law is given priority over EU law. Was that what the Supreme Court did? If one looks at the Supreme Court's reasoning, there are no statements to the effect that it believed that the directive provided insufficient protection to

139 Case C-286/02 *Bellio*, ECLI:EU:C:2004:212, para. 54.
140 Case C-306/12 *Spedition Welter*, ECLI:EU:C:2013:650, para. 31.
141 High Court 16 December 1999 *Coastal Line Container Terminal Ltd v Services Industrial Professional Technical Union* [2000] 1 IR 549 at 561; Supreme Court 5 March 2015 *Thompson v Dublin Bus* [2015] 3 JIC 503.

fundamental rights and that it applied a national constitutional provision instead. It rather appeared to be the step from what national law stipulated (or, perhaps more accurately: what it did *not* stipulate) to the powers envisaged by the directive that was considered to be too drastic; it was thus attempted to (also) draw a link with an interpretative argument. It would indeed be relevant if the rejection of a consistent interpretation was not solely based on the national fundamental right, but this was rather the immediate cause leading to the higher demands placed on the national provision's wording. Yet, another important factor is that the ECJ's *Bellio* judgment concerned a nearly identical provision and that it was found by the ECJ that this could authorise similar actions. So then the relevant question becomes: can national courts, if a consistent interpretation would entail an interference with a national fundamental right, apply higher standards than EU law itself on the foreseeability of the fundamental rights interference by law? I believe that the answer should be no as there was not a clear discrepancy between EU and national law so that, effectively, national law would demand a higher standard for interferences with fundamental rights than EU law. It was argued in chapter 2, subparagraph 5.4 that it follows from Article 52(1) of the Charter that limitations to fundamental rights must satisfy a 'quality of the law' test, i.e. they must be clear and accessible, and should meet the requirement of foreseeability. Although the Supreme Court's judgment was delivered before the Charter became legally binding, it could be argued that the same requirements are applicable when fundamental rights are protected as general principles of law.[142] Accordingly, even though the ECJ has not explicitly confirmed this position, it would in principle make sense if national courts would take a more restrictive approach to consistent interpretation when interpreting a national provision limiting a fundamental right that also finds protection under EU law as the Charter requires that this limitation – deriving from the national provision – must be sufficiently foreseeable. This is not problematic as such. However, this line of reasoning presumes an interpretative gap between EU and national law and I also submitted that a qualification applies if the national provision does not – in a significant way – deviate from the corresponding provision in the directive. And in this regard the close proximity between the relevant provision of Irish law and EU law in the case *Albatros Feeds Ltd v Minister for Agriculture and Food* is recalled. Although the point was not explicitly addressed, I do not consider it very likely that the ECJ would have concluded that the provision contained in the EU law decision interfered with fundamental rights as their interference was not clearly foreseen by that provision. In fact, the ECJ's considerations seem to indicate quite clearly that the actions carried out fell within the scope of the provision contained in the decision. Since the provision of Irish

142 See Article 6(3) TEU and, in relation to the test to be applied for limitations to the right to property, Case 44/79 *Hauer*, ECLI:EU:C:1979:290, para. 17 *et seq.* See, more generally, Case C-368/95 *Familiapress*, ECLI:EU:C:1997:325, para. 26; Case C-274/99 P *Connolly*, ECLI:EU:C:2001:127, para. 42; Joined Cases C-465/00, C-138/01 and C-139/01 Österreichischer *Rundfunk*, ECLI:EU:C:2003:294, para. 76 *et seq.*

law was very close to the EU law provision, it can be said that the Supreme Court's position would *de facto* require that national courts are permitted to provide more far-reaching protection under national law. And this is something which EU law does not permit, at least not in the type of situation occurring before the Supreme Court. For this I refer, again, to the ECJ's *Melloni* judgment and the two exceptions to the rule that national law cannot set fundamental rights standards higher than the Charter (see, further, chapter 2, subparagraph 5.4). This, together with the ECJ's *Bellio* judgment, makes it very difficult to justify the Supreme Court's judgment from an EU law perspective. I also want to put forward that the fundamental right to property was of paramount importance for the course adopted by Fennelly J,[143] and the strict requirements concerning foreseeability of the interference are a direct consequence of the presence of this national fundamental right. For these reasons, the Supreme Court's judgment raises an incompatibility with the duty of consistent interpretation. Implicitly, the judgment seemed to call into question the appropriateness of the EU law provision as a legal basis for the concerned actions (which would interfere with a fundamental right). But the Supreme Court avoided such a consideration, which would have constituted a more obvious challenge to the validity of EU law and would cleary have required a preliminary reference. Instead it was attempted to present the rejection of a consistent interpretation as being based not only on fundamental rights, but also on genuine interpretative concerns. However, as I explained, this does not convince.

A similar approach can be witnessed in the subsequent High Court judgment in *EPA v Greenstar Holdings Ltd* concerning the question whether a landfill operator could be required to use a certain portion of collected charges only for the closure, restoration, remediation and aftercare of the landfill. Although Finlay Geoghegan J. had already concluded that there was in her opinion no incompatibility between the national provisions and the directive, she added that, even if this were otherwise, the former could not be given a consistent interpretation (note that these considerations regarding the directive were thus *obiter*). Clearly reiterating the precedent set by *Albatros Feeds Ltd v Minister for Agriculture and Food* regarding the protection of the fundamental right to property, it was found that:

> 'Once paid, the money is part of the business receipts and *prima facie* is the property of the landfill operator. A person, whether legal or natural, is entitled to the benefit of its property and to use it as it sees fit, save as may be restricted by law. Any such restriction imposed by statute, in accordance with the principles of legal certainty, must be in clear and precise terms. There is nothing in the wording of s. 53A of the 1996 Act which could justify an interpretation that it imposes a restriction on the use to which a landfill operator could put a part of charges imposed and collected by it pursuant to section 53A. Accordingly, this

143 The same view was expressed in High Court 14 October 2016 *Bookfinders Ltd v Revenue Commissioners* [2016] IEHC 569 at para. 29.

> Court is precluded by the Supreme Court judgment in *Albatross Feeds* from so interpreting s. 53A, irrespective of a different interpretation of Article 10 of the Landfill Directive to the one set out in this judgment. It follows that a question on the interpretation of the Landfill Directive is not necessary to enable me give judgment on the preliminary issue'.[144]

> Interestingly, this argument was thus not only used to reject a consistent interpretation, but also to deny the necessity of referring questions for a preliminary ruling. As this argument was put forward by some of the German superior courts on more than one occasion, I discussed this issue in a separate subparagraph of the chapter that examines the German superior courts' perspective (chapter 3, paragraph 4). There, I argued that courts cannot easily conclude that it is not necessary to make a reference to decide the dispute before them because in their view national law can in any event not be interpreted in conformity with the directive. The same applies here.

It is noted that the implementing measures that were interpreted in *EPA v Greenstar Holdings Ltd,* are not an example of *verbatim* transposition.[145] Therefore, the judgment is in this respect not subject to the same criticism as *Albatros Feeds Ltd v Minister for Agriculture and Food.* The case provided an excellent opportunity to ask the ECJ to elucidate the role played by fundamental rights as a limitation to the duty of consistent interpretation. But unfortunately that opportunity was not taken up.

3.4. INCIDENTAL INTERFERENCES WITH THE TRADITIONAL APPROACH AND A TRINITY OF IRISH LEGAL CULTURE

Subparagraph 3.2 contained a few examples of case law that clearly showed the consequences of the shift in approach, i.e. a shift away from the literal approach, which is, or has remained, the dominant method for interpreting Irish law. There was the judgment in *EPA v Harte Peat Ltd.* Although the structural priority which the judgment conferred on consistent interpretation has remained a somewhat isolated position, it did provide a clear example of supremacy of the duty of consistent interpretation. The Supreme Court's judgment in *Nathan v Bailey Gibson Ltd* is an emphatic example of a transgression of the traditional interpretative rules, as well as the judgments in *Health Service Executive v Sallam* and *SIAC Construction Ltd v National Roads Authority.* In those judgments the Irish superior courts permitted a more far-reaching interference with the concerned provisions' wording in order to enable a consistent interpretation. It is pointed out that, as I searched for conflicts of interpretation, the focus has been on the more controversial cases, and it should

144 High Court 8 April 2014 *EPA v Greenstar Holdings Ltd* [2014] 4 JIC 802 at para. 70.

145 Compare, on the one hand, Article 10 of Council Directive 1999/31/EC of 26 April 1999 on the landfill of waste, *OJ* 1999, L182/1 and, on the other hand, Article 53A of the Waste Management Act 1996.

not be overlooked that it is relatively rare that national interpretative rules are interfered with as a result of the duty of consistent interpretation. The dominance of case law in which the duty of consistent interpretation is applied in relation to implementing legislation might be an explanation for this as it can be presumed that it will then be easier to adopt a consistent interpretation without interfering with the traditional approach.[146] It is also pointed out that an application of the duty of consistent interpretation will sometimes adapt the interpretation that would have followed on the basis of a traditional approach but this does not necessarily mean that there was a conflict. I think that the judgment in *Eircom Ltd v ComReg* provides a good example of this.

Referring to the *contra legem* limitation, the Irish superior courts have on a number of occasions rejected a consistent interpretation. In this respect the courts' approach is to a large extent explained by a 'trinity of Irish legal culture'. First, the *contra legem* limitation is normally understood as referring to the clear wording of the concerned provision. This follows on from an important aspect of Irish legal culture: the dominance of a literal approach under the common law method of legal reasoning which can, in my view, ultimately be traced back to Ireland's historical experiences with parliamentary sovereignty and the latter's conferral of strict legislative supremacy. While I am convinced that this first aspect is compatible with the ECJ's case law, there are other aspects of the Irish superior courts' case law relating to the *contra legem* limitation that seem to be problematic from the perspective of the supremacy of EU law. This brings me to the second part of the trinity: the Irish legal system's dualist approach to international law.[147] This feature emerged in the judgment in *EPA v Neiphin Trading Ltd.* Even though the case was concerned with an interpretation of implementing legislation and it was beyond dispute that there was an implementing objective, the High Court was only prepared to accept that the Oireachtas had been willing to take over the objective of implementing the 'polluter pays principle' contained in the directive in as far as national law positively confirmed such an intention. This can be seen as reflecting the dualist approach to the extent that the latter requires '(…) that the courts are only empowered to base their decisions on international sources if these have been re-enacted by the laws of that State'.[148] I argued that the partitioning of the implementing objective and requiring positive confirmation of separate objectives in national law is incompatible with the presumption formulated in the ECJ's *Wagner Miret* and *Pfeiffer* judgments. The third aspect is the protection of fundamental

146 See also High Court 3 March 2011 *EPA v Neiphin Trading Ltd* [2011] 2 IR 575 at para. 67. See, further, O'Reilly (n. 36), p. 346.

147 M. Claes, *The National Courts' Mandate in the European Constitution* (Hart Publishing 2006), p. 208; Phelan (n. 21), p. 534; Sterck (n. 18), p. 111.

148 Claes (n. 147), p. 30. At p. 169, Claes also explains that the international norm is made into a national norm and that it is the latter that is recognised. From this perspective, it would also make sense to focus only on the intentions expressed by the national legislature.

rights under the Constitution, another central feature of Irish legal culture. This aspect was clearly at work in the Supreme Court's judgment in *Albatros Feeds Ltd v Minister for Agriculture and Food,* where Fennelly J. considered that the protection of the fundamental right to property placed more demanding requirements on the provision's wording before it could be interpreted as permitting certain powers – which could infringe upon that right – required by EU law. While it appeared from the court's reasoning that the argument concerning fundamental rights was applied in tandem with the interpretative argument concerning the provision's text, I argued that there was almost no difference between EU and national law on the material point so that, on balance, the Supreme Court appeared to place higher demands on the foreseeability of an interference with a fundamental right and that this would be incompatible with EU law. The ECJ's case law has not so far explicitly addressed the question whether national courts can invoke fundamental rights as a limitation to the duty of consistent interpretation. The fundamental right to property could be relevant in as far as limits to fundamental rights should in principle meet the test of foreseeability which, in turn, could affect the scope that is available under the traditional interpretative methods. However, in the specific circumstances of the case (the national provision constituted a *verbatim* transposition) the Supreme Court appeared to challenge the supremacy of EU law as its approach to the test of foreseeability boiled down to an application of higher national fundamental rights standards.

In addition to these judgments that are reflective of Irish legal culture, there was also the Supreme Court's judgment in *Harding v Cork County Council (No 5).* There, Kearns J. concluded, albeit *obiter,* that the national provision did not permit further interpretation, even though there was arguably grammatical ambiguity. I think that it was not only the difference in wording between the national provision and the directive, but also an interpretation based on the surrounding provisions and the derived legislative intent that prevented a consistent interpretation. While it may be asked whether the Supreme Court tried hard enough to adopt a consistent interpretation, and the judgment broadened the scope of the *contra legem* limitation beyond an incompatibility with the provision's clear wording, I do not see this judgment as a clear violation of the duty of consistent interpretation.

4. AN AFTERTHOUGHT: AN EXPLANATION FOR MORE AND LESS FAVOURABLE ATTITUDES TOWARDS THE DUTY OF CONSISTENT INTERPRETATION?

While the Interpretation Act 2005 was intended to clarify that courts were in certain circumstances allowed to adopt a purposive approach to interpretation

– which was in part inspired by the Irish courts' approach to the interpretation in conformity with EU law – it has also been understood as reaffirming and fixating the dominance of the literal approach. I already pointed out that Edwards J. implied in his judgment in *EPA v Neiphin Trading Ltd* that the introduction of the Interpretation Act 2005 may have removed the flexibility of the interpretative rules at common law, previously used by the Irish superior courts to depart from a literal interpretation in favour of a consistent interpretation.[149] The Interpretation Act 2005 commenced on 1 January 2006. On 16 June 2005, the ECJ's *Pupino* judgment was delivered, which established that national courts are not required to adopt a *contra legem* interpretation. Arguably, these two developments both emphasised the restrictive side to the interpretative process. So while there may not have been crystal-clear directions for the Irish courts – from both the EU as well as national law perspective – as to the reconciliation of the duty of consistent interpretation and national interpretative rules pre-2006, it was now made explicit by the Interpretation Act 2005 which approach courts should follow. And, additionally, the *contra legem* limitation made it clear that it is not necessarily incompatible with EU law if a consistent interpretation is rejected.

Interestingly, judgments such as *Murphy v An Bord Telecom* Éireann and *Nathan v Bailey Gibson Ltd,* both considered as emphatic examples of the duty of consistent interpretation having priority over national interpretative rules, but also for example the judgment in *SIAC Construction Ltd v National Roads Authority,* were all delivered before 2005. And the delivery of the Supreme Court's judgment in *Albatros Feeds Ltd v Minister for Agriculture and Food* in 2006, which adopted a more restrictive approach with regard to the duty of consistent interpretation, was followed by a series of judgments rejecting a consistent interpretation – some being more cogently reasoned (from the perspective of the duty of consistent interpretation) than others.[150] I admit that it is difficult to simply contribute this to the introduction of the Interpretation Act 2005 and the *contra legem* limitation. Nevertheless, the High Court's judgment in *EMI Records (Ireland) Ltd v UPC Communications Ireland Ltd* is a good example showing how these developments have made it easier to reject a consistent interpretation – albeit for good reasons on that particular occasion. As I argued in subparagraph 3.1.2, the High Court in that judgment interpreted section 5 of the Interpretation Act 2005 as normally permitting the courts to apply a purposive interpretation, but prohibiting such if this would give rise to a manifest violation of the text, involving a transgression of the court's own competences. A few paragraphs later, reference was made to the ECJ's *Pupino* judgment and it was pointed out that national courts are not required

149 High Court 3 March 2011 *EPA v Neiphin Trading Ltd* [2011] 2 IR 575 at para. 67.
150 See, for example, Supreme Court 2 May 2008 *Harding v Cork County Council (No 5)* [2008] 2 ILRM 251; High Court 3 March 2011 *EPA v Neiphin Trading Ltd* [2011] 2 IR 575; Court of Appeal 16 December 2016 *Smith v Meade* [2016] 12 JIC 1608.

to adopt a *contra legem* interpretation.[151] So, on the one hand, non-negotiable limits to interpretation were derived from section 5 of the Interpretation Act 2005 and, on the other hand, there was an explicit exception under EU law that could be invoked for applying that limitation. In addition to that, the High Court's judgment in *EPA v Neiphin Trading Ltd* clearly shows what further adverse effects the introduction of the Interpretation Act 2005 may have had for the scope to adopt a consistent interpretation, if section 5 is interpreted as requiring that, even in cases concerning implementing legislation, only the intentions of the Oireachtas that find expression in the domestic legislation can be decisive.

I must make it clear that a shift whereby more emphasis is placed on limits derived from the national interpretative rules is in my opinion not good or bad as long as the requirements under Articles 288 TFEU and 4(3) TEU are respected. However, the point is that I did encounter a difference in attitude if some of the earlier judgments applying the duty of consistent interpretation are compared to the post-2006 case law and in this paragraph I have attempted to find a rational explanation for this difference.

5. CONCLUSION

The Irish courts' traditional approach to interpretation is aimed at identifying the legislature's intention. This also means that the principal constraint placed upon the Irish courts is that they should not perform legislative functions, a limitation that is ultimately of a constitutional nature. At the beginning of this chapter it was seen that the common law method of legal reasoning has been characterised as pragmatic, containing a degree of flexibility and room for further development of the interpretative rules but also as adopting a textualist and formalist approach to interpretation. This is confirmed by my sketch of the Irish courts' traditional approach under the rules at common law. A literal interpretation is the dominant approach for ascertaining the legislature's intention. Under the rules at common law, the flexible nature was primarily reflected in the indeterminateness of the threshold for proceeding to a more purposive approach: the finding that a literal interpretation would produce an ambiguous or absurd result. The drawing of the exact contours is a matter that was to a large extent left to the discretion of the courts who could determine whether it would be appropriate to depart from a literal interpretation in the specific circumstances of the case. But even if they proceeded in this way, they did not drift too far away from the legislation as such: they would typically take into account guidance offered by the structure of the legislation, surrounding provisions, the long title of the legislation and, albeit to

151 High Court 11 October 2010 *EMI Records (Ireland) Ltd v UPC Communications Ireland Ltd* [2010] IEHC 377 at paras. 96, 103.

a lesser extent, legislative history. There is broad support for the view that the legislature's intention is not to be ascertained on the basis of parliamentary history. Also, if the gap between a particular interpretation and the provision's wording is simply too large, the Irish courts will not discard the literal interpretation, no matter how absurd or ambiguous, as they feel that they would thereby transgress their own competences. Partly as a result of the influence of EU law on Irish law, the courts had started to make use of purposive criteria more often. Although it has not changed the dominance of the literal rule, the introduction of the Interpretation Act 2005 aimed to consolidate the trend towards a more purposive approach, yet thereby also fixated the courts' appraisal to what extent it might be appropriate to look at such criteria.

The Irish superior courts recognise that the duty of consistent interpretation has its legal basis in EU law, more specifically Articles 288 TFEU and 4(3) TEU while, in as far as the provisions were adopted by the legislature to implement the directive, a further reason to apply the obligation is found in the traditional teleological approach to interpretation. Since the Irish superior courts' case law does not support a view whereby the latter is an imperative for proceeding to an application of the duty of consistent interpretation, the position is in conformity with EU law requirements in this respect.

The determination of the relationship between EU and national law requires that a conflict of interpretative rules can be identified (or, perhaps, a potential conflict in as far as the theory of constitutional pluralism is concerned). This can be the result of national interpretative methods requiring an approach that falls short of the obligations under the duty of consistent interpretation, or where the duty of consistent interpretation is applied in a manner that interferes with the outer limits of the national interpretative rules.

As Edwards J. observed in his judgment in *EPA v Neiphin Trading Ltd*, the Irish courts have to interpret national law in accordance with well established traditional interpretative rules and, in as far as the duty of consistent interpretation applies, they simultaneously have to do so with due regard to that obligation. He also pointed out that in most of the judgments delivered so far, this has not resulted in significant difficulties since most of the time the Irish courts were required to apply the duty of consistent interpretation in relation to implementing legislation, so that the objectives of the directive and the intention of the Oireachtas coincided. He is probably correct in this regard. Be that as it may, the legislative framework that provided the background for the High Court's judgment in *Murphy v An Bord Telecom* Éireann had also been intended to implement EU law (what is now Article 157 TFEU), but there were nevertheless serious interpretative difficulties. The High Court's judgment was the first occasion at which an Irish superior court applied the duty of consistent interpretation, and Keane J.'s approach remains one of the most striking examples of the conflict between the traditional common law method of legal reasoning and the exigencies of the duty of consistent interpretation, highlighting the textualist and formalist nature of the former as well as its flexible nature as provoked by the latter. This resulted in a fundamental shift in approach that permeated the Irish superior courts approach to the duty of consistent interpretation. While there was clearly a different perspective in Dublin compared to Luxembourg on how interpretation should be approached, the High Court recognised the different context within which EU law operated and adapted its approach to these circumstances by relaxing the rigidity of the literal approach, thereby enabling a more effective application of the duty of consistent interpretation. This was possible as the approach to interpretation under the rules at common law was of a flexible nature in the sense that they were not codified and could be adapted to such changing circumstances. The Supreme Court's judgment in *Nathan v Bailey Gibson Ltd* was the first judgment where the firepower of the duty of consistent interpretation was really tested in a context of directives. In a spirit similar to the judgment in *Murphy v An Bord Telecom* Éireann, the conflict of interpretations was resolved in favour of a consistent interpretation.

However, in the period that followed, examples of decisions supporting the theory of supremacy of EU law grew thinner (exceptions are to be found in the judgments in *Health Service Executive v Sallam* and *SIAC Construction Ltd v National Roads Authority*; and, to some extent, *EPA v Harte Peat Ltd*). Moreover, in a number of important judgments, the Irish superior courts started to follow a more restrictive line in their approach to the duty of consistent interpretation. This started with the Supreme Court's judgment in *Albatros Feeds Ltd v Minister for Agriculture and Food* concerning an important feature of Irish legal culture. I noted that Fennelly J.'s judgment (with whom the other judges agreed) goes beyond the scope of the established limits to the duty of consistent interpretation and submitted that – even though the ECJ's case law has not yet explicitly addressed the concerned point – the approach to the requirements that limitations to fundamental rights must fulfil, in that particular case, appeared to be incompatible with EU law. The more restrictive line adopted by the Supreme Court was continued by the High Court in its judgment in *EPA v Neiphin Trading Ltd.* That judgment provides authority for the position that, even though an implementing objective was identified, the directive's objectives were only taken into account in as far as national law positively confirmed that the Oireachtas had the intention to implement the concerned objective. The objective to implement the directive was as it were replaced by and subdivided into the different objectives pursued by the directive, each of which requiring such positive confirmation. Also here an important feature of Irish legal culture played a role, namely the legal system's dualist approach to international law. Finally, there is the Supreme Court's judgment in *Harding v Cork County*

Council (No 5). There, Kearns J. rejected, albeit *obiter*, the possibility to adopt a consistent interpretation, holding that such an interpretation would be *contra legem*. His judgment departed from the Irish superior courts' prevailing view on the meaning of the *contra legem* limitation as the national provision's wording did not as such seem to prevent further interpretation and I believe that he also relied on the broader scheme of the legislation (i.e. a systematic interpretation) for reaching his conclusion. It is observed that also in *Albatros Feeds Ltd v Minister for Agriculture and Food* and *EPA v Neiphin Trading Ltd* reference was made to the *contra legem* limitation, and also on these occasions there was a somewhat unusual application of that limitation. In the former case, there was a contradiction as a result of what national law *did not* say. The same is true for the latter case, and it must be added that, also in that judgment, other interpretative criteria than a grammatical interpretation were essential for rejecting a consistent interpretation. These judgments reflect an understanding of *contra legem* that is not necessarily confined to an incompatibility with the provision's text. The ECJ's case law has not yet made it clear whether it shares this broader view which, arguably, would entail that so far as possible and *contra legem* largely become each other's mirror image. However, there is also a distinction between these cases and the judgment in *Harding v Cork County Council (No 5)*. While it may be asked whether it was tried hard enough to obtain a consistent interpretation, there was not, unlike these other judgments, an incompatibility with the duty of consistent interpretation.

In paragraph 4 I argued that the adoption of a stricter line in the courts' case law is not entirely coincidental and can be traced back to two developments occurring around the same time. This line was adopted after the introduction of section 5 of the Interpretation Act 2005 and the ECJ's establishment of the *contra legem* limitation. While the former for the first time codified, at least to some extent, the interpretative rules that are to be applied by the Irish courts and therefore arguably removed some of the pre-existing flexibility, the latter made it clear that national courts were sometimes permitted to hold that a consistent interpretation was simply not possible.

On balance, although there are emphatic precedents supporting the theory of supremacy of EU law, and while this initially seemed to accurately reflect the Irish superior courts' response to the challenges that accompanied the need to reconcile well established traditional interpretative rules with the duty of consistent interpretation, this has become the more isolated position and matters have become more nuanced. The examples have become few and far between, nearly all of them occurring before the introduction of the Interpretation Act 2005, and the Supreme Court has since taken a more restrictive approach towards the duty of consistent interpretation. The question is whether this means that the Irish courts have adopted the perspective of national constitutionalism. Subject to the obvious qualification that it is difficult to reduce an entire body of case law to one model, there are nevertheless important similarities. First, a characteristic of national constitutionalism is that, ultimately, a Member State's constitution, or other national acts of similar authority, remain the ultimate source of application of EU law. While it was seen that the Irish superior courts refer to Articles 288 TFEU and 4(3) TEU as the legal basis for the duty of consistent interpretation, it must not be overlooked that, notwithstanding Ireland's benevolent constitutional accommodation of EU law, its smooth operation is in the end enabled by and subject to these constitutional arrangements and EU law provisions only become effective on the basis of the European Communities Act 1972. Admittedly, the latter provisions are not referred to when the Irish courts apply the duty of consistent interpretation, but it is nevertheless something which is, at a minimum, not inconsistent with the theory of national constitutionalism. Secondly, it is recalled that national constitutionalism does not mean a wholesale rejection of supremacy of EU law. Quite to the contrary, there is in general an acceptance of supremacy of EU law; it is not even excluded that certain constitutional provisions may need to be set aside. The only exception to this is where the operation of EU law violates fundamental constitutional provisions. Ireland's willingness to intervene in such circumstances was already seen in a judgment delivered outside the context of the duty of consistent interpretation: the Supreme Court's judgment in *SPUC (Ireland) Ltd v Grogan,* where the operation of EU law threatened to violate the constitutional right to life. Now, consider the situation in Ireland with regard to the duty of consistent interpretation. Although there will not normally be a conflict, when this does arise, there is authority for the position that fundamental aspects of the Irish legal system restrict the duty of consistent interpretation. Nevertheless, a conclusion that the theory of national constitutionalism provides the most adequate theory from the Irish superior courts' perspective sits somewhat uneasily with the fact that the High Court in *EPA v Neiphin Trading Ltd* and the Supreme Court in *Albatros Feeds Ltd v Minister for Agriculture and Food* (as well as the judgment in *Harding v Cork County Council (No 5)*), did not seem to have had the intention to depart from their obligations under the duty of consistent interpretation. There was an attempt to align the reasoning for the rejection of a consistent interpretation with the ECJ's framework – and in respect of the judgment in *Albatros Feeds Ltd v Minister for Agriculture and Food* it is noted that, in principle, and notwithstanding my conclusion that in the specific circumstances of the case the rejection of a consistent interpretation could not be reconciled with the framework for the duty of consistent interpretation, it would be desirable if the impact of a consistent interpretation on constitutionally guaranteed rights would be recognised as a relevant factor. Of course, subjective intent cannot cure a violation of the requirements under the duty of consistent interpretation. Yet, this does show that, if a preliminary ruling would establish that the current position adopted by the Irish superior courts is indeed in violation of the duty of consistent interpretation, they are probably not necessarily unwilling to reconsider their approach in light of the requirements under EU law. A further consequence that can be derived from this, is that the Irish superior courts' position might be more adequately explained by the theory of constitutional pluralism. This theory maintains the starting point that there are in certain areas of the law conflicting positions, yet has the additional benefit that it encompasses a school of thought that is more focussed on recognising the importance of, and providing the theoretical building blocks for, conflict avoidance. It does not seem unlikely that if the ECJ were to determine that the Irish courts have incorrectly applied the duty of consistent interpretation, there would be scope for reconciliation. The ECJ's reaction to the judgment in *SPUC (Ireland) Ltd v Grogan* and the subsequent constitutional amendments enacted by Ireland are a useful example of mutual responsiveness to the legitimate concerns underlying the conflicting positions. However, it is noted that it was the Irish Government that was responsible for the Member State's contribution to this reconciliation. The Supreme Court has not yielded so far when it comes to the protection of fundamental rights protected under the Constitution.

CHAPTER 5
THE DUTCH SUPERIOR COURTS' PERSPECTIVE

1. INTRODUCTION

The Dutch legal order is well known for its rich tradition of being open to international law. This is perhaps the result of an interplay between a progressive school of thought and some of the country's characteristics.

> This is described in more detail by Claes and De Witte. 'Part of the explanation may be the historical tradition of the Dutch school of international law. It may be tempting to draw a straight line from Grotius' *Mare Liberum* to the radical version of *pacta sunt servanda* espoused by Dutch internationalist doctrine. Since Grotius' time, this idealist attitude was in the best national interest. The traditional receptivity to international rules, and willingness to co-operate with foreign nations is clearly in the interest of a small trading nation, that is too small to preserve its independence on its own, and needs open borders for its prosperity'.[1]

In line with (or perhaps it is more accurate to say: as a result of) the Dutch legal order's internationalist spirit, EU law was in general received without major difficulties.[2]

The Dutch legal order's openness towards international law is reflected in the relatively unique Articles 93 and 94 of the Dutch Constitution that were introduced with the constitutional revisions of 1953 and 1956:

> Article 93 provides that provisions of treaties and of decisions by international institutions, which may be binding on all persons by virtue of their contents shall become binding after they have been published. Article 94 provides that statutory regulations in force within the Kingdom shall not be applicable if such application is in conflict with provisions of treaties that are binding on all persons or of decisions by international institutions.

---

1 M. Claes and B. De Witte, 'Report on the Netherlands', in: A.-M. Slaughter, A. Stone Sweet and J.H.H. Weiler (Eds.), *The European Courts & National Courts – Doctrine and Jurisprudence* (Hart Publishing 1998), p. 189.

2 Ibid, p. 171.

Although the constitutional provisions concern international law in general and are not specifically directed towards EU law, and while they were introduced before the ECJ's landmark judgments in *Van Gend & Loos* and *Costa v ENEL*,[3] they were enacted to take into account in particular the new supranational features of the European Coal and Steel Community (which established a common market in coal and steel, and in certain respects laid down the supranational architecture that was further developed in the subsequent Treaty establishing the European Economic Community) and proved to be perfectly suitable for the reception of those landmark judgments.[4] Be that as it may, since autonomy and supremacy are widely accepted as inherent features of EU law, there is some discussion in Dutch legal scholarship whether Articles 93 and 94 of the Constitution are at all necessary in the context of EU law. But since this is in my opinion primarily a theoretical discussion which is moreover not immediately relevant for the discussions in this chapter, it will not be repeated here.[5] For present purposes, another matter is probably more important, namely that Articles 93 and 94 do not seem to be directly relevant for a duty of consistent interpretation (including the obligation to interpret national law in conformity with directives, as established in the ECJ's *Von Colson and Kamann* judgment,[6] but the term is used here to refer in a more general sense to an interpretation in conformity with any rule of international law). This appears, first, from a decision by the Dutch Supreme Court (Hoge Raad; hereinafter HR) interpreting national law in conformity with international law that was adopted before the introduction of those provisions into the Constitution – indicating that this is not conditional upon the existence of those provisions.[7] Secondly, the qualification 'that are binding on all persons' coincides with the provision having direct effect – in fact, in the context of Articles 93 and 94 of the Constitution, the Dutch courts have started to apply the test developed under EU law whether the invoked provision is 'unconditional and sufficiently precise', to

3 Case 26/62 *Van Gend & Loos*, ECLI:EU:C:1963:1; Case 6/64 *Costa v ENEL*, ECLI:EU:C:1964:66.

4 B. De Witte, 'Do Not Mention the Word: Sovereignty in Two Europhile Countries – Belgium and The Netherlands', in: N. Walker (Ed.), *Sovereignty in Transition* (Hart Publishing 2003), p. 362.

5 The majority view is that Articles 93 and 94 of the Constitution are superfluous in the context of EU law: on account of the autonomous nature of the EU legal order, direct effect and supremacy apply *qua* EU law. This view was confirmed in HR 2 November 2004, ECLI:NL:HR:2004:AR1797, *NJ* 2005/80 (*Rusttijden*). See further Claes and De Witte (n. 1), p. 183-4. Cf. L.F.M. Besselink and others, *De Nederlandse Grondwet en de Europese Unie* (Europa Law Publishing 2002), p. 31-2, 37, where it is argued that, among others, the discussions on the constitutional revisions of 1953 and 1956, as well as the subsequent constitutional revisions in 1983 made it clear that Articles 93 and 94 *were* considered to be relevant for the application of (then) ECSC and EC law in the Dutch legal order. A different view would therefore be incompatible with the intentions behind the Constitution. Also, in L.F.M. Besselink and C.R.A. Swaak, 'The Netherlands' Constitutional Law and European Integration' (1996/1) *European Public Law*, p. 36, it is argued that the ECJ's judgments in *Van Gend & Loos* and *Costa v ENEL* do not in fact require that *compatible* constitutional provisions are disposed of.

6 Case 14/83 *Von Colson and Kamann*, ECLI:EU:C:1984:153.

7 See HR 3 March 1919, ECLI:NL:HR:1919:126, *NJ* 1919/371 (*Grenstractaat Aken*).

other rules of international law than EU law.[8] So, leaving aside the point whether those provisions are necessary at all in the context of EU law, it is in any event clear that they are not concerned with a duty of consistent interpretation. It must at the same time be made clear that this has not stood in the way of Dutch courts applying a duty of consistent interpretation.[9] In this regard it has been argued that it follows from the unwritten principle of Dutch constitutional law, laying down the monistic attitude towards international law, that the courts must seek an interpretation that is in conformity with international law,[10] even where that law does not have direct effect.[11]

It has been put forward that the Dutch courts, before the ECJ's *Von Colson and Kamann* judgment, were willing to inform themselves about the meaning of the underlying directive when they were applying implementing legislation, and that in particular for the HR's case law regarding turnover tax this also resulted in interpretations aimed at conformity with the directive.[12] It is submitted that this would be a rather logical approach that does not require an express obligation of consistent interpretation for its legitimation. It would also not be surprising taking into account the Dutch legal order's traditional openness to international law and the national courts' familiarity with consistent interpretation in the general international law context. However, while I must admit that I did not examine this matter extensively, legal scholarship does not seem to provide many references to judgments applying a consistent interpretation in the period before the ECJ's judgment. It is therefore difficult to say how widespread this practice was and just how far the Dutch courts were willing to go in order to align national law with the directive.

I have now arrived at the point in the story where the Dutch courts' practice in the area of EU law faced the introduction of the obligation to interpret national law in conformity with directives on account of the ECJ's *Von Colson and Kamann* judgment. This chapter discusses the Dutch superior courts' (i.e. the HR; the Administrative Jurisdiction Division of the Council of State (Afdeling

8 HR 1 April 2011, ECLI:NL:HR:2011:BP3044, *NJ* 2011/354 (*Clara Wichmann/Staat*); HR 10 October 2014, ECLI:NL:HR:2014:2928, *NJ* 2015/12 (*Rookverbod*).

9 See, for example, HR 23 April 1974, ECLI:NL:HR:1974:AB5708, *NJ* 1974/272; HR 16 November 1990, ECLI:NL:HR:1990:ZC0044, *NJ* 1992/107, para. 3.2.3; ABRvS 24 February 2003, ECLI:NL:RVS:2003:AH9582, *AB* 2003/327; ABRvS 4 June 2008, ECLI:NL:RVS:2008:BD3121, *AB* 2008/229; CBb 24 December 2009, ECLI:NL:CBB:2009:BL9703; ABRvS 20 March 2013, ECLI:NL:RVS:2013:BZ4937, *AB* 2013/359.

10 J.H. Jans and M.J.M. Verhoeven, 'Europeanisation via Consistent Interpretation and Direct Effect', in: J.H. Jans, S. Prechal and R.J.G.M. Widdershoven (Eds.), *Europeanisation of Public Law* (Europa Law Publishing 2015), p. 74.

11 Besselink and others (n. 5), p. 29.

12 See the interview with Koopmans, reported in A. Ottow and S. Van Woensel, 'Interview met mr. T. Koopmans' (1987/3) *Ars Aequi*, p. 142-3. See also M.H. Wissink, *Richtlijnconforme interpretatie van burgerlijk recht* (Kluwer 2001), p. 30.

Bestuursrechtspraak van de Raad van State; hereinafter ABRvS); and the Trade and Industry Appeals Tribunal (College van Beroep voor het bedrijfsleven; hereinafter CBb) perspective on that obligation.

> The jurisdiction of the Dutch superior courts was discussed in detail in the introductory part of this book. Here it is briefly recalled that the HR carries out review in cassation of judgments by the lower ranking courts in civil, criminal and tax disputes – it is, again, pointed out that I only look at the former and the latter. Where appropriate, I will specify if it was the Civil or Tax Chamber of the HR that delivered the judgment. The ABRvS is the highest appeal court having general jurisdiction in administrative law disputes. Unless one of the two specialised administrative law appeal courts has jurisdiction, the ABRvS is the competent court. One of these specialised courts is the CBb, entertaining jurisdiction in socioeconomic administrative law (the other is the Central Appeals Tribunal which is, however, not included in the research).

I first examine on which legal basis the Dutch superior courts proceed when they apply the duty of consistent interpretation. Secondly, the scope for, and limits to, a consistent interpretation from the perspective of the Dutch interpretative rules are examined. In addition to this, and by way of an afterthought, I make some observations with regard to the importance of an argumentation elucidating a court's decision to accept or reject a consistent interpretation.

2. THE LEGAL BASIS FOR THE APPLICATION OF THE DUTY OF CONSISTENT INTERPRETATION

There are two reasons why the perspective on the legal basis for the duty of consistent interpretation is relevant. First, it is as such an argument in favour of a particular theory for the relationship between EU and national law. Secondly, it can be an indication for an approach to the duty of consistent interpretation that further supports, or challenges, a particular theory.

In the previous paragraph I mentioned that some authors adopted the position that, *prior* to the delivery of the ECJ's *Von Colson and Kamann* judgment, Dutch courts already looked at the underlying directives when they were interpreting national provisions implementing them. I provided that it would be a logical step for the Dutch courts to do so. In the early years *after* the ECJ's seminal judgment, the Dutch courts delivered two judgments that continued, and confirmed, this kind of approach. This case law also provided an insight into the legal basis on which the courts proceeded. The clearest example is a judgment of the HR, delivered only a month after the ECJ's *Von Colson and Kamann* judgment (therefore the HR was, formally, subject to the duty of consistent interpretation, although it may be asked to what extent the judges sitting in the HR were at the time fully aware of this new obligation; in any event no reference was made to the brand new judgment), it was held that an interpretation deviating from the directive must be rejected as it must be presumed that the legislature would not have intended to confer a divergent meaning on the national provision having an implementing objective.[13] And in a judgment from 1987 the HR considered that it followed from a historical interpretation that the legislature had intended to introduce a legislative scheme that conformed entirely to the directive, so that the directive must be looked at for determining the correct meaning.[14] The references to the legislature's intention (i.e. an implementing objective) continued throughout the nineties in the HR's case law.[15]

Around that time, the ABRvS had mostly been silent on what it considered as the legal basis when applying the duty of consistent interpretation. However, this changed in 2000 with the *Buitengebied Texel* judgment. The effect of directives in the national legal order was discussed in a more general way and, referring to the ECJ's *Von Colson and Kamann* and *Marleasing* judgments, the ABRvS held that in applying national law, the national court called upon to interpret it is required to do so, as far as possible, in the light of the wording and the purpose of the directive *in order to achieve the result pursued by the latter.*[16] This copied the well known sentence from the *Marleasing* judgment.[17] It could perhaps be argued that the ABRvS was not here providing its own vision on the legal basis for the duty of consistent interpretation, but simply recalled the ECJ's proclamation of that obligation – which happened to contain, in the final part, a reference to the legal basis – and nothing more. However, it would not then have been necessary to include the final part of the sentence ('in order to achieve the result pursued by the latter'). In the absence of an indication to the contrary, it must be presumed that the ABRvS does not add superfluous words to its judgment and that they reflect the view of the ABRvS. In two important judgments delivered in 2007 and 2008, the HR also referred to the objective of achieving the result pursued by the directive for the legal basis of the duty of consistent interpretation, adding a logical reference to Article 288 TFEU.[18]

---

13 HR 2 May 1984, ECLI:NL:HR:1984:AW8625, *BNB* 1984/295.

14 HR 24 April 1987, ECLI:NL:HR:1987:AG5584, *NJ* 1987/660 (*Ubbink Isolatie/Dak- en Wandtechniek*), para. 3.5.

15 HR 29 December 1995, ECLI:NL:HR:1995:ZC1943, *NJ* 1996/418 (*Buyck/Van den Ameele*), para. 3.4; HR 19 September 1997, ECLI:NL:HR:1997:ZC2435, *NJ* 1998/6 (*Assoud/SNS*), para. 3.4.2.

16 ABRvS 31 March 2000, ECLI:NL:RVS:2000:AB1152, *AB* 2000/302 (*Buitengebied Texel*), para. 2.6.2.7. The same considerations are found in ABRvS 13 November 2002, ECLI:NL:RVS:2002:AF0314, *AB* 2003/26, para. 2.2.5.

17 Case C-106/89 *Marleasing*, ECLI:EU:C:1990:395, para. 8.

18 HR 10 August 2007, ECLI:NL:HR:2007:AZ3758, *AB* 2007/291 (*Wandelvierdaagse*), para. 3.4; HR 6 June 2008, ECLI:NL:HR:2008:BD3139, *AB* 2008/214 (*Joustra*), para. 3.3.1.

The *communautaire* legal basis – which was seen to have been gradually taken over by the Dutch superior courts – has remained dominant to this day. In addition to further judgments referring to Article 288 TFEU and/or the objective of achieving the result pursued by the directive,[19] the HR's and ABRvS's case law now also refers to Article 4(3) TEU and the full effectiveness of EU law for the legal basis.[20] The CBb has referred to the objective of achieving the result pursued by the directive,[21] but has also delivered a judgment that placed more emphasis on the national rules having an implementing objective.[22] However, I should add that the legal basis for the duty of consistent interpretation has been discussed in the CBb's case law on only a few occasions. It is therefore difficult to discern a clear position, and the contribution to the current discussion is of limited value from a quantitative point of view.

I conclude that the Dutch superior courts' prevailing view is that the legal basis for the duty of consistent interpretation must be found in EU law. The courts most frequently refer to Articles 288 TFEU and 4(3) TEU and the objective of achieving the result pursued by the directive. They normally pick one of these whereas I argued in paragraph 3.2 that the more satisfactory approach would be to base the duty of consistent interpretation on Articles 288 TFEU and 4(3) TEU together (ideally in combination with the full effectiveness of EU law). Nevertheless, it is submitted that the severity of this issue should not be blown out of proportion. The ECJ does not consistently make this reference either.[23] It would probably place too high an expectation on the national courts to require them to consequently use such a reference.

A final important remark that must be made here is that the Dutch courts refer directly to the EU law provisions constituting the obligation's legal basis; it follows from the Dutch constitutional setting for the reception of EU law that no intermediary in national law is required for this.

Since the Dutch courts recognise the legal basis for the duty of consistent interpretation provided by EU law, there seems to be a willingness to accept the obligation's binding nature and autonomous position under EU law – presumably also as far as more intervening aspects of that obligation are concerned. Their

19 ABRvS 11 June 2014, ECLI:NL:RVS:2014:2120, *AB* 2014/320, para. 2.7; ABRvS 1 April 2015, ECLI:NL:RVS:2015:999, *M en R* 2015/92, para. 2.6; ABRvS 3 May 2017, ECLI:NL:RVS:2017:1175, *JGR* 2018/2, para. 4.2.

20 HR 5 April 2013, ECLI:NL:HR:2013:BZ1780, *NJ* 2013/389 (*Albron/FNV c.s.*), para. 3.4.2; ABRvS 29 April 2015, ECLI:NL:RVS:2015:1361, para. 7; ABRvS 7 June 2017, ECLI:NL:RVS:2017:1520, *AB* 2017/249, para. 9.

21 CBb 6 November 2009, ECLI:NL:CBB:2009:BK2641, *AB* 2010/215, para. 6.3.1.

22 CBb 5 June 2014, ECLI:NL:CBB:2014:206, *AB* 2014/345, paras. 3.5.1-3.5.3.

23 See, for example, Case C-12/08 *Mono Car Styling*, ECLI:EU:C:2009:466, para. 60; Case C-53/10 *Mücksch*, ECLI:EU:C:2011:585, para. 32.

perspective on the legal basis is therefore in line with the theory of supremacy of EU law.

3. THE SCOPE FOR, AND LIMITS TO, A CONSISTENT INTERPRETATION FROM THE PERSPECTIVE OF THE DUTCH SUPERIOR COURTS

On the one hand, the duty of consistent interpretation was characterised as an interpretative rule. On the other hand, the existing theories on the relationship between EU and national law require that there is a conflict or, in the context of constitutional pluralism, perhaps a potential or looming conflict. If the two are combined, this means that a conflict on the level of interpretative rules needs to be identified for the existing theories to come into play. The existence of a conflict can be the result of either an incompatibility with the obligation to interpret national law so far as possible, or the national interpretative rules. The scope and meaning of the former were already discussed in chapter 2. In this chapter I discuss the latter to acquire a better understanding of the Dutch superior courts' traditional approach to interpretation (i.e. the approach adopted in a purely internal context). I then proceed to the main part of this paragraph which examines when a conflict of interpretative rules arises, how the Dutch courts resolve such a conflict, and which theory most adequately explains the adopted solution. Before proceeding to this analysis, it is first pointed out, by way of example, that there is not a conflict if a consistent interpretation turns out to be identical to the interpretation that follows from a traditional approach to interpretation:

> In its judgment of 30 June 2011 the CBb had to determine whether the appellant was correct in arguing that the reference to 'financial instrument' in the concerned national provision had to be interpreted in accordance with the meaning conferred to it in another piece of legislation. Such an interpretation would have entailed that deposits were not covered, a result that was incompatible with the applicable directive. The CBb held that the appellant's argument should be rejected: the relevant provision had an implementing objective, its wording was nearly identical to the corresponding provision in the directive, and there were no objective indications in the relevant legislation that the legislature had intended to confer a meaning that deviated from the directive. The CBb added that an anomaly would arise if the interpretation argued for by the appellant was accepted as the national provision would then have become pointless.[24] On account of the latter argument, it is unlikely that, in the absence of the duty of consistent interpretation, the CBb would have followed the appellant's argument.

24 CBb 30 June 2011, ECLI:NL:CBB:2011:BQ9755, *JOR* 2011/260, para. 6.4.

> The Nature Conservation Act contained an exception to the obligation to carry out an 'appropriate assessment' in the sense of the Habitats Directive[25] in relation to nitrogen deposition if, on balance, such deposition decreased under the new plan. One of the questions addressed by the ABRvS in this regard was whether the factual situation pertaining at the time of the adoption of the new plan, or the effects permitted to occur under the previously adopted plan, provides the relevant frame of reference. The ABRvS considered that the first option provides the relevant frame of reference. This was in line with earlier decisions and compatible with the wording of the concerned provision of national law. It added that it was also under an obligation to interpret national law so far as possible in conformity with the Habitats Directive and that this was achieved through the adopted interpretation. Finally, it provided that this outcome found support in a letter sent by the Minister discussing the interpretation of the concerned national provision.[26] It can therefore be said that all arguments pointed in the same direction.

But also if the national courts go a little bit further, and even if the adopted consistent interpretation entailed an adaptation of a traditional interpretation, this does not automatically mean that there was a conflict. While the identification of a conflict presupposes some kind of adaptation, this does not hold true the other way around. Hence, it is necessary to acquire a precise understanding of the interpretative scope, more specifically the interpretative discretion, that is available in a traditional context.

3.1. THE TRADITIONAL APPROACH TO INTERPRETATION

3.1.1. A Considerable Degree of Interpretative Autonomy

According to Wiarda the Dutch courts' traditional approach to interpretation transformed from being governed by dominant heteronomous aspects (heavily influenced by Montesquieu's doctrine of separation of powers) to more autonomous aspects. This meant that an interpretation derived from the provision's text only had become less forceful and that the focus shifted towards determining the 'true meaning' of the provision's words – by also looking at the purpose and principles behind that rule.[27] It is sometimes, but not always, expressly added that this concerns the purpose and principles strived for by the *legislature*.[28] The degree to which the courts must remain as closely as possible to the objective indications of the legislature's will is a matter that touches upon a variety of aspects regarding the approach to interpretation and will become clearer as the discussion unfolds.

---

25 Council Directive 92/43/EEC of 21 May 1992 on the conservation of natural habitats and of wild fauna and flora, *OJ* 1992, L206/7.

26 ABRvS 1 April 2015, ECLI:NL:RVS:2015:999, *M en R* 2015/92, para. 2.6.

27 G.J. Wiarda, *Drie typen van rechtsvinding* (W.E.J. Tjeenk Willink 1999), p. 38.

28 See R.E.C.M. Niessen, *Rechtsvinding in belastingzaken* (Sdu 2009), p. 18. Cf. T. Groenewegen, *Wetsinterpretatie en rechtsvorming* (BJu 2006), p. 8.

The Dutch courts apply the grammatical, historical, systematic and teleological interpretation to determine a rule's meaning. Importantly, there is broad acknowledgment that the framework is of a flexible nature: there is no fixed weight among the methods and each of the methods should be taken into account if it provides a relevant insight.[29] However, this flexibility does not mean that statutory interpretation is an uncontrolled process. If the interpretative methods point in the same direction and provide a clear answer to the question which interpretation needs to be adopted, the courts must simply accept the clear guidance offered by the interpretative criteria.[30] When matters are not so straightforward, the difficulties of not having a clearly delineated interaction between the four interpretative methods emerge. There is in this regard a sliding scale regarding the degree to which the interpretative criteria limit the courts' autonomy.

Taking these general characteristics into consideration, I will now discuss the individual interpretative methods. Grammatical interpretation is the starting point and the argument seems to carry a certain weight. One could in this regard speak of the 'presumptive force' of grammatical interpretation: in the absence of sufficiently compelling arguments to the contrary, an argument that is correctly based on the provision's wording can as such justify that that interpretation is followed. The reason behind the force of this argument is that it enjoys a strong legitimation since it makes an appeal to the authority of the author of the text that is being interpreted, i.e. the legislature.[31] But the described approach means, at the same time, that, even if the provision initially seemed to be clear on account of a grammatical interpretation, the courts should normally not stop there; they must consider that meaning in light of the other interpretative methods if they provide a relevant insight – and the courts' practice shows that they normally do so.[32] The other interpretative methods can confirm, but also undermine, the provision's textual meaning. It is uncontroversial that the meaning derived from a grammatical interpretation, even if it is clear, is not sacrosanct. If the other interpretative methods clearly indicate a different meaning, the words can be departed from (obviously the threshold for applying the other methods becomes lower as the words provide less guidance; provisions that are of a flexible *casu quo* general nature are the clearest example of norms leaving a large measure of discretion to the courts[33]). This

---

29 P. Scholten, *Mr. C. Asser's Handleiding tot de beoefening van het Nederlands Burgerlijk Recht. Algemeen Deel** (Kluwer 1974), p. 35-6; J.B.M. Vranken, *Mr. C. Asser's handleiding tot de beoefening van het Nederlands burgerlijk recht. Algemeen deel*** (Kluwer 1995), para. 217; Groenewegen (n. 28), p. 188; C.E. Smith, *Regels van rechtsvinding* (BJu 2007), p. 172; M.H. Wissink, 'Interpretation of Private Law in Conformity with EU Directives', in: A.S. Hartkamp and others (Eds.), *The Influence of EU Law on National Private Law* (Kluwer 2014), p. 148.

30 Wiarda (n. 27), p. 19.

31 H.T.M. Kloosterhuis, 'Argumentatieve analyse van taalkundige argumentatie bij de interpretatie van rechtsregels' (2009/2) *Rechtsgeleerd Magazijn Themis*, p. 75. Cf. the case note by Ortlep in *AB* 2016/175, which seems to assign an even more superior position to grammatical interpretation.

32 Groenewegen (n. 28), p. 86; Niessen (n. 28), p. 14.

33 Wiarda (n. 27), p. 27.

may involve a minor alteration of the text but, in the context of private law, it has been submitted that an outcome whereby important parts of the text are ignored, is not per se excluded.[34] In a judgment from 2011, the Civil Chamber of the HR stated that a provision's formulation is not always decisive for the meaning that should be attributed to it (even if the provision was recently enacted).[35] However, it would in my opinion be incorrect to derive from this the general conclusion that arguments on the basis of a grammatical interpretation may frequently be put aside. Before a particular interpretation is adopted it should normally be checked whether it does not do too much violence to the wording.[36] This is an additional way of looking at grammatical interpretation, where it performs a gatekeeper role. In this role it does not assign a specific and fixed meaning, but rather determines the range of meanings that are still permissible. This role occupies a prominent place in the approach to grammatical interpretation in civil law in particular. Arguably, it increases the scope for further interpretation. Especially where an interpretation would transgress the scope of a provision's text, the principle of legal certainty comes into play as a limitation.[37] It needs to be emphasised that, if the just discussed perspective on grammatical interpretation is adopted (i.e. grammatical interpretation as a method imposing outer limits), it remains exceptional for courts to choose an interpretation of a rule that is not in line with its wording.[38]

An interpretative method that is also frequently applied is the historical interpretation.[39] Historical interpretation includes the explanatory memorandum and the parliamentary proceedings. Niessen points out that, while there may be some discussion about the extent to which this always offers a reliable tool for accurately determining the legislature's intention (primarily because of the variety of actors involved in the preparation and discussion of new legislation, which may

---

34 Scholten (n. 29), p. 40; A.S. Hartkamp, *Mr. C. Assers Handleiding tot de beoefening van het Nederlands Burgerlijk Recht. 3. Vermogensrecht algemeen. Deel I. Europees recht en Nederlands vermogensrecht* (Kluwer 2018), para. 183.

35 HR 9 December 2011, ECLI:NL:HR:2011:BU7412, *NJ* 2013/273, para. 3.5. See further HR 9 December 1994, ECLI:NL:HR:1994:ZC1573, *NJ* 1995/224, para. 3.3.

36 Scholten (n. 29), p. 36; C.E. Smith, 'Het woord als grenswachter: functies van taalkundige interpretatie voor de rechtsvinding (2009/2) *Rechtsgeleerd Magazijn Themis*, p. 70.

37 Groenewegen (n. 28), p. 95, 97, with reference to HR 27 September 1996, ECLI:NL:HR:1996:ZC2151, *NJ* 1997/624, para. 3.3 (the argument based on a historical interpretation was rejected: it could not be accepted from the point of view of legal certainty as it would do too much violence to the provision's text). See also Concl. A-G Wattel, ECLI:NL:PHR:2006:AU8201, para. 6.1, in HR 2 June 2006, ECLI:NL:HR:2006:AU8201, *BNB* 2006/282.

38 See also Scholten (n. 29), p. 40; Wissink (n. 29), p. 148. In Groenewegen (n. 28), p. 220, it is submitted that the Dutch courts display a larger degree of restraint when it comes to a transgression of the outer limits of a rule's clear meaning.

39 See Groenewegen (n. 28), p. 101, who describes it as one of the most frequently used interpretative methods. See, for example, HR 9 April 1999, ECLI:NL:HR:1999:ZC2891, *NJ* 2000/688, para. 5.2; ABRvS 11 May 2000, ECLI:NL:RVS:2000:AA6110, para. 2.2.1-2.2.2; HR 10 August 2001, ECLI:NL:HR:2001:AB3115, *BNB* 2001/351, para. 3.6 *et seq*; HR 20 February 2007, ECLI:NL:HR:2007:AZ0213 (*Samir A.*). See also W. Snijders, 'Parlementaire geschiedenis: zin en onzin' (2008/6774) *Weekblad voor Privaatrecht, Notariaat en Registratie*, p. 845.

have as a consequence a plurality of ideas being expressed[40]), it is nevertheless, next to the provision's wording, the primary source indicating such intention.[41] Similar to grammatical interpretation, this confers upon it a certain authority.[42] But the threshold for a departure from an interpretation based on a historical interpretation is arguably lower if compared to grammatical interpretation. Even if a matter was explicitly discussed by the legislature, this does not exclude the possibility that the courts take a different position.[43] It can in my opinion be said that the usefulness of a historical interpretation is even more dependent on the extent to which it provides a clear and coherent answer for the proceedings to which it is applied. An additional factor that must be taken into account for a historical interpretation is that the weight of this argument decreases as its age increases.[44]

It can be assumed that the view, that the strength of the argument depends on its aptitude to provide a clear answer in the current proceedings, also applies in relation to systematic interpretation, which attempts to understand the meaning of an individual provision by looking at its place and function in the larger legal context of which it is a part.

The other interpretative methods *can* provide relevant input in the context of teleological interpretation, which is aimed at determining the purpose of the legislation.[45] But as the application of this method involves looking at the societal needs which the provision (or, sometimes, a particular vision on what an area of the law as a whole aims to achieve, such as the protection of employees in the context of labour law[46]) was intended to meet, there is often an autonomous

---

40 See also Vranken (n. 29), paras. 142-3 (who, by the way, characterises this method as the most controversial one).

41 Niessen (n. 28), p. 15.

42 See also Wissink (n. 29), p. 150, where it is provided that a historical interpretation is an authoritative argument.

43 Vranken (n. 29), para. 152. For examples see HR 24 January 1996, ECLI:NL:HR:1996:AA1820, *BNB* 1996/138, para. 3.10; HR 20 November 2001, ECLI:NL:HR:2001:AB2809, *NJ* 2003/632 (*Mensenroof*).

44 Ibid, para. 150. See also Snijders (n. 39), p. 845 confirming the unfixed weight of arguments based on historical interpretation.

45 Groenewegen (n. 28), p. 169-70 provides examples where grammatical, historical and/or systematic interpretation were used to determine a provision's purpose (reference is made to: HR 18 June 1993, ECLI:NL:HR:1993:ZC1008, *NJ* 1993/614 (*Rietveld/Gemini ziekenhuis*), para. 5.1; ARRvS 26 January 1993, ECLI:NL:RVS:1993:AN3013, *AB* 1993/238, para. 2). See also Niessen (n. 28), p. 16, referring to HR 30 January 2009, ECLI:NL:HR:2009:BH1174, *BNB* 2009/95, para. 3.3.3 (where the historical interpretative method was used to discover the rule's ratio). See also HR 26 February 2016, ECLI:NL:HR:2016:335, *AB* 2016/175 (*X/ASR*), para. 3.7.3. The same point is made in Smith (n. 29), p. 166; J.W.A. Fleuren, 'Wetshistorische interpretative en "de bedoeling van de wetgever"', in: P.P.T. Bovend'Eert and others (Eds.), *De staat van wetgeving. Opstellen aangeboden aan prof. mr. C.A.J.M. Kortmann* (Kluwer 2009), p. 163 *et seq*.

46 R.A.A. Duk, *De Hoge Raad en rechtsvinding in het arbeidsrecht* (BJu 2013), p. 86.

element to it.[47] And the method cannot only build upon the other methods, but may also be dismissive of them: if it is found that they do not accurately reflect the true, contemporary, purpose of the legislation, a teleological interpretation can also go against one or more of the other interpretative criteria (including textual arguments).[48] Conversely, the teleological method can also be overruled itself.[49] The Dutch courts frequently apply the teleological method.[50]

In light of the relative weight of, and the lack of a clear priority among, the interpretative methods, other tools have been sought to scrutinise the courts' approach to interpretation. The first is of a substantive nature and well known: no matter which interpretative method is applied, the courts must respect the prerogatives of the legislature, in particular the prerogative to make choices of a political nature, in accordance with the doctrine of separation of powers.[51] The second tool is of a more procedural nature. The fact that – with the exception of the more straightforward interpretative questions – the weight of one argument needs to be viewed in the light of other relevant arguments and the specific circumstances of the case, increases the importance of explaining carefully the interpretative choices made by the court. It is therefore sometimes suggested that the Dutch courts should apply a 'discursive substantiation requirement'.[52] This would require them to engage in an open confrontation of *all* the relevant arguments, so that their choices become more explicit and verifiable.[53] In other words, it is a kind of procedural minimum guarantee aimed at ensuring that the courts do not exceed the limits of their autonomy. But it is emphasised that, if the interpretative methods do not unambiguously guide the judge towards a particular decision, arguably, more than one justifiable outcome remains and this is not changed by such a

47 Scholten (n. 29), p.116-20. The importance of considering a provision in the societal context within which it was introduced is also mentioned in Smith (n. 29), p. 97.

48 HR 9 December 1994, ECLI:NL:HR:1994:ZC1573, *NJ* 1995/224, para. 3.3. See also J.G.H. Altena-Davidsen, *Het legaliteitsbeginsel en de doorwerking van Europees recht in het Nederlandse materiële strafrecht* (Kluwer 2016), p. 210-1, with reference to among others HR 21 April 1998, ECLI:NL:HR:1998:ZD1030, *NJ* 1998/782, para. 5.2.2 (which is an excellent example showing not only the setting aside of certain arguments based on a historical interpretation, but also the role played by a grammatical interpretation, and demands regarding the operability of the rule, for determining its purpose).

49 See, for example, ABRvS 11 May 1996, ECLI:NL:RVS:1996:AN5165, *AB* 1996/410.

50 Groenewegen (n. 28), p. 167.

51 Vranken (n. 29), para. 241; Wiarda (n. 27), p. 79; Smith (n. 29), p. 47; J.C.A. De Poorter, 'Rechtsvorming door de bestuursrechter: Over grenzen van de rechtsvormende taak, rechterlijke dialogen en de Grondwet', in: A. Kristic, A. Meuwese and G. Van der Schyff (Eds.), *Functies en betekenis van de Grondwet: een dialogisch perspectief* (Wolf Legal Publishers 2011), p. 139; Altena-Davidsen (n. 48), p. 215.

52 See Vranken (n. 29), para. 227 *et seq*; R. Ortlep, 'Optimaliseren rechtseenheid tussen de hoogste bestuursrechters', in: E.M.H. Hirsch Ballin, R. Ortlep and A. Tollenaar, *Rechtsontwikkeling door de bestuursrechter. VAR-reeks 154* (BJu 2015), p. 122 *et seq.*

53 Ortlep (n. 52), p. 122 *et seq.*

procedural guarantee. The judge must then make a decision (and must do so in a well-reasoned manner, to which the guarantee would contribute).[54]

3.1.2. Some Specific Remarks Regarding Public Law

On account of the measure of autonomy that the Dutch courts enjoy when it comes to interpreting a provision one or the other way, it may be asked whether they enjoy a similar degree of autonomy when interpretative rules are applied in the area of public law. Wiarda recognised that his arguments were to a large extent derived from the civil law context and that, as a result of the nature of this area of the law (Wiarda highlights the less peremptory nature of civil law norms), traditionally, the courts enjoy a larger measure of autonomy, and that this is probably different for the area of public law.[55] In response to a new edition of an authoritative work on the approach to interpretation in Dutch law, Vranken's contribution to the Asser series, one of Scheltema's first responses as an administrative lawyer was that it was striking to see how much room is left to the courts.[56] The civil law perspective has been dominant for legal scholarship's discussion about the Dutch courts' approach to interpretation. While the previous subparagraph is intended as a general sketch of the approach to interpretation, I must admit that it builds to a large extent on the existing work in this field and, therefore, it may inadvertently have a civil law bias. Taking notice of Wiarda's recommendation, I therefore want to pay separate attention to the interpretative method that seems to be the most prominent method requiring a differentiated approach in the context of public law: grammatical interpretation. The reason behind this is that there is a different kind of legal relationship between the parties in public law proceedings, which is characterised by an uneven balance of power between the State and individuals. This has as a consequence that the legality principle occupies a far more prominent role in public law, which in turn means that individuals are to a larger extent protected by the wording of the applicable rules – which is facilitated by the fact that these rules are designed to clearly state the individual's rights and obligations (open concepts such as reasonableness and fairness, which are key to private law, are less common).[57] This applies first and foremost to criminal law, but also to the area of tax law and, albeit to a lesser extent, administrative law. Be that as it may, even in the HR's case law in the area of criminal law there are examples relativizing the importance of textual limitations[58] – albeit that it is in principle not permitted

54 Scholten (n. 29), p. 54; Vranken (n. 29), para. 217 *et seq;* De Poorter (n. 51), p. 149. See also Duk (n. 46), p. 17, where the importance of a well-reasoned judgment is emphasised.

55 Wiarda (n. 27), p. 61.

56 M. Scheltema, 'Hoe groot is de rechterlijke vrijheid', in: E. Van de Griend (Ed.), *Rechtsvinding: gedachtenwisseling over het nieuwe Algemeen Deel van de Asser-serie* (W.E.J. Tjeenk Willink 1996), p. 21.

57 De Poorter (n. 51), p. 126, 130.

58 See, for example, HR 31 March 1998, ECLI:NL:HR:1998:ZD1165, *NJ* 1998/780; HR 12 June 2007, ECLI:NL:HR:2007:BA0426, *NJ* 2007/347. See further the case note by 't Hart in *NJ* 1995/292;

to proceed to an analogous application of substantive criminal law.[59] It can be assumed that, compared to criminal law, the legality principle does not require a stricter approach in tax and administrative law. Be that as it may, compared to *civil law*, the Tax Chamber of the HR and the ABRvS seem less inclined to depart from a provision's clear wording.[60] I am not aware of any analysis concerning the CBb in this regard, but I can think of no *a priori* reason why the characterisation of public law and the use of a grammatical interpretation would not also apply to this court.[61]

With regard to administrative law specifically, an additional element is the separation of powers between the judiciary and the executive. A large number of administrative law provisions confer a measure of discretion upon the executive for determining how certain evaluative terms are to be interpreted, and in which situations it makes use of the competences provided for in the concerned provision. The administrative law courts would then apply a marginal test in

---

N. Rozemond, 'Waar ligt de grens van het legaliteitsbeginsel?', in: P.C. Boogert and T. Kooijmans (Eds.), *Over de grens van het legaliteitsbeginsel* (Gouda Quint 2000), p. 42; J. De Hullu, *Materieel strafrecht. Over algemene leerstukken van strafrechtelijke aansprakelijkheid naar Nederlands recht* (Kluwer 2015), p. 103. Nan derives from the HR's case law in the area of criminal law that a grammatical interpretation is not sacrosanct, J.S. Nan, *Het lex certa-beginsel* (Sdu 2011), p. 35.

59 See Altena-Davidsen (n. 48), p. 212. See also C.P.M. Cleiren, 'Het legaliteitsbeginsel', in: Th. A. De Roos and M.A.H. Van der Woude (Eds.), *Jurisprudentie Strafrecht Select* (Sdu 2008), p. 294, but note her qualifying remarks, pointing out that it is sometimes difficult to separate between an analogous application (not permitted) and a far-reaching extensive interpretation (permitted).

60 Niessen (n. 28), p. 31, 33-5, 40, where, in the first place, it is confirmed that also in tax cases there is not always a strict adherence to the text (see also C. Maas, 'Beslissen of motiveren? Over het gebruik van taalkundige argumenten in het fiscale recht' (2014/7071) *Weekblad fiscaal recht*, p. 1384 *et seq*). At the same time, the important weight of the legality principle in tax cases is emphasised. It is also mentioned that, while the prevailing view in legal scholarship dismisses a prohibition to apply tax law by analogy, no examples of an *expressis verbis* application of that technique were found in the HR's case law in tax cases. With regard to administrative law, I refer in the first place to R.J.N. Schlössels, 'Bestuursrechter, procesrecht en methoden van rechtsvinding: rechtsvinding in het bestuursprocesrecht', in: L.E. De Groot-Van Leeuwen and J.D.A. Den Tonkelaar (Eds.), *Rechtsvinding op veertien terreinen* (Kluwer 2012), p. 86, 102. He makes the point that the ABRvS's case law with regard to *procedural* administrative law also applies more autonomous interpretative methods to reach a decision. However, in relation to *substantive administrative law*, Schlössels mentions that, on account of the legality principle (as well as the discretion enjoyed by the executive, which is discussed separately), it may be asked whether a more autonomous approach to interpretation is suitable here. Even clearer is Groenewegen (n. 28), p. 93, which refers to a number of examples where the ABRvS departed from the provision's text. Yet, having examined the ABRvS's case law on this point, it is concluded that, generally, the ABRvS is less likely to depart from the provision's text if compared to the HR (presumably the author based his conclusion on the HR's case law in general, and did not separately consider the comparison in view of the case law of the HR's Tax Chamber).

61 It is noted that the CBb has, unlike the ABRvS, accepted an application *contra legem* of the principle of legitimate expectations. In Ortlep (n. 52), p. 113, it is submitted that it may be because of the nature of the proceedings before the ABRvS, which frequently involve the interests of third parties, that this court has been unwilling to depart from the relevant provision's wording. One might see in this general characterisation (i.e. involvement of third parties) an argument why the CBb is not always bound to the text to the same extent as the ABRvS. However, it is submitted that further research is required before it can be concluded that the CBb's case law is characterised by a more lenient approach to grammatical interpretation in comparison to the ABRvS.

such circumstances.[62] In relation to substantive administrative law (in contrast to procedural administrative law), it has been argued that there are therefore reasons to assume that the courts have a less autonomous position as regards interpretation in those cases.[63] However, there is broad acknowledgment that a more reserved attitude is only appropriate as far as the application of the facts to the legal framework, and the consequences deriving therefrom, are reviewed, and not for the determination (i.e. interpretation) of the parameters of the legal framework as such.[64] Perhaps even more importantly, deference by the legislature to the position of the executive does no longer seem to be justified if this would result in a violation of the directive. On balance, I believe that this aspect of administrative law adjudication is neither likely to have a significant impact on the approach to interpretation nor should it be permitted to do so.

3.1.3. *The Role Played by the Principle of Separation of Powers between the Legislature and the Judiciary*

As regards the question which principles guide the courts when determining the correct meaning of a rule, it is submitted that – especially compared to Germany and Ireland – the objective of determining the intention of the legislature does not seem to be a very explicit consideration.[65] In the Dutch courts' case law one does not really find references to constitutional or other provisions from which the courts derive points of guidance for the required approach to interpretation.[66] The amount of freedom that the courts enjoy in this regard will vary depending on the interaction between the circumstances of the case and the extent to which the interpretative methods provide a clear answer. Nevertheless, it is clear from the weight of grammatical interpretation, the frequent use of historical interpretation, the substantive limitation derived from the legislature's prerogatives, and the circumstance that, often, teleological interpretation involves, or can involve, the use of heteronomous interpretative criteria, that respect for the constitutional

62 It is noted that the 2017 annual report of the Council of State (p. 61) provides that it no longer uses the term 'marginal test' (*marginale toetsing*) and emphasises that public authorities never carry out public law competences in complete freedom, but that their discretion is always subject to certain limitations.

63 Schlössels (n. 60), p. 86. See also De Poorter (n. 51), p. 127; J. Uzman, 'Commentaar bij Taco Groenewegen', in: E.T. Feteris and others (Eds.), *Gewogen oordelen. Essays over argumentatie en recht* (BJu 2012), p. 95.

64 R.M. Van Male, 'Van motiveringscontrole naar bestuursrechtelijke rechtsvinding' (2007/10) *Nederlands Tijdschrift voor Bestuursrecht*, p. 392-4; J.C.A. De Poorter and H.J.Th.M. Van Roosmalen, 'Motivering van rechtsvormende uitspraken door de Afdeling bestuursrechtspraak' (2009/8) *Nederlands Tijdschrift voor Bestuursrecht*, p. 219-27; T. Groenewegen, 'Interpretatie in het bestuursrecht en de trias politica', in E.T. Feteris and others (Eds.), *Gewogen oordelen. Essays over argumentatie en recht* (BJu 2012), p. 90.

65 In T. Koopmans, 'De constitutionele kant van de rechtsvinding', in: E. Van de Griend (Ed.), *Rechtsvinding: gedachtenwisseling over het nieuwe Algemeen Deel van de Asser-serie* (W.E.J. Tjeenk Willink 1996), p. 1, it is observed that this dimension is often also missing in legal scholarship's discussion of the Dutch courts' approach to interpretation.

66 Although Articles 11 to 13 of the General Provisions Act provide norms that relate to the process of interpretation, they do not offer concrete interpretative rules and are rarely referred to when the Dutch courts elaborate on their approach to interpretation.

position of the legislature needs to be considered as one of the primary factors explaining the approach to interpretation.[67]

3.2. THE RESERVED APPROACH À LA *PINK FLOYD*

Arguably, it would not be irrational to presume on the basis of the preceding subparagraph that the Dutch courts enjoy wide powers when it comes to interpreting national law in conformity with the directive and that this results in an unproblematic and forceful application of the remedy. However, these expectations were not really reflected in the HR Civil Chamber's *Pink Floyd* judgment which, for a long time, was the leading case in the Netherlands on the duty of consistent interpretation.[68]

> In the Pink Floyd judgment, the HR was asked whether a rule stipulating that, when a copy is brought into circulation by, or with the consent of, the holder of the copyright, the latter has exhausted his exclusive right, could be geographically limited so as to cover only EU-wide exhaustion, rather than worldwide exhaustion. The appellant submitted that the Rental Rights Directive[69] required the former interpretation. However, the HR, without in fact having discussed the correctness of the appellant's submission, rejected a consistent interpretation, primarily putting forward that a consistent interpretation was grammatically impossible. The main reason why it was grammatically impossible was, in turn, that the national rule did not refer to a particular territory, which was viewed by the HR as making it clear that the rule provided for worldwide exhaustion.[70] On account of the existence of some grammatical ambiguity, it may be asked whether the HR tried hard enough to adopt a consistent interpretation.[71] Wissink also does not understand the emphasis placed on the wording of the national rule, but adopts a more moderate view, pointing out that Dutch intellectual property law always presumes worldwide exhaustion unless the concerned rule specifically states otherwise (note that, unlike the provision's text, the latter point was not relied upon by the HR in its judgment).[72] By the way, it is also interesting to mention that, despite the provision's text being neutral on this point, a lower ranking court *did* accept that a rule contained in another piece of Dutch intellectual property legislation only provided for EU-wide exhaustion. However, unlike the rule with which

67 See also Kloosterhuis (n. 31), p. 75; Niessen (n. 28), p. 14-5.

68 Admittedly, before the *Pink Floyd* judgment, the HR delivered judgments that showed a more far-reaching approach to the duty of consistent interpretation, see e.g. HR 13 September 1991, ECLI:NL:HR:1991:ZC0328, *NJ* 1992/225 (*Dekker*).

69 Council Directive 92/100/EEC of 19 November 1992 on rental right and lending right and on certain rights related to copyright in the field of intellectual property, *OJ* 1992, L346/61.

70 HR 25 October 1996, ECLI:NL:HR:1996:ZC2177, *NJ* 1997/649 (*Pink Floyd*), paras. 3.3-3.4.

71 The case note by De Wit under *IER* 1995/30, criticises the view that the wording of the rule on exhaustion that was interpreted by the HR in its *Pink Floyd* judgment categorically prevented an interpretation providing for EU-wide exhaustion only.

72 Wissink (n. 12), p. 162.

the HR's *Pink Floyd* judgment was concerned, this particular rule had been introduced to implement a directive.[73]

In his work discussing the HR's application of the duty of consistent interpretation in the first decade or so after its introduction, Wissink took the view that the HR normally adopted a somewhat reserved and national law-oriented approach, primarily applying the obligation as a 'means of choice' (i.e. the obligation is only used to make a choice if the provision can be interpreted in more than one way).[74] Altena sees the HR's *Pink Floyd* judgment as a good example of this reserved approach.[75]

So a rather gloomy outlook then for the scope to bring national law in conformity with the directive through the duty of consistent interpretation, with adherence to the traditional interpretation setting the tone? Not quite.

3.3. THE ROLE PLAYED BY THE PRESUMPTION TO COMPLY IN RELATION TO GRAMMATICAL AND HISTORICAL INTERPRETATION

The first area of the Dutch courts' case law that showed a bolder approach to the duty of consistent interpretation is found by looking at judgments applying the presumption. Altena has also observed that these judgments, and in particular the HR's *Wandelvierdaagse* judgment, paved the way for a stronger approach towards consistent interpretation across the board.[76] The characteristics of the Dutch interpretative framework seem to make it easier to establish a 'structural prioritisation'. As Wissink explains, if national courts normally apply interpretative methods in a flexible manner, a fixation of these rules can be seen as an effect of the duty of consistent interpretation.[77]

The presumption has been around since the very inception of the duty of consistent interpretation in the Dutch legal order. In a judgment delivered in 1984 (i.e. well before the ECJ's *Wagner Miret* and *Pfeiffer* judgments[78] establishing the presumption as a matter of EU law), it was argued before the HR that the Law on turnover tax could be applied if it was established that there was an undertaking in the sense of that legislation, and that this was so notwithstanding the fact that

73 District Court The Hague 7 July 1995, ECLI:NL:RBSGR:1995:AK3535, *IER* 1995/30.
74 Wissink (n. 12), p. 167.
75 J. Altena-Davidsen, 'The Netherlands', in: C.N.K. Franklin (Ed.), *The Effectiveness and Application of EU and EEA Law in National Courts* (Intersentia 2018), p. 81-3.
76 Ibid, p. 83.
77 Wissink (n. 12), p. 114.
78 Case C-334/92 *Wagner Miret*, ECLI:EU:C:1993:945, para. 20; Joined Cases C-397/01 to C-403/01 *Pfeiffer*, ECLI:EU:C:2004:584, para. 112.

the concerned party did not possess the quality of taxable person as stated in the Sixth Directive.[79] This was rejected by the HR, holding that it must be presumed that the legislature did not have the intention to confer a different meaning on the term used in the Law on turnover tax (which has an implementing objective) that deviated from the term taxable person contained in the directive.[80] Arguably, it was quite logical to approach the matter in the way that the HR did, and this did not bring about a change to the traditional framework of interpretative methods (by the way, the judgment contained no signs that the HR consciously applied the duty of consistent interpretation as established in the ECJ's *Von Colson and Kamann* judgment).

The HR has provided a number of instructive judgments applying the presumption of the intention to comply that took the approach to consistent interpretation a step further. The concerned line in the HR's case law started with the *Wandelvierdaagse* judgment which concerned proceedings in the area of tax law and the interpretation in conformity with the directive was relied upon by the Member State against an individual (the same applies, by the way, for the HR's *Joustra* judgment delivered not long thereafter). This is perhaps not the most obvious setting for a landmark judgment pushing the boundaries of consistent interpretation. It showed that the pronounced vertical legal relationship that characterises this area of the law is not necessarily an obstacle for the introduction of a more far-reaching approach. However, the ABRvS and CBb have not, or at least not yet, followed the HR's approach.

3.3.1. *Applying the Presumption (1): A Structural Prioritisation of the Implementing Objective and Grammatical Interpretation as an Outer Limit*

The relevant passage of the *Wandelvierdaagse* judgment reads as follows:

> 'Het is vaste rechtspraak van het Hof van Justitie van de Europese Gemeenschappen dat de nationale rechter bij de toepassing van bepalingen van nationaal recht, ongeacht of zij van eerdere of latere datum dan de richtlijn zijn, deze zo veel mogelijk moet uitleggen in het licht van de bewoordingen van een op het betrokken gebied geldende richtlijn, teneinde het hiermee beoogde resultaat te bereiken en aldus aan artikel 249, derde alinea, EG te voldoen (…). Dit brengt mee dat de nationale rechter bij de uitlegging en toepassing van het nationale recht ervan moet uitgaan dat de staat de bedoeling heeft gehad ten volle uitvoering te geven aan de uit de betrokken richtlijn voortvloeiende verplichtingen (HvJ EG 16 december 1993, Wagner Miret, C-334/92, Jurispr. blz. I-06911).

79 Sixth Council Directive 77/388/EEC of 17 May 1977 on the harmonization of the laws of the Member States relating to turnover taxes – Common system of value added tax: uniform basis of assessment, *OJ* 1977, L145/1.

80 HR 2 May 1984, ECLI:NL:HR:1984:AW8625, *BNB* 1984/295.

> Evenbedoelde verplichting kan mitsdien niet afstuiten op het resultaat van een wetshistorische uitlegging van de betrokken nationale bepaling, indien de bewoordingen van die bepaling een uitlegging toelaten die deze bepaling in overeenstemming doet zijn met de richtlijn. Het beginsel van de rechtszekerheid verlangt in dat geval niet dat de justitiabele die reden vindt zich nader te oriënteren omtrent de betekenis en reikwijdte van de wettelijke bepaling, met voorbijgaan aan het bepaalde in artikel 249 EG moet kunnen afgaan op uitsluitend de gevolgtrekkingen die hij meent te kunnen baseren op toelichtingen en uitlatingen die zijn gegeven of gedaan in het proces van het tot stand brengen van de wettelijke regeling. Dit is slechts anders indien in zulke toelichtingen of uitlatingen ondubbelzinnig uitdrukking is gegeven aan de welbewuste bedoeling om de nationale regeling te doen afwijken van hetgeen waartoe de richtlijn zou verplichten of de vrijheid zou laten.'[81]

The above considerations provided that, first, it follows from the national courts' duty of consistent interpretation that when they interpret national law it must be presumed that the legislature intended to comply with the directive. Secondly, as a consequence, consistent interpretation is not frustrated by a concrete interpretation derived from a historical interpretation if the provision's wording leaves room for the consistent interpretation. Thirdly, in those circumstances, the principle of legal certainty does not require protection of individuals who consulted a rule's parliamentary history to determine their legal position and acted accordingly. This would only be different if the relevant rule's parliamentary history contains statements that unequivocally express a conscious intention of the legislature to depart from the directive. With regard to the first point, it is mentioned that this made it clear that the approach relies on the ECJ's *Wagner Miret* judgment (to which the HR referred) and the presumption established therein that the legislature intends to comply with the directive.[82] The second point tells something about the effect of the presumption, which is twofold. On the one hand, a concrete legislative intention incompatible with the implementing objective is in principle set aside. On the other hand, in a situation such as the present one (i.e. where a historical interpretation produces arguments opposing a consistent interpretation, yet the presumption applies), grammatical interpretation only stands in the way of consistent interpretation if it does not leave room for such an interpretation.[83] In this regard the HR's approach can be distinguished from those of Advocate-General De Wit, and the Regional Court of Appeal whose judgment was reviewed, who determined what in their view was the single most accurate grammatical interpretation – and were persuaded that this required that a consistent

---

81 HR 10 August 2007, ECLI:NL:HR:2007:AZ3758, *AB* 2007/291 (*Wandelvierdaagse*), para. 3.4.

82 Case C-334/92 *Wagner Miret*, ECLI:EU:C:1993:945, para. 20.

83 It is probably correct that this does not mean that, if there is not also the opposing argument derived from parliamentary history, consistent interpretation nevertheless always requires that such an interpretation is compatible with a grammatical interpretation. See also Wissink (n. 29), p. 152.

interpretation be rejected.[84] As regards the third point, this could be interpreted as an indication that the presumption only applied because the relevant legislation has an implementing objective. The *Wandelvierdaagse* judgment was not very clear in that regard in my opinion. However, subsequent case law confirmed that this is indeed a condition for the presumption to apply in the first place.[85] This is in line with the ECJ's case law as well (chapter 2, subparagraph 4.2.2). This means that, if the legislation did not have an implementing objective in the first place, or if it is rebutted by an unequivocal expression of a conscious intention of the legislature to depart from the directive, the presumption does not apply. In relation to the latter, I want to point out that, as there does not yet seem to have been a situation where the legislature expressed such an unequivocal intention, it appears to be a rather theoretical possibility that the presumption would not apply once a general implementing objective is established.[86] The exception would in my opinion be applied if it was for example acknowledged by the legislature that the directive does not permit other exceptions than the ones stated therein, but decides that it is nevertheless expedient to add an additional exception.

> It is recalled that the ECJ's *Björnekulla* judgment provided that national courts are required to examine the possibility to interpret the applicable rules in a manner that is in conformity with the directive, notwithstanding opposing arguments derived from the *travaux préparatoires.*[87] It has been put forward that the rule laid down in the HR's *Wandelvierdaagse* judgment corresponds to the *Björnekulla* judgment.[88] I am inclined to accept this view. Although the ECJ's judgment does not literally make the point that, if a consistent interpretation is grammatically possible, courts should proceed to such an interpretation and must disregard the rule's parliamentary history if necessary, the ECJ's judgment in my opinion clearly implies that if national law provides a route to consistent interpretation and the only argument against such an interpretation is based on the rule's *travaux préparatoires,* the latter must be disregarded. However, I should point out that none of the HR's judgments applying the presumption referred to the ECJ's *Björnekulla* judgment.

---

84 Concl. A-G De Wit, ECLI:NL:PHR:2007:AZ3758, paras. 7.2, 7.7, in HR 10 August 2007, ECLI:NL:HR:2007:AZ3758, *AB* 2007/291 (*Wandelvierdaagse*); Regional Court of Appeal Arnhem 2 March 2006, ECLI:NL:GHARN:2006:AV6387, para. 4.6. See also the case note by Widdershoven in *AB* 2007/291, para. 4 (agreeing with the HR's approach); Altena-Davidsen (n. 75), p. 84.

85 HR 21 September 2012, ECLI:NL:HR:2012:BW5879, *AB* 2012/367 (*ACI Adam e.a./Stichting De Thuiskopie*), para. 5.1.3; HR 17 January 2014, ECLI:NL:HR:2014:88, *NJ* 2015/304 (*Ryanair Ltd/PR Aviation*), paras. 3.4.2, 3.5.2.

86 Case note by Widdershoven in *AB* 2007/291, para. 3.

87 Case C-371/02 *Björnekulla,* ECLI:EU:C:2004:275, para. 13.

88 Case note by Widdershoven in *AB* 2012/367, para. 3; Wissink (n. 29), p. 151; M.J.M. Verhoeven and J.H. Jans, 'Doorwerking via conforme interpretatie en rechtstreekse werking', in: S. Prechal and R.J.G.M. Widdershoven (Eds.), *Inleiding tot het Europees bestuursrecht* (Ars Aequi Libri 2017), p. 73; Altena-Davidsen (n. 75), p. 84.

What are the consequences of the above for determining the relationship between EU and national law under the duty of consistent interpretation? I agree with Wissink, who characterises this area of the case law as a 'modification of the general interpretative framework'.[89] But it is important to be specific here, as the *Wandelvierdaagse* judgment made two points: first, it significantly reduced, to the benefit of a consistent interpretation, the role played by arguments derived from parliamentary history and, secondly, grammatical interpretation was applied as an outer limit. It must be examined whether there was a conflict of interpretative rules for each of them separately. As regards the first point, the approach can be contrasted with an earlier decision by the HR where it held that, since the legislature in the Law on turnover tax had opted for a system that deviated from the directive, there was no room to adopt a consistent interpretation. That conclusion was reached notwithstanding the implementing objective of the national provision under consideration.[90] This supports the conclusion that the rule established in the HR's *Wandelvierdaagse* judgment entailed a departure from the traditional approach consisting of a structural prioritisation of the intention to implement the directive. However, the question is: was this adaptation in *conflict* with the national interpretative rules? That question was already examined in chapter 3, subparagraph 3.2.2 where a similar situation arising in the German superior courts' case law was discussed. It suffices here to refer to the argumentation provided there and to point out that – perhaps even more clearly – the Dutch courts' traditional interpretative framework can be characterised as a normally flexible system and that exceptions to the prioritisation are even more clearly limited to situations where the legislature expressed in parliamentary history the unequivocal intention to go against the directive. While it is not unconceivable that the legislature expressed in parliamentary history an understanding of the directive that turned out to be incorrect, there does not yet seem to have been a situation where the legislature expressed an intention to depart from the directive. An application of the exception thus remains a rather theoretical possibility.[91] I conclude that this constellation supports the theory of supremacy of EU law. Secondly, can the same be said in relation to the effect of the presumption on grammatical interpretation? Here, the *Wandelvierdaagse* judgment's approach is more nuanced. I do not think that there was a structural prioritisation. Importantly, the judgment shows that the courts are still required to examine whether grammatical interpretation permits a consistent interpretation, which criterion was not *de facto* set aside.[92] And while

89 Wissink (n. 29), p. 151.

90 HR 7 December 1994, ECLI:NL:HR:1994:AA2977, *BNB* 1995/87 (*Grasland*), para. 3.3. It must be pointed out that the legislature had not intentionally departed from the directive (see *Kamerstukken II* 1967/68, 9324, 3, p. 33).

91 Case note by Widdershoven in *AB* 2007/291, para. 3.

92 See also HR 6 June 2008, ECLI:NL:HR:2008:BD3139, *AB* 2008/214 (*Joustra*), where the presumption applied but a consistent interpretation of some of the relevant provisions was rejected on account of a grammatical interpretation.

this aspect of the *Wandelvierdaagse* judgment comes close to the German Federal Court of Justice's *Heininger* judgment establishing the 'negative test' approach (which takes a particular result as its starting point, i.e. the interpretation prescribed by the directive, and, instead of asking what the most accurate interpretation of the national provision is, asks whether that provision does not oppose the desired interpretation, see chapter 3, subparagraph 3.2.1), I am not convinced that the HR's judgment should be placed in the same category. Certainly, it is more common to apply a grammatical interpretation in order to determine the most exact meaning of the provision's wording (so here it could be argued that there was an adaptation) but, referring to subparagraph 3.1.1, it seems that it is not entirely uncommon to view grammatical interpretation as an outer limit. It is also pointed out that it is quite normal that consistent interpretation to some degree adapts the application of the national interpretative method. If this were otherwise, the obligation would be without effect. So not each decision that is somehow different from a traditional interpretation and prioritises another, less natural, reading, confirms the theory of supremacy of the duty of consistent interpretation. Of course, these points must equally be taken into account for the negative test approach identified in the German chapter. But importantly, in the *Heininger* judgment the justification for the adaptation was not primarily based on the provision's implementing objective which, however, was seen to be the case for the *Wandelvierdaagse* judgment. I think the impact of this argument explains the approach adopted in the latter judgment. A second distinction is that in the *Heininger* judgment and subsequent judgments the negative test approach was stated far more explicitly and, thirdly, the approach is more well-established (I only found a few other judgments in Dutch case law applying the approach[93]). Admittedly, there is not a clear dividing line for when case law can be said to support the negative test approach, but I nevertheless believe that the German and Dutch case law must on this point be placed on the opposing sides of that line. In one of the other Dutch judgments applying an approach in line with the negative test approach, there was not an implementing objective, this brings it closer to the German side of the line.[94]

3.3.2. *Applying the Presumption (2): A Decline of the Significance of Grammatical Interpretation?*

It was already in 2001, before the HR's *Wandelvierdaagse* judgment, that Wissink argued that, if the legislature has misunderstood the directive, this does not necessarily preclude the adoption of a consistent interpretation. This will only be so, if the legislature's incorrect understanding manifested itself in the enacted

---

93 Dutch judgments similar to the concerned part of the *Wandelvierdaagse* judgment's approach are found in CBb 5 June 2014, ECLI:NL:CBB:2014:206, *AB* 2014/345, para. 3.5.3; ABRvS 1 April 2015, ECLI:NL:RVS:2015:999, *M en R* 2015/92, para. 2.7.

94 This is the judgment of 1 April 2015.

provision in a way that makes it impossible to adopt a consistent interpretation.[95] This turned out to be precisely the tenor of the *Wandelvierdaagse* judgment. After all, grammatical interpretation remained a relevant criterion that was not simply set aside by the presumption. It has also been put forward by for example Jans that, while he believes that in principle a consistent interpretation is to be given priority and can force the national courts to depart from the interpretation that would have followed on the basis of a traditional approach, it must nevertheless respect the limits of grammatical interpretation.[96] It now needs to be examined whether all this has changed with the HR's subsequent judgment in *Albron/FNV c.s.* It is noted that, unlike the *Wandelvierdaagse* judgment, this judgment was delivered in civil law proceedings (and, accordingly, issued by another chamber of the HR).

The case concerned two deviations from the Transfers of Undertakings Directive[97] in the Dutch implementing rules. It used the term 'employer' instead of 'transferor', and only referred to 'contract of employment' and not also to 'employment relationship'. In the case's relevant circumstances, this raised an issue with regard to the applicability of the rules.

> The respondent in the review proceedings was employed by, and had an employment contract with, Heineken Nederlands Beheer B.V., but was, within the group of companies, detached to Heineken Nederland B.V., the operating company supplying catering services. The catering activities were transferred to a third party. As the respondent was not employed by the latter company, a dispute arose as to whether those employees who were assigned to it, automatically became staff members of the transferee.

The Regional Court of Appeal whose judgment was being reviewed had referred questions for a preliminary ruling to the ECJ, whose ruling made it clear that the directive applied to a situation such as the one in the main proceedings, and thus required that the employees were able to rely on the protection conferred upon them by the directive in case of a transfer of undertaking. In the follow-up decision, the Regional Court of Appeal decided that the respondent's situation could be brought within the scope of the Dutch rules on transfers of undertakings through a consistent interpretation. That decision was upheld by the HR. It first reiterated in general terms the kind of approach that national courts must adopt when they interpret national law in conformity with directives, mentioning in particular the presumption that the legislature intends to comply with the directive. It then

95 Wissink (n. 12), p. 157, who refers to HR 20 October 1995, ECLI:NL:HR:1995:ZC1846, *NJ* 1996/330 (*Van Asseldonk/Ter Schure*) as a clear example confirming this point.

96 This view was already espoused in his case note in *M en R* 1995/57. See also the case note by Jans in *M en R* 2010/43, para. 1. See further Altena-Davidsen (n. 48), p. 260.

97 Council Directive 2001/23/EC of 12 March 2001 on the approximation of the laws of the Member States relating to the safeguarding of employees' rights in the event of transfers of undertakings, businesses or parts of undertakings or businesses, *OJ* 2001, L82/16.

continued by examining the ground of appeal concerning the rule's parliamentary history. The legislature had in the explanatory memorandum elaborated his choice to only use the term contract of employment, and it was clear that he had willingly decided not to use the term employment relationship in addition to this. However, the reason for this choice was that the legislature believed that the term contract of employment already covered all the situations to which the directive was intended to apply, and that the additional term employment relationship was merely introduced to facilitate the application of the directive in Member States with a different kind of labour law system. Taking this into consideration, the HR concluded that it had not been established that the legislature had not wanted to duly implement the directive into national law. The argument based on parliamentary history was therefore dismissed. The next ground of appeal that was addressed concerned the wording of the national provision, which deviated from the directive on two points (as discussed above). The HR provided two interesting statements in this regard. First, referring to a previous judgment (that was delivered in a purely internal context and also by the HR's Civil Chamber) it considered that a provision's formulation is not always decisive for the meaning that should be attributed to it (even if the provision was recently enacted).[98] Secondly, referring to the presumption of the intention to comply, its general observations concerning the duty of consistent interpretation and the circumstance that the case is concerned with the interpretation of legislation that was specifically enacted for the purpose of transposing a directive intended to confer rights on individuals,[99] it held that there was all the more reason not to confer a decisive role upon the national provision's text. Unlike the judgment of the Regional Court of Appeal, the HR did not discuss in detail in what way the text of the concerned provision was actually in line with the directive but rather emphasised the point that other considerations should come into play when determining the limits of a provision's text and that this may be a reason to conclude that these limits should not be drawn too narrowly.[100] Accordingly, the second ground of appeal was also dismissed.[101] A similar decision was adopted in a HR judgment of 14 April 2017 (this case also concerned the use of the term 'contract of employment', however, the discussion focussed on grammatical interpretation and the presumption only and, similarly, the HR appeared to believe that a consistent interpretation could be achieved by adopting an extensive interpretation of the text).[102]

---

98 Reference was made to HR 9 December 2011, ECLI:NL:HR:2011:BU7412, *NJ* 2013/273, para. 3.5. See further HR 9 December 1994, ECLI:NL:HR:1994:ZC1573, *NJ* 1995/224, para. 3.3.

99 This clearly referred to Joined Cases C-397/01 to C-403/01 *Pfeiffer*, ECLI:EU:C:2004:584, para. 112.

100 Cf. Regional Court of Appeal Amsterdam 25 October 2011, ECLI:NL:GHAMS:2011:BU1290, *NJ* 2012/163, para. 2.6 (the judgment under review). Advocate-General Wissink did discuss in detail in what way a grammatical interpretation could be made compatible with the interpretation required by the directive, see the Concl. of A-G Wissink, ECLI:NL:PHR:2013:BZ1780, paras. 2.14, 2.52-2.56, 2.59.

101 HR 5 April 2013, ECLI:NL:HR:2013:BZ1780, *NJ* 2013/389 (*Albron/FNV c.s.*), paras. 3.6.5-3.7.

102 HR 14 April 2017, ECLI:NL:HR:2017:689, paras. 3.3.2-3.3.7.

It is interesting to compare the HR's judgment in *Albron/FNV c.s.* with the ABRvS's judgment of 26 April 2017.[103] The ABRvS found that the Dutch implementing legislation provided for a more extensive exclusion from an entitlement to residence for the purpose of family reunification than permitted by the directive. A consistent interpretation was rejected because it would be incompatible with a grammatical interpretation of the concerned provision, which clearly conferred the more extensive powers on the competent public authority. While the ABRvS did not rely on the provision's parliamentary history to justify its decision, the references to parliamentary history in the judgment clearly showed that the legislature had wanted to adopt the more extensive exclusion ground. Yet, interestingly, it was also provided by the legislature that this was believed to be in conformity with the directive.[104] This calls to mind the line adopted in the HR's *Wandelvierdaagse* judgment, which had been delivered in tax law proceedings and therefore can be said to have paved the way for applying the presumption in a vertical relationship. Since the text also raised questions as far as concerns the possibility to adopt a consistent interpretation, it also calls to mind the judgment in *Albron/FNV c.s.* However, it is recalled that the latter judgment was delivered in civil law proceedings. In any case, the ABRvS did not mention the presumption or the HR's judgments. It could be derived from the judgment that, even if it is established that the legislature wanted to comply with the directive, the ABRvS draws a line if consistent interpretation is not grammatically possible.

Although there is not, or perhaps not yet, extensive case law on this point, it follows from the above that the HR considers that there is, on the basis of the *national* interpretative rules, scope to adopt a liberal approach to the limits imposed by a provision's wording, which approach also takes into account indications derived from other interpretative criteria. The adopted position is in line with what was mentioned in relation to the traditional approach to interpretation in subparagraph 3.1.1. There is thus not a departure from the national interpretative rules. While the HR pointed out that there was all the more reason to adopt a flexible approach to grammatical interpretation when an implementing objective is established and the presumption applies, a structural prioritisation cannot be discerned at this point. Such a prioritisation could be established if the HR's case law showed that it is prepared to take a more flexible approach with regard to the provision's wording in for example all cases to which the presumption applies and where the applicable directive confers rights on individuals. A number of HR judgments delivered before the judgment in *Albron/FNV c.s.* oppose such a conclusion.[105] I conclude that further case law is necessary before it can be said that the HR is always prepared

---

103 ABRvS 26 April 2017, ECLI:NL:RVS:2017:1109, paras. 3.1-3.7.

104 *Kamerstukken II* 2007/08, 31549, 3, p. 8.

105 I refer in particular to HR 20 October 1995, ECLI:NL:HR:1995:ZC1846, *NJ* 1996/330 (*Van Asseldonk/Ter Schure*), para. 3.5; HR 5 June 2009, ECLI:NL:HR:2009:BH2815, *NJ* 2012/182 (*De Treek/Dexia*), para. 4.7.4.

to adopt a liberal approach to grammatical interpretation and to allow other interpretative criteria to further determine the scope available for interpretation (or that it will only refuse to do so in very limited categories of cases). It is pointed out that, while it is not possible to identify a conflict as a result of a structural prioritisation, this does not exclude the possibility that the individual decision entailed a transgression of the Dutch interpretative rules. This will be discussed further in the next subparagraph. The ABRvS's case law is even more scarce on the point discussed here, and also less permissive. The ABRvS does not seem to be prepared to adopt an interpretation that would be clearly incompatible with the limits of the provision's wording.

3.4. TRANSGRESSIONS OF NATIONAL INTERPRETATIVE RULES?

Even if a consistent interpretation requires a significant modification of the traditional interpretation, it would appear from the discussion in subparagraph 3.1 that it cannot lightly be concluded that this resulted from a conflict with the traditional interpretative rules, and it would seem difficult to point out at what point exactly such a conflict arises. Indeed, since the Dutch interpretative rules offer quite some degree of flexibility, it is more difficult to find cases in which there was a clear transgression of those rules. However, it appeared from subparagraph 3.1.1 that, if all the interpretative criteria clearly point in a particular direction, this curtails the discretion enjoyed by the courts, especially if a grammatical interpretation makes it unambiguously clear what meaning is to be conferred upon the provision. It is examined whether the Dutch superior courts have found arguments that enable them to go beyond such limits, especially limits imposed by a grammatical interpretation, and to what extent this must be viewed as the result of a conflict of interpretative rules. A distinction is made in this regard between legislation that does, and legislation that does not, have an implementing objective.

3.4.1. The Intention to Implement the Directive

In its judgment in *Beets-Proper/Van Lanschot Bankiers*, delivered in 1987, the HR interpreted the national provision in conformity with the directive relying on the argument that the former was intended to implement the latter.[106] Two things must be mentioned here. In the first place, the consistent interpretation entailed a restrictive interpretation of the national provision. Secondly, the HR's judgment did not refer to an obligation qua EU law to interpret national law in conformity with directives. It rather seemed to be the national provision's genealogical place in the legal order, stemming from the directive, that caused the HR to use the directive in

106 HR 21 November 1986, ECLI:NL:HR:1986:AG5465, *NJ* 1987/351 (*Beets-Proper/Van Lanschot Bankiers*), para. 2.1.

order to determine the meaning of the implementing provision. The argument that the national provision was intended to implement the directive was thus already used in the period immediately after the ECJ's *Von Colson and Kamann* judgment and in a way which gave a 'twist' to the meaning of the national provision. However, it is submitted that it must be presumed that there is not normally a transgression of the national interpretative rules if the adopted interpretation was first and foremost arrived at by placing reliance on the national legislature's intention (which is then viewed as an aspect of historical and/or teleological interpretation).

If, in addition to the national provision having an implementing objective, other interpretative methods appear to be compatible with a consistent interpretation, it is unlikely that such an interpretation entails a transgression of the Dutch interpretative rules – even if this causes the provision of national law to have a meaning that is not immediately obvious on account of an isolated, traditional, approach to interpretation.[107] A step further is the CBb's *IMC Securities* judgment, where the adopted consistent interpretation was clearly incompatible with a grammatical interpretation, yet supported by the provision's implementing objective (which was put forward as the main argument for the adopted interpretation) as well as concrete statements from the explanatory memorandum on the relevant point (leading to an interpretation whereby the prohibition 'to maintain' (*houden*) the price of financial instruments at an artificial level was interpreted to mean quite the opposite, namely that it is not required that the price is maintained for a certain duration and that it is also prohibited 'to bring' (*brengen*) the price to an artificial level, such as the sudden fluctuation in the price which had occurred in the current situation).[108] And in three HR (Civil Chamber) judgments, and another judgment by the CBb, where it was established that the legislature had intended to implement the directive, so far as possible went quite far indeed.

> I first mention the HR's judgment in *Buyck/Van den Ameele.*[109] When the legislature adopted measures to implement the Transfers of Undertakings Directive,[110] it was overlooked that Dutch law would not protect the employee against dismissal if the nullity of the dismissal was not invoked on time. This was found to be incompatible with the directive. The incompatibility was resolved through a consistent interpretation. It cannot be doubted that this entailed an interpretative stretch as the text of the national provision seemed to point in the direction of the incompatible interpretation and a historical interpretation was also in line with the incompatible interpretation. However, it is noted that the historical interpretation did not make it clear whether the legislature had

107 See, for example, ABRvS 15 June 2016, ECLI:NL:RVS:2016:1773, para. 4; ABRvS 12 October 2017, ECLI:NL:RVS:2017:2771, paras. 5.2-5.3.

108 CBb 22 February 2012, ECLI:NL:CBB:2012:BV6713 (*IMC*), para. 4.2.

109 HR 29 December 1995, ECLI:NL:HR:1995:ZC1943, *NJ* 1996/418 (*Buyck/Van den Ameele*).

110 Council Directive 77/187/EEC of 14 February 1977 on the approximation of the laws of the Member States relating to the safeguarding of employees' rights in the event of transfers of undertakings, businesses or parts of businesses, *OJ* 1977, L61/26.

envisaged the difficulties that could arise if the employee did not invoke the nullity in time.[111] Arguably, this created scope for further interpretation, which was facilitated by the argument that the legislature had intended to implement the directive.

Secondly, there is the judgment in *Stichting De Thuiskopie/Opus Supplies Deutschland e.a.* The judgment concerned the question who could be held responsible for payment of the compensation owed to copyright holders resulting from the exception for copying for private use. In particular, it needed to be determined how the term 'importer', used in the Dutch implementing legislation, should be interpreted. It was clear that a broad interpretation of that term, which would also cover the respondent in the proceedings before the HR, did not follow from a grammatical interpretation of the national provision. I should add that historical and systematic arguments appeared to oppose a consistent interpretation as well, at least if a traditional approach was adopted.[112] However, the HR was uncertain if this was compatible with the directive and referred questions for a preliminary ruling. The ECJ's ruling emphasised that Member States who have introduced an exception for copying for private use have an obligation of result to ensure that copyright holders actually receive the compensation, and that '[i]t is for the national court, where it is impossible to ensure recovery of the fair compensation from the purchasers, to interpret national law in order to allow recovery of that compensation from the person responsible for payment who is acting on a commercial basis'.[113] When the case returned to the HR its considerations focussed on the determination that a restrictive interpretation of importer would lead to the prohibited 'impossibility' to recover the compensation mentioned by the ECJ. It then simply provided that importer should be interpreted so as to cover the respondent. It thus opted for the broad interpretation.[114]

The HR's judgment in *Albron/FNV c.s.* was already discussed in subparagraph 3.2.2, where I argued that the HR did not confer a structural priority on consistent interpretation in that case. Yet, this cannot change the fact that the consistent interpretation adopted by the HR was difficult to reconcile with a traditional interpretation of the concerned rule. I already discussed the discrepancy between the interpretation required by the directive, and grammatical and historical interpretation. It should be noted that, in addition to this, a systematic interpretation did not seem to support a consistent interpretation either (the terms employer and employee would be given a meaning that deviated from the meaning conferred on those terms in the title of the Civil Code of which the provision interpreted by the HR is a part).[115] However, the concerned provision did have an implementing objective.

---

111 *Kamerstukken II* 1979/80, 15940, 3-4, p. 8.

112 Concl. A-G Langemeijer, ECLI:NL:PHR:2009:BI6320, paras. 3.18-3.23, in HR 20 November 2009, ECLI:NL:HR:2009:BI6320, *NJ* 2009/581.

113 Case C-462/09 *Stichting De Thuiskopie,* ECLI:EU:C:2011:397, para. 41.

114 HR 12 October 2012, ECLI:NL:HR:2012:BW8301, *NJ* 2012/586 (*Stichting De Thuiskopie/Opus Supplies Deutschland e.a.*), para. 2.4.

115 R.M. Beltzer and I.A. Haanappel, 'Het Hof van Justitie en zijn benigna interpretatio van werkgever en werknemer' (2011/1) *Arbeidsrechtelijke Annotaties*, p. 76-7.

> Finally, there is the CBb's judgment of 5 June 2014. The court admitted that a literal reading of the provision of the Telecommunications Act required that any electronic mail with a commercial purpose must contain an address through which the recipient can cease such mail. However, it considered that the corresponding provision in the directive only applied this requirement to mail that constituted direct marketing. The mail in question was clearly of a commercial nature, but was not considered by the CBb as marketing since the parties previously concluded a contract with regard to these mails. The grammatical incompatibility was surpassed by the provision's implementing objective.[116] It may also be asked to what extent this outcome was compatible with the explicit intention of the legislature to adopt a broad approach to the mail that would be covered by the requirement.[117]

In the above four judgments, there was in each case a larger or smaller discrepancy with the national provision's wording as well as one or more of the other interpretative criteria or simply all the other interpretative criteria. It is in my opinion beyond doubt that the approach to consistent interpretation in each case required an adaptation of the traditional approach, the latter having led to a different outcome. It could perhaps be argued that, on some occasions, the adjustment was less far-reaching: in *Stichting De Thuiskopie/Opus Supplies Deutschland e.a.* the provision's wording was not entirely incompatible, and while the systematic argument was difficult to discard, the historical argument lost some of its weight as the legislature did not seem to have envisaged the kind of situation that gave rise to the dispute. However, can the same be said for the other judgments? Or is it not possible to escape the conclusion that there was a conflict of interpretative rules? This depends on how one views the court's use of the argument that the legislation was intended to implement the directive. In my opinion it is difficult to view this as an interference on behalf of the duty of consistent interpretation. I think it refers first and foremost to a route in national law supporting a consistent interpretation. In this regard it should also be taken into account that the argument that the national provision has an implementing objective was already used in an early judgment such as *Beets-Proper/Van Lanschot Bankiers*, and no reference was made to the duty of consistent interpretation *qua* EU law, indicating that the HR was acting in accordance with, and on the basis of, national interpretative rules. In such a situation, i.e. where arguments recognised by the national interpretative rules are used, it must be presumed that there was not a transgression of these rules. The above four judgments do not warrant a different conclusion. Consider, the judgment in *Albron/FNV c.s.*,[118] where the adopted consistent interpretation departed in a significant way from an isolated, traditional, interpretation. The legislature had opted for the term 'employer' instead of 'transferor', and only

116 CBb 5 June 2014, ECLI:NL:CBB:2014:206, *AB* 2014/345, paras. 3.5.1-3.5.3.

117 See the case note by Sauter in *AB* 2014/345, paras. 3, 5.

118 By the way, it is again recalled that a similar decision was adopted in HR 14 April 2017, ECLI:NL:HR:2017:689, paras. 3.3.2-3.3.7.

referred to 'contract of employment' and not also to 'employment relationship'. The choice for this formulation fitted the existing system of the Civil Code, and the explanatory memorandum elaborated on this decision. However, a further interpretation by the ECJ of the corresponding provision in the directive showed that the legislature's understanding of the directive had been incorrect. Is it then inexplainable that the courts rely on the provision's implementing objective (which in the *Albron/FNV c.s.* judgment, as well as the other cases discussed, was clearly stated in the explanatory memorandum) to reshuffle the balance between the interpretative methods, producing an outcome that meets this objective? Wissink points out, with regard to the provision's text – and it seems to me that the same applies *a fortiori* for the other interpretative methods – that '(...) whether the wording of a rule is "clear" or not cannot be derived only from its plain meaning, but must be judged with reference to, inter alia, parliamentary intent'.[119] I agree, and I also want to recall here that the discussion of the traditional approach to interpretation in subparagraph 3.1.1 showed that there is not a fixed hierarchy between the different interpretative methods, that their weight depends on the circumstances of each case, and that grammatical interpretation is not sacrosanct. I conclude that, if it is established that parliamentary intent is aimed at implementing the directive, it follows from Wissink's observations and subparagraph 3.1.1 that the answer to the question asked is that it is not inexplainable and that it is not necessary to view the *Albron/FNV c.s.* judgment, or any of the other judgments, as a transgression of the Dutch interpretative rules. Admittedly, the argument of the provision having an implementing objective was not advanced by the HR in *Stichting De Thuiskopie/Opus Supplies Deutschland e.a.* It rather seemed to apply the ECJ's preliminary ruling directly to the case before it and forgot to explain to what extent the required interpretation could be accommodated by national law. Nevertheless, as I already observed, it could be argued that, compared to the other three judgments, the arguments opposing a consistent interpretation were the least compelling in this case.

It can be concluded that, when an implementing objective is established, there is always an argument supporting consistent interpretation. Moreover, judged by the Dutch courts' application of this argument it carries a lot of weight. Verhoeven and Jans are surely correct in providing that the argument that the concerned provision was intended by the legislature to implement the directive is an important factor enabling consistent interpretation.[120] The reason behind this is, in my opinion, that it has its basis in national law and reflects the intention of the legislation.

So when an implementing objective is established the approach to consistent interpretation can go quite far without this leading to a conflict. A final remark

119 Wissink (n. 29), p. 150-1. See also Hartkamp (n. 34), para. 185.
120 Verhoeven and Jans (n. 88), p. 70. See also Hartkamp (n. 34), para. 185.

that is necessary, is that the establishment of an implementing objective does not always save the national rule from being incompatible with the directive. There is extensive case law in which a consistent interpretation was rejected even though the rule had an implementing objective. In those cases the main argument to reject a consistent interpretation was that such an interpretation would exceed the limits of a grammatical interpretation. This is in line with the picture of the Dutch superior courts' application of the limits to the duty of consistent interpretation that will be provided in subparagraph 3.5.[121] Such different outcomes are not incoherent: the discretion enjoyed by the Dutch courts entails that, within certain limits, they can arrive at different conclusions. As long as the requirements imposed by the duty of consistent interpretation are respected, no issue under EU law arises.

3.4.2. Consistent Interpretation of Non-Implementing Legislation

A logical question following from the previous part, pointing out that a conflict is unlikely if the duty of consistent interpretation is applied to legislation having an implementing objective, is whether the same can be said if the legislation does not have such an objective. In other words, can one find examples of far-reaching interpretations of national law in this category? The Dutch superior courts have frequently adopted a consistent interpretation of national law which did not have an implementing objective. In three judgments from the ABRvS and one from the CBb, general, to some extent flexible, provisions were used as a steppingstone to read in the more specific requirements contained in the directives. One of them, the ABRvS's *Buitengebied Texel* judgment, is mentioned by way of an example as it clearly illustrates this point:[122]

> The ABRvS considered that the Nature Conservation Act did not contain provisions that were explicitly adopted to implement the requirements of

121 A rejection of a consistent interpretation, even though it was clear that the rule had an implementing objective, can be seen in HR 20 October 1995, ECLI:NL:HR:1995:ZC1846, *NJ* 1996/330 (*Van Asseldonk/Ter Schure*), para. 3.5; HR 6 June 2008, ECLI:NL:HR:2008:BD3139, *AB* 2008/214 (*Joustra*), paras. 3.2, 3.3.2-3.3.3; HR 5 June 2009, ECLI:NL:HR:2009:BH2815, *NJ* 2012/182 (*De Treek/Dexia*), para. 4.7.4; ABRvS 25 November 2009, ECLI:NL:RVS:2009:BK4312, *M en R* 2010/43, para. 2.5.1; ABRvS 3 April 2012, ECLI:NL:RVS:2012:BW1435, para. 2.2.5; ABRvS 11 June 2014, ECLI:NL:RVS:2014:2120, *AB* 2014/320, para. 2.7; ABRvS 26 April 2017, ECLI:NL:RVS:2017:1109, paras. 3.1-3.7.

122 Additionally, there is the judgment in ABRvS 28 July 2004, ECLI:NL:RVS:2004:AQ5732, *M en R* 2004/104, m.nt. J.H. Jans. The case is viewed by Jans as far-reaching since the entire legal framework of the directive was read into the national provision. He concludes that, apparently, the ABRvS did not consider this to be a transgression of interpretative rules. The next judgment is, ABRvS 28 February 2007, ECLI:NL:RVS:2007:AZ9494, *AB* 2007/183 (*Fortis*), para. 2.11. See also the case note by Jans and Verschuuren in *M en R* 2007/45, para. 2. And, finally, consider the judgment delivered in CBb 12 September 2016, ECLI:NL:CBB:2016:270. The CBb did not discuss to what extent the requirements of the applicable directive could be read into national law. This is to some extent compensated by the judgment that was appealed (see District Court Rotterdam 4 August 2011, ECLI:NL:RBROT:2011:BR4191, para. 2.3.10) – albeit that the district court's reasoning was also not particularly elaborate.

> the Habitats Directive to avoid the deterioration of the natural habitats and that there were also no other legislative provisions applicable that formed an implementation of the requirements deriving from Article 6(2) of the Habitats Directive. Nevertheless, in as far as the habitats were also designated as national natural sites, it considered it possible to give a consistent interpretation to Articles 12 and 16 of the Nature Conservation Act, which were aimed at the protection of such sites and laying down the requirement to obtain a permit for any actions that could potentially be harmful to the ecological values for which the area was designated.[123]

As the national provisions were not clearly incompatible with the directive, it is presumed that the national courts could reach their decision without transgressing the Dutch interpretative rules. These judgments are also good examples showing that administrative law is not only made up of highly detailed provisions, leaving almost no scope for further interpretation but that, similar to civil law it also contains provisions of a more general nature, whose flexibility can be utilised for an interpretation in conformity with the directive.

At first sight, it would seem that a different conclusion needs to be drawn in relation to the HR's *Dekker* judgment. The HR concluded that, if a violation is established of (then) Article 1637ij of the Civil Code prohibiting discrimination between men and women as regards the conclusion of a contract of employment, this is sufficient to establish the employer's civil liability, and grounds of exemption applicable on the basis of (then) Article 1401 of the Civil Code (now Article 6:162 of the Civil Code) must be disregarded.[124] Article 1637ij did, but Article 6:162 does not (and Article 1401 did not), have an explicit implementing objective. It needs to be pointed out that Article 6:162 is a central provision of the Dutch Civil Code. It is sometimes necessary to determine how other provisions of law interact with these central provisions, in which regard the courts should take into account the specific circumstances of the case before them. This is no different when the national provision was introduced to implement a directive. Whenever provisions of national law implement a directive, it is likely that they are applied in combination with one or more existing provisions that occupy a central position in a particular legal area for putting into effect the claims advanced.[125] The HR had to determine how Article 1637ij interacted with Article 6:162. To be sure, an initial reading of both provisions might support the conclusion that Article 1637ij placed no restrictions on Article 6:162, so that the latter is fully applicable, including the grounds of exemption. Yet, this outcome would disregard that the former was

123 ABRvS 31 March 2000, ECLI:NL:RVS:2000:AB1152, *AB* 2000/302 (*Buitengebied Texel*), m.nt. Ch. Backes, para. 2.6.2.9.2. Backes's view that the ABRvS correctly decided that, as far as concerns the areas designated as national natural sites, there was sufficient scope for a consistent interpretation is also found in the case note by Jans in *M en R* 2000/105.

124 HR 13 September 1991, ECLI:NL:HR:1991:ZC0328, *NJ* 1992/225 (*Dekker*), para. 2.1.

125 Wissink (n. 12), p. 258, 271.

introduced to implement the directive. If this objective is taken into account, together with the fact that the directive did not permit that the establishment of civil liability was made subject to the grounds of exemption under Dutch law,[126] a different kind of arrangement would also seem justifiable, especially if it is taken into account that Dutch liability law recognises a number of exceptions to the applicability of the grounds of exemption contained in Article 6:162.[127] So, briefly put, it would then be Article 1637ij's implementing objective in combination with the possibility to adjust the interaction with Article 6:162 to the circumstances of the case, that allows the conclusion that there was not a conflict of interpretations. As an aside, and noting that it is immaterial for whether or not there was a conflict of interpretations, it is observed that the HR's *Dekker* judgment fits in well with the rule established in the ECJ's subsequent *Pfeiffer* judgment that national courts are obliged to apply a technique available under national law if this enables them to adopt a consistent interpretation.[128]

Another case where it was less clear that there was not a transgression – but where such a conclusion is in the end not persuasive – is the ABRvS's judgment of 1 April 2015. This case was already discussed earlier on in this paragraph as far as concerns the question what provides the relevant frame of reference for the determination whether a new plan on balance leads to a decrease of nitrogen deposition on the relevant site. There, I argued that the interpretation consistent with the directive did not really differ from a traditional interpretation. Yet, the ABRvS also had to decide which mitigating measures could be taken into account for determining whether a new plan requires an appropriate assessment in the sense of the Habitats Directive. It held that it is not permitted to take into account mitigating measures adopted externally, i.e. outside the company with which the new plan is concerned; the relevant provision of national law only covered measures adopted internally, i.e. within the activities of the concerned company.[129] It is noted that the provision mentioned mitigating measures in general, and in a case note under the judgment, the ABRvS was criticised for deviating from the provision's wording by adopting a restrictive interpretation.[130] While it would certainly have been reasonable to adopt a broader interpretation, the ABRvS invoked two arguments to justify the more restrictive interpretation. First, a broader interpretation would have been incompatible with another provision in the concerned legislation, which stipulated that, if new plans are likely to have a significant effect on a Natura 2000 site (a European ecological network of special areas of conservation), this means that

126 See in this regard the ECJ's ruling, requested by the HR in the proceedings discussed here, Case C-177/88 *Dekker*, ECLI:EU:C:1990:383.
127 G. Betlem, 'Een vierde type van rechtsvinding' (1991/34) *Nederlands Juristenblad*, p. 1370; Wissink (n. 12), p. 271.
128 Joined Cases C-397/01 to C-403/01 *Pfeiffer*, ECLI:EU:C:2004:584, para. 116.
129 ABRvS 1 April 2015, ECLI:NL:RVS:2015:999, *M en R* 2015/92, para. 2.7.
130 See the case note by Kaajan in *M en R* 2015/92, para. 6.

an appropriate assessment in the sense of the Habitats Directive is required. As external mitigating measures fall outside the scope of the plan as such, they cannot therefore be taken into account at the stage of determining whether an appropriate assessment must be carried out. This seems to be a compelling systematic argument as this provision implemented a key requirement of the Habitats Directive. A broad approach to mitigating measures would therefore vitiate this provision and its attempt to correctly implement the directive. Secondly, the ABRvS explicitly provided that the adopted interpretation was not incompatible with the text of the provision on mitigating measures.

3.5. LIMITS TO THE APPLICATION OF THE DUTY OF CONSISTENT INTERPRETATION

The Dutch superior courts recognise two types of limits to the application of the duty of consistent interpretation. First, it can be considered that an interpretative method, or a combination of interpretative methods, stands in the way of a consistent interpretation. As will be seen, the limits of a grammatical interpretation occupy a dominant role here. Sometimes, this is relied upon in combination with the legislature's intention. Surprisingly, the Dutch courts hardly ever refer explicitly to the limitation of a *contra legem* interpretation when they encounter limits of this kind. Secondly, the Dutch superior courts may find a limitation in the consequences that a consistent interpretation would have for the concerned individual. In this regard the principle of legal certainty plays a dominant role – which is also sometimes referred to in the context of the first kind of limitation. The prominent role played by legal certainty is also a feature that is emphasised by Dutch legal scholarship.[131]

The Dutch superior courts have not so far rejected a consistent interpretation with reference to the limits of their judicial function (i.e. the principle of separation of powers) or the protection of fundamental rights. However, with regard to the former, it is noted that it could be argued that this principle is never entirely absent when courts need to determine what is still a valid interpretation of the law.[132] And some judgments rejecting a consistent interpretation have been interpreted as implicitly referring to the limits of the judicial function.[133]

---

131 J.M. Prinssen, *Doorwerking van Europees recht. De verhouding tussen directe werking, conforme interpretatie en overheidsaansprakelijkheid* (Kluwer 2004), p. 51-2; Altena-Davidsen (n. 75), p. 88.

132 Wissink (n. 12), p. 246. See also Verhoeven and Jans (n. 88), p. 69-70.

133 Case note by Jans under ABRvS 31 March 2000, ECLI:NL:RVS:2000:AB1152, *M en R* 2000/105 (*Buitengebied Texel*) (characterising the limits to consistent interpretation as being of a constitutional nature); H.F.M.W. Van Rijswick (Ed.), *EG-recht en de praktijk van het waterbeheer* (STOWA 2008), p. 62 (discussing ABRvS 11 May 1996, ECLI:NL:RVS:1996:AN5165, *AB* 1996/410).

3.5.1. *The Prominence of the Limits of Grammatical Interpretation*

Perhaps not entirely unexpectedly, the limits of the national provision's wording is by far the most important reason to reject a consistent interpretation.[134] The ABRvS has provided in a more general way that the extent of the implementing deficit is a determining factor when national law is interpreted in conformity with the directive.[135] Also, even though subsequent case law learned that the HR does not hold the view that compatibility with the provision's wording is always a necessary condition for consistent interpretation (note that this position applies to the HR's Civil Chamber), case law applying the presumption (see subparagraph 3.3.1) showed that, notwithstanding the applicability of the presumption, the grammatical interpretative method can nevertheless produce an insurmountable obstacle to a consistent interpretation – and it is safe to say that it is unlikely that grammatical interpretation will play a less prominent role if the presumption does not apply.

Most of the time, the Dutch superior courts' considerations regarding grammatical interpretation will be less didactical and more case-specific, and the importance of this criterion can then only be deduced from the fact that it produced a compelling reason to reject a consistent interpretation. These judgments can also be interpreted as an implicit reference to the *contra legem* limitation.[136] On a number of occasions the Dutch superior courts referred explicitly to the *contra legem* limitation without, however, actually proceeding to an application of this limitation to reject a consistent interpretation in the case before them; it was mentioned either as part of a more general discussion of their obligation to interpret national law in conformity with the directive, or it came to the conclusion that the limitation was not violated.[137] There have in fact been remarkably few judgments which explicitly referred to this limitation as part of the reasoning *and* proceeded to an application of this limitation in order to reject a consistent interpretation. This is not difficult to understand for the period before the ECJ's *Pupino* and *Adeneler*

134 The importance of this limitation is also recognised in Dutch legal scholarship. I already referred to the position adopted by Jans in his case note in *M en R* 1995/57 and *M en R* 2010/43, para. 1, as well as Altena-Davidsen (n. 48), p. 260.

135 ABRvS 15 December 1994, ECLI:NL:RVS:1994:AN4903, *AB* 1996/29. See, in a similar vein: ARRvS 6 March 1986, ECLI:NL:RVS:1986:BP8194, *M en R* 1987/6 (*Rotganzen*).

136 ABRvS 13 November 2002, ECLI:NL:RVS:2002:AF0308, *AB* 2003/26, para. 2.2.6; ABRvS 7 December 2005, ECLI:NL:RVS:2005:AU7583, *AB* 2006/67 (*Boxtel*), para. 2.2.4, and see in particular para. 7 of the case note by Widdershoven; HR 6 June 2008, ECLI:NL:HR:2008:BD3139, *AB* 2008/214 (*Joustra*), paras. 3.2, 3.3.2-3.3.3, see in particular para. 2 of the case note by Widdershoven; HR 5 June 2009, ECLI:NL:HR:2009:BH2815, *NJ* 2012/182 (*De Treek/Dexia*), para. 4.7.4, see in particular Concl. A-G De Vries Lentsch-Kostense, para. 6.23; CBb 17 June 2015, ECLI:NL:CBB:2015:214, *AB* 2015/297, see in particular the case note by Ortlep.

137 HR 21 September 2012, ECLI:NL:HR:2012:BW5879, *AB* 2012/367 (*ACI Adam e.a./Stichting De Thuiskopie*), para. 5.1.2; HR 5 April 2013, ECLI:NL:HR:2013:BZ1780, *NJ* 2013/389 (*Albron/FNV c.s.*), paras. 3.4.4, 3.7; HR 17 January 2014, ECLI:NL:HR:2014:88, *NJ* 2015/304 (*Ryanair Ltd/PR Aviation*), para. 3.5.2; ABRvS 15 June 2016, ECLI:NL:RVS:2016:1773, para. 4.

judgments (establishing the *contra legem* limitation),[138] but the limitation is also hardly mentioned in subsequent judgments rejecting a consistent interpretation (although, as pointed out, there seem to have been plenty of *implicit* references to that concept). When this *does* happen, it is found that the interpretation would be *contra legem* as a result of the national provision's incompatible wording (which view also ties in with the implicit references and some,[139] but not all,[140] of the views expressed in the context of the traditional approach to interpretation).

> In the ABRvS's judgment of 11 June 2014, for example, the procedure for obtaining a water permit had not been coordinated with the procedure for the environmental permit. This was consistent with the Water Act, but contrary to the IPPC Directive.[141] Having referred to the *contra legem* limitation, a consistent interpretation was dismissed: this would require that the relevant provision of the Water Act did not only apply to discharges, but also to abstractions and infiltrations, and such an extensive interpretation was held to be clearly incompatible with the unambiguous wording of the national rule, which only mentioned the former.[142]

> In a judgment of 13 June 2014, the issue was that the Consumer Credit Act made applicability of an exception contained in the directive[143] subject to an additional condition that no purchase offers to participate in the concerned credit transaction were directed to the public. The Civil Chamber of the HR deemed it impossible to adopt a consistent interpretation: disregarding the additional condition would contravene the rule's unambiguous wording and would be *contra legem*.[144]

Often the limits of grammatical interpretation will not be the only reason that could support the rejection of a consistent interpretation. Arguably, if there is an incompatibility with the directive on account of the national provision's wording, it is not surprising to see that the legislature's elucidation of that rule in for example the explanatory memorandum confirms the incompatibility. After all, the former

---

138 Case C-105/03 *Pupino*, ECLI:EU:C:2005:386, para. 47; Case C-212/04 *Adeneler*, ECLI:EU:C:2006:443, para. 110.

139 Smith (n. 36), p. 69-70.

140 Wiarda (n. 27), p. 39; Groenewegen (n. 28), p. 89, referring to the (outer limits) of a rule's meaning.

141 Directive 2008/1/EC of the European Parliament and of the Council of 15 January 2008 concerning integrated pollution prevention and control, *OJ* 2008, L24/8.

142 ABRvS 11 June 2014, ECLI:NL:RVS:2014:2120, *AB* 2014/320, para. 2.7. It is noted that the ABRvS also referred to another provision in the Water Act from which it was clear that the legislature distinguished between, on the one hand, discharges and, on the other, abstractions and infiltrations. The ABRvS also applied the *contra legem* limitation in its judgment of 3 April 2012, ECLI:NL:RVS:2012:BW1435, para. 2.2.5. An extensive interpretation of national trade mark law was dismissed in District Court The Hague 6 February 2019, ECLI:NL:RBDHA:2019:930, para. 4.11 (the term 'shape' would have to be interpreted as also encompassing 'another characteristic').

143 Directive 2008/48/EC of the European Parliament and of the Council of 23 April 2008 on credit agreements for consumers and repealing Council Directive 87/102/EEC, *OJ* 2008, L133/66.

144 HR 13 June 2014, ECLI:NL:HR:2014:1385, *NJ* 2015/477, para. 3.5.4.

is intended as an accurate reflection of the legislature's intention. Both the limits of grammatical interpretation as well as arguments derived from a historical interpretation can then be invoked to reject a consistent interpretation.[145] An example where the additional argument was based on a systematic interpretation can also be found.[146] And the ABRvS's *De Ingelsche Waarden* judgment rejected a consistent interpretation relying on systematic-teleological arguments: the scheme of the applicable legislation was based on the issuing of permits with an unlimited duration, which caused it to be incompatible with the directive which envisaged a system of permits with a limited duration.[147]

I believe that the above is an accurate reflection of the general approach taken by the Dutch superior courts *vis-à-vis* the limits to the duty of consistent interpretation. I find nothing in the general approach that urges me to conclude that there exists in this regard an incompatibility with the national courts' obligations under the duty of consistent interpretation. While the ECJ has so far not provided a clear definition of the *contra legem* limitation, this limitation has so far primarily been linked to the clear wording of the text.[148] In chapter 2, subparagraph 5.5, I noted that the ECJ's case law has not yet unambiguously stated whether the *contra legem* limitation can be conceptualised in a broader way, accommodating an array of limitations that the national courts run into on account of national interpretative rules. I argued that such a conceptualisation would result in *contra legem* becoming to a large extent identical to the dispensational side to 'so far as possible'. However, it should be clear that the Dutch case law does not support such a broader view and it is not really an issue in Dutch law.

Without prejudicing the conclusion that the Dutch courts' application of the limits to the duty of consistent interpretation generally complies with EU law, it needs to be said that two points require some further attention. First, in two judgments from the CBb interpreting the term 'connection' (in the context of the Law on

145 HR 20 October 1995, ECLI:NL:HR:1995:ZC1846, *NJ* 1996/330 (*Van Asseldonk/Ter Schure*), para. 3.5; ABRvS 29 May 2001, ECLI:NL:RVS:2001:AN6786, *RAwb* 2001/98, paras. 2.4-2.5. See also ABRvS 26 April 2017, ECLI:NL:RVS:2017:1109, paras. 3.1-3.7 (discussed in subparagraph 3.3.2).

146 This is the ABRvS's judgment of 11 June 2014 discussed above.

147 ABRvS 5 December 2007, ECLI:NL:RVS:2007:BB9488, *AB* 2008/18 (*De Ingelsche Waarden*), para. 2.2.8.

148 In Case C-176/12 *AMS*, ECLI:EU:C:2014:2, paras. 39-40, for example, the ECJ did not question that the *contra legem* limitation was invoked, which seemed to have been the result of the wording of the relevant national provision. See also, albeit before the introduction of the limitation that a *contra legem* interpretation is not required, Case C-111/97 *EvoBus Austria*, ECLI:EU:C:1998:434, para. 20. The ECJ's Advocates General, as well as EU legal scholarship, have predominantly interpreted the *contra legem* limitation as referring to the limits of the provision's text: Opinion of AG Jacobs in Case C-456/98 *Centrosteel*, ECLI:EU:C:2000:137, para. 32; Opinion of AG Van Gerven in Case C-271/91 *Marshall II*, ECLI:EU:C:1993:30, para. 41; Opinion of AG Elmer in Case C-168/95 *Arcaro*, ECLI:EU:C:1996:107, paras. 39-41; Opinion of AG Bot in Case C-441/14 *Ajos*, ECLI:EU:C:2015:776, para. 68. See further S. Prechal, *Directives in EC Law* (OUP 2005), p. 207. Cf. Wissink (n. 29), p. 146.

electricity), it focussed on a traditional approach, after which it was concluded that there was no room to take into account a potentially divergent position under the directive. It is argued that this approach is not correct: the domestic framework did not seem to have been so clear-cut that any further interpretation was *a priori* excluded and, logically, it must first be determined what the directive actually says before it can be concluded that the gap between the directive and national law is too large.

The CBb rejected the respondents' argument that the directive used different terminology than the national implementing legislation, and that the latter was not permitted to stand in the way of the operation of the directive. The CBb simply provided that the duty of consistent interpretation cannot have the effect of setting aside the clear terms of national law. Additionally, it referred to a segment of the national rule's parliamentary history, which was considered to support the wording of the rule.[149] It is argued that the CBb fell short of its obligations under the duty of consistent interpretation by rejecting such an interpretation without even looking at the directive, and in particular by not asking itself the question whether the directive may have required a different outcome. The determination of the extent to which a consistent interpretation is possible always requires that a comparison is made between the national provision and the relevant provision from the directive. It is a comparative exercise, whose outcome cannot, in principle, be determined after having examined just one of two relevant provisions. The fact that the concerned provision seemed to have a clear meaning on the basis of a traditional approach to interpretation, is not necessarily the end of the matter.[150] In order to contribute to the obligation of implementing the directive, and to enhance the effectiveness of directives more generally, the duty of consistent interpretation also requires national courts to reconsider the interpretation that a traditional approach prescribes. Also, the finding that a particular interpretation turned out to be incompatible with the directive can often have a profound impact on the previously adopted views regarding the national provision's meaning. Especially where the rule has an implementing objective. In this regard it should be pointed out that the term 'connection' was introduced in legislation implementing one of the predecessors of the directive that was invoked by the respondent, and while the legislature recognised that the used terminology was different from the directive, it was also emphasised that this was not believed to prejudice the full effect of the directive.[151] Since it cannot cure the discussed inadequacy of the approach adopted by the CBb in these two judgments, I will not further explore whether a consistent interpretation would actually have been possible. It suffices here to conclude that there were signs that the national legal framework did not seem to have been so clear-cut that any further interpretation was *a priori* excluded. This is not a condition for the main point – i.e. that the CBb should have first examined the necessity to

149 CBb 23 July 2012, ECLI:NL:CBB:2012:BX4127, paras. 6.1.1, 6.1.5; CBb 17 June 2015, ECLI:NL:CBB:2015:214, *AB* 2015/297, para. 5.2.

150 See also Wissink's critical remarks on approaching harmonious interpretation as a 'two-staged-exercise', Wissink (n. 29), p. 145. It is mentioned that in the two judgments discussed, matters are probably even worse as the CBb never really seemed to have entered the second stage at all.

151 *Kamerstukken II* 1997-98, 25621, 3, p. 23.

examine the possibility of a consistent interpretation by looking at what the directive says – to apply, but it does reinforce this point. I conclude that the CBb's judgments were in any event incompatible with the duty of consistent interpretation from a procedural (instead of substantive) point of view (i.e. the national court reached its conclusion without taking the steps prescribed by EU law that are intended to facilitate finding a route to a consistent interpretation – it thus concerns the line of argumentation followed).[152]

The second point requiring further attention is that, while I believe that the limits of a grammatical interpretation in principle provide a legitimate reason for rejecting a consistent interpretation, this ground should not be applied too easily. The HR's *Pink Floyd* judgment, which was discussed in subparagraph 3.2 provides an example of this. Consider also the ABRvS's judgment of 25 November 2009.

The ABRvS's judgment of 25 November 2009 concerned the extent to which the location of experiments with genetically modified organisms must be made available. Article 56 of the Law on environmentally hazardous substances provided that certain information (which included the information on the locations with which the dispute before the ABRvS was concerned) must be kept secret if such a decision is justified in view of the protection of company secrets. However, the provision of the directive which Article 56 intended to implement requires that the information is made available. The ABRvS concluded that it was not possible to arrive at an interpretation of national law whereby the location of the experiments may never be kept secret.[153] At first sight, such a conclusion appears quite logical, taking into account the imperative way in which Article 56 was formulated. However, this decision was criticised by Jans, who points out that the directive *also* made it clear that the locations of experiments with genetically modified organisms are not company secrets. Also, the condition in Article 56 that the protection of company secrets must be justified, provides the competent authority with some discretion, which could be used to secure compliance with the directive. Jans emphasises that it is not decisive that this interpretation would deviate from the traditional interpretation of the concerned provision. He questions whether the ABRvS made enough of an effort in this case to interpret national law in conformity with the directive.[154]

3.5.2. *The Principle of Legal Certainty*

Before going into the main topic of this subparagraph, i.e. legal certainty as a self-standing limitation, I want to submit two preliminary observations. First, in its *Pink Floyd* judgment, the HR also considered that the principle of legal certainty prevented it from adopting a consistent interpretation: such an interpretation was not to be expected on account of the provision's wording and could not therefore be relied

152 A judgment that suffers from a similar flaw as the one that I identified in relation to the CBb's judgment is HR 20 October 1995, ECLI:NL:HR:1995:ZC1846, *NJ* 1996/330 (*Van Asseldonk/Ter Schure*), para. 3.5.

153 ABRvS 25 November 2009, ECLI:NL:RVS:2009:BK4312, *M en R* 2010/43, para. 2.5.1.

154 Case note by Jans in *M en R* 2010/43, para. 1.

upon against individuals to whom the national rule on exhaustion of copyright was addressed. Here, the reference to legal certainty provided an additional argument, consequential to the result prescribed by national interpretative methods: it was linked to the extent to which consistent interpretation departed from the meaning that could reasonably be expected on the basis of an application of the traditional interpretative methods. Such use of the principle of legal certainty corresponds to an application of the *contra legem* limitation, which was later established by the ECJ (on the basis of the principle of legal certainty). In this regard it is interesting to point out that the Regional Court of Appeal whose judgment was being reviewed in the HR's *Pink Floyd* judgment *did* consider that it was prevented from adopting a consistent interpretation as it would then be required to interpret national law *contra legem.*[155] Leaving aside the question whether the HR was correct in coming to the conclusion that the principle of legal certainty (understood in the way that was just mentioned) stood in the way of a consistent interpretation, such use of the principle thus seems to correspond with the *contra legem* limitation that was subsequently recognised under EU law. It will be seen that the principle of legal certainty has also been applied in a different way, i.e. as a limitation to consistent interpretation that is not strictly (or, as regards the *Fortis* judgment that will be discussed further below, perhaps, less strictly) linked to the scope offered by the national interpretative methods. This line of the Dutch superior courts' case law has so far only manifested itself in judgments delivered by the ABRvS. There thus exists a difference in approach to the limits that are derived from the principle of legal certainty between the HR and the ABRvS.[156] The HR's *Albron/FNV c.s.* judgment also considered the principle of legal certainty. It was argued before the HR that there existed a *communis opinio* in the lower courts' case law and legal scholarship supporting a particular interpretation (opposing the consistent interpretation). The principle of legal certainty was also mentioned in the same breath with the *contra legem* limitation but the former clearly performed a different function than in the *Pink Floyd* judgment. The HR curtly concluded that both were not violated by the adoption of a consistent interpretation.[157]

As a second preliminary observation, it is pointed out that the ABRvS does not in general exclude the possibility of adopting a consistent interpretation where such an interpretation can be said to have adverse consequences for individuals that were difficult to foresee; legal certainty is not an absolute limitation to a consistent interpretation.[158] This is clear from two judgments which provide an example of a consistent interpretation in the context of judicial implementation (i.e. where the directive has in principle been implemented correctly but it must be made sure

155 Regional Court of Appeal The Hague 1 June 1995, ECLI:NL:GHSGR:1995:AK3519, para. 16.
156 See also Altena-Davidsen (n. 75), p. 88, who argues that the legal relationship central to the case is a distinguishing factor as far as the limits to the duty of consistent interpretation are concerned.
157 HR 5 April 2013, ECLI:NL:HR:2013:BZ1780, *NJ* 2013/389 (*Albron/FNV c.s.*), para. 3.7.
158 Cf. Altena-Davidsen (n. 48), p. 260, although, if I am correct, this is more a normative standpoint.

that terms derived from the directive remain in line with the ECJ's case law).[159] In both cases an unexpected interpretation of terms in national law implementing a directive had (considerable) negative consequences for the legal position of the concerned individuals.

> These cases also show that if the duty of consistent interpretation is applied in the context of judicial implementation, this does not per se mean that no interpretative difficulties can arise. In the first judgment, the ABRvS took into account the ECJ's further interpretation of the corresponding term contained in the directive, which entailed that, years after the implementation of the directive it turned out that a permit had been required for certain activities, as a consequence of which administrative enforcement action could now be taken.[160] And in the second judgment, a consistent interpretation gave rise to a different understanding of the term waste, which had consequences for a permit relating to such activities that had become final, which seemed to deprive the permit of most, or perhaps even all, of its purpose (a specific issue in that case was that the permit used the term waste, which was understood as referring to the corresponding provision in Dutch law which, in turn, implemented the directive).[161]

Although this has been subject to criticism from the perspective of legal certainty,[162] it is pointed out that a meaningful application of the duty of consistent interpretation always requires the courts to deviate, to some extent, from the traditional understanding of national provisions, and that, most of the time, it will be unlikely that such a move was entirely foreseen by the addressees of that rule. This is inescapable if it is accepted that the duty of consistent can adversely affect the legal position of individuals[163] – which is recognised as a central feature of this obligation and constitutes the main distinction with direct effect.

Turning to the main topic of this subparagraph, i.e. legal certainty as a (more) self-standing limitation, I should start with the ABRvS's *Fortis* judgment first. While legal certainty was only relied upon implicitly in that judgment, Widdershoven correctly observes that there was a clear link with that principle.[164]

---

159 For another example, see ABRvS 28 July 2004, ECLI:NL:RVS:2004:AQ5732, *M en R* 2004/104.

160 ABRvS 2 November 2000, ECLI:NL:RVS:2000:AN6579, *AB* 2001/51, para. 2.1.1.

161 ABRvS 20 June 2001, ECLI:NL:RVS:2001:AB2437, *AB* 2001/260, paras. 2.6, 2.8.1-2.8.2.

162 Case note by Jongma and Tieman in *AB* 2001/260, para. 2. See also Verhoeven and Jans (n. 88), p. 67 (although they do not seem to attach to this the conclusion that the adopted consistent interpretation was not possible).

163 See also the case note by Widdershoven in *AB* 2007/183, para. 5.

164 Case note by Widdershoven in *AB* 2007/183, para. 4. See also Verschuuren and Jans (*M en R* 2007/45, para. 2); Zijlmans (*JM* 2007/65). Widdershoven also remarks that the judgment touches upon the legality principle (which, in turn, is closely linked to legal certainty), too. See in this regard also ABRvS 31 March 2010, ECLI:NL:RVS:2010:BL9657, paras. 2.6-2.6.2, where, albeit less explicitly, the same line was adopted as in the *Fortis* judgment and the ABRvS considered that the concerned administrative authority was not *competent* to make an assessment of the effects of the proposed activities as there was not a requirement to obtain a permit in the first place.

> Article 19d of the Nature Conservation Act provided that it is prohibited to carry out projects or perform other operations without a permit or in contravention of the conditions or restrictions attached to that permit if, having regard to the goal of conservation, the quality of natural habitats and the habitats of species, *that were designated in accordance with Article 10a of the Act*, could, as a result of those projects or operations, deteriorate, or a significant disturbance to the species for which the area was designated is caused. Article 10a clearly referred to an appointment by the Minister. Only once this additional appointment had been made were projects and operations prohibited unless a permit was issued for them. As no appointment had yet been made, the prohibition did not apply. This was contrary to the Habitats Directive, which did not make the applicability of its protective regime conditional upon such an additional appointment. However, the ABRvS ruled that it is not permitted to extend the scope of the prohibitory provision contained in Article 19d(1) of the Nature Conservation Act, which is coupled to a requirement to obtain a permit, through a consistent interpretation, while this extension is not foreseeable by the addressees of that norm. The ABRvS also took into account that, if the concerned prohibition is violated, the competent authority can apply administrative enforcement and that such a violation constitutes an economic criminal offence ('*economisch delict*').
>
> According to the ABRvS, this must be contrasted with the situation where the prohibition and the corresponding obligations for the individual already existed and where the existing framework is merely modified by the consistent interpretation. The *Fortis* judgment confirmed that it is possible to modify *existing* obligations on the basis of the directive as it was held that the obligations stated in Article 16 of the Nature Conservation Act *did* apply to some of the areas for which a permit had been granted to carry out certain activities, yet the substance of the obligations was ('merely') modified in order to provide for the protective regime of the Habitats Directive.[165]

So the tenor of the ABRvS's *Fortis* judgment was that it was not permitted to broaden the scope of a prohibitory provision, which simultaneously entailed an extension of the requirement to hold a permit for certain activities, on the basis of a consistent interpretation, while such a broadening was not foreseeable by the addressees of the national provision. It is submitted that there were thus two factors carrying the rejection of a consistent interpretation in the judgment. This understanding of the judgment entails that, first, it was a significant, yet not decisive, factor that the consistent interpretation concerned the scope of a prohibition, but that, secondly, the outcome of the *Fortis* judgment must also be understood in the light of the clear incompatibility as a result of the explicit requirement of an appointment (the unforeseeability of the required interpretation). An understanding of the judgment whereby a consistent interpretation is not permitted to interfere with the interpretation of a prohibitory provision whatsoever (so that the limitation applies even though the interpretative gap is rather small) is difficult to reconcile with the finding that legal certainty cannot impose an absolute obligation (see the

165 ABRvS 28 February 2007, ECLI:NL:RVS:2007:AZ9494, *AB* 2007/183 (*Fortis*), paras. 2.10-2.11.

just discussed ABRvS judgment of 2 November 2000 concerning the meaning of the term 'discharge' and the ABRvS judgment of 20 June 2001 concerning the meaning of 'waste') – but note that this position may be different for criminal law provisions, where the limitation in EU law has a related, yet not identical, legal basis (see chapter 2, subparagraph 5.1.1 and the discussion further below). It also ties in with the general characteristic of legal certainty as a flexible principle which does not require that it is safeguarded at all costs.[166] If this interpretation of the *Fortis* judgment is followed, it is also in line with the ECJ's case law.[167]

> Three further points corroborating the suggested interpretation are mentioned. First, two case notes under the ABRvS's *Fortis* judgments also seem to take the position that, while the consequence that a consistent interpretation would broaden the scope of the prohibition provided an important argument against such an interpretation, it was also relevant that the consistent interpretation clearly deviated from the result prescribed on the basis of the provision's wording.[168] Secondly, although I admit that this cannot be decisive for the issue under consideration, it is noted that it has been observed in relation to the HR's general approach to interpretation that this court (or at least the Civil Chamber of that court) sometimes also looks at the consequences of one or the other interpretation when determining which interpretation is preferable.[169] The ABRvS pointing out that a consistent interpretation would entail a broadening of a prohibitory provision can also be understood in this way. Finally, the suggested view connects well with the characteristics of the traditional approach to interpretation in the field of administrative law. The discussion on the traditional approach to interpretation in subparagraph 3.1.2, learned that the legality principle occupies a far more prominent role in public law, which in turn means that individuals are to a larger extent protected by the wording of the applicable rules.[170] It seems to me that this applies in particular to administrative law provisions establishing a prohibition (hence the necessity to take this into account as a relevant circumstance). At the same time, it was made clear that, also in administrative law, interpretative arguments rarely have absolute priority (hence the rejection of viewing the *Fortis* judgment as introducing such a strict priority in relation to prohibitory provisions).

But what about the consideration in the *Fortis* judgment that a violation of that prohibition is subject to administrative enforcement and can be sanctioned as an economic offence? I should immediately point out that this merely provided an additional argument for rejecting a consistent interpretation. If this were otherwise, the approach does not seem to be in conformity with EU law. As

166 Prechal (n. 148), p. 207.

167 See in particular Case C-321/05 *Kofoed*, ECLI:EU:C:2007:408, para. 45; Case C-53/10 *Mücksch*, ECLI:EU:C:2011:585, para. 34.

168 Verschuuren and Jans (*M en R* 2007/45, para. 2); Zijlmans (*JM* 2007/65); cf. Widdershoven (*AB* 2007/183, paras. 1, 4).

169 Wissink (n. 29), p. 147-8, referring to HR 9 December 2011, ECLI:NL:HR:2011:BU7412, *NJ* 2013/273, para. 3.7, and p. 154-5 for a discussion on the role that this argument plays in the HR's application of the duty of consistent interpretation.

170 See in this regard, in particular, Scheltema (n. 56), p. 22; De Poorter (n. 51), p. 138.

Widdershoven cogently explains, the ABRvS seemed to make an implicit reference to the limitation established in the ECJ's *Kolpinghuis* judgment, prohibiting the determination or aggravation of criminal liability. Outside the area of criminal law, the duty of consistent interpretation can be applied to impose obligations additional to those already existing under national law considered in isolation. The individual must then surely comply with the unfavourable, additional, conditions and Widdershoven also believes that a violation of these conditions can be remedied through administrative enforcement. However, it follows from the *Kolpinghuis* judgment that such a violation may not be criminally prosecuted or sanctioned. Widdershoven predicted that, while there is not yet explicit authority on this point in the ECJ's case law, it would also not be permitted to impose an administrative fine having the character of a criminal charge in the sense of Article 6 of the ECHR.[171] The latter point is discussed next. Subsequently, I return to the point regarding administrative enforcement.

As regards the point that it is only the imposition of a criminal sanction that is prohibited, see also the CBb's judgment of 21 September 2015 where national law was given a consistent interpretation so as to allow regulatory authorities to demand copies of documents.[172] The adoption of a consistent interpretation was not very difficult in this case. However, it could be argued that, taking into account the specific circumstances of the case, supplying the copies entailed a real risk that an administrative fine would be imposed. Apparently the CBb did not see in this a reason to set limits to the duty of consistent interpretation, which I believe should indeed be viewed as a separate matter. As the case before it did not concern the imposition of such a fine, I believe that the CBb acted correctly.

Notwithstanding the absence of authority on this point in the ECJ's case law, the ABRvS's *Mandemakers* judgment of 4 March 2009 rejected a consistent interpretation as it provided the basis for the administrative fine (i.e. an administrative sanction) imposed on the appellant. The first point that is of interest here, is what provided the legal basis for this rejection. The ABRvS simply referred to the principle of legal certainty and the ECJ's *Kolpinghuis* judgment and considered that the limitation established in that judgment also applied to the case before it.[173] It was seen in chapter 2, subparagraph 5.1.1 that the *Kolpinghuis* judgment prohibited both the establishment of criminal liability where it is not clearly foreseen in the law, as well as a retroactive application of criminal law. Although this is not explicitly mentioned in the judgment, it is observed that the ABRvS encountered the first limitation. At the time that the judgment was delivered, the analogy with the *Kolpinghuis* judgment was not self-evident and the ABRvS should have asked

171 Case note by Widdershoven in *AB* 2007/183, para. 5.

172 CBb 21 September 2015, ECLI:NL:CBB:2015:288, *AB* 2016/52, para. 4.4. Cf. District Court Rotterdam 5 September 2012, ECLI:NL:RBROT:2012:BX6988, para. 6.1. However, in the latter judgment the directive was not invoked.

173 ABRvS 4 March 2009, ECLI:NL:RVS:2009:BH4621, *AB* 2009/156 (*Mandemakers*), para. 2.6.2.

the ECJ for a preliminary ruling on such a fundamental point. However, in the meantime, Article 49 of the Charter enshrining the principle of legality of criminal offences has entered into force, which has also been relied upon by the ECJ as a legal basis for the prohibition to determine or aggravate criminal liability.[174] On the basis of Article 52(3) the scope of that provision must be interpreted in harmony with Article 6 of the ECHR, and the latter also encompasses administrative fines qualifying as criminal sanctions.[175]

The *Mandemakers* judgment is also of interest for another reason. It can be seen as an example where, had a consistent interpretation actually been applied, this would have been in the context of remedial interpretation.[176] However, I do not think that, similar to the interpretation of the *Fortis* judgment proposed by me, the extent of the interpretative gap played a role of importance here for rejecting the consistent interpretation. The judgment contains no indications that it did. If the *Mandemakers* judgment can correctly be viewed as falling in the same line as the ECJ's *Kolpinghuis* judgment, the consequence that an interpretation in conformity with the directive would be decisive for the imposition of a fine carries far more weight and will usually be a sufficient reason for rejecting a consistent interpretation. *A fortiori* in situations where there is a clear discrepancy between the directive and national law, *but also in situations where the adjustment of the traditional interpretation would have been more modest.* If I am correct, this is an important distinction with the *Fortis* judgment.

> I should also refer to the CBb's *IMC* judgment (see also subparagraph 3.4.1).[177] In this case an administrative fine had been imposed on the appellant. This was based on an interpretation of national law which took into account the meaning of the corresponding provision in the directive. While it could be argued that the CBb applied the duty of consistent interpretation in the context of judicial implementation (in any event the national implementing legislation and the directive largely used the same terminology), a preliminary reference was necessary in order to clarify how broad the term had to be interpreted that determined the liability of the appellant, and this deviated considerably from what the text of the concerned national provision seemed to provide. Following the appellant's argumentation on this point, the CBb looked at the *lex certa* principle, but came to the conclusion that the principle was not violated.

174 Case C-7/11 *Caronna*, ECLI:EU:C:2012:396, para. 55.

175 See in particular Case C-524/15 *Menci*, ECLI:EU:C:2018:197, paras. 26-33 (see also the case note in M. Vetzo, 'The Past, Present and Future of the *Ne Bis In Idem Dialogue between the Court of Justice of the European Union and the European Court of Human Rights*: The Cases of *Menci, Garlsson* and *Di Puma*' (2018/2) *Review of European Administrative Law*, p. 55 *et seq*). For an application of the criteria from the ECtHR's case law, see Case C-489/10 *Bonda*, ECLI:EU:C:2012:319, para. 36 *et seq*; Case C-617/10 Åkerberg *Fransson*, ECLI:EU:C:2013:105, paras. 33-5. See further A.J.C. De Moor-Van Vugt and R.J.G.M. Widdershoven, 'Bestuurlijke handhaving', in: S. Prechal and R.J.G.M. Widdershoven (Eds.), *Inleiding tot het Europees bestuursrecht* (Ars Aequi Libri 2017), p. 289.

176 Case note by Widdershoven in *AB* 2009/156, para. 4.

177 CBb 22 February 2012, ECLI:NL:CBB:2012:BV6713 (*IMC*), para. 4.3.

> Admittedly, the rule's explanatory memorandum clearly referred to the broader interpretation. Yet, since the Dutch language version of the directive used the same terminology as the implementing provision, and some of the other language versions supported a more narrow interpretation, it was not certain that the legislature had been correct in his observations in the explanatory memorandum until the ECJ delivered its preliminary ruling. It suffices here to refer back to the discussion in subparagraphs 3.3 and 3.4 to demonstrate that, had the ECJ decided differently (i.e. confirming the more narrow interpretation that seemed to follow from a grammatical interpretation), it would be all but certain that an incompatible interpretation based primarily on a historical interpretation would prevail under these circumstances. The judgment illustrates the CBb's approach to the *lex certa* principle, and also shows that it may not always be self-evident that no interpretative difficulties can arise if a case is an example of, or is close to, judicial implementation.

In order to complete the discussion on the use of the principle of legal certainty in the Dutch superior courts' case law applying the duty of consistent interpretation there is, last but not least, the ABRvS's *KOMO* judgment. This judgment took things even further by holding that a consistent interpretation was impossible as such an interpretation cannot provide the basis for administrative enforcement (which concerns administrative action that is not of a punitive nature).[178] That decision again relied on the ECJ's *Kolpinghuis* judgment. The ABRvS acknowledged that the proceedings before it were in no way concerned with criminal law, yet it referred to the *Mandemakers* judgment and considered that it can be assumed that there exists not only a limitation with regard to administrative fines but also, as in this case, *enforcement.* It is important to emphasise that the competent public authority's options for responding to a violation of the concerned national provision were not limited to administrative fines; the applicable enforcement regime also stated administrative enforcement.[179] I have two objections against the position adopted in this judgment. First, I do not see on what basis the ABRvS deemed it possible to connect the situation before it to the ECJ's *Kolpinghuis* judgment (which is based on the principle of *nullum crimen, nulla poena sine lege,* i.e. a specific enunciation of the principle of legal certainty in criminal law).[180] Secondly, the effectiveness of EU law directives would be significantly decreased if the duty of consistent interpretation, which is perhaps the primary tool for ensuring their effect in the Member States' legal orders,[181] is able to confer a different meaning on provisions of national law, but it would not be permitted to enforce this if individuals did not comply with the modified understanding of national law. This would mean that legislative

---

178 ABRvS 8 June 2016, ECLI:NL:RVS:2016:1613, *AB* 2016/273 (*KOMO*), para. 10.3.

179 See Article 120 jo. 120b of the Housing Act.

180 An extension of the limitation laid down in the ECJ's *Kolpinghuis* judgment to administrative enforcement is also rejected in the case note by Widdershoven in *AB* 2007/183, para. 5.

181 U. Everling, 'Zur Auslegung des durch EG-Richtlinien angeglichenen Rechts' (1992/3) *Zeitschrift für Unternehmens- und Gesellschaftsrecht*, p. 395; Wissink (n. 12), p. 49; G. Betlem, 'The Doctrine of Consistent Interpretation – Managing Legal Uncertainty' (2002/3) *OJLS*, p. 399.

amendments correctly implementing the directive are still required in order for the result prescribed by the directive to be enforced in practice. For these reasons, I am of the opinion that the ABRvS's *KOMO* judgment raises an incompatibility with the requirements imposed by the duty of consistent interpretation.

3.6. GENEROUS INTERPRETATIVE RULES BUT ALSO NEW LIMITS

The sketch of the traditional approach to interpretation at the beginning of this paragraph provided three important lessons. First, it was seen that Dutch law offers a flexible framework of interpretative rules. A fixation of those rules would therefore be a deviation from the norm whereas the same characteristic makes it difficult to discern to what extent a consistent interpretation entailed a conflict with national interpretative rules. Secondly, grammatical and historical interpretation most frequently underpin the adopted interpretation. Thirdly, the broad interpretative room enjoyed by the Dutch courts is more narrow in the area of public law compared to private law – albeit that there is also a considerable number of provisions in administrative law specifically, containing discretion.

Despite the seemingly accommodating framework, the HR's *Pink Floyd* judgment – which was for a long time considered as the leading case in the Netherlands – showed a reserved approach to the duty of consistent interpretation. A more forceful application of the obligation was seen in the HR's *Wandelvierdaagse* judgment requiring that, if an implementing objective can be established, a rule's parliamentary history is to be set aside and grammatical interpretation is to function as an outer limit. I argued that this judgment must be viewed as a structural prioritisation fixating an otherwise flexible system. However, since it only provided for priority of a consistent interpretation in relation to an incompatible historical interpretation, a conflict of interpretations could only be established for this part of the judgment (and not the HR's approach to grammatical interpretation and I also argued that the negative test approach did not apply to this part). The HR's judgment in *Albron/FNV c.s.* also provided interesting material for this part of the analysis, but I arrived at the conclusion that the judgment did not, in the end, establish a structural prioritisation of consistent interpretation over the limits of grammatical interpretation. The ABRvS's and CBb's case law do not show a conflict as a result of the procedural steps that are taken to determine whether or not a consistent interpretation is possible.

I encountered quite a few examples where it can be said that the adopted consistent interpretation deviated from the interpretation that would have followed on account of a traditional interpretation of the concerned national provision (see e.g. the HR's judgments in *Buyck/Van den Ameele*, *Stichting De Thuiskopie/Opus*

Supplies Deutschland e.a. and *Albron/FNV c.s.*, as well as the CBb's judgment of 5 June 2014 concerning the Telecommunications Act). While at first sight the cases perhaps give the impression that there existed a conflict, I argued that they do not necessarily have to be viewed in that way. First and foremost, the national provisions relevant to these disputes on each occasion had an implementing objective, which largely explains the deviation from the interpretation that the interpretative methods would otherwise have prescribed. I argued that it must be presumed that there was not a conflict of interpretations if a consistent interpretation is primarily based on the rule having an implementing objective. In my opinion the Dutch framework of interpretative rules offered sufficient flexibility in the discussed cases to view the provision's wording in the light of parliamentary intent, which showed that the rules were adopted to implement the directive. Since the finding of an implementing objective so often (but note that I also encountered a number of judgments where a consistent interpretation was rejected despite the presence of an implementing objective) removed the tension with national interpretative rules that would otherwise have existed, it was a logical step to search for transgressions of the national interpretative rules in judgments adopting a consistent interpretation where this argument was not available. However, the analysis revealed that the number of judgments in which the Dutch courts depart from the national interpretative rules then becomes a lot thinner. And in the two discussed cases where there was a remarkable contrast, there were other reasons than supremacy of EU law explaining the adopted approach. Notably, on both occasions there was also, albeit indirectly, a link with an implementing objective.

There are two types of limitations. First, there are the limits that are based on the national interpretative methods as such. Here, the limits of a grammatical interpretation are by far the most important. *Contra legem* is also interpreted as referring to the limits of this method. If other arguments are added, these are usually arguments based on a historical interpretation. Although there are of course always judgments that raise some questions, on balance, this aspect of the Dutch superior courts' case law is unproblematic. The only exceptions to this are, in my opinion, two judgments delivered by the CBb concerning the interpretation of the term 'connection' in the Law on electricity. I argued that it failed to interpret national law so far as possible in conformity with the directive by rejecting a consistent interpretation without having even looked at the directive and basing its interpretation on an isolated examination of national law. There are, in the second place, limits that concern the consequences that a consistent interpretation would have for the concerned individual. In this regard the principle of legal certainty plays a central role as a self-standing limitation. I proposed a reserved interpretation of the ABRvS's *Fortis* judgment, which does not raise an incompatibility with the limits to the duty of consistent interpretation under EU law. The ABRvS's *Mandemakers* judgment certainly broadened the scope of the limitation established in the ECJ's

Kolpinghuis judgment by applying it to administrative fines, having the character of a criminal charge in the sense of Article 6 ECHR, as well. Although the ABRvS should have referred preliminary questions to the ECJ, there are in my opinion sufficient connecting points in EU law for the limitation introduced by the ABRvS. However, the ABRvS's *KOMO* judgment, which further extended the *Kolpinghuis* judgment's line of reasoning to administrative enforcement (which is not of a punitive nature) exceeded the limits to the duty of consistent interpretation.

4. AN AFTERTHOUGHT: THE IMPORTANCE OF WELL-REASONED JUDGMENTS

In some of the judgments adopting a consistent interpretation it was completely left to the reader to find out what might have been the justification for such an interpretation. In this regard I once again recall the two judgments of the ABRvS adopting a consistent interpretation in the context of judicial implementation.[182] After the ABRvS had determined the correct interpretation of the directive, this was simply imported into the national provision without any further clarification. While there were compelling reasons in support of a consistent interpretation (no grammatical incompatibility, the presence of an implementing objective), there were also concerns from the perspective of the principle of legal certainty. I think that the ABRvS took the position that there were no serious interpretative obstacles to a consistent interpretation, and that it was therefore not necessary to provide a further explanation. In its judgment of 28 July 2004, the ABRvS appeared to put the interpretation of provisions having a general, flexible, character, into the same category. Without any further explanation, detailed requirements stipulated in the directive (which had not yet been implemented) were read into the requirement to assess applications for a permit in the light of the protection of people and the environment.[183] The same thing occurred in the ABRvS's judgment of 7 April 2004 which, by the way, concerned a similarly formulated national provision.[184] It is more difficult to find a distinguishing factor for the judgment of 2 December 1991 – which again did not state the reasons underlying consistent interpretation – concerning a consistent interpretation of the conditions to take action against birds causing damage or nuisance to their surroundings.[185] With regard to the HR's case law, it is observed that it sometimes appears to simply take over the ECJ's preliminary ruling in the follow-up decision without explaining how this

182 ABRvS 2 November 2000, ECLI:NL:RVS:2000:AN6579, *AB* 2001/51, para. 2.1.1; ABRvS 20 June 2001, ECLI:NL:RVS:2001:AB2437, *AB* 2001/260, paras. 2.6, 2.8.1-2.8.2.

183 ABRvS 28 July 2004, ECLI:NL:RVS:2004:AQ5732, *M en R* 2004/104, m.nt. J.H. Jans, paras. 2.3, 2.4.2. Jans primarily criticises the ABRvS's judgment for the absence of any explanation as to why a consistent interpretation was deemed possible.

184 ABRvS 7 April 2004, ECLI:NL:RVS:2004:AO7095, *AB* 2004/460, para. 2.7.2.

185 ARRvS 2 December 1991, ECLI:NL:RVS:1991:AN2626, *AB* 1992/475.

outcome is accommodated through an interpretation of national law.[186] What all these judgments have in common is that it becomes more difficult to identify what motivated the courts to adopt a particular decision. In the above, I already mentioned that, due to the flexibility of the interpretative framework, in Dutch law it is not always easy to discern if there is a conflict of interpretative rules. This becomes even more difficult if courts do not always make explicit the reasons underlying their decision. It leaves one searching for connecting points in the law while remaining attentive to grounds arguing against the adopted interpretation. Only those who are an expert in the concerned area of law will feel truly confident in doing so. The difficulty of identifying whether traditional interpretative limits are upheld is not merely something that is of academic interest (or, indeed, the interest of the author): even though the interpretative discretion of Dutch courts is not constitutionally conditioned, it affects the relationship between the legislature and the judiciary, and it seems to me that this demands that it can be verified to what extent a judicial decision goes beyond the accepted limits of statutory interpretation. The principles of legality and legal certainty demand that the courts make use of techniques of statutory interpretation in a foreseeable way and in a manner that does not do too much violence to the wording of the legislation. One final remark. Of course there are reasons in favour of a concise style of legal reasoning. For example: unnecessary elaborations may have unintended and unforeseen consequences, and a weighing of all the different points of view may cause the judgment to become less compelling.[187] But it is submitted that these considerations also require that a judgment clearly states which arguments carried the most weight.

The rigour of a judgment's reasoning becomes even more important if a consistent interpretation is rejected. My analysis of the case law permits the conclusion that the Dutch superior courts share this view. There are of course more and less convincing arguments; for this I refer to my observations regarding the Dutch superior courts' approach to the limits of the duty of consistent interpretation. It could be argued that there exists a relationship between the impact and consequences of a particular decision and the demands that are placed on a judgment's reasoning.[188] From this perspective, the terse reasoning of the ABRvS's *Mandemakers* and *KOMO* judgments, broadening the limits to the duty of consistent interpretation, is somewhat disappointing.

---

186 See HR 12 October 2012, ECLI:NL:HR:2012:BW8301, *NJ* 2012/586 (*Stichting De Thuiskopie/Opus Supplies Deutschland e.a.*), para. 2.4; HR 20 January 2017, ECLI:NL:HR:2017:59, *NJ* 2017/63. It is noted that both cases concerned horizontal legal relationships, so the HR could not have applied the remedy of direct effect instead of consistent interpretation.

187 See, among others, F. Bakels, 'Totstandkoming en uitleg van uitspraken van de Hoge Raad' (2015/11) *Ars Aequi*, p. 938; Ortlep (n. 52), p. 123.

188 See also Ortlep (n. 52), p. 124 mentioning the judgment's relevance for the development of the law as a differentiating factor. I think it is clear that the two ABRvS judgments clearly come within this category.

5. CONCLUSION

At the very beginning of this chapter I noted that, in line with the Dutch legal order's internationalist spirit, EU law was in general received without major difficulties. Does this also apply to the Dutch superior courts' application of the duty of consistent interpretation? And what does that mean for determining the relationship between EU and national law (supremacy of EU law, national constitutionalism or constitutional pluralism) in the context of the duty of consistent interpretation?

In the years immediately following the delivery of the ECJ's *Von Colson and Kamann* judgment (and perhaps even on a few occasions before that date) the Dutch superior courts interpreted national law in conformity with directives in order to give effect to the legislature's stated implementing objective of the concerned national provisions. The ABRvS first started to recognise the *communautaire* legal basis for consistent interpretation, which was gradually taken over by the other superior courts. Nowadays the prevailing view is that the legal basis for the duty of consistent interpretation is to be found in Articles 288 TFEU and 4(3) TEU and the objective of achieving the result pursued by the directive – although I should add that the Dutch courts normally just pick one of these, which overlooks the added value of individual parts and their collective meaning.

The discussion of the scope for, and limits to, a consistent interpretation from the perspective of the Dutch superior courts, the principal part of the chapter's analysis, started out by briefly looking at the Dutch courts traditional approach to interpretation (i.e. the approach applied in a purely internal context). The sketch of the traditional approach provided three lessons that are important for the determination which theory is the most adequate for understanding the relationship between EU and national law under the duty of consistent interpretation. First, it was seen that Dutch law offers a flexible framework of interpretative rules. A fixation of those rules would therefore be a deviation from the norm whereas the same characteristic makes it difficult to discern to what extent a consistent interpretation entailed a conflict of interpretative rules. Secondly, grammatical and historical interpretation most frequently underpin the adopted interpretation. Thirdly, the broad interpretative room enjoyed by the Dutch courts is usually more narrow in the area of public law compared to private law. The most important conclusion that needs to be drawn here is that the Dutch interpretative rules offer a generous framework for applying the duty of consistent interpretation.

If this characterisation is taken into account, it was somewhat surprising to see that the case law initially took a more reserved approach to the duty of consistent interpretation. However, a bolder approach was adopted in the HR's

Wandelvierdaagse judgment (which concerned proceedings in a tax law dispute) in as far as it introduced, as a matter of principle, that a rule's parliamentary history is to be set aside if an implementing objective is established. Such a structural prioritisation has not, or at least not yet, been taken over by the ABRvS and CBb. None of the superior courts has gone so far to adopt a similar principled change in attitude in relation to grammatical interpretation. The generosity of the Dutch interpretative rules is most clearly reflected in the HR's case law, which provides the most prominent examples of far-reaching interpretations bringing national law in conformity with the directive. In my opinion there were a fair number of judgments where the adopted consistent interpretation departed from the conventional approach to interpretation, setting aside arguments that would not otherwise have been set aside (e.g. the HR's judgments in *Buyck/Van den Ameele*, *Stichting De Thuiskopie/Opus Supplies Deutschland e.a.* and *Albron/FNV c.s.*, as well as the CBb's judgment of 5 June 2014 concerning the Telecommunications Act). Yet, 'so far as possible' arguably goes quite far in the Dutch superior courts' case law on account of the flexibility of the interpretative rules. This significantly raises the threshold for concluding that there was a conflict as a result of a violation of the Dutch interpretative rules. Even more importantly, if a judgment approached this threshold, consistent interpretation was on each occasion supported by the argument that the legislation was adopted to implement the directive. It was seen that this is an effective argument enabling a consistent interpretation (although I also discussed some judgments where a consistent interpretation was rejected despite the presence of an implementing objective). The argument has been used by the Dutch courts for a long time, presumably even before the introduction of the ECJ's *Von Colson and Kamann* judgment, to determine the meaning of implementing provisions (see in particular the HR's judgment of 2 May 1984, but also the judgments in *Ubbink Isolatie/Dak- en Wandtechniek* and *Beets-Proper/Van Lanschot Bankiers*). When Dutch courts use this argument, they are not departing from the national interpretative methods but they follow a route to consistent interpretation using a well-established technique in Dutch law (this can be categorised as historical, systematic and/or teleological interpretation). Taking into account the high threshold as a result of the Dutch framework's flexibility and the prominent role of the rule's implementing objective, I concluded that there were no transgressions of national interpretative rules establishing a conflict. There are also judgments adopting a consistent interpretation of non-implementing legislation. However, the number of judgments in which the Dutch courts depart from the national interpretative rules then becomes a lot thinner. And in the two discussed cases where there was a remarkable contrast, there were other reasons than supremacy of EU law explaining the adopted approach. Notably, on both occasions there was also, albeit indirectly, a link with an implementing objective.

Turning to the question whether there has been a conflict as a result of the Dutch superior courts going beyond the limits recognised under EU law, it is necessary to distinguish between two types of limitations. There are, in the first place, the limits that are based on the national interpretative methods as such. Within this first category, a consistent interpretation was most of the time rejected as it would exceed the limits of a grammatical interpretation. If other arguments are added, these are usually arguments based on a historical interpretation. The *contra legem* limitation is rarely relied upon explicitly to reject a consistent interpretation. If this does happen, reference is made to the limits of a grammatical interpretation. However, it follows from the HR's *Albron/FNV c.s.* judgment that, in civil law, the limits of a grammatical interpretation should not be approached in a restrictive way so that the conclusion that an interpretation is *contra legem* is in principle not solely based on an isolated grammatical interpretation. I concluded that, in general, the approach to the limits of the duty of consistent interpretation in this first category is not incompatible with EU law. I only found an exception to this in two CBb judgments interpreting the term 'connection' in the context of the Law on electricity. The CBb only looked at the concerned provision from the perspective of national law, and since it believed that this produced a 'clear' meaning, it was found that it was not necessary to examine what the directive required (as was suggested to it by the respondent). The questions whether there was a discrepancy and, if applicable, how large the interpretative gap actually was, and whether there was room to reconsider the interpretative arguments based on a traditional approach in this light, were side-lined. While there is a connection between the limits of the interpretative methods as such and the principle of legal certainty (see the HR's *Pink Floyd* judgment), that principle has primarily been applied as a self-standing limitation, which provides the second category of limitations. This line of the ABRvS's case law started with its *Fortis* judgment. Suggesting a modest interpretation of the judgment (it was a relevant, yet not decisive, factor that the court was asked to extend the scope of a prohibitory provision, and without the additional grammatical concerns a consistent interpretation would not have been rejected), I believe that there was not an incompatibility with the requirements imposed by the duty of consistent interpretation. The ABRvS's *Mandemakers* judgment certainly broadened the scope of the limitation established in the ECJ's *Kolpinghuis* judgment by applying it to administrative fines having the character of a criminal charge in the sense of Article 6 ECHR, as well. Nevertheless, there are in my opinion sufficient connecting points in EU law supporting the conclusion that there was not a violation on this point. However, this cannot be said for the ABRvS's *KOMO* judgment which considerably extended the prohibition to determine or aggravate criminal liability on the basis of a consistent interpretation by applying the same limitation to administrative enforcement.

In summary, it can be said that the Dutch superior courts' approach to the duty of consistent interpretation is characterised by the prominence of grammatical interpretation, the impact of a rule's implementing objective, and limits based on the principle of legal certainty.[189] While the duty of consistent interpretation sometimes requires the courts to take an approach that deviates from a conventional application of the interpretative methods, the general patterns that were sketched in subparagraph 3.1 can be recognised. From this point of view, it is also not surprising to see that the ABRvS is more inclined to reject a consistent interpretation if this requires a significant departure from the provision's wording, and that the principle of legal certainty occupies a more central role in its jurisprudence. As the CBb is also an administrative law court one might expect to see a more reserved approach there as well, but such a view does not find clear support in the court's practice; this court sometimes adopted a consistent interpretation that stretched the limits of the national interpretative rules (see, in addition to the *IMC* judgment, its judgment of 5 June 2014 concerning the Telecommunications Act).

The question which theory on the relationship between EU and national law characterises the Dutch courts' approach to the duty of consistent interpretation has not really occupied the minds of Dutch legal scholarship. This can be seen as a reflection of its relative lack of enthusiasm in engaging with the question who holds ultimate authority in Europe and for developing mechanisms aimed at safeguarding precious constitutional sanctuaries from Europe. Having completed my analysis of the case law, I can think of another reason why this is so. If there is one thing characterising the interaction of EU and national law in the Dutch superior courts' application of the duty of consistent interpretation, it is the harmonious relationship that exists between the two.[190] To be sure, the structural prioritisation established in the HR's *Wandelvierdaagse* judgment supports the theory of supremacy of EU law. Yet, I do not have the impression that this was a painful genuflection by the HR, and legal scholarship's response to this move has generally been approving. Even more importantly, for the remaining part, the Dutch superior courts have found ways to fulfil their obligations without transgressing the discretion conferred upon them by national interpretative rules. This harmonious picture is not disturbed by the Dutch superior courts' approach to the limits to the duty of consistent

---

189 These are also the three key themes identified by Wissink for describing the HR's approach to the duty of consistent interpretation (Wissink (n. 29), p. 148-55). It must be noted, however, that Wissink to some extent relativizes the role played by grammatical interpretation. Grammatical arguments must in principle be considered in the light of the other interpretative criteria and the former does not independently determine what is and what is not a permissible interpretation. In that regard it should be taken into account that he looks at the duty of consistent interpretation from a civil law perspective. Cf. for example the view put forward by Jans who proposed a liberal approach to the duty of consistent interpretation, but also emphasised that consistent interpretation always requires a grammatical possibility. This, in turn, is explained by the administrative law perspective that he adopts.

190 See also Altena-Davidsen (n. 75), p. 99.

interpretation. Some judgments are more convincing than others when it comes to rejecting a consistent interpretation – and the manner in which that conclusion was reached. The most conspicuous example – and the most threatening in terms of the effective application of directives – is provided by the ABRvS's judgment applying the ECJ's *Kolpinghuis* judgment by analogy to administrative enforcement (and as regards administrative fines the ABRvS is advised to refer a preliminary question; while I strongly encourage national courts to take an active role in interpreting EU law, the preliminary reference procedure was designed to produce uniform answers to such fundamental questions). Be that as it may, I strongly believe that the ABRvS intended to faithfully apply the duty of consistent interpretation. Instead of putting national constitutional provisions before the requirement of a consistent interpretation, it sought to justify its decision by drawing a connection with the limits to the duty of consistent interpretation recognised by EU law. It did not succeed on this point, but at the same time it is difficult to see this as expressing support for the theory of national constitutionalism. I only ask here: which national constitutional principle did the ABRvS invoke on this point?

In an epilogue to Wiarda's famous book on legal interpretation describing the transformation from a more heteronomous style of interpretation to a more autonomous one, Koopmans discerns a similar pattern as a result of the influence of EU law on national courts.[191] At least in the context of the duty of consistent interpretation, I do not think that this autonomy primarily exists *vis-à-vis* the law (the legislature) in a pluralistic legal order, but rather towards a single legal order and/or legislature (i.e. either the national or EU legal order/legislature).[192] The viewpoints from both legal orders are recognised, yet there is no strict adherence, or submission, to one of either legal orders – which is not incompatible with requiring that significant weight is conferred on the argument that a particular interpretation is consistent with the directive.[193] The Dutch superior courts' perspective shows that the duty of consistent interpretation has the potential to enable courts to mediate seemingly conflicting claims by EU and national law, thereby preventing a more serious conflict between the two systems. It is then a potent example of successful adjudication in a pluralistic legal order.[194] This is achieved not only by the duty of consistent interpretation affording a degree of autonomy to the national courts in carrying out their obligations; it must be recognised that the flexibility of the Dutch interpretative framework is an important facilitating factor here as well. Mutual

191 See the epilogue by Koopmans in Wiarda (n. 27), p. 60.
192 See also R. Barents, 'Enkele kanttekeningen bij de autonomie van de nationale rechter in het Unierecht' (2013/4) *Trema*, p. 130, observing that courts may have become more autonomous in relation to national law, but not in relation to EU law.
193 See Wissink (n. 12), p. 144-5.
194 See also M. Brenncke, *Judicial Law-Making in English and German Courts* (Intersentia 2018), p. 268.

flexibility leads to a smooth application of the duty of consistent interpretation. To quote Cruijff: '*Dat is logisch*'.

CHAPTER 6
CONCLUSION

1. INTRODUCTION

If one jumps immediately from the list of cases to the German Federal Court of Justice's (Bundesgerichtshof; hereinafter BGH) *Quelle* judgment adopting an interpretation consistent with an EU law directive in contravention of the national provision's clear wording and, while browsing further through the book, spots the Dutch Supreme Court's (Hoge Raad; hereinafter HR) *Pink Floyd* judgment rejecting a consistent interpretation of a provision which arguably contained some ambiguity, it is tempting to wonder whether both cases were actually applying the same rule of EU law.[1] Having learned that this was indeed so and that both courts claimed to be applying an obligation *qua* EU law to interpret national law 'so far as possible' in conformity with the directive, one might then be tempted to wonder whether there is at all, on the level of EU law, a kind of mechanism at play structuring the obligation's interaction with national rules relevant in an interpretative context, or whether the scope to adopt such an interpretation is entirely left to the discretion, and benevolence, of the national courts. Indeed, on this point, the duty of consistent interpretation may disappoint those who are first and foremost familiar with interactions between EU and national law in the context of direct effect, for which the rule of supremacy of EU law provides a clear-cut conflict rule. Taking into account that a number of authors have argued that the duty of consistent interpretation is the primary tool for ensuring the effect of directives in the Member States' legal orders, it is surprising that it is relatively unknown how this interaction takes place. Going beyond individual judgments, I ventured to explore whether, adopting a perspective that takes into account the requirements imposed by the ECJ and the overall picture of the case law in three Member States, enabled me to draw a conclusion on the extent to which the existing theories on the relationship between EU and national law could be applied to the relationship between the two legal orders in the context of the duty of consistent interpretation. For this purpose, the following research question was adopted:

1 BGH 26 November 2008 *Quelle*, BGHZ 179, 27; HR 25 October 1996, ECLI:NL:HR:1996:ZC2177, *NJ* 1997/649 (*Pink Floyd*).

> To what extent are supremacy of EU law, national constitutionalism, or constitutional pluralism adequate theories for understanding the relationship between EU and national law under the duty of consistent interpretation, taking into consideration, first, the requirements that are imposed by EU law on national courts and, secondly, the approach adopted by superior courts in Germany, Ireland and the Netherlands to determine whether it is possible to interpret national law in conformity with an EU law directive?

It was logical to start my attempt to answer the research question by looking at, and acquiring a better understanding of, the framework for the duty of consistent interpretation composed by the ECJ. The findings of this examination are presented in the first part of the conclusion, together with the German, Irish and Dutch approach to the question what so far as possible does, and does not, require them to do. This first part constitutes a necessary (and instructive) step to answering the research question. I also sum up the areas of the duty of consistent interpretation that have not yet been settled by ECJ case law and my own views on the route that could be taken in relation to these areas. The second part then analyses to what extent supremacy of EU law, national constitutionalism or constitutional pluralism provide adequate theories for understanding the relationship between EU and national law under the duty of consistent interpretation. This part attempts to assess to what extent the existing theories are universalizable and can be applied – albeit, perhaps, in a slightly modified form – to other areas of EU law than for example direct effect, or that they reveal gaps in our knowledge and do not sufficiently explain certain interactions between EU and national law. These findings also make it possible to further reflect on the meaning of those theories for the application of EU law by national courts in general (in particular their meaning beyond the more well known context of direct effect, to which they are often linked). A third and final part is added for it will be seen that, although the existing theories are very valuable for understanding the interaction between the duty of consistent interpretation and national rules of interpretation, they do not adequately reflect the interaction between the two as far as concerns the day-to-day application of the obligation. The third part further discusses this missing piece in the puzzle of the relationship between EU and national law under the duty of consistent interpretation.

2. SYNTHESIS OF WHAT 'SO FAR AS POSSIBLE' REQUIRES (AND WHAT IT DOES NOT)

This paragraph summarises and puts together the findings of the chapter discussing the ECJ's composition of a framework for the duty of consistent interpretation and the individual national chapters. The ECJ's case law clearly identifies the legal basis for the duty of consistent interpretation, its temporal scope and object. These resolved issues are discussed first. However, I observed that the large open space created by the ECJ's *Von Colson and Kamann* judgment's instruction to interpret national law so far as possible in conformity with EU law has only partly been filled by providing a number of methodological instructions and some guidance in relation to the limits to the duty of consistent interpretation.[2] And even these instructions do not always offer clear lines; they often consist of little more than a few rough sketches that need to be further drawn in by the national courts. It is attempted to complete the picture by putting together the findings derived from the individual national chapters. This is done in the second subparagraph. The third subparagraph discusses the national courts' own answers to the open-textured question how far they should go in order to obtain an interpretation in conformity with the directive. Fourthly, I briefly sum up the points which have not yet received a clear answer in the ECJ's case law and could give rise to interesting questions in the future. This also includes my own views on how these matters could be resolved.

2.1. THE RESOLVED ISSUES

2.1.1. Legal Basis

The ECJ views Articles 288 TFEU and 4(3) TEU, with the inclusion of the principle of effectiveness, as providing the legal basis for the duty of consistent interpretation. The reference to Article 288 TFEU positions the obligation as an extension of the legislature's obligation to implement the directive through the adoption of legally binding measures; national courts must also play their part in implementing the directive (but it is noted that a consistent interpretation will not suffice in itself to fully implement the directive if the underlying provisions were clearly not sufficiently in line with the directive). Although the obligation's purpose therefore primarily refers to the implementing objective contained in Article 288 TFEU, 4(3) TEU is indispensable as it contributes a more appropriate basis for the 'interventionist aspect' of the duty of consistent interpretation. In line with this I argued that the inclusion of Article 4(3) TEU also confers upon the duty of consistent interpretation the capacity to overrule national rules if necessary. The added value of the principle of effectiveness (which, in this particular context, refers to the idea that the authorities of Member States are required to ensure the effective protection of EU law rights and, more generally, the effective enforcement of EU law), whose relevance for the legal basis was first mentioned in the ECJ's *Pfeiffer* judgment,[3] is to a lesser extent immediately apparent. However, in addition

2 Case 14/83 *Von Colson and Kamann*, ECLI:EU:C:1984:153.

3 Joined Cases C-397/01 to C-403/01 *Pfeiffer*, ECLI:EU:C:2004:584, para. 114.

to pointing out the similarities between this principle and Article 4(3) TEU, I argued that inclusion of this principle 'bolstered' the legal basis for the duty of consistent interpretation, and that it was necessary in order to extend the duty of consistent interpretation to the area of framework decisions based on the former Third Pillar of the Treaties.

The national courts' prevailing view regarding the legal basis largely corresponds with that of the ECJ, albeit that it sometimes took a while before a clear position emerged. Also, the national courts do not consequently state both Articles 288 TFEU and 4(3) TEU (ideally also with a reference to the full effectiveness of EU law) as the legal basis, but neither does the ECJ. It should be noted that in Germany and Ireland the operation of EU law, and therefore also the provisions on which the duty of consistent interpretation is based, is controlled by national instruments acting as a conduit.

The only more serious divergence regarding the legal basis for the duty of consistent interpretation can be found in the German Federal Fiscal Court's (Bundesfinanzhof; hereinafter BFH) case law. This court has adopted a more nationally-oriented approach relying on the legislature's implementing intention to apply the obligation and subsuming it under traditional national interpretative methods (it is pointed out that this line of reasoning is not entirely alien to some of the courts from the other Member States as well, although the view is mostly found in older judgments, or as an additional argument).

Another competing vision stems from legal scholarship and concerns the supremacy of directives. Adherents of the theory of supremacy of EU law (as a hierarchical model, see chapter 1, subparagraph 1.3.1) put forward that the duty of consistent interpretation can be directly based on the supremacy of the applicable directive. On this hierarchical conception of the relationship between EU law directives and national law, it is nothing more than logical that the incompatible, hierarchically inferior, norm is interpreted in conformity with the hierarchically superior norm.[4] I argued that, while directives produce certain legal effects in the national legal orders even before they are implemented, or correctly implemented, into national law (to acquire their full effect), EU law has never unambiguously stated that, outside the context of direct effect, this legal effect is that the directives are hierarchically superior, i.e. that they enjoy supremacy, *vis-à-vis* national law. Apart from the fact that supremacy of EU law has never been mentioned by the ECJ as the legal basis for the duty of consistent interpretation, such a vision does not therefore appear to me to be theoretically sound. The consequences of the rejection

4 This view is espoused in K. Lenaerts and T. Corthaut, 'Of Birds and Hedges: The Role of Primacy in Invoking Norms of EU Law' (2006/3) *ELRev*, p. 293.

of this view on supremacy in the context of the duty of consistent interpretation are discussed further in subparagraph 3.2.

2.1.2. Temporal Scope

The ECJ's *Adeneler* judgment clarified that the duty of consistent interpretation does not apply before the directive's transposition period has expired. Yet, after the directive has entered into force, national courts are under an obligation to refrain from adopting any measures that could seriously compromise the result prescribed by the directive.[5] The judgment's considerations confirmed the linkage between the obligation and the objective of implementing the directive.

Since the national courts' activities before expiry of the transposition period are not therefore subject to the duty of consistent interpretation, the obligation's temporal scope was not a point of special interest for the national chapters.

2.1.3. Object

The ECJ's *Marleasing* judgment made clear that the duty of consistent interpretation applies to national law '(…) whether the provisions in question were adopted before or after the directive (…)'.[6] And in the ECJ's *Pfeiffer* judgment it was held that the duty of consistent interpretation '(…) requires the national court to consider national law as a whole in order to assess to what extent it may be applied so as not to produce a result contrary to that sought by the directive'.[7]

Adherents of the theory of supremacy of EU law will again put forward that, since directives are part of the national legal orders and occupy a superior position therein, it is self-evident that any rule of national law must be interpreted in conformity with them – and presumably view these judgments as a confirmation of their position.[8] However, I submitted that the theory of supremacy of EU law is not needed to explain the obligation's scope since Articles 288 TFEU and 4(3) TEU (with the inclusion of the principle of effectiveness) by themselves have legal effect in the national legal orders and this is not confined to implementing legislation only. Also, parity with the legislature's position, which can fulfil its obligations through pre-existing legislation, requires that national courts should also be able to fulfil their own obligations by implementing pre-existing legislation in conformity with directives.

5 Case C-212/04 *Adeneler*, ECLI:EU:C:2006:443, paras. 113-5, 122-3.
6 Case C-106/89 *Marleasing*, ECLI:EU:C:1990:395, para. 8.
7 Joined Cases C-397/01 to C-403/01 *Pfeiffer*, ECLI:EU:C:2004:584, para. 115, referring to Case C-131/97 *Carbonari*, ECLI:EU:C:1999:98, paras. 49-50, where the same point was made, albeit by using different words.
8 See the Opinion of AG Van Gerven in Case C-106/89 *Marleasing*, ECLI:EU:C:1990:310, para. 9.

The national chapters provide ample examples where the duty of consistent interpretation was applied to non-implementing legislation and/or pre-existing legislation. The only more serious (but isolated) divergence regarding the object of the duty of consistent interpretation can be found in the *Gasversorgung II* judgment where the BGH appeared to consider the absence of an implementing objective as such a relevant reason to reject a consistent interpretation.[9]

2.2. DRAWING IN THE SKECTHED LINES

It can be seen that the national sphere does not occupy a very dominant role in relation to the above discussed issues. This is not surprising since the national courts were given clear instructions on these points (and they have not seriously contested these elementary aspects of the duty of consistent interpretation). The scope of the national sphere increases for the issues discussed in this subparagraph as the ECJ's case law leaves a measure of discretion to the national courts. The discretion afforded by the ECJ can be explained by the decisive role which national interpretative rules play for the determination of the issues discussed here. From the EU law perspective the issues discussed below are therefore, at least to some extent, intentionally left unresolved. The national courts' discretion has been curtailed, positively, through specific methodological instructions, and, negatively, through limits to the duty of consistent interpretation.

2.2.1. The Interpretative Selection Rule

The ECJ's *Océano* judgment introduced the interpretative selection rule.[10] This neither affects the range of interpretations that are available according to national interpretative rules nor does it impose a hierarchy between the applicable national interpretative methods, but it *does* prescribe that, if the provision of national law is open to more than one interpretation, priority must be given to the one that is in conformity with the directive.

The first thing that comes to mind in the context of the interpretative selection rule is that it resembles the well established technique in German law of *verfassungskonforme Auslegung* (the requirement to adopt an interpretation that is

9 BGH 28 October 2015 *Gasversorgung II*, BGHZ 207, 209, para. 44. It is noted that constitutional complaints against a similar judgment were rejected in BVerfG 17 November 2017, NJW-RR 2018, 305, paras. 38, 40.

10 Joined Cases C-240/98 to C-244/98 *Océano*, ECLI:EU:C:2000:346, para. 32. See also Case C-212/04 *Adeneler*, ECLI:EU:C:2006:443, para. 124; Case C-414/07 *Magoora*, ECLI:EU:C:2008:766, para. 44; Case C-305/08 *CoNISMa*, ECLI:EU:C:2009:807, para. 50; Case C-594/10 *Van Laarhoven*, ECLI:EU:C:2012:92, para. 37; Case C-124/12 *AES-3C Maritza East 1*, ECLI:EU:C:2013:488, para. 53.

in conformity with the German Constitution if a lower-ranking provision allows more than one interpretation). In the chapter discussing the German superior courts' perspective it was seen that both German legal scholarship and the German superior courts are attracted to the idea of drawing an analogy between *verfassungskonforme Auslegung* and the duty of consistent interpretation. Although, at first sight, it raises the question whether such an analogy sufficiently encourages the German courts to explore the outer limits of their interpretative rules to adopt a consistent interpretation, it was seen that this concern is not justified.

> Judgments within this category provide that the duty of consistent interpretation is subject to the general rules of interpretation, the national provision being open to more than one interpretation and there being room for further interpretation. The provision's wording and legislative intent are primarily referred to by the German courts when they translate these general considerations to more concrete limits. On balance, the approach does not seem to be that different from, and hence not more restrictive than, case law that does not draw the analogy. That does not alter the fact that I encountered judgments which, in my opinion, were incompatible with the duty of consistent interpretation (see the German Federal Labour Court's (Bundesarbeitsgericht; hereinafter BAG) judgment of 18 February 2003 concerning the classification of on-call duty and the BFH's judgment of 15 February 2012 incorporating the duty of consistent into the systematic-teleological interpretative method). Yet, I also pointed out that I am not convinced that this was an immediate consequence of the analogy drawn with *verfassungskonforme Auslegung* per se. Also, while judgments drawing the analogy rejected a consistent interpretation relatively often, I argued that this can be explained by the courts wanting to explain that they would have done the same thing in a similar, purely internal, situation.

Reference to *verfassungskonforme Auslegung* is therefore a sign that a consistent interpretation will not be adopted, but it is not a sign that the court falls short of its obligations under the duty of consistent interpretation.

2.2.2. The Presumption of the Intention to Comply

The presumption that the legislature intended to comply with its obligations under the directive was introduced in the ECJ's *Wagner Miret* judgment,[11] and reiterated in its *Pfeiffer* judgment.[12] It follows from these judgments that the presumption applies when there is an actual indication of legislative intent to comply with the directive. Furthermore, I interpret the ECJ's *Björnekulla* judgment as providing that incompatible intentions arising from the *travaux préparatoires* must be rejected in favour of a consistent interpretation if the concerned national provision has an implementing objective and where there are otherwise sufficient connecting points

11 Case C-334/92 *Wagner Miret*, ECLI:EU:C:1993:945, para. 20.
12 Joined Cases C-397/01 to C-403/01 *Pfeiffer*, ECLI:EU:C:2004:584, para. 112.

in national law supporting a consistent interpretation.[13] Apart from this, it was left to the national courts to determine the exact scope of the presumption.

Looking at the national chapters, a couple of things stand out. For one thing, the German chapter showed that the scope of the presumption is sometimes interpreted extensively (see e.g. the BGH's judgment of 7 May 2014,[14] where there was only a whiff of an implementing objective, and the BAG's judgment of 24 March 2009,[15] which referred to the ECJ's *Pfeiffer* judgment in the situation where the rule did not have an implementing objective but the explanatory memorandum contained no incompatible indications). In the Irish chapter it was seen that the courts sometimes apply a presumption that, unless clearly stated otherwise, the provision is to have the same meaning as the directive where the same, or similar, *wording* is used. However, the rationale behind this presumption is thus different from the one advanced in the ECJ's *Wagner Miret* and *Pfeiffer* judgments (because it is premised on the similarity of the words used), and in my opinion this part of the Irish superior courts' case law is not intended as a further interpretation of those ECJ judgments. In a judgment from the Irish High Court the presumption of the intention to comply was clearly linked to the establishment of an implementing objective. An implementing objective has been a prerequisite in the Dutch superior courts' case law too.

Moving from the scope of the presumption to its effects, it is pointed out that the preceding chapters provided a few instances where a national court did not mention the presumption while rejecting a consistent interpretation of implementing legislation with reference to the legislature's incompatible concrete intentions (e.g. the intention to confer an entitlement to compensation to one of the parties to a contract). Although I argued in chapter 2, subparagraph 4.2.2 that the ECJ's *Wagner Miret* and *Pfeiffer* judgments in principle seem to oppose that in these circumstances the legislature's incompatible intentions are prioritised, there was at the same time an incompatibility as a result of other interpretative criteria, and I do not believe that this argument can simply be set aside on the basis of the presumption. Nevertheless, it does not seem to be correct if it is not tested how far the presumption can take the courts in their pursuit of a consistent interpretation. On one occasion, the Dutch Administrative Jurisdiction Division of the Council of State (Afdeling Bestuursrechtspraak van de Raad van State; hereinafter ABRvS) prioritised an incompatible intention notwithstanding the legislature's statement that it believed that it acted in conformity with the directive on the relevant point (but note that there was also a grammatical incompatibility in that judgment).[16]

---

13 Case C-371/02 *Björnekulla*, ECLI:EU:C:2004:275, para. 13.

14 BGH 7 May 2014, BGHZ 201, 101, para. 23 *et seq.*

15 BAG 24 March 2009, BAGE 130, 119, paras. 58, 67.

16 ABRvS 26 April 2017, ECLI:NL:RVS:2017:1109, paras. 3.1-3.7.

This can be contrasted with the BGH's *Quelle* judgment which, in a situation where there was a discrepancy between the concrete intention to confer an entitlement to compensation and the *concrete* implementing objective and the legislature indicated that the provision made in pursuit of the concrete intention was considered to be compatible with the directive, used a presumption to prioritise the implementing objective.[17] The approach has subsequently been extended to cover situations where there was not such an explicit discussion on the legislative proposal's compatibility with the directive.[18] Yet, it must be noted that no reference was made to the ECJ's *Wagner Miret* or *Pfeiffer* judgments on these occasions. A presumption has also been applied by the BGH to dispel certain doubts, arising from the explanatory memorandum, regarding the legislature's intention to duly implement the directive (again, no reference was made to the ECJ's case law). In the Dutch superior courts' case law it is familiar to see the presumption – and this time supported by a reference to the ECJ's case law – being applied to the question how an implementing objective must be reconciled with other, conflicting, intentions, too. The prime example here is the *Wandelvierdaagse* judgment. There, the Tax Chamber of the HR considered that, as a matter of principle, a rule's conflicting parliamentary history is to be set aside if an implementing objective is established. Yet, the effect of the presumption is broader as the same judgment established that grammatical interpretation is to function as an outer limit – but nevertheless a limit, which entails that the position adopted is not necessarily incompatible with the just referred to ABRvS judgment – to consistent interpretation.[19] Again relying on the presumption, the judgment in *Albron/FNV c.s.* of the Civil Chamber of the HR viewed it as a *circumstance* supporting a dynamic approach to the limits imposed by the national provision's wording, meaning that, if appropriate, these should be determined in the light of other interpretative criteria as well (but note that this does not go so far that the provision's wording is viewed as being wholly set aside by the presumption and I concluded that there is not yet sufficient authority to make the claim that the HR applies such a dynamic approach in the majority of cases *qua* an obligation under EU law).

The question at what point the presumption is rebutted can be divided into two spheres. First, in relation to the main sphere of legislative intent, German and Dutch courts take the position that the presumption no longer applies if the legislature unequivocally expressed a conscious intention to depart from the directive. Remaining within the sphere of legislative intent, there are three interesting German judgments concerning the role played by legislative inertia for

17 BGH 26 November 2008 *Quelle,* BGHZ 179, 27, paras. 24-5.

18 BGH 21 December 2011 *Bodenfliesen,* BGHZ 192, 148, paras. 31-4. See also BGH 9 April 2002 *Heininger,* BGHZ 150, 248, 256.

19 HR 10 August 2007, ECLI:NL:HR:2007:AZ3758, *AB* 2007/291 (*Wandelvierdaagse*), para. 3.4.

determining intent. It seems that this will depend on the circumstances of the case, but the case law is not entirely consistent.

> In the first judgment, legislative inertia was a reason for the court to conclude that the legislature had consciously refused to amend the national implementing rules to the directive while, in the second judgment, this inertia was not considered to undermine the legislature's intention to implement.[20] While these statements appear contradictory, it needs to be pointed out that, in the first judgment, there was, on the one hand, a preliminary ruling from the ECJ that established the incompatibility and, on the other, the German Government's persisting attitude that the national provision did not require any amendments in light of EU law, whereas, in the second judgment, the incompatibility had only been pointed out by legal scholarship and there had not been any subsequent reiterations of the initial, incompatible, position by relevant authorities. However, the third judgment was similar to the second situation and nevertheless no consistent interpretation (by means of a *Rechtsfortbildung*) was adopted.[21] It should be noted that all three judgments were delivered by different courts.

The final point within the sphere of legislative intention is provided by the High Court's judgment in *EPA v Neiphin Trading Ltd.* It provides authority for the position that, even though an implementing objective was identified, the directive's objectives were only taken into account in as far as national law positively confirmed that the Oireachtas (the Irish Parliament) had the intention to implement the concerned objective. The objective to implement the directive was as it were replaced by and subdivided into the different objectives pursued by the directive, each of which requiring such positive confirmation. The High Court did not mention the presumption under EU law, but it follows from my discussion regarding the scope of the presumption that it applied on account of the national provision having an implementing objective.[22] The High Court's approach violated the integrity of the presumption of the intention to comply. Secondly, in relation to the sphere of the national provision's wording, the High Court, in another judgment, stated that where the national provisions have an implementing objective '(...) the Court must presume, in the absence of explicit wording to contrary effect, that the legislative purpose is to give full and accurate effect to the provisions of the Community measure (...)' (it is noted that no reference was made to the *Wagner Miret* or *Pfeiffer* judgment).[23] Admittedly, both the German as well as the Dutch courts have also rejected a consistent interpretation of a provision having an implementing objective on account of its incompatible wording, but

20 Cf. BFH 15 February 2012, BFHE 236, 267, paras. 23-7; BVerwG 31 January 2017, Beck online Rechtsprechung 2017, 103948, paras. 29-32.

21 BGH 3 July 2018, NJW-RR 2018, 1204, para. 14.

22 High Court 3 March 2011 *EPA v Neiphin Trading Ltd* [2011] 2 IR 575 at paras. 107, 110-1.

23 High Court 4 December 2009 *MST v Minister for Justice, Equality and Law Reform* [2009] 12 JIC 403 at para. 27.

they have, in the examples examined in the individual chapters, not discussed this in the context of an interpretative presumption.

2.2.3. A Reinforced Obligation when Interpreting Implementing Legislation?

Leaving aside the impact of the presumption of the intention to comply, which is also premised on the finding of an implementing objective and was discussed separately, the most remarkable 'shifts' (*vis-à-vis* the traditional approach to interpretation, i.e. the approach adopted in a purely internal context) were witnessed when the national courts applied the duty of consistent interpretation to implementing legislation. Yet, the ECJ's case law only reservedly addresses this aspect of interpretation by providing that the obligation applies in particular to implementing legislation. In chapter 2, subparagraph 4.2.2, I explained that this consideration must be viewed as a mere prognosis. It can therefore be asked to what extent far-reaching examples of a consistent interpretation are necessarily retraceable to this soft point of guidance and it could perhaps be argued that this part of the national case law is more appropriately discussed in subparagraph 2.3. However, since there is a connecting point in the ECJ's case law, I have decided to include it here.

In Germany and the Netherlands, a similar pattern emerges. The argument that the concerned provision is intended by the legislature to implement the directive carries a lot of weight and is an important factor enabling consistent interpretation (yet, it must be acknowledged that this argument is not a panacea: there are also several examples in which a consistent interpretation of implementing legislation was rejected). Courts in both Member States take into consideration the national provision's genealogical place in the legal order, stemming from, and intended to implement, the directive. The argument thus enters the stage through a systematic, and in particular, a historical or teleological interpretation. Importantly, the argument reverberates through other, opposing, interpretative arguments as well, causing them to be reconsidered in a new contextual setting characterised by the alarming discovery that there is a looming conflict between the directive and national law.

> What explains the strength of this argument? It is apparent from discussions on the duty of consistent interpretation in German legal scholarship that, even those who argue that the obligation cannot affect the traditional interpretative approach, nevertheless consider it legitimate that, if an implementing objective is established, this is taken into account by means of the above mentioned interpretative criteria. There was already German case law adopting a consistent interpretation of implementing legislation before the introduction of the ECJ's *Von Colson and Kamann* judgment. There are indications that the same applies for the Netherlands. In any case the Dutch courts applied a consistent interpretation to implementing legislation just after the introduction of the ECJ's *Von Colson and Kamann* judgment (and it may be asked whether the

judges sitting in court were at the time fully aware of this brand new obligation). In other words, such an argument is not perceived of as a 'foreign invader' into the national interpretative framework in both Member States. Secondly, use of this argument resonates well with the main objective of interpretation in Germany (i.e. identifying legislative intent) and, albeit less explicitly, this objective is arguably an important consideration in the Dutch setting as well.

In the German chapter it was seen that the pivotal requirement for adopting a *Rechtsfortbildung* (a further development of the law by the courts), a technique which considerably increases the scope to adopt a consistent interpretation, is that a *Regelungslücke* (a legislative gap or lacuna) is established. This, in turn, requires that an implementing objective can be established. However, this means at the same time that the German courts are more likely to encounter obstacles to a consistent interpretation when this argument is not available.

Turning to Ireland, I wish to refer to the observations by Edwards J. in his judgment in *EPA v Neiphin Trading Ltd,* providing that applying the duty of consistent interpretation has not resulted in significant difficulties for the Irish courts since the obligation has primarily been applied in relation to implementing legislation, so that the objectives of the directive and the intention of the Oireachtas coincided.[24] It follows from Barrett J.'s considerations in *EPA v Harte Peat Ltd* that the requirement of adopting a consistent interpretation is to be treated as enjoying priority, *if* the national provisions have their genesis in EU law.[25] However, apart from a judgment delivered on the same day by the same judge, this position has not been confirmed elsewhere. Compared to German and Dutch courts, it is more common to look at the act as a whole (instead of for example the explanatory memorandum) and to derive therefrom that it follows the same approach as the directive and/or that there was an implementing objective.[26] This is not surprising, however, on account of the Irish courts' traditional approach to interpretation.

2.2.4. Option under National Law Becomes an Obligation Qua EU Law

This instruction, which derives from the ECJ's *Pfeiffer* judgment, has not really been extensively discussed in the examined national courts' case law. However, the Irish Supreme Court applied the same technique to reach a consistent interpretation in *Nathan v Bailey Gibson Ltd.*[27] In a general sense, it can be said that the national courts do not exclude one or more interpretative tools that are available to them in a purely internal context. More specifically, it was seen that the German courts

---

24 High Court 3 March 2011 *EPA v Neiphin Trading Ltd* [2011] 2 IR 575 at para. 71. See also S. O'Reilly, 'The Private Enforcement of European Community Laws in the Irish Superior Courts' (2009/31) *Dublin University Law Journal*, p. 346.

25 High Court 30 May 2014 *EPA v Harte Peat Ltd* [2015] 1 IR 462 at paras. 12, 26.

26 See High Court 6 October 1998 *Watson v EPA* [2000] 2 IR 454 at 478.

27 Supreme Court 29 February 1996 *Nathan v Bailey Gibson Ltd* [1998] 2 IR 162 at 174-8.

have also applied the technique of *Rechtsfortbildung* to obtain an interpretation in conformity with the directive. It could also be argued that the HR's *Dekker* and *Albron/FNV c.s.* judgments[28] (adjusting the interaction between a specific provision and a more general provision extending to many areas of civil law to the circumstances of the case, and a liberal approach to the limits of grammatical interpretation, respectively) provide an example of the ECJ's point of guidance.

2.2.5. Verbatim *Transposition*

It is recalled that I concluded in chapter 2, subparagraph 4.3.3, that the ECJ's *Spedition Welter* judgment must be interpreted as excluding the possibility for national courts to claim that the national provision's wording cannot accommodate a consistent interpretation if the directive was transposed *verbatim.*[29] The only case that I discussed that can be directly linked to this judgment was the follow-up judgment delivered by a lower ranked court.

> The Landgericht Saarbrücken, which made the reference for a preliminary ruling resulting in the ECJ's *Spedition Welter* judgment, in its follow-up judgment repeated the most important part of the ECJ's judgment and then simply concluded that, accordingly, the claims representative was authorised to accept service of judicial documents (which was the result prescribed by the directive).[30] The argumentation is not particularly elaborate, but it seems to be clear that it did not find any difficulty in adopting a consistent interpretation.

However, there have been some judgments in which the applicable legislation could be characterised as representing a *verbatim* transposition. They indicate that the courts in that situation do not normally have many difficulties in adopting a consistent interpretation, but also shows that it is not completely self-evident that a consistent interpretation can be adopted.

> The Supreme Court clearly dealt with a *verbatim* situation in *Thompson v Dublin Bus,*[31] and in this regard it formulated the presumption that, if the legislature had the intention to depart from or go beyond the directive, it would have clearly expressed this intention so as to remove any doubt. This presumption was already discussed above. In the Supreme Court's judgment in *Albatros Feeds Ltd v Minister for Agriculture and Food* the national provision was also very similar to the directive – at least as far as the material point in that case was concerned there was no distinction – but a consistent interpretation was rejected. I put forward that a distinguishing factor between these cases might be found in the interference of such an interpretation with fundamental

28 HR 13 September 1991, ECLI:NL:HR:1991:ZC0328, *NJ* 1992/225 (*Dekker*), para. 2.1; HR 5 April 2013, ECLI:NL:HR:2013:BZ1780, *NJ* 2013/389 (*Albron/FNV c.s.*), para. 3.7.

29 Case C-306/12 *Spedition Welter,* ECLI:EU:C:2013:650, para. 31.

30 LG Saarbrücken 15 November 2013, not reported.

31 Supreme Court 5 March 2015 *Thompson v Dublin Bus* [2015] 3 JIC 503. See also High Court 16 December 1999 *Coastal Line Container Terminal Ltd v Services Industrial Professional Technical Union* [2000] 1 IR 549 at 561.

rights protected under the Constitution (this issue is further discussed in subparagraph 2.3). Also, although this concerns the use of identical terms (instead of an entire provision), Dutch case law in which the duty of consistent interpretation is applied in the context of judicial implementation (this concerns the situation where the directive has, in principle, been implemented into national law correctly, and is used as a standard for interpretation with the national courts adjusting their interpretation of the implementing measures to the interpretation of the directive by the ECJ, see also chapter 2, paragraph 6) supports the view that they then automatically follow the interpretation given to those terms in the ECJ's case law. This automatic incorporation of the EU law meaning is sometimes criticised from a perspective of legal certainty as an unexpected interpretation of terms in national law implementing a directive can have (considerable) negative consequences for the legal position of the concerned individuals.[32]

2.2.6. *Determining or Aggravating Criminal Liability and Legitimate Expectations Outside the Area of Criminal Law*

The ECJ's *Kolpinghuis* judgment established a prohibition to determine or aggravate criminal liability on the basis of a consistent interpretation.[33] This means, first, that it is not permitted to establish criminal liability where this is not clearly foreseen in the law (this refers to requirements imposed by *lex certa*) and, secondly, that criminal law may not be applied retrospectively. In the *Kolpinghuis* judgment, the prohibition was based on the principles of legal certainty and non-retroactivity. The ECJ later specified the legal basis by referring to the principle that a provision of the criminal law may not be applied extensively to the detriment of the defendant (*nullum crimen, nulla poena sine lege*).[34] After the introduction of the Charter, it has also referred to Article 49(1) of this instrument (enshrining the principle of legality of criminal offences).[35] The second limitation addresses the temporal effect of legislation. In the ECJ's *Klohn* judgment, *which was delivered outside the context of criminal law*, it was seen that EU law in principle requires that national legislation adopted to implement the directive applies immediately to future effects of situations which arose under previous national rules. The ECJ proceeded to an examination of the merits of the argument advanced on the basis of the principle of legitimate expectations, thus recognising that it could, potentially, be a relevant limitation to the duty of consistent interpretation. However, applying a detailed analysis whether the principle could be relied upon in the proceedings before the national court, the ECJ concluded that the argument based on the principle should be rejected, leaving no scope for the referring court to carry out its own assessment in the light of the facts of the case. There was on that occasion thus no exception to the basic rule of immediate effect.

---

32 Case note by Jongma and Tieman in *AB* 2001/260, para. 2.
33 Case 80/86 *Kolpinghuis*, ECLI:EU:C:1987:431, para. 13.
34 Joined Cases C-74/95 and C-129/95 *Criminal proceedings against X*, ECLI:EU:C:1996:491, para. 25.
35 Case C-7/11 *Caronna*, ECLI:EU:C:2012:396, para. 55.

Since criminal law is not included within the scope of this research, it has not occupied a prominent place in the preceding chapters. However, the case law of the ABRvS contains two lines that are premised on an analogy with the prohibition laid down in the *Kolpinghuis* judgment (to be more specific: it addressed the first component derived from *lex certa*). First, in its *Mandemakers* judgment it held that this prohibition must also be applied in the situation where consistent interpretation leads to the imposition of an administrative fine which qualifies as a criminal charge.[36] The *Mandemakers* judgment also shows that the prohibition can be applied even if the interpretative gap between EU and national law is itself of a more modest nature; the circumstance that a fine is imposed as such reduces the scope for a consistent interpretation. Since there is a connecting point in EU law on the basis of the Charter and the broad interpretation of the concept 'criminal charge' under Article 6 ECHR, I do not think that the ABRvS violated the limits to the duty of consistent interpretation provided by EU law (be that as it may, the ABRvS should have referred preliminary questions to the ECJ on this point). Secondly, the same cannot be said for the ABRvS's *KOMO* judgment, which extended the analogy with the prohibition to determine or aggravate criminal liability even further by applying it to administrative enforcement (which is not of a punitive nature).[37]

In the German Federal Administrative Court's (Bundesverwaltungsgericht) judgment of 7 July 2016, it mentioned that a violation of the concerned provision could lead to an administrative fine and emphasised that the limits of the provision's wording therefore required extra consideration (it is noted that the BVerwG concluded that in the case before it a consistent interpretation would not exceed this threshold).[38] I also encountered a judgment delivered by one of the lower ranking courts confirming this position. However, unlike the ABRvS, these judgments did not draw an analogy with the ECJ's *Kolpinghuis* judgment.

> This could be seen as an indication that, unlike the ABRvS, it is not of the opinion that the situation where consistent interpretation could give rise to the imposition of an administrative fine is subject to the same limitations that apply for the determination or aggravation of criminal liability. Yet, an important distinction with the ABRvS's judgment is that the latter directly addressed the question whether it had been permitted to impose a fine. This point was not at stake in the cases delivered by the German courts.

The review of administrative fines is in Germany conferred upon the senate of the BGH dealing with criminal law. As this part of the BGH's jurisdiction is not included in the analysis, it has not been the subject of a comprehensive examination and I

---

36 ABRvS 4 March 2009, ECLI:NL:RVS:2009:BH4621, *AB* 2009/156 (*Mandemakers*), para. 2.6.2.
37 ABRvS 8 June 2016, ECLI:NL:RVS:2016:1613, *AB* 2016/273 (*KOMO*), para. 10.3.
38 BVerwG 7 July 2016, BVerwGE 155, 381, para. 26.

did not encounter judgments that concerned the question whether a fine could be imposed as a result of a consistent interpretation. However, it is noted that there is in fact support in legal scholarship for an analogous application of the limits concerning criminal liability to administrative fines. Further research is necessary before a less tentative conclusion can be drawn as to whether or not the position in Germany is similar to that of the ABRvS. It is quite logical that a position similar to the *Mandemakers* judgment was not discerned in the Irish courts' case law: it follows from a combined reading of Articles 34(1) and 37 of the Irish Constitution that administrative fines are not allowed in the first place. Offences can be *prosecuted* by administrative authorities (for example, the European Communities (Processed Animal Products) Regulations 2000, with which the Supreme Court's judgment in *Albatros Feeds Ltd v Minister for Agriculture and Food* was concerned, stipulated that the contravention of some of its provisions constitutes an offence and that the Minister may bring and prosecute proceedings for an offence) but are only *imposed* by courts after a conviction.

Finally, section 5 of the Irish Interpretation Act 2005 is generally understood as codifying the development in Irish law whereby the courts more frequently departed from the literal approach to interpretation and started to apply more purposive criteria. However, this provision excludes from its scope provisions relating to the imposition of a penal or other sanction. It is noted that this also seems to reflect concerns relating to the *lex certa* principle.

With regard to the temporal effect of legislation outside the area of criminal law, and the role played by legitimate expectations in that regard, it is noted that the BAG's judgment of 23 March 2006 and the subsequent BVerfG judgment, as well as the German superior courts' case law discussing the limits to a *Rechtsfortbildung*, have recognised legitimate expectations as a relevant limitation to the duty of consistent interpretation. However, they have not so far relied on the EU law principle but on the national variant, which is protected under the German Constitution. The matter will therefore be discussed in subparagraph 2.3.

2.2.7. Res Judicata *as a Separate Limitation to the Duty of Consistent Interpretation?*

The ECJ's *Klohn* judgment clearly accepted the principle of *res judicata* as a limitation to the duty of consistent interpretation. In line with earlier applications of this principle outside the scope of consistent interpretation it is, in principle, left to the national courts to determine whether this requirement is violated. I put forward that it is more appropriate to view the *res judicata* limitation as a limitation on the result prescribed by EU law (and its deference to national procedural autonomy) and not as a limitation on the interpretative process carried out in the context of the duty of consistent interpretation. Surely, a consistent interpretation must also respect the principle of *res judicata*, but this would not be any different if EU law would have been invoked by means of direct effect.

2.2.8. *No Requirement to Adopt a* Contra Legem *Interpretation*

In relation to directives, this limitation was first mentioned in the ECJ's *Adeneler* judgment.[39] This limitation finds its legal basis in, and must be viewed as a specific enunciation of, the principle of legal certainty. So while the exact scope of *contra legem* is to a large extent determined by the national courts, it has its origins in EU law, which justifies the ECJ exercising a degree of control over the outer limits of its meaning. It is clear from the ECJ's case law that *contra legem* can be invoked when the national court is prevented from adopting a consistent interpretation on account of the outer limits of the national provision's wording. But in the *Impact* judgment the ECJ was open to the referring court's suggestion that the adoption of a consistent interpretation might be *contra legem* on account of a national interpretative rule that was established on the basis of case law (precluding, in principle, the retrospective application of legislation). And in the *Klohn* judgment reliance on the principle of *res judicata* was also discussed with reference to the *contra legem* limitation.[40] This indicates that *contra legem* might also be given a broader meaning. The ECJ has also restricted the scope of *contra legem*. In the *Ajos* judgment, it made it clear that national courts may not dismiss a consistent interpretation only because the relevant provision had been consistently interpreted in a way that is incompatible with EU law.[41]

It was submitted that it is not yet clear whether the ECJ views the *contra legem* limitation as primarily referring to limitations derived from a provision's wording, or whether it has a broader meaning. If the latter view would be correct, and this would go so far that all kinds of interpretative obstacles deriving from national interpretative rules are brought within its scope, it may be asked whether the limitation would not lose its independent meaning and becomes a synonym for the dispensational side inherently present in 'so far as possible'.

Divergent positions are adopted in the three examined Member States with regard to the meaning of the *contra legem* limitation. In Germany there exists a dichotomy between implementing and non-implementing legislation. With regard to the former, it follows from the BGH's *Quelle* judgment that the *contra legem* threshold is not yet reached merely because of an incompatibility with the provision's text, but instead refers to the limits attached to *Rechtsfortbildung*.

---

39 Case C-212/04 *Adeneler*, ECLI:EU:C:2006:443, para. 110, referring to Case C-105/03 *Pupino*, ECLI:EU:C:2005:386, para. 47.

40 Case C-268/06 *Impact*, ECLI:EU:C:2008:223, para. 103.

41 Case C-441/14 *Ajos*, ECLI:EU:C:2016:278, paras. 33-4. Subsequently confirmed in Case C-414/16 *Egenberger*, ECLI:EU:C:2018:257, paras. 72-3; Case C-68/17 *IR*, ECLI:EU:C:2018:696, para. 64.

> There is the requirement to examine whether a consistent interpretation can be acquired by means of a *Rechtsfortbildung*. This automatically means that an interpretation exceeding the limits of a provision's wording is not necessarily prohibited. Instead the *contra legem* limit refers to what is no longer methodologically permissible according to national interpretative rules. It can be deduced from the subsequent paragraphs of the BGH's *Quelle* judgment that these limits are violated if a consistent interpretation would depart from the conditions for establishing a *Regelungslücke* (but as the result of a consistent prioritisation of the legislature's implementing objective, this is not likely to occur in relation to implementing legislation – yet, compare the BGH's judgments of 5 October 2017 and 3 July 2018) or a number of specific limits that apply in relation to *Rechtsfortbildung* which, broadly speaking, refer to the separation of powers and legal certainty.[42]

Importantly, subsequent case law from the BGH and BAG shows that, if the national provision does *not* have an implementing objective, first, a *Rechtsfortbildung* is not adopted since there is only a (clear) legislative intention that is not in line with the directive (hence, the required *Regelungslücke* cannot be identified) and, secondly, the courts then fall back on the conventional limits to interpretation, in which regard they are in particular required to take into account the outer limits of a grammatical interpretation.[43] If the case law on the limits to consistent interpretation in the context of *Rechtsfortbildung* and otherwise (i.e. *Auslegung*, for this distinction, see further chapter 3, subparagraph 3.1) is looked at jointly, it can be said that, in principle, the German courts are required to respect a provision's text and the intention of the legislature, but if a *Regelungslücke* is identified, the former no longer constitutes an absolute limitation, the focus then shifts to the other criteria mentioned.[44] The Irish superior courts' prevailing view is that the *contra legem* limitation prohibits an interpretation that is incompatible with the national provision's wording (including not only contradictory statements, but also, on one occasion, a lack of clear statements supporting the position derived from the directive). However, exceptionally, the courts have also relied on arguments of a different kind when invoking the *contra legem* limitation: the purpose and broader scheme of the legislation and jurisprudentially developed rules. The difference with the German courts is that, here, an understanding of *contra legem* that is not linked to the provision's text is not used to increase the scope for consistent interpretation, but to bring additional arguments within the sphere of that limitation, thereby increasing the scope to *reject* a consistent interpretation. Finally, the Dutch superior

42 BGH 26 November 2008 *Quelle*, BGHZ 179, 27, paras. 21-2, 29-35.

43 BAG 17 November 2009 *Urlaubsentgelt*, BAGE 132, 247, paras. 28-9; BGH 16 May 2013 *Interprofessionelle Sozität*, NJW 2013, 2674, paras. 28, 42-3.

44 BAG 23 March 2006, BAGE 117, 281, para. 26. This is also supported by BAG 17 November 2009 *Urlaubsentgelt*, BAGE 132, 247, paras. 28-31; BGH 16 May 2013 *Interprofessionelle Sozität*, NJW 2013, 2674, paras. 28, 42-3. See also C.-W. Canaris, 'Gemeinsamkeiten zwischen verfassungs- und richtlinienkonformer Rechtsfindung', in: H. Bauer and others (Eds.), *Wirtschaft im offenen Verfassungsstaat* (C.H. Beck 2006), p. 58, pointing out that the same limits are applied in the context of *verfassungskonforme Auslegung* (including references to case law).

courts simply view the *contra legem* limitation as referring to the outer limits of the provision's text. It is noted that, while not actually referring to the *contra legem* limitation, the HR's *Albron/FNV c.s.* judgment indicated a lenient approach, at least in respect of civil law proceedings, to the question when a consistent interpretation goes beyond the national provision's wording.

On balance, it can be said that in particular the German courts, but seemingly this can also apply to the Dutch courts in certain situations (but presumably only in a civil law context), have adopted a view on *contra legem* that is more favourable than viewing this limitation as a mere reference to what is still grammatically possible. This is of course compatible with the latter view and unproblematic from the perspective of EU law. The Irish courts have sometimes taken a broader, i.e. less permissive, view on *contra legem* which resonates the position in the ECJ's *Impact* and *Klohn* judgments (which, perhaps not entirely by coincidence, originated in a reference for a preliminary ruling by the Irish Labour Court and Supreme Court respectively).

2.3. THE NATIONAL COURTS' OWN FURTHER INTERPRETATION

Although it follows from the above that many aspects of the national courts' application of the duty of consistent interpretation can somehow be connected to instructions provided by the ECJ's case law, the latter does not exhaustively prescribe how far national courts are required to go to bring national law in conformity with the directive. If this were otherwise, the ECJ would probably be forced to exceed its own competences. The purpose of this subparagraph is not to summarise and compare all the individual interactions between the duty of consistent interpretation and national interpretative rules on the basis of the national chapters. Instead, I will point out some of the general threads that can be gleaned from these chapters.

The German and Irish chapters both showed a remarkable development. In the former, it was seen that the BGH changed its approach to interpretation to the benefit of a consistent interpretation by taking the directive as its starting point and – openly acknowledging that it departed from the most natural reading of the concerned provision – applying the grammatical interpretative method as an outer limit. In other words, a consistent interpretation should be adopted as long as the provision's wording did not oppose such an interpretation.

> The Dutch superior courts' case law, in particular the HR's *Wandelvierdaagse* judgment, shows some signs of this approach, but they are less compelling: there was not an equally clear discrepancy with the conventional approach to

interpretation and, importantly, a key condition for the approach was that an implementing objective could be identified, which indicates that there was not a conflict.

In the Irish chapter, it was seen that there was an important shift in approach starting with the High Court's judgment in *Murphy v An Bord Telecom* Éireann.[45] This entailed that the strict textualist approach to interpretation was relaxed in favour of a more purposive approach aimed at putting into effect the objectives of the directive. This shift in approach has characterised the Irish superior courts' approach towards the duty of consistent interpretation for a considerable time and has produced some interpretations that clearly deviated from a traditional interpretation of the law. However, I also identified a more reserved trend in the case law and argued that this can be traced back to two developments occurring around the same time: the introduction of section 5 of the Interpretation Act 2005, which lays down instructions for the construction of acts and statutory instruments, and the ECJ's establishment of the *contra legem* limitation.

Another example of a favourable approach is provided by the use of flexible *casu quo* general provisions to adopt a consistent interpretation. All of the national chapters contain examples that show that such provisions are often capable of accommodating a consistent interpretation without any real difficulties. At the same time, in private law, an area riddled with provisions of this kind, this does not seem to go so far that they always provide a rule to fall back on if more specific provisions cannot accommodate a consistent interpretation.[46]

While it is a resolved issue that the duty of consistent interpretation also applies to legislation that does not have an implementing objective, the majority of the methodological instructions positively steering the national courts' approach, pertains to legislation which *does* have this objective. There is not any further guidance concerning the question just how far the national courts should go when interpreting non-implementing legislation. Although the case law of all the examined superior courts contains examples adopting a consistent interpretation of such legislation, and it can even be said that the adopted interpretations sometimes departed from the traditional meaning of the national provision, I have not come

45 High Court 11 April 1988 *Murphy v An Bord Telecom* Éireann [1989] ILRM 53 at 59, 61.

46 M.H. Wissink, 'Interpretation of Private Law in Conformity with EU Directives', in: A.S. Hartkamp and others (Eds.), *The Influence of EU Law on National Private Law* (Kluwer 2014), p. 155-7. He refers, among others, to the HR's *Pink Floyd* judgment, which I discussed in chapter 5, subparagraph 3.3.1. The HR was not only invited to examine the possibility of acquiring a consistent interpretation through the specific rule concerning the exhaustion of copyright, but also on the basis of Article 6:162 of the Civil Code (concerning liability for unlawful acts). The HR rejected the latter argument as well, pointing out that this would violate the prohibition to impose obligations on an individual on the basis of a directive and that a consistent interpretation requires that the outer interpretative limits are not exceeded.

across any judgments where they exceeded the limits of national interpretative rules for this purpose. This could be explained by the fact that there are no specific instructions deriving from EU law requiring them to push the interpretation of national law beyond its conventional limits. Another reason could be that there are less connecting points in the national interpretative methods encouraging the court to go a step further (such as the argument that the legislation was intended to implement the directive).

The presence of the national courts' own further interpretation is felt in particular with regard to the limits to the duty of consistent interpretation. This is not surprising since, apart from the prohibition to determine or aggravate criminal liability, and now also legitimate expectations (but note that the latter limitation has only been introduced recently), the ECJ's case law does not offer much guidance (it is noted that the principle of *res judicata* has also been applied as a limitation to the duty of consistent interpretation, but I argued that this is first and foremost a limitation on the result prescribed by EU law and that it must be viewed as a product of national procedural autonomy). The meaning of the *contra legem* limitation, discussed in subparagraph 2.2.8 is actually also primarily based on the national courts' own further interpretation (but was discussed there as it is also a further interpretation of the ECJ's rough sketch). Particularly the Dutch, as well as the German, limits are also often discussed without a reference to the *contra legem* limitation. The superior courts' perspectives also produced limits that I have not yet mentioned and which therefore – advertently or inadvertently – do not seem to connect, or are more difficult to connect, to the ECJ's instructions. This is sometimes problematic. In two different situations, national fundamental rights played an important role for the rejection of a consistent interpretation. Notwithstanding its conclusion that a consistent interpretation was methodologically possible, the BAG rejected such an interpretation on account of the principle of legitimate expectations, which is protected under the German Constitution. While the ECJ's *Klohn* judgment has recently (i.e. before the German case law referring to legitimate expectations) provided some support for the view that this may be a relevant limitation, it referred to the *EU law* principle as the relevant benchmark for determining whether restrictions applied to the duty of consistent interpretation (this is also consistent with the approach towards the other limitations: see the limitation laid down in the *Kolpinghuis* judgment and the *contra legem* limitation). As regards the BAG's judgment specifically, I submitted that the fact that a consistent interpretation was solely rejected on account of the principle of legitimate expectations and the difficulties which the BAG's concerns against the retroactive operation of the law raise in the specific context of consistent interpretation, make it less likely that such an approach to the principle of legitimate expectations will find acceptance in the ECJ's case law. However, importantly, a similar judgment became the subject of a constitutional complaint and was annulled by the German Federal Constitutional

Court (hereinafter; BVerfG) so that it no longer represents good law. The BVerfG provided that the BAG should have first consulted the ECJ through the preliminary reference procedure to obtain clarification. At the same time, the BVerfG did not unambiguously exclude the possibility to apply the national principle of legitimate expectations in case it is found that the EU law principle offers insufficient protection. In that regard the above identified concerns pertaining to the BAG's position apply *mutatis mutandis.* However, since there is now some support in the ECJ's case law for the view that the principle of legitimate expectations could be a relevant limitation with regard to consistent interpretation and the BVerfG has pointed out the obligation to refer preliminary questions before a consistent interpretation is rejected on this ground, I also think that there is a possibility that the two positions could in the future be reconciled. This requires that it is recognised that the EU law principle provides the relevant benchmark and the German courts must be willing to adhere to the guidelines provided by the ECJ for the substantive test whether the principle is violated – which certainly seems to be less accommodating than the one applied in the BAG's judgment. Secondly, the Supreme Court's judgment in *Albatros Feeds Ltd v Minister for Agriculture and Food* (subsequently reiterated by a High Court judgment) indicated that there is less scope to interpret national provisions in conformity with the directive in order to create powers whose application would interfere with fundamental rights protected under the Irish Constitution. Interestingly, the judgment indicates a link with the requirement that interferences with fundamental rights must be clearly foreseen by law (the foreseeability requirement). This, in turn, enables the identification of a common feature underpinning both the German case and the Supreme Court's judgment: as the former concerned the principle of legitimate expectations and the latter the requirement of foreseeability, both can be traced back to the principle of legal certainty. Similar to what was observed in relation to the German case, it is argued that, if the limitation applied by the Supreme Court were to find acceptance, it should, contrary to what was in fact done, be reframed as an issue concerning fundamental rights protected by EU law, in particular the requirement of foreseeability. I argued that it would be conceivable that the duty of consistent interpretation is interpreted by the ECJ as requiring that fundamental rights protected by EU law are taken into account. Fundamental rights can be directly relevant for the interpretative process; see Article Article 49 of the Charter enshrining the principle of legality of criminal offences, whose effect coincides with the limits established in the *Kolpinghuis* judgment. They can also be indirectly relevant. In particular as a result of Article 52(1) of the Charter, which provides that limitations to fundamental rights must be provided for by law, limitations must be sufficiently foreseeable. That requirement also applies to national courts when they are acting within the scope of EU law and justifies a stricter approach to interpretation where the required interpretation of the national provision entails a limitation to a fundamental right. The judgment in *Albatros Feeds Ltd v Minister for Agriculture and Food* related to this type of situation in which fundamental rights can play a role. However, in relation to the Supreme Court's judgment there are some concerns. It was submitted that, since the EU and national law provisions were very close and an ECJ judgment seemed to indicate quite clearly that the former provided a sufficiently clear legal basis for the actions that were disputed in the Supreme Court's judgment, the fundamental rights protection offered by EU law was implicitly challenged and the national standards in terms of foreseeability prioritised. In this regard there seems to be an incompatibility with EU law.

However, limits not clearly connected to the framework provided by EU law are not always problematic. The Dutch chapter provided an example where the rejection of a consistent interpretation was in part based on the consideration that the dispute concerned the scope of a prohibition addressed to individuals in administrative law, which was viewed as requiring a more restrained approach. I pointed out that there is a link with the principle of legal certainty here (as well as the legality principle). However, while the ECJ's case law refers to the principle of legal certainty, it has only derived specific limitations from this principle, and has not so far recognised the point raised by the ABRvS as a relevant factor. It should also be recalled that the duty of consistent interpretation applies to the situation that a Member State relies on a directive against an individual. But then again, it needs to be emphasised that it does not necessarily follow from the Dutch judgment that the fact that the provision's scope was extended was as such a decisive factor for rejecting a consistent interpretation and I contended that it is therefore possible to reconcile the judgment with the ECJ's case law. It was already seen in subparagraph 2.2.6 that the ABRvS extended the limitation established in the ECJ's *Kolpinghuis* judgment to administrative fines as well as enforcement. Those judgments also invoked the principle of legal certainty but this should be understood in light of the judgments' references to the *Kolpinghuis* judgment and was therefore intended as an extension of an existing limitation instead of the introduction of a new one.

As a final remark, it may be added that concerns relating to legal certainty (and in particular non-retroactivity) were also behind the Danish Supreme Court's considerations in the *Ajos* case that it did not deem it possible to adopt a consistent interpretation of national law as this would set aside well established case law conferring another, incompatible, interpretation, on the relevant provision. I endorsed the ECJ's *Ajos* judgment, but also discussed a number of situations for which it is not immediately obvious that case law cannot have an influence on the question whether a consistent interpretation is possible (see chapter 2, subparagraph 5.2.2).

2.4. LOOKING AHEAD

Having discussed the ECJ's instructions on the application of the duty of consistent interpretation, the national superior courts' interpretation of elements containing a larger or smaller degree of discretion, as well as the national courts' own further interpretation of the obligation, this subparagraph gives an overview of some of the more pressing issues regarding the duty of consistent interpretation that were identified in the above analysis as well as my own views on how these issues could be resolved.

On the basis of the ECJ's *Spedition Welter* judgment, it is not entirely clear whether it should be interpreted as removing the national court's freedom to determine whether a consistent interpretation can be adopted if the national provision literally took over the directive, or whether it only precluded the rejection of a consistent interpretation on the basis of the national provision's wording. In chapter 2, subparagraph 4.3.3 I proposed the latter interpretation. A further question is whether the instruction provided in the *Spedition Welter* judgment also applies to individual terms. Dutch case law applying the duty of consistent interpretation in the context of judicial implementation already adopted such an approach (albeit that the judgments were delivered some time before the *Spedition Welter* judgment and could not therefore have applied the judgment's reasoning).

The BAG's judgment of 23 March 2006, the subsequent BVerfG judgment and the Supreme Court's judgment in *Albatros Feeds Ltd v Minister for Agriculture and Food* raise the question whether fundamental rights can be invoked as a limitation to the duty of consistent interpretation. I submitted that the concerned rights must also be protected under EU law (in this regard it is noted that the principle of legitimate expectations *is* protected as a general principle of EU law but *not* as a fundamental right in EU law). Also, in general, such concerns are more likely to qualify as an exception to the duty of consistent interpretation if they are linked to arguments that are found in the interpretative sphere and can be related to the national courts' discretion under the duty of consistent interpretation. I refer to the previous subparagraph for comments on the way in which fundamental rights could be relevant as a limit to the duty of consistent interpretation.

So far, the ECJ has derived the limitations concerning criminal liability and the *contra legem* limitation from the well known phrase that 'the duty of consistent interpretation is limited by general principles of law, particularly those of legal certainty and non-retroactivity' (as regards the former, it is noted that the limitation concerning criminal liability is based on the legality principle in criminal law, more specifically *lex certa*). It also seems to have recognised that the principle of legitimate expectations may provide a relevant limitation. Which further limitations could be derived from those principles?[47] The limitation discussed in the ABRvS's *Fortis* judgment was also linked to the principle of legal certainty and I put forward that there is something to be said for the position that national courts are not required to adopt a consistent interpretation if such an interpretation is difficult to reconcile with the provision's text and when a prohibitory provision is being interpreted (without the nature of the concerned provision being a decisive factor). Furthermore, I agreed with the extension of the limitation laid down in the *Kolpinghuis* judgment to administrative fines constituting a criminal charge but dismissed the further extension of this limitation to administrative enforcement in general. The above mentioned phrase concerning the limits to the duty of consistent interpretation appears to refer to general principles of law in general. It could therefore be asked whether other principles than legal certainty can be invoked by the national courts to reject a consistent interpretation (see chapter 2, subparagraph 5.3).[48] Since the ECJ's as well as the national courts' case law do not really provide any useful guidance on this point, it is difficult to make recommendations. At the same time, it can be said that, apparently, it is not a very pressing issue.

Finally, does the *contra legem* limitation only encompass the situation where there is a grammatical impossibility, or does the concept have a broader meaning? Both the ECJ's as well as the national courts' case law does not provide a clear-cut answer to this question. From an EU law perspective it is of course unproblematic if, on their own initiative, national courts go further than what appears to be grammatically possible and thereby *increase* the scope to adopt a consistent interpretation. However, alternatively, an understanding whereby *contra legem* is not necessarily linked to the limits of a grammatical interpretation, can also entail that national courts invoke additional reasons to reject a consistent interpretation and thereby *reduce* the obligation's scope. If the ECJ would permit all kinds of interpretative obstacles deriving from national interpretative rules to be brought within the scope of the *contra legem* limitation, it may be asked whether the limitation would not lose its independent meaning and become a synonym for the dispensational side inherently present in 'so far as possible'. At the same time this would have as a consequence that national courts surrender a significant part of the discretion that they currently exercise: if reasons for rejecting a consistent interpretation are 'Europeanised' they are simultaneously brought under the control and ultimate authority of the ECJ – at least as far as concerns their outer limits. In other words: the large open space created by the ECJ's *Von Colson and Kamann* judgment would be narrowed down considerably.

---

47 See also C.N.K. Franklin, 'Synthesis', in: C.N.K. Franklin (Ed.), *The Effectiveness and Application of EU and EEA Law in National Courts* (Intersentia 2018), p. 57.

48 See S. Prechal, *Directives in EC Law* (OUP 2005), p. 204-5, for a list of general principles that could be relevant.

3. THE FIT BETWEEN CONSISTENT INTERPRETATION AND THEORIES ON THE RELATIONSHIP BETWEEN EU AND NATIONAL LAW

A German, Irishman and Dutchman walk into a bar... This sounds like the beginning of a joke, but once I add that this scene is actually intended to illustrate the difficulties of disentangling the complex interactions between EU and national law in the context of the duty of consistent interpretation, that will probably take all the fun out of it for most people (but, hopefully, arouses the interest of the audience at which this book aims). The German is familiar with, and adheres to, the normative framework offered by *verfassungskonforme Auslegung*, and might argue that the duty of consistent interpretation is merely a means to make a choice between the interpretations that remain after an examination of national law in accordance with a conventional approach (but note that another adherent of this analogy might even come up with a different answer). The Irishman might contend that his courts are bound by a strict literal approach to interpretation and only if ambiguity remains as a result of grammatical interpretation is there scope to consider the purpose behind the legislation, in which regard the requirements of the directive could come into play. However, he adds that there even exists case law supporting the view that the latter is only possible if the specific objectives from the directive were taken over by the Oireachtas. The Dutchman listens with growing amazement and then objects that there is always a degree of competition between the different interpretative methods and the duty of consistent interpretation simply means that national courts must choose the interpretation that is in conformity with the directive and can even force the national courts to depart from the interpretation that would have followed on the basis of a traditional approach. All of them can refer to judgments from their own national courts to support their arguments,[49] and to make things even more complicated judgments are pointed out which originate from the interlocutor's Member State and undermine his position.[50]

When an attempt is made to disentangle a complex issue, they key is to find the right angle to sort out the seemingly incongruous facts with which one is confronted. In my opinion the right angle for understanding the way that consistent interpretation works was to ask how the two constituent dimensions interact with each other.

49 See BAG 30 March 2004, BAGE 110, 122, para. 47; High Court 4 March 1986 *Murphy v An Bord Telecom* Éireann [1986] ILRM 483 at 486-7; HR 5 April 2013, ECLI:NL:HR:2013:BZ1780, *NJ* 2013/389 (*Albron/FNV c.s.*), paras. 3.6.5-3.7.

50 BAG 24 March 2009, BAGE 130, 119, para. 67; Supreme Court 29 February 1996 *Nathan v Bailey Gibson Ltd* [1998] 2 IR 162 at 174-8; CBb 23 July 2012, ECLI:NL:CBB:2012:BX4127, paras. 6.1.1, 6.1.5; CBb 17 June 2015, ECLI:NL:CBB:2015:214, *AB* 2015/297, para. 5.2.

The next logical step was then to look at the existing theories that aim to describe the relationship between EU and national law: supremacy of EU law, national constitutionalism, and constitutional pluralism. I discuss the adequacy of each of those theories and then take stock of what has been discovered. As this also reflects upon the theories themselves and the discussion on the explanatory value of those theories for how EU law is applied in the Member States' legal orders (in particular beyond the more familiar context of direct effect), the results of this research also permit further reflection on this point. However, it is first necessary to explain what kind of conflict there is between EU and national law in the context of the duty of consistent interpretation. This is necessary since chapter 1, subparagraph 1.3 showed that the existing theories take as a starting point that there is a conflict of norms.

3.1. A CONFLICT OF INTERPRETATIVE RULES

It is not difficult to agree that there is a conflict of norms where a directive provides that a contract is void and national law does not. The theory of supremacy of EU law and, should the application of the provision in the directive impinge upon national constitutional provisions, national constitutionalism and constitutional pluralism, each prescribe a different approach to the resolution of such a conflict. However, I already argued in the conclusion to chapter 2 that the starting point is different for the duty of consistent interpretation. It is aimed at the *prevention* of a conflict between the directive and national law. Therefore, the paradigmatic situation in which the existing theories have been applied to directives cannot simply be transplanted to the context of consistent interpretation. This raised an issue which, at least at first sight, might appear to make an inquiry into the adequacy of the existing theories on the relationship between EU and national law pointless. Yet, moving from the focus between directives and national law to Articles 288 TFEU and 4(3) TEU, and drawing inspiration from the idea of viewing the duty of consistent interpretation as an interpretative rule,[51] I found a way through which the existing methods could still be of value. This views the duty of consistent interpretation as a binding legal norm – as far as its binding nature is concerned it is not different from the above mentioned rule in the directive stipulating when a contract is void. This equation with legal norms contained in (for example) a directive is justified as the duty of consistent interpretation is also based on legal norms, namely Articles 288 TFEU and 4(3) TEU (with the inclusion of the principle of effectiveness). The difference lies in the nature and effects of the norms. The duty of consistent interpretation operates at the level of interpretative rules, does not impose an obligation of result and is inherently not unfettered taking into account the semantic limits of the term 'interpretation' whereas the example

51 Canaris (n. 44), p. 45 *et seq.*

from the directive operates at the level of substantive rules, prescribes a particular result and must be given effect regardless of the impossibility to accommodate the result under national law. The approach advocated by me does not undermine the coherence of the existing theories; it does not depart in a significant way from the conventional understanding and application of those theories. What changes, however, is the kind of norm to which they are applied. It is this element that requires a slight adjustment of the familiar perspective.

One might perhaps object that the duty of consistent interpretation only imposes clear obligations with regard to the resolved issues that were discussed in subparagraph 2.1 and that it is only in relation to those outer limits that a conflict can be identified with the required degree of precision. In my opinion such a view fails to appreciate two things. First, ECJ judgments such as *Dominguez* and, even more clearly, *Ajos,* show that, also with regard to discretionary aspects (i.e. the scope of the *contra legem* limitation), Articles 288 TFEU and 4(3) TEU do not simply defer to whatever national law produces but set an autonomous standard (even though its exact scope may only receive further clarification at a later point in time).[52] But, as the second argument will show, things can even be taken a step further. This requires me to turn to the national courts' role in the context of the duty of consistent interpretation. It can be said that the duty of consistent interpretation is an 'inherently contestable concept'.[53] It possesses different connotations, depending on the time and place in which it is used. The latter is clear from the differences between Member States as to how far the duty of consistent interpretation requires them to go. But there have also been differences in approach within a single Member State over the course of time. Compare, for example, the approach adopted by the HR's *Pink Floyd* judgment with its subsequent *Wandelvierdaagse* judgment. Consider also the shift in approach after the ECJ's preliminary ruling in the case of *Murphy v An Bord Telecom* Éireann before the High Court – which may, in turn, be compared to the High Court's judgment in *EPA v Neiphin Trading Ltd.* Different positions adopted by the national courts exist alongside each other without, in principle, one being a more faithful rendition of the duty of consistent interpretation than the other. The curious thing about this norm is that, within certain limits to which all courts are bound equally, the meaning ascribed to 'so far as possible' at a particular time and place is at *that* moment, and for the judge sitting in court, the only correct meaning. Nevertheless, this diversity does not mean that

52 It is also possible to mention the ECJ's *Marleasing* judgment in this regard, which seemed to be an indirect response to the House of Lords's judgment in *Duke v. Reliance Systems Ltd* [1988] AC 618 (Lord Templeman), 638-9, 641, based on the recognition that the unfettered application of national methodology might result in too far-reaching restrictions on the effectiveness of the duty of consistent interpretation.

53 B. Clarke, 'Eccentrically Contested Concepts' (1979/1), *British Journal of Political Science,* p. 123-4, who introduced this as a variant to Gallie's 'essentially contested concepts' (W.B. Gallie, 'Essentially contested concepts', in: M. Black (Ed.), *The importance of language* (Cornell University Press 1962), p. 121-46).

there is not a binding legal norm. Actually, rules of this kind are quite common as far as concerns for example defences to maintain national rules contrary to EU law (think of the justification grounds for the free movement provisions, or perhaps even Article 4(2) TEU requiring the EU to respect the national identities of the Member States), the main difference of course being that the duty of consistent interpretation imposes a positive obligation.

3.2. SUPREMACY OF EU LAW

In chapter 1, subparagraph 1.3.1, it was seen that supremacy can be defined as the capacity of an EU law norm '(...) to overrule inconsistent norms of national law (...)'.[54] I also alluded to the definition provided by Prechal, which she attuned to the reality that EU law does not only take effect through direct effect, but also through consistent interpretation:

> '(...) supremacy entails the obligation to resolve the conflict in favour of the Community law provision, either by setting aside the conflicting rule of national law, or by national law being consistently interpreted with Community law'.[55]

However, these definitions primarily emphasise the conflict resolution function of supremacy.[56] Chapter 1, subparagraph 1.3.1 also pointed out that a distinction has been drawn between supremacy as a hierarchical model and supremacy as a conflict resolution model. For the sake of convenience, I thereafter simply referred to supremacy of EU law. However, in the following parts it is again necessary to distinguish between both models.

Primarily looking at the systemic features of both models, but also – albeit that they have not so far provided a detailed and comprehensive description of their desired approach – some indications, if applicable, as to the consequences of a model for the application of the duty of consistent interpretation, an attempt is made to determine the fit with the encountered practices.

3.2.1. Supremacy (1): Interpretation in Conformity with Supreme Directives?

The most familiar view on the supremacy of EU law and the duty of consistent interpretation is provided by the hierarchical model, based on the notion that

54 B. De Witte, 'Direct Effect, Primacy, and the Nature of the Legal Order', in: G. De Búrca and P.P. Craig (Eds.), *The Evolution of EU Law* (OUP 2011), p. 323.

55 S. Prechal, 'Direct Effect, Indirect Effect, Supremacy and the Evolving Constitution of the European Union', in: C. Barnard (Ed.), *The Fundamentals of EU Law Revisited* (OUP 2007), p. 38.

56 This also follows from De Witte's assertion that the principle of supremacy only requires the disapplication, and not the invalidity (which is typically viewed as a characteristic of the hierarchical model), of the incompatible national provision, see De Witte (n. 54), p. 341.

directives are a supreme source of law in relation to national law. Hence, the latter should be interpreted in conformity with the former. This model has something to say for it as the mere fact that the national courts proceed to interpreting their laws in conformity with the directive suggests that they recognise the superiority of the latter norm. Yet, this does not of course exclude that there are alternative reasons why the national courts proceed in this way. More importantly, the hierarchical model attracts insuperable defects in terms of its theoretical underpinning. The model does not only presuppose that directives are viewed as being part of the national legal orders (this is seen as being self-evident by this model as the national legal orders are part of the same hierarchy) but also – and this is where it goes wrong – assumes that the entire body of EU law enjoys supremacy and, since directives are part of EU law, they naturally enjoy supremacy too.[57] Interestingly, the discussion on the theoretical foundations for the German courts to apply *Rechtsfortbildung* in the context of the duty of consistent interpretation (chapter 3, subparagraph 3.8) revealed that, at least in Germany, directives are not seen as fully effective norms in the national legal orders (directives occupy a markedly different position than the Constitution and therefore the theoretical underpinning of *verfassungskonforme Rechtsfortbildung* cannot be extended to consistent interpretation in EU law) – save for the situation where they have direct effect – and, hence, cannot establish the normative gap required for this technique to be applied. However, directives do produce effects in the national legal order, indirectly, through the provisions of Articles 288 TFEU and 4(3) TEU, which requires the courts to look, within the realm of national law, for an intention of the national legislature to implement the directive, which *does* provide the support necessary for a *Rechtsfortbildung.* Zooming out from Germany, it was seen in Chapter 2, subparagraph 2.3, why the hierarchical model's claim that directives enjoy supremacy should be rejected and I briefly recalled my findings in subparagraph 2.1. I refer to those observations, which can only lead to the conclusion that this view on supremacy and consistent interpretation does not provide an adequate theory.

3.2.2. *Supremacy (2): Articles 288 TFEU and 4(3) TEU as a Supreme Interpretative Rule*

Since I just provided that the hierarchical model is inadequate in relation to the duty of consistent interpretation, it follows that, if supremacy of EU law is to provide an adequate theory, it must therefore be understood in a narrower sense, i.e. as a conflict resolution model. An important virtue of this way of looking at the role played by supremacy is that it is not plagued by the issue facing the hierarchical model, where the link between supremacy and directives was a prerequisite for establishing the legal basis for consistent interpretation.

---

57 See Opinion of AG Van Gerven in Case C-106/89 *Marleasing*, ECLI:EU:C:1990:310, para. 9; M. Claes, *The National Courts' Mandate in the European Constitution* (Hart Publishing 2006), p. 115; Lenaerts and Corthaut (n. 4), p. 289.

Just as was done for the hierarchical model, a distinction is made between the applicability and the rank of directives in the national legal order. So, to start with the former, Articles 288 TFEU and 4(3) TEU (with the inclusion of the principle of effectiveness) are binding norms that apply within the national legal orders *qua* EU law and stipulate an interpretative rule. This is sufficient for the duty of consistent interpretation to apply; the supremacy view on the relationship between EU and national law conceptualises the EU legal order as autonomous and thus capable of directly creating legal obligations binding in the national legal orders.[58] So the national courts can simply apply the duty of consistent interpretation on this footing. It is reiterated – perhaps unnecessarily – that the difference with the hierarchical model is that the separate question of effect (i.e. supremacy) was there an indispensable step for proceeding to an application of consistent interpretation in the first place.

Turning to the second point, i.e. the rank of Articles 288 TFEU and 4(3) TEU, it is noted that, as part of EU primary law, these provisions moreover enjoy supremacy by nature (again, the difference with the general (i.e. excluding the question of direct effect) position of directives is noted). How does this capacity manifest itself in the context of consistent interpretation? To answer this question, it is first necessary to discard a misunderstanding with regard to the effect of supremacy. It has been put forward that '[s]upremacy can (...) be used to denote the supremacy of Community-consistent interpretation over national techniques and canons of construction'.[59] This transposes the role played by supremacy in the context of direct effect to consistent interpretation. It is asked which interpretation is consistent with the directive and conflicting national interpretative methods are simply set aside. Conferring such a meaning on supremacy disregards the fundamental role played by national courts and interpretative rules for determining whether a consistent interpretation can be adopted.[60] Since the aim is to determine which theory is the most adequate for understanding the encountered practices of consistent interpretation, it is perhaps even more important that the ECJ's as well as the national courts' case law stand in flat contradiction to such a view on the role played by supremacy.

It is therefore necessary to find a more fitting view on supremacy in the context of consistent interpretation. This can be achieved if the obligation is first and

58 M. Kumm, 'Who is the Final Arbiter of Constitutionality in Europe?: Three Conceptions of the Relationship between the German Federal Constitutional Court and the European Court of Justice' (1999/2) *CMLRev*, p. 369; M. Poiares Maduro, 'Contrapunctual Law: Europe's Constitutional Pluralism in Action', in: N. Walker (Ed.), *Sovereignty in Transition* (Hart Publishing 2003), p. 504; De Witte (n. 54), p. 352.

59 Claes (n. 57), p. 116, with reference to M.H. Wissink, *Richtlijnconforme interpretatie van burgerlijk recht* (Kluwer 2001), p. 121 *et seq*, who, however, does not agree with this way of looking at the duty of consistent interpretation.

60 See also Wissink (n. 59), p. 130, 132.

foremost understood as an interpretative rule. It requires, at a minimum, that national courts make an effort to find a route through which national law can be given a specific meaning, namely the one prescribed by the directive. However, it is not the envisaged result that is superior, but the methodological route that needs to be applied to the examination whether this result can be obtained through interpretation. If the theory of supremacy of EU law is understood in this way, the ECJ's, as well as the national superior courts', case law contains a number of indications supporting the theory.

First, I put forward that, as a necessary prerequisite, the addition of Article 4(3) TEU provides a justification for a potential interference by the duty of consistent interpretation with the interpretation of national law. Building on this basis, the ECJ's case law outlining the methodological instructions puts this promise into effect. The interpretative selection rule, the presumption that the legislature intends to comply with the directive (and its further articulation with respect to *travaux préparatoires* in the ECJ's *Björnekulla* judgment), and the pre-emption of the grammatical interpretation in relation to *verbatim* implementing measures, all indicate that the duty of consistent interpretation has the capacity to potentially interfere (in a significant way) with national interpretative rules. The ECJ's interventionist attitude in the ECJ's *Dominguez* and *Ajos* judgments goes in the same direction. These indications of consistent interpretation possessing the potential of supremacy are not reduced by the limits to the obligation that have been recognised by the ECJ. The prohibition with regard to criminal liability and the *contra legem* limitation are both based on, and are ultimately controlled by, EU law itself. The same applies in relation to the limits mentioned in the ECJ's *Klohn* judgment. Moreover, I argued that an application of the *contra legem* limitation must respect the ECJ's positive methodological instructions.[61]

Nevertheless, no matter how far-reaching the ECJ's case law might be, if national courts are somehow able to evade a conflict through a creative application of their interpretative rules, the theory of supremacy has no role to play. Also, unilateral proclamations by the ECJ indicating supremacy constitute only one side to the story if it actually *does* come to a conflict and the national courts' response must

61 Cf. M. Dougan, 'When Worlds Collide! Competing Visions of the Relationship between Direct Effect and Supremacy' (2007/4) *CMLRev*, p. 947, who views the *contra legem* limitation as standing in flat contradiction to a supremacy approach to the duty of consistent interpretation. However, I should point out, first, that Dougan appears to apply an understanding of supremacy which requires that all arguments standing in the way of conformity with the directive are simply set aside. Secondly, consistent interpretation is viewed in light of the broader hierarchical model of supremacy, which also encompasses that supremacy, in itself, is capable of precluding the application of national norms incompatible with allegedly hierarchically superior directives. In light of the wide possibilities to enforce the directive under that scenario, it indeed becomes difficult to understand the rationale behind the *contra legem* limitation. Yet, again, this is not the view propagated by me (and, for the sake of completeness: in the end also not by Dougan himself).

be examined in turn. Therefore, if supremacy is to be an adequate theory for understanding the relationship between EU and national law in the context of the duty of consistent interpretation, it is also required that examples can be identified in the national courts' case law in which a conflict actually occurs and, moreover, was resolved in favour of EU law.[62]

When is there a conflict in the context of the duty of consistent interpretation? This requires that it is examined when there is a conflict between the duty of consistent interpretation and national rules of interpretation. The first step in this examination consists of the identification of an adaptation of the traditional interpretation or interpretative process (i.e. the outcome or approach that would have been followed in a purely internal context). However, this first step is not sufficient for establishing a conflict, which requires that the adopted interpretation cannot be reconciled with the national interpretative rules. Since, in contrast to substantive national rules, national interpretative rules usually contain a larger or smaller degree of discretion, it proved more difficult to determine exactly when such a confict can be identified. It was for each national chapter necessary to first acquire a better understanding of the scope that is available on the basis of a traditional approach. Nevertheless, I discovered three different situations in the national superior courts' case law where such a conflict could be identified and was resolved in favour of a consistent interpretation. There are, in the first place, the BGH's judgments taking the directive as its starting point and – openly acknowledging that it departed from the most natural reading of the concerned provision – applying the grammatical interpretative method as an outer limit. In other words, it is asked whether grammatical interpretation does not *oppose* a consistent interpretation. This has been labelled by Brenncke as the 'negative test approach'.[63] The Dutch superior courts' case law, in particular the HR's *Wandelvierdaagse* judgment, shows some signs of this approach but, as I explained in subparagraph 2.3, it is less clear that there was a conflict. Secondly, there is the 'shift in approach' that occurred in the Irish superior courts' case law. The paradigmatic example of this is the judgment in *Murphy v An Bord Telecom* Éireann. There, the strict textualist approach to interpretation to which the Irish courts were accustomed was relaxed in favour of a more purposive approach aimed at putting into effect the objectives of the directive. The same approach was followed in subsequent judgments which clarified that the shift had been inspired by the courts' understanding that they operated in a different context when EU law is applicable and that the adaptation of their approach would be necessary to ensure a smooth alignment of the interpretation of national law with the directive.[64] This shift in approach underpinned a number

62 This is described as the bi-dimensional character of supremacy in J. Weiler, 'The Community System: the Dual Character of Supranationalism' (1981/1) *YEL*, p. 267, 275-6.

63 M. Brenncke, *Judicial Law-Making in English and German Courts* (Intersentia 2018), p. 291.

64 High Court 2 October 1987 *Lawlor v Minister for Agriculture* [1990] IR 356 at 375; High Court 21 June 1994 *Bosphorus Hava v Minister for Transport* [1994] 3 CMLR 464 at 469-70.

of interpretations in conformity with the directive that clearly deviated from, and would have been incompatible with, the pre-existing state of affairs under the interpretative rules at common law (but note the difference in tone in subsequent judgments discussed in the part on national constitutionalism). The identification of this shift in approach was facilitated by the fact that, compared to Germany and the Netherlands, the Irish interpretative rules are of a more formal nature, which renders identifying changes to the interpretative approach more feasible (by the way, the openness to change, in the sense of a modification of the system as such, is also a recognised feature of the common law method of legal reasoning). By contrast, if the national interpretative framework is normally of a flexible nature and does not tolerate a fixation of the weight that is to be ascribed to interpretative methods, it is more likely that the third situation, a structural prioritisation, arises. Such a prioritisation was explicitly acknowledged in the HR's *Wandelvierdaagse* judgment, requiring that the intention to implement the directive is prioritised over opposing, more specific, intentions (e.g. the intention to confer an entitlement to compensation to one of the parties to a contract). Albeit less explicitly, the same prioritisation, was seen in the German case law. In a similar vein, the implementing objective has been invoked to dispel doubts about the precise meaning that the legislature intended the adopted provision to have. Furthermore, it should be noted that this systematic prioritisation has been an indispensable tool for justifying a *Rechtsfortbildung* in conformity with directives.

3.3. NATIONAL CONSTITUTIONALISM

This theory was described as rejecting the idea that EU law autonomously determines its legal effect in the national legal orders; a Member State's constitution, or other national acts of similar authority, remain supreme and constitute the ultimate source of application of EU law.[65] It is accepted that EU law takes precedence over 'ordinary' national law and perhaps even certain constitutional provisions, but not over the fundamental provisions of the constitution.[66]

A question that immediately arises with respect to the model of national constitutionalism, which rejects the capacity of EU law to autonomously prescribe its applicability in the distinct Member States' legal orders, is whether it offers an adequate explanation for the national courts proceeding to a consistent interpretation on the basis of Articles 288 TFEU and 4(3) TEU (with the inclusion of the principle of effectiveness). However, in the end, this position does not lead to significant practical difficulties. The applicability of EU law, as well as its supremacy over ordinary national law, is recognised on the basis of national

65 Kumm (n. 58), p. 366; Maduro (n. 58), p. 505; De Witte (n. 54), p. 356.
66 De Witte (n. 54), p. 355-6.

instruments approving these obligations. In other words, on balance, the same result is achieved, but the source from which the obligations flow is different from the theory of supremacy of EU law discussed above.[67] It was seen in the German and Irish chapter that the operation of EU law, and therefore also the provisions on which the duty of consistent interpretation is based, is controlled by national instruments acting as a conduit.

To what extent are the examples of conflicts of interpretations discussed in the previous subparagraph compatible with this perspective as well? An incompatibility does not arise merely because a conflict of interpretative rules was decided to the benefit of the duty of consistent interpretation if this is merely an example of supremacy over 'ordinary' national law. I do not think that the examples of supremacy deriving from the Dutch case law go beyond this point. It is more difficult to be certain on this with regard to the Irish superior courts' shift in approach, the BGH's case law reflecting the 'negative test approach' as well as the German superior courts prioritisation of the objective to implement the directive in general. As regards the latter, it should be added that there clearly seem to be constitutional tensions when the legislature's implementing objective is used to justify the adoption of a *Rechtsfortbildung*. This technique already permits the courts to go beyond the outer limits of the national provision's text – thus raising sensitive legal-political questions concerning the demarcation of the court's competences *vis-à-vis* the legislature – and on one point of view case law adopting a consistent interpretation in the context of *Rechtsfortbilding* permits that the legislature's clear intentions are even further negated. In any case, if the academic reception to the German superior courts' approach to *Rechtsfortbildung* in the context of the duty of consistent interpretation is compared with the other examples derived from German case law, as well as those from Ireland and the Netherlands, the amount of opposition in relation to the former could be taken as a sign that this approach definitely stirred a more fundamental concern under German law.

So while this model is presumably to an important extent, albeit not entirely, compatible with case law conferring supremacy on the duty of consistent interpretation, it may offer *additional* explanatory value when it comes to case law rejecting a consistent interpretation if this is based on constitutional limitations. After all, national constitutionalism requires that such limits are upheld notwithstanding their incompatibility with EU law. Especially in Germany, but also Ireland and – albeit less prominently – arguably the Netherlands as well, the limits to interpretation can be viewed from the perspective of the relationship between the legislature and the courts and, accordingly, as a matter that is evidently of a constitutional pedigree. However, it would in my opinion not be correct to

67 Ibid, p. 354 who derives the applicability, as well as supremacy, of EU law obligations from the national constitutional clauses regarding limitations on sovereignty.

regard every rejection of a consistent interpretation as support for the theory of national constitutionalism. First, it does not need to come to a conflict with the duty of consistent interpretation if the rejection is based on good reasons and is compatible with the requirement to interpret national law so far as possible. This formulation, and its further interpretation in the ECJ's case law, confers a large measure of discretion on the national courts so that a degree of restraint is required and it would only be appropriate to accuse national courts of a violation of the duty of consistent interpretation if they clearly failed to fulfil their obligations. If this high threshold is not met, a rejection of a consistent interpretation is still a faithful application of that obligation. Most of the national case law rejecting a consistent interpretation – referring to the *contra legem* limitation or otherwise – can be qualified in this way. A further qualification can be found in the fact that, even if national courts *do* transgress the outer limits of the duty of consistent interpretation, most of the time, the argumentation for rejecting a consistent interpretation will not be dictated by the national constitution – which hardly ever prescribes a specific and detailed outcome – or a desire to reassert its superiority over EU law, but is more likely to result from an incorrect understanding of the scope of the duty of consistent interpretation. Finally, if there *is* a genuine constitutional concern, EU law will most of the time not require that a consistent interpretation is adopted notwithstanding the finding that such an interpretation would clearly transgress the constitutionally guaranteed limits of the judicial function (which brings us back to the first qualification!).[68] While it is pointed out that the German superior courts' case law showed two dubious examples where the presumption of the intention to comply was left unapplied, I am hesitant to conclude that these judgments support the theory of national constitutionalism if the above qualifications are taken into account. However, I do believe that the BGH's *Gasversorgung II* judgment and the BFH's judgment of 10 August 2016 can be brought within this category (falling short of the requirement to utilise the scope for *Auslegung* and *Rechtsfortbildung* respectively).

Taking the above into consideration, most judgments rejecting a consistent interpretation are equally compatible with a theory of supremacy of EU law as well as national constitutionalism and cannot, therefore, tip the scale in favour of one of them. However, in addition to the two just referred to BGH and BFH judgments, three further exceptions should be noted. There is in the first place the BVerfG's judgment concerning the question whether a consistent interpretation that would be methodologically possible could nevertheless be rejected on account of the principle of legitimate expectations (an unforeseen retroactive application of the law). This principle is protected under Article 20(3) of the Constitution. On the one hand, the BVerfG made it clear that the rejection of a consistent interpretation on the basis of the principle of legitimate expectations is not only a matter of

68 Consider, for example, BAG 10 December 2013, BAGE 146, 384, paras. 32-4.

national law, and that this requires consideration of the position under EU law. At the same time, however, the BVerfG did not seem to exclude entirely the possibility to apply the national principle of legitimate expectations.[69] If this is taken into account, the judgment could be viewed as an example supporting the theory of national constitutionalism. However, I believe that, compared to the second and third example, the BVerfG's judgment is more ambiguous in this respect. While the BAG's judgment that constituted the subject of the constitutional complaint applied the national principle to the detriment of a consistent interpretation and hence provided support for the theory of national constitutionalism even more clearly, this is not taken into account for the present discussion as this position was annulled by the BVerfG. The principle of legitimate expectations also reoccurs as a limitation to a *Rechtsfortbildung*, although it has never been applied by the German superior courts in that context. Be that as it may, it is clear that it is considered possible to apply this limitation. Secondly, there is the High Court's judgment in *EPA v Neiphin Trading Ltd* providing authority for the position that, even though an implementing objective was identified, the directive's objectives were only taken into account in as far as national law positively confirmed that the Oireachtas had the intention to implement the concerned objective. I argued that the position adopted by the High Court reflects Ireland's dualist approach to supranational law, as it is consistent with such a view to recognise only the national re-enactment – and the intentions expressly articulated therein – of the international norm. Notwithstanding the identified incompatibility, it should also, however, be mentioned that the High Court's more general observations explicitly stated that it did not intend to dispose of the more purposive and teleological approach, which it normally considered to be the appropriate approach in a context of consistent interpretation. Thirdly and finally, there is the Supreme Court's judgment in *Albatros Feeds Ltd v Minister for Agriculture and Food* indicating that there is less scope to interpret national provisions in conformity with the directive in order to create powers whose application would interfere with fundamental rights protected under the Irish Constitution. According to the judgment's reasoning the fundamental rights concern was not the sole reason for rejecting a consistent interpretation and the judgment also put forward grammatical arguments against a consistent interpretation. Nevertheless, it was submitted that the fundamental rights concern was in fact decisive for the rejection of a consistent interpretation and that the protection afforded by the Supreme Court to national fundamental rights was incompatible with EU law.

Leaving the theory of national constitutionalism behind us, I want to briefly address the primacy model. It is appropriate to do so here since chapter 1, subparagraph 1.3.2, showed that, on close inspection, primacy is on some points similar to the theory of national constitutionalism. It is important to emphasise

69 BVerfG 10 December 2014, ZIP 2015, 335, paras. 14, 37 *et seq.*

that this view is based on an understanding of primacy that is to be distinguished from supremacy. This differs somewhat from the dominant use of the term, which applies it as a synonym for supremacy. As far as concerns the applicability of the duty of consistent interpretation in the national legal orders, the primacy model takes a route similar to national constitutionalism.[70] Yet, the primacy model is in my opinion significantly impaired by a conceptual difficulty when it comes to explaining that national rules must yield where they conflict with EU law. According to the primacy model, a condition for this is that the provision of EU law has direct effect.[71] I am not sure to what extent this takes into account that there may also be a conflict between interpretative rules in the context of consistent interpretation – or whether it only recognises the existence of a conflict between two substantive provisions. However, the required link with direct effect either means that application of the duty of consistent interpretation in a conflictive situation operates through the intermediary of direct effect of Articles 288 TFEU and 4(3) TEU,[72] or that, indeed, those EU law provisions are not capable of producing a binding legal norm that may conflict with national rules. Both positions are in my opinion not very attractive and are not to be preferred. Against the background of the degree of explanatory value offered by the other theories, I do not, for this reason, see any added value in endorsing the primacy model.

3.4. CONSTITUTIONAL PLURALISM

The theory of constitutional pluralism became acutely relevant with national constitutional courts' judgments, in particular those of the BVerfG, highlighting the risk of constitutional conflict as a result of incommensurable claims of ultimate authority of EU law and national constitutional law. It is in my opinion therefore evident that the theory can only be meaningfully applied to situations where such a conflict occurs, or where positions are adopted under EU and national law that indicate a *potential* conflict. Constitutional pluralism could be described as the neutral bystander's perspective on a conflict that emerges from the two above discussed theories. Yet, there is not a fit between constitutional pluralism and the judgments discussed under the theory of supremacy of EU law where national courts went beyond their own interpretative limits to adhere to the claims of the duty of consistent interpretation. After all, no conflicting positions remained in these examples. However, the case law discussed under the theory of national constitutionalism mentioned five situations where a rejection of a consistent interpretation was based on arguments that relate to constitutional concerns and

70 M. Avbelj, 'Supremacy or Primacy of EU Law – (Why) Does it Matter?' (2011/6) *ELJ*, p. 754 who, discussing the primacy model, seems to derive the applicability of the duty of consistent interpretation from the Member States' voluntary agreement to obligations arising under EU law.
71 Ibid, p. 751.
72 See also Dougan (n. 61), p. 946.

seemed to be in conflict with the national courts' requirements under the duty of consistent interpretation. It is emphasised that it is not always *certain* that the ECJ and the national courts adopt conflicting positions on the points raised in those judgments as the ECJ was not given the opportunity to declare its position. Nevertheless, as the ECJ's case law currently stands, there is sufficient reason to presume such a conflict. Hence, this line in the case law on the duty of consistent interpretation also fits in with theories on constitutional pluralism.

In the debate on the theory of constitutional pluralism, a school of thought developed that acknowledges the potential for constitutional conflict, but focusses on developing principles to avoid the actual occurrence of such conflict and/or making sure that the conflicting claims do not cause the legal orders to become incoherent and disintegrated. In this regard, Maduro, a prominent representant of this school of thought, highlights the importance of (i) respect for the identity of the other's legal order, (ii) an obligation to reason and justify decisions in the context of a coherent and integrated legal order, and (iii) an obligation to reason and justify decisions in a manner that could be universalisable, for which it must be based on reasoning that could be applied by any other national court. These ideas resonate well with principles underlying the duty of consistent interpretation. There is, in the first place, a kind of 'mutually assured discretion'[73] between EU and national law, more specifically the duty of consistent interpretation and national interpretative rules, which reduces the scope for conflict. At the same time, it must be admitted that this discretion is most of the time not exercised to avert imminent constitutional conflict. Secondly, the Irish judgments that were identified as constituting a conflict were reasoned in terms that evinced a certain commitment to the duty of consistent interpretation, taking into account and discussing the ECJ's case law as well. So while some determinations were found to be incompatible with that case law, there is at the same time a commitment to the EU legal order and an attempt to fit in the national decision with the language familiar from the ECJ's case law. Admittedly, the same cannot be said for some of the BFH's judgments rejecting a consistent interpretation and showing no signs that it was attempted to align this rejection as far as possible with the requirements put forward by EU law. Yet, this can in turn be contrasted with the BVerfG's judgment regarding the principle of legitimate expectations, where it was pointed out that national courts should first participate in a dialogue with the ECJ in order to take its position into account as it was recognised that the matter also affected the normative claims made by the duty of consistent interpretation under EU law. Especially since the ECJ does not seem to wholly exclude the relevance of legitimate expectations in relation to the limits to the duty of consistent interpretation, the positions adopted in German law and

73 For this term see M. Goldmann, 'Constitutional Pluralism as Mutually Assured Discretion: The Court of Justice, the German Federal Constitutional Court, and the ECB' (2016/1) *MJ*, p. 119.

EU law are now less far apart and could be reconciled if the German courts have to deal with claims based on legitimate expectations in future cases.

It can therefore be said that, although there is a fit between these judgments and the model of national constitutionalism, the model of constitutional pluralism offers an additional nuance, which I think makes it an even more attractive perspective for the interpretation of those judgments seeking to reconcile the views held in EU and national law.

3.5. BALANCE

It is recalled that supremacy as a hierarchical model and primacy are impaired by conceptual shortcomings. These theories are therefore abandoned, which means that the theories of supremacy as a conflict resolution rule, national constitutionalism and constitutional pluralism remain. It is also recalled that I conceptualised the duty of consistent interpretation as an interpretative rule prescribing a methodological route that national courts must follow when they examine to what extent national interpretative rules can accommodate an interpretation that complies with the directive. Finally, as the remaining theories all refer to an actual or imminent conflict, only case law satisfying this condition could be decisive for the conclusion which theory is the most adequate.

I discovered three different situations in the national superior courts' case law where such a conflict could be identified and was resolved in favour of a consistent interpretation, thus supporting the theory of supremacy. These situations reflect general trends in the national superior courts' case law and are therefore supported by a larger body of case law. At the same time, the theory of supremacy cannot explain the instances of national courts rejecting a consistent interpretation on grounds with a national constitutional pedigree. Especially since the theory of national constitutionalism recognises the supremacy of EU law in 'ordinary' situations (albeit on the basis of a different source) and only makes an exception to this rule if the operation of EU law presents a threat to fundamental provisions of the constitution, this theory appeared to provide a more adequate theoretical model for understanding the relationship between EU and national law. Yet, it was seen that the judgments where national constitutional considerations were prioritised over consistent interpretation did not wholly repudiate the obligations which the latter imposes and in fact sought to align their reasoning with the EU law framework for the duty of consistent interpretation, or alluded to reconciliatory strategies. I argued that the theory of constitutional pluralism, and in particular the school of thought developed under that theory focusing on conflict avoidance principles, offers an even more appropriate model for understanding these particular judgments. The theory of constitutional pluralism does not fit in, however, with judgments in which the national superior courts yielded to the supremacy of EU law (this also applies, albeit to a lesser extent, to the theory of national constitutionalism).

It can therefore be said that all three theories possess *some* explanatory value. Viewed from the perspective of the ECJ's and Dutch case law, supremacy of EU law is clearly the most adequate theory. For the overall picture, for which the German and Irish case law also come into the equation, the answer is more nuanced. National constitutionalism and constitutional pluralism have the benefit that they pay heed to parts of other theories as well (supremacy of EU law, and supremacy of EU law and national constitutionalism respectively). The reality of the other theory, or theories, is acknowledged but, acting as a kind of matryoshka, an additional layer is added to reflect other realities as well. Constitutional pluralism has a slight advantage over national constitutionalism in this regard. Compared to those two theories, supremacy of EU law is more linear and one-dimensional and contradicts some of the case law from the German and Irish courts. Be that as it may, if one looks at the entire body of case law that was examined, it is observed that judgments supporting the theory of supremacy of EU law are part of a well established approach whereas the judgments that are only explainable on account of national constitutionalism and/or constitutional pluralism are of a more incidental nature. *Without denying the added value of those latter theories*, it would, in my opinion, be incorrect to view them as the centre of gravity when it comes to explaining the relationship between EU and national law. That role is more appropriately conferred upon supremacy of EU law. This conclusion is evidently true in relation to constitutional pluralism, which is first and foremost based on the idea of a persisting actual or imminent constitutional conflict which, fortunately, remains the exception.[74] Therefore, it is not the most adequate theory explaining the relationship between EU and national law under the duty of consistent interpretation. Surely, most of the judgments supporting supremacy of consistent interpretation are probably also reconcilable with national constitutionalism and it cannot be denied that in Germany and Ireland national instruments approving the obligations on which the duty of consistent interpretation is based are ultimately necessary. Yet, on balance, this theory is in my opinion not more adequate than supremacy of EU law. Once EU law has gone through the national conduit permitting its applicability in the national legal order, the case law of the courts in those Member States directly refers to the EU law provisions on which they act and normally recognises the supremacy of the requirement to interpret national law in conformity with directives. This is therefore, also under a theory of national constitutionalism, the main position. Also, I already pointed out that

74 See also, in a more general sense, J. Baquero Cruz, 'Legal Pluralism and Institutional Disobedience in the European Union', in: M. Avbelj and J. Komárek (Eds.), *Constitutional Pluralism in the European Union and Beyond* (Hart Publishing 2012), p. 265; P. Eeckhout, 'Human Rights and the Autonomy of EU Law: Pluralism or Integration?' (2013/1) *Current Legal Problems*, p. 183.

the theory of national constitutionalism is not a *perfect* fit for the judgments in which a consistent interpretation was rejected on grounds related to national constitutional concerns. To be sure, in the final decision concerns related to the national constitution prevailed but there were also signs of an attempt to align the reasoning with the EU law framework for the duty of consistent interpretation, or an allusion to reconciliatory strategies. So while the theory of supremacy of EU law does not provide a satisfactory explanation for every single resolution of a conflict between the duty of consistent interpretation and national interpretative rules, on balance, this theory has the highest explanatory value.

3.6. REFLECTIONS ON THE PERENNIAL QUESTION OF THE RELATIONSHIP BETWEEN EU AND NATIONAL LAW

I concluded that all three theories on the relationship between EU and national law possess some explanatory value as regards the interaction between those two legal spheres in the context of the duty of consistent interpretation. The novelty of this finding is that all of the theories make an appearance in the context of consistent interpretation. The fact that those theories have explanatory value for the relationship between EU and national law is nothing new. This relationship is the subject of an ongoing discussion whose relevance has not abated, even after so many years since the opening gambit in the ECJ's *Costa v ENEL* judgment.[75] The instructions from Luxembourg on the duty of consistent interpretation and the national courts' application of this obligation are only a modest piece in this larger puzzle. Nevertheless, the findings of my examination of the duty of consistent interpretation from the perspective of theories concerning the relationship between EU and national law make it possible to reflect further on the role played by the theories of supremacy of EU law, national constitutionalism and constitutional pluralism for the application of EU law.

First, the examination in the current research provides the important reminder that one should not mistake the forest for the trees. It was seen that German and Irish case law provided examples where the actors holding ultimate authority to interpret the national constitution challenged the supremacy of EU law. However, I also argued that this remains the exception and that the examples providing support for the theory of supremacy of EU law are more extensive and well-established. I think it can be presumed that this is not fundamentally different outside the context of consistent interpretation. The obligation to review national legislation for its compatibility with EU law and to set aside conflicting national provisions has by and large been accepted by the national courts, and challenges to EU law

75 Case 6/64 *Costa v ENEL*, ECLI:EU:C:1964:66.

are of a more incidental nature.[76] The former is sometimes overshadowed by the latter since they usually raise a less fundamental issue (or, more specifically: the issue is no longer considered to be fundamental, yet it should not be forgotten that for some national courts acceptance of their EU law mandate required a serious genuflection to the exigencies of EU law) but this does not change the important role played by supremacy of EU law for the day-to-day application of EU law. By the way, it is noted that the amount of attention which such opposing national court judgments receive indicates that it is generally accepted that the norm is that EU law takes priority.

Secondly, notwithstanding the relatively few occurrences of actual conflict between EU and national law, the existing theories of course provide conflicting visions on the source from which EU law derives its validity in the national legal orders, how a conflict between EU and national (constitutional) law is to be resolved, and who holds ultimate authority for deciding this. In the context of the duty of consistent interpretation, this was exemplified by the discussion what constitutes the legal basis for the duty of consistent interpretation and the BAG's judgment of 23 March 2006 and the BVerfG's subsequent judgment in a similar case. In as far as these different theories on the relationship between EU and national law do not lead to an actual conflict, they exist alongside each other and offer a useful and rational explanation for the incompatible positions held by the ECJ and the national court but also for the divergences in the approach to EU law by courts from different Member States (reflecting their adherence to different theories). From this perspective the question is not so much which theory is the most adequate, but they rather complement each other. The BVerfG's *Lisbon* judgment and its predecessors provide excellent examples how a court can expound on a theory such as national constitutionalism and/or constitutional pluralism, further defining its attitude towards EU law, without there being a direct conflict. The analysis of the duty of consistent interpretation showed that the theory of constitutional pluralism is particularly of added value in as far as it offers a school of thought that is focussed on recognising the importance of, and providing the theoretical building blocks for, conflict avoidance. Unfortunately, there have also been examples where the national court's considerations concerning the relationship between EU and national law were of less didactical value and where there was at the same time a direct confrontation.[77] When such a conflict arises supremacy of EU law and national constitutionalism describe the respective positions of the ECJ and the national court whereas constitutional pluralism could be described as the neutral bystander's perspective on the conflict – which confers a degree of legitimacy on

76 Claes (n. 57), p. 149.
77 ÚS 31 January 2012, Pl. ÚS 5/12 (*Landtová*); Højesteret 6 December 2016, *Sag 15/2014* (*Ajos*), I refer here to the judgment's considerations concerning the application of EU law on the basis of the general principle of EU law prohibiting discrimination on grounds of age.

both theories but also dismisses their claims of absolute superiority. In that sense the former two theories are of a different nature than the latter.

Thirdly, the theory of direct effect and supremacy of EU law are often coupled.[78] This makes sense if the conflict rule model is applied since supremacy must then make an appearance each time that EU law is directly relied upon.[79] Weiler puts forward that the two concepts are analytically tightly connected '(...) by the Court's vision of the exigencies of a cohesive and integral legal order and its insistence on the principle of uniform interpretation and application of Community law (...)'.[80] This understanding of supremacy, whereby it is linked with direct effect, has led to it being understood as requiring absolute uniformity all of the time. Perhaps the view on the effect of supremacy in the context of consistent interpretation mentioned in subparagraph 3.2.2, whereby national interpretative rules must be set aside in as far as they are incompatible with the interpretation prescribed by EU law, is also influenced by this dominant perspective on supremacy. The current research shows that supremacy of EU law has a broader meaning: it is also applicable in the context of consistent interpretation where it confers priority on Articles 288 TFEU and 4(3) TEU (with the inclusion of the principle of effectiveness) to resolve a conflict of interpretative rules to the benefit of the duty of consistent interpretation. The effect of supremacy is then much more nuanced. On the one hand, it does not force the national court to reach a particular interpretation regardless of the scope that is available under national law to do so but it requires the court to take into account certain methodological obligations which facilitate a consistent interpretation of national law. On the other hand, courts can, within certain limits, provide different answers to the question just how far the duty of consistent interpretation requires them to go, which reflects and respects the different interpretative contexts in which they operate. There is, in other words, not a requirement of strict uniformity. Moving away from the specific relationship between direct effect and supremacy, I think that, in a more general way, it can be said that this research showed that, in addition to supremacy of EU law, also the use of the theories of national constitutionalism and constitutional pluralism is not restricted to a context wherein EU law enters the stage by means of direct effect.

Notwithstanding the added value of an enriched understanding of supremacy of EU law and the finding that it has a meaning that is more encompassing than the function which it carries out in relation to direct effect, I believe that the traditional understanding of supremacy will continue to occupy a more prominent position (albeit not an exclusive position). The situations in which national courts apply supremacy of EU law to set aside a specific, substantive rule of EU law (for example

78 See, for example, De Witte (n. 54), p. 323.
79 Prechal (n. 55), p. 53.
80 Weiler (n. 62), p. 276.

a provision of a directive) are far more common than national courts setting aside a conflicting national interpretative rule that conflicts with the duty of consistent interpretation. If the remedy of direct effect is applied there is no question that there is a conflict between EU and national law and this logically leads to the question which norm must yield. From the perspective of EU law, it is then self-evident that EU law must be given supremacy. However, as will be further discussed in the next paragraph, in the context of the duty of consistent interpretation it is not only intended to avoid a conflict between the substantive provision of the directive and the norm of national law, but even with regard to the preceding phase in which it is asked whether a consistent interpretation can be adopted, a conflict of interpretative rules can most of the time be prevented through the mutually assured discretion between the duty of consistent interpretation and national interpretative rules.

4. ADAPTATIONS AND THE DAY-TO-DAY APPLICATION OF THE DUTY OF CONSISTENT INTERPRETATION

The finding that, on balance, and notwithstanding the added value of the other theories, supremacy of EU law has the highest explanatory value, requires a qualification of its own. The above reached conclusion in subparagraph 3.5 is certainly correct as far as concerns the question how *conflicts* between the duty of consistent interpretation and national interpretative rules are resolved. However, this raises the question to what extent the presence of such a conflict is representative for the overall picture with regard to the national courts' application of the duty of consistent interpretation. As I mentioned at the beginning of paragraph 3, the key was to find the right angle to sort out the seemingly incongruous facts resulting from diverse applications of the duty of consistent interpretation. To be sure, a careful analysis of the relationship between EU and national law in the context of the duty of consistent interpretation, forcing me to determine the precise impact of the duty of consistent interpretation on the national interpretative process, procured further insight into how things work. Yet, I have to admit that it also had the side effect that I found out that, actually, most of the time, an application of the duty of consistent interpretation does not lead to such a conflict. This is self-evident when the adopted consistent interpretation turns out to be identical to, or merely confirms, the interpretation that follows from a traditional approach to interpretation. The same holds true if the national provision is open to more than one interpretation and the duty of consistent interpretation is applied as a means of choice. The analysis has paid little attention to such cases since the lines along which these cases are decided are quite predictable and this area of the case law does not raise significant questions. Moreover, the impact of the duty of consistent interpretation is only marginal. The same cannot be said, however, for a large number of judgments where the duty of consistent interpretation had the effect of forcing an adaptation of the traditional interpretation, or where the court took a slightly different approach to interpretation than usual. Importantly, also in this respect, most of the time, the adaptation did not go so far that it can be said that a conflict arose. From the point of view of scale, such adaptations that fall short of a genuine conflict are more representative of the national courts' case law regarding consistent interpretation.

Since the existing theories on the relationship between EU and national law cannot explain the above mentioned adaptations (as they relate directly, or more indirectly, to situations of conflict), how must this be viewed? It is submitted that there is then an 'ordinary' application of the duty of consistent interpretation. The crux of the matter, as well as the obligation's success in reconciling a looming conflict between the directive and national law, is to be found in the latitude available under national interpretative rules, the responsiveness of certain interpretative methods to changing circumstances and, more generally, the national courts' willingness to look further than a traditional interpretation and search for routes to adopt one that is consistent with the directive. It is no coincidence that the most serious clashes as a result of national interpretative rules *not* being able to accommodate the requirements of the duty of consistent interpretation all concerned rules that are of a more determinate and absolute nature: fundamental rights and instructions based on the Irish Interpretation Act 2005. There is then less scope for the national court to manoeuvre.

As was already pointed out, discretion is not only to be found in the national interpretative rules but also in the duty of consistent interpretation. And as I noted in the Dutch chapter, mutual flexibility leads to a smooth application of the duty of consistent interpretation. Within certain limits, multiple approaches can exist alongside each other, without one necessarily being a better or worse rendition of what the obligation requires. At the same time, the required flexibility and resultant diversity may come at the expense of predictability of judicial decisions (as the example of three people walking into a bar showed). I believe that this uncertainty can be diminished if legal scholarship keeps track of the ECJ's case law, but in particular the attitudes of national courts with regard to their obligation to coordinate the duty of consistent interpretation and national interpretative rules. As is apparent from the analyses in this book, this is not a static doctrine but a dynamic process, and it is therefore necessary to remain attentive to changes in attitude. But it is also pointed out that a degree of uncertainty is something inherent to legal interpretation, whether one looks at adjudication in an EU law context or otherwise. The identification of outer interpretative limits helps reducing this uncertainty and it is therefore of particular importance to know under which circumstances they remain a reliable bulwark. Should judges, lawyers and citizens be confronted with new questions resulting from the duty of consistent interpretation that challenge the durability of these bulwarks of the national interpretative rules, the answer to the question which theory on the relationship between EU and national law is the most adequate one facilitates answering such fundamental questions.

SAMENVATTING

1. INLEIDING

Op 6 december 1984 schorste het Duitse arbeidsgerecht (*Arbeitsgericht*) in Hamm de behandeling van de voor hem aanhangige procedure en besloot prejudiciële vragen voor te leggen aan het Europees Hof van Justitie (HvJ). Er bestond voor de verwijzende rechter geen twijfel over de vraag of verzoeksters, twee vrouwelijke sollicitanten, slachtoffer waren geworden van discriminatie op grond van het geslacht. Echter, in de onderhavige zaak bood het Duitse recht enkel de mogelijkheid een vergoeding van zogenaamde vertrouwensschade toe te kennen (de schade ontstaan doordat erop werd vertrouwd dat de totstandkoming van de arbeidsverhouding niet zou worden gehinderd door een discriminatoire behandeling). De verwijzende rechter vroeg of een sanctie van dien aard conform de gelijke behandelingsrichtlijn was. Dat bleek niet het geval te zijn, maar die onverenigbaarheid kon niet via rechtstreekse werking worden verholpen omdat niet aan de voorwaarden voor toepassing daarvan was voldaan. Het HvJ introduceerde echter een nieuwe verplichting voor de nationale rechters: de verplichting om het nationale recht zoveel mogelijk conform de EU-richtlijn uit te leggen. In zijn einduitspraak passeert de Duitse rechter de argumenten op basis van een wetshistorische en systematische interpretatie van de nationale bepaling ten gunste van de richtlijnconforme interpretatie.

Hoe zag het Duitse arbeidsgerecht de relatie tussen de verplichting tot richtlijnconforme interpretatie en nationale rechtsvindingsregels? Die vraag geeft aanleiding tot de vervolgvraag of er überhaupt een regel voorhanden is die de aanspraken van eerstgenoemde en laatstgenoemde coördineert. Het is dan logisch te kijken naar de drie gevestigde theorieën over de relatie tussen Unierecht en nationaal recht: voorrang van Unierecht, nationaal constitutionalisme en constitutioneel pluralisme. En indien is onderzocht in hoeverre deze theorieën een adequate verklaring bieden voor de wijze waarop het HvJ en nationale rechters richtlijnconforme interpretatie benaderen, dan biedt dit ook direct inzichten met betrekking tot de vraag wat de toepasbaarheid is van de drie theorieën buiten de context waarin zij al langer bekend zijn binnen het juridische debat, oftewel de context van rechtstreekse werking. De centrale vraag in dit proefschrift is:

> In hoeverre bieden de theorieën van voorrang van Unierecht, nationaal constitutionalisme of constitutioneel pluralisme een adequate verklaring voor de relatie tussen Unierecht en nationaal recht in het kader van de verplichting tot richtlijnconforme interpretatie, rekening houdende met, allereerst, de verplichtingen die het Unierecht in dit verband oplegt aan de nationale rechters en, ten tweede, de toepassing van deze verplichting door hoogste rechterlijke instanties in Duitsland, Ierland en Nederland?

Een belangrijk onderdeel van het theoretisch kader voor dit onderzoek zijn de theorieën van voorrang van Unierecht, nationaal constitutionalisme en constitutioneel pluralisme. Eerstgenoemde brengt met zich mee de verplichting om een conflict tussen Unierecht en nationaal recht te beslechten in het voordeel van de Unierechtelijke bepaling, ofwel door middel van rechtstreekse werking, ofwel door middel van conforme interpretatie. Deze definitie presenteert voorrang als (enkel) een conflictregel. Het hiërarchische model gaat verder en neemt tot uitgangspunt dat het Unierecht is geïntegreerd in de nationale rechtsordes, welke samen een eenheid vormen waarbinnen al het Unierecht voorrang heeft ten opzichte van het hiërarchisch ondergeschikte nationale recht. Nationaal constitutionalisme verschilt van voorrang van Unierecht wat betreft de basis voor de voorrang van het Unierecht op nationaal recht dat geen constitutionele rang inneemt – die basis berust op de nationale constitutie – en in zijn afwijzing van voorrang van Unierecht op nationaal constitutioneel recht. De theorie van het constitutioneel pluralisme, tot slot, is voortgekomen uit, en beoogt een oplossing te bieden voor, de omstandigheid dat de twee voorgaande theorieën beide het laatste woord claimen bij een conflict tussen Unierecht en nationaal constitutioneel recht en zij slechts op basis van de logica van de eigen rechtsorde volledige gelding kunnen hebben. De belangrijkste uitgangspunten van deze derde theorie zijn, allereerst, dat twee of meer autonome en gelijkwaardige constitutionele rechtsordes naast elkaar bestaan, zodat geen van beide absolute en onvoorwaardelijke superioriteit kan claimen en, ten tweede, dat op enigerlei wijze de overlappende rechtsordes concessies zullen moeten doen. De drie theorieën gaan allen uit van de situatie dat er een normconflict (of in het geval van constitutioneel pluralisme wellicht ook een potentieel conflict) is tussen Unierecht en nationaal recht. Het dient onderzocht te worden in hoeverre zich dit laat vertalen naar de context van richtlijnconforme interpretatie.

2. DE CONSTRUCTIE VAN EEN KADER VOOR RICHTLIJNCONFORME INTERPRETATIE DOOR HET HVJ

2.1. *De rechtsbasis voor richtlijnconforme interpretatie*

Het HvJ verwijst vanaf de introductie van de verplichting tot richtlijnconforme interpretatie naar artikelen 288 Verdrag betreffende de werking van de Europese Unie (VWEU) en 4(3) Verdrag betreffende de Europese Unie (VEU) voor de rechtsbasis van de verplichting. Daar is later, vanaf het arrest *Pfeiffer*, de volle werking van het Unierecht als grondslag aan toegevoegd. De heersende opvatting is dat richtlijnconforme interpretatie dient te worden gezien als onderdeel van de verplichting voor lidstaten om de richtlijn in het nationale recht te implementeren. In dat verband treedt vooral artikel 288 VWEU op de voorgrond. Echter, een eventuele inmenging ten opzichte van nationale rechtsvindingsregels kan beter worden gelegitimeerd op basis van artikel 4(3) VEU, welke bepaling ook aan de basis stond voor de verklaring in het arrest *Costa t. ENEL* dat Unierecht voorrang heeft op nationaal recht. De volle werking van het Unierecht en artikel 4(3) VEU hangen nauw samen en overlappen elkaar deels. Daarnaast kan in de toevoeging van eerstgenoemde het schragen van de rechtsbasis voor conforme interpretatie worden gezien en was zij nodig om destijds de verplichting tot conforme interpretatie van toepassing te doen zijn voor kaderbesluiten aangenomen onder de voormalige 'derde pijler' van de Verdragen. Een benadering van voorrang volgens het hiërarchische model baseert conforme interpretatie rechtstreeks op de hogere rang van richtlijnen, welke rang dan logischerwijze betekent dat het ondergeschikte nationale recht conform de hogere regel dient te worden uitgelegd. Het HvJ heeft echter nooit uitgesproken dat richtlijnen in algemene zin – dus afgezien van bijvoorbeeld de situatie waarin aan richtlijnbepalingen rechtstreekse werking wordt verleend – voorrang genieten. De rechtsbasis die het hiërarchische model voorstaat vindt dus geen steun in de bestaande jurisprudentie.

2.2. *Welke inspanning vergt 'zoveel mogelijk' richtlijnconform interpreteren?*

Door sommige auteurs is wel betoogd dat absolute voorrang zou moeten worden toegekend aan het argument dat een bepaalde uitleg van nationaal recht conform de richtlijn is en iedere onverenigbare nationale regel daarvoor dient te wijken. Dit lijkt echter niet te sporen met de fundamentele rol die in de jurisprudentie van het HvJ wordt toebedeeld aan nationale rechters en nationale rechtsvindingsregels. Het standpunt dat de werking van de verplichting tot richtlijnconforme interpretatie volledig wordt beheerst door nationale rechtsvindingsregels dient echter ook te worden verworpen. Er is brede consensus dat de verplichting tot richtlijnconforme interpretatie grenzen kan stellen aan de toepassing van nationale rechtsvindingsregels. De verplichtingen die richtlijnconforme interpretatie met zich meebrengt zijn nader uitgewerkt in de jurisprudentie van het HvJ. De daaruit voortvloeiende kaders begrenzen de autonomie waarover nationale rechters beschikken wanneer zij de verplichting tot richtlijnconforme interpretatie ten uitvoer brengen. Brenncke spreekt in dit verband van '*bounded internal European legal pluralism*'.

Allereerst is wat betreft het voorwerp van conforme interpretatie geoordeeld dat het gehele nationale recht in beschouwing dient te worden genomen bij de beoordeling of conforme interpretatie mogelijk is. Zulks volgt mijns inziens niet uit de voorrang van richtlijnen tegenover al het nationale recht, maar uit het feit dat de werking van artikelen 288 VWEU en 4(3) VEU qua werking niet beperkt zijn tot omzettingsrecht.

Ten tweede heeft het HvJ een aantal nadere methodologische instructies geformuleerd. Zo formuleerde het HvJ een interpretatieve voorrangregel ten gunste van een richtlijnconforme interpretatie (indien de nationale bepaling meer dan één interpretatie toelaat, waarvan er tenminste één conform de richtlijn is, dient die interpretatie te worden gevolgd). Ook overwoog het HvJ dat bij de uitleg van omzettingsrecht de rechter ervan uit dient te gaan dat de wetgever de bedoeling heeft gehad ten volle uitvoering te geven aan de richtlijn. Deze twee instructies wijzen erop dat het HvJ richtlijnconforme interpretatie ziet als een verplichting die onder bepaalde omstandigheden voorrang boven nationale rechtsvindingsregels geniet. Hoewel de jurisprudentie van het HvJ wellicht soms de indruk zou kunnen wekken dat een verdergaande verplichting tot richtlijnconforme interpretatie van toepassing is waar het omzettingsrecht betreft, wordt hier naar mijn mening slechts een prognose uitgesproken ten aanzien van het mogelijke resultaat. Dit is dus geen voorbeeld van voorrang van Unierecht, hetgeen evenmin het geval is voor de aanwijzing dat interpretatiemogelijkheden die beschikbaar zijn naar nationaal recht steeds dienen te worden aangewend bij het onderzoek naar de mogelijkheid tot richtlijnconforme interpretatie.

Ten derde rijst de vraag of het HvJ in bepaalde gevallen het te bereiken uitlegresultaat dwingend voorschrijft. Naar mijn mening is dat in beginsel niet het geval en wordt de nationale rechter slechts gewezen op het te bereiken uitlegresultaat, gekoppeld aan een prognose. Een stap verder is de benadering zoals in het arrest *Dominguez* waarbij de conclusie van de nationale rechter dat geen richtlijnconforme interpretatie mogelijk is niet zonder meer wordt aanvaard. Ook het arrest *Spedition Welter*, betreffende de interpretatie van nationaal recht dat letterlijk de bewoordingen van de richtlijn overnam, bevat elementen van voorrang van Unierecht voor zover grammaticale argumenten tegen een richtlijnconforme interpretatie worden geëcarteerd.

Op basis van de analyse van de jurisprudentie van het HvJ kan worden geconcludeerd dat de verplichting tot richtlijnconforme interpretatie een interpretatieve norm is die voorrang geniet boven nationale regels voor zover zij onverenigbaar zijn met de positieve instructies die door het HvJ werden geformuleerd.

2.3. *Grenzen richtlijnconforme interpretatie*

De verplichting tot richtlijnconforme interpretatie wordt begrensd door EU-rechtsbeginselen. Op basis van het rechtszekerheidsbeginsel en het verbod van terugwerkende kracht, en meer in het bijzonder het strafrechtelijk legaliteitsbeginsel (*nullum crimen, nulla poena sine lege*), werd in het arrest *Kolpinghuis* geoordeeld dat richtlijnconforme interpretatie niet bepalend kan zijn voor het vestigen of verzwaren van strafrechtelijke aansprakelijkheid. Het dient te worden benadrukt dat, afgezien van strafrechtelijke aansprakelijkheid, er geen verbod is om via richtlijnconforme interpretatie verplichtingen aan particulieren op te leggen. Wel wordt op basis van het rechtszekerheidsbeginsel een belangrijke begrenzing gevonden in het verbod om nationaal recht *contra legem* uit te leggen. De *contra legem*-grens ziet vooral op interpretatiemoeilijkheden die verband houden met de bewoordingen van de nationale bepaling, maar zij is ook toegepast op een nationale ongeschreven interpretatieregel en het beginsel van *res judicata*. In het arrest *Ajos* oordeelt het HvJ dat het niet is toegestaan enkel op basis van vaste nationale rechtspraak een bepaalde uitleg als *contra legem* te bestempelen. Hier ziet men, net als in het arrest *Dominguez*, de kritische houding terug van het HvJ ten aanzien van het standpunt van de verwijzende rechter dat conforme interpretatie niet mogelijk zou zijn. In het arrest *Klohn* werden het Unierechtelijke vertrouwensbeginsel en het beginsel van *res judicata* als grenzen op richtlijnconforme interpretatie erkend. Hoewel het HvJ zich hierover nog niet heeft uitgelaten, werd door mij betoogd dat fundamentele rechten – als EU-rechtsbeginselen of rechten beschermd door het EU-Handvest (hierna: Handvest) – een grens kunnen opleveren voor de verplichting tot richtlijnconforme interpretatie. Dit is al aan de orde voor de begrenzing van vestiging of verzwaring van strafrechtelijke aansprakelijkheid op basis van het strafrechtelijk legaliteitsbeginsel (zie inmiddels tevens artikel 49(1) van het Handvest). Maar ook fundamentele rechten die niet in dezelfde mate raken aan interpretatievraagstukken zouden op een meer indirecte wijze relevant kunnen zijn. Indien een richtlijnconforme interpretatie bijvoorbeeld het recht op eigendom inperkt verlangt artikel 52(1) Handvest dat die beperking bij wet is gesteld, hetgeen onder meer vereist dat de beperking duidelijk en toegankelijk, en voldoende voorzienbaar is. Onder verwijzing naar het arrest *Melloni* kan worden gesteld dat het in beginsel de Unierechtelijke variant van een fundamenteel recht dient te zijn waarop een beroep wordt gedaan als begrenzing van richtlijnconforme interpretatie. Benadrukt dient te worden dat de genoemde grenzen op de verplichting tot richtlijnconforme interpretatie voortvloeien uit het Unierecht zelf en de ruimte die nationale rechters hebben om een richtlijnconforme interpretatie af te wijzen wordt gecontroleerd door het Unierecht. De geïdentificeerde grenzen zijn dan ook niet onverenigbaar met de theorie van voorrang van Unierecht.

3. HET PERSPECTIEF VAN DE DUITSE RECHTER

3.1. *De rechtsbasis voor richtlijnconforme interpretatie*

Ofschoon door Duitse rechters aanvankelijk verschillend werd gedacht over wat de rechtsbasis vormt voor de verplichting tot richtlijnconforme interpretatie, is dit naar elkaar toegegroeid en wordt nu in de regel verwezen naar de artikelen 288 VWEU, en/of 4(3) VEU, en/of de volle werking van het Unierecht. De geïdentificeerde rechtsbasis ondersteunt een visie op de relatie tussen Unierecht en nationaal recht die wordt beheerst door voorrang van Unierecht. Dit vergt een kanttekening: het federale hof voor fiscale zaken (*Bundesfinanzhof*) beroept zich nog vaak op de omzettingswil van de wetgever.

Duitsland kent een dualistische benadering van het internationale recht. Dit betekent dat de Unierechtelijke bepalingen die de rechtsbasis voor richtlijnconforme interpretatie vormen onderdeel werden van het Duitse recht via de Duitse wet tot goedkeuring van het Verdrag van Lissabon.

3.2. *Ruimte voor, en grenzen van, richtlijnconforme interpretatie*

Een interpretatief conflict doet zich voor indien sprake is van een onverenigbaarheid met de verplichting tot richtlijnconforme interpretatie of nationale rechtsvindingsregels. Om een onverenigbaarheid met laatstgenoemde vast te stellen is een preciezer begrip vereist van de rechtsvindingsregels in Duitsland. Die regels worden beheerst door artikel 20(3) ('*die Rechtsprechung sind an Gesetz und Recht gebunden*') en artikel 97(1) ('[d]*ie Richter sind unabhängig und nur dem Gesetze unterworfen*') van de Grondwet. Belangrijkste doel is het achterhalen van de wil van de wetgever, zoals die tot uitdrukking komt in de bewoordingen en de context van de te interpreteren bepaling. Hiertoe hanteert de Duitse rechter het grammaticale, wetshistorische, systematische en teleologische uitlegcriterium. De rechter beschikt over veel vrijheid bij de rechtsvinding en de constitutionele bepalingen stellen slechts buitengrenzen. De Duitse rechtsvindingsleer en de rechtspraak onderscheiden *Auslegung* (wetsinterpretatie) en *Rechtsfortbildung* (rechtsvorming). Laatstgenoemde vereist dat een *Regelungslücke* wordt vastgesteld (een leemte in de wet in weerwil van de bedoelingen van de wetgever) en is daarnaast onderworpen aan een aantal specifieke grenzen.

De Duitse jurisprudentie bevat twee voorbeelden van voorrang van richtlijnconforme interpretatie. Allereerst is er jurisprudentie waarin niet wordt onderzocht welke uitleg het beste aansluit bij de aanwijzingen die voortvloeien uit de nationale uitlegcriteria, maar in plaats daarvan de richtlijn tot uitgangspunt wordt genomen en de vraag wordt gesteld of nationale uitlegregels zich niet verzetten tegen het richtlijnconforme uitlegresultaat. Die benadering geeft blijk van de overtuiging dat richtlijnconforme interpretatie, welke verplichting zijn basis vindt in de artikelen 288 VWEU en 4(3) VEU, een superieure positie inneemt ten opzichte van (bepaalde) nationale rechtsvindingsregels, vergelijkbaar met de positie onder de figuur van grondwetconforme interpretatie (*verfassungskonforme Auslegung*) gebaseerd op de superieure positie van de grondwet in de Duitse rechtsorde. Ten tweede is er jurisprudentie die laat zien dat systematisch voorrang wordt verleend aan de bedoeling van de wetgever om de richtlijn om te zetten boven andere, daarmee onverenigbare, doelstellingen. Een dergelijke systematische voorrang wijkt af van de structuur van Duitse rechtsvindingsregels (het gewicht dat aan een bepaald argument toekomt ligt niet vast en hangt af van de omstandigheden van het geval). Laatstgenoemde techniek wordt ook veelvuldig ingezet om de inzet van een richtlijnconforme *Rechtsfortbildung* te rechtvaardigen (zie de uitspraak in *Quelle* van de hoogste federale rechter in burgerlijke en strafzaken (*Bundesgerichtshof*)).

Uiteraard is er ook jurisprudentie waarin een richtlijnconforme interpretatie wordt afgewezen. Dergelijke afwijzingen vallen qua aanleiding uiteen in twee categorieën: grenzen van de rechterlijke functie (en dan met name vanwege grenzen die voortvloeien uit een grammaticale interpretatie en een afwijkende bedoeling van de wetgever) en (de qua omvang beperktere categorie) bescherming van fundamentele rechten. Zo'n afwijzing betekent niet zonder meer dat de verplichting tot richtlijnconforme interpretatie wordt geschonden. Het HvJ heeft immers erkend dat die verplichting niet onbegrensd is. De meeste uitspraken waarin een conforme interpretatie wordt afgewezen kunnen op die wijze worden verklaard. Echter, in twee onderzochte uitspraken was het twijfelachtig of de benadering verenigbaar was met de aanwijzing dat bij de uitleg van omzettingsrecht de rechter ervan uit dient te gaan dat de wetgever de bedoeling heeft gehad ten volle uitvoering te geven aan de richtlijn. Echter, er waren zwaarwegende argumenten tegen een richtlijnconforme interpretatie en ik aarzel om in de uitspraken een voorbeeld van nationaal constitutionalisme te zien. Daarnaast zijn er twee uitspraken waarin de rechter niet volledig de naar nationaal recht beschikbare ruimte benutte om via een *Auslegung* of *Rechtsfortbildung* een richtlijnconform uitlegresultaat te bereiken – en, aldus, het nationale recht niet zoveel mogelijk richtlijnconform interpreteerde. Deze uitspraken kunnen worden gezien als voorbeelden die de theorie van nationaal constitutionalisme steunen, maar in één geval waren er ook aanwijzingen in de richting van de theorie van constitutioneel pluralisme (hoewel de uitvoering naar mijn oordeel tekortschoot, werd in één van de uitspraken getracht voor de afwijzing van een conforme interpretatie aan te knopen bij de criteria ontwikkeld in de jurisprudentie van het HvJ). Tot slot is er belangwekkende jurisprudentie op het gebied van het vertrouwensbeginsel. Het federale hof voor arbeidsrechtszaken (*Bundesarbeitsgericht*, hierna BAG) oordeelde dat, ofschoon een conforme interpretatie interpretatief mogelijk was, het nationale vertrouwensbeginsel zich hiertegen verzette. Die benadering onderschreef duidelijk de theorie van nationaal constitutionalisme. Een gelijkluidende beslissing werd vernietigd door het Federaal Constitutioneel Hof (*Bundesverfassungsgericht*, hierna: BVerfG) waarin het benadrukte dat de afwijzing van een conforme interpretatie niet enkel een kwestie van nationaal recht is, maar ook onderhevig is aan het Unierecht en het BAG de zaak dus prejudicieel had moeten verwijzen. De overwegingen van het BVerfG sluiten evenwel niet zonder meer uit dat het nationale vertrouwensbeginsel wordt toegepast (terwijl daarvoor naar mijn oordeel geen ruimte zou zijn op basis van het Unierecht). In deze benadering herkent men het constitutioneel pluralisme. De grens van het nationale vertrouwensbeginsel komt ook terug in het kader van de grenzen van *Rechtsfortbildung* – hoewel de grens in die context tot nu toe nog niet werd toegepast.

Zoals gezegd bieden de Duitse rechtsvindingsregels van zichzelf al de nodige manoeuvreerruimte voor de rechter, hetgeen het eenvoudiger maakt nationaal recht richtlijnconform te interpreteren. Desalniettemin zoekt de Duitse rechter de grenzen regelmatig op en zijn er voorbeelden waarin dit aanleiding gaf tot een conflict dat in het voordeel van richtlijnconforme interpretatie werd beslecht. Ondanks incidentele afwijkingen van de verplichting tot richtlijnconforme interpretatie ligt, voor wat betreft het antwoord op de geïdentificeerde conflicten, het zwaartepunt dus bij voorrang van het Unierecht.

4. HET PERSPECTIEF VAN DE IERSE RECHTER

4.1. De rechtsbasis voor richtlijnconforme interpretatie

De Ierse rechter verwijst voor de rechtsbasis voor conforme interpretatie naar artikelen 288 VWEU en 4(3) VEU. Voor zover de te interpreteren regelgeving een omzettingsdoel heeft volgt bovendien uit een toepassing van het teleologische interpretatiecriterium dat dient te worden gezocht naar een uitleg die in overeenstemming is met de richtlijn, zonder dat dit een noodzakelijke voorwaarde is om richtlijnconform te interpreteren. De geïdentificeerde rechtsbasis ondersteunt een visie op de relatie tussen Unierecht en nationaal recht die wordt beheerst door voorrang van Unierecht.

Ierland kent een dualistische benadering van het internationale recht. Dit betekent dat de Unierechtelijke bepalingen die de rechtsbasis voor richtlijnconforme interpretatie vormen onderdeel werden van het Ierse recht via artikel 2 van de European Communities Act 1972.

4.2. Ruimte voor, en grenzen van, richtlijnconforme interpretatie

Een interpretatief conflict doet zich voor indien sprake is van een onverenigbaarheid met de verplichting tot richtlijnconforme interpretatie of nationale rechtsvindingsregels. Om een onverenigbaarheid met laatstgenoemde vast te stellen is een preciezer begrip vereist van de rechtsvindingsregels in Ierland. Voor de Ierse rechter is het belangrijkste doel van interpretatie het vaststellen van de bedoeling van de wetgever. Hij dient ervoor te waken dat de bevoegdheden van de wetgever worden doorkruist. Dit is een grens van constitutionele aard.

Een beschrijving van de Ierse interpretatiebenadering vereist een bespreking van de interpretatieregels op basis van het gemene recht (*common law*). Die regels voorzien in een pragmatische, enigszins flexibele (in die zin dat de regels openstaan voor een nadere uitwerking) benadering, maar worden tevens gekenmerkt door legisme en formalisme. Rechters dienen in beginsel een letterlijke interpretatie van de relevante bepaling te volgen. De flexibiliteit van de regels onder het gemene recht uitte zich onder andere in de rechterlijke beoordelingsruimte wanneer een (gematigde) doelmatige interpretatie was toegestaan. De letterlijke benadering is dominant gebleven met de invoering van de Interpretation Act 2005 waarmee een aantal regels omtrent de te volgen interpretatiebenadering werd voorgeschreven. Die wet streeft een gematigde doelmatige wetsinterpretatie na maar legt wel vast wanneer het rechters is toegestaan rekening te houden met dit uitlegcriterium.

De uitspraak van de rechter in eerste aanleg (*High Court*) in *Murphy v An Bord Telecom Éireann* biedt een treffend voorbeeld van de verschuiving in de interpretatiebenadering onder het gemene recht als gevolg van de vereisten van richtlijnconforme interpretatie, in die zin dat doelmatige interpretatie een prominentere rol opeiste ten koste van een letterlijke uitleg. Die verschuiving heeft lange tijd de Ierse benadering van conforme interpretatie gekenmerkt en werd mogelijk gemaakt door de flexibiliteit van het gemene recht om zich aan te passen aan nieuwe ontwikkelingen. Zij is een voorbeeld van voorrang van richtlijnconforme interpretatie. De genoemde verschuiving werd opgevolgd door een periode volgend op de introductie van de Interpretation Act 2005 waarin er minder uitspraken vielen te bespeuren die deze welwillende benadering volgden en een tendens waarneembaar was richting een terughoudender toepassing van conforme interpretatie. Twee uitspraken zijn naar mijn mening onverenigbaar met de Unierechtelijke verplichtingen die op de Ierse rechter rusten en tonen gelijkenissen met de theorie van nationaal constitutionalisme. Zo stelde het Ierse Hooggerechtshof (*Supreme Court*) naar mijn oordeel verdergaande eisen aan een beperking van het door de Ierse grondwet beschermde recht op eigendom dan het Unierecht toestaat, hetgeen in die zaak van doorslaggevend belang was voor de afwijzing van een richtlijnconforme interpretatie. En in *EPA v Neiphin Trading Ltd* koos de rechter in eerste aanleg – onder invloed van het Ierse dualistische denkmodel – een benadering waarbij uit de ter omzetting van de richtlijn aangenomen bepalingen expliciet dient te blijken dat specifieke doelstellingen uit de richtlijn zijn overgenomen door de nationale wegever. Ik betoogde dat dit onverenigbaar is met de presumptie dat de wetgever de bedoeling heeft gehad ten volle uitvoering te geven aan de richtlijn.

De Ierse rechtspraak biedt dus een genuanceerd beeld. Er zijn aanwijzingen in de richting van voorrang van Unierecht, maar zeker ook nationaal constitutionalisme. Bovendien is een lezing van de uitspraken van het Ierse Hooggerechtshof en de rechter in eerste aanleg in *EPA v Neiphin Trading Ltd* mogelijk waardoor beide niet per definitie onverzoenbaar zijn met de theorie van constitutioneel pluralisme. Er leek geen intentie te zijn om bewust af te wijken van Unierechtelijke verplichtingen en indien uit bijvoorbeeld een prejudiciële beslissing de onjuistheid van de eerder ingenomen positie zou blijken, sluit ik het niet uit dat de Ierse rechter bereid is om op zoek te gaan naar manieren om een conflict tussen de nationale constitutionele vereisten en de vereisten die het Unierecht stelt te vermijden.

5. HET PERSPECTIEF VAN DE NEDERLANDSE RECHTER

5.1. *De rechtsbasis voor richtlijnconforme interpretatie*

Voorafgaand aan het arrest *Von Colson en Kamann,* en tot in de loop van de jaren negentig, zag men regelmatig de overweging dat een interpretatie die afwijkt van de richtlijn moet worden verworpen omdat ervan dient te worden uitgegaan dat de wetgever bij de aanpassing van het nationale recht aan de richtlijn daarvan niet heeft willen afwijken. Vervolgens was het de Afdeling Bestuursrechtspraak van de Raad van State (hierna: ABRvS) die voor de verplichting tot conforme interpretatie wees op de verplichting om het door de richtlijn voorgeschreven resultaat te bereiken. De communautaire rechtsbasis werd overgenomen, en aangevuld met verwijzingen naar artikelen 288 VWEU, 4(3) VEU en de volle werking van het Unierecht, door de andere hoogste rechters. De genoemde Unierechtelijke bepalingen zijn – als gevolg van de heersende constitutionele visie op de werking van het Unierecht in de Nederlandse rechtsorde – rechtstreeks van toepassing in de Nederlandse rechtsorde.

5.2. *Ruimte voor, en grenzen van, richtlijnconforme interpretatie*

Een interpretatief conflict doet zich voor indien sprake is van een onverenigbaarheid met de verplichting tot richtlijnconforme interpretatie of nationale rechtsvindingsregels. Om een onverenigbaarheid met laatstgenoemde vast te stellen is een preciezer begrip vereist van de rechtsvindingsregels in Nederland. Nederlandse rechters hebben (met name in het privaatrecht) een flexibel rechtsvindingsinstrumentarium tot hun beschikking staan. Beslissingen worden het vaakst geschraagd met grammaticale en wetshistorische argumenten. In de jurisprudentie zijn weinig aanwijzingen te vinden dat de Nederlandse rechter zich voor de te kiezen interpretatiebenadering laat leiden door constitutionele of andere bepalingen. Echter, de argumenten die het meest het interpretatieproces beïnvloeden, maar ook de door Nederlandse rechters aangehaalde overweging dat bepaalde keuzes voorbehouden zijn aan de wetgever, wijzen erop dat eerbiediging van de constitutionele positie van de wetgever een cruciale factor is.

Een voorbeeld van voorrang van Unierecht kan worden bespeurd in de uitspraak van de Hoge Raad in *Wandelvierdaagse,* waarin systematisch voorrang wordt verleend aan de bedoeling van de wetgever om de richtlijn om te zetten boven andere, daarmee onverenigbare, wetshistorische argumenten. Er is geen systematische voorrang ten opzichte van het grammaticale interpretatiecriterium. Wel is er ruime jurisprudentie waaruit blijkt dat Nederlandse rechters bereid zijn tot een verstrekkende toepassing van de verplichting tot richtlijnconforme interpretatie, waarbij ook ten opzichte van het grammaticale interpretatiecriterium veel ruimte wordt genomen. Die benadering kan echter worden verklaard door het flexibele rechtsvindingsinstrumentarium en het krachtige argument dat de nationale bepalingen het doel hebben de richtlijn om te zetten (als onderdeel van een wetshistorische, systematische en/of teleologische interpretatie). Indien het argument van de omzettingsstrekking niet beschikbaar is, worden de uitspraken waarmee wordt afgeweken van de interpretatiebenadering in een zuiver nationale context een stuk schaarser. Ook dient te worden opgemerkt dat de ABRvS terughoudender is wat betreft afwijkingen van de bewoordingen van de regel (voor het College van Beroep voor het bedrijfsleven lijkt dit niet zozeer het geval te zijn).

De rol die in de onderzochte uitspraken wordt toebedeeld aan nationale uitlegcriteria (soms in combinatie met de wil van de wetgever) als grens op de verplichting tot conforme interpretatie is, afgezien van kleine uitzonderingen, verenigbaar met de jurisprudentie van het HvJ. Er is belangwekkende jurisprudentie van de ABRvS waarin het rechtszekerheidsbeginsel als een meer zelfstandige norm (lees: grens) wordt gehanteerd ten opzichte van conforme interpretatie. In de zaak *Fortis* zou een richtlijnconforme interpretatie hebben geleid tot de uitbreiding van een verbodsbepaling die is gekoppeld aan een vergunningplicht, terwijl deze uitbreiding niet kenbaar was voor adressanten van de verbodsbepaling. Reeds deze laatste toevoeging wijst erop dat niet enkel de uitbreiding van de verbodsbepaling, maar eveneens grammaticale moeilijkheden, in de weg stonden aan een richtlijnconforme interpretatie. Ik zie dan ook geen onverenigbaarheid met het Unierecht. In *Mandemakers* werd de *Kolpinghuis*-grens door de ABRvS uitgebreid naar bestuurlijke boetes. Daarvoor bestaat geen precedent in de jurisprudentie van het HvJ, maar er zijn voldoende aanknopingspunten (artikel 49 Handvest en de ruime uitleg die door het Europees Hof voor de Rechten van de Mens wordt gegeven aan het begrip *criminal charge* in artikel 6 EVRM). Echter, in de zaak *KOMO* werd de *Kolpinghuis*-grens doorgetrokken naar bestuurlijke handhaving (niet van punitieve aard); voor een dergelijke uitbreiding zijn geen aanknopingspunten in het Unierecht aan te wijzen.

Er is sprake van een harmonieuze relatie tussen de verplichting tot conforme interpretatie en Nederlandse rechtsvindingsregels. In de meeste gevallen is het mogelijk om tegemoet te komen aan de verplichting zonder dat daarmee grenzen van nationale rechtsvindingsregels worden overschreden. Zoals opgemerkt is er jurisprudentie waarin wel degelijk voorrang werd verleend aan conforme interpretatie (zie de uitspraak in *Wandelvierdaagse*), maar dit is de uitzondering en stuitte niet op fundamentele bezwaren. Ook is er jurisprudentie waarin de rechter niet voldeed aan de verplichting tot richtlijnconforme interpretatie. Ik zie daarin echter geen ondersteuning voor de theorie van nationaal constitutionalisme (of constitutioneel pluralisme). Ik heb de indruk dat die uitspraken eerder berusten op een onjuiste interpretatie van de Unierechtelijke verplichting, dan dat bewust de voorrang van het Unierecht (in casu artikelen 288 VWEU, 4(3) VEU en de volle werking van het Unierecht) wordt afgewezen. Zulks zou dan dienen te geschieden op basis van Nederlandse constitutionele bepalingen en/of beginselen, maar de uitspraken geven er op geen enkele manier blijk van dat de rechter zich door dergelijke overwegingen liet leiden. Het geheel overziend kan worden gesteld dat de Nederlandse jurisprudentie een krachtig voorbeeld biedt van de wijze waarop op harmonieuze wijze in een pluralistische rechtsorde – die de nationale rechter kan confronteren met tegengestelde posities in bijvoorbeeld een richtlijn en nationaal recht – via richtlijnconforme interpretatie de op het eerste gezicht tegengestelde posities met elkaar in overeenstemming worden gebracht, zodat een (ernstiger) normatief conflict wordt voorkomen.

6. CONCLUSIE

6.1. Een conflict tussen interpretatieve normen

In hoeverre kan er in het kader van richtlijnconforme interpretatie sprake zijn van een normatief conflict? De theorieën voorrang van Unierecht, nationaal constitutionalisme en constitutioneel pluralisme nemen dit immers allen als uitgangspunt. In de situatie waarin bijvoorbeeld de richtlijn de nietigheid van een overeenkomst, en nationaal recht het tegenovergestelde, voorschrijft, zal door niemand worden betwist dat sprake is van zo'n normatief conflict. Echter, richtlijnconforme interpretatie beoogt nou juist conflicten tussen de richtlijn en nationaal recht te voorkomen. Voor een begrip van conforme interpretatie dient dan ook niet de werking van de theorieën over de relatie tussen Unierecht en nationaal recht ten aanzien van het conflict tussen de richtlijn en nationaal recht als uitgangspunt te worden genomen. Dit conflict is slechts de aanleiding die de artikelen 288 VWEU en 4(3) VEU (en het beginsel van de volle werking van het Unierecht) activeert, welke bepalingen aan de basis staan van een interpretatieve norm: de verplichting tot richtlijnconforme interpretatie. Die norm doet qua verbindendheid niet onder voor de zoeven genoemde richtlijnbepaling. De verbindendheid ziet op de methodologische aanwijzingen ontleend aan de artikelen 288 VWEU en 4(3) VEU. Maar het is ook een bijzondere norm qua aard en het effect dat zij sorteert: zij is toegespitst op (nationale) rechtsvindingsregels, legt geen absolute resultaatsverplichting op (uiteraard wordt wel voorgeschreven dat de na te streven interpretatie diegene is die conform de richtlijn is, maar dat is iets anders) en is, in het verlengde hiervan, inherent begrensd. Wat dus verandert is het type norm waarop de theorieën over de relatie tussen Unierecht en nationaal recht worden toegepast, zonder dat een dergelijke toepassing mijns inziens de coherentie van die theorieën in gevaar brengt.

Betoogt zou kunnen worden dat de verplichting tot richtlijnconforme interpretatie slechts een bindende norm oplevert voor zover door het HvJ duidelijke aanwijzingen zijn vastgesteld (zoals bijvoorbeeld de aanwijzing dat de verplichting van toepassing is op al het nationale recht). Dit miskent evenwel twee punten. Allereerst wordt geen afbreuk gedaan aan de verbindendheid van een norm in het geval de reikwijdte van die norm (nog) niet volledig is uitgekristalliseerd. Ten tweede dient weliswaar te worden toegegeven dat voor belangrijke aspecten die zien op de toepassing van conforme interpretatie veel beoordelings*ruimte* wordt toegekend aan de nationale rechter, hetgeen de vraag zou kunnen opwerpen of wel sprake is van een autonome, bindende, Unierechtelijke norm, maar hier wijs ik op de gedachtenvorming met betrekking tot 'wezenlijk betwistbare begrippen' (*inherently contestable concepts*). Hoe ver de nationale rechter exact gaat bij het richtlijnconform interpreteren kan in de loop der tijd veranderen en verschilt per lidstaat – soms zelfs tussen verschillende rechterlijke instanties in dezelfde lidstaat. Verschillende toepassingen bestaan dus naast elkaar en het Unierecht lijkt die ruimte bewust te bieden. Die diversiteit doet recht aan de verschillende rechtsvindingstradities en opvattingen omtrent interpretatie, en is onontkoombaar. Zij doet geen afbreuk aan de verbindendheid van de norm.

6.2. *Richtlijnconforme interpretatie en theorieën over de relatie tussen unierecht en nationaal recht*

Ik kom terug op de vraag in hoeverre de bestaande theorieën de interactie tussen Unierecht en nationaal recht in het kader van conforme interpretatie kunnen verklaren. Indien voorrang wordt opgevat als een hiërarchisch model zou kunnen worden opgemerkt dat het feit dat de rechters van de lidstaten het nationale recht conform richtlijnen uitleggen erop wijst dat zij aan laatstgenoemde binnen hun rechtsorde een superieure rang toekennen. Dwingend is die opvatting echter niet. Voor de afwijzing van het hiërarchische model is nog belangrijker dat het voor zijn theoretische onderbouwing ten onrechte uitgaat van de gedachte dat al het Unierecht, en dus ook richtlijnen steeds (dus los van rechtstreekse werking) voorrang genieten. Voorrang kan ook als een conflictregel worden beschouwd en in dat verband hoeft geen beroep te worden gedaan op een link tussen voorrang van Unierecht en richtlijnen. De rechtsbasis wordt gevonden in de artikelen 288 VWEU en 4(3) VEU (en de volle werking van het Unierecht). Dit biedt een voldoende verklaring voor de *toepasselijkheid* van de verplichting tot conforme interpretatie. Wat betreft de *werking* van conforme interpretatie ten opzichte van nationale rechtsvindingsregels wijs ik erop dat de artikelen 288 VWEU en 4(3) VEU tot het primaire Unierecht behoren en dus van nature voorrang genieten voor zover zich een conflict voordoet met regels afkomstig uit de nationale rechtsordes.

De jurisprudentie van het HvJ biedt een aantal voorbeelden die de theorie van voorrang, opgevat als conflictregel, ondersteunen. Ik wijs er in dit verband op dat artikel 4(3) VEU een eventuele inmenging ten opzichte van nationale rechtsvindingsregels legitimeert. Meer concreet lijken de aanwijzingen inzake de interpretatieve voorrangregel, dat de rechter ervan uit dient te gaan dat de wetgever de bedoeling heeft gehad ten volle uitvoering te geven aan de richtlijn, en de interpretatie van nationaal recht dat letterlijk de bewoordingen van de richtlijn overnam, de potentie te hebben om (in verregaande mate) in te grijpen in de toepassing van nationale rechtsvindingsregels. Tot slot kan worden gewezen op de kritische houding van het HvJ in de arresten *Dominguez* en *Ajos*. Tegelijkertijd is het noodzakelijk naar de nationale jurisprudentie te kijken, zodat kan worden vastgesteld of, en zo ja wanneer, zich daadwerkelijk conflicten voordoen en, indien zulks het geval is, of zij in het voordeel van het Unierecht worden opgelost. Voor het identificeren van een conflict is een noodzakelijke, maar ontoereikende, stap dat wordt nagegaan of de toepassing van nationale rechtsvindingsregels werd aangepast aan de vereisten van een richtlijnconforme interpretatie. Er is echter pas sprake van een conflict indien de toepassing van de verplichting tot conforme interpretatie onverenigbaar is met de nationale rechtsvindingsregels. Het onderzoek leverde drie situaties op waarin dat het geval was. Allereerst is er jurisprudentie waarin niet wordt onderzocht welke uitleg het beste aansluit bij de aanwijzingen die voortvloeien uit de nationale uitlegcriteria, maar in plaats daarvan de richtlijn tot uitgangspunt wordt genomen en de vraag wordt gesteld of nationale uitlegregels zich niet verzetten tegen het richtlijnconforme uitlegresultaat. Ten tweede de verschuiving in de interpretatiebenadering als gevolg van de vereisten van richtlijnconforme interpretatie, in die zin dat doelmatige interpretatie een prominentere rol opeiste ten koste van een letterlijke uitleg (ingeluid in de zaak *Murphy v An Bord Telecom Éireann*). Ten derde is er jurisprudentie die laat zien dat systematisch voorrang wordt verleend aan argumenten die een richtlijnconform uitlegresultaat mogelijk maken.

De theorie van het nationaal constitutionalisme roept op twee punten vragen op. Allereerst liet ik zien dat de nationale rechters voor de rechtsbasis van conforme interpretatie voornamelijk verwijzen naar het Unierecht. Dit is evenwel geen onoverkomelijk probleem omdat de bepalingen van het Unierecht in lidstaten als bijvoorbeeld Duitsland en Ierland hun werking hebben via nationale goedkeuringswetten en dus zou kunnen worden gesteld dat zij uiteindelijk op een nationale wettelijke basis berusten. Ten tweede wees ik op drie situaties waarin voorrang wordt verleend aan conforme interpretatie. Het zou afbreuk doen aan de verklarende waarde van de theorie van nationaal constitutionalisme indien met die voorrang eveneens nationale regels of beginselen *van constitutionele aard* opzij zouden worden gezet. In Nederland denk ik niet dat dit het geval is. Voor Duitsland en Ierland is dit twijfelachtiger, ik wijs hier bijvoorbeeld op de voorrang die wordt verleend aan het argument dat de wetgever de bedoeling had de richtlijn getrouw om te zetten ter rechtvaardiging van een *Rechtsfortbildung*. De meerwaarde van de theorie van nationaal constitutionalisme zou met name gezocht kunnen worden in jurisprudentie die een richtlijnconforme interpretatie afwijst. Hier dient te worden opgemerkt dat de meeste afwijzingen verenigbaar zijn met de grenzen van conforme interpretatie die door het Unierecht zijn erkend, of zijn ingegeven door overwegingen die niet van constitutionele aard zijn. Maar voor Duitsland en Ierland geldt dat in een aantal gevallen de afwijzing wel kan worden teruggevoerd op constitutionele bepalingen of beginselen.

De drie situaties waarin voorrang wordt verleend aan conforme interpretatie sluiten niet aan bij de theorie van constitutioneel pluralisme: er was weliswaar een conflict, maar dit lijkt nu te zijn beslecht in het voordeel van conforme interpretatie (hoewel uiteraard nooit kan worden uitgesloten dat op een later moment toch meer belang wordt gehecht aan nationale constitutionele argumenten). De jurisprudentie waarin een conforme interpretatie werd afgewezen en die in de richting van de theorie van nationaal constitutionalisme wezen, dienen ook hier genoemd te worden. Immers, mijn analyse was dat de gekozen benadering onverenigbaar was met de eisen die het Unierecht stelt, zodat verondersteld kan worden dat zich twee conflicterende posities voordoen. De theorie van het constitutioneel pluralisme zou vooral van meerwaarde kunnen zijn doordat in wetenschappelijke beschouwingen op dit onderwerp uitgangspunten zijn geformuleerd om de (potentieel) conflicterende posities in goede banen te leiden en te voorkomen dat zij leiden tot een incoherente en gedesintegreerde rechtsorde. Die uitgangspunten zijn in sommige – maar niet alle – voorbeelden die tevens steun boden aan de theorie van nationaal constitutionalisme terug te vinden.

Uit het bovenstaande volgt dat alle theorieën iets toe te voegen hebben indien wordt gezocht naar een verklaring voor de relatie tussen Unierecht en nationaal recht in het kader van richtlijnconforme interpretatie. Het voordeel van nationaal constitutionalisme en constitutioneel pluralisme is dat zij, als een soort matroesjka, delen van (een) andere theorie/theorieën onderkent/onderkennen, maar daar een laag aan toevoegen waarmee ook rekening wordt gehouden met feiten waarvoor geen adequate verklaring kan worden gevonden op basis van de andere theorie/theorieën. Desalniettemin blijven de uitspraken waarvoor enkel nationaal constitutionalisme en constitutioneel pluralisme een passende verklaring bieden beperkt. Indien naar de gekozen benaderingen in geval van een interpretatief conflict worden gekeken ligt het zwaartepunt eerder bij voorrang van het Unierecht.

6.3. *Beschouwingen op de eeuwige vraag van de relatie tussen unierecht en nationaal recht*

Allereerst herinnert het onderzoek eraan dat de uitzondering de regel bevestigt. Hoewel een aantal spraakmakende uitspraken werd besproken die aansloten bij de theorieën van nationaal constitutionalisme en/of constitutioneel pluralisme, blijft dit de uitzondering en dient niet over het hoofd te worden gezien dat in de meeste gevallen nationale rechters de voorrang van het Unierecht onderkennen. Ten tweede kunnen de besproken theorieën elkaar aanvullen, en bieden zij de verschillende actoren de mogelijkheid om te gaan met de moeilijkheden van een geïntegreerde rechtsorde door haar te benaderen vanuit de eigen visie op de relatie tussen de samenstellende delen. Dit neemt niet weg dat de verschillende theorieën uiteindelijk een andere visie hebben op de vragen waarop het gezag van het Unierecht berust, hoe een conflict tussen dat recht en nationaal (constitutioneel) recht moet worden beslecht, en wie daarover het laatste woord heeft. Indien zo'n conflict zich voordoet beschrijven voorrang van Unierecht en nationaal constitutionalisme de posities van respectievelijk het HvJ en de nationale (constitutionele) rechter, terwijl constitutioneel pluralisme het best kan worden gezien als het perspectief dat wordt geboden door de neutrale toeschouwer van het conflict. Ten derde ziet men in de literatuur regelmatig een verknoping van voorrang en rechtstreekse werking. Daarvoor bestaan ook goede redenen van zowel empirische als theoretische aard. Tegelijkertijd heeft dit de negatieve bijwerking dat voorrang regelmatig wordt vereenzelvigd met de idee van absolute uniformiteit in de toepassing van het Unierecht. Het onderzoek laat zien dat voorrang een ruimer bereik heeft dan rechtstreekse werking en dat in de context van conforme interpretatie de werking van voorrang genuanceerder is dan bij rechtstreekse werking. Ook de theorieën van nationaal constitutionalisme en constitutioneel pluralisme spelen niet enkel een rol wanneer Unierecht het toneel betreedt via rechtstreekse werking.

6.4. *De 'gewone' toepassing van richtlijnconforme interpretatie*

Tot slot dient één kanttekening te worden geplaatst bij de zojuist beschreven bevindingen van mijn onderzoek naar de relatie tussen Unierecht en nationaal recht in de context van conforme interpretatie: in de meeste onderzochte gevallen was geen sprake van een interpretatief conflict, zodat de theorieën over de relatie tussen Unierecht en nationaal recht niet aan bod komen. Dat geen sprake is van een conflict is evident indien conforme interpretatie wordt gehanteerd om de uitleg van een bepaling te bevestigen die tevens wordt ondersteund door nationale interpretatiemethoden, of wanneer die interpretatiemethoden nou juist geen duidelijkheid bieden en conforme interpretatie wordt aangewend om de knoop door te hakken. Echter, er zijn ook vele voorbeelden waarin geen sprake was van een conflict terwijl de verplichting tot conforme interpretatie ertoe leidde dat een interpretatie werd gegeven die afweek van de interpretatie waarvoor de nationale interpretatiemethoden het meeste steun boden. Wanneer een dreigende onverenigbaarheid tussen de richtlijn en nationaal recht op deze manier kan worden voorkomen werkt conforme interpretatie optimaal. Al deze gevallen zijn voorbeelden van een 'gewone' toepassing van de verplichting waarbij zich dus geen conflict voordoet.

Zoals eerder door mij werd opgemerkt zijn het niet enkel nationale rechtsvindingsregels die ruimte bieden aan de verplichting tot conforme interpretatie, maar is dit ook omgekeerd het geval (wanneer laatstgenoemde uitmondt in een afwijzing van een richtlijnconforme interpretatie is dit uiteraard niet optimaal aangezien een conflict tussen de richtlijn en de nationale bepaling blijft bestaan en om een andere oplossing vraagt; tegelijkertijd dient het Unierecht die ruimte te laten om te voorkomen dat conforme interpretatie een onwerkbaar instrument wordt dat niet meer door de nationale rechters wordt geaccepteerd). Die wederzijdse flexibiliteit kan ten koste gaan van de voorspelbaarheid van rechterlijke beslissingen. Een zekere mate van onvoorspelbaarheid is evenwel inherent aan rechtsvindingsprocessen. Het is daarom nuttig te weten waar de uiterste grenzen van Europese en nationale rechtsvindingsregels liggen. Indien de toepassing van de verplichting tot richtlijnconforme interpretatie op dergelijke interpretatieve verdedigingsmuren stuit – er aldus sprake is van een interpretatief conflict – is het van groot belang om te begrijpen welke theorie over de relatie tussen Unierecht en nationaal recht het best weergeeft wat de meest waarschijnlijke uitkomst zal zijn van een dergelijk conflict.

LIST OF CASES

EUROPEAN COURT OF JUSTICE

Case 26/62 *Van Gend & Loos*, ECLI:EU:C:1963:1
Case 6/64 *Costa v ENEL*, ECLI:EU:C:1964:66
Case 14/68 *Walt Wilhelm*, ECLI:EU:C:1969:4
Case 11/70 *Internationale Handelsgesellschaft*, ECLI:EU:C:1970:114
Case 41/74 *Van Duyn*, ECLI:EU:C:1974:133
Case 33/76 *Rewe*, ECLI:EU:C:1976:188
Case 45/76 *Comet*, ECLI:EU:C:1976:191
Case 52/76 *Benedetti*, ECLI:EU:C:1977:16
Case 106/77 *Simmenthal*, ECLI:EU:C:1978:49
Case 44/79 *Hauer*, ECLI:EU:C:1979:290
Case 8/81 *Becker*, ECLI:EU:C:1982:7
Case 14/83 *Von Colson and Kamann*, ECLI:EU:C:1984:153
Case 152/84 *Marshall I*, ECLI:EU:C:1986:84
Case 235/84 *Commission v Italy*, ECLI:EU:C:1986:303
Case 314/85 *Foto-Frost*, ECLI:EU:C:1987:452
Joined Cases C-201/85 and C-202/85 *Klensch*, ECLI:EU:C:1986:439
Case 14/86 *Pretore di Salò*, ECLI:EU:C:1987:275
Case 80/86 *Kolpinghuis*, ECLI:EU:C:1987:431
Case 157/86 *Murphy*, ECLI:EU:C:1988:62
Case 103/88 *Costanzo*, ECLI:EU:C:1989:256
Case C-177/88 *Dekker*, ECLI:EU:C:1990:383
Joined Cases C-297/88 and C-197/89 *Dzodzi*, ECLI:EU:C:1990:360
Case C-322/88 *Grimaldi*, ECLI:EU:C:1989:646
Case C-106/89 *Marleasing*, ECLI:EU:C:1990:395
Case C-213/89 *Factortame*, ECLI:EU:C:1990:257
Joined Cases C-6/90 and C-9/90 *Francovich*, ECLI:EU:C:1991:428
Case C-159/90 *SPUC*, ECLI:EU:C:1991:378
Case C-165/91 *Van Munster*, ECLI:EU:C:1994:359
Case C-338/91 *Steenhorst-Neerings*, ECLI:EU:C:1993:857
Case C-91/92 *Faccini Dori*, ECLI:EU:C:1994:292
Case C-334/92 *Wagner Miret*, ECLI:EU:C:1993:945
Case C-382/92 *Commission v United Kingdom*, ECLI:EU:C:1994:233
Case C-421/92 *Habermann-Beltermann*, ECLI:EU:C:1994:187
Case C-46/93 *Brasserie du Pêcheur*, ECLI:EU:C:1996:79

Case C-312/93 *Peterbroeck*, ECLI:EU:C:1995:437
Case C-365/93 *Commission v Greece*, ECLI:EU:C:1995:76
Case C-28/95 *Leur-Bloem*, ECLI:EU:C:1997:369
Joined Cases C-74/95 and C-129/95 *Criminal proceedings against X*, ECLI:EU:C:1996:491
Case C-168/95 *Arcaro*, ECLI:EU:C:1996:363
Case C-284/95 *Safety Hi-Tech*, ECLI:EU:C:1998:352
Case C-300/95 *Commission v United Kingdom*, ECLI:EU:C:1997:255
Case C-368/95 *Familiapress*, ECLI:EU:C:1997:325
Case C-53/96 *Hermès*, ECLI:EU:C:1998:292
Case C-129/96 *Inter-Environnement Wallonie*, ECLI:EU:C:1997:628
Case C-111/97 *EvoBus Austria*, ECLI:EU:C:1998:434
Case C-131/97 *Carbonari*, ECLI:EU:C:1999:98
Case C-185/97 *Coote*, ECLI:EU:C:1998:424
Case C-215/97 *Bellone*, ECLI:EU:C:1998:189
Case C-262/97 *Engelbrecht*, ECLI:EU:C:2000:492
Joined Cases C-270/97 and C-271/97 *Sievers*, ECLI:EU:C:2000:76
Joined Cases C-240/98 to C-244/98 *Océano*, ECLI:EU:C:2000:346
Case C-456/98 *Centrosteel*, ECLI:EU:C:2000:402
Case C-144/99 *Commission v Netherlands*, ECLI:EU:C:2001:257
Case C-274/99 P *Connolly*, ECLI:EU:C:2001:127
Case C-481/99 *Heininger*, ECLI:EU:C:2001:684
Case C-12/00 *Commission v Spain*, ECLI:EU:C:2003:21
Case C-129/00 *Commission v Italy*, ECLI:EU:C:2003:656
Joined Cases C-465/00, C-138/01 and C-139/01 *Österreichischer Rundfunk*, ECLI:EU:C:2003:294
Case C-207/01 *Altair Chimica*, ECLI:EU:C:2003:451
Joined Cases C-397/01 to C-403/01 *Pfeiffer*, ECLI:EU:C:2004:584
Case C-8/02 *Leichtle*, ECLI:EU:C:2004:161
Case C-60/02 *Criminal proceedings against X*, ECLI:EU:C:2004:10
Case C-286/02 *Bellio*, ECLI:EU:C:2004:212
Case C-371/02 *Björnekulla*, ECLI:EU:C:2004:275
Case C-105/03 *Pupino*, ECLI:EU:C:2005:386
Case C-188/03 *Junk*, ECLI:EU:C:2005:59
Case C-235/03 *QDQ Media*, ECLI:EU:C:2005:147
Case C-144/04 *Mangold*, ECLI:EU:C:2005:709
Case C-212/04 *Adeneler*, ECLI:EU:C:2006:443
Case C-316/04 *Stichting Zuid-Hollandse Milieufederatie*, ECLI:EU:C:2005:678
Case C-208/05 *ITC*, ECLI:EU:C:2007:16
Joined Cases C-222/05 to C-225/05 *Van der Weerd and Others*, ECLI:EU:C:2007:318
Case C-321/05 *Kofoed*, ECLI:EU:C:2007:408
Case C-356/05 *Farrell*, ECLI:EU:C:2007:229

Case C-432/05 *Unibet*, ECLI:EU:C:2007:163
Case C-55/06 *Arcor*, ECLI:EU:C:2008:244
Case C-246/06 *Navarro*, ECLI:EU:C:2008:19
Case C-268/06 *Impact*, ECLI:EU:C:2008:223
Joined Cases C-383/06, C-384/06 and C-385/06 *Vereniging Nationaal Overlegorgaan Sociale Werkvoorziening*, ECLI:EU:C:2008:165
Case C-404/06 *Quelle*, ECLI:EU:C:2008:231
Joined Cases C-378/07 to C-380/07 *Angelidaki and Others*, ECLI:EU:C:2009:250
Case C-414/07 *Magoora*, ECLI:EU:C:2008:766
Case C-12/08 *Mono Car Styling*, ECLI:EU:C:2009:466
Case C-305/08 *CoNISMa*, ECLI:EU:C:2009:807
Case C-456/08 *Commission v Ireland*, ECLI:EU:C:2010:46
Joined Cases C-65/09 and C-87/09 *Weber*, ECLI:EU:C:2011:396
Case C-115/09 *Trianel*, ECLI:EU:C:2011:289
Case C-462/09 *Stichting De Thuiskopie*, ECLI:EU:C:2011:397
Case C-53/10 *Mücksch*, ECLI:EU:C:2011:585
Case C-282/10 *Dominguez*, ECLI:EU:C:2012:33
Case C-489/10 *Bonda*, ECLI:EU:C:2012:319
Case C-594/10 *Van Laarhoven*, ECLI:EU:C:2012:92
Case C-617/10 *Åkerberg Fransson*, ECLI:EU:C:2013:105
Case C-7/11 *Caronna*, ECLI:EU:C:2012:396
Case C-97/11 *Amia*, ECLI:EU:C:2012:306
Joined Cases C-359/11 and C-400/11 *Schulz*, ECLI:EU:C:2014:2317
Case C-399/11 *Melloni*, ECLI:EU:C:2013:107
Case C-124/12 *AES-3C Maritza East 1*, ECLI:EU:C:2013:488
Case C-131/12 *Google Spain*, ECLI:EU:C:2014:317
Case C-176/12 *AMS*, ECLI:EU:C:2014:2
Case C-306/12 *Spedition Welter*, ECLI:EU:C:2013:650
Case C-18/13 *Maks Pen*, ECLI:EU:C:2014:69
Joined Cases C-131/13, C-163/13 and C-164/13 *Italmoda*, ECLI:EU:C:2014:2455
Case C-497/13 *Faber*, ECLI:EU:C:2015:357
Case C-395/14 *Vodafone*, ECLI:EU:C:2016:9
Case C-441/14 *Ajos*, ECLI:EU:C:2016:278
Case C-505/14 *Klausner Holz Niedersachsen*, ECLI:EU:C:2015:742
Case C-187/15 *Pöpperl*, ECLI:EU:C:2016:550
Case C-524/15 *Menci*, ECLI:EU:C:2018:197
Case C-605/15 *Aviva*, ECLI:EU:C:2017:718
Case C-414/16 *Egenberger*, ECLI:EU:C:2018:257
Joined Cases C-569/16 and C-570/16 *Bauer*, ECLI:EU:C:2018:871
Case C-684/16 *Max-Planck-Gesellschaft*, ECLI:EU:C:2018:874
Case C-42/17 *M.A.S. and M.B.*, ECLI:EU:C:2017:936
Case C-68/17 *IR*, ECLI:EU:C:2018:696

Case C-122/17 *Smith*, ECLI:EU:C:2018:631
Case C-167/17 *Klohn*, ECLI:EU:C:2018:833
Case C-378/17 *Minister for Justice and Equality and Commissioner of the Garda Síochána*, ECLI:EU:C:2018:979

CZECH REPUBLIC

ÚS 31 January 2012, Pl. ÚS 5/12 (*Landtová*)

DENMARK

Højesteret 6 December 2016, *Sag 15/2014* (*Ajos*)

GERMANY

BVerfG 17 June 1953 *Armenanwalt*, BVerfGE 2, 336
BVerfG 17 May 1960, BVerfGE 11, 126
BVerfG 30 June 1964, BVerfGE 18, 97
BVerfG 15 December 1965 *Wencker*, BVerfGE 19, 342
BVerfG 14 February 1973 *Soraya*, BVerfGE 34, 269
BVerfG 19 June 1973, BVerfGE 35, 263
BVerfG 29 May 1974 *Solange I*, BVerfGE 37, 271
BVerfG 11 October 1978, BVerfGE 49, 304
BVerfG 11 June 1980, BVerfGE 54, 277
BVerfG 22 October 1985, BVerfGE 71, 81
BVerfG 23 October 1985, BVerfGE 71, 108
BVerfG 14 January 1986, BVerfGE 71, 354
BVerfG 22 October 1986 *Solange II*, BVerfGE 73, 339
BVerfG 8 April 1987 *Kloppenburg*, BVerfGE 75, 223
BVerfG 3 October 1989, BVerfGE 81, 29
BVerfG 3 April 1990, BVerfGE 82, 6
BVerfG 31 May 1990, BVerfGE 82, 159
BVerfG 10 July 1990, BVerfGE 82, 286
BVerfG 23 October 1991 *Eilversammlungen*, BVerfGE 85, 69
BVerfG 3 June 1992, BVerfGE 86, 288
BVerfG 20 October 1992, BVerfGE 87, 209
BVerfG 30 March 1993, NJW 1993, 2861
BVerfG 12 October 1993 *Maastricht*, BVerfGE 89, 155
BVerfG 24 May 1995, BVerfGE 93, 37
BVerfG 20 March 2002, BVerfGE 105, 135

BVerfG 30 March 2004 *Geldwächse,* BVerfGE 110, 226
BVerfG 30 June 2009 *Lisbon,* BVerfGE 123, 267
BVerfG 6 July 2010 *Honeywell,* BVerfGE 126, 286
BVerfG 25 January 2011, BVerfGE 128, 157
BVerfG 25 January 2011, BVerfGE 128, 193
BVerfG 4 April 2011, NJW 2011, 1723
BVerfG 19 July 2011, BVerfGE 129, 78
BVerfG 26 September 2011, BVerfGK 19, 89
BVerfG 10 January 2012 *Delisting,* BVerfGE 132, 99
BVerfG 19 March 2013, BVerfGE 133, 168
BVerfG 26 August 2014, NJW 2014, 3504
BVerfG 10 December 2014, ZIP 2015, 335
BVerfG 23 May 2016, ZIP 2016, 55
BVerfG 17 January 2017, BVerfGE 144, 20
BVerfG 17 November 2017, NJW-RR 2018, 305

BAG 14 March 1989, NJW 1990, 65
BAG 30 August 1989, BAGE 62, 338
BAG 21 May 1992, BAGE 70, 238
BAG 5 March 1996, NJW 1996, 2529
BAG 11 December 1997, BAGE 87, 303
BAG 18 February 2003, DB 2003, 1387
BAG 18 September 2003, BAGE 107, 318
BAG 30 March 2004, BAGE 110, 122
BAG 23 March 2006, BAGE 117, 281
BAG 26 April 2006, BAGE 118, 76
BAG 1 February 2007, Beck online Rechtsprechung 2011, 72103
BAG 22 March 2007, NZA 2007, 1101
BAG 24 March 2009, BAGE 130, 119
BAG 17 November 2009 *Urlaubsentgelt,* BAGE 132, 247
BAG 23 June 2010, BAGE 135, 34
BAG 20 September 2011, NZA 2012, 326
BAG 10 December 2013, BAGE 146, 384
BAG 18 October 2016, Beck online Rechtsprechung 2016, 74836

BFH 20 January 1988, BFHE 152, 556
BFH 18 April 1991, RIW 1991, 782
BFH 30 July 1992, Beck online Rechtsprechung 1992, 7770
BFH 12 March 1998, BFHE 185, 308
BFH 2 April 1998, BFHE 185, 536
BFH 23 October 2003, BFHE 203, 531
BFH 8 September 2010, BFHE 231, 343

BFH 29 June 2011, BFHE 233, 470
BFH 15 February 2012, BFHE 236, 267
BFH 16 May 2012, BFHE 238, 468
BFH 13 May 2013, BFHE 241, 1
BFH 22 August 2013, DStR 2013, 2757
BFH 2 July 2014, Beck online Rechtsprechung 2014, 96183
BFH 19 January 2016, ZIP 2016, 1378
BFH 10 August 2016, BFHE 255, 300
BFH 12 October 2016, BFHE 255, 457
BFH 26 July 2017, DB 2017, 2395
BFH 22 November 2018, DStR 2019, 265

BGH 14 February 1974, DB 1974, 1280
BGH 19 May 1981, BGHSt 30, 105
BGH 22 May 1989 *Kochs Adler*, BGHZ 107, 296
BGH 9 March 1993, NJW 1993, 1594
BGH 10 November 1997, NJW 1998, 1071
BGH 5 February 1998, NJW 1998, 2208
BGH 29 November 1999, NJW 2000, 521
BGH 9 April 2002 *Heininger*, BGHZ 150, 248
BGH 29 April 2003, ZIP 2003, 1692
BGH 19 October 2004, ZIP 2004, 2373
BGH 20 January 2005, NJW 2005, 1508
BGH 14 February 2006, NJW 2006, 1340
BGH 16 August 2006, NJW 2006, 3200
BGH 26 November 2008 *Quelle*, BGHZ 179, 27
BGH 14 January 2009, NJW 2009, 1660
BGH 7 July 2010 *Heinrich Heine*, NJW 2010, 2651
BGH 21 December 2011 *Bodenfliesen*, BGHZ 192, 148
BGH 16 May 2013 *Interprofessionelle Sozietät*, NJW 2013, 2674
BGH 8 January 2014, NVwZ 2014, 1111
BGH 7 May 2014, BGHZ 201, 101
BGH 17 December 2014, NJW 2015, 1023
BGH 29 July 2015, ZIP 2015, 61
BGH 28 October 2015 *Gasversorgung II*, BGHZ 207, 209
BGH 12 October 2016, NJW 2017, 1093
BGH 5 October 2017, MDR 2017, 13
BGH 3 July 2018, NJW-RR 2018, 1204

BSG 23 October 1958, NJW 1959, 167

BVerwG 2 July 1975, BVerwGE 49, 60

BVerwG 23 January 1992, BVerwGE 89, 320
BVerwG 18 December 1997, NJW 1998, 3433
BVerwG 29 January 2004, Beck online Rechtsprechung 2004, 21828
BVerwG 3 December 2009, Zeitschrift für deutsches und internationales Bau- und Vergaberecht 2010, 262
BVerwG 31 March 2011, BVerwGE 139, 272
BVerwG 29 September 2011, NVwZ 2012, 176
BVerwG 20 December 2012 *Mücksch*, NVwZ 2013, 719, 723
BVerwG 18 April 2013, NJW 2013, 2457
BVerwG 5 September 2013, BVerwGE 147, 312
BVerwG 22 October 2015, NVwZ 2016, 308
BVerwG 7 July 2016, BVerwGE 155, 381
BVerwG 31 January 2017, Beck online Rechtsprechung 2017, 103948
BVerwG 21 August 2018, DÖV 2019, 79

RG 28 October 1919, RGZ 97, 43

OLG Karlsruhe 5 September 2007, NJW-RR 2008, 1016

OLG München 8 December 2016, Beck online Rechtsprechung 2016, 21199

ArbG Hamm 6 September 1984, ZIP 1984, 1525

LG Saarbrücken 15 November 2013, not reported

IRELAND

Supreme Court 31 January 1946 *The People (Attorney General) v Kennedy* [1946] IR 517
Supreme Court 27 July 1970 *East Donegal Co-op Livestock Mart Ltd v Attorney General* [1970] 1 IR 317
Supreme Court 1 April 1971 *Rahill v Brady* [1971] IR 69
Supreme Court 19 January 1979 *DPP v Flanagan* [1979] IR 265
Supreme Court 4 December 1981 *Inspector of Taxes v Kiernan* [1981] IR 117
Supreme Court 17 June 1983 *Campus Oil Ltd v Minister for Industry and Energy* [1983] IR 82
Supreme Court 7 July 1988 *McGrath v McDermott* [1988] IR 258
Supreme Court 19 December 1989 *SPUC (Ireland) Ltd v Grogan* [1990] 1 CMLR 689
Supreme Court 26 May 1993 *Howard v Commissioners of Public Works* [1994] 1 IR 101
Supreme Court 29 February 1996 *Nathan v Bailey Gibson Ltd* [1998] 2 IR 162
Supreme Court 15 May 1997 *Re The Employment Equality Bill 1996* [1997] 2 IR 321

Supreme Court 4 February 1998 *Telecom Éireann v O'Grady* [1998] 3 IR 432
Supreme Court 29 July 1998 *DPP (Ivers) v Murphy* [1999] 1 IR 98
Supreme Court 11 July 2001 *Crilly v T & J Farrington Ltd* [2001] 3 IR 251
Supreme Court 11 April 2002 *Maguire v Ardagh* [2002] 1 IR 385
Supreme Court 21 February 2003 *O'Connell v EPA* [2003] 1 IR 530
Supreme Court 26 July 2006 *Albatros Feeds Ltd v Minister for Agriculture and Food* [2007] 1 IR 221
Supreme Court 2 May 2008 *Harding v Cork County Council (No 5)* [2008] 2 ILRM 251
Supreme Court 14 December 2011 *O'Flynn Construction Ltd v Revenue Commissioners* [2011] IESC 47
Supreme Court 10 May 2012 *Kadri v Governor of Wheatfield Prison* [2012] IESC 27
Supreme Court 5 March 2015 *Thompson v Dublin Bus* [2015] 3 JIC 503
Supreme Court 23 June 2015 *National Asset Management Agency (NAMA) v Commissioner for Environmental Information* [2015] 2 ILRM 165

Court of Appeal 16 December 2016 *Smith v Meade* [2016] 12 JIC 1608

High Court 4 March 1986 *Murphy v An Bord Telecom Éireann* [1986] ILRM 483
High Court 12 February 1987 *Crotty v An Taoiseach* [1987] IR 713
High Court 2 October 1987 *Lawlor v Minister for Agriculture* [1990] 1 IR 356
High Court 11 April 1988 *Murphy v An Bord Telecom Éireann* [1989] ILRM 53
High Court 14 April 1989 *Greene v Minister for Agriculture* [1990] 2 IR 17
High Court 12 October 1990 *Condon v Minister for Agriculture* [1993] Irish Journal of European Law 151
High Court 7 October 1992 *Nathan v Bailey Gibson Ltd* [1993] ELR 106
High Court 21 June 1994 *Bosphorus Hava v Minister for Transport* [1994] 3 CMLR 464
High Court 4 November 1994 *Mulcahy v Minister for the Marine*, not reported
High Court 6 May 1997 *Ni Eili v EPA* [1997] 2 ILRM 458
High Court 6 October 1998 *Watson v EPA* [2000] 2 IR 454
High Court 7 May 1999 *Maher v An Bord Pleanála* [1999] 2 ILRM 198
High Court 16 December 1999 *Coastal Line Container Terminal Ltd v Services Industrial Professional Technical Union* [2000] 1 IR 549
High Court 31 July 2002 *Wicklow County Council v Fenton (No 2)* [2002] 4 IR 44
High Court 1 September 2003 *O'Shea v Kerry County Council* [2003] 4 IR 143
High Court 16 July 2004 *SIAC Construction Ltd v National Roads Authority* [2004] IEHC 128
High Court 21 July 2005 *Hanrahan Farms Ltd v EPA* [2012] 3 IR 417
High Court 29 July 2005 *Eircom Ltd v ComReg* [2007] 1 IR 1
High Court 23 November 2006 *BUPA Ireland Ltd v Health Insurance Authority* [2006] IEHC 431

High Court 26 April 2007 *Sweetman v An Bord Pleanála* [2008] 1 IR 277
High Court 6 October 2008 *Monahan v Legal Aid Board* [2009] 3 IR 458
High Court 4 December 2009 *MST v Minister for Justice, Equality and Law Reform* [2009] 12 JIC 403
High Court 11 October 2010 *EMI Records (Ireland) Ltd v UPC Communications Ireland Ltd* [2010] IEHC 377
High Court 3 March 2011 *EPA v Neiphin Trading Ltd* [2011] 2 IR 575
High Court 22 November 2011 *JC Savage Supermarket Ltd v An Bord Pleanála* [2011] IEHC 488
High Court 2 March 2012 *Dowling v Minister for Finance* [2012] IEHC 89
High Court 26 October 2012 *Minister for Justice and Equality v Doyle (No 2)* [2012] IEHC 451
High Court 19 November 2013 *Sandymount and Merrion Residents Association v An Bord Pleanála* [2013] 11 JIC 1904
High Court 8 April 2014 *EPA v Greenstar Holdings Ltd* [2014] 4 JIC 802
High Court 9 May 2014 *Health Service Executive v Sallam* [2014] 5 JIC 905
High Court 30 May 2014 *EPA v Harte Peat Ltd* [2015] 1 IR 462
High Court 30 May 2014 *OCS One Complete Solution Ltd v Dublin Airport Authority PLC* [2014] IEHC 306
High Court 6 July 2016 *Revenue Commissioners v Canada Life Ltd* [2016] IEHC 499
High Court 12 May 2016 *KRA v Minister for Justice and Equality* [2016] IEHC 289
High Court 14 October 2016 *Bookfinders Ltd v Revenue Commissioners* [2016] IEHC 569

THE NETHERLANDS

ARRvS 6 March 1986, ECLI:NL:RVS:1986:BP8194, *M en R* 1987/6 (*Rotganzen*)
ARRvS 2 December 1991, ECLI:NL:RVS:1991:AN2626, *AB* 1992/475
ARRvS 26 January 1993, ECLI:NL:RVS:1993:AN3013, *AB* 1993/238
ABRvS 15 December 1994, ECLI:NL:RVS:1994:AN4903, *AB* 1996/29
ABRvS 11 May 1996, ECLI:NL:RVS:1996:AN5165, *AB* 1996/410
ABRvS 31 March 2000, ECLI:NL:RVS:2000:AB1152, *AB* 2000/302 (*Buitengebied Texel*)
ABRvS 11 May 2000, ECLI:NL:RVS:2000:AA6110
ABRvS 2 November 2000, ECLI:NL:RVS:2000:AN6579, *AB* 2001/51
ABRvS 29 May 2001, ECLI:NL:RVS:2001:AN6786, *RAwb* 2001/98
ABRvS 20 June 2001, ECLI:NL:RVS:2001:AB2437, *AB* 2001/260
ABRvS 13 November 2002, ECLI:NL:RVS:2002:AF0308, *AB* 2003/26
ABRvS 24 February 2003, ECLI:NL:RVS:2003:AH9582, *AB* 2003/327
ABRvS 7 April 2004, ECLI:NL:RVS:2004:AO7095, *AB* 2004/460
ABRvS 28 July 2004, ECLI:NL:RVS:2004:AQ5732, *M en R* 2004/104
ABRvS 7 December 2005, ECLI:NL:RVS:2005:AU7583, *AB* 2006/67 (*Boxtel*)

ABRvS 28 February 2007, ECLI:NL:RVS:2007:AZ9494, *AB* 2007/183 (*Fortis*)
ABRvS 5 December 2007, ECLI:NL:RVS:2007:BB9488, *AB* 2008/18 (*De Ingelsche Waarden*)
ABRvS 4 June 2008, ECLI:NL:RVS:2008:BD3121, *AB* 2008/229
ABRvS 4 March 2009, ECLI:NL:RVS:2009:BH4621, *AB* 2009/156 (*Mandemakers*)
ABRvS 25 November 2009, ECLI:NL:RVS:2009:BK4312, *M en R* 2010/43
ABRvS 31 March 2010, ECLI:NL:RVS:2010:BL9657
ABRvS 3 April 2012, ECLI:NL:RVS:2012:BW1435
ABRvS 20 March 2013, ECLI:NL:RVS:2013:BZ4937, *AB* 2013/359
ABRvS 11 June 2014, ECLI:NL:RVS:2014:2120, *AB* 2014/320
ABRvS 1 April 2015, ECLI:NL:RVS:2015:999, *M en R* 2015/92
ABRvS 29 April 2015, ECLI:NL:RVS:2015:1361
ABRvS 8 June 2016, ECLI:NL:RVS:2016:1613, *AB* 2016/273 (*KOMO*)
ABRvS 15 June 2016, ECLI:NL:RVS:2016:1773
ABRvS 26 April 2017, ECLI:NL:RVS:2017:1109
ABRvS 3 May 2017, ECLI:NL:RVS:2017:1175, *JGR* 2018/2
ABRvS 7 June 2017, ECLI:NL:RVS:2017:1520, *AB* 2017/249
ABRvS 12 October 2017, ECLI:NL:RVS:2017:2771

CBb 6 November 2009, ECLI:NL:CBB:2009:BK2641, *AB* 2010/215
CBb 24 December 2009, ECLI:NL:CBB:2009:BL9703
CBb 30 June 2011, ECLI:NL:CBB:2011:BQ9755, *JOR* 2011/260
CBb 22 February 2012, ECLI:NL:CBB:2012:BV6713 (*IMC*)
CBb 23 July 2012, ECLI:NL:CBB:2012:BX4127
CBb 5 June 2014, ECLI:NL:CBB:2014:206, *AB* 2014/345
CBb 17 June 2015, ECLI:NL:CBB:2015:214, *AB* 2015/297
CBb 21 September 2015, ECLI:NL:CBB:2015:288, *AB* 2016/52
CBb 12 September 2016, ECLI:NL:CBB:2016:270

HR 3 March 1919, ECLI:NL:HR:1919:126, *NJ* 1919/371 (*Grenstractaat Aken*)
HR 23 April 1974, ECLI:NL:HR:1974:AB5708, *NJ* 1974/272
HR 2 May 1984, ECLI:NL:HR:1984:AW8625, *BNB* 1984/295
HR 21 November 1986, ECLI:NL:HR:1986:AG5465, *NJ* 1987/351 (*Beets-Proper/Van Lanschot Bankiers*)
HR 24 April 1987, ECLI:NL:HR:1987:AG5584, *NJ* 1987/660 (*Ubbink Isolatie/Dak- en Wandtechniek*)
HR 16 November 1990, ECLI:NL:HR:1990:ZC0044, *NJ* 1992/107
HR 13 September 1991, ECLI:NL:HR:1991:ZC0328, *NJ* 1992/225 (*Dekker*)
HR 18 June 1993, ECLI:NL:HR:1993:ZC1008, *NJ* 1993/614 (*Rietveld/Gemini ziekenhuis*)
HR 7 December 1994, ECLI:NL:HR:1994:AA2977, *BNB* 1995/87 (*Grasland*)
HR 9 December 1994, ECLI:NL:HR:1994:ZC1573, *NJ* 1995/224

HR 20 October 1995, ECLI:NL:HR:1995:ZC1846, *NJ* 1996/330 (*Van Asseldonk/Ter Schure*)
HR 29 December 1995, ECLI:NL:HR:1995:ZC1943, *NJ* 1996/418 (*Buyck/Van den Ameele*)
HR 24 January 1996, ECLI:NL:HR:1996:AA1820, *BNB* 1996/138
HR 27 September 1996, ECLI:NL:HR:1996:ZC2151, *NJ* 1997/624
HR 25 October 1996, ECLI:NL:HR:1996:ZC2177, *NJ* 1997/649 (*Pink Floyd*)
HR 19 September 1997, ECLI:NL:HR:1997:ZC2435, *NJ* 1998/6 (*Assoud/SNS*)
HR 31 March 1998, ECLI:NL:HR:1998:ZD1165, *NJ* 1998/780
HR 21 April 1998, ECLI:NL:HR:1998:ZD1030, *NJ* 1998/782
HR 9 April 1999, ECLI:NL:HR:1999:ZC2891, *NJ* 2000/688
HR 10 August 2001, ECLI:NL:HR:2001:AB3115, *BNB* 2001/351
HR 20 November 2001, ECLI:NL:HR:2001:AB2809, *NJ* 2003/632 (*Mensenroof*)
HR 2 November 2004, ECLI:NL:HR:2004:AR1797, *NJ* 2005/80 (*Rusttijden*)
HR 20 February 2007, ECLI:NL:HR:2007:AZ0213 (*Samir A.*)
HR 12 June 2007, ECLI:NL:HR:2007:BA0426, *NJ* 2007/347
HR 10 August 2007, ECLI:NL:HR:2007:AZ3758, *AB* 2007/291 (*Wandelvierdaagse*)
HR 6 June 2008, ECLI:NL:HR:2008:BD3139, *AB* 2008/214 (*Joustra*)
HR 30 January 2009, ECLI:NL:HR:2009:BH1174, *BNB* 2009/95
HR 5 June 2009, ECLI:NL:HR:2009:BH2815, *NJ* 2012/182 (*De Treek/Dexia*)
HR 1 April 2011, ECLI:NL:HR:2011:BP3044, *NJ* 2011/354 (*Clara Wichmann/Staat*)
HR 9 December 2011, ECLI:NL:HR:2011:BU7412, *NJ* 2013/273
HR 21 September 2012, ECLI:NL:HR:2012:BW5879, *AB* 2012/367 (*ACI Adam e.a./Stichting De Thuiskopie*)
HR 12 October 2012, ECLI:NL:HR:2012:BW8301, *NJ* 2012/586 (*Stichting De Thuiskopie/Opus Supplies Deutschland e.a.*)
HR 5 April 2013, ECLI:NL:HR:2013:BZ1780, *NJ* 2013/389 (*Albron/FNV c.s.*)
HR 17 January 2014, ECLI:NL:HR:2014:88, *NJ* 2015/304 (*Ryanair Ltd/PR Aviation*)
HR 13 June 2014, ECLI:NL:HR:2014:1385, *NJ* 2015/477
HR 10 October 2014, ECLI:NL:HR:2014:2928, *NJ* 2015/12 (*Rookverbod*)
HR 26 February 2016, ECLI:NL:HR:2016:335, *AB* 2016/175 (*X/ASR*)
HR 20 January 2017, ECLI:NL:HR:2017:59, *NJ* 2017/63
HR 14 April 2017, ECLI:NL:HR:2017:689

Regional Court of Appeal Amsterdam 25 October 2011, ECLI:NL:GHAMS:2011:BU1290, *NJ* 2012/163

Regional Court of Appeal Arnhem 2 March 2006, ECLI:NL:GHARN:2006:AV6387

Regional Court of Appeal The Hague 1 June 1995, ECLI:NL:GHSGR:1995:AK3519

District Court The Hague 7 July 1995, ECLI:NL:RBSGR:1995:AK3535, *IER* 1995/30
District Court The Hague 6 February 2019, ECLI:NL:RBDHA:2019:930

District Court Rotterdam 4 August 2011, ECLI:NL:RBROT:2011:BR4191
District Court Rotterdam 5 September 2012, ECLI:NL:RBROT:2012:BX6988

UNITED KINGDOM

House of Lords 22 April 1982 *Garland v British Rail Engineering Ltd* [1983] 2 AC 751, 771
House of Lords 11 February 1988 *Duke v Reliance Systems Ltd* [1988] AC 618
House of Lords 26 November 1992 *Pepper v Hart* [1993] AC 593
House of Lords 19 October 1995 *Webb v Emo Air Cargo (U.K.) Ltd (No 2)* [1995] 1 WLR 1454
Supreme Court 30 May 2012 *Assange v Sweden* [2012] 2 AC 471

Court of Appeal 27 April 1978 *Shields v E Coomes (Holdings) Ltd* [1978] 1 WLR 1408, 1415
Court of Appeal 25 July 1979 *Macarthys Ltd v Smith* [1979] ICR 785, 789

Employment Appeal Tribunal 30 October 2009 *EBR Attridge Law LLP v Coleman* [2010] IRLR 10

CURRICULUM VITAE

Sim Haket obtained his Master's degree in European Law at Utrecht University in 2012 (cum laude). This was followed by an internship at the Ministry of Economic Affairs, where he worked for SOLVIT, an EU-wide network which helps citizens and businesses in enforcing their EU law rights in other Member States. He then returned to Utrecht University and worked as a junior lecturer, teaching courses on EU law, international law and administrative law. In 2014 he commenced his doctoral research for the Montaigne Centre for Rule of Law and Administration of Justice. During the research Sim visited the European Court of Justice, Heidelberg University and University College Dublin. In the academic year 2015-2016 he chaired the faculty's PhD council. Since 2017 he is a staff member of the journal 'Overheid & Aansprakelijkheid' (contributing summaries of Dutch case law concerning State liability). Since September 2019 Sim is assistant professor in constitutional law at Utrecht University.

www.ingramcontent.com/pod-product-compliance
Ingram Content Group UK Ltd.
Pitfield, Milton Keynes, MK11 3LW, UK
UKHW051920100926
8556IPUK00021B/1276

9 781780 68879